PEWS, BENCHES & CHAIRS

F. Gardam

The Georgian box pews at Torbryan, Devon (above) which (right) encase fifteenth-century oak benches.

The creation of eighteenth-century box pews from medieval benches was not uncommon. As one Victorian writer put it, quoted on page 221:
the solid open benches of earlier date, were gradually raised higher and higher by additional framing; and the proper direction of the pews, which even at first was preserved, and made to face the altar, became disregarded, and by cutting away the middle framing, two pews, and more often benches, were thrown into one, and cross seats were added. Thus came into existence the high square pews of our own days.... An illustration of another example will be found in Figure 2 in Chapter 18 (page 278).

Those restoring churches in Victorian times often made careful use of such earlier material when creating seating, as discussed, for example, in Chapters 8, 12, 16 and 18.

PEWS, BENCHES and CHAIRS

*Church seating in English parish churches
from the fourteenth century to the present*

edited by
Trevor Cooper and Sarah Brown

The Ecclesiological Society · 2011

© Copyright the authors 2011, except where stated. All rights reserved.

ISBN: 978-0-946823-17-8

Published 2011 by the Ecclesiological Society
c/o The Society of Antiquaries of London
Burlington House
Piccadilly
London
WIV 0HS

The Ecclesiological Society is a registered charity
Charity No. 210501

www.ecclsoc.org

The views expressed in this publication are those of the authors, and do not necessarily represent those of the Ecclesiological Society or its officers.

Front cover. The church of St Peter & St Paul, Kedington, Suffolk. This fine unrestored church is awash with seating from a range of periods. In the photograph can be seen open benches of Perpendicular date, later box pews, the Barnardiston family pew of the early seventeenth century (which is partly made up from the medieval rood screen) and, in the chancel, wooden chairs of a type common in churches from the mid nineteenth century onwards.

Rear cover. Oil painting, *The Free Seat*, painted 1869 by James Lobley (1829–88). In this context 'free' meant the seat was available for anyone, though in practice largely used by the poor; this is in contrast to 'appropriated' seating which was reserved for the use of particular individuals, often those relatively well-established in society. (Oil on panel, 55 cm x 85 cm; © Birmingham Museums & Art Gallery)

Contents

Preface   *vii*
Acknowledgements   *ix*

Part 1: CONTEXT

1 Introduction: Pews – understanding significance, recognising need *by Sarah Brown*   1
2 Liturgy and spaces: some recent trends *by Peter Moger*   9
3 The Temple of His Presence *by Peter Doll*   13
4 Pews in Norwegian churches *by Oddbjørn Sørmoen*   19
5 How many seats in church? *by Trevor Cooper*   37

Part 2: HISTORY: TO THE NINETEENTH CENTURY

6 Seating in the nave of the pre-Reformation parish church *by P. S. Barnwell*   69
7 Medieval benches and bench ends of Somerset: towards an archaeological approach *by Jerry Sampson*   87
8 Assessing and evaluating English pews: three case studies *by Charles Tracy*   111
9 Order and place in England, 1580-1640: the view from the pew [excerpt] *by Christopher Marsh*   131
10 Post-Reformation church seating arrangements and bench assembly notation in two North Devon churches *by Francis Kelly*   149
11 'To take theire plases wheare they shall not offend others': the 1635 reseating of Puddletown church, Dorset *by Bob Machin*   171
12 The pews at St Mary, Newent, Gloucestershire *by Hugh Harrison*   183

Part 3: HISTORY: THE NINETEENTH CENTURY

13 Patterns of church seating from Waterloo to 1850, and the role of the Cambridge Camden Society *by Christopher Webster*   197
14 Victorian guidance on seating from the Incorporated Church Building Society   211
15 Movable benches or chairs? Correspondence in *The Ecclesiologist* 1854–6   237
16 'The same fashion as the present ancient seats': G. G. Scott and the reseating of medieval churches *by Suzanna Branfoot*   257

17 Some seating designs in churches by
    John Hayward of Exeter *by Jo Cox* — 267
18 Church seating: a view from Suffolk
    by James Bettley — 277
19 Victorian church seating: variations upon a theme
    by Geoff Brandwood — 281
20 Spoiled for choice: seating from the catalogue
    by Geoff Brandwood and Trevor Cooper — 303
21 Machine carving of Victorian pew ends: some
    initial findings *by Jo Cox* — 323

Part 4: CONSIDERING CHANGE
22 Seats in church *by Robert Maguire* — 335
23 Pews: the view from a DAC secretary
    by Jonathan MacKechnie-Jarvis — 351
24 The appropriate alternatives to fixed seating
    by Anthony Russell — 359
25 Pew platforms *by Will Hawkes* — 367
26 Assessing the importance of Victorian and other
    congregational seating *by Roy Porter* — 371
27 Considering changes to church seating
    by Trevor Cooper and Sarah Brown — 385
28 Pews: why do they matter? *by Trevor Cooper* — 401

Part 5: CASE STUDIES
29 Case studies — 411

Part 6: POSTSCRIPT AND FURTHER READING
30 Postscript: One hundred years hence
    by Trevor Cooper — 457
    Further reading — 477

Notes on Contributors — 483
Index — 487

Preface

The question of pew removal is a matter on which many people, whether churchgoers or not, have strong views: indeed its grip on the public imagination is such that it formed a subplot in the popular BBC Radio programme, *The Archers*. The arguments about pews in fictional Ambridge merely reflected the many genuine and difficult discussions taking place up and down the country.

During informal (and lively) discussion of these matters at meetings of the Council of the Ecclesiological Society – of which both editors are members – it became clear that in many ways we lacked enough background information on church seating to take an informed view of the general issues. At the same time we were aware of a great deal of research activity that deserved an airing. Hence the idea for this book.

Our subject is congregational seating, and we have restricted our scope to Church of England parish churches – there is certainly a need for a study of nonconformist and Roman Catholic seating, but we have not attempted that here. Furthermore, our attention has been on seats as seats, rather than the adornment of the bench ends which support them; nor have we looked at seating in the chancel, a rather different topic. Even with these constraints there is still a great deal to say, and we have looked for authors who could tackle the subject from many different angles. It is perhaps worth saying that we did not attempt to impose any uniformity on our authors, and the chapters will be found to vary greatly in their style, their length, and the way they approach their topic.

From the beginning we wanted to tackle head on the issues related to the removal of pews, and the relative merits of pews, movable benches and chairs. To that end we commissioned a number of chapters from those who have a case to argue, and there is an entire section of the book devoted to the possibility of changing seating, together with a series of case studies of churches which have (or in some cases, have not) changed their seating arrangements. We have found this material helpful and enlightening, and hope that others find the same.

However it is important to emphasise that we as editors do not agree with everything that is written here, and that nothing in the book reflects the views of the Ecclesiological Society, which (unlike the original Society of the same name) has no corporate stance on these matters. We should also say that authors are expressing their personal views rather than writing on behalf of any organisation, so that the only weight to be attached to any statement in this book derives from the authority of the individual who wrote it. Furthermore, our selection of authors was made simply on the basis of their having something interesting to say, and was not dependent on their views – to put it bluntly, there is in the production of this volume no agenda, covert or overt, promoting a particular future for church seating: the only agenda is to provide factual information, and encourage reasoned and informed debate.

One of the least important matters for debate, but one on which we have discovered that our authors are not slow to express an opinion, is the use of the word 'pew'. Some are happy to use it for any benched wooden seating. Others argue that it should be reserved for seating with doors, and use the word 'bench' if there are no doors. We have not imposed consistency here, but have allowed authors to follow their own preference, seeing our editorial role as ensuring there was no resulting ambiguity. For what it is worth, there is evidence as early the mid-1840s that the word 'pew' was sometimes being used of church seating without doors.[1]

We are very grateful to our authors, without whom this book would not have existed. We also wish to acknowledge significant financial assistance from English Heritage. In addition, part of the cost of publication has been defrayed by a donation from the estate of the late Dr James Johnston, who was Secretary of the Society until his untimely death. We like to think he would have enjoyed this book.

Trevor Cooper and Sarah Brown

---

1 In 1846, in the title of a series of publications, 'Working Drawings of Ancient Pews or Open Seats' (*Oxford Society for Promoting the Study of Gothic Architecture. The Rules, List of the Members, and Catalogue of the Library, Drawings, and Engravings* (Oxford, 1846), 36).

Acknowledgements

The Society wishes to acknowledge significant financial assistance in the publication of this volume, from English Heritage (given to support the publication in Chapter 19 of research commissioned from Dr Geoff Brandwood), and from a donation from the estate of the late Dr James Johnston.

Most of the photographs were taken by, and are copyright of, the authors. We are grateful to them and to other individuals and institutions for permission to reproduce images in their possession for which they retain copyright, as follows (images are listed by chapter number followed by figure number): Clifford Ball: 8.8, 8.9; P. S. Barnwell: 6.3, 6.6, 6.7; James Bettley: 18.1–5; reproduced with the permission of Birmingham Libraries & Archives: 20.6–13; Birmingham Museums & Art Gallery: rear cover; Joanna Booth: 29.15a; The Bodleian Library, University of Oxford (the image is from The John Johnson Collection of Printed Ephemera): 20.3; Geoff Brandwood: 19.1, 19.4, 19.5a &b, 19.6–15; Suzanna Branfoot: 16.1–11; The Bridgeman Art Library: 30.2; Sarah Brown: 1.1–4; David Bryan: 29.11; Church of England, Church Buildings Council: 25.1–2, 26.1–5, 26.7; Churches Conservation Trust: 8.5, 26.6; City of London, London Metropolitan Archives: 30.15; The church authorities, St Clydog's, Clodock: 30.6; Trevor Cooper: front cover, 1.5, 10.6, 10.7, 10.12, 11.1–3, 11.6–9, 21.5, 22.3–5, 22.6, 29.4d, 30.4, 30.5, 30.16; *Country Life*: 11.5; Jo Cox: 17.1–11, 21.1–4; Geoff Crawford: 30.10; Richard Davies: 29.6; courtesy of the Devon and Exeter Institution: 14.1–3; Diocese of St Edmundsbury and Ipswich / James Halsall: 29.7; Peter Doll: 3.2–4; Dorset County Museum: 11.4; John Earl: 30.14; East Sussex Record Office (ref: KIR/29/31): 14.4; English Heritage / Derek Kendall: 19.5c, 19.16; reproduced by permission of English Heritage.NMR: 8.A12, A13; Hugh Harrison: frontis, 10.25, 12.1–19, 29.2, 29.15b&c; the PCC of St Nectan's Church, Hartland (digitised by S. J. Hobbs): 10.2; Hartland Digital Archive / S. J. Hobbs: 10.10, 10.11; S. J. Hobbs: 10.1, 10.8; Hymns Ancient & Modern: 30.17; JUPITERIMAGES via www.clipart.com: 30.1; Francis Kelly: 10.9, 10.14, 10.17, 10.19, 10.20, 10.22–24; The church authorities, St Mary's, Kirtlington: 29.13; Simon Knott, www.norfolkchurches.co.uk: 29.9; Lambeth Palace Library: 30.3; Leicester County Council Museums Service: 30.5; Tim Lomax, used by kind permission: 2.1; Jonathan MacKechnie–Jarvis: 23.1–3; Methodist Property Office: 29.5; Nicholas Meyjes: 22.4, 22.5, 22.7; The New York Public Library, Astor, Lenox and Tilden

Foundations: 20.2; C B Newham: 6.1–2, 6.5, 10.5, 10.13, 10.15b, 10.16, 10.18, 10.21; Special Collections, Princeton Theological Seminary Libraries: 20.4; reproduced with permission of *Punch Ltd.*, www.punch.co.uk: 30.9; Redgrave Church Heritage Trust / Bob Hayward: 29.10; Riksantikvaren: 4.1–7 (photos: Oddbjørn Sørmoen), 4.8 (photo: Eva Smådahl), 4.9 (photo: Aage Blegen); Riksantikvaren / Gurly Engelsen: 4.A1–A4; Riksantikvaren / Jens Christian Eldal: 4.A5; Anthony Russell: 24.1–4; Mark Russell–Smith: 29.15d&e; Chris Rutter: 29.14b–d; John Salmon: 29.3a; Jerry Sampson: 7.1–15; SAVE Britain's Heritage: 28.1; Charles Smith: 29.3b–j; The church authorities, St Margaret's, Thorpe Market: 29.9; Take a Pew: 29.1; Jonathan Taylor: 8.1; John Thewlis: 29.4a–c; Charles Tracy: 8.2–4, 8.6, 8.7, 8.A1–A10; V&A Images/Victoria and Albert Museum, London: 20.5; The Victoria and Albert Museum, London: page 238, 30.11, 30.12; Dave Walker (www.cartoonchurch.com): cartoons on page 37; John Ward: 3.1; Watts & Co., London: 20.14; John Whybrow: 22.1; The church authorities / P. H. Townsend, St Mary's, Willand: 29.8. We have attempted to secure the permission of all copyright holders to reproduce images. We apologise for any breach of copyright and will correct the matter in any future edition.

Chapters 2, 8, 9, 11, 25 and the first case study in Chapter 29 first appeared in whole or in part in other publications. They are reproduced here by kind permission of the original publishers and authors. The chapters concerned provide details of the original publication and a copyright notice. We are also grateful to the National Churches Trust for providing initial, unadjusted data from their Survey 2010, used in Chapter 5.

Part 1

CONTEXT

1. Introduction: Pews – understanding significance, recognising need

Sarah Brown

MANY TYPES OF CHURCH FURNISHING have been subject to rapid and dramatic changes of taste and fashion over the centuries, but few more so than church seating. The advantages and disadvantages of pews – by which I refer to fixed wooden bench seating – a subject of much current debate and the catalyst for this book, have been discussed for over one hundred and sixty years, exposing preoccupations with comfort, convenience and flexibility that are reassuringly familiar.

The pressure for change

The history of church furnishing in the centuries since the Reformation of the mid sixteenth century and probably before has been one of evolution and change. For many churches in the twenty-first century the need for further change is of paramount concern – and, as Oddbjørn Sørmoen shows in his chapter on Norwegian churches (Chapter 4), this is an issue not restricted to England. The pew has become the focus around which the campaign for change has recently coalesced.[1] Pew removal is essential to the liturgical transformation advocated by Richard Giles: 'Flexible seating is therefore essential if a real process of liturgical formulation is going to be stimulated every time the assembly meets for worship. Not only do we need to break free from centuries of captivity in serried ranks of pews, but we need also to be frequently ringing the changes in our seating plan to denote different 'moods' of the assembly appropriate to different seasons of the Church's Year'.[2] In 2007 Roy Strong was prepared to go even further, advocating a bonfire of 'utterly awful kipper coloured choir stalls and pews' in pursuit of the restoration of community space.[3] These pressures for change are explored in Chapters 2 and 3 by Peter Moger and Peter Doll.

Both English Heritage and those denominational agencies for whom it is an increasingly pressing issue are responding to this by an active and imaginative engagement with re ordering proposals emerging from churches, as can be seen in the case studies presented at the end of the book (Chapter 29). (As yet, however, there is little evidence that pews are regarded as a problematic issue in the Catholic Church.) National guidelines are now widely available, and will be found in the list of further reading at the end of this book. Furthermore, since at least 2005 English Heritage has commissioned systematic research to inform the debate and evaluation of the significance of church seating, some of the results of which are published here for the first time in the chapter on Victorian seating by Geoff Brandwood (Chapter 19). The principle of acceptable change, sometimes extensive, if informed by research and justified by understanding has gained ground in recent years. Milestone publications have included Kate Clarke's *Informed Conservation* of 2001 and English Heritage's *Conservation Principles* of 2008.[4] In line with this approach, in this book Roy Porter in Chapter 26 explicitly addresses the significance of church seating, whilst we have attempted to synthesise and condense much of this recent thinking in Chapter 27 on 'Considering changes to church seating', which we hope will be of immediate practical value.

Taking a historical view

The evaluation of pews and decisions concerning what we can afford to lose without irreparable damage to our ecclesiastical heritage must be rooted in a balanced understanding of the history of church seating. Our medieval forebears, unused to universal pewing, would probably have found the sparsely seated interiors advocated by some anti-pew campaigners far less surprising than many of us do today. Medieval worshippers were used to moving about relatively freely in the naves of their churches, and it is probably only in the later Middles Ages that fixed seats began to be provided for the laity in any numbers. P. S. Barnwell explores the evidence for this elsewhere in this volume (Chapter 6), whilst Jerry Sampson discusses the archaeology of some of this early seating, and shows how it can tell the story of multiple changes (Chapter 7). There is, of course, a general presumption in favour of retention of surviving medieval schemes. After the Reformation fixed congregational seating became ever more widespread, as the liturgy shifted its emphasis from the celebration of the Eucharist to congregational participation and the ministry of the Word. The habit of regularly occupying the same pew, in arrangements often determined by family association and social and gender segregation, was established at an early date. Historians of the early modern period have found the documentary sources relating to sixteenth- and seventeenth-century church seating to be a fruitful source for the exploration of the social history of the parish, as in Chapter 9 by Christopher Marsh, although relatively few physical signs of these earliest schemes have survived. A forlorn inscription in the church of St Leonard, Flamstead, Hertfordshire (Fig. 1), recalls long-lost Elizabethan parochial seating.[5] Lost cathedral seating is recorded in the seventeenth-century inscription on the memorial to Elihonor Sadler (d.1622) in the south nave aisle of Salisbury Cathedral, who had served God from the same pew in the nave for over fifty years. The chapters by Charles Tracy, Francis Kelly,

Fig. 1: Inscription at St Leonard, Flamstead, Hertfordshire, recording the burial in 1598 at 'this seats end' of 'our neighbor & frind olde John Grigge'.

Bob Machin and Hugh Harrison (Chapters 8, 10–12) describe some of the survivors from this period, and show how the physical evidence can tell us about the original form and planning of the seating.

The majority of medieval parish churches survived the Reformation structurally unchanged, so that our understanding of the impact of the Reformation and Elizabethan Settlement on our churches is informed by our knowledge of the layout of furniture and fittings. The furnishings of a church like Walpole St Peter in Norfolk, for example, illustrates these transformations in microcosm (Fig. 2). From the late Middle Ages survive elaborate late-fifteenth-century stalls, associated with a truncated painted rood screen. From the seventeenth century is the pulpit of 1620, situated half way down the nave, and of the same date are the rows of simple open benches which fill the nave at the pulpit's foot. In the eighteenth century the pews were adapted and extended by the addition of doors and the provision of new box pews (Fig. 3) at the west end of the nave. The survival of such an accretive collection of seating of different dates is not common and it was perhaps the open nature of the bulk of the nave seating that saved Walpole St Peter from wholesale re-pewing in the nineteenth century.[6]

It was, of course, the eighteenth- and early-nineteenth-century closed box pew (or 'pue') that attracted the ire of the nineteenth-century ecclesiological reformer, and the box pew became a symbol of all that was wrong with the church of the long eighteenth century, the subject of Christopher Webster's contribution to this volume in Chapter 13. In his influential tract on the history of pews published in 1841, the Revd John Mason Neale asked rhetorically: 'For what is the history of pues, but the history of the intrusion of human pride, selfishness and indolence into the worship of God'.[7] The war waged against the box pew by the Cambridge Camden Society (and others) was extraordinarily

Fig. 2: Walpole St Peter, Norfolk, the late-fifteenth-century stalls in the chancel.

successful and by 1847 the Society was already able to anticipate complete success in banishing the box pew from the English parish church.[8] In 1991 Nigel Yates estimated that there were only 210 pre-Tractarian interiors surviving in England.[9] In the twenty-first century we tend to find the box-pewed interior charming and characterful, and some churches would be of limited architectural interest without these furnishings. It has to be said that while the relative rarity and charm of many box pews should ensure their preservation, there are many cases in which the inflexibility of a box-pewed interior has made modern worship and church expansion problematic.[10]

The triumph of ecclesiology in the nineteenth century has meant that many thousands of our churches of all dates and styles of churchmanship are now filled, some would say strait-jacketed, by row upon row of eastward-facing fixed pews – some of which, as Jo Cox discusses in an exploratory article in Chapter 21, may have been machine-carved, whilst, as Geoff Brandwood and Trevor Cooper show in Chapter 20, much may have been straight from the catalogue. But it was not all hack work, nor was it necessarily destructive of older seating: Suzanna Branfoot in Chapter 16 discusses how G. G. Scott responded creatively and sensitively to the medieval pews he found, and James Bettley in Chapter 18 explains how Victorian restorers in Suffolk paid their respects to earlier work, whilst in Chapter 17 Jo Cox describes how architect John Hayward produced designs for new pews to meet each of his client's different requirements. Nevertheless, the sheer quantity and rigid arrangement of Victorian seating cannot be overlooked: it might be exemplified by the interior of St Botolph, in Boston (Fig. 4). I know nothing of the history of this set of pews, and have no idea how they are viewed by

INTRODUCTION: PEWS – UNDERSTANDING SIGNIFICANCE, RECOGNISING NEED

Fig. 3: Walpole St Peter, Norfolk, eighteenth-century box pewing at the west end of the nave.

members of the congregation, but in terms of sheer acreage, they have an extraordinary impact on the church interior. And the east-facing pew is far from confined to the interiors of the Established Church. By the end of the nineteenth century it had come to dominate the nonconformist and Catholic interior. It has formed our idea of a 'normal' or stereotypical church (Chapter 30).

There can be little doubt, therefore, that while historical precedent supports change, in seeking to implement it within a framework of informed understanding we are faced with the sheer weight of numbers and the overwhelming ubiquity of the nineteenth-century pew. In Chapter 5 Trevor Cooper estimates there are are up to four million sittings in Church of England churches alone, the majority of which will be Victorian pews.

Victorian debates and their relevance

The historical long view can provide encouragement in engaging with some of the most pressing contemporary issues. For example, comfort, or rather the lack of it, is often the ground on which removal of pews is advocated. William Butterfield, was one of the most important architects to consider the question of pew design and comfort.[11] One of his articles on this topic, and its accompanying illustration, is reprinted in Chapter 14 which explores Victorian guidance emanating from the influential Incorporated Church Building Society. Treating all worshippers as male and of the same size and build, Butterfield summarised his views in the following words:

> In extricating ourselves from the pews system, we have not, I think, shown as much practical sense as Englishmen are usually credited with. A hassock is a stumbling block. It is always in different stages of decay,

Fig. 4: St Botolph, Boston, Lincoln, view looking east, an example of a fully-pewed nave.

raggedness and nastiness. The knee should be lifted about 5 inches above the floor in kneeling. This allows the foot to remain at a comfortable angle . . . The height of a seat-back which will meet the case of a person when thus kneeling, is the most suitable and convenient height for him when sitting. It leaves the bones of the shoulders at liberty to move freely above it . . . there is thus no need for a sloping back when the shoulders are thus free . . . I have shown the hat of each person deposited on the further side of his own kneeling board , in full view of the person to whom it belongs and entirely free of the possibility of it being kicked by the person to whom it does NOT belong.[12]

While we might find Butterfield's comments of little help in adapting seats for twenty-first century needs, we could be reassured by the fact that the search for an appropriate level of comfort and convenience has been a long-standing pre-occupation.

Perhaps surprisingly, the same can be said of the debate on pews versus chairs. As Geoff Brandwood reminds us (Chapter 19), Butterfield's All Saints, Margaret Street in London (completed 1859) was provided with movable chairs from the beginning, causing considerable debate. Chairs were used in other Victorian churches, such as G. E. Street's important church of St James, Kingston, Dorset, completed in 1880 (Fig. 5), where the church guide today speaks warmly about the flexibility that chairs bring.[13] Indeed, almost as soon as they had seen off the box pew, the members of Cambridge Camden Society (by then renamed as the Ecclesiological Society) were arguing with fervour the relative merits of the bench versus the chair, as can be seen in Chapter 15 in this book where we reprint a lengthy though anonymous

INTRODUCTION: PEWS – UNDERSTANDING SIGNIFICANCE, RECOGNISING NEED

Fig. 5: *St James, Kingston, Dorset (G. E. Street, completed 1880). The nave had chairs from the beginning.*

correspondence on the issue from the years 1854–6. Two totally opposing view points appeared in *The Ecclesiologist* in 1854.

> Seat your worshippers each on his own chair, and you must crowd them to the detriment both of the decorum or worship or else you must fritter away ground area... Chairs, if of one size, must be made so as to contain without inconvenience the average of fat and not of thin sitters (letter from *A Committeeman*).

> Chairs are the right thing, – if only we could learn how to use them. Enlarge your church or divide and multiply your services, only do not cramp and destroy the life and elasticity of your worship for the sake of a little more 'accommodation' (letter from *Londinensis*).[14]

In this book Anthony Russell and Jonathan MacKechnie-Jarvis both contribute to the pews versus chairs debate (Chapters 23 and 24), as does Trevor Cooper more obliquely in Chapter 28, and Robert Maguire from first principles in Chapter 22. In this context Will Hawkes makes some important but easily overlooked practical points regarding the floor of the church when removing pews (Chapter 25).

The future
It would be ahistorical and artificial to allow a particular liturgical and theological outlook to freeze-frame our churches in one

7

worshipping moment in time. An unchecked and unconscious series of changes to our churches and their furnishings has bequeathed to our conservationist age a serendipitous collection of survivors. The choices we make in how and what we preserve in the future will be difficult and must be made with care. The pewing issue is now widely recognised as central to our future use of church buildings. By refusing to accept further change we would be denying some churches a future – a high price to pay for conserving the past. To allow a wholesale removal of historic seating schemes would be equally unconscionable, squandering the massive investment of materials, craftsmanship and the evidence of parochial history and devotion that make so many of our church interiors both distinctive and beautiful. It is the hope of the editors that this book will both encourage and inform this important debate.

Notes

1 Half in jest, the editor of *Current Archaeology* has proposed the formation of a new campaigning group, the 'Pew Preservation Society'. 'Odd Socs', *Current Archaeology* 50 (2008), 214.
2 Richard Giles, *Repitching the Tent: Reordering the church building for worship and mission* (Norwich 1996), 175.
3 Roy Strong, 'The Beauty of Holiness and its Perils: What is to Happen to 10,000 Parish Churches?', Gresham College Special Lecture 2007, transcript available at www.gresham.ac.uk/printtranscript.asp?EventId=604 (accessed 16 October 2009).
4 Kate Clarke, *Informed Conservation* (London, 2001); English Heritage, *Conservation Principles: Policies and Guidance for the Sustainable Management of the Historic Environment* (Swindon, 2008), available at www.englishheritage.org.uk/server/show/nav.9181 (accessed 16 October 2009).
5 N. Pevsner and B. Cherry, *Buildings of England: Hertfordshire* (Harmondsworth, 1977), 141–42. The church is best known for its exceptional wall-paintings. The inscription is entirely overlooked in the Pevsner entry.
6 N. Pevsner and Bill Wilson, *The Buildings of England: Norfolk 2: North-West and South*, 746–47.
7 [J. M. Neale], *The History of Pues; A Paper Read Before the Cambridge Camden Society. ... With an Appendix Containing a Report Presented to the Society on the Statistics of Pews, etc.* (Cambridge, 1841).
8 'If we cannot yet announce that every battlemented enclosure, every towering partition, has been levelled with the dust, we may confidently affirm that so many breaches everywhere appear... that no reasonable doubt can now be entertained of a complete and speedy victory' (*The Ecclesiologist* 3 (1847), 187).
9 Nigel Yates, *Buildings, Faith and Worship* (Oxford, 1991), 192–229.
10 Parishioners at St Mary's Church, Lydiard Tregoze (Wiltshire), for example, struggle to accommodate a growing congregation within the fragility of the historic pewed interior, the subject of an unpublished report for English Heritage by Hugh Harrison in 2004. Copies on deposit with the Church Buildings Council and National Monuments Record, Swindon.
11 Paul Thompson, *William Butterfield* (London, 1971), 482–86.
12 William Butterfield, 'Church Seats' published in the *Church Builder* 1885, 77–82, reprinted on pages 231-35 below.
13 Terry Hardy, *St James, Kingston: a Jewel in the Purbeck Hills* (2009), 3.
14 *The Ecclesiologist* 15 (1854), 89–93, quote on p. 90, and 157–161, quote on pp. 158–59. Reprinted below, pages 239–44.

2. Liturgy and spaces: some recent trends

Peter Moger

THE CHANGING ARRANGEMENT of church buildings over time offers a fascinating commentary on the development of Christian worship. The Reformation saw east-facing altars give way to communion tables placed lengthways in the chancel. The eighteenth-century fashion for box pews and three-decker pulpits reflected the stress on preaching at the time. The ornate sanctuaries and elevated high altars of the late nineteenth century grew out of Anglo-Catholic concerns to restore the sacramental dimension to worship.

A major twentieth-century development was that of the Eucharist taking centre-stage. The 'Parish Communion Movement' led to churches (across all traditions) making Holy Communion the main Sunday service. Practically, this meant the installation of nave altars, a presiding priest facing the congregation, and attempts to articulate spatially 'the Lord's people gathered around the Lord's table on the Lord's day'.

Another important feature of late-twentieth-century worship was the influence of Charismatic renewal within the historic churches. This led to greater freedom and informality, with the exercise of the Holy Spirit's gifts, and changes in musical style (hymns and choirs giving way to songs and mixed vocal and instrumental groups). Choir stalls were removed to accommodate music groups and interiors were often reordered to enable greater informality (Fig. 1).

This article is reproduced from the Conservation Bulletin, *Issue 61 (Summer 2009) by kind permission of the author and English Heritage. Text copyright ©Peter Moger 2009.*

Revision of liturgical texts

The Church of England has always articulated its theology through its worship – and in particular, through liturgical texts. Apart from the proposed 1928 revision of the Prayer Book, its liturgy remained virtually unchanged from 1662 until 1966. Then, in common with other churches – significantly the Roman Catholic Church after Vatican II – a comprehensive programme of liturgical revision began. This addressed the shape, structure and language of worship. These revisions were drawn together in the *Alternative Service Book* of 1980, which remained in use for twenty years.

Anglican worship continues to develop. Perhaps the most striking feature today, compared with a generation ago, is the sheer variety of types and styles on offer – both between parishes and within parishes. The post-modern context we now inhabit accepts diversity (and choice) as a norm. The Church of England's most recent liturgical revision has sought to address this while still uniting the church through common liturgical structures and core texts. These principles underpin *Common Worship: Services and Prayers for the Church of England* (2000–2008). Within this resource, there are several significant trends, all of which impact on the ordering of buildings.

The centrality of baptism

Recent thinking stresses the centrality of baptism – the sacrament that confers Christian identity. Historically, fonts have been at the church door – symbolising the entry of the new Christian into the Church. Renewed interest in baptism has brought two developments. One is a growth in the number of baptismal pools, recalling ancient practice and reflecting a shift towards immersion baptism (principally for adults but also for infants). The second is the strategic placing of the font at the west end of the building, to ensure its immediate visibility as a reminder of baptism (as in the recent example at Salisbury Cathedral).

Seasons, movement and senses

There was little official provision for the celebration of the seasons of the Christian Year before the 1980s. *Common Worship* offers extensive seasonal material, which has been enthusiastically adopted. Prime examples include:
- Ash Wednesday service with imposition of ashes
- Palm Sunday procession with dramatic reading of the Passion
- Eucharist of Maundy Thursday with foot-washing
- Easter Vigil with lighting of the Paschal Candle and renewal of baptismal vows
- Carol services and processions in Advent.

Many seasonal services involve significant movement within the liturgy. A Palm Sunday procession begins outside and moves into church, representing Christ's entry into Jerusalem. An Advent procession typically involves west–east movement, illustrating progression from darkness to light. At baptism, too, movement to and from the font is encouraged. Within all traditions, there is a growing use of 'prayer stations' at points around the building, and the concept of 'liquid worship' depends on the ability of a congregation to 'flow' from one worship station to another within a service.

Traditionally, in Anglican services, worshippers' participation is auditory: they listen and respond! A greater proportion of people, though, prefer to engage visually, and far more still are kinaesthetic learners. The imposition of ashes on Ash Wednesday and foot-washing on Maundy Thursday make a genuine impact on those who prefer to engage in worship other than through words. These traditional ceremonies, now reclaimed as part of the official liturgy of the Church of England, are just part of a burgeoning of multi-

Fig. 1: Musicians lead singing at an informal Anglican service – an example of the influence of Charismatic renewal within historic churches. (© Tim Lomax. Used by kind permission)

sensory worship which spans the traditions. These developments raise serious issues for church ordering, not least where existing furniture is fixed! It is hard to seat twelve people in a circle for foot-washing if there is no available space. Likewise, a procession to the font is difficult if the aisle width is narrow.

One sign of the impact of technology on worship is the growing numbers of screens in churches for projection of text and image. There are clear benefits from their use, but also questions to be asked, both aesthetic and liturgical – does, for instance, the person controlling the projector become the effective 'leader' of screened worship?

Domestication

Some reorderings are clearly motivated by a desire to make church buildings more 'user-friendly'. While buildings should aid mission, questions need to be asked about their primary purpose as worship spaces. Are they 'houses of God' (places of holiness) or 'meeting places for God's people' (places of homeliness)? Strong views (not always in line with the perceived Evangelical/Catholic divide) are held on both sides of the debate, but it is clear that there are moves towards the 'domestication' of church interiors. At the same time, there is evidence of reaction, with a growing following for emerging forms of worship in which mystery is a core element.

The current diversity in worship is both exciting and bewildering for those attempting informed decisions about the ordering of worship space. What remains to be seen is how many of the current trends will endure in a culture in which the rate of change is ever-increasing.

3. The Temple of His Presence

Peter Doll

THE GOTHIC REVIVAL continues to have a profound impact on our expectations of the appearance of a church. In 2000, the Ecclesiological Society's conference of a few year's earlier led to the publication of a volume on the Cambridge Camden Society entitled *'A Church as it Should Be'*, which reflected how far that Society's ecclesiological assumptions have shaped the definition for many churchgoers – and, probably, for even more no-longer-churchgoers – of what a church should look like.[1] A church of which I was until recently vicar, St Michael and All Angels, Abingdon, was a typical example of such a building. It is set alongside an attractive Victorian park; its design (cruciform, with nave, transepts, and chancel distinguished by a dwarf screen) came from the office of Sir G. G. Scott, and it was built between 1864–7.

The late Nigel Yates pointed out in his penultimate book, *Liturgical Space*,[2] that although the early Camdenians had railed against the prevalence of pews filling church interiors, by the 1870s churches were being built in which the rules of ecclesiology in relation to the position of font, altar, and pulpit were strictly applied, but which were themselves crammed full of pews. St Michael's was one such church. Some pews had been removed over the years (from the crossing and from the area in the south-west corner to which the font had been moved) but by and large the church retained its Victorian, intensively-seated appearance (Fig. 1). Not only could the seating accommodate

Fig. 1: St Michael and All Angels, Abingdon, before the recent changes. © John Ward, all rights reserved: www.flickr.com/photos/oxfordshirechurches

numbers far in excess of our usual Sunday congregation (around 70), it also effectively constrained the shape of our worship and other potential uses of the building.

The processional form of the church

One reason the Camdenians railed against pews was that they effectively choked the symbolic expressiveness of the building. Each Gothic church was built as a microcosm, a universe in miniature, bringing together earth (in the nave) and heaven (in the chancel), each distinguished but also joined by the rood and its screen. The sacrifice of the cross unites earth and heaven and shows God's people the way from one to the other. Further, the entire Christian life is encompassed by the building and by the eucharistic liturgy which the church is designed to show forth: from the font by the entrance, to the liturgy of the word in the nave (exemplified by the pulpit) and then through the screen to the heavenly banquet of the Eucharist at the altar in the chancel.

The pew-crammed interior imposes a largely static setting for what was originally a mobile, processional journey from earth to heaven. Unfortunately, reorderings of older churches since Vatican II and even new church designs have continued to assume a static congregation, preferring to bring the altar to the people, rather than the people to the altar.

The processional form of the Gothic church did not, of course, arise out of a vacuum. Most of our premodern churches are modelled ultimately on the Temple of Solomon. As in the Temple, our historic and historically-informed churches shape our pilgrim journey with a sequence of foci pointing to the way God covenants with us. The font at the entrance to church (like the Temple's great bronze basin known as 'the Sea') speaks of his prevenient grace meeting us on our way to cleanse us. The nave ('the Holy Place'), with its focus the lectern/pulpit/ambo, symbolises the earthly created order, the fitting place for the liturgy of the Word of God made flesh. The rood screen, like the Veil of the Temple, is the liminal sign of our citizenship in both earth and heaven, paradoxically uniting the discrete spaces of chancel and nave while asserting the integrity of each. The chancel stands as the Holy of Holies, where the worship of earth is united with that of heaven, the altar being the place where the one eternal sacrifice of Christ's self-offering to the Father is re-presented on earth.

Worship at St Michael's

The community at St Michael's developed an approach to worship with the intention of working with the symbolic richness of the building rather than being constrained by the pews. We tried to make the hallmark of our liturgy common prayer expressed through common actions and common foci: rather than the congregation being mostly passive spectators at a ritual performed by the clergy on their behalf, we wanted the whole community to be consciously celebrating the liturgy together. Thus the defining action of 'The Gathering' is the congregational procession to the baptistery at the door of the church; its defining focus is the font. (This focus is further expressed by the sprinkling of the congregation with blessed water from the font as a sign that our penitence and God's forgiveness are a renewal of our baptismal covenant.) The common action of the Liturgy of the Word is the gathering back in the nave, and the common focus is the lectern/pulpit. Here the clergy seating is on a level with the rest of the congregation: in the words of liturgical historian Robert Taft, 'All are on an equal footing before the Word of God, all are in need of its purifying effect before approaching the Eucharistic table'.

The defining action of the Liturgy of the Eucharist is the congregational movement into the chancel, and the common focus is the altar. By inhabiting together the chancel space, the 'heavenly' place in the Gothic church, we express our unity with the angels and the saints in the feast of the kingdom. There is one further common focus – on the eschaton or second coming of Christ, expressed by all facing east together. For the priest to go around the altar to face the people would effectively close the circle and declare the journey at an end. To face east together is to acknowledge that the completion of the pilgrimage is in God's future and is dependent on Christ's coming in glory.

After making the stational liturgy a regular part of our worship for several years, doing our best to work around the constraints of the pews, our architect told us that the joists under the wooden sections of our floor were unsound and needed replacing. Since all the pews would need to come up with the floor and many of them were worm-eaten and structurally unsound, the church council took the decision to replace the pews with movable wooden chairs. Not only would this change enable us to use the church flexibly in our worship, it would also allow us to offer the nave of the church for use as a community space – a lunch club for the elderly; toddlers', children's and youth groups; concerts; a meeting space for local groups. Although some members of the congregation expressed disquiet over the use of the church for secular activities, most felt that the medieval example of using church naves as community centres (see, e.g. Sir Roy Strong, *A Little History of the English Country Church*)[3] was a precedent worth emulating. Theologically it was felt inappropriate to suggest that God was interested only in our prayers and not in the rest of our lives; it was argued that a powerful statement of incarnational faith could be made by bringing the everyday life of our community into close contact with the sacred liturgical space.

In addition we sought to use the opportunity presented by the removal of the pews to articulate more carefully and even expand the symbolic reference of the building. Before the reordering, the tabernacle for the Blessed Sacrament was kept on a shelf on the wall to the right of the high altar. This was an unworthy and undignified provision. The tabernacle has now been placed on a stone plinth on a small wooden platform (both of these original to the building and recovered and 'recycled' from other uses) under the centre of the north transept window. The equivalent space in the south transept now has a servery where refreshments are provided after the liturgy.

The expansion of symbolic reference came with the installation of the 24-foot diameter labyrinth, inspired by examples in Chartres and other cathedrals (Figs. 2 & 3). Originally, we envisaged that it would be used primarily as means

Fig. 2: St Michael's after the introduction of chairs in the nave, and the creation of the labyrinth at the west end. The processional form of the church, from font, to pulpit, to altar is evident. The cleared spaced in the transepts can just be glimpsed, that in the north for the Blessed Sacrament, that in the south for refreshments.

Fig. 3: When appropriate, the chairs can be arranged choir-wise.

of spiritual exploration and prayer by individuals and groups (as indeed it has been) and as a sign of Christian life as a pilgrimage. A fuller appreciation of the medieval understanding of the labyrinth has helped us appreciate its deeper symbolic significance. The imagery and texts associated with the medieval French and Italian labyrinths consistently referred to Theseus and the Minotaur, because Theseus was seen as a precursor of Christ, the strong man who descended into the depths of hell, fought and conquered Satan, and emerged victorious leading those who had been imprisoned by sin and death (1 Peter iii. 18–21). This theology of dying, descending, and rising again is also expressed in the sacrament of baptism (Romans vi. 3–4), so the close conjunction of the two has become an apt expression of the living out of the gift of baptism in the life of the church. Happily, we were able to find a labyrinth design that not only reflected this tradition but also had an impeccable local pedigree – in an early-eleventh-century manuscript from Abingdon Abbey of Boethius *De consolatione philosophiæ*. When the nave seating is arranged choir-wise (Fig. 4), the labyrinth with a legilium at the centre also becomes an effective focus of the liturgy of the Word.

'A church as it should be'

The removal of the pews gave the community at St Michael's the opportunity to engage more deeply with the sacred geography of their church building, to deepen their experience of worship, and to transform themselves in Christ for ministry and mission to the community. It is no exaggeration to say that St Michael's has been literally and metaphorically 'set free' to renew its life. It has

Fig. 4: Coffee after the service, the labyrinth in use.

deepened the community's identity as a pilgrim people, as the Body of Christ through baptism, and as a priestly people called to serve God in all his people. This setting free is true not simply for the congregation – I think it is true also for Scott's building. The old pews had tyrannised and choked and darkened the space, masking the graceful proportions and details and the processional rhythm of the nave piers, all now revealed in the renewed space. We believe St Michael's is in every sense 'a church as it should be' for the twenty-first century.

Notes
1. Christopher Webster and John Elliott (eds.), *'A Church as it Should Be': The Cambridge Camden Society and its Influence* (Stamford, 2000).
2. Nigel Yates, *Liturgical Space: Christian Worship and Church Buildings in Western Europe 1500–2000* (Aldershot, 2008), 121–22.
3. Roy Strong, *A Little History of the English Country Church* (London, 2007).

4. Pews in Norwegian churches

Oddbjørn Sørmoen

THE QUESTION of relevant furnishing in churches is as old as the Church itself; and the current discussion about what is appropriate and acceptable for a church in our time is not confined to the British Isles. Norway is also, perhaps surprisingly for many, facing a battle between pews and chairs. The discussion is often regarded as being between conservative preservationists and progressive charismatic believers, but the question is far more complex than this.

Churches have always been fitted out to suit the relevant kind of service and liturgy, be it Anglican, Roman Catholic, Lutheran or any other. In spite of all the theological differences, the same *stylistic* changes have through the centuries swept over all the denominations approximately at the same time, although the consequences for the fittings were different due to the variety of liturgical practices. The question of pews versus chairs that sweeps over the different denominations, however, is not primarily about visual style – but the style of celebration.

Norwegian churches

Except for the two hundred years after the Black Death (1349/50), churches have been built in Norway at all times since the eleventh century. There are today 1,600 Lutheran churches in Norway for a population of 4.5 million, of whom about 80% are members of the State church, the Church of Norway. On average, 95 individuals attend every service, according to national church statistics for 2007.

The oldest and internationally most famous church buildings are the medieval wooden stave churches, of which some are up to 800 years old. The number of remaining stone churches from the same period is less than 200, the most common building material by far being wood. After a law was passed in 1851 requiring that one third of the congregation should have a seat in the local church, the biggest church building boom since the middle ages started, lasting till the first decades of the twentieth century. There are also a number of churches being built today, some of high architectural quality.

New liturgy

At present there is an organised renewal of the liturgy in the Lutheran Church of Norway, which was initiated in 2003. The renewal, or rather reform, covers all aspects of the liturgy, from the use of the sacred room and the position of the altar, to the liturgical texts, music and hymnbooks. This year (2009) a variety of proposals are being tried out all over the country, and the assessment will be closed in September 2009.

The basic ideas of the renewal are a greater variety of services, involving the congregation more than before, and more adapted to local needs; and celebrating the Eucharist *versus populum* (facing the congregation) although it has by no means in modern times been celebrated facing east to the same extent as in the Tridentine mass. The waves of the international liturgical movement which spread out from Vatican II in the 1960s, have finally reached the shores of Norway.

The demand for change, however, came long before the present idea of a new liturgy. A congregation is no island but a part of wider church movements and trends. Quite often the new ideas come with a change of clergy. He or she did not 'grow up' with the old church, and lacks the intimate feeling for the local history and the local sacred room. Some times the 'dear old church' seems outdated compared to fresh ideas.

No uniform international trends

For someone who tries to keep up with what goes on internationally in contemporary church architecture and also in different denominations, it is easy to see that there is no uniform movement against the use of pews. Many of the new 'church icons', like Richard Meyer's Jubilee Church in the suburb Tor Tre Teste in Rome, 2003, have contemporary designed pews.

Mortensrud parish church, 2002, in one of the more recent suburbs of Oslo, is a celebrated piece of architecture, designed by the architects Jensen & Skodvin, well represented in international magazines and books about contemporary church architecture. The project was carried out in close cooperation with the congregation, which explicitly asked for pews (Figs. 1 & 2). They wanted a church 'where people want to get married', a church open to everyone, including those who want to remain anonymous. The pews were made in spite of strong opposition from the official Church Building Consultant, employed by the Ministry of Culture and Church, who was an advocate for the inclusive, flexible way of celebration.

Mortensrud is the exception rather than the rule: one dominant feature of Norwegian churches built in the last 25 years is the lack of pews and the presence of chairs, as if it were a

Figs. 1 & 2: The celebrated Mortensrud parish church in Oslo, architects Jensen & Skodvin, 2002. The church was built in close cooperation between the architects and the congregation, deliberately with pews.

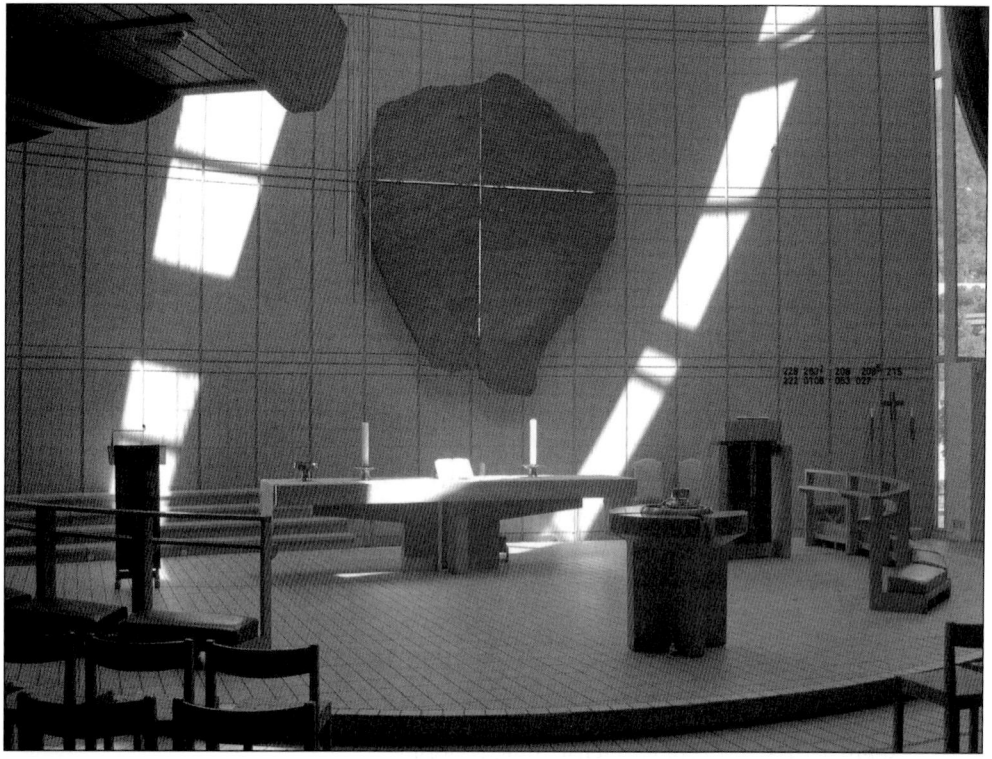

Figs. 3 & 4: Fyllingsdalen parish church in Bergen, architect Hjertholm, 1976. A highly sensitive interior concept where flexibility is paramount and chairs have always been inevitable.

credo (Figs. 3 & 4). It seems that many equate pews with traditionalism; a forward looking congregation feels there should be 'new wine in new bottles'!

Seating comfort

Nobody denies that old pews *may be* uncomfortable, though they are not necessarily so. The Directorate for Cultural Heritage, which is involved in advice and decision-making in churches of heritage value, has published guidelines for adjusting old church pews, to make them more comfortable to sit on without ruining the often characteristic style (see appendix). With good craftsmanship and sensible demands, it is often possible to make sufficient adjustments without reducing much of the historic value of the pew or the church interior. In Norwegian churches the ends are the most important part of the pews, seen from the heritage point of view. Very often simply providing cushions, either individual or covering the whole seating, is the best means of improving comfort.

When the seating becomes a symbol

Looking at the trends of the last 30 years, the question of comfort does does not often seem to be the crucial factor. This is about something else, something more symbolic; a question of 'what a church should be'. The image of the church should fit the liturgical ideals, and these often come from other sources than traditional church architecture. They often, but not always, come from expanding American charismatic movements, where liturgy in the traditional sense hardly exists. A characteristic of these temples is often the big open hall, the totally flexible room, similar to a modern concert venue with a stage in the front, where the pastor and a band can move freely. The 'heavy' symbolic architecture becomes an obstacle.

These churches have cut their formal links with the two-thousand-years-old liturgical tradition, perhaps because modern man does not comprehend the rituals or because they have a vision of the 'original' biblical service. The dioceses with a traditionally strong link with the USA, the 'bible belt' in the south and west of Norway, seem to have more confrontations with the heritage authorities because of this. The possible temperature of the discussion is illustrated by the fact that at a church building conference last year the Directorate for Cultural Heritage was compared with the 'movements that turn the cross upside down', because of a dispute about the protection of church pews.

Another inspiration is the Lutheran liturgical movement much present in Northern Germany and Sweden. Here the idea of taking out the pews completely to be able to celebrate the service in the centre of the nave, with chairs in half circles on the northern and southern side, is the extreme example.

Why pews can be important

Most people appreciate the significant differences in the design of a pew and a chair. Some people also see symbolic differences, like the 'individual' chair and the pew of 'fellowship', or the 'flexible' chair and the 'rigid' pew. However these symbols are in themselves not important from a Norwegian heritage or design point of view.

For the interior of a historic church, however, the difference between the pew and the chair does matter, especially if the pew or the chair is a part of the historic fabric or character. If it is a part of the historic fabric, be it the original or from a period of a major conscious 'recreation' or restoration, the particular chairs or pews are regarded as very important. To change the seating would be a grave intrusion in the historic building, its design and character (Figs. 5 & 6).

There are also examples, especially from the period between the wars and the 1950s, when the historical 'character' was recreated with the original reredos and rood screen, returned from a museum, when the complementing pews were neither original nor exact copies but the design and position was a reflection of the original. In these examples it is the 'period colour', the 'character' rather than the actual fabric that is important. It is much easier to make adjustments to, and remove parts of, these pews than if they were originals.

The pew has a uniform visual stability. This often contributes considerably to the character of the room. The pews usually cover a large proportion of the floor space and fill the room visually. If this is an important part of the historic room, one cannot just remove them, and pretend they have not been there. They were purposely built as pews and have been a part of the total design and history of the church since it was new.

The aim is in some cases to preserve the individual pew, though in Norway usually the question is not 'collecting valuable individual pieces', but protecting the more of less complete interior or the character of the interior.

How to adjust without losing tradition

If we put to one side the question of comfort, the debate is really not so much about pews or chairs, but about flexibility or better use of space. The character of the services has usually changed since the church was built. More often the use of choirs, drama

Figs. 5 & 6: Bragernes parish church in Drammen, architect Norgrenn, 1869/71. In a neo-gothic interior like this, a change from pews to chairs will ruin the interior. Temporary removal of pews for concerts or special services is, however, possible.

groups and greater inclusion of the congregation demand more space. The dramaturgy of funerals and confirmations is also different from what it once was.

Knowing the history of the building is always a key to finding solutions, even if not all the solutions lie in history. Remarkably often one can see that the interior has changed through the ages. In Norwegian churches some of the pews were directed towards the pulpit in the nave and not toward the chancel, especially in the eighteenth and nineteenth centuries. In many churches the pews were changed completely in the nineteenth century, for reasons of taste or style. The 'old' pews were reintroduced in the early twentieth century. Knowing this history makes it more likely that one can make adjustments again. In *Vår Frue*, Our Lady, in Trondheim the front pews were, in a reordering in 2008, simply turned towards the aisle and the new movable *versus populum* altar (Fig. 7); a significant change of the liturgy did not mean a dramatic change of the interior.

Permanent or temporary removal of pews may also be possible, depending on the size of the church. The character is

Fig. 7: Vår Frue in Trondheim, c.1200. A reordering of the existing pews gave the flexibility needed for a new liturgy. A new 'light' mobile altar is seen to the left.

Fig. 8: Bodø Cathedral, architects Blakstad & Munthe-Kaas, 1956. Some of the front pews in this enormous cathedral have been replaced with chairs for flexibility. The chairs fit in better with the period character than in most other churches. The small number of chairs minimises the intrusion.

usually not 'ruined' by removing one or two pews in the front or back, to give more space for the new more flexible services (Fig. 8). Turning the space underneath the gallery into a café or introducing chairs instead of pews does more harm to the historic character.

The need for flexible furnishing is usually not constant. Often there is a need for more space at the time of concerts and alternative furnishing at special events. Some churches have cut their long pews up into shorter sections, which are much easier to handle and rearrange (Fig. 9).

It is frequently not the furnishing that needs flexibility, but the liturgists themselves. Why not tailor the service and liturgy to take advantage of the specific room? Every church has its own

Fig. 9: Fet parish church, architect Schüssler, 1890. The front pews have been made shorter to give the required flexibility and to make rearrangement quick and easy for special services, concerts and funerals.

qualities. Movements in the room and alternative ways of using the space during the service offer new aspects to the celebration.

Sharing understanding

In Norway working with new liturgy in traditional churches has brought together different specialists like theologians, liturgists, art historians, architects and congregations. The aim has been to understand better the others' arguments and reasons. This has been very fruitful for those involved: new knowledge is found, alternatives appear and people appreciate and understand more of their history. This way of working does not solve all problems but enriches everybody and teaches the deeper meaning of both the building history and the liturgy.

❖ ❖ ❖

APPENDIX: Norwegian guidance on adapting pews

Prepared by the Norwegian Institute for Cultural Heritage Research, NIKU, on behalf of the Directorate for Cultural Heritage.

This extract and loose translation has been prepared by the Ecclesiological Society, not by the original authors. In matters of importance, the original should be consulted. The original document (in Norwegian) may be found at http://tinyurl.com/lpqurh, or at the full website address: www.riksantikvaren.no/?module=Webshop;action=Product.public Open;id=88;template=webshop

The Society is grateful to the Norwegian Directorate for Cultural Heritage (Riksantikvaren) for allowing it to make use of this article (for which the Directorate retains copyright); for copies of and permission to reproduce the images in the appendix; and for a speedy and helpful response to our queries.

Introduction

For centuries church benches have been an integral element of [Norwegian] church interiors, but there are frequent complaints that they are uncomfortable to sit on. This briefing suggests various measures that may make them more comfortable. The briefing was first published in September 2000, and a new edition released in 2005.

History and importance of pews in Norway

[This section is not included in this translated extract.]

Issues with chairs

Plans for the replacement of church benches with chairs must be considered in conjunction with the heating system. We need to limit the extent to which we heat our churches if we are to put a stop to the damage caused by dry air, which is close to destroying much church art and many old church interiors throughout the country. We need to use heating systems that provide heat directly to people instead of heating up the entire church, and it is also important that the periods during which the heating is switched on are as short as possible. The only known solution is to use radiant elements mounted under bench seats. There are heating systems which give greater flexibility in the placement of benches or chairs, but they are slow at the beginning and end of each heating cycle, and therefore cannot be justified because they make for unnecessarily long heating periods, and this creates dry air with the risk of damage to valued cultural resources.

Making old benches more comfortable

Many people complain that old church benches are painful, and some people even say that this keeps them away from church. However, there are many things that can be done to rectify the problem.

Cushions

First one should see whether loose seat cushions can improve the situation. Seat cushions are available on the market both for an entire bench and single seats. They are specially designed and adapted for benches, and are usually of a quality that will withstand wear and tear for a long time.

A Norwegian manufacturer of individual cushions also sells racks for stacking cushions and pads at the entrance of the building, so that people can take one or more as desired, both to sit on and for their back. The rack makes it easy to keep track of the items.

With the use of individual cushions, care must be taken that they are not left on a heater under the bench, creating a fire hazard. It is therefore of advantage if they are relatively heavy and equipped with a slip-resistant surface.

Before filling the church with cushions, be aware that increasing the quantity of fabric in the building can degrade the acoustics, particularly with respect to music. The organist should therefore be consulted.

For all types of bench cushions the general rule is that they should be made in natural materials such as wool or leather, and that the colour selected should be harmonious and discreet in its relation to the colour of the bench. It appears that red bench cushions are particularly popular, but this colour should generally be avoided. There is, after all, no requirement that seat cushions in a church should be ornaments to compete with the far more important liturgical fixtures and fittings.

If you choose a leather cover, it must be regularly maintained, so that it does not become dry and cracked. To maintain the leather, you can use the same materials as for saddles, which can be obtained from dealers in riding equipment and from furniture stores. Or you can obtain advice from a leather supplier or a saddler. These materials will also usually act as cleaning agents.

Modification

A more extensive intervention is modification of the bench. The reasons for rebuilding the bench and the appropriate solutions vary so much that it is not possible to give anything other than general advice, based on the most common issues.

A general rule is that you should use professionals as planners and consultants, usually interior designers with knowledge of chair proportioning, or expert furniture joiners. The task is usually too complex for amateurs if you are to get results which satisfactorily meet all the various requirements.

Another rule is that one should always take the time to create one or more test benches before investing time in a larger number.

Often the biggest problem is that the seat depth is too small to provide good support under the thighs. This is often combined with the fact that the seat is horizontal, or worse, tilting forwards. This can be solved in many places by creating a projection at the front of the seat, or by placing a 'seating board' or cushion on the old seat, arranged to tilt slightly backwards. If the wood of the seat is sufficiently thick, the desired slant of the seat can also be achieved by planing the wood away to achieve a more comfortable angle.

In other cases it may be necessary to disassemble and put the bench together again with the seat placed at a correct angle.

If the seat has a rounded front edge, it will be necessary to cut or plane this into a straight edge before adding any projection to the front of the seat, and then to finish off the new work by providing a rounded edge similar to the one the bench originally had.

Adding a projection to the front of the seat may have the drawback that there then is too little space between the benches. In this case, one must reduce the number of benches to obtain enough space. Today's standard distance is 100 cm between each bench back. In old churches it is usually far less.

An increase in height can make the seat too high for most people. In this case, the problem can be solved by cutting the bench ends off at their bases. One should then replicate the specific profiles and designs that previously gave character to the foot of each bench end, to preserve its aesthetic qualities.

The angle of inclination of the back of the bench is often less important than people think, as long as it is not completely vertical. In any case, first try making changes to the seat alone. If this is not sufficient, a narrow and thin, fixed lumbar pad can often solve the problem. This cushion must integrate with the structures and lines that already give character to the back of the bench.

More dramatically, you may have to disassemble the bench and then put it together again with the back rest at a better angle. The use of a new lumbar back board will allow the original bench to be preserved to a greater extent.

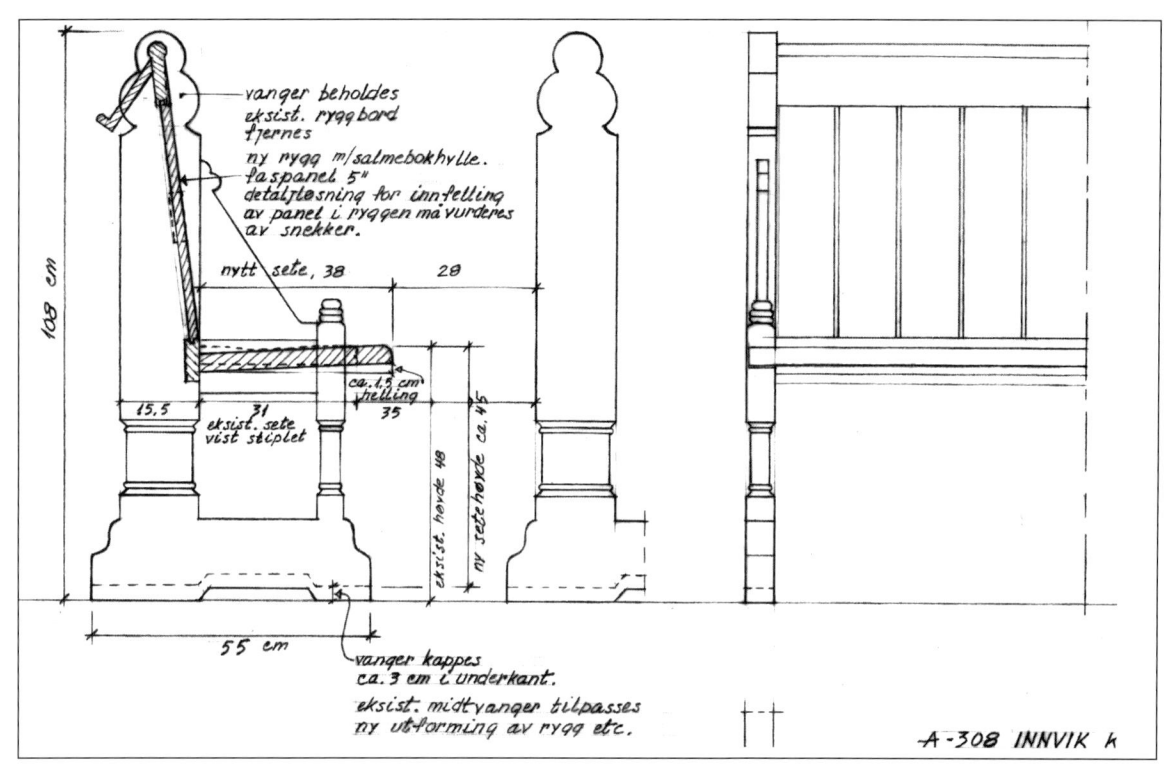

Fig. A1: Aurland Church. For these characteristic bench ends, a proposal to create new seats and back, with maximum reuse of materials.

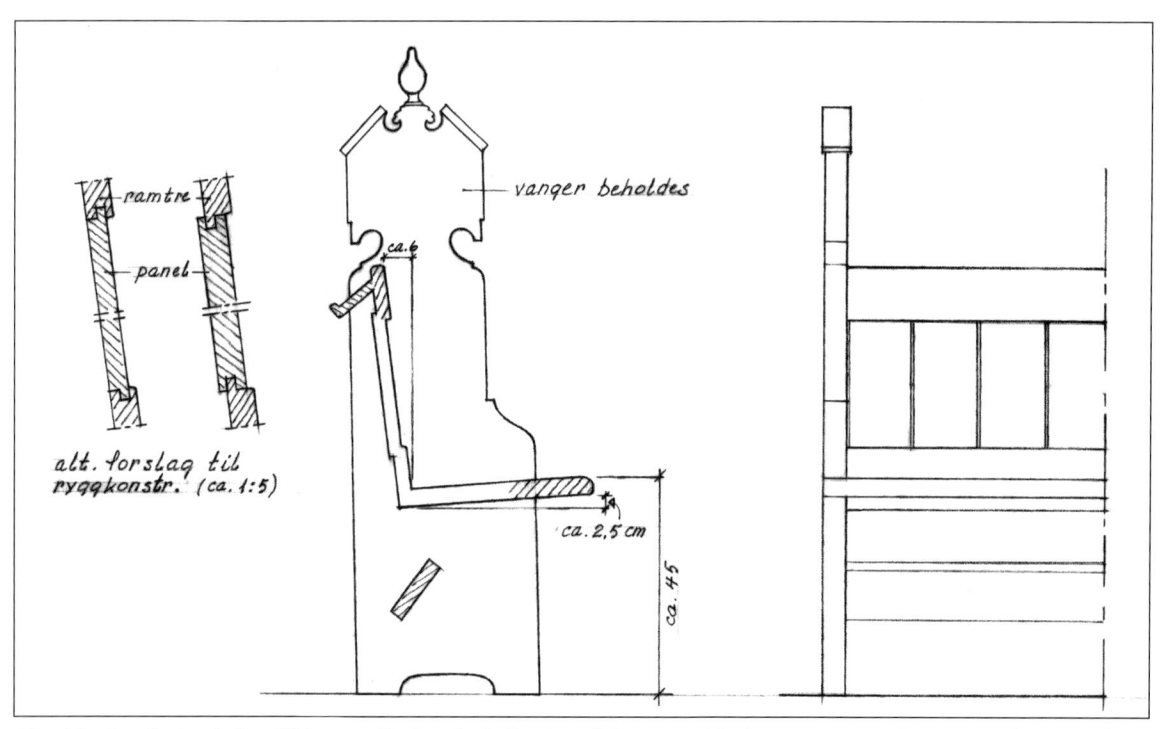

Fig. A2: Innvik church. In addition to adjusting the inclination of the seat and back, it was proposed to remove about 3cm from the foot of the bench end, so that the seat is lowered.

PEWS IN NORWEGIAN CHURCHES (APPENDIX)

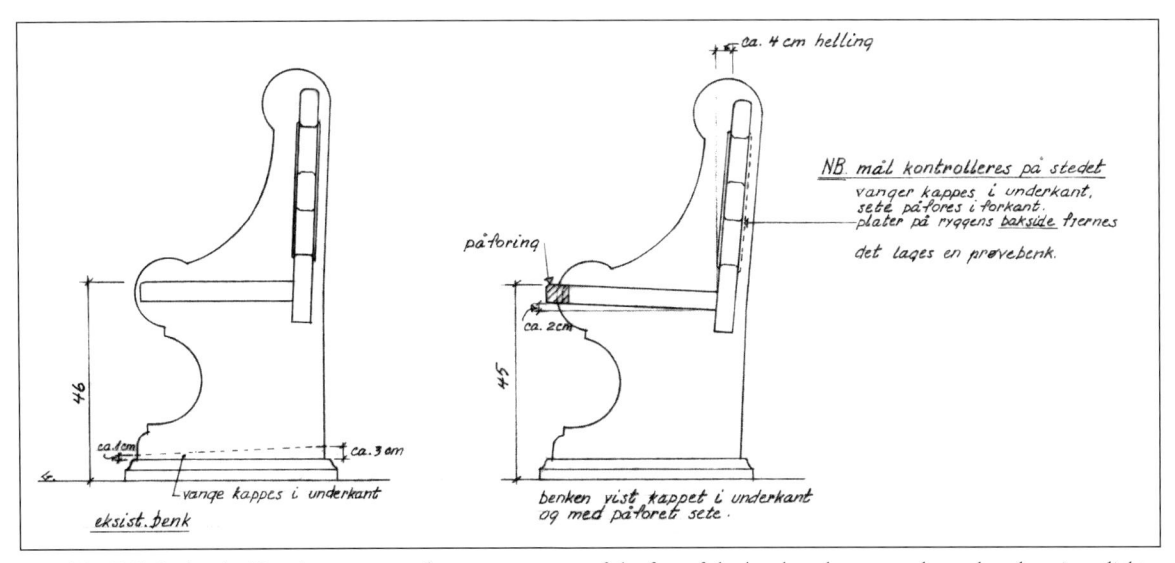

Fig. A3: Råholt church. Here it was proposed to cut away part of the foot of the bench end at an angle, so that there is a slight tilt backwards.

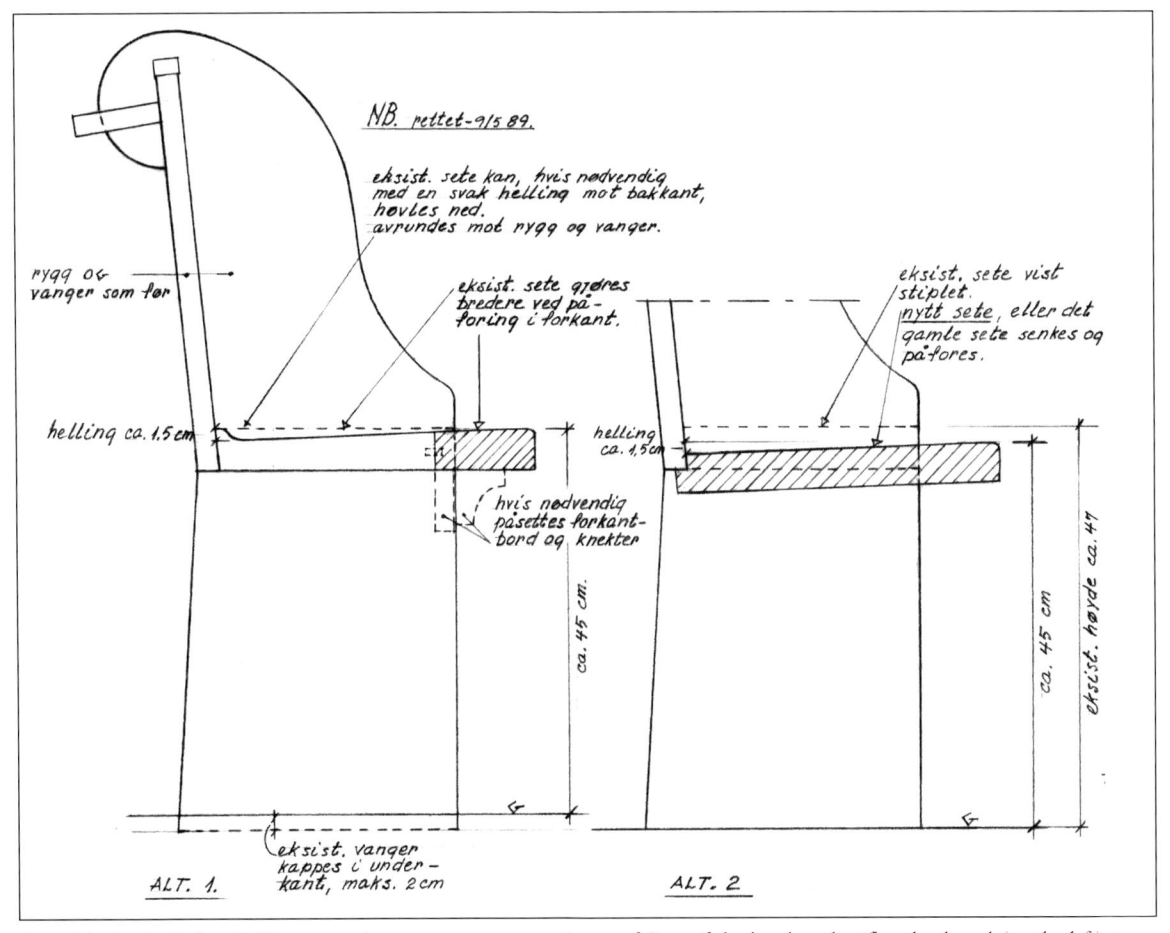

Fig. A4: Sauland church. The proposal was to remove a maximum of 2 cm of the bench end at floor level, and (on the left) to add a projection to the front of the seat, or, alternatively (right), to fix a new seat. The back of the bench is not changed.

For less valuable benches, it may in some cases be appropriate to allow the seat back to be replaced with entirely new material. But only in exceptional cases has it been possible to recommend that an old bench end be replaced, and then usually with a close replica.

Extensive repair of old church benches can be relatively expensive, but usually much cheaper than full replacement. An option that costs less and ensures that some benches remain preserved in their original condition, is to repair only a proportion of the benches. You might choose to do work on the benches in the front half of the church, thus solving the common problem of most people sitting at the back.

Some places have used a cheap and easy solution to improve their comfort, by tipping benches backwards by cutting the foot of the bench ends at an angle, thus making the bench tilt. The result has usually been that the bench loses its sense of vertical balance, and there is a weird kind of streamlined effect, as though the bench were racing down the aisle (see case study below). Although comfortable, this cannot be regarded as successful in the context of a fine church interior.

As a rule, there will be a need for a combination of one or more of the solutions that are suggested here. It will usually not be helpful to force any of these solutions on old church benches where they do not fit. The way a bench is altered must be based on the kind of bench and its structure and design. It is particularly important to find a comprehensive solution: one that provides the desired functional result, while preserving the bench's original character, and artistic and historical qualities.

[A paragraph on obtaining permission from the authorities has been omitted in this translated extract.]

The drawings

[The drawings reproduced here are details from four of the seven drawings on the Directorate's website, using high-resolution versions of the images kindly provided by the Directorate.]

The drawings (Figs. A1–A4) show how small changes can make church benches more comfortable, without to any appreciable degree losing their original look and feel. The most significant measures are to introduce a recumbent backrest and a tilting seat with larger surface area. These proposals, or a combination of them, may suggest ideas to other churches. As a rule, most of the original parts of the benches are reused, to take account of economic and conservation considerations. Before

Fig. A5: Three benches at St Petri church in Stavanger (1866). See text for discussion.

setting to work in earnest, it is appropriate to create a test bench, so that the effect can be evaluated and any necessary adjustments incorporated in the remaining benches.

The drawings were created by Gurly Engelsen, Directorate for Cultural Heritage, in the 1970s and 1980s.

Case study: St Petri Church

Because of their special construction and design the benches in the church of St Petri in Stavanger (1866) were a particular challenge (Fig. A5). To the left is a bench as originally designed. To the right is a bench where the annoying lumbar rail (positioned at the height of the lower back) has been removed, and the bench has been tilted backwards and the seat moved forward.

However, with the diagonal angling, the bench is now tilted and out of balance, and there is a somewhat odd and rather unpleasant effect – the bench looks as though it has been streamlined for racing down the aisle. Furthermore, the removal of mouldings at the base has made the foot of the bench look very clumsy.

In the middle is a test of the final solution, one that proved to be both easy and affordable. A new, padded seat has been placed on top of the old, and this provides a slight tilt backward. The back rail has been replaced with a padded, wider board, which removed the problem the rail was causing. The cushions are made of brown leather, custom made to match the bench's original paint scheme (imitation oak), as this colour scheme was soon to be recreated on the bench. With this solution the old benches remain preserved in their entirety, while the new items are supplementary and could be removed without causing any more damage.

5. How many seats in church?

Trevor Cooper

As this is a complex chapter with much detailed information, I have begun with a summary.

Summary

HUGE EFFORTS were put into church building and enlargement during the nineteenth century in England to cope with the near quadrupling of the population during the century, and the shift from country to town. In the Church of England the pressure to add more seats was at least partly shaped by the grant system, which rewarded the number of sittings inserted into a building. This favoured pews, with their higher capacity, over chairs. A further pressure for pews rather than chairs in all denominations was the 'appropriation' of seating, whereby places were set aside for particular individuals: this requires fixed, rather than movable, seating. Although appropriation declined in the nineteenth century, in the Church of England about one in six seats were still appropriated at the start of the First World War; the practice has since died out.

Unfortunately, in both the Church of England and the nonconformist denominations, more seats were provided than were needed, and with a fall in churchgoing many of these churches were becoming empty by the end of the nineteenth century. Since that time many nonconformist and Church of England churches have closed. But there are still far fewer Sunday worshippers in each church building than in the mid nineteenth century – for example, in the Church of England, 217 worshippers per building in 1851, 60 per building today; in the Methodist church, 97 in 1851, 40 today.

In the Church of England, the number of seats has fallen from a peak of nearly seven million in the early 1900s to something under four million today. Although some of this reduction is due to church closure, or replacement with a smaller building, the majority is due to thinning out of seats in existing churches, for example by partial removal of pews, or by their complete replacement with chairs. Even so, the Church of England is still heavily over-pewed, and is able to seat three or four times as many people as actually attend on a given Sunday, and more than twice as many as attend at Easter. This is an average, of course, and some churches will be fuller than this, and some emptier. This level of over-provision probably encourages churches to remove pews to free up space.

Yet despite perceptions, evidence presented here suggests that the number of churches carrying out pew removal in any given

Pews allowed seating to be 'appropriated' (reserved for the use of particular individuals).

Churches were suffering from overcapacity by the end of the nineteenth century, and were becoming relatively empty.

Graph 1: Number of churches in England, 1851 and at present. There are more CofE churches than in 1851, about the same number of nonconformist churches overall, and many more Roman Catholic churches. Individual denominations within nonconformity show different patterns, represented here by two examples, Methodists and Baptists.

Graph 2: Number of all-age Sunday worshippers per church building in England, 1851 and at present. It is notoriously difficult to define and measure church attendance, so the precise numbers need to be treated with caution, but the general pattern is clear – there are fewer people per building now than in 1851, implying that buildings are today functioning well below their seating design capacity. Note that the data understates the number of people in 1851, as it only counts attendance at one service, the best attended one on Census Sunday 1851.

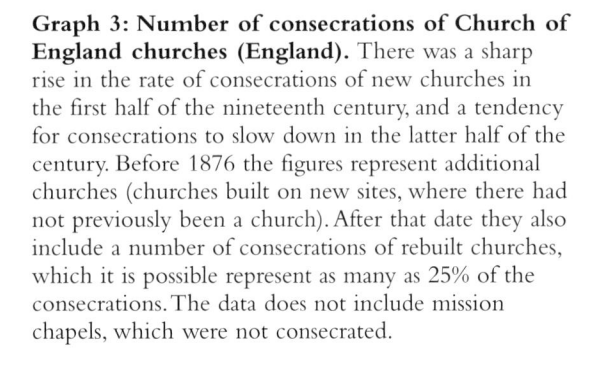

Graph 3: Number of consecrations of Church of England churches (England). There was a sharp rise in the rate of consecrations of new churches in the first half of the nineteenth century, and a tendency for consecrations to slow down in the latter half of the century. Before 1876 the figures represent additional churches (churches built on new sites, where there had not previously been a church). After that date they also include a number of consecrations of rebuilt churches, which it is possible represent as many as 25% of the consecrations. The data does not include mission chapels, which were not consecrated.

Graph 4: Number of Church of England churches in England. The number of Church of England churches rose slowly before the middle of the nineteenth century and then more sharply. The peak appears to have occurred in the middle of the twentieth century. The broad shape of the graph is almost certainly correct, but it should be noted that the data up to and including 1941 overlooks mission chapels, whilst at the same time the figures for 1876–1941 are inflated through the inclusion of any rebuilt churches which were consecrated.

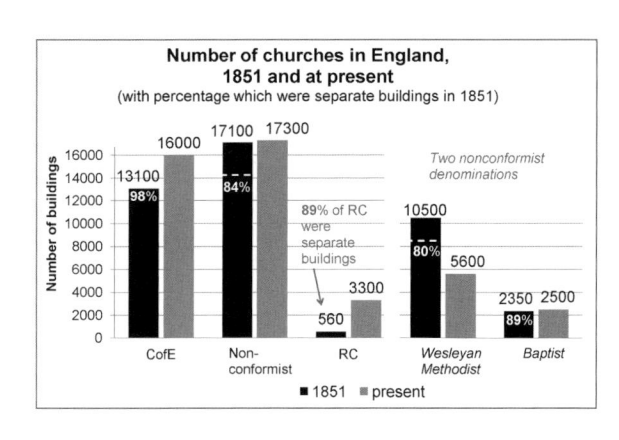

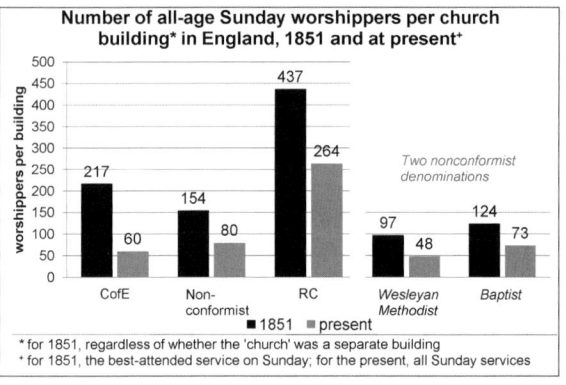

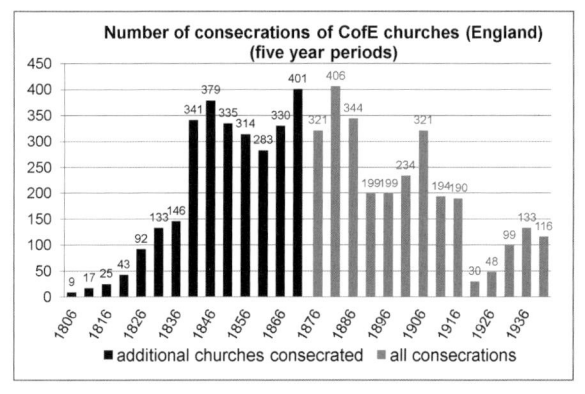

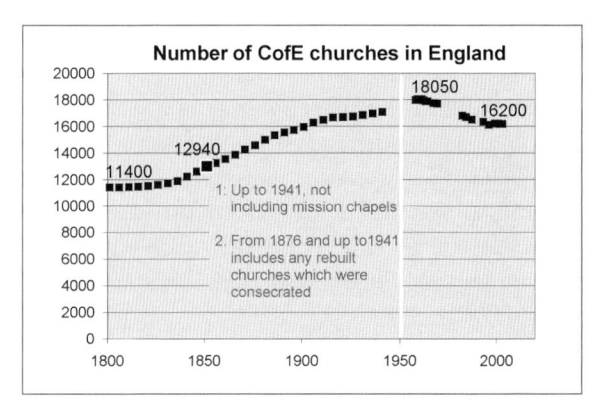

year has been quite small: the recent average rate of *complete* pew removal in Church of England churches is less than one half of one per cent per annum (0.2% for rural areas, twice this for urban areas). The rate of *partial* pew removal has been between 1% and 2% per annum. These rates may be increasing.

The story of the Roman Catholic church is completely different. Starting from a very low base in the early nineteenth century, the number of churches increased right through to the 1980s; since then there there has been a relatively sharp reduction in the number of buildings. Although the number of worshippers at Roman Catholic churches is approximately the same as at Church of England churches, they have about five times fewer church buildings, fitting their congregations in by making use of each building several times on Saturday evening and Sunday. Probably for this reason, there appears to be far less pressure to remove pews in these churches than in Church of England or nonconformist buildings. However, Roman Catholic churches have recently been closing at a relatively fast rate.

❖ ❖ ❖

Purpose

THIS CHAPTER DISCUSSES the number of pews and other seating in churches in England, looking both at trends since the early nineteenth century, and at the current position. Since the number of pews is closely related to the number of church buildings, this too is discussed in some detail, together with levels of attendance to gauge whether the number of sittings is in balance with the number of attendees. Most of the chapter is devoted to the Church of England, finishing with a brief discussion of nonconformity and Roman Catholicism.

Sources for all the graphs and tables are given at the end of the chapter. The word 'pew' is used in a general way to refer to any benched wooden seating (rather than limiting the expression to box pews with doors). The word 'church' is taken to include 'chapel'. The facts and figures refer to England unless otherwise stated. Until 1920 the Church of England was the established church in Wales as well as England, and this should be borne in mind whenever figures are quoted for both England and Wales.

Introduction

The population of England more than doubled in the fifty years from 1801, from 8.3 million to 16.8 million. Over the next fifty years it nearly doubled again, reaching 30.5 million in 1901.[1] This huge increase, together with a shift from country to town, led during the nineteenth century to new churches being built in large numbers, and many existing churches being enlarged.

Our earliest national snapshot of the number of churches dates from 1851, from the Religious Census held on 30 March that year (and never to be repeated). The results are shown in Graph 1, together with the number of churches today. It will be seen that, despite subsequent closures, the Victorian building boom means that in England today there are nearly a quarter more Church of England church buildings than in 1851. The position is very different for the Roman Catholics, who have about six times as many churches as in 1851. It is difficult to be as certain of the number of nonconformist church buildings today, but there are probably slightly more than in 1851 though spread over more denominations.

In passing we should note that the 1851 figures include some buildings described as 'not separate' – these would be rented rooms and public halls, rather than separate church buildings specifically designed for worship. Not many Church of England congregations met in such buildings, but for the nonconformists and Roman Catholics they made up a significant proportion.[2]

Church building continued throughout the nineteenth century. It accelerated from about the middle of the century even though by that time many churches were far from full (Table 1, see right hand column). As Robin Gill has shown in a seminal study, this drive to attract worshippers through increasing the supply of churches led to serious over-provision during the latter part of the century.[3] A further factor was that during this period there was a fall in the level of churchgoing as a proportion of the overall population. Thus by the close of the century many churches were becoming rather empty.[4] New churches certainly could not guarantee a congregation – 'the appearance of disappointing failure [is] suggested by the spectacle of services scantily attended' as one Church of England organisation commented sadly about the small congregations in new church buildings in 1882.[5]

The number of people going regularly to church on Sunday has since dropped further, the exception being Roman Catholic attendance where Victorian and later immigration has had a substantial impact, though even there the number of buildings has outpaced the growth in the number of attendees. The net effect is that there has been a sharp drop since 1851 in the number of Sunday service worshippers at each building (Graph 2). As a result, many churches are today being used by fewer people than they were designed for; and they have much more space than is needed to seat their congregations.

In short, the huge efforts put into church building and enlargement during the nineteenth century in England meant

Table 1: Seats in churches in England and Wales in 1851: number of sittings, proportion of free (i.e. not appropriated) seats, and occupancy (including Sunday School children)

	Number of sittings (million)	Percent of sittings free (i.e. not appropriated)	Percentage occupancy (all-age) at busiest service on Census Sunday 1851	Note
Anglican (CofE)	5.3	46%	56%	1
All nonconformists	4.7	48%	67%	
Roman Catholic (RC)	0.19	51%	134%	2
Total and average	**10.2**	**47%**	**62%**	
Total and average excl. RC	*10.0*	*47%*	*61%*	3
Of the nonconformists:				
Welseyan Methodists	2.2	49%	n/a	
Independents	1.1	41%	n/a	
Baptists	0.75	50%	n/a	
Calvinistic Methodists	0.25	39%	n/a	
other nonconformists	0.40	62%	n/a	4

All figures rounded. 'Not available' indicated by 'n/a'.

Notes: 1. Note that at this date, the Church of England was the Established Anglican church in both England and Wales. For about 20% of the CofE sittings it is not possible to distinguish whether sittings were free or not. The figure of 46% is based on those where such distinction is possible. This problem occurred only to an insignificant extent with other denominations.

2. The RC had more than 100% of their sittings occupied at their busiest service. This may indicate people standing, or may show the difficulties in collecting number of attendances when there were multiple services.

3. This row excludes RC data. Although the RC occupancy is very high, the number of RC sittings is quite small, so does not much affect the overall average occupancy.

4. The 'other' nonconformists included groups such as the Quakers and Brethren with very high levels of free seating, and the Scottish Presbyterian churches in England and Wales, with very low levels.

that the Victorians provided far more church seating than was needed. This overcapacity and the subsequent attempts to deal with it are explored in more depth in the remainder of the chapter, focusing on the Church of England.

The Church of England: churches and attendance

It is only in the last fifty years that the number of Church of England churches has been routinely counted. It is surprisingly difficult to find out how many there were in each diocese before the late 1950s, not least because the church authorities were far more interested in the number of sittings than the number of churches. The best that can be done for the period from 1800 to the 1950s is to use the number of buildings recorded in the Religious Census of 1851 as a starting point, and adjust it backward and forward by using the number of church consecrations each year. Consecrations are shown in Graph 3,

Graph 5: Number of Incorporated Church Building Society grants, cumulative. The number of grants in England and Wales given by the Incorporated Church Building Society (ICBS) for enlarging and reseating Anglican churches far outstripped the number of grants for new buildings or for rebuildings. There were periods of acceleration and deceleration which occurred at different times for each type of activity. This data does not represent all activity, as many churches did not receive grants from the ICBS.

Graph 6: New mission chapels supported by the Incorporated Church Building Society. The ICBS created a special fund for supporting the building of mission chapels in England and Wales. There is a busy period of building in the latter part of the century, tailing away towards the end of the century, then picking up after the turn of the century (the same late increase is shown in Graph 12). The Society was short of cash for making grants for this purpose, and it is not known what proportion of new mission chapels they supported. Those shown here total nearly 800 over the period.

Graph 7: Percentage of Church of England sittings in England which were not appropriated (i.e. were 'free'). The meaning of 'free' and 'appropriated' is discussed in the text. During the seventy years from the middle of the nineteenth century, the proportion of free sittings in Church of England churches rose considerably, but nearly one in six (16%) were still appropriated at the outbreak of the First World War.

Graph 8: Percentage of free seats in Incorporated Church Building Society grants. The grants given by the Incorporated Church Building Society for additional seating in Anglican churches in England and Wales supported an increasing proportion of free seats during the course of the century, as appropriation went out of fashion and those who had rights in existing pews were more willing to give them up.

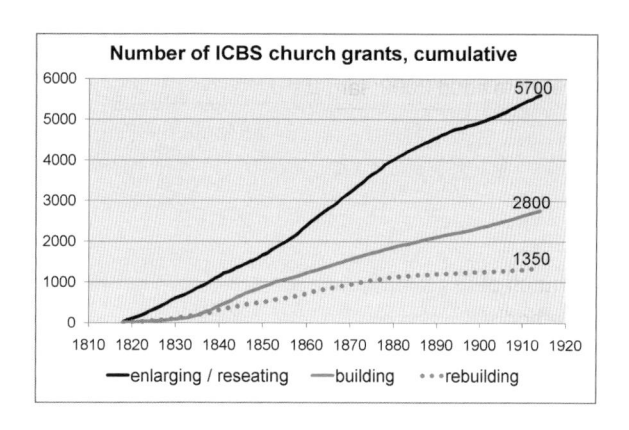

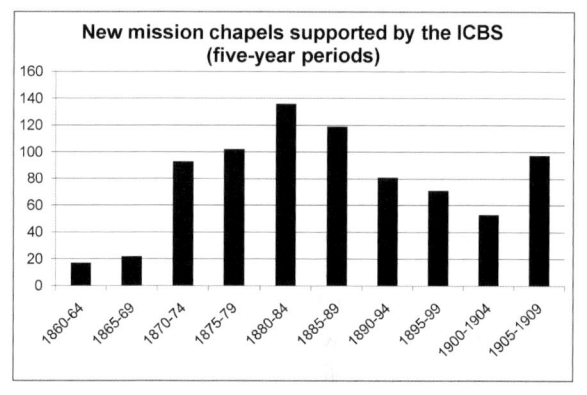

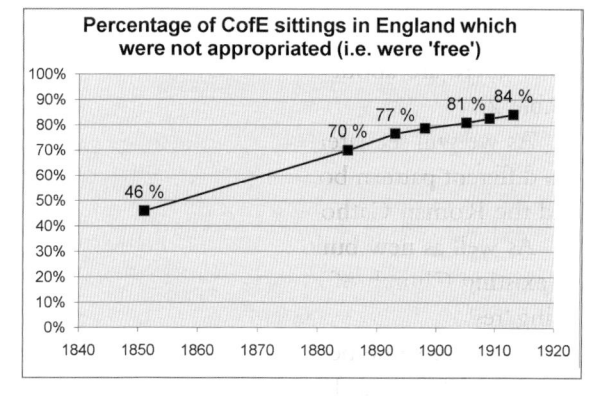

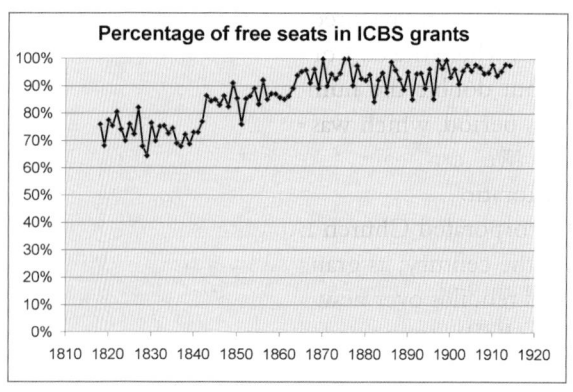

Table 2: Number of listed places of worship (POWs) in England
Data provided 2009; larger numbers rounded

	All POW	Listed POW			
		Total listed	by grade of listing		
			I	II*	II
Church of England	16000	12020	4020	4230	3780
Methodist Church	5350	550	3	31	515
Roman Catholic	3230	570	22	98	448
Baptist Union	1950	250	0	11	235
United Reformed	1470	260	0	19	243
Other Christian	? 9000	860	30	120	710
Total Christian POW	**? 37000**	**14500**	**4070**	**4510**	**5930**
Non Christan faiths		52	3	15	34

from which can be seen the surge in new buildings in the middle years of the century. As shown in Graph 4, in 1851 there were just under 13,000 Anglican churches in England, representing an increase of about 1,500 since the beginning of the century. Numbers then grew faster through the second half of the nineteenth century, followed by slower growth later. A peak of about 18,000 buildings was reached by the middle of the twentieth century, since when the number has shrunk, so that today there are about 16,000, three-quarters of which are listed (Table 2).

As we will see later, this steady rise and subsequent gentle fall is a different pattern both from the nonconformist denominations and the Roman Catholics.

As well as new buildings on new sites, a much larger number of existing Church of England churches – often medieval – were being 'restored' and extended and enlarged during the nineteenth century, with some being pulled down and rebuilt.[6] For example, between 1840 and 1875 approximately 5,300 medieval parish churches were restored or rebuilt in England (only counting those cases where the cost of the work was more than £500), which was about double the number of churches on new sites built during this period, which was of the order of 2,500.[7]

We can gain further insight into the large number of restorations by inspecting the grant-giving activities of the Incorporated Church Building Society (ICBS) during the course of the century; its grants show a similar dominance of restorations and rebuilds over new building (Graph 5). This is not to claim that the ICBS supported every project:[8] early in the century the Church Commissioners' new churches were not supported by the

ICBS,[9] whilst later the ICBS was low on funds, and was cautious about giving grants to churches in those dioceses which did not support it in return. Additionally, there were always some patrons and donors who would wish to go it alone, without asking for financial support from the ICBS. So the amount of new church building and restoration nationally will be understated by the ICBS figures, but the overall pattern – showing the number of restorations and rebuilds as far greater than the number of new buildings – is almost certainly representative.[10]

One form of new Victorian church building often overlooked is the mission chapel, sometimes known as a 'mission room' or 'mission hall'. This was a popular form of building by both Anglicans and nonconformists in towns in the latter part of the nineteenth century, often built to provide informal services on Sunday or weekday evenings for the labouring poor who would have felt ill at ease attending, for example, Matins or Evensong in the parish church. (Church of England mission chapels, which were typically not consecrated, are different from chapels of ease, which are consecrated churches providing the routine Sunday services but without full parochial status.)

Graph 6 shows the number of new mission chapels grant-aided each year by a special ICBS fund, totalling nearly 800 in the fifty years up to 1910. Some, probably a large number, were built without grant aid from the ICBS, so this understates the overall number, which is not known. However, as discussed later, by the end of the century mission chapels were providing almost 10% of the total available seating in Church of England churches; this suggests that they might have consisted of something like 10% of the building stock (depending on their average size), and this would suggest there were more than 1,500 of them.

Some mission chapels later became chapels of ease or parish churches in their own right, but as patterns of worship and evangelism changed others were closed or sold, with many shutting up shop in the early and middle decades of the twentieth century.[11] They have been little studied, and are often overlooked.[12]

The number of Anglican churches has been reduced considerably from its peak, but not as fast as routine church attendance has been dropping. As a result, the number of Sunday attendees per church building has fallen. On the day of the Religious Census in 1851, the number of adults attending the best-attended service in each Church of England church averaged about 170 per church (217 if Sunday School children are included). Today, the average attendance on Sunday is just over 50 per church (60 if children are included) (Graph 2).

Pews in the Church of England

The remainder of our discussion of the Church of England concentrates on seating, rather than buildings. As well as using national data, in the latter part of this section we will use the diocese of Derby as a case study (the diocese is almost identical geographically to the county of Derbyshire). Derby has been chosen not because it is a typical diocese (even if such a thing existed), but because more raw data is available than for many dioceses – figures for seating capacity and attendance for individual churches have been published for 1823, 1851 and the present, and seating capacity can be gleaned for many of the churches from national reports of 1886 and 1889.[13] The Derbyshire data allows additional types of analysis, and has raised new questions.

Free and appropriated seating in the Church of England

In the nineteenth century, many churches of all denominations provided a mixture of 'free' seating (available for anyone to use) and appropriated seating (where each pew was restricted to the use of certain individuals). As can be seen in Table 1, the proportion of free seating in 1851 was fairly similar across the denominations, a little under one half. The remainder was appropriated. Appropriation requires fixed seating, one reason for the popularity of pews as against chairs.[14]

In nonconformist and Roman Catholic churches, seating was normally appropriated by members of the congregation paying an annual subscription or 'rent', allowing adherents to show commitment and give financial support to the work of their church, an important source of revenue for the non-established denominations, which had no income from the State. The renting of seats has now, of course, largely died away.

The situation in the Church of England was more complicated: some seats were rented, especially in new churches; but other appropriated seats were reserved not through any financial arrangement, but through long-standing custom.[15] Commonly this would be through seats being attached to a particular building in the parish, in which case the pew owner might then have no especial loyalty to the church, merely possessing a pew through the accident of occupancy of a particular building; he or she might even be a dissenter and rarely attend. Sometimes ownership of a pew was treated as a freehold which could be bought and sold like any other property.

As discussed by Christopher Webster in Chapter 13, from early in the nineteenth century through to its end there was a growing (though contested) movement in the Church of England towards making all seating free, to avoid the waste of appropriated

Table 3: Proportion of free seats in CofE churches in larger settlements in 1875
(England and Wales, settlements with population of 2000 people or more)

Size of church (number of sittings)	Number of churches of this size	Proportion of seats which were free				Total
		less than 1/4	between 1/4 and 1/2	between 1/2 and all	all	
200 or fewer	23	4%	4%	13%	78%	100%
201-500	370	8%	16%	15%	60%	100%
501-1000	1125	9%	31%	25%	35%	100%
over 1000	698	11%	45%	27%	17%	100%
overall results	*2216*	*9%*	*33%*	*24%*	*34%*	*100%*

All relevant parishes were circulated. The response rate for this question was 79%. Figures are rounded.

pews being left empty when their owner was not present, and to make the Established church open to everyone. As a result of the continuing pressure for change, the overall proportion of Church of England seats which were free gradually rose (Graph 7), though as late as 1914 (the last year for which data is available) about 16% of seats were still appropriated. This relatively high figure explains why a significant number of pews still show the remains of row-numbers or name-badge holders on their bench ends. Anecdotal evidence suggests the practice of appropriation died away swiftly in the 1920s and 1930s.

This nineteenth-century shift in attitude to appropriated seating can be seen in the grants given by the ICBS for new seats (Graph 8). This organisation had an obligation to support the provision of free seating, with at least one half of the seats it grant-aided being free. At the beginning of its life about three-quarters of grant-aided seats were free, rising during the century to something closer to one hundred per cent, an indication of increasing willingness on the part of other funders and existing pew holders to support entirely free seating when a church was being repewed.

There is a useful snapshot from 1875, when the largest parishes in England and Wales, those with a population of 2000 people or more, were asked the proportion of free seating in their churches.[16] The results are shown in Table 3. There is an obvious pattern: the larger the church, the smaller the proportion of seats which were free. Overall about one third (34%) of the churches in these larger parishes had entirely free seating, but this dropped to half that figure (17% of churches) for those churches which could seat more than one thousand people.

Why should larger churches have been more likely to have had appropriated seating? Some – but by no means all – of these appropriated seats in larger churches will have been in the new buildings raised with the assistance of the Church Building Commission in the three decades or so from 1818 up to the mid 1850s, when it supported, to a greater or lesser extent, the building of 612 churches. In order to support the costs of the clergy and running the building, the Commission deliberately created a mixed economy of both free and rented seats in its new churches (the so-called 'Commissioners' Churches'), and the proportion of free seats it supported hovered between about 50% and 70%. In the earlier years of the century some Commissioners' churches were veritable giants, and though in the light of experience they became smaller as the century wore on (Graph 9), as discussed later in this chapter the later ones were still larger than average, in order to fit the particular situations for which they were built. Between them, these Commissioners' churches held about 525,000 sittings, some 10% of all Church of England sittings in 1851 (the overall number of sittings is discussed later in the chapter). Only 59% of this mass of sittings were free when created, and this goes part of the way to explaining why in 1875 it was found that larger churches were more likely to have appropriated seats.[17] However, there must be additional factors at play here, although I am not sure what they are.

Some ten years later, in 1886, the number of rented seats (forming a subset of all appropriated seats) was investigated by Parliament. The results distinguished between 'new' and 'old' churches, and though the terms are not defined, 'new' seems to mean, more or less, 'built on a new site within the past one hundred years or so'. The results are shown in Table 4, and it is abundantly clear that by this date at least, the majority of churches had no rented seats. Renting was largely confined to new churches, with just under one half (45%) of these buildings stating that they rented some or all of their seats, an important corrective to assumptions which are sometimes made about Victorian arrangements.

Table 4: Proportion of CofE churches with rented sittings in England in 1886

	Proportion of churches who responded that:		Number of churches
	some seats rented	NO seats rented	
New churches	45%	55%	3121
Old churches	4%	96%	8034

For 'old' and 'new' churches, see text.
The final column is the number of churches which responded to the survey.

Graph 9: Average number of sittings in churches funded by the Commissioners. The Church Commissioners for England and Wales initially built some extremely large buildings, to provide maximum accommodation in areas short of church accommodation. Over the next few decades, Commissioners' churches tended to become smaller.

Graph 10: Number of sittings in Church of England churches in England. The number of sittings, including seats in mission chapels, peaked in the early twentieth century at just under seven million (a slightly inflated figure) and has since fallen back to something nearer three and a half or four million (estimated). There are weaknesses in the data, but the general trends are likely to be reliable.

Graph 11: Number of new sittings grant-aided by the Incorporated Church Building Society and Church Commissioners. The first half of the nineteenth century saw the greatest rate of new sittings created in Anglican churches in England and Wales, and thereafter the rate was reasonably steady until a further drop towards the end of the century. As explained in the text, there is some degree of double-counting for a period after, say, the early 1830s, indicated on the graph by declining shades of grey for the Commissioners' contribution towards seating.

Graphs 12, 13 and 14 are shown in logical sequence here, but are discussed out of sequence in the text.

Graph 12: Sittings in Church of England churches in England, by type of building. A high proportion of the overall number of sittings were found in mission chapels between the late nineteenth century and first quarter of the twentieth century. The accommodation provided by these chapels peaked a little before the First World War, and then fell significantly.

This graph is discussed on page 53.

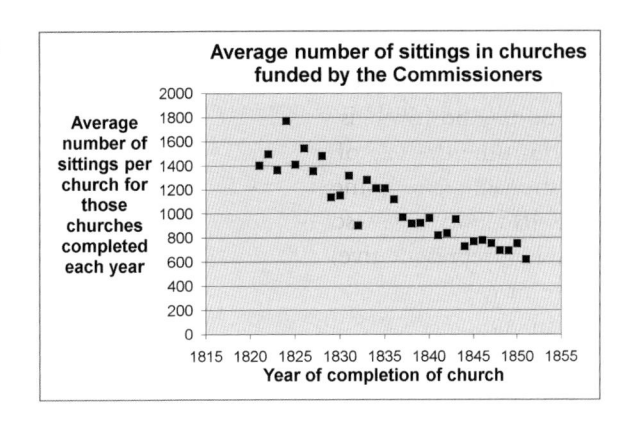

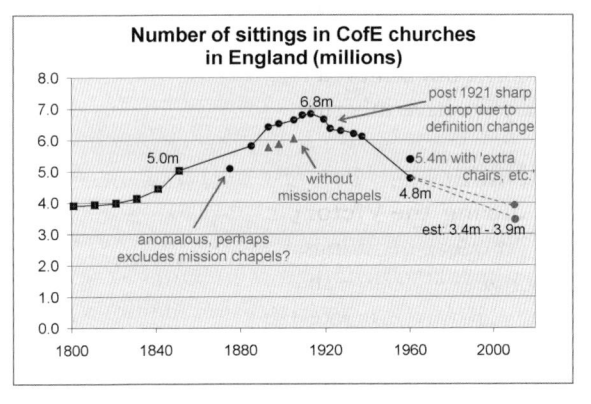

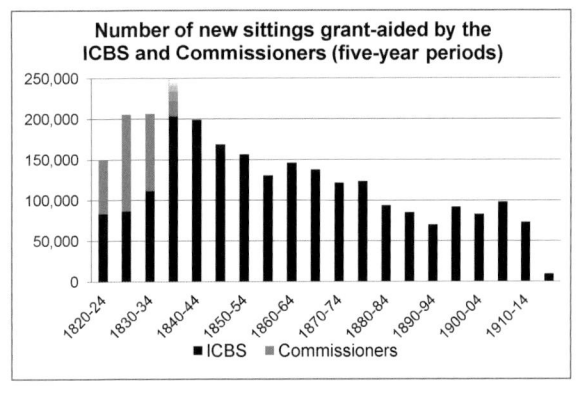

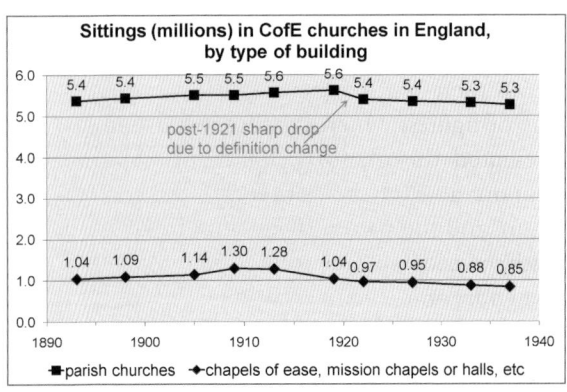

The survey also asked whether churches had seats which were saleable, or had been sold. Here the number of churches responding positively is very low (at 108, about 1% of the sample). By this time the sale of seats was widely regarded as being legally questionable, and some of the respondents explained that their seats had once been sold but no longer were, so (assuming the sample is representative) it seems that by this date the practice had more or less come to an end.

In summary, during the nineteenth century there was a continual reduction in the proportion of appropriated seats in Church of England churches, but they had by no means disappeared by the First World War. Importantly, appropriation requires fixed seating, and renting encourages as much seating as possible, both achieved through pews rather than chairs. This is the legacy we have inherited.

Rise in the number of Church of England sittings during the Victorian period

The number of sittings in the Church of England over the past two hundred years is shown in Graph 10 (note that the figures for today are my estimates). This is the pattern over time for the country as a whole, and there will be major local variations, both in terms of absolute numbers of seats, and the number of seats as a percentage of the population.[18] The graph shows that the net gain during the nineteenth century was – approximately – 2.6 million sittings, an increase of some two-thirds. This is the *net* result: the number of new seats must have been greater than this, as during this period some seats were being lost through the removal of galleries, the ejection of seats from chancels and chapels, and the removal of utilitarian seating for the poor.

When was the busiest time for the creation of new sittings? It is difficult to say, though the ICBS data does provide a clue. Over the one hundred years from its foundation in 1818, the ICBS helped provide some 2.8 million additional seats. The pattern of this support is shown in Graph 11, which also includes the 525,000 completely new sittings provided by the Church Building Commission (though after the early 1830s until the early 1850s there will be increasing double counting between the two sets of figures, which I have tried to allow for in the way I have presented the graph).[19] As discussed earlier, the ICBS did not support all churches undertaking work, so that both the total figure and the pattern over time of Graph 11 needs to be treated with considerable caution, and probably the most that can be drawn from it is to say that new sittings continued to be provided in large numbers throughout the century, and that the latter half of the century may have seen a slightly slower rate than the first

Graph 13: Percentage of churches in each size band in Great Britain, interim results. These interim results are from the yet unpublished National Churches Trust Survey 2010. We are grateful to the Trust for providing these early, unconfirmed findings. They show that the size distribution of Church of England and nonconformist churches are broadly equivalent, whilst Roman Catholic churches are more likely to fall into the larger size bands.

This graph is discussed on page 55.

Graph 14: Church of England churches in England: seating capacity and all-age attendance, various years. Church attendance is difficult to measure. Nevertheless, the graph is useful in highlighting how the Church of England not only has more seats than it needs on Sunday, but the proportional excess of capacity is greater than in the past.

This graph is discussed on page 57.

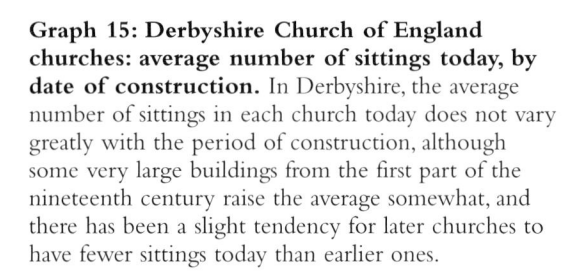

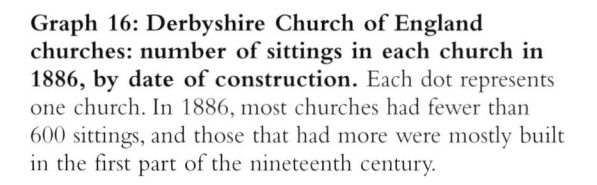

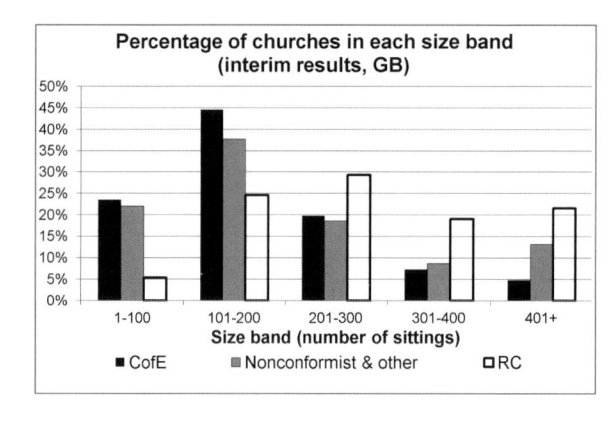

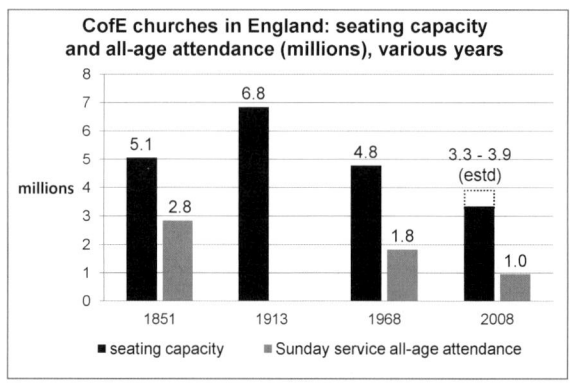

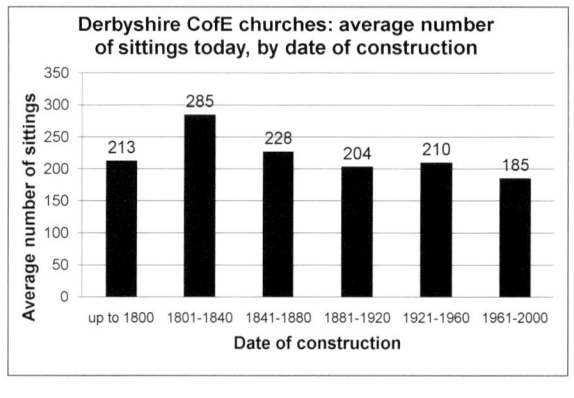

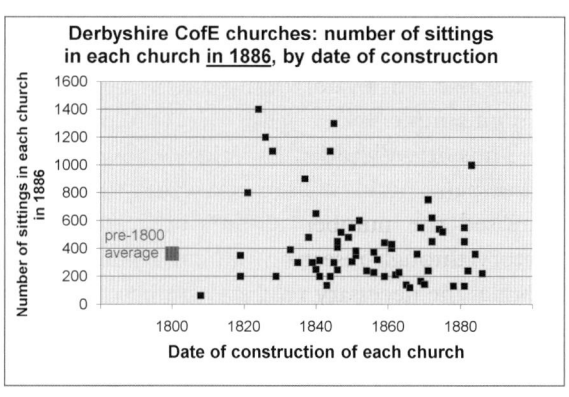

Graph 15: Derbyshire Church of England churches: average number of sittings today, by date of construction. In Derbyshire, the average number of sittings in each church today does not vary greatly with the period of construction, although some very large buildings from the first part of the nineteenth century raise the average somewhat, and there has been a slight tendency for later churches to have fewer sittings today than earlier ones.

Graph 16: Derbyshire Church of England churches: number of sittings in each church in 1886, by date of construction. Each dot represents one church. In 1886, most churches had fewer than 600 sittings, and those that had more were mostly built in the first part of the nineteenth century.

half. If the very large Commissioners' churches are stripped out, the graph of new sittings broadly agrees with the two graphs of schemes shown on page 283.

The fundamental point is the huge, and successful, effort put into increasing the available accommodation in Church of England churches. Although the number of seats did not keep up with population growth, it was not for want of trying, and there was some anguish at the constant dropping behind: 'great as have been these efforts, there can be no doubt that they have fallen very far short of the requirements', as one Church of England report put it in 1875, and went on to regret – in what today seems a somewhat surreal comment – that 'the Church [of England] does not now provide for the simultaneous worship of more than one third of the population'.[20]

Number of sittings in each Church of England church building

Victorian churches tend today to be have more seats than older ones, or those built since.[21] This can be seen in Derbyshire in Graph 15. But these figures include all the changes of the last one hundred years. In Derbyshire, the data also allow us to quantify the size difference *before* the changes of the twentieth century, using data collected in 1886. Most of those built after the middle of the nineteenth century were in the size band 200–600, but in the earlier period 1820–c.1845 about one half of the new churches were very large indeed, with more than 600 sittings. Some of these large churches were probably Commissioners' Churches. In 1886, the average number of sittings for churches built before 1800 was about 360, whilst for those built between 1800 and 1886 the average was about 440 (Graph 16).[22]

We can also carry out a before and after comparison for cases in Derbyshire where a replacement church building was erected on an existing church site (Graph 17). This shows that in 1886, a church which had been built since 1823 to take the place of an existing church almost always had more sittings than the church it replaced. This is in no way surprising, of course – indeed, it may be the least surprising statement in the entire book – but has not (as far as I am aware) been generally confirmed before with a random sample.

Thus new Victorian churches were larger than churches from earlier periods. It is usually also assumed that *existing* churches increased the number of their sittings during the nineteenth century, through reseating and enlargement. The Derbyshire data provides the necessary random sample to explore this idea, and the detailed results are distinctly surprising. My analysis looked at the number of seats in individual churches in 1823 and in the very

Graph 17: Derbyshire Church of England churches: number of sittings for replacement churches built between 1823 and 1886. Each dot represents a replacement church building, put up between 1823 and 1886 to replace an existing church building. Most of them are above the diagonal line, indicating that most of the new churches were larger than the one they replaced.

Graph 18: Derbyshire Church of England churches: comparison of number of sittings in 1823 and 1886 in individual churches not totally rebuilt. Each dot represents one church. Those below the line had fewer sittings in 1886 than in 1823. Some churches gained seating, some lost it.

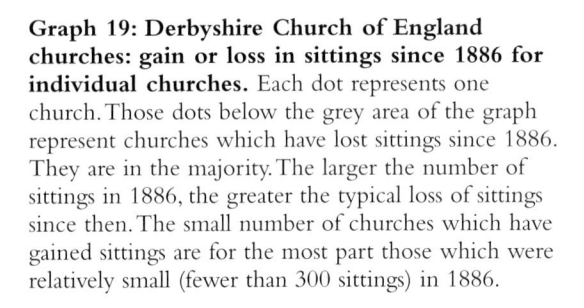

Graph 19: Derbyshire Church of England churches: gain or loss in sittings since 1886 for individual churches. Each dot represents one church. Those dots below the grey area of the graph represent churches which have lost sittings since 1886. They are in the majority. The larger the number of sittings in 1886, the greater the typical loss of sittings since then. The small number of churches which have gained sittings are for the most part those which were relatively small (fewer than 300 sittings) in 1886.

Graph 20: Derbyshire Church of England churches: percentage in each size band. Today, nearly half the Church of England churches in Derbyshire (42%) have between 101 and 200 sittings.

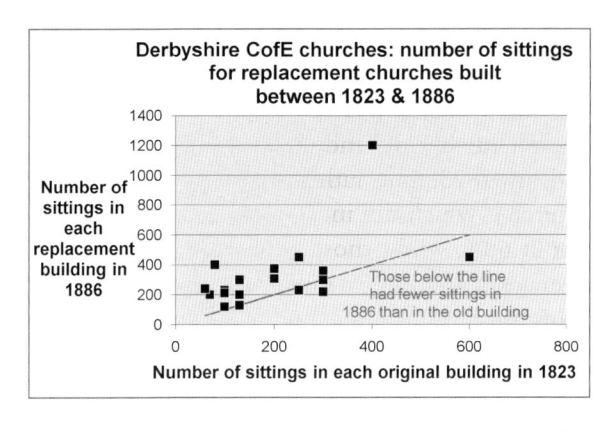

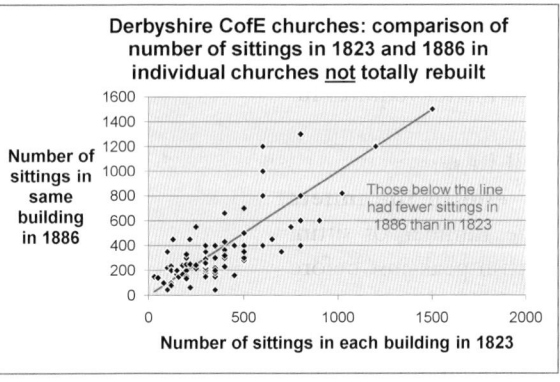

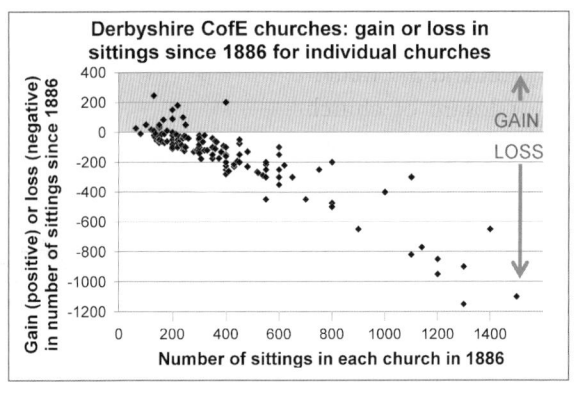

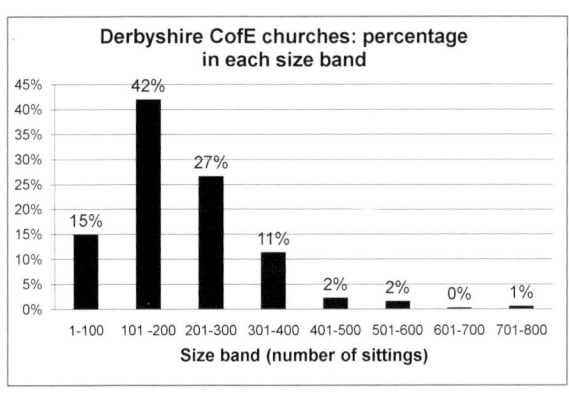

same churches in 1886, excluding those which had been completely rebuilt in the intervening period (though including the many which had had extensions). It turns out that some of these churches did indeed have more sittings in 1886 than they did in 1823, but rather more had fewer (Graph 18). Those churches which did increase their sittings did so by an average of about 60%, whilst those who reduced their sittings did so by an average of about 36%; the overall result is a net gain of about 13%. This is a most surprising finding. If it is correct, and if it is generalisable across the country (which, of course, it may not be) it means that during the nineteenth century some churches were indeed greatly increasing their accommodation, but a significant number of others had cut back on their capacity well before the century was out, and that the overall result was a smallish net gain. The matter requires further research.[23]

Fall in number of Church of England sittings since the end of the nineteenth century

The number of sittings in the Church of England reached a flattish peak just before the First World War, at about 6.8 million. By 1960 the number had dropped considerably, with a reported number of 4.8 million. Some of this drop of two million was due to a tightening up in the method of counting in the early 1920s, but most of the reduction was real enough. Since then I estimate that the number of sittings has fallen further, to between 3.4 million and 3.9 million.

Closure of churches is one way in which seating has been reduced. For example, since 1960 about one in ten churches have closed, and although about one third as many new churches have been built, these tend to be smaller than the ones that have closed. Not a great deal is known about church closure before 1960, but Graph 12, covering the period 1893 to 1937, is suggestive. In this forty year period, the number of sittings in parish churches dropped by just 6% from its peak of about 5.6 million, and much of this probably arose from the tightening up of definitions after 1921, and perhaps also some thinning out of seats. In contrast, seating in chapels of ease and mission chapels combined dropped by a much more significant 35% from the peak of about 1.3 million, suggesting that these buildings – probably mostly the mission chapels – were being closed.

However most of the loss of seating since the pre First World War peak is not due to closure, but due to individual churches reducing their number of sittings. We can see this in Derbyshire (Graph 19) where most surviving churches have fewer sittings than in 1886, except for some of the smallest churches. (This graph only includes churches which have not been replaced with

Table 5: Percentage of CofE churches removing pews each year
Period: 2000–2008; results for seven English dioceses

Diocese	Percentage of churches with pews removed per annum	
	Total pew removal	Other pew removal
	%	%
Bury St Edmunds	0.12	1.10
Derbyshire	0.17	2.20
Ely	0.17	1.46
Exeter	0.13	1.29
Lichfield	0.10	0.93
Manchester	0.44	n/a
Southwark	0.41	1.12
Average	*0.20*	*1.29*

Note: The average in the bottom row is weighted by the number of churches in each diocese

a new building since 1886.) Overall, since 1886 these Derbyshire churches have each shed about 40% of their seating, on average. This is a huge drop. It is not known if this reduction since late Victorian times has occurred over the rest of the country, but I suspect that it has.

The removal of sittings continues today. In 2009 I contacted all the Church of England dioceses in England and asked them for their rate of pew removal since the year 2000. The seven replies I received are summarised in Table 5. Based on this data, a reasonable estimate is that in rural areas roughly two Church of England churches per thousand (that is, 0.2%) have been losing all their pews each year, whereas in urban areas it has probably been about double this rate. Given the publicity and concern which total pew removal has created, this is surprisingly low, and it may be that general perceptions are confused by the much faster rate at which pews are being *partially* removed, which has been rather higher at ten or twenty churches per thousand per year (between 1% and 2% per year). In addition, many Church of England churches (about three quarters) are listed buildings (Table 2), and the consultation process involves many stakeholders, so proposals to remove pews are very public, and may affect perceptions of the frequency of pew removal.

However it should be noted that these figures are based on only a sample of dioceses, and (perhaps more importantly) that this is the average rate of loss over the last decade. I rather think matters are now accelerating.

How full are Church of England churches today?
As mentioned above, I estimate the number of sittings in Church

of England churches today as between 3.4 million and 3.9 million. This is a huge number. To put it in context, it is about four times the number of cinema seats in the UK, and nearly twice as many people as can squeeze into the stadia of all 116 clubs in the top five tiers of the English Football League.[24] In addition there are the seats provided by nonconformist and Roman Catholic churches – a back-of-the-envelope calculation suggesting five million between them.[25]

The implication of my estimate for the Church of England is that each church can today seat between about 200 and 250 people, on average. The only national information available to check my estimate is the initial, unadjusted data from the yet unpublished National Churches Trust Survey 2010 (Graph 13). We are grateful to the Trust for providing these early findings to enable them to be used in this chapter. It will be seen that their data is in line with the average seating capacity of 200–250 which I am suggesting (my estimate was made before I saw the Survey data).

The number of Church of England worshippers of all ages on a typical Sunday in England is about 960,000, so a seating capacity of 3.4m–3.9m means that churches are on average less than one third full, perhaps as little as a quarter full. Even at Easter, the number of worshippers (approximately 1.4m) is fewer than one half the number of seats.[26] These are averages, of course, and some churches will be much fuller than this. On the other hand, some will be emptier.

My estimate is broadly in line with data I published for the diocese of Manchester a few years ago. With much of that diocese being urban, the average church is quite large, and holds about 360 people. Average attendance a decade ago was about 80 per church, so the seating in each church was a little under one quarter utilised.[27]

As I have shown elsewhere, churches in rural areas can be much emptier, as for historical reasons their churches provide far more seats per head of population than in urban areas. For example, some groups of churches in rural areas of the diocese of Chelmsford have seats for as many as one in five of the local population, a very large over-provision. Not surprisingly, in these groups of churches, only 15% of their seats are used on Sunday on average.[28]

In Derbyshire the average church holds about 220 people (Graph 20) and average adult Sunday attendance at each church is a little over 50.[29] Thus, on average, Derbyshire churches utilise 21% of their seating (a little less than one quarter) on a typical Sunday. Graph 21 unpicks this average. It shows each individual church, indicating how well occupied the seating is by adults attending

Graph 21: Derbyshire Church of England churches: percentage of sittings used in 2009 (average adult Sunday attendance). Each dot represents one church. The higher up the chart, the fuller it was with adults on a typical Sunday in 2009. About half the churches were less than 20% full.

Graph 22: Derbyshire Church of England churches: percentage of sittings used in 1851 (adults, Census Sunday). As for Graph 21, but this graph represents the situation in 1851. In fact, it understates the number of adults attending church as it only counts attendance at one service, the best attended one.

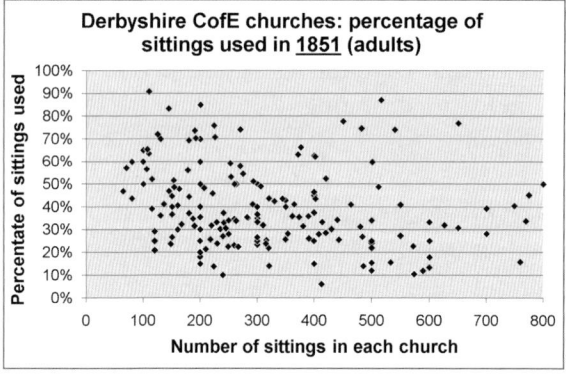

Graph 23: Kent: number of new church buildings, by decade. There was more church building during the second half of the nineteenth century than the first. The Roman Catholics accelerated their building programme, but from a very low base. In every decade, the total of Methodist and other nonconformist building far outstripped Church of England building.

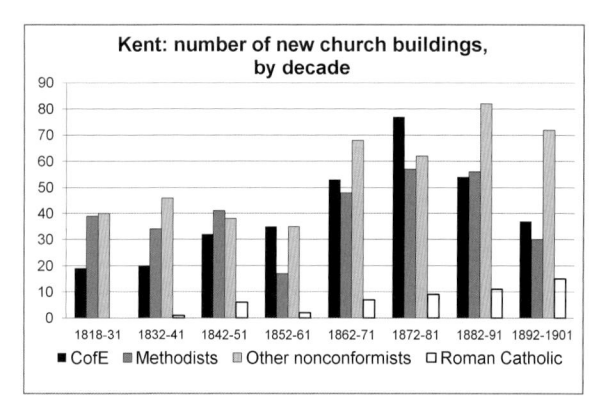

Graph 24: Number of Roman Catholic churches in England and Wales. The number of churches has increased many times over since 1851. In recent years there have been a significant number of closures, though most of these (at least until recently) have not been of parish churches but of other church buildings.

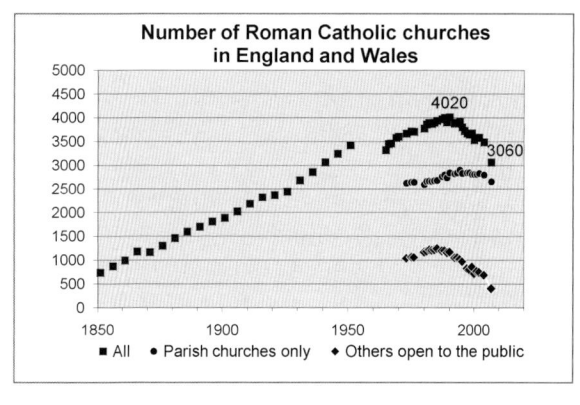

Table 6: Number of churches built in the nineteenth century in Kent and Sussex
Sussex: 1821–1900; Kent: 1818-1901

Denomination		Kent	Sussex
Anglican		327	207
Nonconformist		765	[244]
	Methodist	322	
	Other	443	
Roman Catholic		51	44
Total		**1143**	**[495]**

Note: the figures for Sussex are certainly understated, and probably particularly so for Nonconformist churches, hence this figure is in square brackets

services on a typical Sunday, expressed as a percentage of that church's total seating. The clustering at the lower levels of occupancy is obvious. This is probably not untypical.

It is instructive to compare this with similar Derbyshire data for 1851 (Graph 22).[30] At the best attended service in 1851 the churches were on average about 36% full, if Sunday School children are omitted, about 53% full if they are included. As discussed earlier, it is a myth to suppose that churches were full in mid-Victorian times, but in Derbyshire today they are typically much less full – average seat occupancy has dropped by something approaching one half (1851: 36%; 2008: 21%).

We can carry out the same comparison between 1851 and the present at the national level, including a reasonable estimate of the situation in 1968 (Graph 14). Not too much attention should be paid to the precise figures, which depend on various assumptions, but the broad pattern is clear: the proportional excess of sittings over attendance is today greater than at any time since the mid nineteenth century.

In a nutshell, despite a vigorous reduction in the number of seats since Victorian times, the Church of England is still heavily over-seated. This level of over-provision must surely help explain why some churches are keen to remove pews to free up space for other purposes.

Nonconformist church building and attendance

We finish this chapter with a brief discussion of nonconformity and then Roman Catholicism.

A good starting point is Kent, where one very determined author has managed the feat of tracking the dates of build of all new nineteenth-century church building over the entire county. A plot of the dates of building shows that churches and chapels were being raised during the whole century (Graph 23), with

Table 7: Churches, sittings and attendance in 28 large towns in England, 1851 and 1881

	1851	1881	Increase number	Increase percent
Population	947,000	1,982,000	1,035,000	109%
Number of churches				
CofE	204	456	252	124%
Free	432	1110	678	157%
RC	28	60	32	114%
Total / average	*664*	*1626*	*962*	*145%*
Number of sittings				
CofE	178,000	281,000	103,000	58%
Free	224,000	507,000	283,000	126%
RC	12,000	30,000	17,000	142%
Total / average	*415,000*	*818,000*	*404,000*	*97%*
Percentage of population attending church (total of morning and evening)				
CofE	13.8 %	12.7 %		
Free	20.6 %	20.4 %		
RC	2.8 %	2.3 %		
Total / average	*37.2 %*	*35.4 %*		

Based on Gill, Table 8. The towns were: Barrow, Bolton, Bradford, Burnley, Burslem, Coventry, Darlington, Derby, Gloucester, Gosport, Hanley, Hull, Ipswich, Leicester, Longton, Newcastle-upon-Lyme, Northampton, Nottingham, Peterborough, Portsmouth, Rotherham, Scarborough, Sheffield, Southampton, Stoke-on-Trent, Warrington, Whitehaven, Widnes.

building activity rather greater during the second half. Not surprisingly, as can be seen in Table 6, the number of new Roman Catholic churches was relatively small, whereas the number of nonconformist churches built in that county was more than double the number of Anglican ones; a preponderance of nonconformist buildings is also found in a similar count of new churches in Sussex, even though nonconformist buildings in that county were under-counted.[31]

Because of the large number of nonconformist denominations, their lack of centralisation (in some cases), and their fissiparous nature, there is no country-wide data yet available on the number of nonconformist buildings or their capacity, and there may never be.[32] Overall, though is clear that, during the nineteenth century, the various nonconformist groupings raised more new buildings, and provided more new seats, than the Church of England.[33] Even by 1851 there were in England about one third more nonconformist churches than Church of England ones – in round terms, 17,000 against 13,000 (Graph 1) – though at this date they provided slightly fewer sittings (Table 2): about 4.7 million as against 5.3 million.[34]

Over the coming years nonconformists built more churches, and added more seats, than the Church of England. Robin Gill has published a wide range of area-based case studies comparing the situation at various dates, and this enables us to understand better what was happening. The results of one of his studies is shown in Table 7, for a group of 28 large towns from up and down the country, comparing the years 1851 and 1881. It will be seen that in these towns the nonconformists started off with more seats than the Church of England in 1851, and during the next thirty years more than doubled this number (from 224,000 to 507,000), whereas the Church of England only added a little more than one half of its 1851 number of seats (from 178,000 to 281,000). Thanks to this increase in provision by the nonconformists at a time when many towns were expanding, the percentage of the population attending their church services hardly changed over the thirty year period.

When necessary, nonconformists can – and do – shut their churches relatively easily.[35] For example, in 1851 there were about 11,000 places in England and Wales used by one branch or another of Wesleyan Methodism, of which some 8850 (about 80%) were separate buildings, rather than (for example) hired halls and rooms. By the time of the re-union of these various Methodist groups in 1932, this number of buildings was said to have shot up to about 20,000. Today there are approximately 6,000, and until recently (and perhaps still) the number was falling by (very approximately) one hundred per year.[36] Many nonconformist denominations saw a rise in the number of church buildings during the nineteenth century and a fall since, but I do not yet have the national data to demonstrate this in any detail. The total number of nonconformist churches today is probably slightly larger than in 1851, though spread over more denominations.

Despite this adjustment, nonconformist churches are emptier than they were, as shown in Graph 2. To take just one denomination, the average number of (Wesleyan) Methodists of all ages attending on a Sunday has fallen from 97 per church building in 1851 (at the best attended service on Census Sunday) to 40 today. This would suggest that these buildings are being used by many fewer people than they were designed for, confirmed in Graph 13 which gives the impression that the typical nonconformist church can seat something between 200 and 300 people. It should be mentioned in passing that later nonconformist churches tended, on average, to be smaller than earlier ones.[37]

As well as closure, anecdotal evidence suggests that nonconformist churches are moving more quickly than Anglican churches to reduce the number of sittings in any given building in order to bring capacity into line with attendance, and to release space for other uses.[38] As a relatively small number, about one in eight, of nonconformist church buildings are listed, and mostly at the lowest grade of listing (Table 2), this sort of reordering is less of an issue than with Church of England churches.

Roman Catholic churches and attendance

The story of church building in the Roman Catholic church is completely different, due not only to the large increase in the number of Roman Catholic worshippers, but also to operating with more worshippers per church.

Starting from a very low base in the early nineteenth century the number of churches increased right through to the 1980s, growing about sixfold (Graph 24). In 1851 there were about 560 Roman Catholic church buildings in England with seats for about 183,000 people, and 243,000 people said to be attending on any particular Sunday. There are now about 3,300 Roman Catholic churches, and the number of people attending Mass is of the order of 875,000 (2006 figure).

The buildings are worked hard: even though typical attendance at Roman Catholic churches today is very approximately the same as for the Church of England on a given Sunday (960,000 in 2008), they have about five times fewer church buildings. The contrast with nonconformist and other churches (with approximately 1,375,000 Sunday worshippers in 2005, and just over 17,000 buildings) is similar though less extreme.[39] In short, there are many more worshippers per Roman Catholic church building than in the other denominations, though the number per building has dropped substantially since 1851 (Graph 2). This high attendance per building may be one reason why there appears to be far less pressure to remove pews from Roman Catholic churches than from those of other denominations, coupled with there being less interest, for theological reasons, in using church buildings for purposes other than worship.

As many churches hold multiple services on a Sunday, the number of seats in any given Roman Catholic building need bear little relationship to the total number of worshippers who use that building for worship, but initial results from the National Churches Trust survey do suggest that Roman Catholic churches can on average seat more people in each building than churches of other denominations (Graph 13).

Since the 1980s Roman Catholic churches have been closed at the relatively high average rate of loss of 10% of churches per decade. It is likely that to some extent this closure is driven by a shortage of priests rather than falling congregations, though the data is not available to explore this properly.

Conclusion

In the past two hundred years the number of churches, and the number of people they could seat, has never been static. As a result of a complex history, which includes enthusiastic (sometimes *over*enthusiastic) building and enlargement, coupled with a long-term downwards drift in routine churchgoing, there is now significant overcapacity in many nonconformist and Church of England churches. Some congregations are happy to live with this, whilst others are actively looking for new ways to make use of the excess space they have inherited. It is against this background that we should understand the calls for changes to seating.

Abbreviations (used in sources and notes)

CBAR **1876** House of Commons, *Church building and restoration. Return to an address of the Honourable the House of Commons, dated 22 February 1876, for Returns showing the number of churches (including cathedrals) in every diocese in England, which have been built or restored at a cost exceeding £500 since the year 1840...* (1876). In contemporary documents this is sometimes referred to as 'Lord Hampton's Report'. **CofE** Church of England **CofE F&F** *Facts and Figures About the Church of England* (Church Information Office, 3 editions of 1959, 1962, 1965) **CofE Statistics** The Church of England (various publishing arms), *Church Statistics* (various years), many available online at www.churchofengland.org/about-us/facts-stats.aspx/ **CofE Yearbook** The Church of England, *The Church of England Year Book* (various years) **Combes** I. A. H. Combes, *Anglican Churches of Derbyshire* (Ashbourne, 2004) **Cooper** Trevor Cooper, *How Do We Keep Our Parish Churches?* (Ecclesiological Society, London, 2004) **Cox** J. C. Cox, *Notes on the Churches of Derbyshire* (4 vols, Chesterfield, 1875-79) **Currie** R. Currie, *Churches and Church-Goers: Patterns of Church Growth in the British Isles Since 1700* (OUP, 1977) **Deficiencies** Lower House of Convocation of Canterbury, *Report of Committee of Deficiencies of Spiritual Ministration*, 1876 **Derby Directory** Diocese of Derby, *Derby Diocesan Directory 2008–2009* (Derby, 2008) **Derbyshire 1823** M. R. Austin (ed.), *The Church in Derbyshire in 1823-4. The Parochial Visitation of the Rev. Samuel Butler, Archdeacon of Derby in the Diocese of Lichfield and Derby*, Derbyshire Archaeological Society Record Series, 1974, v **Derbyshire 1851** Margery Tranter (ed.), *The Derbyshire Returns to the 1851 Religious Census* (Derbyshire Record Society, Chesterfield, 1995) **Elleray** D. Robert Elleray, *The Victorian Churches of Sussex: With Illustrations and a Check-List of Churches and Chapels Erected During the Years 1810-1914* (London, 1981) esp. 42, 43 **Free Seats 1889** *Free Seats in Churches: Return to an Order of the House of Lords, Dated 29th July 1889 for Returns of the 7,703 Old Parish Churches, and the 1,711 New Parish or District Churches .... referred to in the Report of the Select Committee on the Parish Churches Bill, 1886, as Having No Pews or Sittings Rented; with the Answers Received to the Questions of the Committee [The Earl of Selborne] Ordered to Be Printed 13th February 1890* **Gill** Robin Gill, *The 'Empty' Church Revisited* (Aldershot, 2003) **Homan** Roger Homan, *The Victorian Churches of Kent* (Chichester, 1984) **ICBS AR** Incorporated Church Building Society, *Annual Report* (various years) **Mann** Horace Mann, *Census of Great Britain 1851. Religious Worship in England and Wales, Abridged from the Official Report* (London, 1854) **Miele** Chris Miele, '"Their interest and habit": professionalism and the restoration of medieval churches, 1837-77', in Chris Brooks and Andrew Saint (eds.), *The Victorian Church: Architecture and Society* (Manchester University Press, 1995), 151-72 **Port** M. H. Port, *600 New Churches: The Church Building Commission, 1818-1856*, new edn (Reading, 2006) **RC** Roman Catholic **RC Directory** The Roman Catholic Church, *The Catholic Directory* (full title varies, publisher varies, various years) **Report 1886** *Report from the Select Committee of the House of Lords on the Parish Churches Bill (H.L.), Together with the Proceedings of the Committee and an Appendix. Session 1886* **RT6** Peter Brierley (ed.), *UK Christian Handbook Religious Trends No. 6 2006/7* (Christian Research, Eltham, 2006); and similarly for *RT7* (for 2007/8, published in 2008 by Christian Research,

Swindon) **Snell & Ell** K. D. M Snell & Paul S. Ell, *Rival Jerusalems: the Geography of Victorian Religion* (CUP, 2000)

Sources for graphs and tables (with comments)
Graph 1: For 1851, Mann, Table G (the number of 'separate' buildings then estimated by using the separate/not separate ratio for England and Wales jointly in Table A); the count of nonconformist churches excludes overseas and heterodox congregations, the proportion of which forming the 'other' column in Table G was estimated by using Table A. For CofE in 2008, CofE *Statistics* 2008/9; for nonconformist churches in 2005, *RT6*, Table 12.2.3; for Methodists, Baptists and RC in 2006, *RT7*, Tables 9.8.1, 9.2.1, 8.6.1. **Graph 2**: Number of churches (sum of 'separate' and 'not separate' buildings): data as Graph 1. Attendance: for CofE and RC in 1851, best attended service in Mann, Table N; for Methodists and Baptists in 1851, attendance at evening service for England and Wales from Mann, supplement II to Table A, adjusted to strip out Wales in proportion to number of churches in Table N; for CofE in 2008, CofE *Statistics* 2008/9, using all-age Average Sunday Attendance; for nonconformist attendance in 2005, *RT7*, Table 2.24.1; for RC in 2006, *RT7*, Table 8.6.1; for Methodist attendance at the Methodist Church in 2007, 'Methodist Church Connexional Statistics, Statistics for Mission, 2005 to 2007', under 'Attendance' (available at www.methodist.org.uk/downloads/co_871_080408.doc, accessed June 2010), uplifted to allow for other smaller relevant Methodist denominations by using membership ratios in *RT7*, Tables 9.8.1, 9.8.2; for Baptist attendance in 2008, attendance at Baptist Union churches from www.ekklesia.co.uk/node/11446 (accessed June 2010), uplifted to allow for other smaller Baptist denominations by using membership ratios in *RT7*, Tables 9.2.1, 9.2.2. **Graph 3**: For the period up to and including 1871, the figure for consecrations (provided by diocesan registrars) from *Deficiencies*, Appendix A, using the 'additional churches' figure for England & Wales and subtracting the Welsh figures provided (which are for both 'additional churches' and 'churches rebuilt', thus very slightly understating the number of English additional churches). Note: I have not used the figures given in Mann, p. 14 for pre-1851, whose weaknesses he describes and which are commented on critically in *Deficiencies*, 7. For data after 1871, the table 'New Churches, Built or Rebuilt and Consecrated' from CofE *Yearbook*, various years (which will inflate the figures as it includes rebuilds which were consecrated, but understate them as it normally excludes mission chapels – see e.g. the comment for London diocese in CofE *Yearbook* for 1889, page 502). **Graph 4**: For the period before 1958, use the 1851 count in Mann, Table E as a starting point and adjust it backward and forward by the number of consecrations taken from Graph 3 (I have not used Mann's figure for 1831 (p. 13), as the source is not given and it is lower than our other data would suggest). For 1958–1964, CofE *F&F1* (1959) Table 7; CofE *F&F2* (1962); CofE *F&F3* (1965), Table 8. For 1967 and 1969, the CofE *Yearbook* for 1967 & 1970. Remaining years, CofE *Statistics*, various years. **Graph 5:** ICBS *AR* for 1920. **Graph 6:** ICBS *AR* for 1908, 171–91 **Graph 7:** For 1851, Mann, Table A; for other years, CofE *Yearbook*, various years. For the CofE, Mann reports a large number of uncategorised cases (of the order of 20% of the total), as discussed by Snell and Ell, 343–45; to calculate the percentages, I have merely used the 'Free' and 'Appropriated' cases he does categorise and have ignored the uncategorised cases. **Graph 8:** as Graph 5. **Graph 9:** Port, 247. **Graph 10**: For 1851 Mann, Table E, corrected for missing returns by individual diocese. For prior to 1851, Mann, Table 14 (on p. 76) adjusted to exclude Welsh churches by using the 1851 ratio of English/Welsh churches in Table E, corrected for missing returns as previously; there must be some question about the reliability of Mann's pre-1851 figures, given the uncertainty over his other pre-1851 data discussed above under Graph 3. For 1875, *Deficiencies*, Appendix H (using an interpolated figure for Ely); the result is anomalous and may exclude mission chapels, or may not have been corrected for missing returns. For 1885 until before 1960, CofE *Yearbook*, various years (up to 1919 corrected for missing returns): for 1885 there was no disaggregation by building type; for 1893, 1898 and 1905 I used the sum of 'parish churches', 'chapels of ease' and 'mission rooms' but ignored 'other'; for 1909 (following a change in the form of the return in 1906) and 1913, the sum of 'parish

churches' and 'other' (the *Yearbooks* explained that 'other' included chapels of ease, mission rooms and other buildings but excluded the approximately 83,000 seats in chapels royal, peculiars, colleges and public schools, military and naval chapels and chapels for seamen, hospitals, asylums, workhouses, orphanages etc.; it is likely that these were included in the previous definition of category 'other' which I also excluded in earlier years); for 1919, the sum of 'parish churches' and 'mission churches, etc'; for 1922, 1927, 1933 and 1937 the sum of 'parish churches' and 'other consecrated churches, mission chapels etc.'. The apparent decrease in the number of sittings in the years immediately subsequent to 1921 is due to the fact that the figures refer to the 'normal accommodation' instead of, as in years previous to 1922, to 'accommodation', which 'often connoted maximum accommodation, e.g. normal accommodation plus the addition of forms, chairs etc.'. For 1960, CofE *F&F3* (1965), Table 12. For the minimum and maximum estimates of present day sittings I began with the 1960 figures, and then calculated a) the loss of seats from church closures since 1960, assuming either that the closed churches were of average size, or for the ten years from 1960 were smaller buildings seating 200; b) the gain of seats from new church buildings since 1960, assuming they have an average seating capacity either of 150 or 200; c) the loss from pew removal since 1960, either assuming the recent average rate of loss applied throughout that period, or one half of that average. I assumed that 20% of sittings were lost with partial pew removal, 30% with full pew removal. The sources were Cooper, Graph 2.3 (for estimate of new churches); data used for Graph 4 for closures between 1960 and 1969; an EH analysis of closed churches since 1969; and Table 5 for removal of pews. **Graph 11:** For ICBS, as Graph 5; for Commissioners, Port, based on Table 3, p. 247. As discussed in the text, there may be an increasing degree of double counting after the early to mid 1830s, so I have ignored Commissioners' churches after 1840, and shown those for 1835–9 as an uncertain shade of grey. **Graph 12:** CofE *Yearbook*, various years. **Graph 13**: Based on initial, unadjusted data from the yet unpublished National Churches Trust Survey 2010. We are grateful to the Trust for providing these early findings to us to enable them to be used in this chapter. **Graph 14:** Seating capacity: as Graph 10. Attendance: for 1851 and present, as Graph 2; for 1968, CofE *Statistics*, Table 15, using all-age 'usual Sunday attendance' adjusted upwards to be a comparable measure to 'Average Sunday Attendance' (adjusted by the ratio between the two in 2008, from CofE *Statistics 2008/9*). **Graph 15:** Sittings: *Report* 1886 and *Free Seats* 1889; date of construction: Derby *Directory*, checked against Combes (and occasionally Cox) where necessary. **Graph 16:** Sittings today: Derby *Directory*; date of construction: as Graph 15. **Graph 17**: Sittings for 1823: Derbyshire 1823; sittings for 1886: as for Graph 15; date of construction: as for Graph 15. **Graph 18:** As for Graph 17. **Graph 19:** Sittings in 1886: as for Graph 15; sittings in 2008 (from which gain calculated): Derby *Directory*. **Graph 20:** Derby *Directory*. **Graph 21:** Derby *Directory* (using 'usual Sunday adult attendance' for attendance, adjusted upwards to be comparable to adult 'Average Sunday Attendance' by using the ratio between the two for Derbyshire in CofE *Statistics 2007/8*). **Graph 22**: *Derbyshire 1851*. Note: I chose the best attended service, excluding attendance by 'scholars' where the data allowed this, which it almost always did (for the record there were about 26,000 adults and about 13,000 scholars). Where it was given I used the average attendance at best attended service over the previous period, rather than the attendance at best attended service on Census Sunday, as being less subject to the vagaries of a particular day's attendance. **Graph 23:** Homan, 12. **Graph 24**: Currie, 213 (up to 1951); RC *Directory*, various years. **Table 1**: Numbers of sittings, Mann, Table E; proportions free, Mann Table A; attendance at best-attended service, Mann, Table N. I have excluded overseas and heterodox denominations. **Table 2:** raw data from English Heritage (EH), January 2009, available at www.ecclsoc.org by kind permission of EH; this table supersedes the similar table I published in 'Keeping our parish churches: further thoughts', *Ecclesiology Today* 40 (July 2008), 92–98, Table 1. **Table 3:** *Deficiencies*, Appendix F. **Table 4:** *Report* 1886. **Table 5**: personal communication from the DAC Secretaries of the named dioceses; the weighted average was calculated using the number of churches for 2003 in CofE *Statistics 2003/4*. **Table 6:** Homan, p. 12; Elleray, pp. 42, 43. **Table 7**: Gill, Table 8 (my calculations of number of sittings, using his percentages).

Notes

1. By 2001, the population of England was 49.1 million. Julie Jefferies, *The UK Population: Past, Present and Future* (2005), p. 3, available at www.statistics.gov.uk (accessed October 2010).
2. For non-Anglican buildings, the Religious Census asked whether the building was 'separate and entire' and 'whether used exclusively as a place of worship'. For Anglican buildings these questions were not asked, but some responses made it clear to those compiling the statistics that the building was not a separate building. (For facsimiles of the Census forms, see Clive Field, 'The 1851 Religious Census of Great Britain: a bibliographical guide for local and regional historians', *The Local Historian*, Vol. 27 No. 4 (Nov 1997), 194–217, (pp. 216, 217).) It is difficult to gauge the number of 'not separate' buildings today, and I have not attempted to do so in the graph. The so-called 'New' churches frequently meet in rented accommodation, often as a matter of policy: there are about 700 such congregations attached to larger groupings or denominations, and many or all of these will not have a separate building; in addition, there are an estimated 1226 other congregations not attached to a denomination, and some of these will be in the same position (*RT7*, Tables 9.10.1, 9.13.4).
3. Gill points out that the building programme which ultimately led to over-provision was not irrational: building more churches did indeed increase overall attendance, and was known to do so, but this was at the expense of spreading congregations out, so that total fixed costs (e.g. the buildings) rose more quickly than the number of people attending. The fall in the proportion of those attending church made the approach unsustainable (Gill, 100–101).
4. For competitive overbuilding, the decline in attendance, and the resulting overcapacity in the nineteenth century, see Gill, *passim*. Gill is essential reading for anyone working in this field. Given the scope of his research, his demonstration that there was over-provision of seating in the latter part of the nineteenth century (my simplification of his findings) is unlikely to be overturned. However, future work in this area might explore in more depth the accuracy of the number of seats claimed by individual churches; how much of the seating capacity claimed for churches was set aside for children and not suitable for adults, given that Gill's analysis of attendance excludes children (the *Church Builder* in 1864 (no. 9, page 27), suggested that between one fifth and one quarter of overall church seating could sensibly be devoted to children); and the impact of empty appropriated pews on the number of seats practically available. Of course, to the extent that these were constants over the period, they will have no affect on the trends in percentage occupancy found by Gill, even if the absolute occupancy figures change. For the national decline in attendance, see also Callum Brown, *The Death of Christian Britain: Understanding Secularisation 1800–2000* (London, 2001), 162–4; Adrian Hastings, *A History of English Christianity 1920–1985* (London, 1986), 33–40; Robin Gill, 'Measuring church trends over time', in Paul Avis (ed.), *Public Faith: the State of Religious Belief and Practice in Britain* (London, 2003), p. 24.
5. ICBS *AR* for 1882, 8.
6. *Deficiencies*, p. 8, makes it clear that there was no systematic record kept of restorations.
7. The *CBAR*, 1876 collected retrospective information for the period 1840–75, and although its focus was on cost rather than number, it reported on the number of restorations and new churches built in 17 dioceses. These sample results can be uplifted in several different ways to allow for the other dioceses, and these approaches give a central estimate of about 5,300 restorations and 2,600 new buildings in England alone (the range of estimates for new buildings comparing reasonably well with the figures of 2,363 consecrations shown on Graph 6, derived from a different source); and 6,000 restorations and 2,900 new buildings in both England and Wales. Note that Chris Miele's statement that there were more than 7,000 restorations in England and Wales during the period is incorrect (Miele, 156), as he overlooked the fact that the figure of 7,144 which he was using (from the summary section of *CBAR*) included 11 dioceses where the figure included new builds within the restoration figure, thus inflating it (and in addition the summary figure for London is misleading). My estimate of around 6,000

restorations in England and Wales is probably the best that can be done with the data.

8 In the period 1840–75 there were perhaps 2,900 churches built in England and Wales, and some 6,000 restorations (see previous note). During this period the ICBS supported approximately 1370 new buildings, 770 rebuildings, and 2550 enlargements and reseatings (ICBS *AR* for 1920). From this I deduce (somewhat cautiously) that during this period the ICBS gave grants to about one half of the churches being built or undergoing change.

9 In its early years the Commission built new churches using its own funds, voted by Parliament, and up to the end of the 1820s or early 1830s there was little overlap between the ICBS and Commissioners' grant giving (to give a feel for the figures, about 208 Commissioners' churches were built in the period up to 1834, for example). However the Commissioners' average grant shrunk very significantly after the mid 1830s, and their grants tended to become part of a formal approval process rather than paying for much of the building, and some of their later churches were also supported by the ICBS. (Port, 247, 253, 272; M. H. Port, personal communication.)

10 We cannot deduce the overall national pattern from the ICBS data, as we do not know whether the proportion of church work being supported by its grants was constant during the century. Data is available for six dioceses in *CBAR*, 1876 which provides both the date at which work was carried out at each church and characterises it as a restoration or new build, and in an important article Chris Miele has used this information to demonstrate a difference between types of diocese regarding the dates at which restoration and new builds flourished. However the overall national pattern cannot be derived from this limited and unrepresentative sample of dioceses. (Miele, 159 and Figs. 63 and 64; note that Fig. 65 incorrectly states that the necessary date data is available for the diocese of St Asaph.)

11 See e.g. Trevor Cooper, '"Worthy of the age in which we live": churches and chapels in Salisbury', *Ecclesiology Today* 37 (for December 2006, published January 2007), 5–44, (pp. 29–32), *passim*.

12 There is a list of inner London mission chapels and their accommodation and attendance in *The Religious Census of London* (London, 1888), and there may be similar material in other religious censuses of the late nineteenth and early twentieth century. I have not yet explored this data.

13 Full bibliographic details of these various sources are listed above under 'abbreviations'. Note that the 1886 and 1889 reports are national documents between them listing more than 11,000 churches, in which the Derbyshire churches can often (but not always) be identified. The dates of many of the Derbyshire buildings are given in the Derby *Directory*, and in addition for this information I have often used Combes, which is unusually complete and helpful in this respect, and Cox (especially where questions of Victorian restoration versus rebuild arose). Useful background on early nineteenth century religion in Derbyshire will be found in the introduction to *Derbyshire 1823*; M. R. Austin, 'Religion and society in Derbyshire in the Industrial Revolution', *Derbyshire Archaeological Journal* [*DAJ*], 93 (1974), 75–89; M. Tranter, 'Landlords, labourers, local preachers: rural nonconformity in Derbyshire, 1772–1851', *DAJ*, 101 (1981), 119–38.

14 For recent general discussion of free and appropriated seating, see e.g. Snell and Ell, Chapter 10 and for the Anglican church, Roger Lee Brown, *Pews, benches and seats, being a history of the church pew in Wales* (Welshpool, 1998), *passim*. For the need for fixed seating for appropriation, see p. 226 in this volume. If chairs are battened together, it is possible to use them as appropriated seating.

15 There were many complexities to appropriation, including other non-financial routes (such as a faculty), not explored here.

16 *Deficiencies*, 11 and Appendix F. The questionnaire was also sent to 'a few other parishes with scattered population'. There was a high response rate (2216 responses = 79%) for the question on free seating.

17 Figures for Commissioners' churches based on Port, 247; the figures do not quite agree with Port, 276.

18 Most or all of the sources I have used here could be disaggregated to the level of individual diocese, which would almost certainly reveal significant differences between dioceses. The variations in seating over a similar period of time have been explored for Kingston-upon-Hull in Gill, Table 10.
19 See note 9 above.
20 *Deficiencies*, 8. For repeated expressions of concern, see also the ICBS *ARs* of the latter decades of the century.
21 I have previously demonstrated (Cooper, Graph 5.4) that in the diocese of Manchester, churches built in Victorian times now have more sittings than churches which were built before or after that period.
22 The median pre 1800 was 286; post 1800 it was 360.
23 Gill gives totals for seating by geographical area, but his published data does not allow the seating of individual church buildings to be tracked through time.
24 Cinemas in the UK in can seat 865,599 people (2008 figure, sourced from 'UK Cinema Sites, Screens and Seats 2000–2009' on the website of the Cinema Exhibitors' Association Limited, www.cinemauk.org.uk (accessed December 2010)). The relevant football stadia in England can accommodate 2,199,896 people (from 'List of football stadiums in England', article in Wikipedia, http://en.wikipedia.org/wiki/List_of_football_stadiums_in_England (accessed December 2010)).
25 The figure of five million is obtained by multiplying the number of nonconformist and Roman Catholic churches by an assumption about the average number of seats per church building, itself based on inspection of Graph 13.
26 Using the adult Average Sunday Attendance for 2008, and Easter Day/Eve all age attendance for the same year (from CofE *Statistics*).
27 Cooper, 46.
28 Cooper, 47.
29 See the notes on the source of Graph 21 for the source of 'Average Sunday Attendance'.
30 I used '*average* best-attended service' rather than '*Census Sunday* best-attended service' wherever this former figure was available, as being less subject to the vagaries of a particular day's attendance.
31 Elleray, 42, 43.
32 There is a revealing snapshot in *Deficiencies*, page 14, where in 1875 in the nearly 2,800 parishes which had a population of more than 2,000 people, there were more than 9,300 nonconformist places of worship – more than twice as many buildings as the CofE were using, even allowing for mission chapels, etc. Unfortunately is not possible to scale this data up to estimate the number of nonconformist buildings in the whole of England at this date.
33 To compare the CofE and nonconformist rate of building (and/or the provision of additional seats) in explicitly defined geographical areas, see Gill Tables 1, 2, 5, 7, 8, 12, 13, and 15, and the section on conurbations in Table 3.
34 In 1851, for England: CofE, 13,098; nonconformist etc., 17,058; RC, 558; the remainder of relatively orthodox Christian, 143 (sources as per Graph 1). My count of 'nonconformist etc.' buildings included only those used by free, reasonably-orthodox Christian congregations, not of overseas origin.
35 There is a useful brief case-study of nonconformist closure in Gill, 29–31 (and see also 50–52). Debt is a major driver.
36 Mann, Table G; *The Times* (Tuesday 20 Sep 1932), p. 11, col F; *RT*7, Table 9.8.1.
37 Gill, 98–99.
38 See for example Cooper, 'Salisbury', 29–32.
39 For these figures, see the sources for Graph 2 (for nonconformist, *RT*7, 2.24).

Part 2

HISTORY: TO THE NINETEENTH CENTURY

6. Seating in the nave of the pre-Reformation parish church

P. S. Barnwell

THE OUTLINES of the current understanding of the history of medieval seating for the laity in the nave of the English parish church were laid in the nineteenth century. The first work seriously to treat the subject was the *History of Pues*, by the ecclesiologist J. M. Neale, published in 1841.[1] Thereafter, against the background of pressure of space within churches as the population increased during the nineteenth century, the nature of the rights individuals exercised over seats within churches was explored by a number of legal authorities, amongst the most significant of which was the two-volume *History and Law of Church Seats, or Pews*, of 1872, by Alfred Heales.[2] The first volume consists of a meticulous and detailed gathering of documentary evidence for church seats, much of it quoted in full, ranging from the middle ages to the end of the seventeenth century. For its day, before many of the primary sources were known, still less edited and published, it was a remarkable achievement, and the work remains a valuable compendium of references. A comparably authoritative and wide-ranging overview of the physical evidence for medieval seating did not appear for nearly another half century, when Cox's *Bench-Ends in English Churches* was published in the series 'Church Art in England' by Oxford University Press, almost three-quarters of it being a catalogue of examples Cox believed to date from the seventeenth century or earlier.[3] At the same time, Howard and Crossley's *English Church Woodwork* appeared,[4] and gave a summary account of early benches with an emphasis on overall design, accompanied by a series of valuable dimensioned drawings. From then until the late twentieth century there was until recently little work on the subject, and much of what was produced did not go much beyond increasing the number of examples of early seating, repeating received wisdom on the history of seats, and describing and classifying the motifs carved on bench ends.[5] During the last twenty years the study of seating has received impetus from the new angle of women's history: Aston examined the segregation of the sexes in churches before, during and after the middle ages,[6] and, more recently, French has considered ways in which the women of some parishes used seats to express their position within local society (discussed below).[7]

A result of the relatively small amount of work on medieval nave seating, and of its disjointed nature, is that it is not possible to produce a synoptic overview of the subject. What follows is therefore no more than an attempt to elucidate the current state of knowledge concerning some aspects of the topic, and to indicate some which might repay further investigation. The scope of the discussion is limited to seating in the nave and aisles, excluding seats in screened-off chapels and in chancels.

It is generally thought that for most of the middle ages the laity in the nave stood when they were not kneeling. For the aged and infirm various forms of seat might be available. First, the most physically obvious, are low and narrow stone ledges around the walls of naves, and/or broader but often equally low ledges at the bases of some of the piers. Second, there might have been portable stools, which could have been kept in the church or brought from home. Finally, there may be some sets of pews – sometimes occupying part rather than all of the nave – which date from as early as the thirteenth century. These arrangements persisted until at least the late fourteenth century when, in response to an increase in the number and length of sermons, fixed benches or pews began to become more widespread, many churches being furnished with them during the second half of the fifteenth century and the process continuing across the sixteenth-century Reformation. However, while parts of this outline are true, almost every aspect of it poses questions which are unresolved.

Structural seating

One of the most problematic areas is that of stone ledge-seats (Fig. 1). Cox lists a handful of examples at the west of the nave.[8] Although physically removed from the scene of liturgical action in the chancel, and from most of the other devotional foci in the building, seats in such a position would have allowed a view of the rood at the entrance to the chancel and, beyond, to the elevation of the host during mass. Even if not ideal, this could have provided reasonable visual access for the infirm. Elsewhere, and more commonly, the ledges lie along the outer walls of the nave aisles, places from which the rood and high altar could not be seen.[9] By the fourteenth century, the date from which most examples seem to date,[10] aisles were increasingly divided into chapels, screened off from adjacent spaces. The ledges could have provided seats quite intimately placed for all kinds of devotional activity within the chapels, but those outside them, often towards the west of the aisles, were so remote from all the scenes of action within the church that it is not easy to understand how they could have provided those sitting on them with much beyond symbolic presence in the church. While symbolic presence was well understood in the middle ages – witness the potency of images, including effigies of the dead – the ability to *see* the transubstantiated host, the rood, and the images of the saints was so vital that sitting towards the back of the aisle would severely have compromised a major part of the religious experience of the age. The wider ledges found at the bases of some nave piers (Fig. 2) may have been better from this point of view, though many of them would have been divided into sections by the screens around the aisle chapels, and the number of people who could be seated with a view into the chancel was very small; but perhaps all but the most infirm could have turned or moved around at the key moment of the elevation.

It is not, however, clear why many wall and pier ledges should be interpreted as seats. Combined with their less than optimal position, many of the ledges along the walls are so low and narrow that they must always have been uncomfortable. They could perhaps have provided the substructure for long-since removed timber benches resting on them and projecting out further from the walls, but some may, equally, not have been seats at all; they may represent the thinning of the wall above the foundations, or a level from which a wall was rebuilt, a suspicion strengthened by

Fig. 1: Examples of wall-seating? As discussed in the text, each example must be assessed individually. Left, St Mary, Burton, Wiltshire, north aisle wall. Said to be of the thirteenth century, but there is no evidence of the date; on the visible evidence it could have been added at any period after the wall was constructed. Right, St Mary, Over, Cambridgeshire, south aisle window (c.1320–30). This has been interpreted as a seat. But it may be no more than the base of an elaborate recessed window and flanking arches.

Fig. 2: Stone ledges around the bases of piers: are they purpose-built seats or evidence of the lowering of floors? 2a (right): St Benedict, Haltham, Lincolnshire, north arcade, thirteenth century. The crudeness of the ledge compared to the column above suggests this results from the lowering of the floor, as does the ugly and inconvenient square base of the same height upon which the font is elevated.

the fact that at Stogumber, Somerset, there is a similar ledge along the outside of the north nave wall (which Cox interpreted as a seat for outdoor summer sermons).[11] Similarly, some of the ledges around nave piers may result from a lowering of the floor level. Resolution of these problems of interpretation will never be possible for every individual case, but systematic question-led fieldwork to establish the locations, dates, dimensions and exact kinds of ledges of both types would provide the basis for a fresh overall interpretation.

Stools

More flexible than the fixed seats were stools or simple movable forms. There is, however, of their nature, no physical evidence for them, and so little documentary evidence for the contents of parish churches survives from before the late fourteenth century that it provides little assistance. Because the absence of evidence is explicable in its own terms, it is not possible to use it as evidence

Fig. 2b: St Mary, South Creake, Norfolk, early fifteenth century. The ledge is even more crude than at Haltham (Fig. 2a), especially in comparison to the elegance of the arcade above; the faces of the ledge are not even the same width. As at Haltham, the detail of the construction of the base of the font also suggests that the floor has been lowered.

that stools, especially, were rare, and all interpretations of the evolution of seating must bear this carefully in mind. In particular, the innovation of the later middle ages might not have been so much the widespread use of seating, but a shift from stools (or forms) to fixed benches or pews. If correct, this would have significant implications for understanding the nature and evolution of lay religious experience within the middle ages. This point with be touched upon again later.

Fixed benches

The dates of the earliest sets of fixed benches or pews are difficult to assess. The conventional understanding is that the earliest surviving fixed seating dates from the thirteenth century. Amongst the most frequently cited examples are those at Cassington, Oxfordshire (Fig. 3), Clapton-in-Gordano, Somerset (see Figure 3 in Chapter 19, page 285) Mark (also Somerset) and Dunsfold, Surrey (Fig. 4).[12] When the evidence for such an early date is probed, however, doubts begin to arise, since often, as Cautley noted in relation to Suffolk, it seems to rest on no more than crudeness of construction (for a further example, see Figure 2 in Chapter 19, on page 284).[13] In fact such crudeness is not – or at least not always – an indicator of date, for the benches at Dunsfold (one of the only two sets of medieval pews in England to have been tree-ring dated which are recorded in the Vernacular Architecture Group database of dated buildings) are now known to have been constructed of trees felled between 1409 and 1441.[14] The implication of this is that no firm typological development of seats can be arrived at until there has been systematic analysis of their construction accompanied by equally systematic scientific dating of carefully selected examples.

The period at which benches and pews became widespread is no easier to determine, not least since the earlier fixed seats were introduced the more likely it is that the first generation will have become worn out and have been replaced within the pre-Reformation or Reformation periods. The commonly held view that they were rare before the late fourteenth century and only became prevalent in the fifteenth[15] is very largely to be accounted for by the fact that it is the period from which documents of a kind which might refer to seating begin to survive in substantial numbers – wills containing bequests for seats or requests to be buried near particular seats, and, more particularly, churchwardens' accounts, which sometimes refer to the funding or making of seats. The fact that references to seats are not uncommon in the early years of surviving churchwardens' accounts, often in the first half of the fifteenth century, suggests that they had already existed for some time.[16] The nature of early references reinforces the

Fig. 3: St Peter, Cassington, Oxfordshire. Seats said by some to be of the thirteenth century.

suspicion. At Dartmouth, for example, the earliest reference to a seat is in 1438, when a servant paid for the privilege of using a seat: if seats were new, it would have been likely that the wealthy of the parish would have been the first to reserve them in this way, rather than a servant.[17] Another clue comes from St Michael's, Oxford, where the earliest reference to seating (1436–7) is to the construction of seats before Our Lady of Pity, before the St Katherine altar, and behind the north door, the last perhaps suggesting that seats were being fitted into spaces left by earlier partial pewing schemes (see below).[18]

Problems of dating also exist in relation to the sixteenth century, since it is by no means easy to tell from the form of pews themselves whether they were erected before or after the Reformation. The medieval types of pew, with their well-known regional variants – particularly the rectangular bench ends of the south-west of England and the 'poppy-heads' of East Anglia (Fig. 6) – continued uninterrupted throughout the sixteenth century. Of greater assistance are the kinds of ornament on the bench ends, because some motifs were almost certainly used exclusively before the period of reform: such designs include those which feature images of the saints, particularly the Virgin (especially common in East Anglia),[19] or their monograms (such as the crowned 'M' for Mary at St Teath, Cornwall, or the lily and chalice at Morwenstow (Fig. 7a) in the same county), prayers (like the *Ave* at Trent, Dorset and Warkworth, Northamptonshire),[20] as well as symbols of the Passion (Fig. 7b), monks, or elements of the liturgy (such as the procession with holy water at Trull, Somerset,[21] or the chalice and host at Mullion, Cornwall), which were more widespread in the south-west.[22] Moralising themes, such as Reynard the Fox as preacher, were used both before and after the Reformation,[23] though some may have lost or changed their meaning – mermen perhaps ceased to represent Christ (half man and half fish representing the two natures of God) and mermaids became no more than folkloric representations of temptation.[24] Other subjects, such as the wide range of illustrations of daily life or of animals (local, exotic, mythological), as well as geometric or tracery designs, were used before and after the Reformation, though their style may sometimes suggest an earlier or a later date. However, the evolution of style was not synchronous with that of ecclesiastical reform, so that renaissance and arabesque designs were used on either side of the 1530s, which has led to debate as to how much earlier they had been current (see Figure 6b).[25]

Only rarely, as at North Cadbury, Somerset, is a date carved into the bench ends or backs. More common are heraldic devices and rebuses, which can sometimes be linked to specific individuals and therefore provide an indication of the period in which the seats were made: one well-known example is the elephant and castle on a bench end at Lopham, Norfolk, the badge of the Beaumont family which was associated with the parish from the 1430s to the 1460s.[26] Some devices of this kind record the person or family which paid for the seats, but in other cases they may have designated the place where members of the donor's family sat. It has been suggested that some of the more illustrative west-country bench ends may record groups of people who donated particular pews, the jester, viol player and sword dancers at Altarnun, Cornwall, perhaps indicating patronage by local minstrels or players,[27] but it is equally possible that such people sat in the pews thus decorated. Perhaps, though, it is more likely that such depictions of local life brought the parish community into the church, even when the people themselves were not there, in the same way as the more than representational nature of medieval images brought the saints and the dead into the church;[28] the benches and ends with this kind of decoration could have been a permanent semi-present community of worshippers, constant reminders to the saints represented in the church and above all to the interceding Christ crucified on the rood and living in the reserved sacrament.

The installation of seating

The mechanisms whereby parishes paid for the installation of benches seem to have varied. Sometimes seats, or blocks of seats, were provided by individual donors. One of the best documented examples is at Swaffham, for which the rector, Dr John Bright, in 1454 drew up what is now known as the Black Book of

Fig. 4: St Mary and All Saints, Dunsfold, Surrey. Benches once thought to be early, now dated to the first part of the fifteenth century (see text).

Swaffham, setting out and regularising the administration of the parish, to which were later added the names of significant donors to the church. Many of the benefactions relate to the substantial renewal of the building and its furnishings in the mid to late fifteenth century. Among their number are included the provision of seats on the north side of the 'old' church as far back as the entrance, by Thomas and Cecily Styward; later, the north aisle was rebuilt (or restored), glazed and seated by John and Catherine Chapman, while later still John and Agnes Langman paid for the 'great' seats on both sides of the nave, and Thomas Cocke donated some seats in the south aisle.[29] Similarly, in 1474, William Philpot of Godmersham, Kent, left instructions in his will for the erection at his expense of seats at Elmsted.[30] On other occasions, however, the churchwardens arranged a special collection from parishioners to defray the initial cost, as in 1449 at Thame, Oxfordshire,[31] 1504–5 at St Andrew's, Canterbury,[32] and 1518 at St Mary the Great, Cambridge.[33] Elsewhere, and more commonly in the published churchwardens' accounts, the funding mechanism is obscure, perhaps suggesting that the accounts for, and possibly the management of, such special projects were separate from those of the churchwardens.

Although the Black Book of Swaffham does not record the dates of the benefactions for seats, it is clear that they were made at different times, extending into the 1480s, and that the nave and aisles were not all pewed at once. It was suggested earlier that there are hints of a partial scheme at St Michael's, Oxford, and the bequest of Philpot of Godmersham for Elmsted refers to the building of seats from the painting of St Christopher to the north

Fig. 5: St Mary, Slindon, Sussex. Based on their lack of sophistication, Cox confidently asserted that these 'cannot be later than the close of the thirteenth century' (Cox, Bench-ends, 173), but other authors have placed them in the early fifteenth century.

corner of the stone wall, suggesting the north-west corner of the nave or even the west end of the north aisle, perhaps supplementing earlier seats in the body of the church. It therefore appears that in at least some parishes fixed seats were added as demand arose, some of the laity continuing to stand or use stools. Sometimes, even when the nave was fully pewed, as at Ashby St Ledgers, Northamptonshire, where the nave was furnished in the third quarter of the fifteenth century, the east end was left open so that people could still move forward and kneel at the elevation of the host, and perhaps also to provide space for the gospel procession;[34] it is not known how widespread this was, but the same phenomenon has been noted in Suffolk.[35] Elsewhere, particularly when work on the seats was part of a large-scale late-fifteenth- and early-sixteenth-century refurbishment or rebuilding, seats were supplied throughout at one time, as at Bodmin, where the 1491 contract for new seats stipulates that they should be in four ranges throughout all the body of the church, those in the nave 12½ feet long, those in the aisles 7 feet.[36]

Seats and social status

Where seating was introduced in stages, the question arises as to for whom it was intended and why. Although one persistent interpretation is that it was intended for women, and there is clear evidence in many parishes that women purchased, or had purchased on their behalf, life interests in seats, there is also evidence that many men bought such rights for themselves, though sometimes in lesser number. (It is not clear whether this reflects the widespread post-Reformation pattern of women being more assiduous in church attendance than men.) The published pre-Reformation churchwardens' accounts, which mostly relate to churches in towns, reveal that the balance between men and women varied greatly between parishes, but in very few is there evidence that seats were only intended for women. What is true, however, is that men's and women's seats were often segregated, the women often being placed on the north side of the church.[37] According to the mystical interpretation of Durandus of Mende, writing in the second half of the thirteenth century, the reason was that the weaker women were placed on the north side to be sheltered from worldly temptation which lay to the south (presumably because that was where the entrance usually lay), though sometimes the men stood at the front, at the head of the community and the women at the back.[38] More straightforward is the observation that women seem, not unnaturally, to have been associated with the Virgin, for the north side placed them facing her image on the rood and next to the Lady Chapel which was commonly in the north aisle or north chancel chapel, and there is evidence that, in the few churches where the Lady Chapel was on the south, such as St Lawrence's, Reading, the women also sat on that side.[39] The conventional arrangement is sometimes reflected in the seats themselves, those on the north side of the nave at Wiggenhall St Mary, Norfolk, being decorated with images of Our Lady and those on the south with images of male saints.[40]

Rather than the simple notion that women sat and men stood, what emerges from the churchwardens' accounts is that the purchase of a seat was related to social status, mirroring secular evidence that benches were seen as of higher status than stools,[41] and that in many parishes seats in different parts of the church cost different amounts. In a detailed analysis of the information regarding the sale of seats at St Margaret's, Westminster, French has shown that women, who bought three-quarters of the seats, used them to express their social status, sometimes paying to change seat when their position in the parish changed through marriage, widowhood or, particularly, when their husbands became parish office-holders.[42] Westminster may have been a special place in terms of social structure and custom, but other town parishes, including St Edmund's, Salisbury, and All Saints, Bristol, had a range of seat prices, while at Salisbury and Sherborne there is also

Figs. 6a (right) and 6b (opposite): Styles of bench end. The form and decoration of both these pews could lie on either side of the Reformation.
6a (right): All Saints, Chevington, Suffolk. Typical East Anglian poppy-head bench end. Note the absence of a back below the seat.

evidence for women paying to change seats.[43] Such use of seats as a mark of distinction is an extension of the long-standing principle that the patron of a church or persons of high rank could stand or sit in the chancel.[44] The precise pattern and significance of purchases was specific to each place, indicating that parishes had their own traditions,[45] and the prevalence of such practices in rural parishes is unclear[46] since insufficient numbers of churchwardens' accounts have been analysed on account of most being unpublished. It is, however, possible that some pews were designed to be adapted to higher status as demand increased, for at Stogumber all the bench ends have rebates for doors, though not all ever had them fitted.[47]

The purchase of pews to emphasise social position is paralleled by other aspects of parish life from the late fourteenth to the early sixteenth century, particularly those surrounding funerals and commemoration. The most obvious physical evidence is that of funerary monuments, the forms of which, particularly in the later middle ages, were used to express status.[48] Analysis of surviving monuments, wills and churchwardens' accounts shows that from the early fifteenth century (the period from which documentary evidence survives) burial within the church, which attracted a special fee (usually 6s 8d, sometimes half that for burial in less-favoured areas such as the porch; occasionally, as in the in the City of London parish of St Martin Outwich, with further gradations)[49] was increasingly desired, money and status buying the ability of the dead to be brought into the active remembrance of the living parish community and the presence of Christ within the church. (It may be that the popularity of burial within the church affected the design of some pews, particularly in East Anglia: the absence of backs below the seats may have been intended to enable the digging out of graves without disrupting the blocks of seating – see Figure 6a.) Similarly, churchwardens' accounts reveal that in some parishes funerals and anniversaries could be enhanced by hiring the best cross, best or silver candlesticks, or other 'extras',[50] or by payment for the knelling of the 'great' bell (as opposed to the smaller bells);[51] and in some places there were gradations within such arrangements, St Martin in the Fields, London, having both great and small lights,[52] and Peterborough having different prices for the use of different bells.[53] The fact that parishioners increasingly sought to express their social position in death at the same time as they sought to do so in life by purchasing seats is

Fig. 6b: St Swithun, Launcells, Cornwall. Square-headed bench end typical of the West and South-West.

Fig. 7: Examples of pre-Reformation motifs. 7a: St John the Baptist, Morwenstow, Cornwall. The lily (left) of St Mary, and the chalice (right) for Christ and the Eucharist.
7b: St Sativola Virgin or St Michael, Laneast, Cornwall. The five wounds of Christ.

unlikely to be coincidental, and fits, as French notes in relation to the seating of women, into the increasingly stratified and class-conscious culture in the period after the Black Death, and with the efforts of the Crown to keep the lower orders in their place through sumptuary legislation.[54]

Conclusion

In view of the considerations discussed above, there needs to be further discussion of the function of fixed seating, and the reasons why it spread from at least the first half of the fifteenth century, if not the second half of the fourteenth. The traditional answer, as noted above, is that it is associated with an increase in preaching. While there is little doubt that from the later fourteenth century, and particularly in the fifteenth century, parish sermons became more frequent,[55] they were not an innovation – clergy had been commanded to preach almost throughout the thirteenth century and obliged to deliver at least four sermons a year since 1281[56] – and seem to have been quite short.[57] It is perhaps, therefore, too simple to suggest that preaching was the only reason why fixed seats became fashionable, particularly since it is possible, as argued earlier, that the use of stools was more widespread than has usually been thought. Instead, it may be that several causative factors worked together to produce the conditions which led to the installation of pews.

Such was certainly the case concerning burial within the church and the increase in the number and elaboration of funerary monuments. The causes were partly the consequence of religious belief: the working out of the implications of the 1274 doctrine of Purgatory, and particularly the rise of belief in the efficacy of deceased parishioners 'witnessing' the Mass, encouraged burial within the church and also gave rise to a desire for effigies, both to make the dead more fully present within the church and to prompt remembrance and prayer by the living (a 'good work', from which the living also benefited). At the same time social and economic forces created an increasingly class-conscious society in which, after the middle of the fourteenth century, the lower orders were more prosperous than before and could increasingly afford memorials, driving the wealthy to more elaborate monuments to display their social position.

The picture concerning pews may be at least as complicated. The social culture worked to create a desire to express status by sitting in the relative comfort of a pew, rather than standing or sitting on a stool; then, as pews became more widespread, by sitting in particular places. It may also be that the church authorities used the system of selling seats to maintain order in the church, avoiding the unseemly squabbles about who sat where (cf Chaucer's Wife of Bath, who was 'wrath' and 'out of all charity' with anyone who preceded her to the offertory)[58] of which there are occasional hints in contemporary sources from the late thirteenth century onwards.[59] At the same time, the increased frequency of preaching may have meant that there were more occasions when sitting – whether on a stool or a bench – was desirable. But, in addition, the increasing emphasis on meditative and affective devotion, particularly among women,[60] from the second half of the fourteenth century,[61] and especially of meditation centred on the rood, may have been a stimulus to the creation of seating sufficiently comfortable to aid the concentration needed to attain intense religious experience. If this mix of factors is correct, the precise motivation for, and timing of, the construction of pews will have varied from parish to parish, perhaps particularly between the relatively stable countryside and towns, where the social culture was more fluid and competitive. This slow process was not complete by the Reformation but, unlike the majority of elements of late medieval parish church development, the introduction of seats was not arrested by reform, since some of the conditions which gave rise to it – particularly those related to preaching and the display of social position – remained the same. To understand the chronology will require significantly more pews from across the country, in churches both urban and rural, to be scientifically dated. Dating will also help to test the suggestions made here concerning the reasons for the spread of fixed seats, but the indirect and fragmentary nature of the written sources means that there will always be a significant degree of uncertainty.

Notes

1. [J. M. Neale], *The History of Pues; A Paper Read Before the Cambridge Camden Society. …With an Appendix Containing a Report Presented to the Society on the Statistics of Pews, etc.* (Cambridge, 1841).
2. A. Heales, *The History and Law of Church Seats, or Pews*, 2 vols in 1 (London, 1872).
3. J. C. Cox, *Bench-Ends in English Churches* (London, 1916).
4. F. E. Howard and F. H. Crossley, *English Church Woodwork. A Study in Craftsmanship During the Medieval Period, AD 1250–1550* (London, 1917); a second edition with the same text but more illustrations appeared in 1927.
5. Most notable amongst them are perhaps J. Agate, *Benches and Stalls in Suffolk Churches* (Ipswich, 1980), and J. C. D. Smith, *Church Woodcarvings: A West Country Study* (Newton Abbot, 1969). Smith's later work, *A Guide to Church Woodcarvings: Misericords and Bench-Ends* (Newton Abbot, 1974), although larger in geographical compass, is more slight in terms of analytical and original content.
6. M. Aston, 'Segregation in Church', in W. J. Sheils and D. Wood (eds.), *Women in the Church*, Studies in Church History, 27 (Oxford, 1990), 237–94.
7. K. L. French, '"The seat under Our Lady": gender and seating in the late medieval English parish church', in S. Stanbury and V. Raguin (eds.), *Women's Space: Parish, Space and Gender in the Middle Ages*, (Albany, 2005), 141–60; expanded in idem, *The Good Women of the Parish: Gender and Religion After the Black Death* (Philadelphia, 2008), Chapter 3.
8. Ipsden, Oxfordshire; Brimpton, Somerset; Hemingborough, East Riding of Yorkshire; Middleton, North Riding of Yorkshire (Cox, *Bench-Ends*, 2–4).
9. A selection is listed in J. C. Cox and A. Harvey, *English Church Furniture*, 2nd edn (London, 1908), 262.
10. J. Kroesen and R. Steensma, *The Interior of the Medieval Village Church: Het Middeleeuwse Dorpskerkinterieur* (Louvain, Paris, and Dudley, Ma., 2004), 270.
11. Cox, *Bench-Ends*, 4.
12. See, for example, Cox and Harvey, *English Church Furniture*, 276–79; Howard and Crossley, *English Church Woodwork*, 297, 307.
13. H. M. Cautley, *Suffolk Churches and their Treasures*, 4th edn (Ipswich, 1975), 143.
14. A. K. Moir, 'Tree-ring date lists 2005. List 159: Buildings dated by Tree-Ring Services', *Vernacular Architecture*, 36 (2005), 76. The other dated pews are at Braunton, Devon, some of which were erected after 1475 – see I. Tyres, 'Tree-ring date lists 2005. Tree-ring dates from the University of Sheffield Dendrochronology Laboratory. List 161: General List', *Vernacular Architecture*, 36 (2005), 80, with B. Cherry and N. Pevsner, *The Buildings of England: Devon*, 2nd edn (London, 1989), 208, for the addition of further pews (or the replacement of some?) at various dates in the second half of the sixteenth century. See also Francis Kelly, 'Post-Reformation church seating arrangements and bench assembly notation in two North Devon churches', Chapter 10 in this volume. The annual lists printed in *Vernacular Architecture* also appear in abbreviated but searchable form at http://ads.ahds.ac.uk/catalogue/specColl/vag_dendro/.
15. E.g. Cautley, *Suffolk Churches*, 143.
16. W. J. Hardy, 'Remarks on the history of seat-reservations in churches', *Archaeologia*, 53 (1892), 96–97.
17. H. R. Watkin, *Dartmouth, vol. I: Pre-Reformation*, Parochial Histories of Devonshire, 5 (n.p., 1935), 305.
18. *The Churchwardens' Accounts of St Michael's Church, Oxford*, ed. by H. E. Salter, Transactions of the Oxfordshire Record Society, 75 (Oxford, 1933), 40.
19. Smith, *Guide to Church Woodcarvings*, 21.
20. Cox, *Bench-Ends*, 91–93, 135; Howard and Crossley, *English Church Woodwork*, 316.
21. M. McDermott, 'Early bench-ends in All Saints' Church, Trull', *Somerset Archaeological and Natural History Society*, 138 (1995), 117–30; idem,

'Supplementary notes on the bench-ends in All Saints' Church, Trull, and the wood-carver Simon Warman', ibid., 142 (1999), 329–34.

22 Smith, *Guide to Church Woodcarvings*, 34 and *passim*.

23 K. Varty, *Reynard, Renart, Reinaert and other Foxes in Medieval England: The Iconographic Evidence. A Study of the Illustrating of Fox Lore and Reynard the Fox Stories in England During the Middle Ages, Followed by a Brief Survey of Their Fortunes in Post-Medieval Times* (Amsterdam, 1999), contains examples from as late as the seventeenth century.

24 J. Mattingly, 'The dating of bench-ends in Cornish churches', *Journal of the Royal Institution of Cornwall*, n.s. 2, part 1 (1991), 64.

25 Mattingly, 'Dating of bench-ends', esp. 62–64

26 Cox, *Bench-Ends*, 125.

27 Mattingly, 'Dating of bench-ends', 60.

28 H. Belting, *Likeness and Presence: A History of the Image Before the Era of Art* (Chicago and London, 1994), esp. pp. 308, 351, 362, 410–19; Cf D. Freedberg, *The Power of Images: Studies in the History and Theory of Response* (Chicago and London, 1989), esp. pp. 166–67; K. Kamerick, *Popular Piety and Art in the Late Middle Ages: Image Worship and Idolatry in England, 1350–1500* (Basingstoke, 2002), 9; S. Stanbury, *The Visual Object of Desire in Late Medieval England* (Philadelphia, 2008), 16–17.

29 J. F. William, 'The Black Book of Swaffham', *Norfolk Archaeology*, 33 (1965), esp. 251–52.

30 Quoted in Heales, *History and Law*, vol. 1, 53.

31 W. P. Ellis, 'The Churchwardens' Accounts of the parish of St Mary, Thame, commencing in the year 1442 [Part 4]', *Beds, Bucks and Oxon Archaeological Journal*, 8 (1902), 73–75.

32 C. Cotton, 'Churchwardens' Accounts of the parish of St Andrew, Canterbury, from AD 1485 to AD 1625 [Part I]', *Archaeologia Cantiana*, 32 (1917), 225–26.

33 *Churchwardens' Accounts of St Mary the Great, Cambridge, from 1504 to 1635*, ed. by J. E. Foster, Cambridge Antiquarian Society Publications, Quarto Series, 25 (Cambridge, 1905), 39–41.

34 For evidence that the gospel procession, known from the Customary of Sarum (in *The Use of Sarum*, ed. by W. H. Frere, 2 vols (Cambridge, 1989), vol. 1, 101–02), did occur in ordinary parish churches, see Chaucer, *The Canterbury Tales: The Miller's Tale*, ll. 153–57, where the censer eyed the parish women while censing them at this point in the Mass.

35 Cautley, *Suffolk Churches*, 143, observed the same phenomenon but thought it was for dramatic performances.

36 *The Bodmin Register*, ed. by J. Wallis (Bodmin, 1827–38), 33–35. The same may be true of Glastonbury, where in 1500 the seats were made from new: *St John the Baptist, Glastonbury: Churchwardens' Accounts 1366 to 1587*, ed. by W. E. Daniell (Sherborne, 1902), 45.

37 This issue is most fully explored in Aston, 'Segregation in Church', from which much of what follows is drawn.

38 Durandus of Mende, *Rationale divinorum officiorum*, ed. by A. Davril and T. M. Thibodeau, Corpus Christianorum, Continuatio Mediævalis, 140, 140A, 140B, 3 vols (Turnhout, 1995–2000), bk 1 cap. 1 para. 46. In their translation, first published in 1843, the ecclesiologists Neale and Webb noted that the latter practice was still prevalent in some places, especially Somerset: J. M. Neale and B. Webb, *The Symbolism of Churches and Church Ornaments. A Translation of the First book of the Rationale Divinorum Officiorum written by William Durandus sometime Bishop of Mende*, 3rd edn (London, 1906), 37.

39 Aston, 'Segregation in church', 280. The evidence for Reading comes from C. Kerry, *A History of the Municipal Church of St Lawrence, Reading* (Reading and Derby, 1883), 33, 40, and, from after the Reformation (1572), 78.

40 Cox, *Bench-Ends*, 17.

41 P. Eames, *Furniture in England, France and the Netherlands from the Twelfth to the Fifteenth Century* (London, 1977), 202–03.

42 French, *Good Women of the Parish*, 102–12.

43 St Edmund, Salisbury: *Churchwardens' Accounts of St Edmund and St Thomas, Sarum,*

1443–1702, ed. by H. J. F. Swaine (Salisbury, 1896); All Saints, Bristol: *The Pre-Reformation Records of All Saints' Church, Bristol*, ed. by C. R. Burgess, 3 vols, Bristol Record Society, 46, 53, 56 (Bristol, 1995–2004); J. Fowler, 'Sherborne All Hallows' Church Wardens' Accounts', *Somerset and Dorset Notes and Queries*, 23 (1939–42), 189–94, 209–12, 229–35, 249–52, 269–72, 289–99, 311–14, 331–34.

44 Standing in the chancel permitted: 'Synodal Statutes of Bishop Walter de Cantilupe for the Diocese of Worcester, 1240', in *Councils and Synods with other Documents Relating to the English Church. Volume 2, AD 1205–1313*, ed. by F. M. Powicke and C. R. Cheney, 2 vols (Oxford, 1964), part 1, 294–325, cap. 4 (297); standing or sitting, 'Statutes of Bishop Robert Grosseteste for the Diocese of Lincoln, ?1239', in *Councils and Synods*, part 1, 265–78, cap. 45 (275); 'Synodal Statutes of Bishop Nicholas of Farnham for the Diocese of Durham, 1241x1249', *Councils and Synods*, part 1, 421–35, cap. 47 (433).

45 French, *Good Women of the Parish*, 112–16.

46 French, *Good Women of the Parish*, 100.

47 J. Sampson, 'Medieval benches and bench ends of Somerset: towards an archaeological approach', Chapter 7 in this volume.

48 N. Saul, *English Church Monuments in the Middle Ages: History and Representation* (Oxford, 2009), 57–59 with 37–40.

49 C. W. F. Goss, 'The Parish and church of St Martin Outwich, Threadneedle Street', *Transactions of the London and Middlesex Archaeological Society*, n.s. 6 (1933), 71.

50 E.g. Ashburton: *Churchwardens' Accounts of Ashburton, 1479–1580*, ed. by A. Hanham, Devon and Cornwall Record Society, n.s. 15 (Torquay, 1970); All Saints, Bristol: *Pre-Reformation Records of All Saints'*, vols 1 and, more particularly, 2; St Ewen's, Bristol: *The Church Book of St Ewen's, Bristol, 1454–1584*, ed. by B. R. Masters and E. Ralph, Publications of the Bristol and Gloucestershire Archaeological Society, Records Series, 6 (Bristol, 1967); St Edmund's, Salisbury: *Churchwardens' Accounts of St Edmund*; Walberswick: *Walberswick Churchwardens' Accounts, AD 1450–1499*, ed. by R. W. M. Lewis (London, 1947).

51 E.g. Ashburton, *Churchwardens' Accounts of Ashburton*; St Michael's, Bath: C. B. Pearson, 'The Churchwardens' Accounts of the church and parish of St Michael Without the North Gate, Bath, 1349–1575 [Parts 3 and 4]', *Somersetshire Archaeological and Natural History Society*, 25 (1880) and 26 (1881); St Martin in the Fields, London: *St Martin-in-the-Fields: The Accounts of the Churchwardens, 1525–1603*, ed. by J. V. Kitto (London, 1901); Louth: *The First Churchwardens' Book of Louth, 1500–1524*, ed. by R. C. Dudding (Oxford, 1941); St Lawrence's, Reading: *History of the Municipal Church of St Lawrence*; St Edmund's, Salisbury: *Churchwardens' Accounts of St Edmund*.

52 *St Martin-in-the-Fields*.

53 *Peterborough Local Administration: Parochial Government Before the Reformation. Churchwardens' Accounts 1467–1573 with Supplementary Documents 1107–1488*, ed. by W. T. Mellows, Northamptonshire Record Society, 9 (Kettering, 1937).

54 French, *Good Women of the Parish*, 9–13, 205.

55 H. L. Spencer, *English Preaching in the Late Middle Ages* (Oxford, 1993), particularly 60; J. Hughes, *Pastors and Visionaries: Religion and Secular Life in Late Medieval Yorkshire* (Woodbridge, 1988), 153–54.

56 For the importance of preaching from as early as the twelfth century, see S. Wenzel, *Latin Sermon Collections from Later Medieval England. Orthodox Preaching in the Age of Wycliffe* (Cambridge, 2005), 237–42, 335–36; the thirteenth-century evolution of diocesan and provincial legislation concerning the content of preaching is discussed at pp. 229–36. See also M. Gill, 'Preaching and image: sermons and wall paintings in later medieval England', in C. Muessig (ed.), *Preacher, Sermon and Audience in the Middle Ages* (Leiden, 2002), 158–59.

57 Spencer, *English Preaching*, 16–18.

58 Chaucer, *Canterbury Tales: General Prologue*, ll. 449–51.

59 E.g. 'Synodal Statutes of Bishop Peter Quivel for the Diocese of Exeter, 1287', in *Councils and Synods*, part 2, 982–1059, cap. 12 (1007–8).

60 R. Swanson, *Religion and Devotion in Europe, c.1215–c.1515* (Cambridge, 1995), 303–06.

61 For an engaging introduction to this vast topic, see Hughes, *Pastors and Visionaries*.

7. Medieval benches and bench ends of Somerset: towards an archaeological approach

Jerry Sampson

Introduction

MEDIEVAL BENCHES and their carved bench ends are under considerable and largely unappreciated threat. This threat derives from two sources: the most obvious being the attrition caused by an accelerating trend towards the extensive reordering of the interiors of parish churches; but the more insidious being the widespread misidentification of the surviving medieval corpus. While pressures to modernise church interiors mount, understanding of the remaining heritage of medieval seating remains woefully inadequate.

In the past, studies of seating have tended to concentrate on its relationship to the liturgy for which it was designed, or, where they have set out to examine the carved elements, have taken the figural or symbolic bench ends as their subject to the exclusion of the foliate or geometrical. Only in rare instances have authors considered the benches themselves,[1] or used the carvings to investigate the process of manufacture.[2]

Some examples should make this clear. Between 2003 and 2008, surveys of the benches and bench ends at five churches – Middlezoy, Ashcott, Bishops Lydeard, Clevedon and Stogumber (all in Somerset) – were commissioned from the author of this chapter. Of these five churches, the 1958 Pevsner volumes for Somerset do not mention Ashcott as retaining early seating, and of Middlezoy the entry states merely 'not many survive; some have original poppy-heads'.[3] In fact, Ashcott proves to retain 12 medieval and 14 pre- or early nineteenth-century bench ends as well as medieval panels (probably from bench frontals or backs) reused in the Victorian pulpit; while Middlezoy (Fig. 1) has 36 medieval and 2 seventeenth-century bench ends (the latter identifications confirmed by documentary evidence from the nineteenth-century restoration).

The problems with the present state of knowledge can be further illustrated by considering the bench ends of St Michael's, Othery, on the Somerset Levels.

Somerset is one of the few counties with a monograph devoted to its bench ends,[4] but, while visiting the church at Othery recently, three fine late medieval carved bench ends were found to be unrecorded by its author, presumably because they had previously been identified as Victorian replacements. These ends – depicting St Michael subduing the dragon/devil (Fig. 2), St Margaret (Fig. 3), and an angel holding a scroll at the top of a

Fig. 1: Medieval bench ends at Holy Cross, Middlezoy, Somerset, three from a group of 36 surviving at this church.

foliage panel (Fig. 4a) – are amongst the finest such carvings in the county. The first forms a pair with a poppy-head end bearing a 'pelican' carrying a sheaf of barley (used as the badge of Abbot Bere (1493–1524) of Glastonbury Abbey), the other two are technically identical with other medieval ends in the church. A bench end from the church which is illustrated in the county monograph as being the only medieval example of the representation of a butterfly turns out on close examination to be part of a group carved *c.*1880 by the local self-taught craftsman William Halliday.

The church guide book informs visitors that the medieval bench ends are restricted to the eastern part of the nave, and that the restored ends are to be found at the west end. The opposite is actually the case. Were a reordering of the church imminent, and the published sources taken as the guidelines for its execution, then serious losses of medieval carved work would be inevitable.

As the work of William Halliday at Othery illustrates (Fig. 4b), skilled carvers in the nineteenth century were capable of making reproduction bench ends which are sometimes very difficult to differentiate from original carvings, so that (in addition to the tools provided by stylistic analysis), technical or other features can provide essential markers for their identification.

While the style and extent of surface attrition on these carvings should be enough to identify their period, there are clear markers available from a close examination of the corpus to make a definitive identification. The medieval ends are carved from

Fig. 2: Medieval bench end at St Michael, Othery, Somerset, showing St Michael overcoming the dragon.

Fig. 3: Medieval bench end at Othery, Somerset, showing St Margaret with the dragon.

thicker timber (9.6 to 7.7 cm as against 6.7 to 7.6 cm), they have a chamfer on the inner edge beneath the seat, and are pegged to the top rail with a peg from the western edge, both characteristics which the Victorian ends lack. Also characteristic of the medieval ends is the presence of repairs, usually to the edges, but sometimes renewing more than 50 per cent of the carved face, implying renewals during the nineteenth century, and hence the existence of the bench end for a considerable period prior to that date.

Thus a methodology to correctly identify the early bench ends at Othery was relatively easy to construct: by isolating traits associated with a particular bench end which could be confidently ascribed to either the original seating or a restoration, other bench ends which shared these characteristics could be identified and

Fig. 4: Bench ends at Othery, Somerset. On the left (4a), a medieval bench end with an angel holding a scroll above a foliate panel. On the right (4b), very similar work by the Victorian carver William Halliday.

further traits identified within the more general group thus defined.

In a different set of benches different indicators may apply, but the principle of identifying defining traits remains the same, and this chapter sets out a generalised methodology. Not only does it allow the identification of medieval bench ends, but it may also prove useful in enabling the analysis of the medieval or replacement ends into sub-groups, so that the detailed chronology of the creation or repair of the seating can be reconstructed.

Dimensions

Some of these markers can be very simple. For instance, merely recording the overall dimensions of an assemblage of bench ends in a church usually reveals significant variations which may identify the nineteenth-century renewals, as well as providing

Fig. 5: The diagram in the centre shows a typical medieval bench and bench end in elevation, with a vertical back rest, a horizontal seat, and two structural rails, namely the top rail and the back brace (or 'book rest'). With the standard 'three peg' system, the seat and the two rails are all tenoned into the bench end (the tenons are shown in the diagram as grey elements), and secured by pegs (shaded black in the diagram, and labelled A, B, C). The photographs are of medieval pegging at Holy Cross, Thornfalcon, Somerset, the lettering corresponding to the diagram.

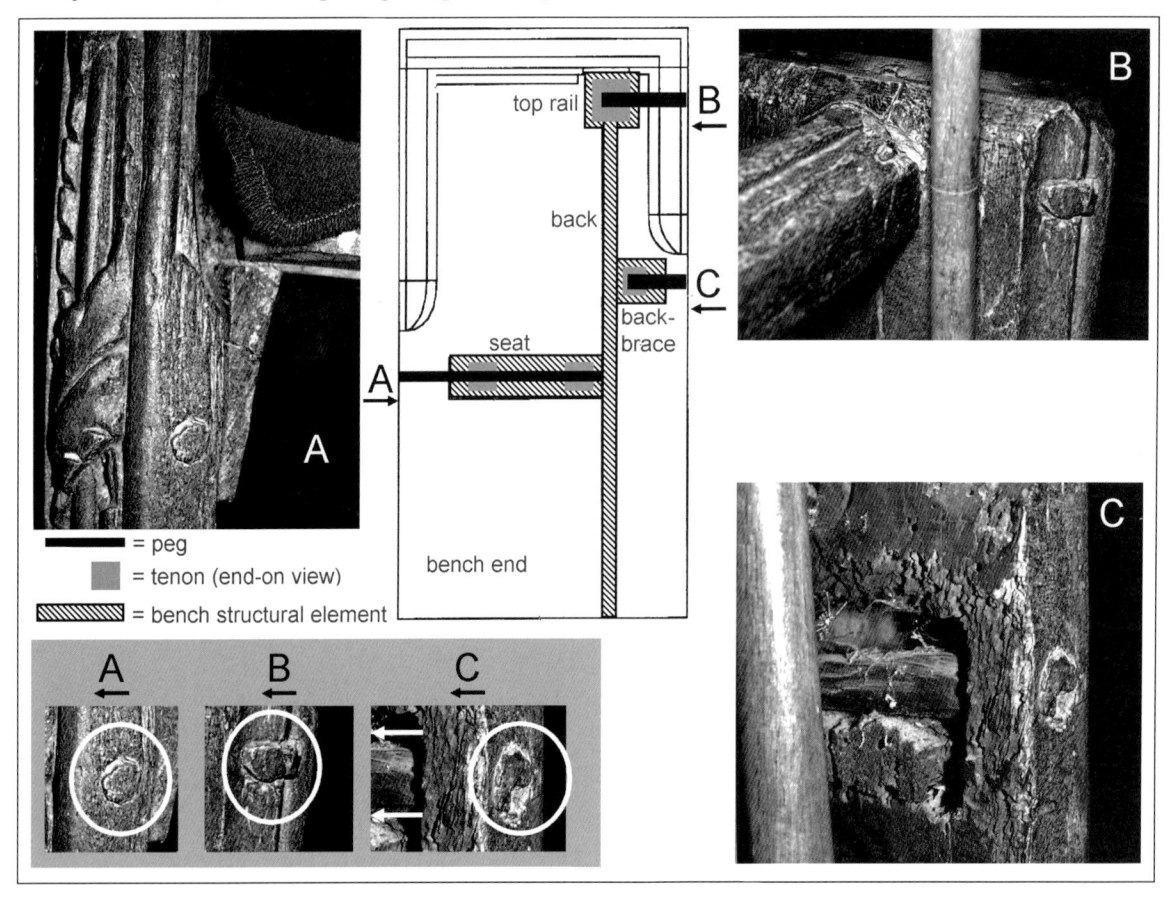

Table: Thickness of timber used for bench ends in some Somerset churches

All measurements in cm

	Medieval	19th century
Bicknoller	7.0 – 8.0	6.5
Bishops Lydeard	8.4 (avg)	6.4 (avg)
Othery	7.7 – 9.6	6.7 – 7.6
Stogumber	7.5 – 9.5	6.0 – 7.9
Stogursey	7.0 – 9.3	6.0
Trull	7.9 – 9.2	6.3 – 7.7

Notes

Bishops Lydeard is here expressed as an average, which makes the differences clearer, but at the cost of hiding the fact that a slight overlap is often apparent, where exceptionally thin medieval bench ends may be marginally thinner than the thickest of the replacements. The nineteenth-century figures for Bicknoller and Stogursey are not averages – the wood was of uniform thickness.

indications of the original distribution of the ends within the medieval nave. The former is usually most apparent in the relative thicknesses of the timber used for the bench ends, later renewals generally being significantly thinner than the medieval timbers, as can be seen in the Table, based on a fairly random group of Somerset churches.

Medieval timbers in Somerset bench ends are generally between 8 and 9 cm thick, and were probably centred on a nominal 3 ins board; whereas most nineteenth-century work is between 6 and 7 cm thick. While some thin medieval boards are thinner than the thickest nineteenth-century renewals, there are almost always other traits which serve to separate these out in other ways. As a general rule, however, the thinnest boards in the corpus will often be found to be associated with post-medieval restorations.

Nineteenth-century restorers generally matched their bench ends very accurately to the medieval corpus, so that heights and widths seldom serve as major indicators of differences in date. However, the medieval workshops had no reason to make their additions to the seating match what was already in existence, and variations in these dimensions are more likely to be indicative of differences in date within the middle ages, or, where contemporary, of having originated from a different position in the church.

At Middlezoy, for instance, two groups of medieval bench ends survive, the most numerous (30 ends) comprising Group 1, but with a set of six forming Group 2, the latter being consistently around 17 ins [43.3 to 44.3 cm] wide and 7.5 to 7.8 cm deep, whereas the Group 1 series are usually between 15.5 ins and 16.5 ins wide and around 6.5 to 7 cm deep. Having first identified the Group 2 ends on the basis of their overall dimensions, further examination showed that they differed also in the heights of the pegging for top rail, back brace and seat, and in the heights of the run-out stops for the mouldings on the inner face; that the top rail was mortised in a different way; the edge-mouldings were different; and the carvings incorporated more foliate elements than the Group 1 ends, probably indicating that they were products of a different early-sixteenth-century workshop.[5]

A single workshop, employing the same carver throughout, executed the benches at Stogumber, but here there is a significant difference in the heights of the ends between the benches east and west of the cross-aisle between the porches: those to the west being around 8 cm shorter than those in the eastern nave (approximately 84 cm high in the west nave, 92 cm high in the east). While at Stogumber this characteristic is probably to do with stressing the social importance of the seats closer to the altar, the reduction in the size of the bench ends in the north aisle at Broomfield probably relates to their function as the seating for the female half of the congregation. Where a medieval seating scheme has been reordered in the nineteenth century, especially where the ends have been fixed to new benches and redistributed around the church, such variations can assist in reconstructing the original positions of the bench ends. The recording of dimensions (including the levels of the original seats) is therefore also significant for the light which such variations shed on the social hierarchies within the late medieval congregation

Pegging

The relative heights of the pegging systems for attaching the end to its bench may prove significant in the same way for tracing the migration of medieval bench ends around a church following reordering, but a more basic trait for identifying renewals is the mere presence or absence of pegging (Fig. 5). Many nineteenth-century restorers followed a 'three-peg' medieval practice by assembling their benches with pegs to fix the tenons of the book rest (back brace) and top rail (both driven from the western edge) and seat (driven from the eastern edge), but this was not always the case, and the absence of pegging is a likely signature of a post-medieval date. It is important when looking for this trait, however, to ensure that the edges of such a bench end have not been pieced-in during later repair – a process which will have erased the visible evidence of the original pegging from a medieval end.

In cases where the benches themselves have been renewed the original ends may have been retained and refixed with nails (as at Middlezoy), or with pegs in different positions at the edge, or with pegs run in from the front (outer face) of the bench end (as at Stogursey, where the renewed top rails have been secured with pegs set longitudinally into the renewed timber and then capped with a rectangular repair). But in these instances there are usually traces of the redundant medieval peg holes – often carefully repaired and therefore sometimes difficult to identify.

The existence of more than one pegging system on the same bench end, is, like the presence of repairs, generally indicative of a pre-nineteenth-century date. This is often the result of a change in the seat height, itself often caused by the destruction of the sill-plate into which medieval bench ends were usually mortised, thereby reducing the effective height of the bench end by 3in or more. Redundant peg-holes are usually accompanied by redundant mortises cut in the reverse (inner face) of the bench end, and these will be discussed more fully below in the context of the renewal of the benches.

Because the loss of the sill-plate was often accompanied by decay to the lower edge of the bench ends, leading to the lower edge being cut down, it is usually preferable to measure the position of the pegs from the top edge (though centuries of handling may have led to the renewal of the top mouldings as well). Like the variations in height and width, variations in the original pegging positions may also be used to establish different medieval workshops or different original locations within the church. The heights of the pegging may have been conditioned by the partitions on the line of the aisle arcades being set out as a single unit and thus establishing the heights for the rail, back brace and seats in the whole bank of seating – thus at Stogumber the north-eastern bank of seats in the nave have the seat-height a clear 6 cm lower than the other areas of seating in the church; if, in a similar situation, the ends had been dispersed around the nave during a nineteenth-century reordering, they could be recognised as a group by their original seat-heights. The eastern south aisle seats at Stogumber were partly cannibalised in the 1873–5 restoration, with four of the ends being resited in the west nave: these were identified as part of the east nave seating by their greater overall height, and as part of the south nave aisle seating by the heights of their pegging.

Occasionally variations in the standard form of the pegging are encountered. At Spaxton, as well as the standard three-peg system discussed so far, there is a group of bench ends at the west end of the south aisle which have a pair of pegs to fix the seat. These exceptionally finely carved bench ends (one of which bears the initials 'I.B.', possibly for John Beny, the carver of the Trull rood-loft in 1539), were subsequently copied, probably in the eighteenth or early nineteenth century, but these copies use the standard three-peg system.

The form of the timber

As with the ends themselves, there is a tendency for the other more structural elements of medieval benches to be made from heavier timbers than their Victorian counterparts. This is particularly true of the back braces (which the Victorians replaced with book rests) and the seats. In both these instances the Victorians usually set these elements into the bench end with a joint which runs the whole width of the timber; whereas the medieval jointing usually consists of two tenons on the seat, and a relatively narrow, usually square tenon on the back brace. Both of these elements are generally around or in excess of 6 cm thick, and seats are usually housed within the width of the bench end or project only a little beyond its edge, often having a square, rather than a curved profile at the corner where they do project. The filled chases of seventeenth-century benches on ends of that date at Middlezoy and Stoke St Gregory are of much lighter construction than the medieval corpus, and tend to be even lighter than the Victorian benches.

Victorian benches, in addition to the characteristic slope of their backs, usually have their backs constructed from vertical planking or planks and muntins (vertical framing members). Medieval bench backs (at least in Somerset) are more commonly made from long horizontal planks, wide enough to construct the full height of the back from two planks – one above and one below the seat. Only in the backs and frontals of the main banks of seats and in the partitions on the lines of the aisles is framed plank and muntin construction used, in the former instances usually with the addition of decorative carved panels.

New benches, old bench ends

Medieval benches, with their straight backs and narrow seats were not constructed for comfort. With vertical backs, projecting top-rails (sometimes with uncomfortable mouldings)[6] and shallow seats, they must have proved a test of patience during the long sermons of the centuries after their manufacture. Where the original seating was decayed the Victorian restorers tended to renew the benches with a sloping back and a wider seat. In such cases, the identification of the medieval corpus often consists simply of identifying those ends which retain on their inner face the neatly filled chases and mortises from which the ancient benches have been withdrawn. In the process bench ends have often been reversed, that is, been used at the opposite end of a bench, with the previous westward edge becoming eastward; in this way, the chases for the new bench do not impinge upon or intersect the old repaired chases, and the repairs occupy what is now the eastern (previously western) half of the inner face.

While the vertical edge mouldings on the front (outer) faces of medieval bench ends in Somerset usually run out just above floor or sill-plate level, where these exist on the inner faces they usually terminate partway down the timber: that on the western edge ending higher, just above the back brace (book rest); that on the eastern edge ending just above the seat. Thus, even where the medieval seat scars are obscured by the extent of Victorian repairs it is often possible to identify the original orientation of the bench end from the relative heights of the run-out stops of the mouldings on the inner face.

It is sometimes the case (as in a few benches at Bicknoller (Fig. 6) and one at Cothelstone) that a medieval end has been

Fig. 6: A medieval bench end at St George, Bicknoller, Somerset, showing the inner face. This bench end has been refixed twice, and bears the scar of its original vertical back, together with that of an earlier Victorian sloping back – both represented by filled chases and mortises. The bench end was reversed (moved to the other end of a bench) before the present sloping back was put in place.
Key: A. Peg to fix medieval top rail. B. Scar of medieval back brace. C. Scar of medieval seat back. D. Moulding run-out, the height of which confirms the bench end has been reversed. E. Scar of the earlier nineteenth-century book rest. F. Scar of the earlier nineteenth-century seat back. G. Present seat back, of later in the nineteenth century.

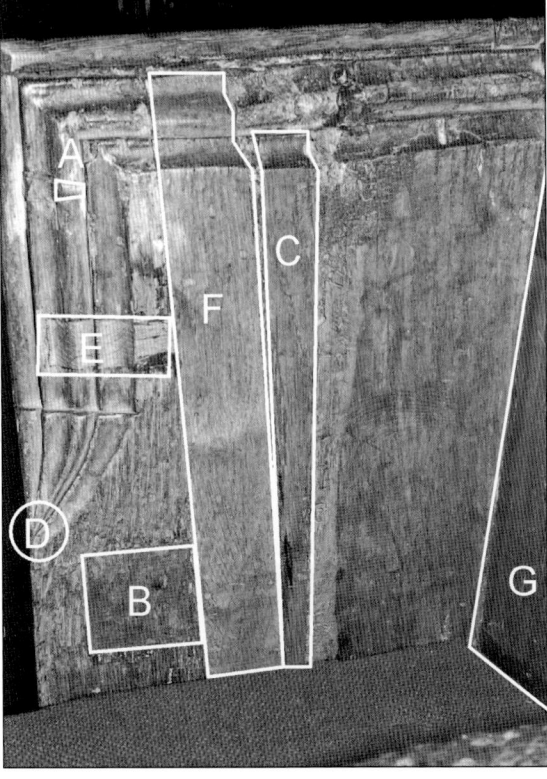

refixed twice, so that its inner face bears the scar of its original vertical-backed bench, together with that of an earlier Victorian sloping back – both represented as filled chases and mortises – and then the present bench. The imprint of the medieval bench means that even where none of the ancient benches survive – as at Ashcott, Bishops Lydeard and Middlezoy (Fig. 7) – their form can be reconstructed from the scars, and this may ultimately prove to be a powerful tool in the analysis of the overall corpus of medieval ecclesiastical seating, since it will provide information on a whole class of lost benches.

In a church which has been reordered and its benches renewed while retaining the carved ends, the relative numbers of originally north- and south-facing ends may indicate the extent of survival of the original seating prior to the restoration. At Bishops Lydeard the relationship of identifiable north- to south-facing ends surviving is 42 per cent to 58 per cent, suggesting that the church was fairly evenly furnished; but at Ottery St Mary twenty of the surviving ends originally faced south and only two faced north – suggesting that only a very restricted number of benches survived outside a bank of seating against a northern wall – the latter probably in the north (Dorset) Aisle.

General repair

Another key sign that a bench end is early is the presence of major repairs, since it is unlikely that oak renewed in the mid to late nineteenth century would require such treatment so soon after manufacture. These repairs have often been carried out with great

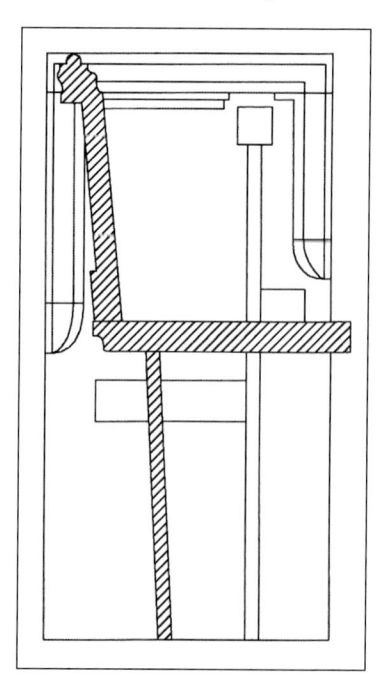

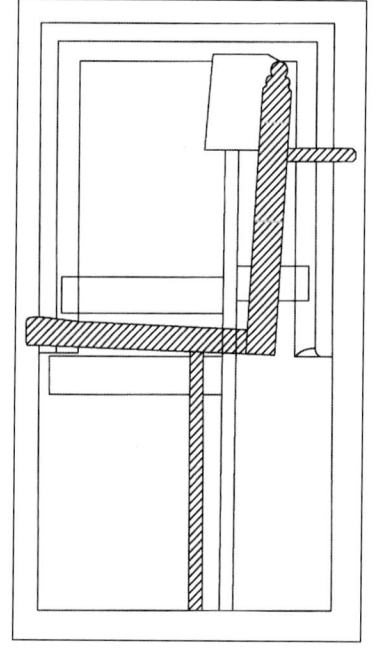

Fig. 7: Elevations of the bench and bench end at St Mary, Bishops Lydeard (left) and Holy Cross, Middlezoy (right), both in Somerset. The current Victorian seating is shown shaded, the medieval elements are unshaded. (To identify the function of each of the medieval elements, see Figure 5.) At both these churches the Victorian seating has a sloping back and seat, whilst the medieval back and seat are vertical and horizontal respectively. At Bishops Lydeard, but not Middlezoy, the bench end has been reversed.

skill, and, after a coat or two of Copal varnish, are often very difficult to detect on superficial examination. This is particularly the case where the edge of the repair has been matched to a feature of the original carving, as when an edge or top-moulding has been renewed using the line of one of the hollows or angles of the mould.

Such repairs should not be confused with the relatively common nineteenth-century practice of carving bench ends from blanks composed of two pieces of oak fixed together with a vertical joint. In these instances it will usually be seen that the two pieces have identical characteristics of surface morphology and carving technique.

It was a relatively common procedure in the nineteenth century to retain the central carved panel from a bench end (or from a bench back or front) and provide it with a new 'frame', replacing the moulded edges and plain base, and providing a new reverse. In this case almost all the diagnostic features for a medieval bench end so far discussed have been erased; indeed it is often difficult in such circumstances to differentiate between a panel originating from the medieval seating and one derived from some other feature, such as the dado of a screen.

While the presence of repairs is usually enough to indicate a pre-nineteenth-century date, their absence is not a sufficient or reliable signature of a nineteenth - or twentieth-century date. While many bench ends have suffered considerable attrition over the centuries, some have survived remarkably unscathed, and other markers must be invoked to make a definitive identification.

The position of repairs can also be significant. As discussed later, they may indicate the former presence of hinges for fixing a door to make a closed pew, or the position of a former hinged or sliding seat.

Surfaces and finish

Grain and colour

Victorian copies are often carved from wood which is of a different quality or species, so that variations in colour and grain can be signs of replacement. Most churches are dimly lit and such variations are difficult to see – indeed, these often show up most clearly in photographs taken under artificial light. Restorers often used red deal for new work, and even after varnishing this usually shows up against the paler oak of the original work.

Accuracy of finish

There is generally a much greater degree of accuracy and crispness of finish in nineteenth century work. This is, however, heavily dependent upon the workshop responsible for the work:

a professional nineteenth-century joinery firm would produce a high degree of finish, but a local craftsman such as William Halliday may leave toolmarks and inaccuracies of line and execution very similar to those on medieval carvings.

Conversion of the timber
Medieval carvers, by contrast to the Victorian joinery workshops, were not averse to leaving traces of their working practice in the form of tool-marks on front or back, or of setting-out lines, and so forth; the line and geometry of their carving were often wanting at the time of production, and time has further affected the surface morphology of many of their products.

Setting-out lines are generally the province of the medieval craftsman, but they can be present on Victorian copies, especially when these are the product of local carvers rather than commercial joiners' workshops. Usually these are restricted to ruled lines, but occasionally lines set out with a compass occur, sometimes with the centres from which the curves were struck still being recognisable.

The medieval carvers were generally careful to prepare their bench ends to a clean finish, even on the reverse, where marks of the pitsaw are sometimes preserved, but where marks of secondary reworking with adze and plane show that the timber was more commonly worked smooth. At Middlezoy the fronts of the carved bench ends suggest that the wood was sanded to remove residual toolmarks, but generally medieval carving preserves the slight 'faceting' of the surface left by the chisel and this is usually clearly visible under raking light.

The extent of wear and tear on the oak is often indicative of greater antiquity, but, again, its absence is not a sufficient signature of a late date. At Clevedon two groups of bench ends of near identical design exist: one (comprising up to seven ends) is heavier in construction and of generally more damaged appearance, and seems certainly medieval; the other has much less surface attrition, and by comparison with Group 1 seems more recent as a result. However, there is a persistent tradition that some of the ends at Clevedon were brought from nearby Wraxall, and it seems likely that the Group 1 ends derive from this source, while the Group 2 ends represent the surviving late medieval bench ends original to Clevedon church, rather than being later copies.

The use of punches and incised 'secondary' detail has not been certainly identified on post-medieval bench end carving, but becomes a hallmark of the medieval Quantock group and its derivatives. For example, square four-point punches, circular punches, dots and the use of the gouge to create wavy-lines or crescents are found on works by Simon Werman (Broomfield and

Trull) and Glosse (Stogursey), showing that these were the common property of more than one Somerset workshop – though, since the square punches must have been custom made, their precise form may serve to identify the work of individual craftsmen. A nine-point punch is used at Ottery St Mary.

Secondary detail – consisting of lightly incised 2-dimensional representations – is also found in work by Glosse at Stogursey, and by other carvers at Bishops Lydeard, Hatch Beauchamp and elsewhere. This too seems to be an exclusively medieval conceit.

Location and assembly numerals

The incised numerals used to identify the position of a component (an assembly numeral) or the position of a bench end (location numeral) do not appear to have been common on the late medieval benches of Somerset. Broomfield and Stogumber both have location roman numerals on bench ends, and there are one or two assembly numbers on bench back planks at Stogumber.[7]

The location numbers, (with no corresponding numbers on the associated benches) at Stogumber are found low down on the inner faces of the ends (several of which are cut by the chase made to locate the bench back, showing that they were incised during the manufacturing process), and these not only identify original ends but also allow the original sixteenth-century configuration of the seating to be reconstructed. These numbers do not run from '1' to '87', but are grouped in sequences corresponding to the ends on a specific bank of seating, sometimes with the ends for both sides of an aisle 'differenced' by the addition of a curved line attached to the main numeral.

In this case the fact that only the ends were numbered shows that the carver was being sent groups of 'blanks' corresponding to the area of seating being worked on by the carpenters' workshop, and that the two were operating as separate workshops. Here, the numbering of the benches in separate blocks shows that the bench end carver was working to a series of 'contracts', the two largest (and probably, therefore, the first) being in the eastern end of the north aisle and the east nave. This sequence is confirmed by the distinct development in the style of the bench ends during the progress of the project (a scheme which may have taken well over a year to complete) – the first group in the east end of the north nave aisle have traits found nowhere else in the church (two have mouldings on the inner face, the northern ends have true tracery in the upper tier of lights and no foliate band between the tiers of lights), while in the west of the nave (the last area to be worked on) five-light designs appear and the upper panel of decoration is more commonly separated from the blind lights beneath.

Fig. 8: A sliding seat at St Peter, Catcott, Somerset (bench on the right). The bench on the left has a slot where there used to be such a sliding seat.

A similar pattern emerges in the location numerals at Broomfield, where two sets of six and one of five consecutive numerals are used, again suggesting that small sets of 'blanks' were being despatched to the carver by the carpenters' workshop. In one set of six (Nos. 18–23)[8] the carving was shared equally between Simon Werman (who signs No. 33) and a highly skilled assistant (who is responsible for a total of thirteen of the bench ends in the assemblage).

At Cheddar there are roman numerals on the upper part of the inner face of the bench ends running into the thirties. These are no longer in order, and in at least one case the numeral is partly cut away by a nineteenth-century repair; however, the character of the numerals and their presence on the visible part of the reverse suggests that they were cut after the benches were assembled, perhaps at the start of the nineteenth century reordering before the benches were dismantled. Original numerals at Monksilver are accompanied by nineteenth-century roman figures cut during the restoration, but the eastern series of the latter are one number higher than the originals, since a bench had been added when the north door was blocked and its gangway was filled with a new seat.

Therefore it would appear that in general location numerals are not a sufficient indicator of pre-nineteenth-century date, and other confirmatory evidence should be sought before accepting such a bench or bench end as medieval. Numerals cut with a scribe are more likely to be medieval than those cut with a chisel or simply scratched into the wood; numbers which are cut through by elements of the (original) bench must, however, have been cut prior to assembly.

Fig. 9: Two close up views of a bench end at St Mary, Stogumber, Somerset. On the left, the neat repair work where there had once been a slot for a sliding seat. On the right, the repair seen from underneath the seat, looking at the inside face of the bench end.

Sliding and hanging seats

At Catcott some of the very plain late medieval or early post-medieval bench ends have small sliding seats (Fig. 8). The plank-seat runs through a slot in the bench end, with its outer end supported on a pair of slightly splayed legs, so that when the seat was not in use it could be slid back beneath the bench out of the way. Others of the bench ends at this church merely retain the letter-box sized slots and these also exist in several of the ends at Chedzoy, and Victorian repairs filling similar slots have recently been identified on 13 of the 33 ends at Stogursey and 11 of the 75 original ends at Stogumber (Fig. 9).

'Hanging seats' or 'flap seats' are well attested in documentary evidence.[9] For example, in 1651–2 the accounts for St Edmund's, Salisbury record payments relating to both hanging and sliding seats:

> Mrs Ann Carter, hanging seat for servant 1s. – Josse, wife of Perigan Dawes, sliding seat before Magistrate's Pew 2s. 6d. – Mrs Battes, widow, a flap seat fixt to her owne for servant 6d.[10]

Fig. 10: Flap seats at two Somerset churches, St Dunstan, Baltonsborough (left) and St Margaret, Tintinhull (right). That at Baltonsborough is raised when not in use, and secured by a catch at the top of the bench end, the legs (which are hinged) lying flat against the seat. The flap seat at Tintinhull is rather less sophisticated – the seat is dropped when not in use, and the iron stay lies along the floor.

Examples of flap seats survive at Baltonsborough and Tintinhull (Fig. 10). At Middlezoy the two seventeenth-century bench ends are decorated only over their upper halves, the lower part of the end remaining uncarved (Fig. 11a). Both have repairs to the sides at the base of the carved area, and it is possible that these relate to the former existence of fixings for hinged subsidiary seats which were part of the original design and obviated the need for the carving where the flaps would have lain. The hinges for a flap seat survive on a bench end at Brompton Ralph (Fig. 11b). At East Quantoxhead several of the bench ends have pairs of (filled) mortises beneath seat level which were probably cut to locate fixed subsidiary seats.

Most of the early documentary references to such subsidiary seats known to the author (as in the instances above) relate to pews on the female (northern) side of the church, and it is of interest to note that all but three of the sliding seats at Stogumber are situated to the north. They were the province of the servants or children of the owners of the benches to which they were attached. Hanging seats could be fixed at the same height as the bench itself, and were probably more suitable for individual servants; whereas sliding seats always had to be positioned below the seat belonging to the bench (necessarily making them lower), and since they could also be longer and accommodate more than one occupant, were better suited to children.[11]

However, flap and sliding seats are known in nineteenth-century seating (as discussed by Geoff Brandwood in Chapter 19, page 294), so their presence is not itself a clear indicator of date.

Fig. 11: On the left (11a), one of two seventeenth-century bench ends at Middlezoy, Somerset. There is no decoration on the lower half of the bench end, and there are repairs to the sides where hinges may have been sited, suggesting there may once have been a flap seat there. On the right (11b), a bench end at St Mary, Brompton Ralph, Somerset, with the remains of two early hinges for a flap seat, about one third of the way up

Fig. 12: Rebates for door hinges on medieval bench ends at two Somerset churches. Left, Lydeard St Lawrence; right, Bicknoller. As discussed in the text, one would expect most doors on medieval bench ends to be added after their initial construction.

Door hinges

Rebates for hinges can indicate the previous existence of a door on a bench end, as for example at Lydeard St Lawrence and Bicknoller (Fig. 12). The conversion of an open bench into a closed pew by the addition of a door is likely to be an adaptation of the seventeenth or eighteenth century, but the form of the bench ends at Stogumber (Fig. 13), where all the ends have been rebated as if to receive doors, but only a maximum of 28 out of more than 80 have in fact received a door, suggests that the idea of attaching doors may have been in the mind of the sixteenth-century workshop which made the benches.

Fig. 13: The remains of a door hinge on the medieval bench end at Stogumber, Somerset. The photo shows the lower part of the bench end, and the pew floor on which it rests. Note that the edge of this bench end, like all the others in the church, has been rebated as if to receive the door, though many of the benches in the church did not have doors fitted.

The Spaxton benches (of which as many as 31 may date from as late as 1561) only have 5 (?+2) ends which bore doors, and the certain attributions are all on the north (female) side of the nave, with doors facing south; at Stogumber the majority of the benches which had doors installed – 20 of the 28 – lie to the north and of these the majority – 16 of the 20 – have doors facing south (towards the men's half of the church). Was modesty (real or feigned) perhaps a factor in deciding to enclose these benches? The eight men's benches with doors are fairly equally divided in this respect: five doors face south, three face north.

Style and motif

Nineteenth-century joinery workshops, having a much wider range than their medieval forebears, being more eclectic, and having the benefit of ecclesiological publications as source material, are likely to be working in styles which are at variance with those of the more localised medieval carvers. The simple 'stock-book' ends produced in many Victorian schemes make little or no pretence at blending in with the surviving medieval carvings.

The incorporation of anachronistic motifs, or of styles originating in other localities can, therefore, be a guide to the presence of renewals. Thus the bench ends at Butleigh resemble medieval bench ends from the midlands, with simple tracery flanked by buttresses, which several commentators have suggested include medieval originals, but these are not stylistically related to the medieval Somerset carving tradition, and (like the mid-nineteenth-century renewal of the nave roof in East Anglian hammer-beam style) are almost certainly intrusive renewals. However, as we have seen, Halliday was copying medieval work at Othery and elsewhere (a good copy of one of the Middlezoy ends occurs amongst his Othery carvings), and where an effort has been made to blend the new with the old real difficulty can occur in detecting any differences in style or motif (as discussed by Suzanna Branfoot in Chapter 16). Indeed, it is possible that in some cases Victorian ends may reproduce lost medieval designs copied from ends which were discarded during the restoration – one Monksilver bench end of the 1840s is a copy of a medieval end at nearby Crowcombe, and it is possible that the end with the sacred monogram in the same church is copied from a lost original. Thus the copies at Stogumber are identifiable largely on the basis of the traits discussed in this chapter, and not their style, where they are exceptionally carefully matched; at Spaxton the copies of the original carvings by I.B. had not previously been identified.

Two of the Stogumber replacements, however, bear motifs which are unlikely to occur in medieval carving: one end bears the chi-rho monogram flanked by alpha and omega, and another has a conventional Latin cross concealed in the foliage. Despite the claims of the county monograph, a depiction of the dove returning to the ark with an olive branch at East Quantoxhead is also stylistically unlikely to be medieval in origin and occurs on an end identifiable by other traits as being of the nineteenth century.

Owners' initials and other inscriptions

Initials 'WL' or 'W' or 'L' occur on 10 of the bench ends at Stogumber, and there are various monograms – 'SW', 'WS', 'H.W.' and 'S.G.' – incised or painted on bench backs; these may relate to the names of the owners of the benches. The 1602 bench ends at Stringston bear initials and what may be the full names of owners, including that of Thomas Pamer (Fig. 14).[12] At Spaxton there are personal and house names neatly incised on several of the back braces. These marks, like those of the hinges for doors, relate to a period when personal ownership of benches was commonplace, and may indicate a pre-nineteenth-century origin for the elements upon which they are found.

At Ottery St Mary the long benches which form part of the 1849–51 restoration under Butterfield have the word 'Free' painted on the backs of the free seats in the western parts of the nave in alternating red and black (which serves as an indicator of the original configuration of the benches).

Other fixtures

Many assemblages show signs of lost fixings for various elements whose purpose is now obscure or may prove impossible to

Fig. 14: Bench ends at St Mary the Virgin, Stringston, Somerset of 1602. The one on the left bears that date and the initial I.W. That on the right also carries various initials, and an inscription probably relating to Thomas Palmer, though it is difficult to interpret.

determine. The former existence of fixtures such as brass plates designating the ownership of the bench is fairly easily identified, but the simple drilled holes occasionally found on the faces of the bench ends could derive from a multitude of causes. Their presence or absence is not a major marker of date – though their presence does tend to suggest that the wood has had an 'extended history' – but it may be worth suggesting a few worth looking for and noting.

Suggestions of the former presence of candle prickets have been noted at Trull, Broomfield, Clevedon (Fig. 15) and elsewhere, taking the form of regular drilled holes in the top of the bench ends and the top-rails of the benches. This seems particularly likely to be the case at Clevedon, since there are traces of candle wax beside the hole in the finial of No. 32. At Clevedon these holes are found in both the Group 1 and 2 (medieval) ends of the centre banks of seating, and in the nineteenth-century Group 4 ends of the northern benches. They appear to form a consistent distribution pattern, so that in the eastern part of the nave every other end had a candle pricket, while to the west only every third end was provided with one (a further indicator of social hierarchy). The Clevedon bench ends also have marks of fixings which may derive from lost gas-lamp fittings. Surviving candle prickets can be seen attached to the box pews of *c.*1827 at Sutton Mallet, the holes in which they are fixed being very similar to those recorded in medieval ends, and in the 1840s benches at Monksilver.

Fig. 15: Three Somerset churches with holes drilled in the top horizontal surface of the bench or pew, almost certainly to hold candle prickets. Left, St Mary and All Saints, Broomfield, looking down on the top rail of the medieval bench; centre, church of the Holy Ghost, Crowcombe, where the hole is drilled into the medieval bench end; right, Sutton Mallet (dedication unknown), where candle prickets still survive in the box pews of about 1827.

The mid-nineteenth-century benches at Butleigh were provided with pairs of L-sectioned battens nailed to the undersides of the seats which serve to neatly secure the brim of a top hat, allowing it to be stored safely out of the way during the service. These battens have also been found fixed beneath the benches at Curry Rivel. At Clevedon there are brass hinged retainers and cast iron drip trays fixed to the fronts of the bench ends for storing umbrellas.

Conclusion

The suggestions outlined above are the first fruits of a limited number of surveys carried out by the author in one area of the country, and they do not pretend to be exhaustive – and the applicability of these techniques to the rich heritage of other counties has yet to be tested. Furthermore, little has been said of the analysis of medieval assemblages of carved bench ends by the more traditional art historical means of style and motif; or of the emerging picture of the pattern of workshops producing seating in medieval Somerset, and their relationship to the carvers producing screens, roofs and other wooden decoration.

As more surveys are undertaken it is expected that other markers and technical features for discriminating ancient and modern will accrue, and further insights into the production of medieval church seating will be gained. Indeed, the most enduring result of such surveys is likely to be our increased information on workshop practice, the social context of the congregational seating, and the long history of alteration and repair.

First, however, it is essential to identify and secure the preservation of the corpus for study.

Notes

1. Mark McDermott, 'Early bench-ends in All Saints' Church, Trull', in *Proceedings of the Somerset Archaeological and Natural History Society*, vol. 138, 117–30; and 'Supplementary notes on the bench-ends in All Saints' Church, Trull, and the wood-carver Simon Warman', ibid. vol. 142, 329–33.
2. Joshua J. Schwieso, 'An unusual bench end in Brompton Ralph Church', in *Proceedings of the Somerset Archaeological and Natural History Society*, vol. 133 (1989), 191–5.
3. Nikolaus Pevsner, *The Buildings of England: South and West Somerset* (Penguin, Harmondsworth, 1958) 237.
4. Peter Poyntz Wright, *The Rural Benchends of Somerset: A Study in Medieval Woodcarving* (Avebury, 1983).
5. Probably the workshop responsible for the benches at Weston Zoyland, Curry Rivel, the main series at Othery, and High Ham.
6. At High Ham two projecting decorative mouldings on the back rail would have rendered the seats exceptionally uncomfortable, and at a later period these have been cut away and are only visible in the outline of the mortise with the bench ends.
7. Such numbering may be a hallmark of the workshop of Simon Werman, since it has also been found on stylistically related work at Monksilver, Cothelstone, Bicknoller, Combe Florey and East Quantoxhead.

8 All the survey catalogues referred to are numbered beginning at the NW corner of the nave, proceed eastwards, and 're-set' at the west end after the easternmost bench of each range of seats.
9 J. Charles Cox, *Bench-Ends in English Churches* (Oxford University Press, 1916) plates on p. 22.
10 Quoted in Cox, *Bench Ends*, 19.
11 At Stogursey bench end No. 28 (the easternmost except for the frontal-end on the south side) has two successive slots at different heights, as if a second seat had been made when the children had grown.
12 The full inscription - 'FORA HOS / OF SER TO / MASPAMER' – is obscure to say the least, but may be intended for: 'For a house of Sir Thomas Pamer'.

8. Assessing and evaluating English pews: three case studies

Charles Tracy

DESCRIBING THE CHANGES that were made to English parish churches over one hundred years ago, Frank Howard and Fred Crossley wrote:

> It is amusing to note how, when an almost complete clearance of the old benches has been made, the few survivors have been relegated to the rear [of the church] for the use of the poorer parishioners, while the aristocracy of the village use the new and hideous seats, or naked chairs, which have taken their place.[1]

This somewhat jaundiced statement was published in 1917 as the wholesale or partial destruction of several of the finest Gothic cathedrals in northern France, along with their historic furnishings, was taking place. The events described by Howard and Crossley and those occurring in First World War France retain a certain currency today. They represent the two extremes of church furnishings lost either voluntarily by those responsible for them or violently against their will. Of course, these are not new concerns: English parish churches have been subject to decay, destruction and reordering since the day they were built.

Naturally, a furniture historian deprecates the degradation of a church's historic environment whatever its cause, but sometimes the evolving liturgy, and perhaps the very survival of the building as a functioning space, has to take precedence. Thankfully, churches continue to be visited by all manner of folk, and church tourism makes a financial contribution to the upkeep of many of them. Moreover, most clergy are aware of their responsibilities in caring for an outstanding collection of historic furnishings.

If, for any number of liturgical or practical reasons, a parish decides that it needs to move or remove an object or group of objects, specialists can be called in to evaluate the artefacts concerned. The clearer understanding of the historical and artistic significance of a church's furniture that such experts can provide is vital to an informed and sensitive reordering debate.

The three case histories discussed below may provide some insights into the delicate and sometimes controversial process of evaluating church furniture. People are often surprised at the specimens of ecclesiastical joinery that are sometimes singled out for preservation. Historicity, artistic quality and conservation are not mind-sets readily accessed by everyone, but, in combination, they will reveal the kernel of a robust significance rating.

A version of this article (without the appendix) was first published in the 2009 edition of Historic Churches *and it is reprinted here with the kind permission of the author and the publisher, Cathedral Communications Limited.*

In general, parishes are unlikely to seek to remove objects of well-established historical or artistic importance. The churchwardens of Fressingfield or Ufford in Suffolk, or Altarnun in Cornwall will know that permission for the removal of their benches would never be granted. As objects of considerable pride in the parish and beyond, their presence is integral to the way that parishioners and visitors experience and enjoy these churches.

More problematic are the sets of furniture which could be designated as having considerable significance or some significance. In these cases there is likely to be a high restoration content. After 400 years or so of constant use, without regular maintenance and repair, original benching would become completely unserviceable.

A valid significance rating usually hinges on an archaeological evaluation of the quality and authenticity of the furniture *en masse*. A sound judgement requires the assessor to burrow beneath the carapace of the furniture's design and decoration. A good bench is a satisfying blend of architectural design, sculptural ornament and skilled joinery. It incorporates several different components: bench ends, seats, seat backs, and fronts. Joinery principles are a key factor in a value assessment. In the highest ranked examples, the quality and refinement of the joinery should be on a par with the design and decoration. If a bench end is decorated, the quality of its carving is as important as its subject matter and iconography. Heraldry on benches can open a window onto patronage and date of manufacture, and supplement the body of information upon which a rating can be based. A grasp of the maker's background, affiliation and level of ability can also be illuminating: the finest church furniture is the product not only of artful execution but also of access to specialist knowledge, aesthetic sensibility and exceptional design skills. A specialist assessor, weighing all these factors together should be able to establish whether the furniture was made by an urban or itinerant workshop, or by the village carpenter.

Ancient benches are nearly always a patchwork of historic restoration, the quality of which can be variable. The ubiquitous Victorian and early-twentieth-century refurbishments usually set a high standard in competency and discernment. At that time great efforts were usually made, as far as contemporary tools would allow, to follow the original construction principles, even when it was feasible only to retain a few of the ancient components. One could describe this factor as 'historical integrity'.

Haddenham

The first of this chapter's case studies concerns St Mary, Haddenham, Buckinghamshire (Figs. 1a & b), where the benches are described in more detail in an appendix to this chapter. Here the monumental late-thirteenth-century village church was found to be still almost fully pewed-out. The parish had proposed to remove most, if not all, of the nave benches. It was suggested that some of the oldest pews could be retained, by being placed 'either along the side walls or along the side of the chancel area'. In fact, they were all of the same age, and comprised a complete set, formerly en-suite with the displaced chancel screen. A compromise along these lines is often proposed, but, in practice, is rarely satisfactory.

The benches in the smaller eastern blocks of the nave showed more evidence of restoration than those in the western block,

Fig. 1a: St Mary, Haddenham, Buckinghamshire. (© Jonathan Taylor)

Fig. 1b: Haddenham, detail of bench end. (© Jonathan Taylor)

which is, perhaps, not surprising. Many are wholly nineteenth-century replacements. A major refurbishment was carried out in about 1860, when the central and side aisle nave flooring was replaced by the red and black encaustic tiles that survive today. The arcaded desk-fronts at the head of each block, as well as the rear seat backs of both blocks, were mostly authentic, with their panels interspersed with plain stiles (the vertical elements) and tracery consistent with late-fifteenth-century designs.

To the untutored eye this might seem to be something of a hodge-podge, but the quality of construction and design of these early-sixteenth-century benches was exceptionally good, and markedly better than that found on most other pews of this date in the same region. It was often necessary to crawl around underneath the benches to assess them, but the joinery practices these efforts revealed were quite sophisticated. They were also an advertisement for the best and most sensitive kind of Victorian restoration. After 500 years the pewed-out nave was still virtually complete, with the central portion of the coeval chancel screen surviving, albeit removed to the west end. The decorative carving on both benches and screen was found to be still completely Gothic in form.

Kildwick

The other two case histories lie on either side of the Pennines. St Andrew, Kildwick, West Yorkshire, possessed a plethora of pew and pew-associated timberwork, most of it *ex situ*. Portions of the mid-nineteenth-century benching at the front of the nave, which the parish wished to remove along with the twentieth-century benching behind it, incorporated decorative panels from the now almost wholly destroyed seventeenth-century box pews (Figs. 2a & b). The chancel choir benches and stalls, which were again a mixture of seventeenth- and nineteenth-century components, were also due for removal (Figs. 3a & b). They contained on their fronts more of this important collection of seventeenth-century West Yorkshire decorative panelling from the same source. Such incorporation is a good example of the Victorians' desire to conserve the art of the past.

It is not possible, in the space of this chapter, to do justice to Kildwick's rare and charming Eltoft family pew of 1633 (Fig. 4), but, in passing, a quotation from Jonathan Swift's withering couplets on such structures, cannot be resisted:

> *A bedstead of the antique mode,*
> *Compact of timber many a load,*
> *Such as our ancestors did use,*
> *Was metamorphosed into pews;*
> *Which still their ancient nature keep*
> *By lodging folks disposed to sleep.*

With regard to the implications of the reordering proposals at Kildwick, it was important to weigh up the value of this collection of vernacular seventeenth-century decorative panelling, incorporated in the assorted mainly nineteenth-century furniture forms. The latter, per se, are of unexceptional artistic value, but, perhaps, deserved to be retained mainly for their utilitarian function as display frames. The same can be said of the mid-nineteenth-century nave front benching, with its display of seventeenth-century panels. The rest of the nave benching was well made, functional, but of little intrinsic interest.

Fig. 2: St Andrew, Kildwick, West Yorkshire. Details of front of nave pewing, showing two dated fragments of the earlier box pews (1691 and 1626).

Fig. 3: Kildwick: decorative seventeenth-century panel assemblages from the box pews, worked into the mainly Victorian chancel choir stalls.

Fig. 4 (left): Detail of the Eltoft family pew at Kildwick. The initials (EE) of Edmund Eltoft and the date of 1638 are inscribed on the entrance door. This is now the only surviving complete item from the church's lost box pew ensemble.

Fig. 5 (right): Oak chest at St John the Evangelist, Leeds (© The Churches Conservation Trust)

Assessing the significance of this eclectic assortment of pews and congregational benching was challenging, but it was clear that the dismantling of the later panel frames would have put at risk the conservation of this uniquely important collection of regional vernacular carved panelling. It is only because this material had been reused in this way, as part of the church's furnishings, that its art-historical value had been overlooked. Such inspired incarceration had saved it from destruction.

The catalogue of an exhibition of oak furniture from Yorkshire churches held at Temple Newsam in 1971 demonstrates the high quality of much of the Kildwick material. The framed three-panelled oak chest from St John, Leeds, which was shown on that occasion (Fig. 5) although similar in design, is, in fact, of inferior quality to the chest at Kildwick. The Leeds chest has similar foliate crosses within a lozenge with exterior lobes, but the latter are cross-hatched, whereas Kildwick's were spiralled. Cross-hatching was not found at Kildwick, although there was some inventive stippling, which probably indicates an early seventeenth-century date. The different dated inscriptions on the Kildwick panelling, meanwhile, demonstrate that the former box pews were supplemented throughout the seventeenth, eighteenth and nineteenth centuries.

Kildwick church, then, contains a superb array of classically-derived, as well as plenty of pseudo-naturalistic, ornament. It is a veritable treasury of Yorkshire decorative vernacular wood carving, mainly from throughout the seventeenth century. As such, it is an important cultural resource which deserves to be better known and more widely studied. With the help of the inscriptions and a comparative analysis, it should be possible to create from this remarkable collection an invaluable chronology of the regional ornament style for the period.

Fig. 6a (left): St Mary the Virgin, Deane, Lancashire. View down the nave from the west end. Note that all the Victorian wooden fittings are stylistically en suite with the earlier material. Fig. 6b (right): view of north aisle benches from west.

Deane

And so, finally, to St Mary the Virgin, Deane, near Bolton, Lancashire. For most of its medieval life this 'long, low and embattled' church was a modest chapel of ease, subject ultimately to Whalley Abbey. The church was fully pewed-out with a mixture of oak benches of the same design but of two different dates, the later being early nineteenth-century (Figs. 6a & b). The original bench ends and seats could be recognised by the thicker scantling (or cross section) of the timbers, and from the fact that they were hand, as opposed to machine, finished (Figs. 7a & b). The profile of all the bench ends was a characteristic pair of reversed scrolls, with a three-quarter round moulding at the top and simple round mouldings on each side. The two campaigns could be recognised most easily from an inspection of these bench tops. The later benches must be the product of the documented 1833 reordering, some of them with brass plates engraved in a copper-plate hand with the name of the lessor of a particular family pew. They also have typically Victorian decorated brass stays and metal troughs (now painted) attached to the ends for the storage of umbrellas. Of the 98 extant benches, 54 are more or less ancient. Unlike the carved ends at Haddenham, Deane's bench ends were plain.

The call for a significance analysis in this case was prompted by the parish's proposed reordering of much of the furnishing. There had been a discussion about the approximate age of the older benches, with proposed datings ranging from late medieval to seventeenth century. In fact, research has turned up another church in Lancashire with a set of benches executed by the same workshop. It is at St Mary and All Saints, Whalley, where the suite of furniture includes the carved arms of the Sherburnes of Stoneyhurst on a bench end originally near their family pew and now mounted on the church wall. Conveniently, this is prominently dated 1638 (Fig. 8). Whether the link with Deane is coincidence, or in some way related to the church's medieval ties with Whalley Abbey, we shall never know. The pew sets are not quite identical. At Whalley the profile of the bench end tops has an extra roll moulding (Fig. 9).

Fig. 7: St Mary the Virgin, Deane. The patina of a seventeenth-century (left) and nineteenth-century (right) bench end.

Fig. 8 (left): The family pew end at St Mary and All Saints, Whalley, Lancashire, displaying the coat of arms of the Sherburnes of Stoneyhurst and dated 1638.

Fig. 9 (right): Whalley, one of the seventeenth-century bench ends in the south aisle, looking south-west. Note the close similarity to the bench ends at Deane. This bench end has a Victorian plate attached indicating it is for the use of the residents of the local almshouse, and an umbrella drip tray beneath. (Both photos © Clifford Ball)

With the 1833 cloned seventeenth-century pews at Deane, we find a nice example of the Victorian historicising tendency, this time applied to a set of early-seventeenth-century benches. By dint of careful observation and research, the argument over dating is settled, and an attractive, although not aesthetically outstanding, set of furniture is found to contain an unexpected historical significance. The decision that is finally taken in Deane's case should now, at least, be better informed, if no easier to arrive at.

❖ ❖ ❖

APPENDIX: The benches at St Mary, Haddenham, Buckinghamshire

Introduction

This appendix briefly discusses the surviving medieval oak benching in the nave of St Mary Haddenham, an architecturally outstanding Buckinghamshire church. It aims to put the benches into a regional and national art-historical context, and discusses the role they played in the original late medieval scheme of furnishing. The findings are not only interesting in themselves, but it is hoped that this discussion will indicate the sort of insights that can emerge when seating undergoes systematic investigation.

For an account of the reordering which the church finally decided upon, see the relevant case study in this book (pages 442–5). A sketch plan of the church is also included there. Note that when the present tense is used in this appendix, it refers to the situation in 2003, when the author carried out an assessment of the benches. The original assessment also commented on the physical condition of the seating and options for change, but these matters are not included here. The photographs of Haddenham in this appendix were taken by the author, but as a record rather than for publication, and allowance should be made for this.

The arrangement of the seating

The seating at Haddenham rests on wooden plinths (sills) in the usual way for this date, although almost all of the plinths seem to have been renewed, presumably in the mid nineteenth century. Much of the seating was probably dismantled at that time. The refurbishment was presumably carried out around 1860 when the nave floors were replaced by the red and black chequer encaustic

Fig. A1a: St Mary, Haddenham, Buckinghamshire, looking west from the chancel step.

Fig. A1b: Looking north-east across the nave.

tiles still *in situ*. The extant wood block floor of the seating may date from this time, or possibly later.

There are twenty-two more or less complete benches in the main space of the nave (Figs. A1a & b), eleven each side, three in the eastern block and eight between the north door entrance way and the west tower. There were other benches in the central block each side at the front of the nave originally, probably bringing the former total for the whole of the central section to twelve each side. From the break in the longitudinal plinths in the front central section it is clear that there has been some disturbance here, and the church reports that benches were removed from the front in the 1980s.

In the side aisles, continuous integral banks of ancient benches survive in the western block, containing six on the north and nine on the south side (Fig. A2). The loss of three benches at the west end on the north side was sustained in the second half of the twentieth century when a panelled vestry was constructed at the back of the north aisle (Fig. A3). With three more ancient benches on the north-east side, somewhat incoherently arranged and much restored, the extant total of side benches amounts to eighteen. The single bench facing north in the south aisle is wholly nineteenth-century in construction.

In summary there were probably in the first place twenty-four benches in the main space, and twenty-six in the side aisles.[2] Based on the conservative supposition that the main nave benches would have accommodated six parishioners, and the side aisle benches five persons, it can be calculated that the nave seating capacity at Haddenham would originally have been in excess of 274 places. Given that the parish population around 1525 was probably little more than 100, such gross over-provision is of some interest.[3]

Fig. A2 (left): The benches in the south aisle, looking west.

Fig. A3 (right): Looking north-west across the rear block north-side benches. In the far north-west corner can be seen the panelled vestry.

Degree of restoration

The western blocks of benches in the central nave appear to be the least disturbed, with the exception of the plinths and most of the seats, and some of the seat backs. The seat plank of the terminal bench on the north side is almost certainly the original one.

The six benches (two pairs of three) at the east end of the nave are much more restored than those in the western block, with many of the bench ends in this eastern area being of the nineteenth century. Here, the bench ends on the north side, the seat backs of the centre pews, and the capping rails on the front, and in the centre benches, are all Victorian, although for the most part the tracery heads have been re-used (Fig. A4). The benches on the south side of this area are more authentic, although the capping rails are also modern. On both sides of this eastern block, the arcaded desk fronts and terminal seat backs are mostly authentic, with their panels interspersed with plain stiles of late-fifteenth-century type tracery.

Fig. A4: A Victorian bench end, retaining the late medieval tracery heads (on the north side of the east-central block of nave benches).

Fig. A5: Treatment of the seat back rest on the back seat of the main nave south-east block.

By contrast with the pews in the western central block, those in the north aisle are comprehensively restored. The south aisle benches however are still in a reasonably authentic state, albeit with a higher restoration content than those in the centre blocks, though the back plank of the terminal seat on this side may be original.

The joinery

From the western central block, we can see that the original quality of construction and design at Haddenham is exceptionally good, and markedly better than that found on most other pews of this date in the same region.

We can take as an example the treatment of the seat backs. The stiles of the fascia panels on the backs of the seat blocks protrude into the other side of the last seats, thus producing on both sides a primitive panel and frame construction (Fig. A5). (The same thing happens on the pew fronts.) The other original seat backs are smooth, their panel joins being almost invisible (where this is not so it is a sure sign that the original seat backs have been replaced). The panels were tongue and grooved, but on the reverse, they appear almost to be of lapped construction. This sophisticated illusion was created by chamfering the panels as they entered the groove and providing a segmental beading at this point which is allowed to die away well above the base of the panel (Fig. A6). This treatment of the seat back is by no means ubiquitous any more, and has been replaced by plain butted and chamfered panels. The conceit used in these benches of a stepped and/or chamfered profile ending in a triangle was much used in oak joinery from the start of the fourteenth century, but was particularly common at the end of the fifteenth century. It is often seen at Haddenham on the inside of the benches, though one has

Fig. A6: Beaded moulding (above the kneeler) on the panel join on the reverse of a seat back (nave south-east block, first opening on right).

Fig. A7 (left): Stepped and chamfered stops, carved in the solid, on the inside of a plain bench end.

Fig. A8: (right): Seat divider on reverse of seat back, with a triangular stop.

to crawl around to find it. It appears on the panels, carved in the solid, on the inside of the squared-up bench ends (Fig. A7) and in a variation on the central stiles on the reverse of the seat backs (Fig. A8). The fact that the craftsman who designed the furniture stipulated the application of a detail like this for use in relatively obscure places, reflects the demands of a fastidious, ambitious and wealthy patron. Were the oak fittings commissioned by a church guild, for instance?

The longest seats in the nave measured 128–133 in x 13½ in x 1½ in. The seat planks were originally wholly unsupported although their replacements were held up by intermittent wooden brackets. A few remain to this day in their original state. The method of their suspension between the seat backs, cut into the stiles and tenoned into the inside of the bench ends, with supporting pieces of wood let in underneath the latter, is judicious.

Art historical significance

The nave at Haddenham presents the rare sight of a completely pewed-out nave with a substantial percentage of the seating still intact after over 500 years, Moreover the rood screen, which was made coevally and *en suite*, has for the most part survived. Proof of its contemporary date is the identical idiosyncratic treatment of the tracery heads on the rood screen and the backs of the pews. One can also point to the use of triple-ball cusps on both components, and many close comparisons in the treatment of figurative and foliate sculpture (Figs. A9a & b).

The decorative carving throughout is still completely Gothic in form, particularly in the use of the voluted-trefoil leaf, which had been used perennially in English church woodwork since the early fourteenth century.[4] The particular fleur-de-lis treatment of the poppy-heads at Haddenham is very unusual (Fig. 10), with the careful balance of formal motifs, and the polygonal collar

Fig. A9: Triple ball and crinkly leaf detail on rood screen (left) and back bench tracery heads (right).

Fig. A10: Two poppy-heads.

below. The quality of the carving at Haddenham is exceptionally good in comparison with other churches in the region. Surprisingly it has not been possible to find any direct comparisons locally, although my researches have not been exhaustive. It is perhaps interesting to note that at Great Tew, Oxfordshire the characteristic undulation on the spandrel leaves found on the rood screen at Haddenham, is echoed on the bench ends.

This late-fifteenth-century woodwork generally conforms to a typical 'Midlands' pattern (Fig. A11).[5] The conformation of the seat backs contrasts with the benches in Norfolk and Suffolk, which use a horizontal plank reaching down only to seat level. Here they reach down to the floor. The typical Perpendicular-style mouldings at Haddenham – triple three-quarter round beading, with smaller similar beading and a generous hollow below on the top rail of the benches, and variations on the same theme on the rood screen – are satisfyingly handled. A similar use of mouldings on top rails can be seen in Oxfordshire (Great Tew,

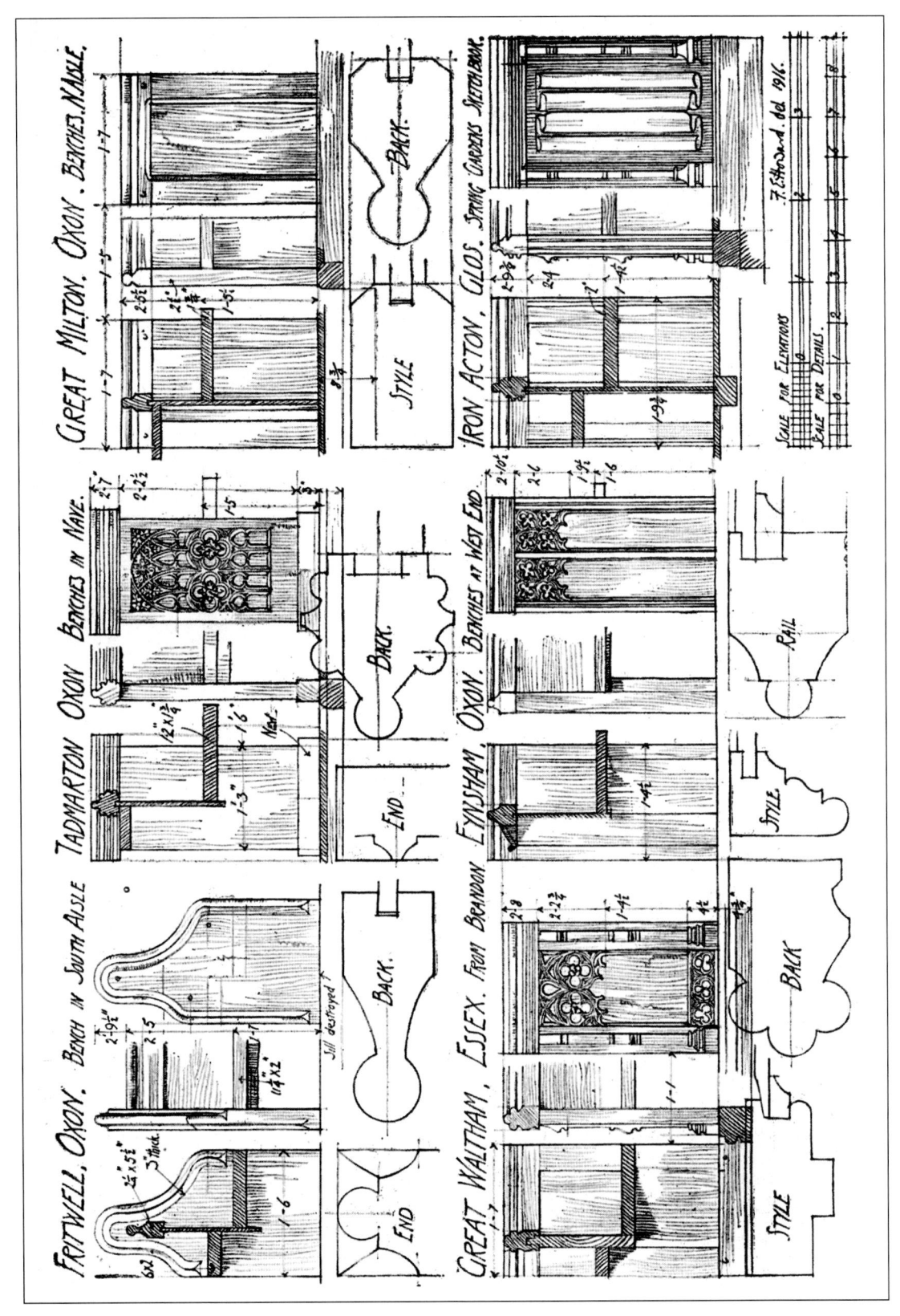

ASSESSING AND EVALUATING ENGLISH PEWS: THREE CASE STUDIES (APPENDIX)

Fig. A11: *Midland types of benches.* (Drawing: F. E. Howard and F. H. Crossley, English Church Woodwork (London 2nd edition, 1927), 303)

127

Fig. A12: Medieval seating at St Michael's, Great Tew, Oxfordshire.

Fig. A13: Medieval seating at All Saints, Landbeach, Cambridgeshire.

Minster Lovell, Steeple Aston), Northamptonshire (Byfield, Ashby St Ledgers) and Cambridgeshire (Landbeach) (see Figs. A12–A17), but these prominent mouldings were commonly used throughout England and Wales towards the close of the fifteenth century. The extant nave seating at Great Tew is a local example of another more or less completely pewed parochial nave.

The superior quality of both design and joinery at Haddenham is highlighted in a comparison with the less ambitious productions in many other parish churches in the region, such as Blunham or Shelton (Bedfordshire) and Guilden Morden (Cambridgeshire). On the other hand the level of competency at Haddenham is still somewhat below what one would expect to find in a greater religious house. Even so only an urban workshop would have had the facilities to plan and execute such a large commission. It would have been well beyond the competency of the village joiner.

By the same token the handling of the double-panelled bench ends at Haddenham represents a noticeable technical advance over most others in the region. They are a composite joined production, stealing a technological advance on the solid ends common in this part of England, although more characteristic of bench ends in the West Country. In the cases of solid ends, an unusually thick piece of timber was required. Locally such bench ends can be seen at Hampton Poyle, Steeple Aston, and Great Tew in Oxfordshire. Framed-up bench ends with single or pairs of tracery heads probably reached the Midlands via Norfolk and Suffolk. Good local examples can be seen at Ashby St Ledgers and

Fig. A14 (left): Two medieval bench ends at St Peter, Steeple Aston, Oxfordshire. See also Figure 1 in Chapter 14, page 215.

Fig. A15 (centre left): Medieval seating at St Kenelm, Minster Lovell, Oxfordshire.

Fig. A16 (centre right): Medieval seating at Holy Cross church, Byfield, Northamptonshire.

Fig. 17 (bottom): Medieval seating at St Leodegarius, Ashby St Ledgers, Northamptonshire.

(Photos: F. E. Howard and F. H. Crossley, English Church Woodwork *(London, 2nd edition, 1927), 41, 311, 312)*

Byfield (Northamptonshire), North Aston (Oxfordshire) and Landbeach (Cambridgeshire).

Conclusion

Although much restored, the Haddenham seating is a remarkably well preserved example of high quality parochial benching of the later English middle ages. It is also an advertisement for the best and most sensitive kind of Victorian restoration. An exemplar of late medieval parochial church patronage and piety in action, the seating also poses questions to the ecclesiologist which are still far from being answered.

Notes

1. F. E. Howard and F. H. Crossley, *English Church Woodwork* (London, 1917), 310.
2. In 1912 the Royal Commission reported that there were eighteen pews in four blocks in the nave, and eleven in two blocks in each aisle. The figure for the central benches falls short of the existing total (twenty-two). Their recorded number of side benches (also twenty-two) accounts for the two blocks at each end and another four, most of which were, presumably, on the north-east side. It is possible one of these benches may have come from the group of presumably four assumed removed in 1860 from the south-east aisle. Cox's description of the benches is based on the above. He mentions a woodcut which I have not seen. (*Royal Commission on Historical Monuments (England,) Buckinghamshire (South)* (1912), 178–79; J. C. Cox, *Bench-ends in English Churches* (London, 1916), 55.
3. See A. C. Chibnall and A. Vere Woodman, 'Subsidy Roll for the County of Buckinghamshire, 1524', *Buckinghamshire Record Society*, 8 (1950), and A. C. Chibnall, 'Muster Certificate for 1522', ibid., 17 (1973). My thanks to Linda Haynes of the Buckinghamshire Information Centre for this information.
4. C. Tracy, *English Gothic Choir Stalls, 1200–1400* (Woodbridge, 1987), 39, note 25.
5. Howard and Crossley, *English Church Woodwork*, 297–304, illustration p. 299.

9. Order and place in England, 1580–1640: the view from the pew [excerpt]

Christopher Marsh

The extract reproduced below is the central portion of an article published by Christopher Marsh in 2005, the last of three he has written on church seating in the early modern period. Here he considers the role of pews in promoting 'order' (in its various senses) in early modern society.

In the introductory section of this essay, not reproduced here, he sets out and then contests certain interpretive models which have been used to analyse early modern social structures. For example, he notes with concern how one such analytical framework directs us toward the view that 'radical, antihierarchical outbursts, and even milder moments of irreverence, represented the bubbling up of real popular feelings, while a general willingness to work cooperatively with hierarchy revealed only a fearful suppression of those feelings'.

In rhetorical vein, he goes on to challenge, 'should we, for example, accept the implied argument that early modern people probably did not actually believe in the existence of a divinely-ordained hierarchy, though they paid the idea public lip-service when private self-interest encouraged it?'

Marsh's view is the opposite: that 'in cultures that set a high store on the omnipotence of God, on communal values, and on reconciliation and the primacy of peace, there are powerful ethical reasons for the avoidance of social fracture that should not be reduced to the imperatives of self-preservation'.

In the extract published here, which follows the introduction sketched above, Marsh illuminates his position with a rich set of very human case studies concerning church seating.

This essay originally appeared in the Journal of British Studies, 44 *(January 2005), 3–26. The extract is reproduced here by kind permission of the author and the publishers, the University of Chicago Press. © 2005 by The North American Conference on British Studies. All rights reserved.*

This article was published in the Journal of British Studies, 44 *(January, 2005), 3–26; here we have reproduced pages 8–20. The other two articles in the series are: Christopher Marsh, '"Common Prayer" in England 1560–1640: the view from the pew',* Past & Present, 171 *(May, 2001), 66–94, and ibid., 'Sacred space in England, 1560–1640: the view from the pew',* Journal of Ecclesiastical History, 33 *(2002), 286–311.*

❖ ❖ ❖

Order and place in England, 1580–1640: the view from the pew [excerpt]

... NO ESSAY on the social order of early modern England is complete without at least a passing reference to pews, and some interesting work has investigated the matter in greater depth[1] ... The following article attempts [to investigate] ... the role of pews in the definition and maintenance of order and [to consider] ... popular attitudes to this role. Its focus is upon the conforming majority of parishioners, rather than upon those – such as the itinerant poor or religious dissenters – whose sense of belonging to the conventional community was more controversial. The essay builds upon previous studies of church seating and social structure by attempting to bring the spiritual and moral dimensions of hierarchy to the fore ... [it] draws on evidence from a number of dioceses but focuses most intensely on the fenland parish of Sutton in the Isle of Ely, which generated some particularly interesting documentation during a succession of Elizabethan and Jacobean pew disputes.[2]

The allocation of places

In most parishes, a lucky few, particularly members of the gentry, occupied seats that they claimed prescriptively and over which they enjoyed special rights, independent of the churchwardens. In many parishes, there were also seats that were customarily linked to particular houses, either as a result of prescriptive titles or simply because the churchwardens allowed and perpetuated less formal connections.[3] The majority of people were more clearly at the mercy of the churchwardens, whose unenviable task it was to manage the seating arrangements and to resolve the inevitable differences of opinion in such a way that the local social order was properly preserved and presented. In a minority of parishes, particularly in market towns, churchwardens organised the collection of pew rents. This system raised money for the church and appeared both rational and practicable. Parishioners could be distinguished from one another on the concrete basis of their graduated payments. Nevertheless, the local officers still had to decide upon precedence within each rent bracket, as Kevin Dillow has pointed out.[4] In most parishes, there were in any case no pew rents, and the wardens were responsible in theory for directing the majority of their neighbours to appropriate 'places' or 'rooms'. In practice, all but a few probably found their own way to positions that were established as theirs by custom, though not by any absolute right. Churchwardens, like historians, deal mainly with the problem cases.

In some parishes, the situation was further complicated by the fact that the churchwardens had fewer places at their disposal than there were members of the congregation. Demographic expansion during this period must have intensified the problem. In 1616, for example, the wardens of Littleport, Isle of Ely lamented that 'there are twentie have noe seates at all, nether can have because there is noe roome in the Church'.[5] Visitors to a parish might also add to the wardens' burden by turning up at church and expecting to be seated. The wardens therefore relied upon there being a proportion of established parishioners who failed to appear on any given Sunday. The rooms of these absentees could then be distributed among those who came to church but had nowhere specific to sit. In the words of one Cheshire woman, 'ytt is and hath bene a usuall thinge amongest the parishioners of Bunburie to enter into and sitt in an other mans seate upon occasion if they finde the same empty and the owners absente'. In Guilden Sutton, Cheshire there was a bench next to the pulpit that was 'estemed and used as a Common seate, for any to sitt in that would'.[6] Overall, it seems unlikely that the seating arrangements in a typical parish church ever remained exactly the same from one Sunday to the next.

It was presumably in reaction to the pressures of office and of socioeconomic change that some churchwardens drew up formal pew plans bearing the names of hundreds of their neighbours. In 1615, a plan devised in Sutton, Isle of Ely was presented to Judge William Gager of the consistory court as the fruit of collaboration between the wardens, their vicar, and nine of the 'better sort of parishioners'. Together, they submitted an 'order ... towcheing the decent placeinge of the parisheners', adding that their chief hope was to promote 'the peace and quiette of the Inhabitants of bothe sexes'.[7] The instinct to set society out on paper was not surprising, but it was often somewhat misguided. It suggests an awareness that the local order was supposed to be static but also a frustration with the difficulties of trying to make it so. In a number of cases, pew plans became as much a part of the problem as a workable solution. They must often have had the effect of reducing the flexibility with which seats could be allotted and thus the capacity of the churchwardens to respond to changes in the local social structure as a result of death, marriage, migration and unstable economic fortunes. It can have been no easy matter to design and execute this response, and it is obviously important to spend some time in examining the criteria upon which thousands of difficult decisions were based. When the churchwardens deliberated over the placement of individual parishioners according to their status, what were the most important guiding principles?

Status was, of course, a complex and many-layered concept, and controversial decisions could convert a church full of Christians into a can of worms. When, in 1701, Richard Gough wrote his famous 'Observations concerning the Seates in Myddle', he pleaded at the outset, 'I hope noe man will blame mee for not nameing every person according to that which hee conceives is his right and superiority in the seats in Church, because it is a thing impossible for any man to know'.[8] Throughout the seventeenth century, however, English churchwardens had to pretend that they were masters of the impossible. When they or their ecclesiastical superiors summarised the task in hand, they spoke of the need to place all parishioners according to pithily paired criteria. In Sutton, the churchwardens in 1615 were to establish the relative 'qualities and worthe' of their neighbours. In Stockport, Cheshire, parishioners were placed according to their 'degree and ability' or, alternatively, their 'ranke and order'. Elsewhere we hear variously of 'callings', 'states', 'merits', 'deserts', 'conditions', 'means' and 'estates', in numerous combinations.[9]

Beneath such terms, an array of more specific criteria was brought into play. Economic wealth was certainly important and had the advantage of being more precisely measurable than many of the other factors. An impression of its practical predominance is conveyed, for example, by the placement of people from Guilden Sutton, Cheshire 'according to their Ranckes, qualities & degrees, and according to the old Rents of the messuages or tenements of the said parishioners situate in the same parish'.[10] The structure of this sentence, however, also seems to imply an awareness that 'Ranckes' and 'Rents' were not synonymous. In Sutton, the men wealthy enough to be taxed at lay subsidy tended to occupy places close to the front of the church. Thirty-eight such taxpayers were named on the plan of 1615, of whom twenty-six sat on the front two seats in one or other of the five blocks of benches. It should be noted, however, that this left twelve taxpayers to take up places lower down the church, including three who sat in the least prestigious of the male seats. From this position, furthermore, they looked at the backs of many neighbours who did not contribute to the subsidies and who, in most cases, must have been economically inferior.[11] Such anomalies were a regular feature of church seating systems and sometimes proved controversial. Economic disability was also a fundamental criterion in the placement of the poor, who often seem to have sat in 'common' seats at the back of the nave, in the belfry, in the aisles, or in the choir. They may have shared such seats with those whose economic prospects were better but whose relative youth prevented them, for the time being, from obtaining places of their own.[12]

Gender was another factor in decisions over the placement of individuals, though the finer details of its operation contain some interesting surprises. In general, men and women sat in separate blocks, as commanded by church leaders. An Oxford cordwainer told the archdeacon's court in 1617 that 'he has heretofore lived in many several counties and towns . . . and he never knew but that the custom in all the said churches was always for men to sit there in seats by themselves apart from the women, and the women likewise by themselves'.[13] Other evidence confirms his observation and reveals that the most common arrangement saw the men seated in blocks at the front of the nave, with the women positioned behind them. In some parishes, however, the sexes sat on different sides of the nave, most often with the men to the south. Again, there were frequent anomalies. In Ely St. Mary's, the front/back segregation was undermined by the existence of some places for women right up to the upper end of the church on the north side. A partial plan for the church at Prestbury, Cheshire in 1628 suggests that mixed seats were quite familiar there. In some parishes, there were instances in which widows retained control of places that had belonged to their husbands. In many more, there were some seats that husbands and wives shared, though this seems to have been common only among the gentry. Even within such seats, the separation of the sexes might be sustained. In 1612, the wives of the Southworth family in Warrington, Lancashire were said to have traditionally sat in 'the heigher end' of the family pew, while their husbands gallantly occupied the lower end.[14] It was a contemporary orthodoxy that a wife derived her social status from her husband. Thus, seating plans that featured married women commonly identified them only as the wives of named husbands. In Sutton, for example, most of the male names listed in 1615 occur twice, but the words 'his wife' are added in the margin alongside references to the pews occupied by women. At first, this looks like unremarkable patriarchal orthodoxy. On closer examination, however, some intriguing differences emerge, and it becomes clear that the status of a wife as understood by the churchwardens was not in fact identical to that of her husband. Edward Kyrbye, for example, occupied a spot near the back of the mens' seats in one column and had only three male neighbours behind him. His wife, however, sat at the front of the women in another column and, on a good day, could glance over her shoulder and see sixty-four other wives. Similar discrepancies applied to many other couples. Moreover, a substantial minority of wives sat in sequences that were not the same as those occupied by their husbands. It is clear, therefore, that many a wife enjoyed or endured a social status that was not wholly dependent upon the 'rank', 'quality', or 'ability' of her husband. The precise placement of individuals was not a merely mechanical, means-tested procedure.

The placement of parishioners, male and female, also took account of their positions on the life cycle. In 1639, the bishop of Chester advised the churchwardens of Guilden Sutton that, in seating their neighbours, they should ensure 'that no servaunts be seated untill all housholders and Masters of Families, and parents be placed each as he deserves'. Nicholas Alldridge has shown how, in St Michael's, Chester, individuals could expect to move closer to the front of the church as they grew older, and the importance of age was implied when witnesses were asked by the church courts which of two rival claimants was 'more ancient'. Where successive plans relating to a single parish have been examined, the same 'upward drift' is evident. Children seem generally to have been seated apart, with the exception of the very young, and, in Puddletown, Dorset, a plan drawn up in 1637 reveals what Dillow calls 'a hierarchy of children ... parallel to, and based upon, that of adults'.[15] Frequently, there were also separate seats for maids and for bachelors. In Ely St. Mary's, the leading men of the parish agreed in 1590 'that all bachelers and boys shall repair and sit in the chauncell where there is formes placed for them to sit upon in pain of being presented by the churchwardens for refusing to sit there'. The distinction between the married and the unmarried was important to both sexes, and in a number of parishes the significance of childbirth was recognised in the provision of a specific seat for the use of mothers who came to be 'churched'.[16]

Words such as 'worth', 'merits', and 'deserts' also suggest that there was a moral and religious element in decisions over the placement of individuals. The evidence, though anecdotal, is considerable. In 1585, the judges in a pew dispute heard by the High Commission found in favour of Mr. Girrie of Little St Mary's, Cambridge, but only after establishing that he was 'a gent[leman] of good reputacon and livinge and of honest behavior and conversacon and well affected to religion'. It was also noted that he 'dwelleth in the best howse in that parishe', but it is clear in this instance that in order to belong to 'the best sorte of people' it was necessary to have mastered at least the basics of orthodox godliness.[17] Richard Roberts of Chatteris, Isle of Ely was presented to the consistory court in 1615 'for that he beinge a brawlinge and contentious fellowe, & but of a meane habilitie, doth sit perkinge in the highest seat in our Church above the best

& ancientest men in our towne'. The dual importance of morality and wealth is nicely illustrated here, though Roberts was difficult to displace because 'the seate he sitteth in is anciently belonginge to his house'. In Colne, Lancashire, the deponents in a case from 1636 were asked about the relationship between one group of claimants and the parish church. Several responded by saying that the men concerned had, among other things, received Holy Communion, baptised their children, and buried their dead in the church.[18] In other words, they had shown themselves to be integrated members of the spiritual community, and this strengthened their claim on the disputed seats. Witnesses might also be asked whether the parties to a dispute had attended church services as they should have done.[19]

In Sutton, a comparison of the 1615 plan with a wide range of other local sources reveals just how seriously some church officers took the subject of moral and religious reputation. The vicar, the churchwardens, and the nine other men who signed or marked the plan made clear attempts to discriminate against those whose behaviour they deemed unacceptable. For example, it is initially difficult to understand why Jeremy Gleadall, a prominent local man who had served previously as churchwarden, was allocated no seat at all. Similarly, the wife of William Gunton was placed some way back in the womens' seats, despite the fact that her husband was a taxpayer and had also held church office. The officers' rationale emerges, however, when the reputation of both individuals for religious nonconformity is recognised. In 1614–15, the churchwardens 'vehemently suspected' that Gleadall was 'of the heresye & scisme of the Novalistes and Puritanes, & sowe the seedes of sedition in the hartes of the kings majesties subjects'. Both he and Gunton's wife were reportedly in the habit of attending sermons given by unauthorised lay preachers in and around the village.[20]

In other instances, the nonconformity noted and punished by the Sutton pew planners was moral rather than spiritual. Most conspicuously, Richard Upchurch, a gentleman, was placed in the very back seat for men on the south side of the church. Again, this seems an extraordinary decision until it is noted from other sources that Upchurch allegedly loved the alehouse, and 'with drinckinge dothe often tymes distemper himselfe that he goeth rayleinge up & downe the streate in the nighte, to the great disquiet of his neighboures beinge in theire beddes, & at reste'. One wonders if the irony of his surname registered with the glovers and poulterers who were now to be his pew fellows. Upchurch was at least given somewhere to sit, unlike William

Bond. This 'common drunckard, swearer and blasphemer of the name of god' was awarded no place at all, though his wife sat near the front of the women.[21] It may well be that the discrepancies already noted between the places occupied by individual men and their wives are frequently accounted for by differing moral and religious reputations.

In contrast, the eleven laymen who compiled or signed the Sutton plan rewarded those – including themselves – who endeavoured to live their lives as loyal members of the Church of England and of orthodox Christian society. Their moral reputations, to judge by the ecclesiastical court records, were generally good (with one exception).[22] Half of these men later made wills, and they were significantly more likely than other Sutton testators of similar rank to register charitable bequests and gifts to the church. Furthermore, they were evidently very well integrated into their local community, and several of them appeared regularly as witnesses to their neighbours' wills in the years between 1617 and 1641.[23] On the plan of 1615, their seats were generally prominent and prestigious. Ten of the eleven occupied places right at the front. The principles applied by these men in devising the plan no doubt seemed to them unquestionably righteous, but their intervention was in a number of instances so provocative that conflict was inevitable, as we shall see.

Several other factors were also taken into account by English churchwardens as they contemplated their difficult decisions. In some parishes, placement was arranged partially according to the street or township in which a person resided. The depth of a family's roots in the locality or the extent to which an individual was permanently resident were also relevant. Many parishes reserved particular seats for the churchwardens and parish clerk, while in towns the mayor and aldermen frequently had specific pews assigned to them. Deafness might also earn its victims places that were close to the pulpit.[24] Overall, it is difficult to resist the conclusion that the churchwardens' weekend job was as difficult and thankless as it was unpaid. They were to make decisions based on a wide range of potentially contradictory criteria. They could not use all of the 'places' in the church, because some were prescriptively claimed and others were attached to specific properties.

They had to think on their feet and make wise use of any places that were vacant because of the temporary absence of their appointed occupants. Lastly, they had to deal with the complaints of that small minority of neighbours who were ready to claim publicly that they deserved something better.

The acceptance and rejection of places

The moment at which the churchwardens felt it necessary to intervene by directing an anxious or angry individual toward a specific place was the principal flash point of the morning. In this instant, the paradox of flux and fixity was at its most acute, and there was plentiful scope for the kind of 'role conflict' discussed by sociologists.[25] Disgruntled parishioners confronted the churchwardens in a variety of ways, most of which can be studied rewardingly by concentrating on Sutton, that laboratory of 'pew rage', during the critical year of 1615. The pew plan drawn up at the start of that year did not meet with universal approval. The most obvious tactic available to those who felt aggrieved was simply to reject the places offered to them. It was reported of Thomas Higham, gentleman, 'that he being appointed & placed to sit in a convenient seate in the Church by the Churchwardens doth refuse to sitt there, & doth abuse the Churchwardens in the Church, in sayeing that they are malipert fellowes and ambitiouse fellowes & have sett there handes with the vicar in this busines'. In this outburst, Higham accused the wardens, explicitly or implicitly, of several things: they had placed their own private interests above those of wider society, they had failed in their duty to define the local links in the chain of being with accuracy and honesty, and they had used their office shamefully in order to insult their social superiors. Despite these charges, the judge commanded Higham to sit where he was told until such time as he proved his case at law.[26] In other parishes, comparably troublesome parishioners declined 'stoutlye & scornfully' to sit where they were told or refused to be 'ordered' for their seats. Some took up their places in defiance of the wardens and simply refused to budge or sat provocatively in rows reserved for members of the opposite sex. In 1601, Robert Banks of Cottenham spurned his appointed place 'but would sit in the lap of Robert Rivers'.[27] His gesture was presumably competitive rather than affectionate.

Back in Sutton, some parishioners drew explicitly on their own patriarchal or paternalistic power and refused seats on behalf of their dependents. The embattled churchwardens told the court that William Oates 'will not suffer his wife to sit in the seate where she was appointed by the Churchwardens, but saith that he will earne money for Mr Chancellor' (in other words, he was prepared to risk litigation). William Gunton, who came from a long line of troublesome spirits, went one better and drew his tenants into the tussle. He was presented 'for interrupting the Churchwardens & troubling them in the Church when they were placing some of theire neighbors in seates convenient . . . , and further saith that he wilbe Churchwarden for his tenantes himselfe, and so caused them to refuse to sitt where the Churchwardens had placed them'. Here, the wardens were being challenged very directly, and Gunton was asserting one hierarchy, which gave a landlord authority over his tenants, against another, which empowered local officeholders to rebuke their neighbours, however wealthy they might be. William Gunton was indeed a formidable figure, for the pew plan indicates that he was in possession of at least four houses within the village. His kinsman, Robert Gunton, made a different type of threat. When the wardens directed him toward a place in the fifth seat for men, he not only refused to occupy it but said that 'rather then [than] he will sitt there, he will goe fourth of the towne'. The declaration may look to us somewhat feeble, but can be read as a direct and deliberate challenge to the wardens, whose job it was to enforce attendance at church. Gunton was threatening to depart symbolically from the hierarchical community, adding spatial insult to verbal injury.[28]

Another tactic was to appeal to higher authority. At some point between 1615 and 1617, a rival group of twelve men sent a petition to Gager, the consistory court judge, complaining angrily about the pew plan that he had ratified. They requested a full review, respectfully informing Gager that he had been deceived by the first group of twelve. The petitioners alleged that the entire plan had nothing to do with the preservation of harmony by the 'better sort', but had instead been a personal attack upon them, designed 'to rent breake and distroie the unitie peace and concord of the said parishe'. Perfectly good pews had been removed and replaced, and several men had thereby been excluded from 'theire olde ancient seates'. All but one of the men who signed the plan had been promoted within the scheme of things as a result. Now, 'some of the cheifest ancient houses in the towne have no seates appoynted at all'.[29] These were sorry times in Sutton.

Neither of the rival groups felt disposed to mention, in the representations they made to Gager, that the dispute had a significant religious and moral dimension.[30] The solidly orthodox and socially well-integrated character of the pew plan's supporters was in stark contrast to the more turbulent temper of their opponents. The antiplan group was in fact a curious coalescence of saints and sinners. On one side, it included Puritan non- or semiconformists, two of whom had daughters named Temperance.[31] On the other, it included a number of men with reputations for illicit sex, the singing of 'filthy songes' on the Sabbath, harbouring unmarried mothers, and drunkenness. Saints and sinners alike had been demoted within the church as a result of their activities.[32] Members of this group were evidently less thoroughly integrated into local society than their enemies and were invited to witness wills with far lower frequency.[33] Seven members of the antiplan coalition later made wills of their own, and none of them left anything to the church.[34] The reticence of all the combatants on these matters seems to reflect an awareness that the appropriate verbal register when appealing to a church court judge was one that emphasised the desirability of peace, unity and concord among Christians, rather than the ecclesiological preferences and moral failings of one's opponents. This meant, however, that Gager had to make decisions on the basis of very partial evidence. Upon receiving the petition from the second group of twelve, he promptly revoked the pew plan and ordered the wardens to return all Sutton's seats to their former state.[35] This handed victory to an unholy alliance of puritans and philanderers.

The Sutton case indicates that individuals on all social levels could feel passionately about where they sat in church.[36] Those who complained about the plan included the gentleman, Thomas Higham, and the alehousekeeper, Henry Blithe. The latter's presence might encourage us to look here for evidence of the 'weapons of the weak' in action. Primarily, however, this was a battle for the front seats in the church, in which a proplan group dominated by solidly prosperous and upwardly mobile yeomen or husbandmen confronted an antiplan alliance whose big hitters were four displaced gentlemen, capable of carrying a handful of poorer men along with them.[37] During the period 1580–1640 as a whole, twenty-eight individuals from Sutton either were involved in disturbances over their placement or signed the protest petition of 1615. From a range of sources, definite status labels can be assigned in nine cases: there were four gentlemen, a yeoman, a husbandman, a chandler with his wife, and our alehousekeeper. Eleven of the remaining miscreants were clearly either yeomen or wealthy husbandman (and their wives in three cases), as indicated by records relating to property, taxation and local officeholding.[38] The remaining eight are difficult to label, but six of them belonged to prominent and prosperous local families such as the Fosters and the Guntons. Overall, therefore, we have a group that covered the local spectrum of status but was heavily dominated by those of middling and higher rank. The statistics compiled by Kevin Dillow on the basis of a much fuller sample tell a similar story for England as a whole. According to his calculations, those presented to the ecclesiastical courts and for whom status labels are known included 31 per cent gentry, 26 per cent yeomen, 17 per cent husbandmen, and 12 per cent craftsmen.[39] It therefore seems that the individuals most likely to confront the churchwardens were those who sat toward the 'upper end' of the church, closer to the chancel than to the font. This fact was noted by the churchwardens of Stoke Edith, Herefordshire who, in 1586, drew up a pew plan in the hope of 'avoiding of controversies that may happen hereafter for challenging the upper seates and kneelings (wch ys a point of mere folly and vayne glory)'.[40] As far as we can tell, those who sat further back did not tend to react aggressively when directed to their places by the churchwardens. As David Dymond has noted, they were 'less quarrelsome than their neighbors'.[41]

Sutton was a hot spot for pew disputes, and immersion in its records can also lead to misleading conclusions about the extent of the problem within most English parishes. Leading local families had a long-established habit of vying for pre-eminence in church, and half of the twenty-eight individuals discussed above had the surnames Gleadall (three), Foster (three), or Gunton (eight). The Guntons had been proudly throwing their neighbours out of pews and storming from the church in outrage since the 1580s.[42] Even in such a turbulent parish, this left an overwhelming majority of people who apparently sat where they were told or who expressed their grievances without the kind of unfettered passion that might land them in the courts. In the deanery of Ely as a whole, confrontations between wardens and parishioners on the subject of seating were significantly less common. Twenty parishes produced only forty-five relevant cases between 1580 and 1640. The 1610s saw eighteen of these cases, with each of the other decades generating between one and nine. The good men and women of Sutton contrived thirteen cases all on their own, concentrated in the 1580s and 1610s. The parishes of Chatteris and Littleport saw five cases apiece, clustered in 1607–15 and 1633–34, respectively. In other words, over half of the disputes took place in a mere three parishes. Nine parishes produced between one and three cases each, and seven witnessed none at all.[43] Furthermore, this was a fenland region with a predominantly pastoral economy and, according to Susan Amussen and others, can be expected to have generated more church seating presentments than an arable area of comparable size.[44] Clearly, 'pew rage' was not rife, despite the well-known economic pressures of the period, and historians – this one included – should be careful about presenting the evidence in concentrated and intoxicating form. We risk writing anti-social history.[45]

Interaction between parishioners

After passing through the porch, parishioners crisscrossed the nave, negotiating a path to their 'places' in the church and in the universal order. As they did so, many minute interpersonal signals must have been sent out. Individuals walked up aisles and along alleys, passing 'superior' and 'inferior' folk as they did so, making and not making eye contact and bodily gestures as appropriate. On Sundays in Sutton in 1615, for example, the labourer Edward Kyrbye could have found his place via two main routes after entering the church through the south door, presumably accompanied by his wife. He might have parted from her immediately and made his way around the back of the church, passing among the parish's more lowly wives before walking up the north aisle, ascending the ladder of female status as he did so, and then finally taking up his place near the back of the men, in the fourth of five 'shorte seates on the Northe side the churche' next to the chapel. Despite his inferior status, this was a symbolic journey upward through local society. Alternatively, he could have led his wife to her position in the best seat for women on the south side, then walked round the front of the church, passing close to the places of three gentlemen and dozens of well-established yeomen or husbandmen (including, ominously, three Guntons), before descending the male social ladder to take up his allotted place. This route took him first up and then down the local hierarchy. Sadly, historians cannot follow sociologists in observing the myriad social encounters that characterised such routine journeys, but we can learn from Erving Goffman that it was these, as much as anything else, that made the social order real by presenting individuals with opportunities to signify their acceptance or rejection of it.[46]

The majority of worshippers found their seats peacefully enough and settled down to begin their devotions or to observe the goings-on around them. Once seated, the model parishioner 'allwayes sufferd her neighbors to passe in & out by her quietly without any disturbance at all', as Jocosam Chelsey of Upton Lovell, Wiltshire put it in 1605.[47] If one's pew fellows did not arrive, however, then neighbours with no places of their own might attempt to occupy the vacant rooms. Some of the unplaced parishioners had already sought and obtained permission to sit in rooms within the special minority of pews that were held by prescription. The generosity of their holders helped to maintain the integrity of the social order, and there is ample evidence to suggest that the codes of paternalism and deference were valued by people on both sides of the equation. In the court records, we quite frequently meet individuals who owed their position within the church to the kindness of a wealthier family. A woman from Colne, Lancashire must have been pleased when, at some date before 1632, Simon Blakey gave her leave to occupy a place in one of his seats. He explained that he could not grant her a room in 'Mistris Towneleys Quire', a still more prestigious location, 'because hee did sitt therin but by leave himselfe'. Clearly, there was an intricate web of patronage in operation here. Many landlords, naturally enough, used such grants not only as a way of building a reputation for generosity but in order to make their interactive power plain to those beneath them. In 1612, for example, a woman from Warrington, Lancashire described the occasion upon which John Southworth had reminded her quite forcefully that her current place in church was his to dispose, 'and because this deponent sould apples hee the saide John saide she . . . should give him everie yeare an apple and aske licence to sitt there because shee should nott Claime anie righte in the same'.[48]

The distinction between occupying a place at the pleasure of its owner and doing so as of right was not invariably clear to all concerned. The situation was further complicated by the way in which deaths, marriages, and comings-of-age could alter the chains of preeminence, again in ways that did not look quite the same to everyone. Lastly, it seems that members of the gentry may have been in the habit of breezing into the church after everyone else had already settled.[49] This had the advantage of ensuring that all eyes were on them and of marking them out as people of unusual privilege. Late arrival, however, also meant that gentlemen ran the risk of arriving at church only to find that others had already occupied their pews. In such situations, the key question was who would 'give place' to whom?

In most circumstances, the issue was probably resolved amicably enough, though our evidence necessarily comes from parishes in which the relationships eventually turned sour. Witnesses from Ashton on Mersey reported in 1631 that they had seen James Massie 'give place' to Sir William Brereton in previous years. In Bunbury, John Reade had received permission to use the Kettle family seat on occasions when it was empty, but Margaret Kettle reported that she had 'sometimes found the sayd Reades wief in the sayd seate who would rise and give place to this deponent'.[50] The records convey an impression of rank upon rank of lesser parishioners watching intently to see who would take precedence in such situations. The status labels of those called upon to give depositions in the diocese of Chester covered the full hierarchical range and included men and women of many ages from twenty-one to ninety-two years.

Sometimes, the tensions that were latent within all such encounters emerged and escalated in spectacular fashion, leaving a trail of vainglory through the records of the church courts in the form of 'instance' litigation. In 1632, for example, the wives of John Martin and John Meacock of Guilden Sutton, Cheshire were in no mood to give place to one another in a prestigious seat for women. The Martins claimed to have occupied the top 'place' in the 'upper end' of this seat for several decades. The Meacocks insisted that this was only because one of their own ancestors had kindly welcomed into the seat an earlier member of the Martin family, who was 'otherwise destitute of a convenient place'. The current goodwife Martin therefore sat in the seat 'without any right or just claime'. Each Sunday, the two wives now confronted one another over who should occupy which place. One week, John Martin claimed, he had positioned himself in the disputed seat, anxious 'to prevent trowble disorder & misdemeanour'. His laudable hopes were comprehensively dashed when John Meacock entered the seat behind 'and laid or tooke hould of bothe the shoulders of the said John Martin . . . and did violently hale and pull him downe backwards'. Meacock told a different story. He emphasised the violence used by Martin's wife against his own, which involved 'treading upon her cloathes & kneeling upon her'. His own action against Martin had been in response to another attack upon his wife and had no other purpose but 'to stay & hinder the said violence and to preserve the kings peace'. The fact that Martin was a churchwarden and Meacock was the village constable must have made this a particularly compelling spectacle for onlookers.[51]

Such litigation was even more heavily dominated by suits involving the gentry and yeomanry than were the 'office' cases referred to earlier.[52] In the instance litigation from the diocese of Chester, there is only one cause that seems to disrupt this pattern. Around 1630, Viscount Cholmondley decided, for reasons unspecified, that he would no longer allow his servant or steward, Thomas Burroughes, to occupy a place in 'the highest or uppermost [seat] save one, on the South side of the middle Ile' in the church at Nantwich, Cheshire. According to Cholmondley, Burroughes was so angered by this act of displacement that he and his sons plotted revenge. Allegedly, they entered the church secretly at night, 'and . . . did then and there with hatchetts, hammers or other Instruments or engins, violently breake the locke of the dore belonging to the said seate'. They then proceeded to pull up some of the boards, disguising the resultant hole in the floor with rushes, 'thinking herby to intrap such as entred into the said seate or pew'.[53] This cunning plan came to nothing, however, for the sexton was looking on.

In the diocese of Chester as a whole, most years in the period 1580–1640 saw fewer than five interpersonal seating disputes, but the 1630s produced between five and twenty such cases each year. This increase reflected a general rise in the total number of instance cases heard but was also the consequence of the Laudian quest for uniformity. Many parishes were ordered to alter their seats so that none was higher or grander than others. The gentry and yeomanry of Cheshire did not welcome this intrusion and often took their frustrations out on one another in the church courts. In 1635, 11 per cent of the 144 instance cases heard in the diocese related to church seating.[54]

❖ ❖ ❖

After further discussion, Marsh concludes his essay: . . . As we have seen, most quarrels occurred among the relatively powerful as they competed for places at the front of the church. To this extent, anxiety over 'order' within the ranks of the gentry and yeomanry may have been fuelled as much by the rivalry of near equals as by the grunts of the many-headed monster (who sat more peaceably at the back). It is an interesting possibility that the 'chain of being' was more problematic for the leaders of local society than it was for men and women of lower rank. Frequently, we have been encouraged by social historians to envisage early modern church services as occasions upon which the 'chief parishioners', from whose ranks the churchwardens were chosen, looked anxiously and critically backward for evidence of disorderly conduct in the body of the congregation. We can end with the provocative suggestion that it may often have been the other way round.

Notes

1 See particularly Susan Dwyer Amussen, *An Ordered Society: Gender and Class in Early Modern England* (New York, 1988), 137–43; Kevin Dillow, 'The Social and Ecclesiastical Significance of Church Seating Arrangements and Pew Disputes, 1500–1740' (D.Phil. diss., University of Oxford, 1990); Robert Tittler, 'Seats of honour, seats of power: the symbolism of public seating in the English urban community, *c.*1560–1620', *Albion* 24, no. 2 (Summer 1992): 205–23; David Dymond, 'Sitting apart in church', in Carol Rawcliffe et al (eds.) *Counties and Communities: Essays on East Anglian History*, (Norwich, 1996); Susan Pittman, 'The social structure and parish community of St. Andrew's church, Calstock, as reconstituted from its seating plan, *c.*1587–8', *Southern History*, 20–21 (1998–99): 44–67; Amanda Flather, 'The politics of space: a study of church seating in Essex, *c.*1580–1640', *Friends of the Centre for English Local History Paper* (Leicester) 3 (1999): 1–55.
2 I am grateful to Jonathan Kelly for allowing me to use the notes that he took while preparing an undergraduate dissertation (1991), under my guidance, on the subject of Sutton. I have, of course, also consulted the original documents.
3 The legal technicalities of church seating are discussed more fully in Dillow, 'Church seating', chaps. 2, 4.
4 Dillow, 'Church seating', 108.

5   Cambridge University Library (CUL), Ely Diocesan Records (EDR), B.2.35, fol. 163r.
6   Cheshire Record Office (ChRO), EDC5, 1620.24, 1639.21.
7   CUL, EDR, B.2.35, fols. 207r–11r. This plan is referred to on a number of occasions in this article, and the reference will not subsequently be repeated.
8   Richard Gough, *The History of Myddle*, ed. David Hey (Harmondsworth, 1981), 78.
9   CUL, EDR, B.2.35, fol. 210 (Sutton) and D.2.18A, flyleaf; ChRO, EDC5, 1632.66 (Stockport), 1611.13, 1631.2, 1632.66, 1636.39, 1636.48, and 1639.21.
10 ChRO, EDC5, 1639.21.
11 I have compared the plan with the following lay subsidy returns: Public Record Office, London (PRO), E179 83/353a, 83/361, 83/172, and 83/387.
12 On seating for the poor, see Paul Griffiths, *Youth and Authority: Formative Experiences in England, 1560–1640* (Oxford, 1996), 105; Dillow, 'Church seating', 154; Claire S. Schen, 'Women and the London parishes, 1500–1620', in Katherine L. French, Gary G. Gibbs, and Beat A. Kümin (eds.), *The Parish in English Life, 1400–1600*, (Manchester, 1997), 258–59.
13 Oxfordshire Record Office, Archdeaconry Papers Oxon, c. 118, fol. 90 (cited by Dillow, 'Church seating', 131).
14 CUL, EDR, B.2.24, fols. 17v–18r, B.2.35, fols. 207–10; Cambridgeshire Record Office (CamRO), P68/611 (Ely); ChRO, EDC5, 1612.19 (Warrington). See also Dymond, 'Sitting Apart in Church', 215–17; Dillow, 'Church seating', 131; and Nesta Evans, 'A scheme for re-pewing the parish church of Chesham, Buckinghamshire, in 1606', Local Historian 22 (1992), 204.
15 ChRO, EDC5, 1639.21; Nicholas Alldridge, 'Loyalty and identity in Chester parishes, 1540–1640', in S. J. Wright (ed.) *Parish, Church and People. Local Studies in Lay Religion, 1350–1750*, (London, 1988), 95; ChRO, EDC5, 1632.66; Dillow, 'Church seating', 138–42.
16 CamRO, P68/611; ChRO, EDC5, 1631.2.
17 CUL, EDR, D.2.18A, flyleaf.
18 CUL, EDR, B.2.35, fol. 27r; ChRO, EDC5, 1636.39.
19 ChRO, EDC5, 1620.21. For cases in which individuals were demoted within the church on moral and religious grounds, see Dillow, 'Church seating', 99–100.
20 For background information on Gleadall and William Gunton, see CUL, EDR, B.2.14, fol. 6v, B.2.29, fol. 25r, B.2.31, fol. 116r; PRO, E179 83/353a. The accusations of nonconformity are in CUL, EDR, B.2.35, fols. 190v, 193r, 194r, and B.2.33, fol. 96v.
21 CUL, EDR, B.2.35, fol. 204r (Upchurch), B.2.30, fol. 31r (Bond).
22 William Thomas was repeatedly accused of incontinence with another man's wife (CUL, EDR, B.2.24, fol. 124v, B.2.33, fol. 98r).
23 CamRO, Ely Consistory Court Probate Register (ECCPR), wills from Sutton. In this period, members of this group appeared as witnesses on thirty-four occasions.
24 ChRO, EDC5, 1631.2, 1632.66, and 1639.21; Alldridge, 'Loyalty and Identity', 95; CamRO, P68/611; CUL, EDR, B.2.35, fols. 207–11r; Tittler, 'Seats of Honour', 217, 222; Evans, 'Scheme for Re-pewing', 204.
25 See Peter Burke, *History and Social Theory* (Oxford, 1992), 48–49.
26 CUL, EDR, B.2.35, fol. 197r.
27 CUL, EDR, B.2.39, fol. 229v, B.2.21, fols. 11v, 93r, B.2.46, fol. 45r, B.2.35, fol. 195r, B.2.18, fol. 126v.
28 CUL, EDR, B.2.35, fol. 197r–v.
29 CUL, EDR, B.2.35, fol. 212r.
30 Flather has also noted seating cases in which religious disagreement was a factor. See 'Politics of space', 37, 51.
31 The daughters are named in CamRO, Ely Consistory Court Wills, William Gunton (1631), and PRO, Prerogative Court of Canterbury Wills, Thomas Jetherell (1619).
32 CUL, EDR, B.2.21, fols. 33v, 36v, 183v, B.2.24, fol. 123v, B.2.29, fol. 142v, B.2.30, fols. 29v, 30r, B.2.35, fols. 191v and 204r; CamRO, Sutton Parish Registers.
33 CamRO, ECCPR, wills from Sutton. Members of the antiplan group witnessed wills on only fourteen occasions in the period 1617–41.

34 In the other group, two out of six testators remembered the church. See CamRo, ECCPR, Robert Gleadall (1641) and John Gunton (1637). Intriguingly, members of the less integrated antiplan group were more likely than their opponents to ask specifically for burial in the church or churchyard at Sutton, perhaps reflecting a high degree of insecurity regarding ecclesiastical placement.

35 CUL, EDR, B.2.35, fol. 214r. Despite this revocation, however, the plan was still referred to in the parish fifteen years later (CUL, EDR, F.5.39, fol. 108r–v).

36 The proprietorial attitude of early modern church-goers to their seats is discussed in Christopher Marsh, 'Sacred space in England, 1560–1640,' *Journal of Ecclesiastical History*, 53, no. 2 (April 2002), 286–311.

37 CamRO, ECCPR, wills from Sutton; PRO, E179 83/353a, 83/361, 83/172, and 83/387.

38 CUL, EDR, B.2.10, D.2.18, B.2.14, B.2.21, B.2.24, B.2.29, B.2.30, B.2.30A, B.2.31, B.2.33, B.2.35, B.2.37, B.2.39, and D.2.51; CamRO, ECCPR, wills from Sutton; PRO, E179 83/353a, 83/ 361,83/172, and 83/387.

39 Dillow, 'Church seating', 204–7. See also Flather, 'Politics of space', 31.

40 Cited in M. Moir, 'Church and society in sixteenth-century Herefordshire' (M.Phil. thesis, Leicester University, 1984), 112.

41 Dymond, 'Sitting apart in church', 220.

42 CUL, EDR, D.2.18, 149r.

43 I have searched the following court books: CUL, EDR, B.2.10, D.2.18, B.2.14, B.2.21, B.2.24, B.2.29, B.2.30, B.2.30A, B.2.31, B.2.33, B.2.35, B.2.37, B.2.39, B.2.43. B.2.46, B.2.47, B.2.52, B.2.53, and D.2.51.

44 Amussen, *Ordered Society*, 141–42.

45 For additional statistics to support these comments, see Dillow, 'Church seating', 191, 196, and Flather, 'Politics of space', 26, 33–34. In contrast, the extent of the problem may be somewhat exaggerated in Amussen, *Ordered Society*, 138.

46 Erving Goffman, *Relations in Public: Microstudies of the Public Order* (Harmondsworth, 1971), 344: 'All behavior of the individual, insofar as it is perceived by others, has an indicative function, made up of tacit promises and threats, confirming or disconfirming that he knows his place'.

47 Wiltshire Record Office, D1/39/2/5, fol. 75r. I am grateful to Eric Carlson for bringing this case to my attention.

48 ChRO, EDC5, 1632.41, 1612.19.

49 E. P. Thompson, *Customs in Common* (Harmondsworth, 1993), 45.

50 ChRO, EDC5, 1631.3, 1620.24.

51 ChRO, EDC5, 1632.30.

52 Dillow, 'Church seating', 191.

53 ChRO, EDC5, 1630.54.

54 For comments on the impact of Laudianism on church seating, see Marsh, 'Sacred space'. My figures on instance cases in the diocese of Chester are based on the EDC5 listings held in the Cheshire Record Office.

10. Post-Reformation church seating arrangements and bench assembly notation in two North Devon churches

Francis Kelly

THIS CHAPTER DISCUSSES RECENT OBSERVATIONS in two churches in North Devon, St Nectan, Stoke, at Hartland and St Brannock, Braunton. Both churches retain impressive blocks of largely original sixteenth-century congregational seating in its intended place, with early assembly notation which has previously been unnoticed and provides insights into the history of the seating. In both cases the notation was discovered as part of an investigation into possible reordering of the seating to fit modern purposes and create space for other uses in addition to now traditional forms of worship

Construction

The benches discussed here are of the recognisable mostly sixteenth-century North Devon/North Cornwall type,[1] though in neither church as refined as the classic examples such as those at St Columb Major, Altarnun or Launcells. The stout oak carpentry is simple and very local. The 4-inch bench ends are square with moulded edges (at Hartland); this is generally enriched in the same manner as the uprights on chancel screens (Braunton and the majority of surviving cases). The ends are twice-tenoned into the sill which is usually moulded and part of a stout floor frame. The seats are 2 inches thick or more and have two chunky tenons secured by single face-driven pegs. The backs are generally made with two framed back boards set in grooves in the ends, and have a moulded top-rail pegged from the rear edge. Behind are the 'book rests'[2] or back braces; these are also thick (2 inches or more) and have one (sometimes two in other churches) similarly chunky tenons single-pegged from the back edge. (For further discussion of the construction of early bench ends, see Chapter 7 by Jerry Sampson in this volume.)

The Hartland benches are relatively short, and the framing is undivided along the length of the bench, apart from the benches at the ends of blocks and the frontals completing the seating blocks. This is unlike most West Country examples where the framing is divided by a central post. For example, at Braunton, because of the length of the benches, the seats have a central 4-inch post. In Hartland some backs are or have been angled for comfort, and further comfort has been provided by simple, narrow kneelers, of nineteenth-century character. Also for comfort, several of the seats have been deepened in both churches.

St Nectan, Stoke, Hartland
Background

The medieval church at Stoke, Hartland, was largely rebuilt in the fourteenth and fifteenth centuries (Fig. 1). It is generous in scale and a veritable treasure house. It lies beyond the tiny township in an exposed situation well in from the cliffs, but as Pevsner points out, 'looks out across a mile of fields towards America'.[3] In an area rich with sixteenth- and early-seventeenth-century seating, Hartland, like nearby Clovelly, stands out for the plainness of the bench ends and for surprising completeness.

A wonderful and very large seating layout dated 1613 survives (Fig. 2), showing how individuals were allocated to places.[4] As with the Puddletown seating of 1635 discussed by Bob Machin in Chapter 11, the plan was the result of a dispute over customary rights and status but, unlike Puddletown, the physical seating at Hartland almost certainly predated the assignment of places. A great deal is known about the history and significance of these seating arrangements, due to the important and detailed research of historian Steve Hobbs (Fig. 3).[5] He has identified each of the names on the plan, and demonstrates how the seating

Fig. 1: St Nectan, Hartland, Devon.

arrangements reflected both the social relationships of the parishioners and the change of social leadership at the Reformation and the weakness of the new owners of Hartland Abbey, to which the church at Stoke had belonged.

In the main part of the church, despite a multiplicity of extra brackets and supports, the seating is largely complete, although the dado panelling was replaced and much of the framework of the floors probably renewed in the restoration of 1848. Much of the seating is thus of the late sixteenth century and early seventeenth century. It is largely plain and mostly oak (with some elm).[6] The bench ends have (later) painted numbers in sequence from front to back in rows (Fig. 3), each row consisting of four benches, one in either aisle and two flanking the nave alley. Until relatively recently the front pews were hard up against the magnificent medieval chancel screen that runs right across the church, leaving only a narrow passage between them and the screen (Figs. 4–7).

There are four areas of nineteenth- and twentieth-century replacement and adaptation (refer to Fig. 3): (i) the south transept (Fig. 3 area B) where stout, matching twentieth-century seating recycles cut-down material said to have been installed in the mid twentieth century from the demolished Methodist Chapel at South-Hole and from St John's Chapel of Ease, both in the extensive parish of Hartland;[7] (ii) at the west end (area C in Fig. 3), probably part of the 1848 restoration, in matching style; (iii) at the north-west end (area D) where fire following a lightning strike early in the twentieth century led to the replacement of the rear section of the north aisle and some seats at the back of the nave; and (iv) most seriously, the adaptation and temporary removal of five rows on both sides of the nave alley in front of the screen (areas E & F), discussed in more detail below.

Antiquarian interest in the seating has in the past centred on the seating in the south chapel (Fig. 3 area A) which includes some bench pews with carved initials 'HP' for Hugh Prust, of the local quasi-gentry family that was prominent at the end of the sixteenth century and start of the seventeenth century.[8] These bench ends have the usual traceried carving and enriched sides and probably date to the mid sixteenth century. These and the other seats in the chapel are not in their historic positions, for although the blocking of the south chapel entrance through the screen might have been intentional, the resultant obscuring of two carved ends, one carrying the traditional *Arma Christi*, clearly cannot be.[9] If they reflect part of the later sixteenth- or early-seventeenth-century arrangements, it is significant that they prevent the south chapel screen doors from functioning – indicating reformed 'auditory' as opposed to circulation or processional needs.

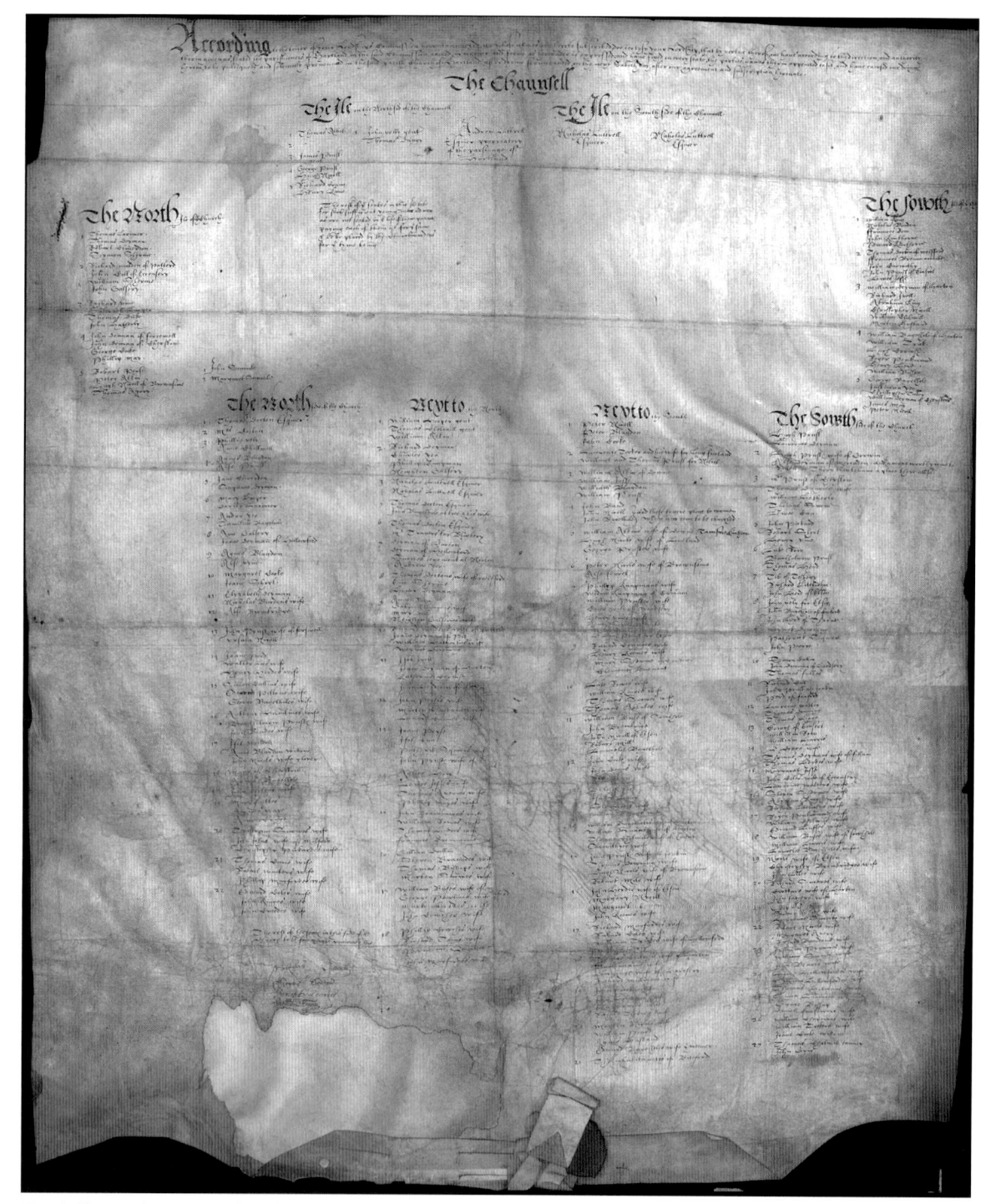

Fig. 2 (this page): Seating plan of 1613 for St Nectan, Hartland, Devon, representing the arrangements agreed that year. The seats themselves almost certainly predate the plan. They are still largely in the position shown on the plan. (Digitised by S. J. Hobbs; © copyright the PCC of St Nectan's church, Hartland)

Fig. 3 (opposite page): Schematic representation (not to scale) of the 1613 seating plan for Hartland, based on the work of Steve Hobbs. The areas marked A – F are for ease of reference in this chapter. The small circles represent female names, the squares represent males. There is a total of 192 females, 128 males (the latter figure including some whose gender is unknown). This is a

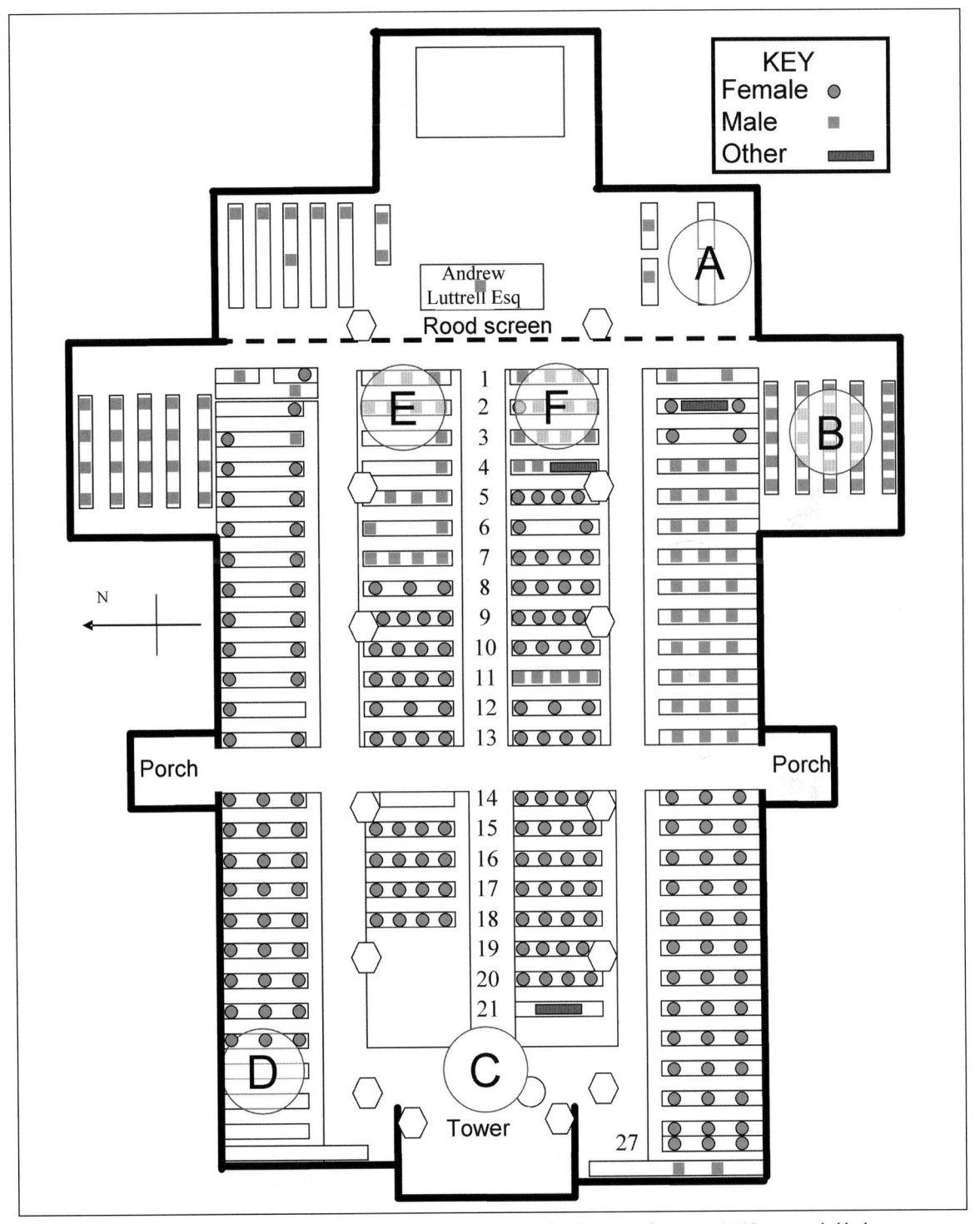

POST-REFORMATION CHURCH SEATING ARRANGEMENTS AND BENCH ASSEMBLY NOTATION IN TWO NORTH DEVON CHURCHES

grand total of 320, though the church today seats about 600, in a parish whose population in 1613 was probably between 1200 and 1500. Those allocations represented by bars were not for individuals but for other uses – in row 2 of the south aisle, the seats were for visitors of the necessary social status (the 'more worthy come to dwell in Church'), row 4 of the south central block was for the ceremony of churching women, and row 21 of the south central block was for 'the inhabitants of Biteford'. (Adapted from page 75 of S. J. Hobbs, St Nectan's, The question of a seat)

PEWS, BENCHES AND CHAIRS

Fig. 4: Interior of St Nectan, Hartland, Devon, showing the screen from the south-west, from a photograph published in 1908. The four rows of benches in the photograph are on the south side of the central alley, butting up against the medieval screen, a position probably occupied since at least 1613. (This corresponds to area F of Fig. 3.) Note the 'hat pegs' on the pew frontal. These pews have particularly rich mouldings to their top rails, a possible sign of status. On the other (north) side of the alley can be seen the Victorian reading desk, lectern and pulpit (at this date against the east side of the pillar) which have replaced some of the earlier pews, and beyond that is the north transept, in the photograph containing seating, today an organ. The seventeenth-century position of the pulpit and reading desk is not known with certainty. (From John Stabb, Some Old Devon Churches, *Vol. I, London, c.1908)*

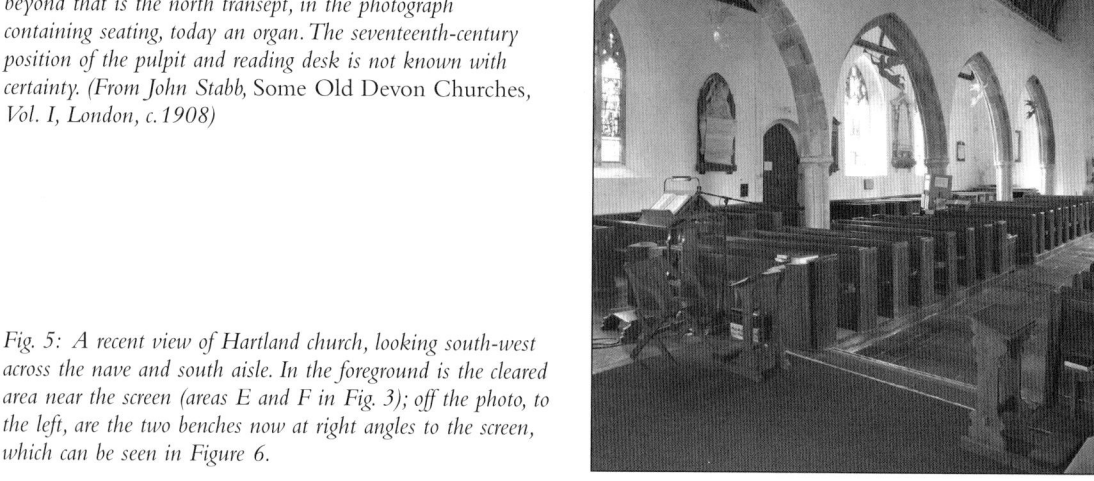

Fig. 5: A recent view of Hartland church, looking south-west across the nave and south aisle. In the foreground is the cleared area near the screen (areas E and F in Fig. 3); off the photo, to the left, are the two benches now at right angles to the screen, which can be seen in Figure 6.

Fig. 6: Hartland, a recent view, looking north-east across the south aisle and nave. The five bench ends facing the camera are rows (from right to left) 6 to 10 (see Figure 3). Rows 1–3 in the body of the nave (the front benches) have been cleared from the church; rows 4 and 5 remain, at right angles to their original position – their backs can be seen in the photograph, near the screen.

Carpenters' assembly notation

What distinguishes Hartland, as with Braunton (discussed below), is that it retains a large number of assembly marks or carpenters' assembly notation, all employing Roman numerals. Although other local sets of church seating retain some evidence of assembly marks,[10] those at Hartland are unusually plentiful and in several sections complete. Oddly, they are not (as at Braunton) underneath the seat or at the base inside the bench end or on the back boards, but on the front (that is, eastern) edge of the bench end, and fairly visible once one has one's eye in (Fig. 8).

The eastern lengths of seating against the outer walls and much of the south aisle retain almost complete sequences of this type of carpenters' notation. That on the south aisle starts with Roman numeral I either side of the cross aisle. Thus the first bench in the south aisle next to the south porch (part of row 13, as located in Figure 3) is numbered I and so on up to the front where row 2 bears the number XII. Elsewhere there are more frequent gaps and anomalies in the number sequence, for instance after number V on row 18 in the south aisle and after II on the nave south section. These minor muddles probably date from the renewal of the floor frames in the 1848 restoration, which might also account for the occasional raising of seats and back braces and the comparatively unworn condition of the square-section sills which bear the bench ends.

The area at the east end of the north aisle is of interest because the seating here is seventeenth-century and appears to have been adapted from cut-down box pews in order to line the ends up with the rest of the church. The ends are panelled with an elegant ebony inlay framing the end and frontal panels (Fig. 9).[11] Despite

Fig. 7: Two bench ends at Hartland, rows 7 and 8 in the southern block in the body of the nave (cf Fig. 6). The benches in the church vary in their details, but these are reasonably typical. The bench ends are tenoned into the sill (thought to have been renewed in 1848), with an early wooden floor flush with the top of the sill, the boards running east-west. The bench ends have simple ovolo mouldings on the outer edge, and a chamfer inside. The top rail of the bench is moulded, and the lower rail (the back brace) is just about wide enough (typically between three and five inches) to function as a book rest, if that were the intention. The corners of the seats are often rounded at the entrance when they have been deepened. The back rest is formed of horizontal boards, tenoned into the top rail and the bench end, and attached to the back brace by nails and pegs. The kneeling rail is almost certainly of later date (perhaps the 1848 restoration).

the adaptation, the bench ends retain numbers on their front edges of the timber. They are made up in three blocks and the carpenters' notation, where it exists, responds to the seat, thus the bench end of row 3 has a Roman III on its eastern edge and IIII on its western edge. This style of numbering continues beyond the cut-down pews up to the cross aisle; it is different from the majority of the numbering in the church, so probably reflects a reordering – perhaps as late as the 1848 restoration.

In general, the assembly and structural relationships of all the benches need more analysis before they will be fully understood.

The current issue

The five rows of benches at the front of the nave were adapted to form choir stalls in the 1950s by being lifted from their (possibly restored) bearers and turned at right-angles to face each other, collegiate style (Fig. 3, areas E & F). These front benches are among the most important from the church. Their top rails have the richest mouldings, a possible sign of status. One of the frontals is exceptional, with what appears to be an early adaptation to provide vertical pegs on the top rail, shaped like hat-pegs though of unknown purpose (Fig. 4), and with incised names and a design for an incised zoomorphic dragon in the smart mid-sixteenth-

Fig. 8: Hartland, examples of the assembly notation. a: Roman numeral XII on the eastern edge of row 2 in the south aisle; b: Roman numeral VII on the eastern edge of row 10 of the north aisle; c: Roman numeral VIII on the western edge of the same bench; d: facing this, the Roman numeral VIII on the eastern edge of the bench end on row 11. Note the last two were presumably intended to define row 8 at one time.

century classicising 'Romayne' style (Fig. 10), very similar to beautiful and fully carved ones at Morwenstow nearby (Fig. 11).[12] Incised names also occur on another end.

More recently three of these five rows of benches were taken out of the church in order to create a stage and altar-pace in front of the screen, and are in safe storage as part of an Archdeacon's Permission for Temporary Reordering.

The parish wish to create more space in front of the medieval chancel screen. This would entail the removal of the remaining front benches. Given that the five front rows of nave benches have already been moved and thus their historic integrity damaged, and given that a nave altar is a reasonable thing to ask for in a church of this length and with such a solid screen, a degree of adaptation is being negotiated. (An alternative, more pragmatic, possibility which has also been suggested is to accommodate flexible worship in the chancel.) The options are reinstatement, removal, further adaptation, or relocation of the historic benches. But the question of how best to reinstate them in any reordering in a position of eminence cannot be ignored. The two relocation options are for them to replace rows 6–11 in order to retain at least a semblance of their sociological significance, or to replace some of the less significant seating at the rear of the nave. The disruption caused by the latter option would clearly be less than the first but could leave them at risk of careless damage during fellowship functions. Other requirements, such as the need to provide a place to serve coffee and concerns about the position of the font against the south-east tower pier, have resulted in this part of the scheme not going ahead. At present plans are being drawn up to reinstate and recycle the benches in a more useful manner. The two best pews with the frontals would frame the dais collegiate-wise in front of the screen, the others being adapted in some manner in the south

Fig. 9: Hartland, north aisle, rows 1 and 2, of different construction from the majority of the seating in the church, with ebony inlay.

Fig. 10: Hartland, row 3, north end of the south central block (now removed from the church; area F in Fig. 3). A zoomorphic design in classicising 'Romayne' style (popular in Devon in the mid sixteenth century) incised on the end of what was a former front bench.
Fig. 11: Similar design to Figure 10, from Morwenstow church.

transept, as part of plans being considered to create space there. This would be at the expense of the current seating in the south transept, which matches the style in the rest of the church but is a twentieth-century arrangement adapting joinery from elsewhere. What is welcome is the aim to recycle the remainder of the historic joinery productively about the church to maintain the tradition.

There have also been suggestions that some of the benching at the front of the south aisle should be moved to ease access, admittedly tight, into the proposed reordered south transept. This proposal has been resisted by English Heritage with the support of the DAC. In addition to the significance of the date, the joinery and the survival of the carpenters' notation as well as the seating numbering, there is another important feature in the two early-seventeenth-century serviceable and picturesque little cupboards fitted below the rail ('book rest') of the frontal (Fig. 12).

Fig. 12: Hartland, row 1 of the south aisle. Left, the frontal with cupboards and sloped book rest; right, the exterior of the frontal.

St Brannock, Braunton

Braunton is famous for retaining its medieval field system in use. Its church is correspondingly special. It is large and wide and has a magnificent very early fifteenth-century roof structure,[13] whilst the structure of the broached spire over the south transept dates to the thirteenth century (both roof and spire are dated from dendrochronological evidence) (Fig. 13).[14] The church is also well known for a complete set of sixteenth-century church seating in two wide blocks each side of the cross aisle (Figs. 14 & 15). As at Hartland there is a slightly deeper pew referred to as the 'Churching' pew and in this case positioned next to the font. There are relevant accounts in the parish records (churchwardens' accounts) but these only survive from 1554; importantly, they include documentary references to the installation or augmentation of seating in about six stages in the later sixteenth century.[15]

The iconography and style of the benches

The point of this note is to draw attention to the survival on most of the benches of a complex corpus of carpenters' assembly notation. First though, it is important to set the context.

The square design of the benches at Braunton resembles that of Hartland, but as with the majority of surviving early North Devon and North Cornwall seating, the bench ends are enriched, some of the edge-carving being undercut; many of the ends bear shields with initials, presumably of donors/owners/renters (Fig. 16).[16] There are it seems two styles of carving and enrichment. The more convincingly pre-Reformation and mid-sixteenth-century examples are now to be found in the south chancel chapel, with two significant ones, previously attached to additional Victorian benches in the nave, now made into a clergy seat (Fig. 17). Nevertheless, most of the remaining seating at Braunton remains typically medieval in character, including traceried framework at head and base of the bench ends, and enrichment of the edges.

The enrichment and the presentation of the subject matter, heraldry and initials in shields are similar to several others in this

Fig. 13: St Brannock, Braunton, Devon. Exterior, from the south. The internal roof structure of the broached spire over the south transept dates from the thirteenth century.

Fig. 14: St Brannock, Braunton, Devon. General view of interior looking east to the medieval screen. The church has about eighty early bench ends.

remote corner of the country, although a little cruder than Kilkhampton or Launcells and certainly not as early as St Columb Major or Woolsery. Some of the bench ends retain conservative iconography of the Passion. The treatment of one of the subjects, the 30 pieces of silver (Fig. 18), stacked in columns and not in a bag, is a feature of the area (as at Kilkhampton and Launcells) – 'typical of the the Duchy' (of Cornwall), as Pevsner puts it in his *Cornwall*.[17] This representation of the subject is rare but does have precedents in later medieval iconography, for example with the coins stacked sideways in the influential early-fifteenth-century psalter, the *Bedford Hours*; so it cannot be regarded as a late (i.e. post-medieval) feature. In general, the iconographical subject matter of the bench ends is characteristically medieval. There has been disfigurement to a few of the faces of saints (Fig.19), which might suggest reforming iconoclasm, but could equally well be accidental damage along a fault-line in the wood.

However, a *later* sixteenth-century date would be consonant with the style of some of the borders; of the hair and dress; and of many of the initials. For example, two benches recycled at an earlier period in the south chapel – including one depicting

Fig. 15: Braunton. a: the north-west block of seating, with one of the early pew frontals in the church. b: a detail of this frontal. The panels cry out for paintings. (15a from J. C. Cox, Bench-ends in English Churches, *London, 1916)*

St Brannock with a tonsure and holding a large chalice with concave facets, which would thus appear pre-Reformation (Fig. 20) – nevertheless have later sixteenth-century-style frames.

Thus it would appear that the apparently medieval iconography cannot be used to date the benches as definitely pre-Reformation. Braunton itself was conservative in its religion in Elizabethan times, continuing to display the holy relics of St Brannock, using copes, chasuble, lights and incense, maintaining a surpliced choir, buying a new organ, and keeping up its guilds and brotherhood days.[18] Instruments of the Passion were uncontroversial as subject matter for sixteenth-century West Country bench ends (Fig. 21). Furthermore, the IHS is discreet and the M's, if they are Marian M's, are uncrowned and similarly discreet; whether symbolic or not they could be taken

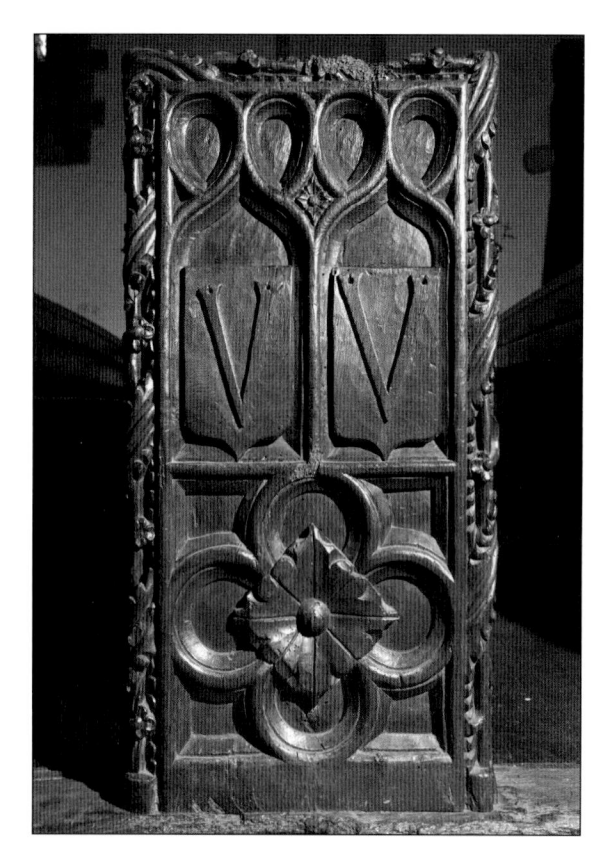

Fig. 16 (left): Braunton, one of a large number of bench ends carrying initials.

Fig. 17 (right): Braunton, pre-Reformation bench end formerly attached to a Victorian pew in the nave, now used to form a clergy seat in the south chapel.

for the initials in shields which make up about 50 per cent of the decoration of the ends.

Tree-ring analysis of one of the pews has sparked further debate. Three planks of one pew were dated (but no bench ends), the results showing that the timber for these planks was felled sometime after *c.*1475. (The dated planks (Fig. 25) were on pew number 3, which is towards the east end of the north aisle.)[19] It seems unlikely that the conversion of the planks entailed the removal of about one hundred year's worth of timber. So does the tree-ring evidence for this seat vindicate a pre-Reformation date for the bench ends, despite the style and uniformity of the pews, and (as about to be discussed) the original or very early bearing sills, and the assembly marking, both of which appear to relate in broad terms to the various documented augmentations of the seating in the later sixteenth century? Might this mean that the some of the augmentations were in fact modifications of existing, pre-Reformation pews, e.g. reseating them?[20] There is not yet a simple answer: the iconography is simple and pre-Reformation but the shape and the style are characteristic of benching throughout the sixteenth century with some obviously pre- and some obviously post-Reformation attributes. Presumably the majority of the bench ends with initials are post-Reformation but it is not certain that the rest are pre-Reformation. A working hypothesis therefore is that the benching has been re-jointed and that in the later sixteenth century a selection of earlier bench ends was reset with new sills and many new benches and back boards to make up the seating referred to in the documents, in this way creating the sense of uniformity which exists today. The likelihood is that the pews span the Reformation period from the early to the later sixteenth century, to some extent therefore providing another instance of continuity of the kind that recent scholarship has been identifying.[21] Hence the importance of research now in train on the parish records which it is hoped will shed light on the owners and thus the dating of the initials on the benches.[22]

Fig. 18 (left): Braunton, bench end with lantern and 30 pieces of silver, bench no. 6 in the south-east block (see Figure 23).

Fig. 19 (right): Braunton, bench end in the north-east block, with two saints, on the left disfigured and unidentified, and on the right St John the Evangelist.

The joinery

An arson attack in July 2003 damaged the pulpit and benches at the front, one of them (fortunately not a significant one) beyond repair. Following the attack, Hugh Harrison established that apart from four Victorian benches at the front, and the loss of the front sills or bearers and parts of their returns, all the remaining seats were on their original bearers and in their original order with carpenters' assembly notation starting with number 1 at the cross aisle up to number 10 at the front.[23]

Fig. 20 (left): Braunton, bench end with St Brannock in a distinctly later-sixteenth-century frame, albeit tonsure and chalice are in a pre-Reformation style.

Fig. 21 (right): Braunton, one of a number of bench ends showing the Instruments of the Passion, here the ladder and hammer.

Based on current evidence, the combination of the original blocks of seating with so much of their carpenters' assembly notation is extremely unusual. Similar numbered joinery at other related churches, such as at Hartland, and in the recycling of numbered joinery at Whimple and Northlew, is nowhere so complete.[24]

This notation is more complex and more varied than at Hartland, with at least three types of chisel marking. All are Roman numerals. The most common is a long, rough, chisel-edge scratching, sometimes across two back boards. There is much use of 'nested' marks (Figs. 22 & 23), as with a Roman VIIII being scratched with four 'glyphs' set inside the V. In the block west of the cross aisle on the south side, the marks are carefully made with a 1-inch gouge, the V's as a result having concave sides (Fig. 24). Thicker, firm, carefully made chisel numbering occurs on the benches of the north side (Fig. 25). These are generally, but not always, balanced by scratch-made numbering on the other end of the bench (normally the north end). The outer ends of the benches on both sides of the nave alley are differenced by a quadrant or semi-circular gouge mark made with a circular gouge. There are very few anomalies, though where they occur these presumably indicate some form of adaptation – for example, the third and fourth and ninth benches on the south side west of the cross aisle; elsewhere there is a satisfying consistency.[25]

The moulded bearers appear original (or sixteenth-century at least), which itself suggests that a uniform pattern of seating, reflected in the present arrangements, was envisaged in advance, as at Hartland. But this is hard to reconcile with the tree-ring dating, the two styles (pre- and post-Reformation) and the augmentations in the later sixteenth century. Dr Hughes's interpretation of the documents, which make at least six references to seating in the later sixteenth century, is that the benches were delivered 'flat-pack' and worked up in batches, probably of one block at a time (as the numbering could bear out) to a pre-arranged scheme in the workshop. (In Chapter 6, P. S. Barnwell finds somewhat similar staged campaigns of seating in the pre-Reformation period.) Against this, the distortions of the planks and bench ends are characteristic of being first used when still green, which could, of course, be explained by earlier material being recycled in a major later sixteenth-century campaign.[26] It is worth pointing out that the screen at Hartland

Fig. 22 (left): Braunton, south-west seating block, bench no. 14, assembly notation: a Roman '9' (with IIII nested in the V).

Fig. 23 (right): Braunton, south-east seating block, bench no. 6, assembly notation: a Roman '7' (with II nested in the V). See Figure 18 for the bench end of this bench.

Fig. 24 (left): Braunton, north-west block, bench no. 16, assembly notation: a 'dished' VIII (the 'V' rotated through ninety degrees, all marks curved).

Fig. 25 (right): Braunton, the assembly mark on the underside of bench no. 3, (east bench on north side). See the text for the date of three planks on this bench.

also has sequenced carpenters' marks, suggesting it too may have been delivered ready for assembly on site.

Changes since the arson attack

Arson meant loss and a great deal of damage and smoke-staining. The organ, the handsome gallery in which it was located and three of the pews on the north side were damaged. Ambitious reordering plans were discussed but a working compromise found, with the Victorian benches removed and the frontals restored on the now surplus Victorian bearers. Two clearly pre-Reformation bench ends that had adorned the Victorian benches have been recycled into a clergy seat. The north transept now has a children's corner and an organ has been restored into a loft above it, with the organ case yet to be funded.

Conclusion

The analytical study of church seating always brings new insights and sometimes surprises. The assembly notation on the benches at Hartland and Braunton needs close examination and reconciliation with the evidence of dismantling and re-erection in both churches and, in the case of Braunton, with the documentary evidence for the augmentation of the church seating in the later sixteenth century and a study of the names behind the initials. The addition of assembly notation to the archaeological study of church seating will enrich our understanding of construction and development over time. Here I have merely drawn attention to a largely unexamined, and potentially fruitful, source of diagnostic information.

Acknowledgements

Hartland is fortunate in having a resident historian and antiquary, Steve Hobbs, Honorary Archivist at Hartland Abbey, and I am grateful to him for his unstinting generosity with the fruits of his researches. He has made a study both of the history of the parish and its documents. This and his recent study of the seating in the church and of the magnificent seating plan of 1613 are available through the Hartland Digital Archive: S. J. Hobbs, St Nectan's, The question of a seat (Oxford University Research Notes 2004–5). Some of the photographs are his. My thanks are due especially to him but also to several other specialists, including Hugh Harrison, Jo Cox and Jo Mattingly for their advice and help. My thanks also to Trevor Cooper for helpful comments on an earlier version of this chapter. The views expressed here are my own.

Notes

1. See J. Mattingly, 'The dating of bench ends in Cornish churches', *Journal of the Royal Institution of Cornwall*, New Series II, vol I, 58–72.
2. These clearly served a primary structural purpose for the back board, and secondary uses no doubt followed simply because they existed. We call them book rests now, but a) they are set rather low, generally about 8–10 inches down from the back rail; b) the question must be asked how many of the congregation in about 1600 would have brought prayer books to church; and c) similar structural device are found on earlier pews. While a shelf in this position could have been an elbow rest, the benches at Hartland, unlike those at Kilkhampton or Clovelly nearby, are too close-spaced to make this practical, let alone comfortable.
3. B. Cherry and N. Pevsner, *Devon* (Penguin, *Buildings of England* series, 2nd edn, 1989), 471.
4. North Devon Record Office HA_PCC_1201-add-1-3.
5. S. J .Hobbs, *St Nectan's, The question of a seat*, (Oxford University Research Notes, privately printed), Hartland Digital Archive, 2004–5. An extract from this work, with details of who sat where and biographical information, can be found at http://genuki.cs.ncl.ac.uk/DEV/Hartland/HartlandSeating.html (accessed 13 Sep 2009).
6. Steve Hobbs, personal communication.
7. Steve Hobbs, personal communication.
8. Hobbs, *St Nectan's, The question of a seat*, especially 140–41 and 272–80 (*passim*).
9. They were presumably elsewhere in the church or possibly, as Steve Hobbs has speculated, from another Prust chapel.
10. Complex series at Northlew; some noted at Morthoe, others at Lansallos (the latter, personal communication Ian Tyers).
11. Steve Hobbs suggests that the use of ebony may be as a memorial, possibly thus reflecting a bequest.
12. Illustrated in Hobbs, *St Nectan's, The question of a seat*, 226–28 and Figs. 57–62. The execution of the lettering suggesting that they were unable to obtain the services of a trained letter-cutter.
13. I. Tyers, *Tree-Ring Analysis of Oak Timbers from St Brannock Church, Braunton, Devon*, English Heritage Centre for Archaeology Report 81/2004, 1–5. His interpretation of tree-ring dating for the roof up to the heartwood-sapwood boundary with allowance for sapwood is that the roof timbers were felled between 1388 and 1413.
14. See I. Tyers et al, *Vernacular Architecture*, 28 (1997), 138–58, and D. H. Miles & M. J. Worthington in S. Pearson, *Vernacular Architecture*, 32 (2001), 76–77.
15. Cherry and Pevsner, *Devon*, 207–08, using the excellent summary based on an examination of parish records by a previous incumbent, the Revd Preb. J. F. Chanter, in Exeter Diocesan Gazette, 'The Church of St Brannock, Braunton',

1934, reprinted by the church 2009. See also P. Hughes, 'An Investigation into the Historical Sources for the Parish Church of St Brannock, Braunton, Devon, with particular reference to the 16th and 17th century furnishings', for Jonathan Rhind Architects, The Old Rectory, Shirwell, Barnstaple, Devon, March 2004.
16 Similar examples notably at Kilkhampton and Launcells in Cornwall and Morthoe, Bickington, and Atherington in Devon.
17 N. Pevsner, *Cornwall* (Penguin, *Buildings of England* series, 1951), 70.
18 Chanter, 'St Brannock', 7 and *passim*.
19 The planks were those numbered VIIII, VIIII & VIIII°, the latter with a circular gouge mark (Tyers, *Tree-Ring Analysis*, 4).
20 It may be relevant that Ian Tyers noted that the bench end from pew '2' is constructed from parts of three other carved ends. He and his colleague, Bob Chappell, noticed that the tenons in some cases betrayed evidence of the bench ends having been dismantled at an earlier date (Tyers, *Tree-Ring Analysis*, 5). Although this probably relates to a regrettable episode in the 1980s when the pew platforms had concrete laid beneath them (John Allan, personal communication), it may represent later sixteenth-century changes, as discussed in the body of the text.
21 Notably since Eamon Duffy's, *The Stripping of the Altars* (New Haven and London, 1993).
22 Steve Hobbs is beginning to study the documents and fabric relating to St Brannock's.
23 For instance, as noted by Ian Tyers, *Tree-Ring Analysis*, 5, the frontal is numbered X and bench 4 is numbered VIII° while the bench end is numbered VIII.
24 The evidence will emerge. Simply talking to professionals in the field has elicited anecdotal evidence of plenty more (e.g. Lansallos church, personal communication, Ian Tyers).
25 Though see note 20.
26 Tyers, *Tree-Ring Analysis*, 5.

11. 'To take theire plases wheare they shall not offend others': the 1635 reseating of Puddletown church, Dorset

Bob Machin

The Church's Restoration
In eighteen-eighty-three
Has left for contemplation
Not what there used to be.
    (John Betjeman, *Hymn*, 1932)

This chapter is reproduced (with different photographs) from the Transactions of the Ancient Monuments Society, *53 (2009), by kind permission of the author and publishers.*

FIRST AMONGST the tasteless Victorian improvements that Betjeman went on to disapprove of were pine bench pews. Therefore, it is a delightful contrast to enter a church which the Victorians forgot. Even if there is not a social hierarchy of eighteenth-century box pews, the ranks of simpler seventeenth-century pews, with their doors and metal furniture, all facing an elevated pulpit, seem so much more suitable for a Reformation Church of England environment. The parish church of St Mary, Puddletown, Dorset is one such, although the rebuilding of the chancel in 1910 is unfortunate.[1] Nevertheless, it is worth visiting because it appears to be the only surviving early-seventeenth-century interior for which there is documentary evidence for what was done, why, and how it was received by the parishioners.

Tensions over seating

Just as many people object to Victorian pine 'free sittings', there were plenty who objected to the reseating of parish churches in the early seventeenth century. Dorset churchwardens' presentments are full of examples. At Ryme Intrinseca in 1609, Susan Husday and Agnes Ploweman were presented 'for contending and strivieing in the Church for a seate: [and] the one thrustinge and pullinge owt the other'. Every Sunday at Lyme Regis in 1631, Hester Jordayne disturbed Ann Gregory, 'and other her pewmates by Continuall Sitting & unseemly & Immodest thrusting of her selfe into their seates, she havinge no right there'. At Folke in 1631, three female servants of William Fauntleroy, Esq., intruded 'themselves into the two former women seates appointed for other of the parishioners and doe disturb them in their seates whereas there is a place allotted for them in their Master's Ile'.

Exactly what the parishioners were arguing about is not always clear, even when we try to read between the lines. Folke was reseated in 1628 and is still largely intact, but there was an earlier dispute over seating. On 3 December 1630, Walter Rideout, gentleman, 'did break open a locke sett uppon the seate appoynted for the churching of women, the seate being locked upp by Mr Dean's direcion, which lock was carried away by him: afterwardes the said seate being againe locked upp by us with an other locke, he ... severall tymes very uncivilly climed over the said seate, and giveth out in speeches that he will sitt in the said seate notwithstanding Mr Deanes order to the contrary'. According to the churchwardens' presentment of the preceding year, everyone had agreed to be seated 'according to their severall rancks & Degrees' except Mr Walter Rideout who had refused two alternative locations – either 'the uppermost seat save one on the north syde of ... the Church' or 'next unto the seate of William Fauntleroy, Esq., in the Ile on the south side'.[2]

The churchwardens at Folke had bent over backwards to accommodate Mr Rideout. But he died an embittered man. The only other thing we know about him is his epitaph, which he himself wrote. He died in 1643, aged eighty-four and the memorial in the church reads:

> Here lyeth a true Christian, now at quiet rest,
> Who whilst he lyved was by the world oprest.
> But praysed be God he hath overcome this evill,
> And vanquished hath the world, the flesh, the devil.

One wonders if Walter Rideout was just a foolish old man or were the three servants of William Fauntleroy just foolish women – like Susan Husday and Agnes Ploweman of Ryme, or Hester Jordayne of Lyme – making mountains out of molehills. However, when one finds hundreds of such disputes about seating, from all over the country, the suspicion grows that these arguments were symptoms of something vitally important to the protagonists.

The Puddletown reseating

When the ministry of the Word replaced the mystery of the Mass at the Reformation, a new 'auditory' layout was required. Most English parish churches were completely refurnished, with a 'three-decker' pulpit and pews. Only a few examples survived Georgian and Victorian restorations, but Dorset is fortunate – the early-seventeenth-century fittings at Folke, Leweston and Puddletown are virtually intact. But Puddletown is unique. As far as can be discovered, this is the only seventeenth-century parish church interior in England where we have both the 1635 fittings and documentary evidence explaining what was done and why (Figs. 1 & 2).[3]

After evening service on Sunday 10 August 1634, the congregation remained seated whilst the churchwardens described a proposal for totally re-fitting the interior. An earlier report had said 'That a maine piller & arech was in Decaye and to be strengthened and that the seats eare not Dessent but mutch out of order and in Decaye and that thear wanted Roome for the parrishoners being Increased'. The starting point was the need to strengthen the north pillar of the chancel arch. In 1505 the west wall of the north transept had been taken down to incorporate it in the new north aisle. It was now realised that this demolished wall had been taking most of the thrust of the chancel arch. The solution proposed by 'skilful workmen' sounds almost as dotty as the cause of the problem – to strengthen the arch by erecting a new screen. This would put the rest of the fittings to shame, so it was further proposed that the church should be 'new Seated throughout' and that there should be 'A gallarie at the weste ende to Receive seates that the church cannott supplie'. Having gone this far, the most important fittings had to be

Fig. 1: St Mary, Puddletown, Dorset, general view from the chancel arch, looking north-west. This view is largely unchanged since 1635, except for the disappearance of the chancel screen. There are pews each side of a central alley in the nave, and a similar arrangement in the north aisle. At the rear, the gallery stretches across the whole church. The font cover can just be seen towards the back of the church on the south (left) of the central alley In the left foreground are the steps up to the pulpit – the present steps are of the early twentieth century, in the place where previously a pew stood, up against the chancel steps. In the right foreground is a small block of pews which also come right up to the chancel steps. Behind those pews is the Earl of Suffolk's pew, with its balustraded top.

replaced: 'A communion table and a frame about yt for the communion and a settle without that'; 'A pulpit and Reading place to be made and advanzed'; and 'A newe cover for the font that is All in Decaie'. All of these improvements were authorised and survive, except that in 1910 the chancel was rebuilt so that its 1635 fittings were re-arranged (Figs. 3–5).

The estimated cost of the work was £130. A levy of five shillings on each of the 240 people to be seated raised £60. The balance of £70 was raised by five ordinary rates on the 129 households. We are told that everyone who paid, 'shall in theire Degree and Ranke be seated and Recorded that hereafter They be not Impeached by any that have not Joyned in the costs of this Worke But such to take theire plases wheare they shall not offend others'.

Fig. 2: The present view from the gallery, looking east. The chancel arrangements are of 1910, when the chancel was lengthened. To the right of the picture is the two-decker pulpit. Immediately to the west of the pulpit are the balustraded pews of the Earl of Suffolk – on the north (left) side of the alley – and the Hastings family (south). A later church plan (1679) shows that the pews to the right (south) of the central alley each sat five people, the smaller pews to the left seating four. This would probably not be too overcrowded by today's standards. In 1635 the north aisle had girls and maid servants sitting in the alley at the 'seat ends' – but no remains of flap or pull out seats can be seen on the ends of the pews, so presumably the young women brought their own stools to sit on.

Fig. 3: The altar and altar rails. The rails are of 1635, and seem to be in their original three-sided arrangement. The gap between the rails and the east wall was introduced when the chancel was lengthened in 1910.

The six principles

All of these proposals were endorsed by the Archdeacon and, according to the inscription on the gallery front, the work was completed within a year (Fig. 6). But although the 'beauty of holiness' was achieved in the church fittings at Puddletown, it caused some unholy dissension within the congregation. Entertaining details of seating disputes, as quoted earlier for other churches, are lacking, but two years after the refitting in 1637, the churchwardens drew up a document headed 'Things propounded and Desired by Lawfull fauour of Authoritie to be furthered and confirmed for the quietinge of the parrishoners in setlinge them in theire proper places and seates in the church'. It contained six principles, a written statement of where each social group should sit, and originally had a seating plan annexed which does not survive.

The first principle was financial: everyone was to pay their contribution to the costs. Those too poor to pay anything could not be excluded from church but they could be stigmatised: 'for the poorer men as undertenants or cottagers that contribut not to the worke they to take theire places in the Belfrie as the like is in other parrishes'. This is a most illuminating remark. The poor were required to stand (in the medieval manner) in the tower opening at the furthest west end of the church (Fig. 5). This was both demeaning and divisive. The fourth principle was related: 'That mens hindes [i.e. servants] and poore undertenants doe putt themselves in their places prepared and assigned and not into the Channsell'. Presumably many of the poor had previously stood around the pulpit and communion rail. That they should continue

Fig. 4: A postcard showing the pulpit and reading desk in the south-east corner of the body of the nave, before the changes of 1910. By this date, the 1635 screen between chancel and nave had gone. It can be seen how close the communion rail was to the chancel step before the chancel was extended in 1910, and how the stairs to the pulpit intruded into the central alley, blocking the journey to the chancel. Between the reading desk stairs and chancel step there was a pew – it can just be glimpsed in the photograph, through the handrail to the pulpit steps; the pew was removed in 1910, and the space taken up with new pulpit steps. The pulpit is a high-quality piece, and seems not to share any design motifs with the other church furniture. In the changes of 1910 it was given a new backing board and a tester, and lost the superstructure shown here (which may or may not be original). The reading desk, shown here with tasselled bible and prayer book, seems to have been left largely unchanged at that time, both as to height and general appearance. To the right of the picture is the Hastings pew, still in place.

to do so in full view of the main body of the seated congregation was now considered either improper or unsightly.

We do not know exactly how many poor there were in Puddletown in 1635, but the estimates for raising the cost of reseating speak of 129 rate-paying households in the parish. The usual multiplier of 4.5 persons per household would give a total population of around 580. The estimates also speak of 240 persons paying five shillings each for a seat. Therefore, 580 minus 240 gives an estimated total of 340 poor. This was more than half the population of the parish, which is an unbelievably high proportion for the seventeenth century. Gregory King's calculations of 1688 led him to believe that half the population of

Fig. 5: The west end in 1910, looking from the south door across the church. The view is largely unchanged today. The font is Norman, with a pyramidal cover of 1635 – a common design for font covers of the time, though this one is notably plain. The pews are arranged to leave a space for the font, though it is not clear whether this is the original arrangement (the 1679 plan appears not to show it). To the left, under the gallery and in line with the central alley, is the door-opening to the 'Belfrie' (the tower) where the poor were placed. The gallery stairs can be seen in the far (north-west) corner.

Fig. 6: The coat of arms on the gallery, bearing the charges of the English sovereigns from 1406/7 until 1603, but no later. The carving is probably therefore older than the gallery. Beneath is the date of the gallery, 1635. The balustrade is of similar design to the altar rails.

England was 'diminuishing the wealth of the kingdom' by earning less than it required for subsistence. The 1672/3 Hearth Tax Assessments from various counties give an exemption rate for the poor of around thirty per cent.

Whatever the real numbers of the poor in early-seventeenth-century Puddletown, it would be physically impossible for more than a score of them to stand at the back of the church. Most of those 'that contribut not to the worke' were not just demeaned – they were, in practical terms, excluded.

The sixth principle dealt with a different financial matter – 'That none be permitted to lett their seates in the Church to Rent'. Pews were either 'private' or 'church' pews. 'Private pews' had been built at their own costs by individuals who had bought a space within the church: they were private property that could be bequeathed or sold. Although Puddletown parishioners had paid for their pews in 1635, they remained parochial property. Pew-holders who were temporarily absent could lend their seats to neighbours or friends, but they could not disrupt the social grading of the seating arrangements decreed by the churchwardens and 'cheef parrishoners'.

The three remaining principles were all concerned with social hierarchy within the building. The third stated 'That menn and woemen be not Intermixed in seates but eyther sorte & sexe to be seated by themselves in theire proper quarters and squadrons'. The separation of the sexes was normal and survived until comparatively recently in some conservative churches. 'The proper quarters' for men and women is readily understood, but their 'proper squadrons' is not so obvious. The villagers were to be divided not only by sex but also by age and socio-economic status. This was also commonplace until well into the nineteenth century. That 'the subordination of ranks is of divine institution and never is more beautifully or harmoniously exhibited than in the House of God, where rich and poor meet together to share the blessings of their common Father' is a commentary from 1840 but the same concept was expressed in innumerable earlier descriptions.

Pride of place at Puddletown went to the two manorial Lords of Puddletown and Waterson – the Hon. Henry Hastings and the Right Hon. Earl of Suffolk. Their superior pews survive immediately beneath the pulpit in the nave (Fig. 7) – the separate pews for their wives in the north aisle have been removed.

Male tenants sat behind their respective manorial lords in the body of the nave with their wives behind them. The division can be seen by the presence of hat pegs in the men's area (Fig. 8). Their sons – 'of best Ranke and estate' – sat with the servants of the manorial lords in a lost pew on the east side of the pulpit (Fig. 4). 'Daughters of the Best ranke' sat with the ladies' maids to the west of the ladies in the north aisle. All other young girls and maid servants sat either at the 'seats ends' in the north aisle or 'in that part of the gallarie ... fitted and prepared for them'. The gallery (Fig. 9) was divided into three parts: one for the overflow of young girls from the aisle, another for 'the newe cottagers that contribute to the worke', and the third for their wives. 'Smaler boyes and scholers' were assigned to the alley 'right before the minister's Pue', on surviving open benches.

Basically, the church was divided into four areas: first, immediately around the pulpit were the manorial lords, their ladies, their maids and the children; second, behind them were their tenants; third, in the gallery were the cottagers; and fourthly, standing in the bell-tower were those few poor people who chose still to come to church. Looking down the church from his pulpit in 1637, the vicar could see that the divine institution of subordinate ranks had been made manifest. Whether or not he thought it beautiful, he knew, as we now do, that it was not achieved harmoniously but only after some acrimonious wrangles.

Fig. 7: The Earl of Suffolk's pew, as seen from the pulpit (with the pulpit candlestick showing in the foreground). Note the carved top to the door of the Suffolk pew, its balustrading, and the panelling covering the lower part of the pillar, the latter a touch of luxury not found in the lower status pews to the rear.

Polarisation

We do not know what the excluded poor thought about the refurnishing of their church. Their opinions were of so little consequence that no literate person bothered to record them. Presumably a few poor continued to attend church, either through piety or to 'earn' the extra charity of bread and fuel doles which some of their wealthier neighbours established from time to time. But the majority only received confirmation of what was already becoming clear in Reformation England, that the poor were now an unwanted surplus population, which those with an economic stake in society would prefer to exclude and forget about.

Those who could afford to pay for the right to sit in their parish church had much to contend about. Some conservatives, such as Walter Rideout, could not accept the changes. Others, like Susan Husday, Agnes Ploweman or Hester Jordayne, felt that they had not received the social recognition that they deserved. The reseating, at Puddletown and elsewhere, reflected a restructuring of traditional society. This brave new world was based primarily upon each person's position on the ladder of wealth. Those who could not contribute financially were to be thrust out – 'as the like is in other parishes'. Those who could afford to pay were seated not according to tradition, birth or the practical contributions they made to community life but according to their financial stake in the parish as manorial lords, tenant farmers or cottagers.

It was a simple polarisation into 'haves' and 'have nots'. We have already heard some of the respectable 'haves' at Puddletown describe themselves as the 'chief parishioners' and those 'of best

Fig. 8: A typical pew, the door open. (This example is in the southern block of pews.) The hinges are original. The pews are uncomfortable, with narrow seats and backrests at right-angles to the seats: to survive, you have to sit somewhat upright. The hat pegs are found in the men's pews throughout the church. The book shelves are early, using hand made nails to attach them to the pew in front; however, from the details of their attachment (which appears to be an afterthought) they are probably not of 1635. (A few otherwise identical pews at the rear of the church do not have them.) The kneeling boards appear to be later than the pews. The pews sit on modern runners, installed in the second half of the twentieth century.

rank and estate'. Elsewhere, in petitions and court judgements, such men called themselves 'the major part' or 'the better sort'. 'Sort' recurs so frequently in sixteenth-century texts that it seems to have replaced the medieval classification into 'ranks and estates'. Sixteenth-century people were either of 'the better sort' or they were not. A 1596 commentator in Devon wrote that 'the gentlemen of the country and some of the better sort' ought to keep hospitality, relieve the poor, and 'be at hand to stay the fury of the inferior multitude if they should happen to break out'.[4]

The mid-seventeenth-century Civil Wars made it necessary to take sides. There has been much debate as to who joined which side and for what reason. But many contemporaries were agreed that, by and large, the royalists were aristocrats, their dependants and 'the needy multitude', whilst parliament had the hearts of 'the yeomen, farmers, clothiers and the whole middle rank of the people'; 'tradesmen and freeholders, and the middle sort of men'; 'the middle sort of people, who are the body of the kingdom'.

All that is lacking here is the term class. It will not be used until the late eighteenth century. But for all practical purposes, a new rural middle class was already established by the mid seventeenth century and had been establishing its values for several generations.

Where, or even whether, one had a seat when the community gathered for worship now depended upon one's ability to pay – in this case five shillings per person and the product of five parish rates per household. It was a simple and rational way to raise money. The appearance of Rate Books among early-seventeenth-

Fig. 9: Open benches in the gallery. These ones are on the north side, near the staircase. In 1635 the gallery was used for young girls overflowing from the north aisle, for the 'new cottagers that contribute to the worke', and for their wives.

century parish records and the frequent appeals to Quarter Sessions against inequitable assessments demonstrates the novelty of the method. The traditional way to raise money for community causes was Church Ales and Revels. These convivial and sometimes boisterous gatherings were now suppressed in the interests of 'law and order'.[5]

The surviving re-fittings at Puddletown, Folke and scores of other places certainly show 'the architectural setting of Anglican worship'.[6] But their ranked seating also shows the pattern of the new social order desired by 'the middling' or 'better sort' of society. This was not achieved without a struggle, but eventually the lower orders were persuaded 'to take theire plases wheare they shall not offend others'.

Acknowledgements
Except for Figures 4 and 5, the photographs are by Trevor Cooper.

Notes
1. For the controversy over the 1910 rebuilding of the chancel see Claudius J. P. Beatty, *Thomas Hardy: conservation architect – his work for the SPAB* (Dorset Natural History & Archaeological Society, 1995), 42–49.
2. Dorset Churchwardens' Presentments are catalogued by year in the Wiltshire Record Office.
3. The Puddletown documents are in the Dorset Local History Centre (formerly the Dorset County Record Office) PE/PUD/CW 5/1 and 5/2.
4. Keith Wrightson, 'Estates, degrees and sorts: changing perceptions of society in Tudor and Stuart England' in P. J. Corfield (ed.) *Language, History and Class* (1991).
5. See D. Underdown, *Revel, Riot and Rebellion* (Oxford, 1985).
6. See the pioneering work by G. W. O. Addleshaw and F. Etchells, *The Architectural Setting of Anglican Worship* (London, 1948) and N. Yates, *Buildings, Faith and Worship: the liturgical arrangement of Anglican churches 1600-1900* (Oxford, 1991, rev. ed. 2000).

12. The pews at St Mary, Newent, Gloucestershire

Hugh Harrison

Introduction

IN JANUARY 1673 the roof of the medieval nave of St Mary's, Newent, Gloucestershire collapsed under the weight of snow, leaving only the chancel undamaged.[1] The pews which were introduced in the subsequent building work form the topic of this chapter, which, it is hoped, will prove of interest not only for the specifics of this particular set of pews, but also as an indication of how an examination of surviving seating can throw light on its history.

A new nave was built in 1675–9, not long after the disaster, designed and constructed by local men, with the carpenter, Edward Taylor, creating innovative roof trusses modelled on those used by Wren at the Sheldonian Theatre in Oxford some thirteen years earlier. These allowed a very wide space to be created, uninterrupted by pillars, creating a nave which is open and spacious. There are giant pilasters around the walls with Ionic capitals; as is common for the period, the pilasters stand on tall plinths to allow for high-backed pews. The walls were originally plastered and there was a plaster ceiling.

Fig. 1: St Mary, Newent, Gloucestershire. The interior facing east, looking along the nave through the chancel arch to the east window. To the south of the chancel is the Lady Chapel. The large openings from the nave into the medieval chancel and chapel were created when the nave was rebuilt at the end of the 1670s. Notice the giant ionic pilasters. The walls were stripped in the nineteenth century.

Fig. 2: The interior looking west, with surviving west gallery at the rear. Some rows of pews have been removed from the front of the church, and the western space under the gallery has been enclosed. There are two alleys or gangways, and a wide central block of pews.

In 1884 Middleton & Son, Cheltenham scraped the walls and removed the plaster ceiling, and made changes to the pewing, as discussed in this chapter. They also removed the 'gallery pews'[2] at the east, whilst the south gallery was removed in the early twentieth century. The west gallery remains, as does the cut-down pulpit (of the late seventeenth century), now in a conventional position in the north-east corner, though earlier it had been on the north side. In more recent years there have been other changes to the nave seating. Some rear pews beneath the west gallery were removed in 1974, with complete clearance of this area when the space was enclosed in 1984. Four rows of seating on the south of the nave were removed in 1995 together with clergy seating and pews in the Lady Chapel, and in 2008 three rows of pews on the north side of the nave were taken out, with their frontal partially reinstated as a screen in front of the pulpit.[3]

Fig. 3: The interior, looking north across the central block of pews.

THE PEWS AT ST MARY, NEWENT, GLOUCESTERSHIRE

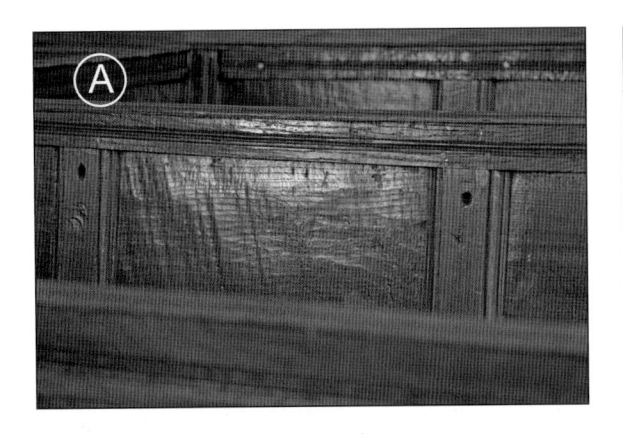

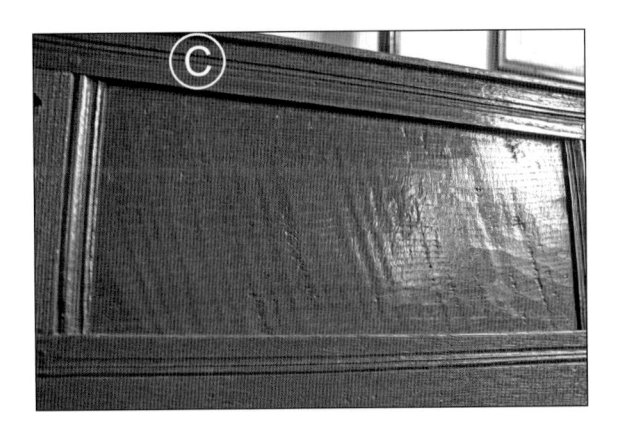

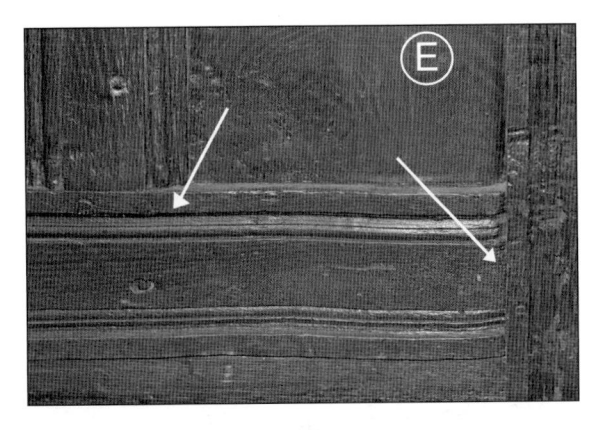

Fig. 4: All these images show evidence of the age of the pews both in original manufacture and subsequent ageing in situ. Torn grain in D and E are the result of none-too-sharp tools; the coarse planing marks seen in A, B, and C would rarely be found in post seventeenth-century work. The ripple in the grain of panels in A and C and deflection of mouldings in D and E are entirely due to timber warping and settling as successive periods of dry and damp create surfaces that reflect internal deflections in the grain. Note the archaic design of the scratch moulds in E which do not intersect at the corners (the arrows point to the scratch mould and the non-intersecting moulds).

Fig. 5: Typical ends to pews. Note that the side margins vary considerably indicating that many of the ends have been altered in width.

Despite these changes, much of the nave is still pewed (Figs. 1–3). The building is listed Grade I, and the listing description of 1954 states that the pews are largely Victorian, 'probably reusing parts of box pews'. The study on which this chapter is based was undertaken to provide guidance on the significance of the pews, as the parish are considering the possibility of reordering the building. The photographs are by the author, and were not intended for publication; it is hoped they will illuminate the points made in the text.

The age and style of the pews

Despite the listing description, close examination of the ageing of most of the seating shows that it cannot be nineteenth century (Fig. 4), and the pew ends with their Mannerist arch panels (that is, using 'classical motifs outside their normal context, or in a wilful or illogical manner') would be unimaginable for the eighteenth century (Fig. 5). Thus the great majority of the pews must date from about 1680, the time of the reconstruction of the church. Also of interest are the raised panels, some rounded to form a cushion mould (Fig. 6). The tenons are typically double-pinned (Fig. 7). Of note is the archaic design of the panelling with scratch moulds throughout, none of which intersect. It is surprising that after installing the revolutionary 'Wren-style' interior, the parish should have installed pews with such old fashioned joinery.

Three distinct arrangements of panelling are still discernible, indicating that originally there were three types of box pew. In the two least common arrangements, there were three rows of panelling, though in each case the bottom panel has largely been cut away to lower the pew. In one of these two arrangements none of the stiles (vertical elements) of the three rows were in vertical alignment with each other, and the bottom row seems to have had panels which were wider than the top row (Fig. 8). In the second arrangement, the top and bottom rows of panelling were vertically aligned, with the middle row having a different alignment (Fig. 9).

The third type of arrangement, of squared-up panelling, forms the vast majority of the seating. In this case the stiles of the surviving top two rows of panelling are in vertical line, one above the other (Fig. 10). No fixing points for seat boards were found on the top two rows of panelling, indicating that (as expected) until the pews were lowered these two rows were originally located above the seat boards. What existed below the present lowest row? In many cases it seems that the bottom edge of the bottom rail has been cut off, and often it is obscured by the variety of infill boards that now fill the gap between the bottom edge of the panelling and the floor. However, in the few places where the bottom edge can be seen, there are no signs of empty mortises or pins. Indeed, the bottom rail seems to be of a slightly different design with no bottom face mould, thus suggesting that this arrangement of panelling has always been only two rows high, with some form of infilling other than panelling below the seat.

Fig. 6a (left): Section through typical panel (seen end on) showing tapered edges to panels, which produces the cushion shape so often found in these pews.

Fig. 6b (right): Front view of the same pew; it has been cut about crudely to make a right-angled return, allowing the section seen in Figure 6a to be seen.

Fig. 7 (top left): Typical construction, with each tenon double pinned.

Fig. 8 (top right): The stiles of the top two rows are not in vertical alignment. The remains of the lowest row of panels, can just be seen beneath the bottom rail. Their stiles are not in alignment with either of the rows above.

Fig. 9 (centre left): Empty mortises (shown by the holes for the pins) in the bottom edge of the bottom rail provide evidence of an original further row of panels beneath the rail. Here the stiles of the bottom row of panels seem to be in line with those in the top row so are much closer together than in the design shown in Figure 8.

Figs. 10a & b (centre right and bottom left): Two examples of the most common form of panel design. The stiles in the top two rows are in vertical alignment. The infill board covers the bottom edge of the bottom rail so it is not possible to tell if there was originally a further panel below

Fig. 11: The remains of a number (probably '3') on one of the pew ends. Note also the old hinge marks.

The pew ends have the remains of painted numbers and the pews once had doors, as evidenced by the remains of hinges (Fig. 11). Thus they were box pews, of the linear rather than square type. The seat boards are of elm. So also are the seat supports, which are generally tenoned into the floor; many of them have a cut-out in the waist, which may have housed a rail, possibly for storing hats during service (Fig. 12). Evidence was found that many (possibly all) of the pews were once lined with red fustian (Figs. 13 & 14).

Fig. 12 (left): Seat support of elm, tenoned into the floor. Note also the notch in the waist of the seat support, possibly to support a rail to hold hats.

Fig. 13 (right): A piece of red fustian caught beneath a pew seat (left of image).

PEWS, BENCHES AND CHAIRS

Fig. 14: The line of holes where fustian was tacked (with one tack hole circled).

Fig. 15: Vertical ghosting marks (difficult to distinguish in black and white reproduction) showing where the seat back panels were originally fixed. The backs have have subsequently been reset at an angle.

Changes to the seating

The seating has been altered. Although the top hinge marks are visible, the bottom ones are not, confirming that the pews have been reduced in height, perhaps by 30–40 cm. The elm seat boards are now supported on softwood bearers fixed to the pew ends with screws, a later arrangement required by the lowering of the pews. Some of the seat supports have also been renewed, in elm to match the others. The seat backs have been re-installed at a slight angle; originally they were vertical (Fig. 15).

These changes were probably carried out as part of the 1884 restoration by Middleton & Son when it was reported that 'The old oak seats have been made uniform, and the doors removed'.[4] It is likely that the seating was thoroughly overhauled. The top rails were probably renewed at this time, as they all fit the present seating arrangement exactly. Considering that the old box pews must have been lowered and the doors removed, this restoration is notable for its modest interference with original material.

Further evidence of the Victorian restoration is found in some new panels along the south wall, and in the divider in the west block. The aspect of the design that distinguishes this divider as a different date is that it is not (as elsewhere) two panels high with infill boards below making up the height, but three panels high of exactly the correct height (Fig. 16). Furthermore many joints in this newer work are not pinned, and those that are have only one pin (Fig. 17).

Fig. 16 (left): A pew-divider in the west block of pews. Note the lack of pins, and the fact that the three panels exactly match the cut-down height of the pews.

Fig. 17 (right): A pew-divider in the west block, with just one pin per tenon.

Fig. 18a (left): Rough housing of seat back into a pew end.
Fig. 18b (right): Rough cut out of seat board over a seat back stile.

The major unresolved question is whether the seating ever faced north. If it did, there are remarkably few signs of alterations when it was turned to face east. It would seem that none of the pews needed altering in length as (virtually) all the seat back panels have end stiles that run top to bottom of each panel, with no sign of the panel-set being shortened. If panel-sets were shortened, an excellent job was done of reducing the length by an exact number of panel's lengths, carefully removing an end stile, cutting back the rails, making new tenons on these rails and then refitting and re-pinning the end stiles. This would be a feat of joinery almost unheard of before, say, the mid or late nineteenth century though of course such early work is not impossible. By comparison, the rough shaping of the seat back panels to the ends and the seat boards to the seat back panels is a much more typical style of alteration up to the mid/late nineteenth century (Fig. 18).

There are three broad possibilities: the seats may always have faced east and never have been turned; they may have been turned to face east but did not need shortening; or they were turned and shortened in a manner unlikely before the mid nineteenth century, and therefore most likely to have been carried out in 1884 (though the general impression is that the work done then was not conservation-minded to that extent). However the brief report of the work quoted above makes no mention of turning the pews in the 1884 work; furthermore, Sir Stephen Glynne at his visit in 1850 although mentioning the pews did not say that they faced north, a feature which if present he might well have commented on.[5] So it may well be that the pews were facing east by 1850, either always having done so, or having been turned at some previous date without shortening.

Fig. 19: A section of floor in front of the nave pews. These oak boards almost certainly date to the same period as the pews.

The floor

The floor is covered by carpet, but it was possible to examine a small section in front of the central block of pews. This consisted of early oak floor boards; flooring of this date and character is a very rare survival (Fig. 19).

As the seat supports are tenoned into the floor boards, the pattern of mortises might well tell the story of any previous seating layout, answering some of the questions raised in this chapter (unless, of course, all the boards have previously been taken up and relaid at random, when no pattern would be visible).

Conclusion

The removal of the wall plaster (possibly moulded and panelled) in the nineteenth century is a regrettable loss as it destroys a major element of the co-ordinated 1679 interior, with the pilasters now visually lost in the hectic pattern of pointing (even simple whitewashing of the walls would improve the coherence of the nave). Nevertheless, the clear rectangular glazing, the pilasters, the pulpit and the pews with their carved end panels create a space that has the feel of an integrated design. As discussed above, far from being Victorian, the evidence of the woodwork shows that most of the pews are of the same period as the rebuilding of the nave, and despite being cut down and losing their doors, have received sympathetic treatment. It is outside the scope of this chapter to comment on the extent of their contribution to the integrity of the interior of the building, but this is clearly a matter which will need consideration when future changes are planned.

Notes

1. This and the next two paragraphs rely heavily on David Verey and Alan Brooks, *The Buildings of England: Gloucestershire 2: The Vale and the Forest of Dean* (Yale University Press, 2002), 601–03. See also both the early-eighteenth-century account reprinted under the entry for Edward Taylor in Howard Colvin, *A Biographical Dictionary of British Architects 1600–1840* (Yale University Press, 1978), and Marcus Whiffen, *Stuart and Georgian Churches: the Architecture of the Church of England outside London 1603–1837* (London, 1948), 20–21.
2. The phrase is Sir Stephen Glynne's, from page 78 of his *Gloucestershire Church Notes* (London, 1902).
3. Recent pew removals described to me by Martin Brown, Church Archivist to whom I am very grateful for providing valuable historic documents and information about the history of the building.
4. *Gloucestershire Notes and Queries,* Vol 3 (1884).
5. He says in his notes for 17 May 1850: 'The nave is pewed in the centre, has a western gallery in which is set up an organ of considerable size, and there are two gallery pews on the east side of the nave, which obstruct the view into the chancel and south aisle, and make it impossible to read the sermon from the altar'. Glynne, *Gloucestershire Church Notes*, 77.

Part 3

HISTORY: THE NINETEENTH CENTURY

13. Patterns of church seating from Waterloo to 1850, and the role of the Cambridge Camden Society

Christopher Webster

Give me leave to say yet more about pews. There can never be enough said; for after seeing very many churches and trying to find out the reason of such falling off in the old ways of Church-worship, and thereby of Church-feeling, I fully believe that most of the mischief comes from pews.[1]

THE QUOTATION is from an influential work published by the Cambridge Camden Society in 1841. This chapter will consider the extent to which that Society was central to the radical developments that took place in patterns of seating between Waterloo and the middle of the nineteenth century.

For the Cambridge Camden Society (later renamed the Ecclesiological Society, the precursor of the present Society of the same name), church seating was a particular concern: some might claim, an obsession. In the forthright language that characterises its published material – language that rarely acknowledged practicalities or pragmatism – uniform, open benches were 'good'; pews (sometimes spelled 'pues') were 'bad': 'from the very first moment of our existence as a Society, we have declared an internecine war against them … we have denounced them as eye-sores and heart-sores'.[2] Although in the twenty-first century 'pew' might be seen as a generic term to describe any fixed seating in a church, for the Society it was a term of abuse reserved for what we would now think of as a Georgian box pew, replete with door and often with cushioned seating.

The Cambridge Camden Society

The Cambridge Camden Society – hereafter the CCS – was founded in 1839 by an earnest group of Cambridge undergraduates intent on the promotion of Gothic architecture, and of church arrangements and furnishings based on those in place before the Reformation. Underpinning this were theological views, and attitudes to ceremonial, not dissimilar to those of the Tractarians and their successors. The influence of the CCS on the style and layout of Anglican churches was huge. Indeed, its prescriptions for the appearance of churches have remained the enduring image of Anglicanism, even for the twenty-first century 'man in the street'. So far as church seating is concerned, its pronouncements on the subject were many as, for the Society, the subject encompassed a much more complex set of issues than the apparently prosaic one of where and on what a worshipper sat, as we shall see. Indeed even its discussion of the materials used for seating was loaded with meaning: sextons were urged to take care of 'the old-fashioned open seats where the poor people sit. These seats, carved in hearty four-inch old English oak, not built of miserable half-inch pieces of deal, are a great deal worthier of your care than the pues … with which your church [is likely to be] infested'.[3]

For convenience, the common physical forms of seating in Anglican churches at the very beginning of Victoria's reign can be divided into four types: (1) pre-Reformation benches, usually of oak and often with handsome carved ends; (2) post-Reformation benches, usually plainer than their medieval counterpart; (3) box pews, predominantly from the Georgian period; (4) simple forms, often backless, often movable, and probably constructed during the previous hundred years. This last type were usually free seats – that is, free for anyone to use. Any of the others, but particularly box pews, might be 'appropriated' – that is, reserved for a particular user, who might pay a rent, or have exclusive use of the pew through another route, such as occupation of a particular property for which the pew was by custom reserved.

Of these four forms of seating, the first two survive to this day in some country churches, but in the larger towns and cities very few medieval churches had not been the subject of reseating in the seventeenth century or, more likely, by the Georgians. It was these churches which were the focus of sustained initiatives to increase the number of church places in the first half of the nineteenth century. Thus by 1839, the date of the inception of the CCS, almost all urban churches, whether medieval or more modern, contained a combination of categories (3) and (4): 'appropriated' box pews, and free seats (Fig. 1).

Fig. 1: Circle of J. Wright, 'By piety's due rites 'tis given / To hold communion with Heaven', print, c.1800. Although clearly a caricature of a church interior and service, it is nevertheless an illuminating record of the period's seating and reveals the division between the wealthier members of the congregation in the box-pews and the poor either on a simple bench or forced to stand. Such arrangements could certainly still be found in some country churches in the middle of the nineteenth century. The gallery on the right is occupied by the band and choir.

What were the CCS's concerns about these patterns of hitherto uncontentious seating? Private seats, usually box pews – 'those monstrous innovations'[4] – failed many a Camdenian test: they lacked medieval precedent; they consumed excessive amounts of space and thus restricted the room available for free seats; they engendered social division and encouraged their owners to look smugly on the humble occupants of the free seats; often the seats were arranged on several sides of the 'box' and thus precluded at least some of their occupants from kneeling to face the altar for the prayers; they represented an unacceptable 'private' domain in God's house. Seating in galleries was equally despised: 'GALLERIES UNDER ANY POSSIBLE CIRCUMSTANCES ARE TOTALLY INADMISSABLE. The greater part of them are, of course, nothing but raised platforms of pues; and everything that has been written about pues is doubly strong against [galleries]'.[5] From them, their occupants could literally look down on the poor. Perhaps contemporary illustrations convey the issues better than words: they reveal a clear physical and visual division between those affluent enough to have a private pew, and the poor condemned to be constantly reminded of their lowly status by their humble benches which lacked comfort and often convenience (Fig. 2). The poor could have been forgiven for feeling they were unwelcome intruders at a form of service intended for their betters. The illustration on the rear cover of this volume makes the point with some eloquence.

An interesting vignette of this attitude is provided by the following: the Incorporated Church Building Society grant application form in the 1830s asked the question 'The Board desire particularly to call your attention to the necessity of providing means for the Congregation to kneel during Divine Service and request to be informed if such provision is to be made in your church for the free seats'. In the form submitted by Tarvin, Cheshire (1833–4), the hand-written answer is 'No particular provision is to be made beyond the flooring', to which another, more politically astute, hand has added 'kneeling boards are provided to all the free seats'.[6]

The early nineteenth century

However, here as in many of the CCS's campaigns, the worst cases were often discussed as though they were the norm, and rarely was there any room for pragmatism. It will be useful to travel back a generation to consider attitudes to seating after Waterloo, a period that saw large sums of money devoted to the issue of church provision, especially in London and in the manufacturing towns of the midlands and north of England.

Fig. 2: St Bride's, Fleet Street, London (Christopher Wren, 1671–8), as it appeared in the early nineteenth century. (G. Godwin, The Churches of London *(1839), vol. II, inconsistently paginated.) This is a typical early-nineteenth-century arrangement of a wide central aisle containing the free benches with box-pews at either side. Although this church offered a fair number of free seats, the social division between the two types of accommodation is explicit.*

A central concern of this period was providing as much accommodation as possible from the limited funds available; not surprisingly, economy was essential. New churches were built and existing ones extended. Nevertheless, additional places barely kept pace with the increasing population and there was much concern that in many locations the poor had only limited access to the established church, and in some places were entirely denied it; one outcome of this, it was believed, was the rise of Nonconformity.[7] The Commissioners of the 1818 Church Building Act provided grants for new churches while extensions were more usually the concern of the Incorporated Church Building Society (ICBS), also established in 1818.[8] Both sets of initiatives, especially those of the ICBS, usually required private subscriptions to supplement a grant.[9] Only very rarely, and in the most affluent of suburbs, was it possible to fund a new church entirely by private subscription.

Once the builders had been paid, running costs were the next issue, for instance the minister's and clerk's stipend as well as maintenance. These all relied heavily – or perhaps entirely – on the annual income from pew rents.[10] Thus, whatever the objections to them by the CCS, the funds generated from pew rents were an absolutely indispensable part of the financial equation when church building initiatives were being assessed. At worst, they were a necessary evil; for many of those involved in church provision, whether as church leaders, clergy, churchwardens, architects or worshippers, they seem generally to have been accepted with few questions. That is not to say that all these constituencies were indifferent to the needs of the poor – far from it – but the novelty in the CCS's argument lay in making an explicit link between the 'excessive' space consumed by the box pews with the insufficient space available for the poor. Conversely, earlier commentators appear to have accepted that any physical disadvantages of private pews were more than off-set by the income they generated; and in an age when inequality was endemic, was there ever likely to be much concern that the well-off were better provided with seats in church than the poor? Rather, for the post-Waterloo generation, insufficient church room for the poor was not a problem for which the rich should be blamed – and, anyway, was it not the rich, they might have argued, who contributed a disproportionately large sum to the Church of England's upkeep? – rather the problem was society's, to be best remedied by building more churches or enlarging old ones.

It will be useful if we look at some examples from the 1815–39 period in more detail. The case of St Stephen, Kirkstall, Leeds, is instructive (Fig. 3). It was designed by R. D. Chantrell and built in 1828–9. The Church Building Commission gave the entire cost of £3,180.[11] It was built to hold 1,000 worshippers, 500 of whom were intended to be in free seats.[12] The plan reveals that there were six large box pews at the eastern end of the ground floor, grouped around the three-decker pulpit, with seats arranged facing in every direction, north, south, east and west. Although they did indeed offer the best view of the pulpit – though a small number of occupants actually had their backs to it – four of the six pews had almost the worst views in the whole church of the altar, and a significant proportion of the seats in these pews had their backs to it. These six pews were likely to have been allocated to the incumbent's family and servants, to the lord of the manor and to one or two other prominent families. The vast majority of the appropriated seats were quite different. They were modest in size and no more than three feet in height; except for those in the north and south galleries, all faced east and in

Fig. 3: St Stephen, Kirkstall, Leeds (R. D. Chantrell, 1827–9), plan. This is typical of the seating arrangements in new post-Waterloo churches.

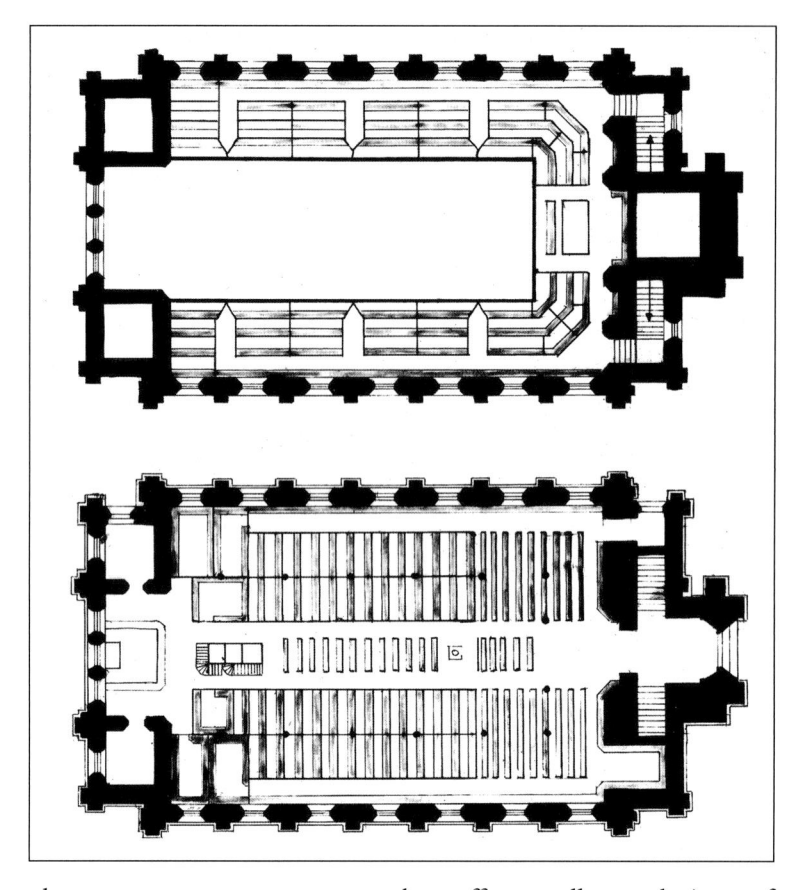

almost every case, were arranged to offer equally good views of the altar as well as the pulpit; they enabled the occupants to turn their heads, if not their bodies, in the direction of the altar during prayers. So far as the free seats are concerned, perhaps the first thing to be noted is how little space seems to be given over to them, considering that half the accommodation was in this category. The free seats consisted of: a series of fixed benches at the west end of the nave, somewhat closer together than the rented seats to their east; a series of movable benches arranged down the central aisle; a continuous fixed 'ledge' along the north, south and west walls of the nave at both ground and gallery levels; a fixed bench behind the organ in the west gallery and on the three sides of the ground floor alcove in the south-west corner. This arrangement was entirely typical of those found in new churches funded by the Commission during the 1818–40 period.

The central concern of the ICBS was how many additional seats would be created by the proposed project. To calculate the outcome accurately, it enquired about the width of each sitting, and the space to be allowed between rows, though, interestingly, there seems to have been no specified minimum until 1842.[13] In general terms, the more additional seats that a project would produce, the more likely it was to be the recipient of ICBS largesse. For the CCS, the ICBS was mistaken in putting increased accommodation above all else: 'Above all, if the Incorporated Society for building and enlarging Churches and Chapels be consulted, care must be taken that the beauty of the building be not sacrificed to the accommodation of worshippers, a fault into which that great Society is – I say it with grief – too apt to fall'.[14]

The funds of the ICBS in this period were more usually devoted to the repair and extension of existing churches than the building of new ones. Where the applicant church had been built within the past 100 years and was a plain rectangle in plan, the end result would differ little from Kirkstall, discussed above. One could point to Francis Goodwin's extension and reseating of St Leonard's, Bilston, Staffordshire of 1827.[15] However, a church with medieval origins and which had undergone perhaps one or two subsequent piecemeal extensions might, by the early nineteenth century, have acquired an incoherent jumble of box pews; the 1834 application for an ICBS grant for All Saints, Leamington recorded that the church had been enlarged in 1808, 1816 and 1829.[16] On one level, maximising the space to increase accommodation might be something of a challenge to the architect; on the other hand, for the ingenious practitioner, it could provide endless opportunities for squeezing in an extra few free seats in order to secure a grant.[17] Children's seats, sometimes recorded as for 'Charity Children' – which could, of course be rather smaller than the standard ones – were a much exploited means of cramming in extra accommodation.[18] At Christ Church, Bermondsey (1846–8), 20 ins x 33 ins was allowed for the adults' seats but just 14 ins x 24 ins for children. On occasions children's seats might take the form of an extra gallery, above a standard one, for instance within a tower; the opportunities they must have presented for misbehaviour need not detain us here.

This pressure to obtain grants by demonstrating increases in seating seems sometimes to have led to exaggeration, perhaps even dishonesty. The case of Hunslet, Leeds is informative. The church received a grant in the 1820s. Hunslet then made a second application in 1843, this time requesting funds for a new church. In seeking to explain that a new church would have much more accommodation than the old one, already enlarged in 1826, the vicar explained that 'the numbers of sittings quoted in the 1826 application were 'never accurate … the chapelwardens exaggerated them' in order to secure a much-needed grant.[19] It may follow, unfortunately, that the drawings that accompanied ICBS applications cannot always be relied upon as an accurate record of the proposed new accommodation and seating arrangements.

The success of the Cambridge Camden Society

A key aspect of the CCS's remarkable success in prosecuting its various causes derived from its ability to claim as its own initiatives that were already well underway at the time of its inception. Certainly this is true of many of its pronouncements about seating.[20] Thus, one can point to a number of 1830s examples of newly built or recently reseated churches where free seats and rented pews were indistinguishable from each other, for example All Saints, Pontefract, West Yorkshire (medieval, repaired and reseated, 1831–3) or Christ Church, Skipton, North Yorkshire (a new church of 1835–9). At the opening of the latter, the *Gentleman's Magazine* noted 'the pews are all single pews, looking eastwards, and convenient kneeling-boards are provided for the free seats'.[21] And certainly by the early 1840s, in the earliest years of the CCS's life, free seats that were simple movable benches or 'shelves' in distant corners – i.e., clearly inferior in both comfort and location to the rented seats – had largely disappeared in new schemes (Fig. 4), and it is questionable whether the CCS can take the credit for this development. In this respect one can point to St Botolph's, Aspley Guise, Bedfordshire (1840–46),[22] or, rather later, St Mary's, Atherston, Warwickshire (1848–50). However, by the mid-1840s, the pervasive influence of the CCS is easily detected; reflecting the new imperative, in 1843, the vicar of Tuxford, Nottinghamshire, wrote to the ICBS seeking a grant for reseating his church: 'the comparatively small number of persons … accommodated appears chiefly attributable to the pewing … I propose to substitute open sittings and stalls for the pews'.[23] Indeed so much had attitudes changed that following the 1854–5 rebuilding of the medieval church at Spofforth, North Yorkshire, it was noted that: 'This church has been rebuilt in the style corresponding with the nave … One unsightly box pew remains in the chancel, claimed by the owner of Rudding Park [the home of the local squire] who will not permit its removal, though a special object of deformity now that the rest of the interior has been properly remodelled'.[24]

Seating was certainly a key concern for the CCS from the beginning and its published opinions on the subject are numerous; a few examples will make the point. *A Few Words to Church Builders* of 1841 was one of its earliest publications. Here, 'Seats' has a separate section in which the 'open wooden seats' or chairs were deemed preferable to pues, the latter being the cause of 'unmixed evil'.[25] The significance of appropriate seating is confirmed by the booklet's 'Conclusion' in which its author confessed: 'If everything else is forgotten and two points only remembered, THE ABSOLUTE NECESSITY OF A DISTINCT AND SPACIOUS CHANCEL, AND THE ABSOLUTE INADMISSIBILITY OF PUES

Fig. 4: St Dunstan in the West, Fleet Street, London (John Shaw, 1831–3). (G. Godwin, The Churches of London *(1839), vol. I, inconsistently paginated.) The church was octagonal in plan and thus had a novel arrangement of seats. The interior is an early example of the move to introduce medieval-type seating in a new church, even in one of distinctly un-medieval plan. The pew ends have a poppy-head motif and, unusually, they were made of oak.*

AND GALLERIES in any shape whatever, I shall be more than rewarded'.[26] In *A Few Words to Churchwardens … Suited to Country Parishes*, first edition also of 1841, can be found, 'pews and galleries … have spoilt more churches than perhaps any other thing whatever; and as to the congregations, it surely looks like selfishness to make one man shut himself up in a comfortable pew, while many can find no room at all'.[27] For its *Churches of Cambridgeshire*, 1845, the Society noted at All Saints, Haslingfield, 'The area of the Nave is filled with its ancient open seats of carved oak, ... for the encroachment of modern pues has here been confined to the chancel and aisles, leaving the nave as a silent ... witness to the superiority of taste and higher sense of propriety which our ancestors possessed'.[28] This is an entirely typical church report in which there is an implicit link between the modern age and a decline in piety.

The cases that most offended Camdenian sensibilities tended to be medieval urban churches which had seen post-Reformation reseatings. Especially where these were piecemeal – 'alterations have taken place from time to time, not on any fixed plan, the convenience of individuals rather than [of] the population as a whole [has been paramount]'[29] – the result might well have been ramshackle. Worse still were those churches with high-sided pews, sometimes topped by crimson velvet curtains on brass rods to give additional privacy to their occupants.

The CCS made much capital from the notorious examples of squire's pews which had their own fire-places and perhaps their own entrance, 'fitted up like drawing rooms',[30] and Neale quotes the case of Tong church where 'the squire has built himself a pew in the Chancel; when the Commandments are begun, a servant regularly enters through the Chancel door with the luncheon tray!'[31] Cases like this might well have been apocryphal and if not, were certainly rare, yet it was precisely this caricature of the Georgian Church of England that found its way into the Victorian and later mythologies. However, of the new, or newly reseated, post-Waterloo churches, private pews, as we have seen, were likely to be much more modest.

Two issues, both of which deserve more attention than can be afforded here, are of relevance to the subject of this chapter. The first concerns materials. While wood was the obvious choice before, during and after the period under discussion, we should not overlook the fact that, in the 1830s, there was much interest in the period's technological innovations; at a time when the art of ecclesiastical woodcarving was both in short supply and expensive, it might be anticipated that alternatives would be developed, for instance materials that could be easily moulded and mass-produced. These we might dismiss today as 'inferior' alternatives, but the period seems to have had a much more positive attitude to them and, to some extent, celebrated their innovative qualities and their potential.[32] Nevertheless, they failed the Camdenian test and were roundly dismissed as 'unreal'.[33] Leeds parish church (1837–41) makes much use of papier mâché and cast iron for the decorative parts of the seating and it is likely that, underneath layers of thick varnish, these materials survive in numerous other churches. The second issue is chancel seating. The CCS's battle for new churches to have long chancels pre-dated agreement about what seating they should contain. By the end of the century, choir stalls were ubiquitous, but before 1850 a variety of alternatives can be found. Interestingly, often it was deemed a convenient location for free seats as the chancel rarely afforded a good view of the pulpit; sometimes a chancel would contain private seats in the form of medieval collegiate stalls, for instance, St Paul's, Armitage Bridge, West Yorkshire (1845–9).

Conclusions

After ten years of vigorous Camdenian campaigning, how can the situation in around 1850 best be summed up? The social divisiveness produced by a combination of appropriated and free seats which were clearly distinguishable was widely recognised, although it would take another ten years or more before Georgian seating would be disappearing on a large scale, and there would be battles over the decades to come about the fundamental principle of appropriation. The worst cases, where box pews were large, high-sided and conspicuous symbols of status, were the first to go.[34] Where they were more modest, change was less radical and it will be instructive for us to imagine what would have happened at Kirkstall, discussed above, had it followed a typical development path.[35] Here, the six box pews at the east end would have been removed altogether to give the chancel arch greater dignity, the free benches in the western third of the nave would have been replaced by seats identical to the appropriated ones further to their east, the free benches placed temporarily down the central aisle removed, and the seats around the outer walls gradually cease to be used as other new churches were built in the area and exploiting corners became less pressing, and as church attendance drifted down.

Fig. 5: St Martin, Stamford (fifteenth century), new seating by Edward Browning, 1844. The seating, all of oak, is of exceptional quality and interest. It replaced the eighteenth-century box pews. The nave is filled with uniform, east-facing, appropriated seats of modest height, but still with doors. The free seats line the north and south walls and face south and north respectively. They too are of oak, and while plainer than the appropriated seats, are still dignified. The arrangement represents a transitional stage on the way to entirely classless accommodation.

Fig. 6: St Stephen, Rochester Row, London (Benjamin Ferrey, 1847–9). (The Builder, viii, 1850, p. 546.) This is a typical late-1840s arrangement of uniform, open, east-facing benches, with no obvious distinction between appropriated and free seats.

As pew rents were abandoned and all the seats became freely available, the former appropriated pews lost the doors that had once defined their owner's rights to become the standard 'free' seats we know today (Fig. 5). This all took time. The system of pew rents continued in some places to the beginning of the twentieth century or later, and diocesan archives reveal the practice of buying and selling pews – or half pews in some cases – carrying on apace after 1850. Although faculties for the removal of box pews are frequent in the middle of the century, privilege was often entrenched and, despite Camdenian successes, examples of faculties to prevent the removal of box pews can also be found after 1850.[36] But by the end of the nineteenth century, very few churches had not been reseated[37] to produce what we now see as the typical Victorian arrangement of dignified ranks of uniform, east-facing fixed benches, each making use of the one in front to provide a hymnbook rest and kneeling board (Fig. 6). Of the seating from the 1815–50 period, very little free seating or seating for children has survived, although where the appropriated seating was modest, as was usually the case, it has survived in large numbers, usually minus the deeply symbolic doors. Galleries do not survive in their original form in large numbers. A small number of modest west galleries continued to be built after 1850, but north and south ones only rarely. Indeed, many galleries were removed in the second half of the nineteenth century, although some were merely truncated to leave just a west gallery as an acceptable compromise if accommodation was still tight; here congregation could at least face east for the prayers – like their colleagues downstairs – in conformity with the CCS's now widely accepted prescription.

How far can the CCS be credited for post-1839 changes? Certainly it speeded the process, but it could be argued that much of it was underway by 1839 and other agencies intent on promoting greater social cohesion would have eventually ensured that, at least in God's house, social inequality was not explicit. Ironically, the few Georgian interiors that survived the modernisers – for instance, St Mary's, Whitby or the chapel at Chislehampton in Oxfordshire – are now the subjects of veneration and we should not overlook the fact that a vast quantity of irreplaceable historic fabric was condemned to bonfires by Camdenian zeal. It is a lesson that surely has wider implications, one that those intent on undertaking reordering in the twenty-first century would do well to remember.

Notes

1. CCS, *A Few Words to Churchwardens … II Suited to Towns and Manufacturing Parishes* (Cambridge, 2nd edn, 1841), 5. Such importance was attached to this statement that it was repeated on the title page of: CCS, *The History of Pews* (Cambridge, 1843). All the CCS pamphlets quoted in this chapter, with the exception of *The History of Pews*, can be found in facsimile in, C. Webster (ed.), '*temples … worthy of His presence': the early publications of the Cambridge Camden Society* (Reading, 2003).
2. *The History of Pues,* 2.
3. CCS, *A Few Words to Parish Clerks and Sextons* (Cambridge, 1843), 5.
4. CCS, *A Few Words to Church Builders* (Cambridge, 1841), 20.
5. CCS, *Church Enlargement and Church Arrangement* (Stevenson et al, Cambridge, 1843), 6. The pamphlet proceeds to catalogue galleries' faults.
6. ICBS, file 01579. The ICBS files are held at the Lambeth Palace Library.
7. Statistics of a parish's population and the number of existing church places, divided between appropriated seats and free one, was a key instrument in the decision-making of the Commissioners administering the 1818 Church Building Act. See M. H. Port, *600 New Churches: the Church Building Commission 1818–1856* (Reading, 2006), especially Chapters 1 and 3.
8. The Church Building Society was founded in 1818, but not incorporated until 1828.
9. In its early years, the Church Building Commission (CBC) often paid the whole cost of a new church, or nearly so. However, from the late 1820s it was usually paying a much smaller proportion of the total.
10. Income from pew rents varied enormously, but typically a pew to hold a family of 4–6 people might cost from a few shillings to a few pounds per year depending upon its prominence within the church. In total, £200 per year might be generated for the church – a very useful sum at a time when a clerk or a curate was unlikely to be paid more than £100 per year – and much more in a bigger church or one in a more fashionable area. Some pews were bought and sold: in the first half of the nineteenth century, a pew might be worth from £10–100, and even more in a fashionable church. Pews available for resale would be advertised in local newspapers.
11. CBC, Kirkstall file, no. 18,274.
12. *Leeds Intelligencer,* 3 April 1828.
13. The ICBS grant application forms required the applicant to state the dimensions on which the calculations of accommodation were based and, presumably, an application where accommodation for individuals was too cramped would be

rejected. 20 ins of seat per worshipper with rows 36 ins apart would be generous; 18 ins x 33 ins was much more usual, for instance at Tarvin, Cheshire, 1833–4 (ICBS, file 01579). In the proposed reseating at St Peter, Barford, Warwickshire (1835–44), the appropriated seats were to be 18 ins x 33 ins, the free seats 18 ins x 31 ins and the children's seats 14 ins x 23 ins (ICBS, file 01869). The 1842 requirement which fixed the minimum distance between rows of pews is reprinted in Chapter 14.

14 *A Few Words to Church Builders* [note 4], 4.
15 ICBS, file 00546.
16 ICBS, file 01697.
17 Occasionally, an ICBS scheme would include a small number of large box pews alongside a larger number of more modest ones, but usually the former can be explained as owners refusing to give up what they claimed as their traditional rights and demanding the reinstatement of their pews as they were before the reseating.
18 Thomas Hardwick's St Marylebone Parish Church of 1813–17 had tiers of seating at either side of the organ, which was placed over the altar, 'for charity schools'. (J. Britton and A. Pugin, *Illustrations of the Public Buildings of London* (London, 1838), vol 1, 133.) However, this was not an ICBS-funded project. Variations on this theme proliferate in ICBS schemes. For instance, St Mary's, Bredbury, Warwickshire (altered 1846–9), had a small gallery which, apparently, could hold 199 children with no obvious provision for adult supervision (ICBS, file 03887).
19 ICBS, file 03292.
20 The point is also made in Simon Bradley, 'The roots of ecclesiology: late Hanoverian attitudes to medieval churches', in Christopher Webster and John Elliott (eds.), *'A Church as it Should Be': the Cambridge Camden Society and its Influence* (Stamford, 2000), 22–45 (pp. 36–40).
21 *Gentleman's Magazine,* 167 (1839), 532.
22 ICBS, file 02723.
23 ICBS, file 03173.
24 ICBS, file 04779.
25 *A Few Words to Church Builders*, 20.
26 Ibid., 30.
27 CCS, *A Few Words to Churchwardens … Country Parishes* (Cambridge, 8th edn, 1841), 11.
28 CCS, *Churches of Cambridgeshire* (Cambridge, 1845), 114.
29 This was said of the eighteenth-century seating in Leeds Parish Church, quoted in W. R. W. Stephens (ed.), *The Life and Letters of Walter Farquar Hook* (London, 1879), vol 1, 381. A similar theme appears in a report on the state of the same church written by the architect Charles Watson in 1810. '[There should be no more] cutting away of pillars and arches for the convenience or enlargement of particular pews; I have never saw a church so much mutilated and disfigured in this respect'. (Quoted in *Leeds Intelligencer*, 25 June 1810.)
30 CCS, *A Few Words to Churchwardens … No. II* (Cambridge, 1843), 381.
31 Quoted in J. White, *The Cambridge Movement,* (Cambridge, 1962), 4.
32 Several articles on the subject of the development of modern materials for mass-produced decoration, although not specifically focused on churches, can be found in editions of J. C. Loudon's *The Architectural Magazine* which ran from 1834–8; for instance: II, 1835, 40–41. The issue is discussed in J. M. Robinson, *The Regency Country House* (London, 2005), 21.
33 'In GOD'S house, everything should be *real*,' thundered *The Ecclesiologist,* 1 (2nd edn), 1843, 11.
34 It is not uncommon to find the oak panelling that once formed the box pews being reused for the new seating. For instance, tall pew doors might be re-used horizontally as the backs of an open pew, adapted for their new role with the addition of a moulded top and hymnbook rest.
35 The discussion about Kirkstall is hypothetical since it was, in fact, the subject of a huge eastern extension in 1863–4. However, the comments are entirely typical of the sort of change that happened in countless other cases.
36 For instance, at Bradford Parish Church in 1853 (West Yorkshire Archives Service, Leeds, RD/AF/2/2a, no. 8).
37 M. Chatfield, *Churches the Victorians Forgot* (Ashbourne, 2nd edn, 1989), lists fewer than 70 substantially unaltered pre-Victorian, 'Prayer-book' interiors.

14. Victorian guidance on seating from the Incorporated Church Building Society

edited by Trevor Cooper

Introduction

THIS CHAPTER REPRINTS a number of Victorian documents on church seating which were published by the Incorporated Church Building Society (ICBS). These represent a significant part of the Society's guidance on general congregational seating published over the course of the nineteenth century.

The ICBS was in business to provide grants for church 'accommodation' (i.e. seating), both in new churches and through the enlargement and reseating of existing churches. It had a particular obligation to provide free seating – that is, seats which anyone could use, as they were not reserved for a particular user – and insisted that a minimum of one half of the seats it helped support were free. The Society's grants never represented a large proportion of a church's budget, and especially so after 1851 when it lost one crucial source of funding. However, it was very influential, partly because of its moral authority, and partly because of its ability to stimulate matched funding through encouraging wealthy donors and autonomous local organisations, of which it helped a large number into existence.[1]

It was respected by all parties within the Church of England, and, from 1848 when its Committee of Architects was established, it was able to call on the free services of some of the most eminent church architects of the time to inspect the plans being put forward for grants: to take a year at random, in 1874 the Committee included G. F. Bodley, David Brandon, Ewan Christian, Benjamin Ferrey, J. L. Pearson, J. P. Seddon, Norman Shaw, G. E. Street, and T. H. Wyatt.

Many thousands of grants were made by the ICBS, and the organisation's voluminous files testify to the attention which it paid to grant applications, and to ensuring that its requirements were met. Its edicts on church seating are likely to have had significant impact on the architects who were commissioning or procuring church seating, who would have had at least half an eye on the requirements of this important funding body. A very great deal of nineteenth-century church seating will therefore have been influenced by the guidance and other documents printed below.

Rules and guidance

Three of the documents printed here were formal guidance notes from the Society to those building, restoring and fitting out the interiors of churches, and were published in 1819, 1842 and 1863. Amongst many other matters, they describe the Society's requirements for church seating.

On this matter the guidance document of 1819 leaves much to the discretion of the architect. In contrast, the guidance notes of 1842 are more directive: they are the first to introduce a minimum size of seating, and also show some ecclesiological influence; it is notable too that the Society offered visitors the chance to inspect at their premises examples of seating which conformed with their requirements.

The requirements for seating in the 1863 Rules are different again from those of 1842, striking in their level of detail and their control of the overall arrangements. Although further research is needed, it seems likely that this was a deliberate response to mounting concern that in order to maximise the size of grant – which depended on the number of additional sittings being provided – churches were being crammed with seating far in excess of what was actually needed. For example, the following comments expressing this concern were made in 1856 by the Secretary of a provincial archaeological society:

> One great evil which both builders and restorers of churches have to guard against is what is called 'accommodation' – the attempt to crowd the greatest number of people into a given space. Two motives lead to this: first, the laudable one of providing room for all who may possibly attend; the second – less commendable – the desire to obtain the largest amount of money-grant from the Church Building Societies. The result is to fill every corner, however inconvenient, with fixed benches, to narrow the passages (the width of which, especially the central one, give such dignity to the building); and, worst of all, by narrowing the seats, to make throughout the church 100 bad sittings instead of 90 good ones, and altogether to prevent kneeling in public worship. There are churches in this town and neighbourhood – fitted up before this point was understood – which almost debar the worshipper from repose of mind or reverence of body, and which it would be well to re-seat entirely anew, with a sacrifice of one-tenth of the present 'accommodation'. The Church Building Societies which give grants according to the number of sittings are mainly responsible for this evil. If they would make the grant for new churches rather dependent on the ground-area, and, in old churches, on the better arrangement, architects and churchwardens would not be driven to the shifts which now disfigure our churches, and which discompose the whole congregation, without really adding to its number. In new churches the whole area need not then be necessarily filled with seats at first, but they might be added as the congregation increased; and thus some of the first expense would be saved, and the congregation really *gathered together*, instead of the scattered segregation, which in a new district church so often strikes us with feelings of formalism and coldness. To

open this question with other Architectural and Church Building Societies, a sub-committee has been appointed this year; and it seems one of those points of practical benefit which it is especially the duty of such Societies as ours to sift and consider.[2]

Note that at the end of these comments the writer mentions that a subcommittee has been set up to discuss with stakeholders the question of seats being crammed in. It may be that the new ICBS Rules which were published in 1863 were the result.

It is worth mentioning that until 1876 it was the policy of the ICBS to reduce its grant by one half when chairs rather than fixed benches were planned. After that the Society announced in its *Annual Report* that it would deal with each case on its merits, though usually making a small reduction in the grant on the grounds that 'chairs are less costly than, and not so durable as, permanent benches'. It is difficult on the available evidence to gauge the strict economic impact of the pre-1876 policy; but, quite apart from rational economics and hard-nosed financial planning, it would not be surprising if this half-grant rule was interpreted as the Society giving a definite message that benches were superior to chairs, as also indicated by the article reprinted below (page 225).

Articles

The five articles reprinted here were written by church architects, mostly eminent; they appeared in the Society's journal, the *Church Builder*, in 1863, 1864, 1884, 1885, and 1899. Although the precise editorial policy of that periodical has not been established, it is unlikely that anything would have been published which went against the Society's broad policy. The 1863 article was used as the opportunity to publicise the new Rules, discussed above.

Medieval exemplars

Within a year or two of the 1842 rules being published, the Society began to advertise working drawings of medieval pewing for architects to use as exemplars.[3] These were mostly from Oxfordshire churches – Eynsham, Great Haseley, Headington, Stanton Harcourt, Steeple Aston, and, in Wiltshire, Great Chalfield. Working drawings of the same pews were also sold by the Oxford Architectural Society,[4] sometimes at least in slightly different versions. They were ephemera, designed to be looked at to provide inspiration, then thrown away, and few copies appear to have survived except by lucky accident (Figs. 1–4).[5] It is noteworthy that pews from some of these churches also figured as woodcuts in works for the more general reader, confirming their popularity in these early days of ecclesiology as examples of normal medieval seating.[6]

Thus from the early 1840s the Society actively promoted these medieval pews as models to be followed. By 1863 the writer of an article which we have reprinted below was able to look back twenty years and say that these exemplar had been widely copied; it will be seen that they are indeed entirely typical of a great mass of standard Victorian seating. Further research is needed, but it does seem that these medieval patterns had a very significant impact – Oxfordshire's medieval seating cloned by the thousand over much of England.

Notes

1. For a discussion of certain aspects of the activities of the ICBS during its first thirty years, see Timothy Parry, *The Incorporated Church Building Society, 1818–1851* (M. Litt Thesis, Trinity College Oxford, Trinity Term 1984); copy in Lambeth Palace Library, class mark: H5194.P2. For the role of the ICBS in encouraging free seating, see Parry's Chapter 2.
2. The speaker was the Revd Thomas James, the Secretary of the Architectural Society of the Archdeaconry of Northampton, reported in *Associated Architectural Societies' Reports and Papers*, 1857 (vol. IV, pt 1), pp. xxxiii–xxxiv.
3. Advertised in the 1844 *Annual Report* of the Society, not in the 1842 *Annual Report*. It has not yet been established whether the drawings were advertised in 1843 (neither Lambeth Palace Library nor the British Library have a copy of the 1843 report).
4. More correctly, the Oxford Society for Promoting the Study of Gothic Architecture. Some, probably all, were produced by Parker, the Oxford publisher. See *Oxford Society for Promoting the Study of Gothic Architecture, The Rules, List of the Members, and Catalogue* . . . (Oxford, 1846), 36; H. Godwin, *The English Archaeologist's Handbook* (London 1867), 6 (I am grateful to Julian Munby, librarian of the (now renamed) Oxford Architectural and History Society, for the latter reference). Variant versions are found at Exeter, for which see note 5.
5. Figures 1–3 are from the scrapbooks of the Exeter Diocesan Architectural and Ecclesiological Society, held by the Devon and Exeter Institution: Box IV Sheet 40; Box IV sheet 42; Box II Sheet125, annotated '100.1'. For different versions of drawings of the Steeple Aston and Great Haseley pews and other relevant drawings, see Box II Sheet 126 annotated '100.4', and Box IV Sheet 44. We are grateful to R. W. Parker for alerting us to this material. Figure 4 is from East Sussex Record Office, KIR/29/31.
6. Woodcuts of Headington and Steeple Aston in J. H. P. (ed.) [i.e. John Henry Parker], *A Guide to the Architectural Antiquities in the Neighbourhood of Oxford* (4 part, Oxford Society for Promoting the Study of Gothic Architecture, 1842–6), 82 and 281. Woodcuts of Great Haseley in Thomas William Weare, *Some Remarks upon the Church of Great Haseley, Oxfordshire*. . . (Oxford, 1840), being No. 1 of 'Memoirs of Gothic Churches read before the Oxford Society for Promoting the Study of Gothic Architecture', p. 23.

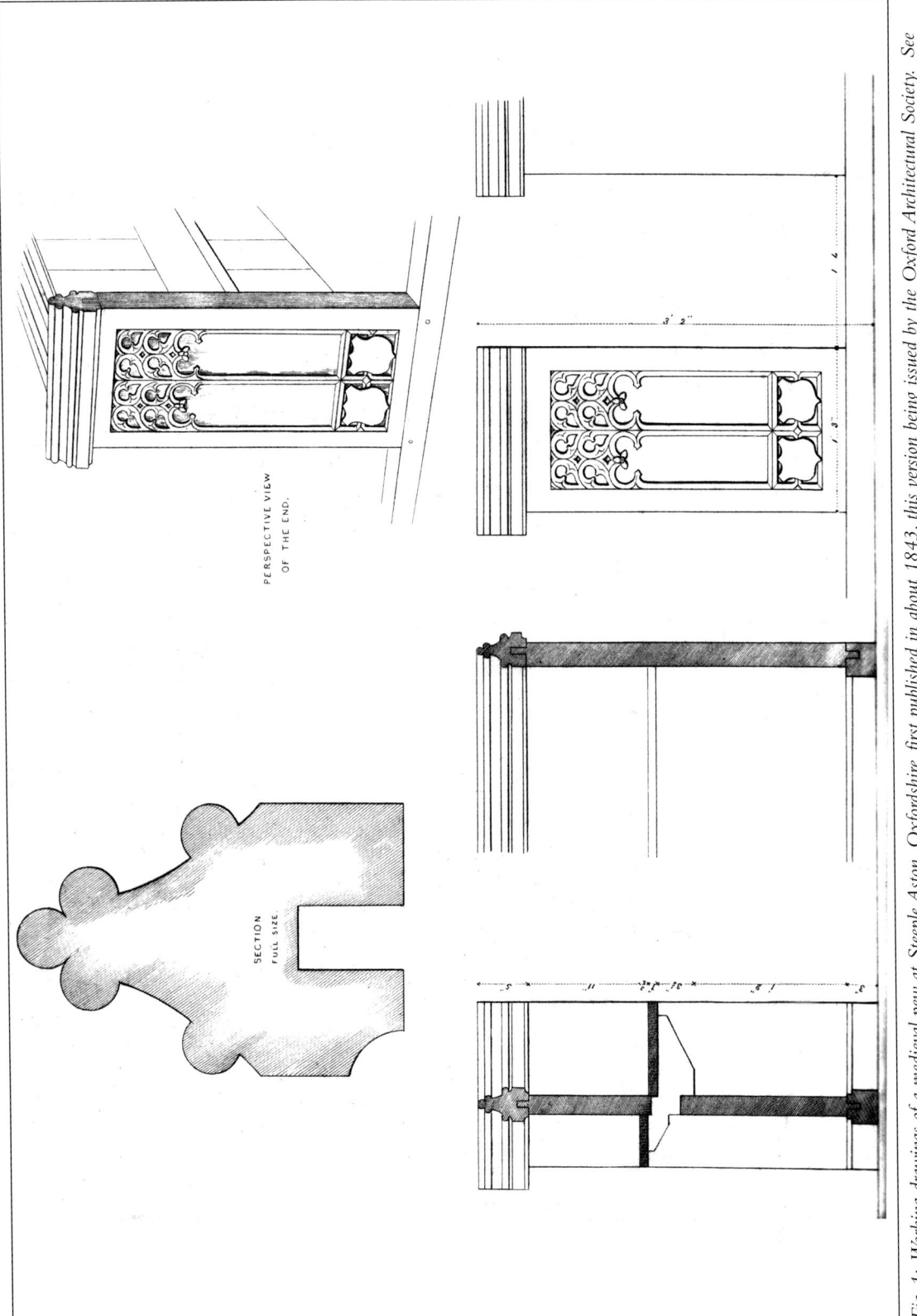

VICTORIAN GUIDANCE ON SEATING FROM THE INCORPORATED CHURCH BUILDING SOCIETY

Fig. 1: *Working drawings of a medieval pew at Steeple Aston, Oxfordshire, first published in about 1843, this version being issued by the Oxford Architectural Society. See also Figure A14 in Chapter 8, page 129.*

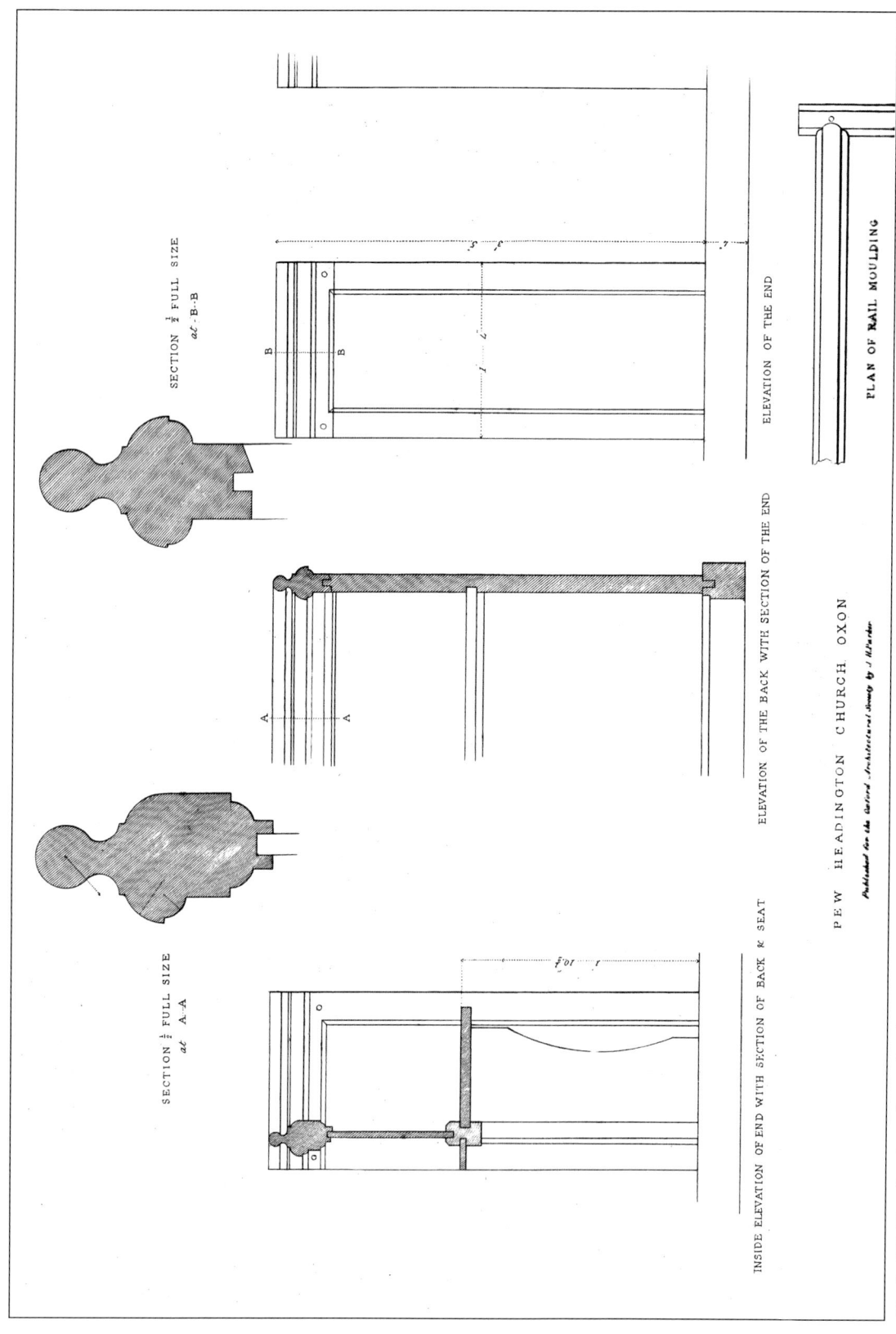

Fig. 2: *Working drawings of a medieval pew at Headington, Oxfordshire, first published in about 1843, this version being issued by the Oxford Architectural Society.*

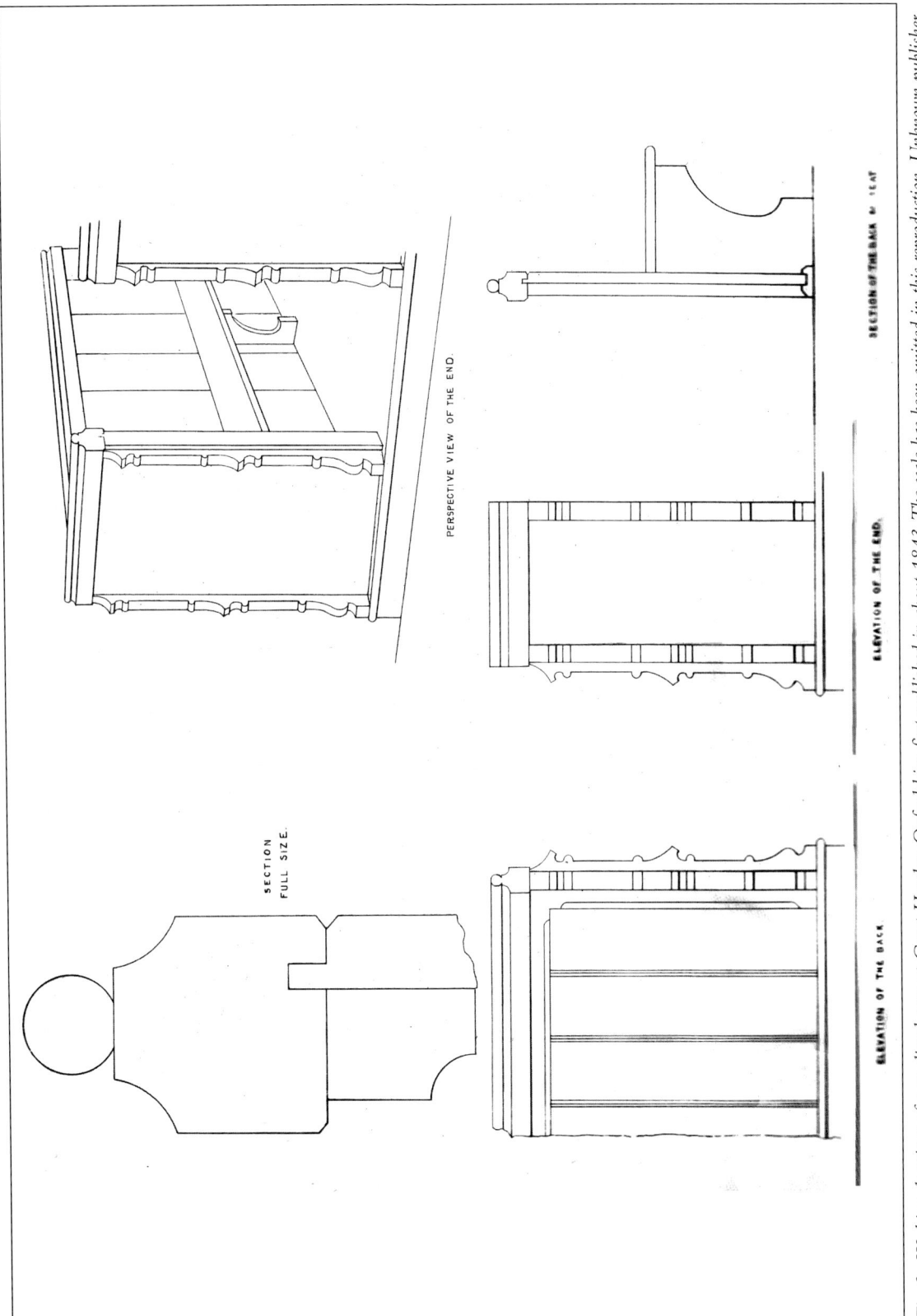

Fig. 3: *Working drawings of a medieval pew at Great Haseley, Oxfordshire, first published in about 1843. The scale has been omitted in this reproduction. Unknown publisher, but probably ICBS.*

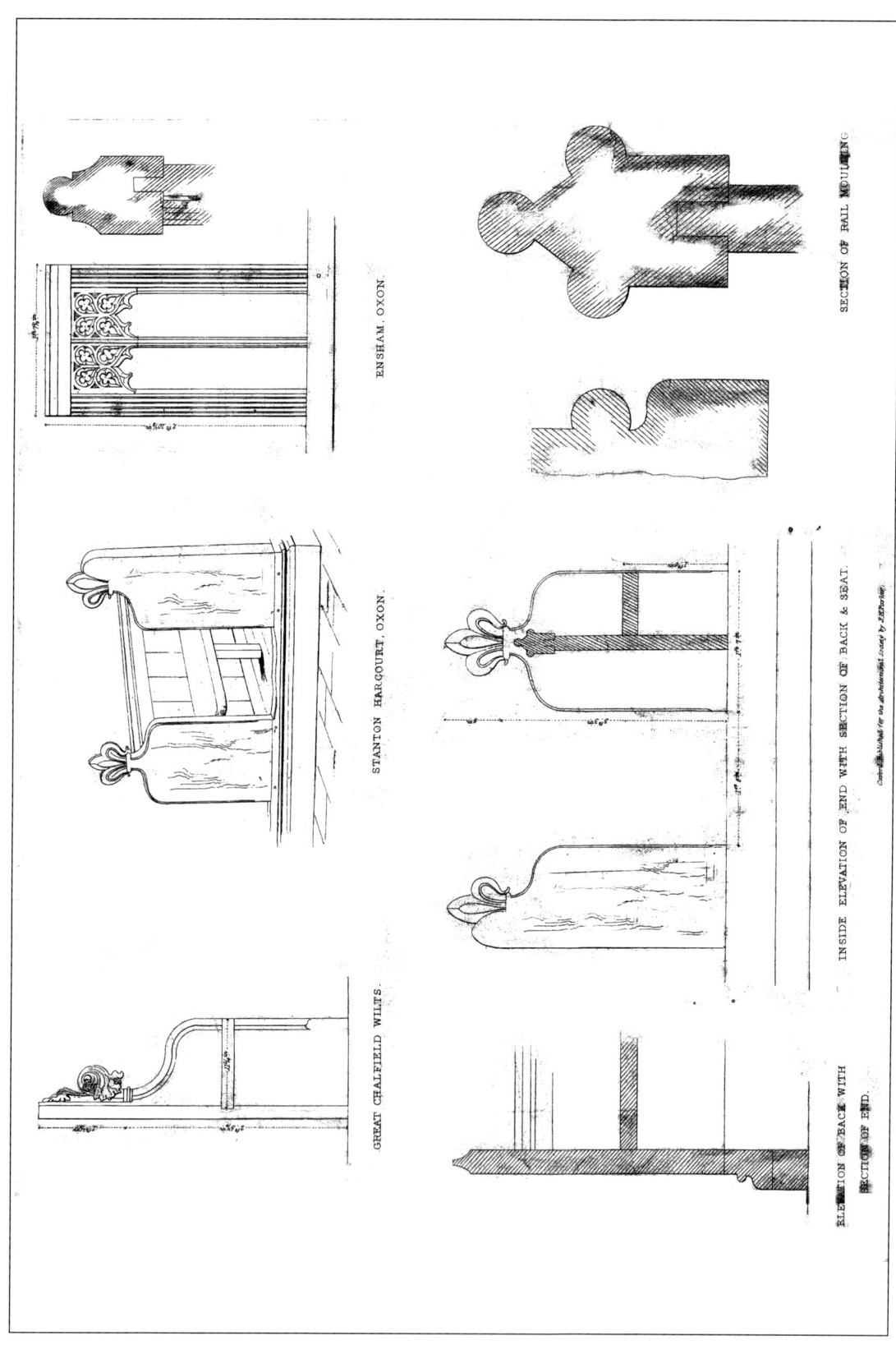

Fig. 4: *Working drawings of medieval pews at Eynsham and Stanton Harcourt, Oxfordshire, and Great Chalfield, Wiltshire. The bottom row of drawings shows details from Stanton Harcourt. First published in about 1843, this version being issued by the Oxford Architectural Society.*

Suggestions (1819) *(extract)*

This first document was published in 1819, soon after the Society's foundation. It was entitled 'Suggestions from the Society for Promoting the Enlargement and Building of Churches and Chapels; for the Consideration of Persons engaged in such undertakings'. The extract below deals with the positioning of congregational seats. On the same topic, though not printed here, there was a brief section on the subject of galleries, supporting their use.

The 'Suggestions' are notable for the requirement that the primary focus should be the pulpit, though seating should not be allowed to block the view of the altar. Pews (that is high seating with doors) were allowed, but only 'as few pews as may be'. Kneeling boards were required.

THE MOST FAVOURABLE position for the Minister is near an end wall, or in a semicircular recess under a half dome. The congregation should all see as well as hear him, therefore no square or round or double pews should be allowed, and as few pews as may be. The rest of the seats, open benches with backs. A narrow shelf fixed behind the back rail will serve at once to strengthen it and to support the prayer-book; under the shelf may be placed pegs, or other conveniences for great-coats and cloaks, sticks and umbrellas; about half-way under the seats may be fixed a shelf for receiving hats. Kneeling-boards should in all cases be provided.

The seats should all be placed so as to face the Preacher, as far as possible. Where the pulpit is placed to the west end, the benches, whether pewed or not, ought to run from E. to W. so that no part of the congregation may turn their backs upon the altar. The pulpit also should be placed so as to intercept the view of it as little as possible.

❖ ❖ ❖

Suggestions and Instructions (1842) *(extract)*

In 1842 an amended set of suggestions were published in the Annual Report, *with the slightly firmer title, 'Suggestions and instructions …'. They were also published separately. The part which dealt with seating (section 17), is reproduced below. In addition, not reproduced here, there was a section on galleries, which is rather more cautious about their use than the 'Suggestions' of 1819.*

A significant ecclesiological change is to require more firmly than the 1819 document that no seating turned its back on the altar, whereas the earlier requirement to focus on the pulpit has disappeared. A central east-west alley is required. The new document points out that more accommodation can be obtained from open benches than from pews. A set of minimum dimensions is published, with a strong steer towards having a low back to the seats. Hassocks are suggested, rather than the previous kneeling boards.

The Society provided models of seating which met these requirements for inspection at their offices, and this offer was repeated in succeeding years.

Section 17: The seats must be so placed as that no part of the congregation may turn their backs upon the altar. There must invariably be an open central passage up the whole length of the Church, from west to east. No square, or round, or double pews can be allowed, and as few pews as may be. Much accommodation is gained by the adoption, instead of pews, of open seats with backs.

The distance from the back of one seat to that of the next must depend in great measure on the height of the backs and the arrangements for kneeling. Where the funds and space admit, convenience will be consulted by adopting a clear width of three feet or even three feet four inches; but the width of two feet six inches in the clear may be allowed if the back of the seat be not more than two feet eight inches in height. This height is in all cases to be preferred, both for convenience and appearance. If a greater height be adopted, the distance from back to back must not be less than two feet eleven inches in the clear. There should not be any projecting capping on the top of the backs. Means for kneeling must in all cases be provided. Hassocks are to be preferred to kneeling boards, especially where the space is narrow.

Twenty inches in length must be allowed for each adult, and fourteen for a child. Seats intended exclusively for children may be twenty-four inches from back to front.

Models of seats for Churches and Chapels, prepared according to the recommendations contained in [paragraph] No. 17 may be inspected at the Society's Office, where their construction will be explained by the Secretary.

❖ ❖ ❖

Seats in churches [with new Rules]
by J. C.

The following article was published in 1863 in the Church Builder, *pages 162–68. It is signed 'J. C.'. This is almost certainly Joseph Clarke, one of the Society's Honorary Consulting Architects, a competent church architect of the time though not widely known today. The article is reprinted here almost in its entirety, the few deletions being indicated by an ellipsis.*

Particular points of interest in the article are the mild embarrassment occasioned by the Society's earlier willingness to support 'high and panelled' pews, a brief description of the mechanics by which people formed box pews from earlier benches (see the frontispiece of this book), mention of the desire to maintain old seating where possible, and the complete ignorance of what makes for a comfortable seat.

In addition there is reference to some lithographs of medieval bench ends published by the Society some years earlier, and the initial copyism that resulted, followed by greater freedom in design. This is discussed in more detail in the introduction to this chapter, where some of the working drawings are reproduced.

The article included a new and very detailed set of Rules regarding church seating (printed on page 224). It is interesting that the minimum distance between rows of seating is two inches greater than in the 1842 'Suggestions'. Square and double pews are banned.

❖   ❖   ❖

AS THE CHIEF AIM of the Church Building Society in its operations is to provide increased Church accommodation, a paper on seats in churches is a proper subject for the pages of the *Church Builder*.

In the early days of the Society the old high square and panelled pews or pens, very narrow and exclusive, were part of its constitution, and those who remember the neat plans then laid before the Committee, and know some of the churches then erected and aided by the liberal grants of the day, are astonished how such a system could have existed so long; yet so it continued till about the year 1840, when attention was drawn in the right direction, and some advance was made towards a better state of things. Then a gradual change began to take place; the cold selfishness of the past gradually gave way under the influence of a revived belief that all are equal in God's House, and that our churches should be fitted up for *devotional* use; and what was at one time weakly viewed as a party symbol, has now become almost universal. The Society ignored the past, and for the future determined by an alteration in its rules that no square or double pews should be introduced in churches aided by its means.

Such being the case now, it is only necessary to say a few words on the manner in which our churches were seated in early times. . . . Weever says, 'Many monuments are covered with seats or pews, made high and easy for parishioners to sit or sleep in, a fashion of no long continuance, and worthy of reformation'. But the fashion unfortunately increased, and in time even these high pews, as well as the solid open benches of earlier date, were gradually raised higher and higher by additional framing; and the proper direction of the pews, which even at first was preserved, and made to face the altar, became disregarded, and by cutting away the middle framing, two pews, and more often benches, were thrown into one, and cross seats were added. Thus came into existence the high square pews of our own days, with their many easy and comfortable nooks and corners, formed, as it would seem, for no other purpose than to encourage sleep.

Whilst with, we trust, better feelings, we are aiming at a more conservative restoration and a more careful preservation of the fabrics and details of our churches, we cannot close our eyes to the fact that a necessity exists in many cases for a proper reseating of our old churches, and we must notice with pleasure a desire arising in so many instances to remodel the churches built in the early times of the Church Building Society.

Where the original benches in old churches can be preserved and restored, either wholly or in part, this should invariably be done; and in the eastern and western counties of England many churches are found where not only the benches remain often very perfect, but the arrangement and accommodation cannot be improved. . . .

These old benches may, in some instances, have been followed as types rather too closely, but still they have been very useful as pioneers in the change which has taken place. It will be remembered that some years since lithographs were circulated by the Society, of ends of benches from churches mostly in Oxfordshire. These were recommended as guides to be followed, and though in a stereotype form, they did some good when the old square pews were beginning to disappear; but now, if the form of church seats takes rather too wide, and in some instances perhaps an eccentric range, it is only a development of their modern use architecturally applied to present requirements. . . .

Unfortunately the modern system of endowing by pew-rents has created in such cases a system of exclusiveness almost as great as that we are endeavouring to overthrow, and leads to new churches being seated, not with reference to devotional worship, but too often with regard to the greatest number of persons who can be crammed in.

The rules of the Church Building Society have been revised with much care [see page 224], and in this revision it has been borne in mind that, whilst too much room must not be thrown away, on the other hand it is obviously wrong so to cramp the space that the services cannot be followed, and the proper posture of devotion assumed.

The question whether the backs of seats should be made to slope or not, seems to raise a question. It is worthy of consideration whether some plan cannot be adopted in imitation of the natural posture of the body whilst sitting. Some architects consider it better to slope the back and not the top rail, as the annexed sketch (Fig. 6); whilst others from experience think that if the seat-board inclines, it is only necessary to slope the back rail, as shown in the rather exaggerated sketch (Fig. 7).

In the second and more important posture of *kneeling* during service; it should be observed a long continuance of this posture needs support, or else much weariness and pain are caused, in some cases so

Fig. 6: The first illustration to the article by Joseph Clarke, published in the Church Builder *of 1863. The illustration on the left is captioned 'Section of seat and book-board'. That on the right was captioned 'Moulding on the back rail; from an ancient example'.*

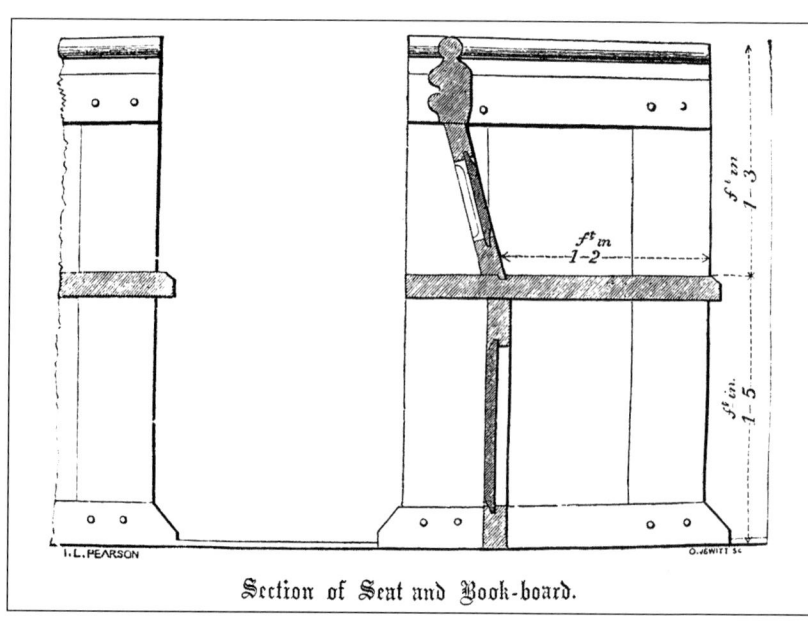

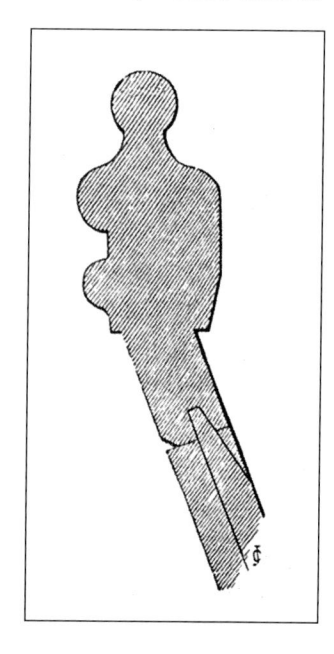

much as to render devotion impossible. And as it is all-important to induce every congregation to kneel, means must be taken to make this position natural.

A low string kneeling-board brought rather forward beyond the line of the back framing seems to give more ease than the usual movable hassocks.

The book-board is unquestionably better placed level with the seat. Its proper use is as a shelf to hold the books, and not, as it is too often made, a resting-board for the arms. When kneeling, the book is better in this position, and in sitting and standing the proper place is in the hands. In the old high pews the book-boards were generally fixed for standing to, and thus in village churches men frequently stood during the service.

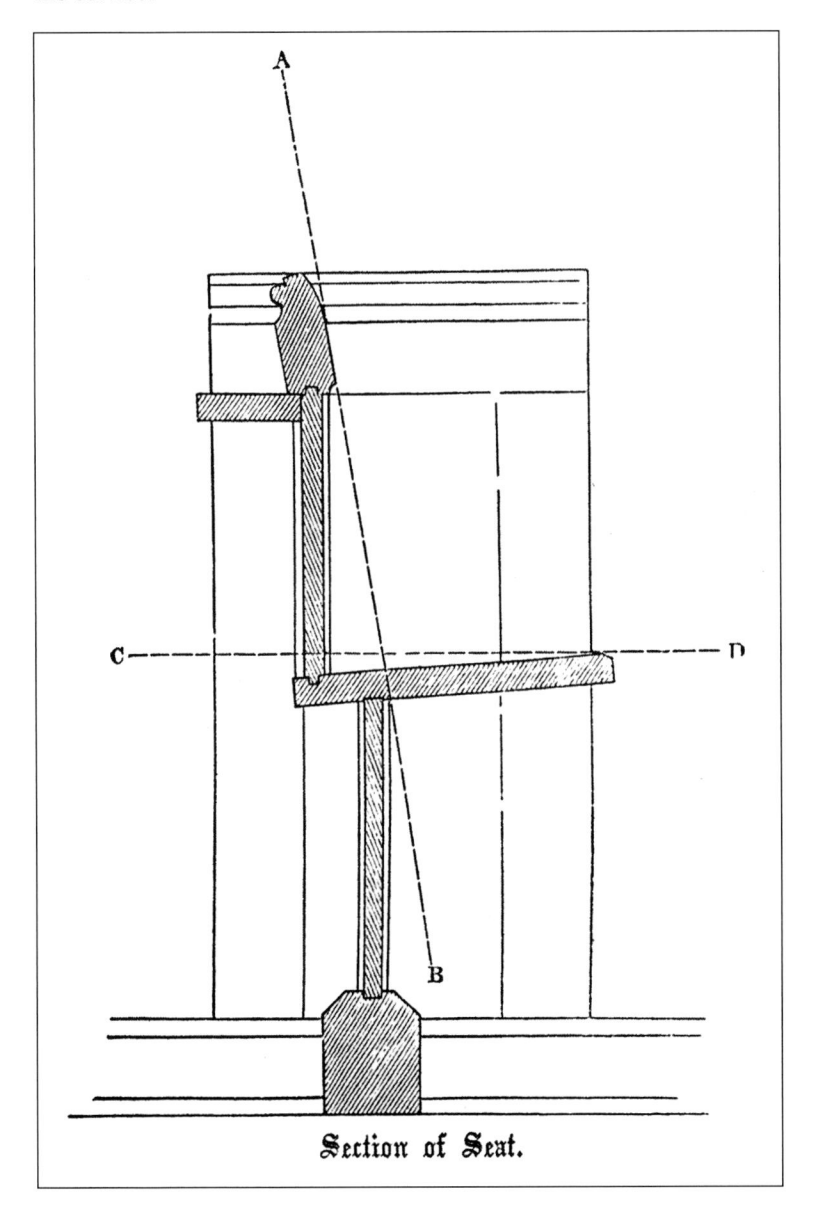

Fig. 7: The second illustration to the article by Joseph Clarke.

The Society's rules respecting seats in churches are as follows:

The seats must be so placed that no part of the congregation shall turn their backs upon the Lord's table, and in the nave and nave aisles should, if possible, face the chancel.

There must be an open passage up the whole length of the centre of the church, from west to east, and from the principal entrance, not less than three feet six inches wide where the width of the nave is under eighteen feet or four feet where this width is exceeded. Side passages must not be less than two feet nine inches in narrow aisles, but three feet where practicable.

A clear space of six feet must be left between the fronts of seats in chancels where the span is under thirteen feet, and not less than eight feet where this span is exceeded.

Square or double pews will not be allowed. The Society strongly recommend the introduction in all cases of low, open seats; doors to the sittings are unnecessary and inconvenient. Under any circumstances the seats throughout the body of the church must be in this respect uniform.

The distance from the back of one seat to that of the next must depend in great measure on the height of the backs. Where the funds and space admit, convenience will be consulted by adopting a clear width of three feet; but a width of not less than two feet eight inches from centre to centre will be allowed if the back of the seat is not more than two feet eight inches in height. This height is in all cases to be preferred, both for convenience and for appearance. If a greater height be adopted, the distance from back to back must be increased one inch at least for every additional inch in height; but under no circumstances must the height exceed three feet. There must not be any projecting capping on the top of the backs. Facilities for kneeling in all cases to be provided. The width of the seat-boards for adults to be not less than thirteen inches.

The seats in the chancel must face north and south, and be so placed as not to interfere with the free access of communicants.

Sittings on movable benches placed in the passages, or on seats with their backs fixed against the north and south wall, are not considered by the Society in the enumeration of sittings to be provided.

Twenty inches in length must be allowed for each adult, and fourteen for a child. Seats intended exclusively for children must be at least twenty-six inches from back to front, and must be provided with backs.

In reseating old churches, where existing widths will not admit of greater length in the seats than sufficient to afford a space of eighteen inches to each adult, such dimension is sanctioned. Wall wainscoting, or wood linings to wall, to be avoided; they confine the damp, and frequently occasion dry rot. Where used, they must be perforated under the seats, to allow the circulation of air. For the same reason tile or cement skirtings are to be preferred. The ends of seats and linings next the walls to be charred, pitched, or painted.

The Incorporated Church Building Society's rules for seating, as published in 1863.

Lastly, in the position of standing, a proper space is necessary between the outer edge of the seat-board and book rest, and each seat must be wide enough to allow of each posture.

The Society lays down a minimum but not a maximum of the dimensions required. Where space can be allowed for three feet from centre to centre of the panelling, it is the width found best to meet all requirements, and under two feet ten inches the cramming system begins.

❖ ❖ ❖

Chairs
by J. C.

*The following year (*Church Builder, *1864, pages 70–74), the same author published a brief article on chairs. Here he appears to be treading carefully, and he more or less limits itself to recommending chairs for filling difficult spaces and providing additional seating. He explicitly confirms the lack of support for the general use of chairs within the ICBS. The version below has been edited to remove less interesting material.*

❖ ❖ ❖

In many churches, chairs may very well be applied; but, unfortunately, until recently they were a novelty in England, and the want of order in the managing and arranging of them led to an opposition which had no real grounds, and is now gradually dying out. For, though a question may arise, which time and other circumstances must decide, how far chairs can be used generally, there is no doubt after even the short experience we have had, that they can be conveniently applied and made applicable in many places where benches could not be introduced.

. . . Chairs may often be introduced into town churches, particularly when, as at the sea-side, there are fluctuating congregations; and there are places in almost every church, where, without destroying the proper devotional arrangements, they can be introduced. Then, in the case of village churches, how charming it is to see the deaf and decrepid drawing round the clergyman, to join in the prayers and hear the service.

In some churches there are narrow aisles, or old chantries, where benches or fixed seats cannot be placed, and here chairs are the only means of providing accommodation . . . chairs are far better than the singular flaps sometimes fixed in the aisles to the ends of pews or benches. If the temper of the times permitted . . . and the idea of 'being seen' at church were extinct, then . . . chairs might more often be introduced, and the architectural beauty of our churches preserved. . . . Again, chairs are very economical. Whilst benches cost from ten to twenty-five shillings each sitting, a chair is not more than from two shillings and sixpence to five shillings.

As a via media between the common use of chairs and fixed benches, it is worth while, in some cases, considering whether the plan of having separate blocks of flooring raised a few inches above the passages, and on which chairs might be placed, surrounded by low rails as in the chapel at Beguinage, at Ghent, might not be adopted.

The Society has on various occasions considered the propriety of permitting the introduction of chairs into churches; and though difficulties arise in their appropriation and arrangement as compared with fixed seats, and the Committee have hitherto thought it undesirable to consent to the proposition generally, yet there are cases where chairs may supplement fixed seats.

The ordinary form of chairs is well known. They should be somewhat lower than the common chair, with a projecting piece at the back, as a rest for the book in kneeling. A double rail may also be placed under the seat for hats. The legs should have some soft substance under, to prevent noise; and the seats may either be of wood or of plaited rush or straw.

❖ ❖ ❖

Church Seats
by William White

The article below is by the well-known church architect William White, who was on the ICBS honorary panel of architects. The article was published in Church Builder *in 1884, pages 108–115. Except for some commercial details of a new type of chair, it has been reprinted in full, with its original illustration.*

The article discusses a number of points, including the suggestion that seating should be level with the floor, and not on pew platforms. One thing which was clearly exercising White was the question of how to make benches reasonably comfortable, a matter on which he held some strong views. In passing he feels the need to defend his proposals against the accusation that he was not replicating the design of medieval benches. Whether or not White was correct in his theories regarding acceptable seating comfort, the general level of ignorance on the topic is striking.

❖ ❖ ❖

THE INTENT OF THIS PAPER is to make a few practical suggestions on the construction of church seats. One of the first principles to be observed is that our back is not properly an arch, but a flexible lever acting from its juncture with its base. The chief support required for any one of natural form and in a healthy condition, is just at the small of the back. This is the one principle which has been the most commonly neglected; and now the architect is told to provide a seat to suit the various descriptions of weakened backs and rounded forms which ought not to exist. An ordinary chair is set before him as his model of perfection and pattern for imitation. But the ordinary chair does not give the required support; the middle rail is absent, or else it recedes so far as to be almost or entirely beyond reach as a support, unless you sit with the bent back or the rounded shoulder, which has been induced by this arrangement, and which indeed has become to very many a second nature. The weariness and discomfort arising from the absence of this support is felt nowhere more than in the ordinary benches and chairs provided for concerts, theatres, and entertainments, or for the use of the poor in the middle passage of the church in fashionable watering-places, where the old state of things holds its own. It is no wonder if church chairs are in bad odour; they are unstable, and far from comfortable. An objection to rush bottoms for chairs has been their tendency to harbour unpleasant companions; but the lighter the chair, the less costly it commonly is, and the more easily removed and packed away when not required for use. Hitherto there has been a difficulty in getting the standard form of a wholesale article of this description altered in the slightest degree without considerable extra cost; and scarcely any of the stock patterns of the great makers have been even tolerably comfortable. Messrs. West and Collier have now undertaken to make an improved chair upon the principles here advocated...

The arrangement and construction of the church bench now demands our attention. For the convenience of a congregation, no less than for general interior effect, the seats ought to be without doors, and should be well divided up by passages. On this account it is commonly objectionable to place the passages against the outer walls of a church with aisles. It is still more objectionable to have the centre of the nave blocked with seats. All the seats should be arranged to face eastwards, except possibly in some cases where the space behind the choir, to the east of the chancel arch, is to be seated. There should be a good cross-passage from north to south, immediately to the west of the choir, as well as from side entrances some way down towards the west end of the church. In no case should there be panels or divisions across, between one seat and another, dividing them in length and preventing access equally from both ends.

The bench end ought to be wide enough to form a finish for the seat and book-board, without the need of these being rounded off at the corners to bring them within its limits. The ancient end was always wide enough to receive them, but then the seat-board would often be only ten or eleven inches wide. The space for entrance between should be not less than fourteen or fifteen inches, and supposing the backs to be thirty-two inches apart, centre to centre, this will leave about seventeen inches for the bench end, which will not be enough properly to take in the seat-board with its partly sloping back besides the thickness of back-framing and the book-board. Thus it often becomes necessary to round off the corners to some extent, unless the benches are made with still wider ends and placed further apart The distance of the seats apart, from back to front, is well regulated by the minimum thirty-two inches, centre to centre measurement, required by the Society. For the *otium cum dignitate* an increased space is desirable. With higher or more sloping backs this greater distance apart becomes really requisite. For Mission Rooms, where further crowding may become absolutely indispensable, three or four inches may be saved.

This is equivalent to an increased accommodation of one seat in eight; but this can be done only with upright backs, and with the omission of book-boards.

The proper section for the bench has been already considered sufficiently under the head of chairs. It will be well now to give a practical illustration of a common form of uncomfortable seat, for the purpose of comparison and contrast with what it ought to be (Fig. 8). In Fig. A (part of Fig. 8) some seats are shown which were put up about forty years ago in an expensively built Memorial Church, but are now happily superseded. Their section is similar to what has been put up by the builder, the churchwarden, and the committee-man of the present day, only that the back is a little higher.

All should be taught from their earliest childhood to sit well back in the seat of a properly formed chair. To those who have acquired the ungainly habit of leaning only from their shoulders or from a bend in their back, an excessive height or an excessive slope may not be of very much consequence. But ordinarily a high or a sloping back will prevent one's sitting far enough back to get the requisite support (as at *d.* in Fig. C.). When a seat back is high and upright, the discomfort is at once attributed only to its not being sloped at all; and a remedy is sought, not by reducing the height, or by sloping only its upper part, but by giving a considerable slope to the whole, which will remedy really but a very small part of the evil; except to those whose backs have become bent to the required extent, they are pre-eminently uncomfortable. I have noticed the curious way in which, after a time, their occupants will change position, first with a foot against the front, or leaning forward, then sitting askew, or bolt upright.

Fig. 8: The illustration to the article by William White, published in the Church Builder of 1884. The illustration is formed of three parts, Figs. A, B, and C. There was no caption.

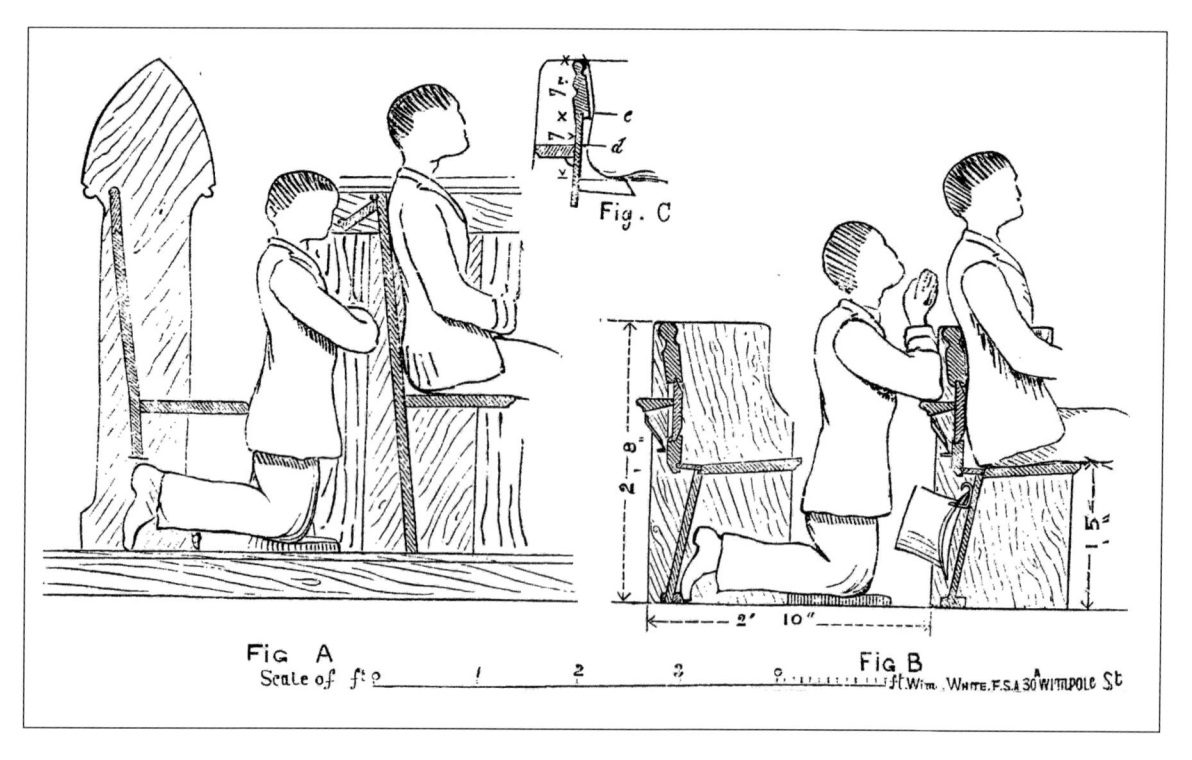

Fig. B. shows the construction of a bench constructed on the principles already laid down as to the convenient rest and support to be afforded to the occupant. Its form may be considered open to the objection of not being in strict accord with the rigid architectural lines of the medieval benches. This objection applies more reasonably and more strongly in cases where remains of the old oak-work are found to justify or to demand an accurate reproduction, or where the unchanged character of the building is such as to require a more scrupulous adherence to medieval form. The medieval benches were moderate in height, and the support came mostly in the right place; but it was not of the right sort, the sharp projecting moulding almost pushing the occupant off the narrow seat. One may oneself be perfectly satisfied with the narrower seat and the medieval top-rail projecting over it into the back, but there are not very many in these days who will patiently and implicitly take on faith that it must be the proper thing, even though it is to be preferred infinitely to a vast number of modern make. For the height of the back, the thirty-two inches regulation measure adopted by the Society must be considered not only ample, but better than more; at the same time it should not be less. The generally received height of eighteen inches for the seat-board then leaves a height of fourteen inches for the support of the back; this may be increased by nearly one and a half inches if the seat-board be reduced to seventeen inches in front, and tipped back three-eighths of an inch.

The height of the backs and ends makes more difference in the general effect of the interior of a church than is usually recognised or supposed. It affects not only the relative proportions in the height of the building and its various parts, but also the sense of elbow-room, and the impression of being cramped and crowded by the seats. On these accounts, as well as on account of the general effect of spaciousness to which it contributes, the flooring of the seats should be level with the pavements, and not be fixed on a raised, platform. For this purpose the flat wood-block flooring, now so generally adopted, is advantageous, apart from its noiselessness and freedom from other objections made to the boarded floor. Stone or tile, or mosaic pavements throughout the church, though excellent aesthetically, are not really to be recommended beneath the seats unless covered with some efficient protection in the form of thick linoleum or other equally objectionable material, to prevent the abstraction of warmth from the feet.

The book-board as a convenient rest for the book when used in standing, sitting, or kneeling, is simply a delusion which has not yet been entirely dissipated. It must be regarded merely as a ledge for the book when not in use. It may, however, be made available as a support and rest for the arms in kneeling though some deprecate its use even for this. In order to afford convenient support, it ought not to be made more than twenty-three or twenty-four inches in height from the kneeling-mat or hassock; if higher than this, the arms and shoulders are forced into a distorted and strained position, and available breadth is lost for convenient kneeling between it and the seat-board, just where room is requisite for the arms and chest. A little space may be gained by fixing the book-board two inches or more below the projecting moulding of the back rail. This also affords additional security against the book being tilted of brushed off accidentally; in no case should it be higher than this.

The disposal of the hat presents a great difficulty. In no case should there be any reasonable excuse or inducement for placing one's 'best topper' behind the heels beneath the seat, where it will inevitably induce a nervous distraction or ill-concealed anxiety for the consequences, and in most cases prevent kneeling altogether. Perhaps the best arrangement for disposing of it is to place a division sloping forwards under the seat, as shown in the section, to receive a hat-peg, which should be fixed, not opposite the occupant, but between two. When this division is fixed upright and only a few inches forward under the seat, it gets dreadfully in the way of the feet of those kneeling in front. This division is, in fact, better omitted altogether, for it is difficult to see what really useful purpose it serves, unless it be made available for the purpose indicated. It forms a dark harbour for dust, which rarely gets swept out, and tends to stagnation of air. A few wood pins or pegs beneath the book-board are useful for sticks and umbrellas placed horizontally. For kneeling, nothing is better than a small pile-mat or thin cushion of carpet. After each service it ought to he hung up by means of a ring or a broad loop to a peg in front, else careless and ignorant people will use it for their feet. Kneeling-stools, if used, should be movable, three and a half to four inches high, so as to get the toes under in standing, and they should have a flat top seven inches wide, which may be covered with pile-carpet or felt and slightly stuffed. These will undoubtedly be used as footstools, and soon become dirty, and on this account it is better to provide likewise a suspended mat, instead of covering them. Some prefer carpet hassocks, these may be three to four inches high; they, too, are commonly used as foot-stools, and cannot so well be hung up out of the way. Some there are who, to this day, require a hassock or book-box ten or twelve inches high, with a sloping top, which allows of a secret semblance of kneeling whilst really sitting. No suggestion need be offered here as to their construction.

The proper construction of the church seat has now been practically explained and illustrated. The impossibility of fitting every one's back to the same form must be abundantly evident; the form suitable to one will be a bitter grief to others, and it would be manifestly of little good to attempt to provide specially for those to whom, from their habit of sitting forward and resting only from their shoulders, a well-formed support has become irksome. All that one can hope for is that, by the full and free discussion of the difficulties, we may be enabled as far as possible to obviate defects and arrive at something like a satisfactory and unanimous conclusion.

❖ ❖ ❖

Church Seats and Kneeling Boards
by William Butterfield

The article below by the high-church architect William Butterfield was first published in the Church Builder *in 1885, pages 77–82. Butterfield was not a member of the ICBS architects' panel, but there was obviously enthusiasm for his article in some quarters at least, for it was republished as a separate pamphlet on several occasions over the following years. Our text is from the third edition of 1889. The line illustration which accompanied his article is also reproduced.*

The article is reproduced here in its entirety. We have drastically abbreviated the preface (though we have included the preface to the first edition which was reprinted in the third edition) as this largely consists of lengthy urgings to the reader to follow Mr Butterfield's wonderful design in every detail and avoid installations not made to the identical specification. Except for a brief section on hassocks, we have entirely omitted the appendix which was mostly puffs from satisfied users (at All Hallows, Tottenham; St Mary the Virgin, Ardleigh, Essex; and the now-destroyed St Mary Magdalen, Old Fish Street, London).

The preface shows that Butterfield's kneeling boards were supported by the ICBS to the extent of keeping specimens at their offices for inspection. How active or unanimous that support was, and whether there was a 'kneeling-board faction' at the ICBS, is not known. In particular the role of Richard Foster, one of the Vice-Presidents of the ICBS, who wrote the preface, has not been explored. It is notable that the publisher of the third separate edition and perhaps the others was not the ICBS, but an independent publisher (Rivingtons).

Butterfield covers a number of points in addition to the question of kneeling. In particular, he inveighs against the idea that church seating has comfort as its overriding purpose.

❖ ❖ ❖

Preface to third edition *(abbreviated)*
The following is the Preface to the First Edition of the Pamphlet: –
TO CHURCH BUILDERS AND CHURCH RENOVATORS

I wish to call attention to the following article by Mr. Butterfield, which appeared in the *Church Builder* for last month.

Full-sized models of the seats and kneeling-boards, as illustrated at the end of this paper, can now be seen at the Offices of the INCORPORATED CHURCH BUILDING SOCIETY, No. 2, Dean's Yard, Westminster, on application to the Secretary, during office hours.

The Society strongly recommends the use of Kneeling-boards, in connection with fixed seats of well-considered proportions.

RICHARD FOSTER. August, 1885.

A third edition being called for, I find it necessary to state that in some Churches, built or reseated during the last few years, various architects, while professing to accept, have attempted to improve on the design for Seats and Kneeling-boards which are recommended in

Mr Butterfield's pamphlet. These attempts, however, have proved complete failures. In many cases the architect tries to give the congregation an easy position for listening to the sermon, by sloping the backs of the seats. This slope is always gained at the cost of room and comfort in kneeling, and is less than no gain to real comfort in sitting. Surely the clergy and architects ought to bear in mind that the first thing to be aimed at is proper kneeling accommodation. They will then find that they have gained all that is necessary to comfort in sitting accommodation. We are constantly told in the Prayer Book to kneel, while sitting is not even mentioned, as being a matter of merely secondary consideration. . .

RICHARD FOSTER

P.S. I have been told sometimes, by clergymen, that in their Churches they cannot afford 3 ft from centre to centre of the seat. Although, where possible, 3 ft is the proper distance for seats to be apart, still, in Mission Chapels, and sometimes in Churches, it is necessary to be content with 2 ft 10 in, or even with 2 ft 9 in. Where such is the case, no seats and kneeling-boards will be found more suitable than those described in this pamphlet. R.F.

Church Seats and Kneeling Boards

IN EXTRICATING OURSELVES from the pew system of thirty or forty years since, we have not, I think, shown as much practical sense as Englishmen are usually credited with. We have not grasped definitely the requirements of the case. We have not sufficiently agreed upon any principles, and have too much seemed to suppose that with the abandonment of pew-doors all was settled. Pew traditions, in consequence, still survive very largely. I will take one point first, viz. that of kneeling, about which the Prayer Book speaks with no uncertain voice. We are still working, in the majority of our rearranged and new Churches, upon the pew tradition of hassocks or carpets, at once dirty, clumsy, untidy, and perishable. No protest has been raised against them, even by our Church Building Societies. If anything within the four walls of a Church should aim at an enduring character, it should be that which concerns kneeling. If anything should be provided, equally serviceable for rich and poor, it should be that which concerns kneeling. The hassock and carpet are the rich man's tradition, and they usually mean appropriation. A hassock is a stumbling-block, even to the youngest and most agile, in entering any seat, and it permanently occupies a large piece of the floor, to the great hindrance of standing with ease and comfort. It is always in different stages of decay, raggedness, and nastiness, and, in town Churches at least, it harbours vermin. It can never be cleaned. The poor man, as may be seen in any Church where some unusual effort has not been made, is not provided with this article. If provided in one generation, the thing will wear out, and for him may never be replaced. I am speaking from a long and large observation. With the abandonment of the pew system, the hassock or rug, in connection with fixed seats, should have ceased to exist altogether.

It is of the first importance that people should learn to abhor anything which is so awkward, perishable, and dirty as a hassock. They must not, however, forget, as some do, that the human body is so constituted that kneeling on the floor for any length of time is not the alternative. Such kneeling strains the joint between the foot and the leg, at the point B B in the accompanying drawing (Fig. 9). It is not a natural posture for that joint. To most people there would be the further objection that the floor must be dirty. The knee should be lifted about five inches above the floor in kneeling. This allows the foot to remain at a comfortable angle with the leg, and at rest. There is no doubt about this.

A level kneeling-board, five inches off the floor, and three and a half inches wide, is the best and most practical provision for kneeling in connection with fixed seats, and it is of fixed seats that I am writing. This board must always be a fixture, and, if kept at a distance of eleven inches from the top-rail of the seat, as shown and figured in the accompanying drawing, it allows the body of a person when kneeling to lean forwards at a convenient and restful angle, and to rest his arms on the capping of the seat back in front of him. The capping should for this purpose be flattened as shown in the half full-sized section at A, or it will cut the arms. The height of the capping of the seat back should not be more than fourteen inches above the seat, or the shoulders of the person kneeling and resting his arms upon it will be forced upwards, and will not be at rest.

The height of a seat back which will meet the case of a person when thus kneeling, is the most suitable and convenient height for him when sitting. It leaves the bones of the shoulders at liberty to move freely above it, as they ought to be able to move, while it gives needful support to the spine. There is no need for a sloping back when the shoulders are thus free. Overmuch effort, as it seems to me, has been often made to produce a too easy and lounging seat for Church use.

Fig. 9: The illustration to the article by William Butterfield, first published in the Church Builder *of 1884. The original caption was 'This design shows the seats as three feet apart, and it is most undesirable that they should be placed closer'. The image is reproduced here at about its original size.*
A photograph of Butterfieldian kneeling boards will be found in Figure 3c in the Case Studies in Chapter 29 (page 419).

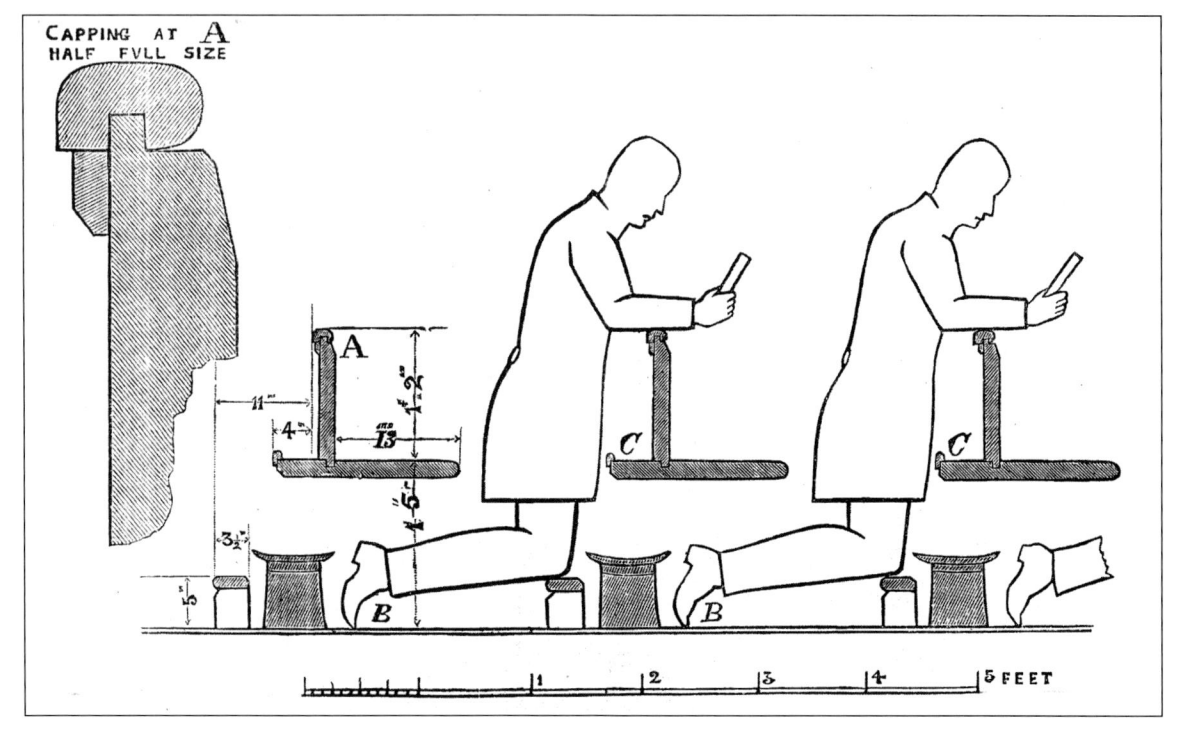

Sitting has been too much first considered, and then kneeling. Lounging is not a seemly and reverent attitude. It destroys all sense of the use and ends for which a Church exists. It is enough, if a Church seat is more easy than an ordinary chair. The old high straight-backed pew-framing was absolutely uncomfortable, and yet we all know how people fought to retain it. There is no need to go to the opposite extreme, and pander to what will promote sleep and lethargy, rather than conduct more befitting the place and occasion.

I have shown the hat of each person deposited on the further side of his own kneeling-board, in full view of the person to whom it belongs, and entirely free of the possibility of its being kicked by the person to whom it does not belong. People have a habit of tucking in the hat under their own seats, which is an entire mistake. The shelf marked C is intended for books when not in use, and should never be higher than the line of the seat, of which it should be a continuation, or it will come to be misunderstood, and used improperly. In countries where fixed seats obtain, as in Germany, and in parts of Italy, fixed kneeling-boards, although much too broad, are never absent. Too great breadth in the kneeling-board prevents a person while sitting from passing his feet over and beyond the kneeling-board, which it is often a great relief to do.

I have had to argue for this sort of Church seat and kneeling-board for the last thirty-five years, and I have never failed to convince entirely those for whom I have worked, however much in the first instance they objected to the idea. I am convinced that no other treatment will ever make kneeling general. "You have made my people kneel," is the message I have received after the system has been long enough in use. "I have become a missionary for your kneeling-boards," was written to me by the strongest objector to them that I have ever met with. But it must never be forgotten, as it is unfortunately always forgotten, that an Englishman does not know how to kneel without patient instruction of a very minute kind. Having given him the means of kneeling, he must be taught how to use it without effort, in a simple, unaffected way, keeping his eyes on his Prayer Book. The joint in the knee should be brought to fit to the front rounded edge of the kneeling-board, so as to avoid kneeling on the hard bone of the knee. Many may be disposed to think that the kneeling-board as figured in the accompanying drawing is too narrow. It is, if anything, too wide – wider than ordinary use requires. Pads are absolutely unnecessary. For the purpose of floor-cleaning, and for other very good reasons, there should be no divisions carried down to the floor beneath the seats. Such divisions harbour dirt, increase a hundredfold the difficulty of washing a floor, and cramp the legs when a person is sitting. A kneeling-board can be cleaned oftener than the floor, and while people are learning to use them properly, it is desirable they should be often cleaned. We cannot educate the people in Church habits as long as no two Churches are fitted upon the same principle.

Appendix by Richard Foster *(extract)*
Mr Butterfield says that one of the bad qualities of hassocks is that they are perishable. It is probably unnecessary to say a word of confirmation

of this, but, in order to show that *hassocks do wear out very quickly*, and that in poor parishes it is difficult to get them replaced, I may mention that I recently received from the clergyman of a poor London parish an appeal for a contribution towards purchasing new hassocks; for, he said, "those which were put in the church two years ago, are all worn out". Mr Hoskins condemns kneeling-pads: and hassocks are of course worse. One cannot but feel, therefore, with the Incorporated Church Building Society, that *kneeling-boards, in connection with fixed seats, and of well-considered proportions, are much to be preferred.*

❖ ❖ ❖

Occasional notes on church furniture and arrangement: No. 1. – PEWS.
by J. T. Micklethwaite

The article below is by the distinguished church architect J. T. Micklethwaite, a member of the ICBS panel of architects. It was published in the Church Builder *of 1899, pages 12–15. The first few paragraphs are not included, as they are merely a brief review of the history of pews.*

Much of what he says here reinforces the general ICBS line, and could have been written at any time within the previous forty years. Perhaps surprisingly at this late date, when church attendance was slipping, he points out that the Society's guidelines are frequently challenged by architects trying to squeeze in more seating.

It is interesting that Micklethwaite quite unaffectedly uses the word 'pew' to refer to a bench, though on first occurrence he clarifies that he is referring to an 'open' pew (rather than a 'box' pew). This of course is the modern ambiguous but perfectly convenient usage of the term.

❖ ❖ ❖

WE HAVE NOW GONE BACK to open pews, and with them we use chairs. Each has its special advantages; for instance, the fixity of the pews, which prevents a zealous but unthinking churchwarden from thrusting six into space only enough for five; and the mobility of the chairs, which allows of them being arranged variously as convenience requires. In a well-appointed and well-served church it is best to use both, there being pews enough for an average congregation, and plenty of room in passages between and beyond them where chairs may be put when they are wanted.

But if we are to have pews they should be such as are convenient for general use, which but few now are. The rules as to pews which have been laid down by the Committee of Honorary Consulting Architects of our Society are probably more often challenged than any of the others. There is a continual struggle to prevent overcrowding and the ill sectioning of seats. Both faults come of the survival of the old view of pews as mere sittings, instead of being places for worshippers, who should kneel and stand as well as sit in them.

To take overcrowding first. The Society requires a spacing of three feet from centre to centre of pews, and no month passes without a request to be allowed to have less, generally on the plea of poverty and the need for many 'sittings'. And for the sake of an additional five or six per cent of *them* it is proposed to spoil all the 'kneelings' in the church. A well-sectioned seat makes the most of the space and may do with rather less than three feet; but seeing the difficulty there is in getting even fairly good sections, no lower standard should be allowed. As to length, the usual practice is better; but still, from time to one finds pews planned of a length to hold, say, six people and a half, which means either the waste of room which might with advantage be put into the open passage or the crowding of seven people into a pew which is too little to hold them.

The most obstinate error about the sectioning of pews is the excessive sloping of the backs and seat-boards. Men seem to look on a pew as a place to lounge in. Infirm folk find such seats troublesome to rise from. And all the slope of the back is so much taken from the working width of the pew. If it were necessary, the amount of it should be added to the normal spacing of three feet. No greater slopes than half an inch in the seat and an inch in the back should be allowed. And even so much is not wanted, for, if the seat-board be broad enough and the back not high enough to reach the shoulder blades, which is now always the case, the back pressure is only on the top rail, and each sitter takes the angle which best suits him.

Book-boards on the top rails are a survival from the box pews, which were made so high that men could read from books so placed. That is not possible now and the book-board at the top not only curtails the kneeling space, but is itself a great inconvenience to kneelers. A shelf about the level of the seat, and sufficient to lay books on when not in use is not in the way and is as useful as one higher up.

Some kneeling-boards seem contrived on purpose to prevent people from kneeling, and not any is generally convenient. It is impossible to contrive a fixed kneeler which shall suit everybody. One wants it forward and another back, and the only right way is to provide movable single kneelers which each can place to suit himself.

Those who are careless about the comfort of worshippers are often very careful about the welfare of hats and umbrellas. As to the former, it ought to be admitted that unless you can put it into a box the only certain protection for a cylinder hat is to hang it up high enough to be out of harm's way. But in practice, with a clean and clear floor and reasonable care on the part of its owner, a hat may generally rest in safety under the seat. He who tries to keep a seat for his hat as well as one for himself is properly served if his neighbour sits on it.

Wet umbrellas should not be brought to the pews, but there should be a stand for them near the church door.

The floors of pews should not be raised above those of the passages, or people using chairs will be at a lower level than those using pews, who may chance to be in front of them. And the reason for forbidding the boarding up of backs below the seats is that the floor may easily be swept and washed.

15. Movable benches or chairs? Correspondence in *The Ecclesiologist* 1854–6

Edited by Trevor Cooper

THE FOLLOWING CORRESPONDENCE appeared in *The Ecclesiologist* between April 1854 and February 1856.[1] It is reprinted here for two reasons. The first is that it gives an insight into the thinking of the time, albeit from the viewpoint of members of the Ecclesiological Society who (in that original incarnation) tended to be of higher churchmanship than average. The second, and more surprising, is that much of it resonates with today's concerns, and it may perhaps be helpful to appreciate that many of the issues we face today are not new – that, as one correspondent put it, 'there cannot be absolute good or bad in either chairs or benches', and that there has always been the need to balance one factor against another.

There is much that is revealing here. We see a nagging worry that churches were off-putting to the poor, both from the formality of church interiors, and the way that fixed seating was subtly appropriated by routine worshippers, making it in practice unavailable for the occasional and uncertain visitor. There was much discussion why churches on the Continent seemed more welcoming, and the extent to which the use of chairs played a part in this. There is a strong concern to encourage kneeling during the service. And there is a rumbling discontent about the pressure to maximise 'accommodation' by cramming seats in, providing far more sittings than were normally needed.

A number of issues are still very much alive today, one hundred and fifty years later. There is discussion about the effect of seating on church architecture, and (perhaps surprisingly) the correspondence shows no blind adherence to the view that because pews were in use in medieval times, they are necessarily the most architecturally appropriate way of seating a church. There is a feeling that interiors need to avoid the impression of fixity and formality, and some discussion of the visual impact of rows of chairs, the effect they have on behaviour, and of the fundamental desirability of self-organising seating arrangements even if they look disorganised. Concerns are expressed about the impact on tiny congregations of having to worship in a church full of fixed seating. The associational differences between chairs and benches are discussed, together with their effect on personal space. In one church where chairs were introduced, there is mention of retaining some benches to 'conciliate prejudice'. There is talk of the difficulties that the elderly may find using chairs to raise and lower themselves. Considerable concern is expressed

A church chair made between 1860–1875 for St Philip's Cathedral, Birmingham, about a decade after this correspondence. Showing Victorian practicality, it has a wide flat top rail for leaning on to pray, a wooden box for hymn books, below which is a hook for a kneeler. At one side there is an iron loop with a dish below to take an umbrella or stick. There is room for the feet when kneeling, and the diagonal braces underneath may be intended to store the hat of the person sitting behind. The solid seat is shaped for comfort in the manner of a Windsor chair. Examples of chairs from a church furnishing catalogue of the 1890s will be found on page 316. (Photo © Victoria and Albert Museum, London)

about the reduced number of people that can be seated on chairs, and whether churches will be able to accommodate everyone at special services.

We find correspondents suggesting the use of portable benches, discussing how many people it takes to shift them, and whether they can be successfully stacked; others puzzle over the visual impact of stacked chairs, and where they are to be stored. Perhaps to our surprise, we find these Victorian correspondents discussing the need for flexibility in the use of church interiors, and waxing lyrical about the way in which chairs and portable benches can be rearranged to meet different needs.

Further research is needed to establish how wide was the interest in chairs at this time, and to what extent it was driven by party. The influential Incorporated Church Building Society did not encourage chairs, though it softened its approach in the mid 1870s, and the need in many churches to provide some appropriated seating, reserved for the use of particular individuals, also encouraged fixed pews.[2] It may well be that enthusiasm for chairs was restricted to those of a high-church disposition,[3] and the correspondence does show that one influence was what had been seen in Roman Catholic churches on the Continent. This would not be a point in favour of chairs for low churchmen, a few at least of whom saw the introduction of chairs as one of many indications of a 'romanising' tendency within the Church of England.[4]

But regardless of the general level of interest, it is a sobering thought that a significant – and influential – body of church opinion was in favour of chairs, and one cannot help but wonder whether the ubiquity of fixed seating in Victorian reorderings may to some extent have been the result of the need to demonstrate to grant-giving societies, other donors, and oneself that one was maximising accommodation, rather than through any deep commitment to pews themselves.

EDITORIAL NOTE: The correspondence has been ruthlessly edited, reducing its length by about one half – not too difficult, given the prolixity of the correspondents. The topic which has been most drastically cut is the comparison with continental practice. I have not indicated where I have cut the text; occasional linking or explanatory material has been put in square brackets. Scholars who wish to recover the entire text in all its Victorian verbosity will need to return to the original publication.

In reading this correspondence it should be recalled that the word 'pews' refers to box pews. Note that some (but not all) of the correspondents assume – without always saying so – that if chairs were to be used, they would be collected individually by each worshipper from the back of the church, rather than being set out in advance.

Notes

1 *The Ecclesiologist*, 15 (NS 12) (1854), 89–93, 157–61, 250–55, 297–99, 389–93; 16 (NS 13) (1855), 5–8, 82–85, 153–5, 330–32; 17 (NS 14) (1856), 21–23.
2 See page 213 above.
3 Roger L. Brown, *Pews, Benches and Seats: being a History of the Church in Wales* (Welshpool, 1998), 54–55.
4 J. T. Wrenford, *Romanizing the Church of England. A Sermon* (London [printed, 1865]), p. 9, referenced in Brown, *Pews*, 55. My inspection of a number of other anti-Romanising pamphlets has not shown similar negative views about chairs, so Wrenford may have been out on a limb – further research is needed.

❖ ❖ ❖

None of the contributors can be identified, but the first letter is from someone who describes himself as a member of the Committee of the Ecclesiological Society, which, he says, is split on the topic of church seating. His preferred solution is portable benching, and he takes a systematic approach to the topic, first laying out his five criteria for successful seating, then demonstrating how badly chairs perform on some of the counts.

DEAR EDITOR – Allow me to renew the question of how the naves of our churches ought to be seated. Pews being now defunct, our choice rests between open fixed benches, open movable benches, and chairs. The first of these expedients meet, I believe, with no genuine support in our Committee, though the circumstances of the times compel us to tolerate its existence in new churches and restorations, from its incomparable superiority over [box] pews. Our private feelings are divided between movable benches and chairs. I propose to offer you some considerations which have determined my individual preference for movable benches.

The requisites which the most perfect system of seating a church should fulfil may be approximately stated as these:

1. Conformity of design with that of the structure.
2. Non-obtrusiveness with respect to the *coup d'œil* of the interior.
3. Accommodation – sufficiently comfortable without luxury – of the worshippers.
4. Economy of space, so as (a) to provide for the largest number of worshippers in a given area with due regard to the means of kneeling, and of decent sitting; and (b) thus to leave as much unoccupied space as possible in the nave.
5. Facility of removal when a more open area should be required for any special occasion.

[Those in favour of chairs] admire, and very rightly, the religious and artistic effect of an open nave – they perceive that pews ruin this effect – and that fixed benches, despite their 'Perpendicular' origin, go very far towards destroying it; and they therefore jump to the conclusion that it is best attained by the method of seating the furthest removed from pews and fixed seats, viz. placing each worshipper on his own individual movable [seat].

The 'frightful contrivance of a seat' referred to by 'A Committee Man', which allowed the user to sit (with the upper seat lowered), or raise the upper seat, turn the chair, and kneel on the lower surface. The picture had been published in 1841 by the Society in their A Few Words to Church Builders.

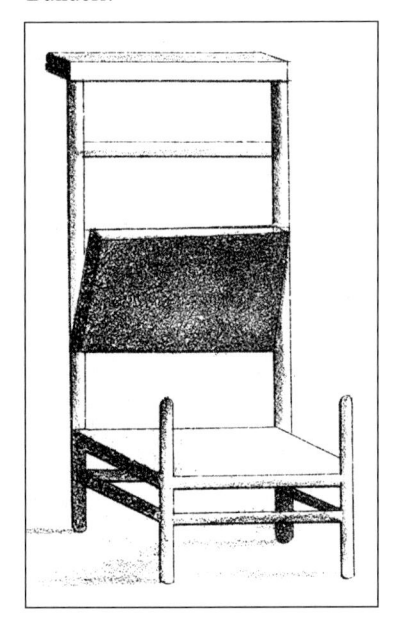

[However] this individualising of seats creates evils of an opposite description, but about as destructive of openness of effect, as the fixed seats of the fifteenth century. Seat your worshippers each on his own chair, and either you must crowd them to the detriment both of the decorum of worship and of their own due comfort, or else you must fritter away ground area. A bench of a certain length will hold more sitters than a range of chairs of the same measure. Make your chairs however square, *pack* them however close – you cannot fit them (without impropriety) so as to hold more than one sitter per chair. These chairs, if of one size, must be made so as to contain without inconvenience the average of fat, and not of thin, sitters. Accordingly every chair which a thin sitter occupies represents in its breadth so much lost space, perhaps in four sitters equal to an entire sitting. Assume then that the *fat* and the thin are equally balanced, and we should find that while each set of chairs crammed ever so closely together can only hold eight persons, a bench of the length of that set, would, without inconvenience of any sort, provide for nine.

But is it [even] possible to secure that the chairs shall be crammed quite close together? Is it even desirable that they should be so? I appeal to your own instinctive feeling to say if there is not involved a sentiment of obtrusiveness, almost of indelicacy, which makes one dislike a stranger sitting in a chair in actual contact with one's own, which in no way exists, against an equally personal proximity to a sitter on the same bench. The reason of this is obvious – the idea of a chair is *isolation* – the idea of a bench *community* – and therefore to make a row of chairs fulfil the duty of mere community shocks the innate ideas of the propriety of things, and is accordingly offensive. Attempt it therefore as you may, you will never succeed in getting your sextons to stick the chairs so as *quite* to touch. Your only expedient would be to lash the chairs together, which to my mind would be simply adopting a very roundabout and clumsy method of making so many benches.

I have I think established that, in point of *latitudinal* accommodation from north to south, chairs are plainly inferior to open benches. I now proceed to show that they are equally wasteful of the *longitudinal* accommodation, from west to east, requisite for *kneeling*.

Here my case is comparatively easy, for it is being established to my hand by the new and growing use in foreign churches. There was (I remember) a time, when we dreamed of spinning chairs round at the different portions of the service, now to sit on them, and then to kneel at them as occasion demanded, and I recollect an engraving of some frightful contrivance of a seat turning on a hinge, with which we were not afraid to decorate one of our earliest tracts [see Figure]. In the meanwhile chair-turning from its manifest incommodiousness and indecency, the noise and confusion which it inevitably creates at the most solemn portions of the service, is going out upon the continent, and the expedient gaining use is to assign to each worshipper *two* chairs – a high one on which he sits looking eastward, and a low one placed before him with the back turned the reverse way at which he has to kneel. Thus *longitudinally* the chair system occupies half as much space again as the bench arrangement, in which the back of each bench becomes the kneeling place of the bench behind it.

In reply it may be urged that this is the fault of the fashion of the chairs, and that they might be so managed that the back of each should be the kneeling place to the worshipper just behind. This suggestion, however, quite overlooks the important consideration that chairs are very easily shaken, shifted, and displaced, even with the best intentions of the most quiet worshipper, and that to give your neighbour immediately behind you the power of so meddling with your chairs voluntarily or involuntarily, is nothing short of securing indecency of public worship.

I have I flatter myself, made out my case for movable benches as against chairs as far as respects the third and fourth *desiderata* of church seating. I return to the two first – conformity of design and non-obtrusiveness – in both which respects the advantage appears to me plainly to lie with the benches.

You must not forget that we are dealing with chairs as a mass – not singly. A single chair, however light may be its design, can carry character, which will be felt as it stands more or less by itself in a room. But mass a body of chairs together, and not only do you not grasp this character, but *the very points which give the single chair its beauty, are deformities in a block of chairs crowded together*.

Benches, on the contrary, are made to be seen and admired in the mass; they are designed to stand in proper line, and their decoration is confined to the bench ends which face gangways; and if their shape is felicitous the more of them there are the more advantageously do they appear. Neither do they give you the idea of a crowd as chairs do, when the eye catches and clings to the unit, and the notion is – 'What a number of chairs to be collected together!' Some such form of thought is the inevitable result of chairing a church, however flimsy each chair may be in its construction; and the whole effect is that of blocking up the nave as completely as could result from any mass of fixed sittings, however heavy they may be.

I need not dwell long on the fifth head – facility of removal – it is self-evident that while two men can remove at one effort any bench if not heavy in its material, they must be occupied for a longer time in clearing away the number of chairs that would represent that bench. Neither need I appeal to any one who has been in a foreign church as to the peculiarly untidy effect of chairs stacked up in a corner.

Under all the five heads then with which I started I have given reasons for the preference of open movable benches over chairs as the furniture of our naves. Benches, I assert, accommodate, under forms the most consonant with the spirit of pointed architecture, the largest number of worshippers on the smallest area. As the result, they leave quite free and open that surplus area of the churches which the chairs from their non-economy of space perforce invade.

But not only does the bench arrangement give a greater feeling of non-confinement throughout the church, but it increases the value of the absolutely free area when that is required for any special occasion. I had lately the opportunity of testing this when attending a funeral, at which the bier was placed in a space cleared to the west of the chancel screen. The entire effect was that of great space, and this effect was manifestly increased by the open area in question having its definite

Two examples of movable benches, from working drawings intended as exemplars, published by the Society in 1847 in their Instrumenta Ecclesiastica *(plate 47). The designs are by William Butterfield. The one with the poppy-head is just over three feet tall, the other is two feet tall. The seats are eighteen inches off the ground. It is suggested that the bench should be about eight feet long. These are heavy items, a long way removed from modern movable benching.*

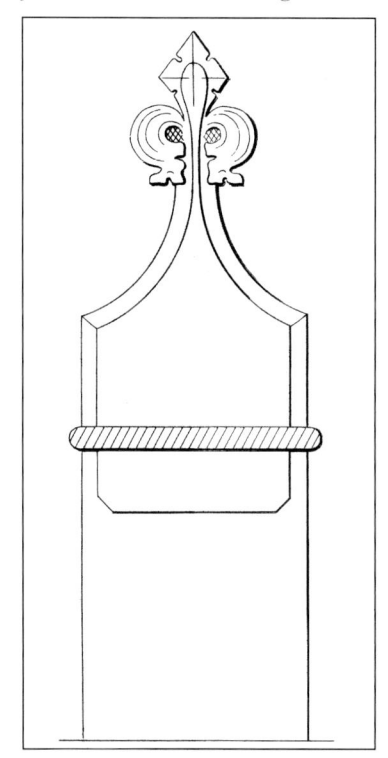

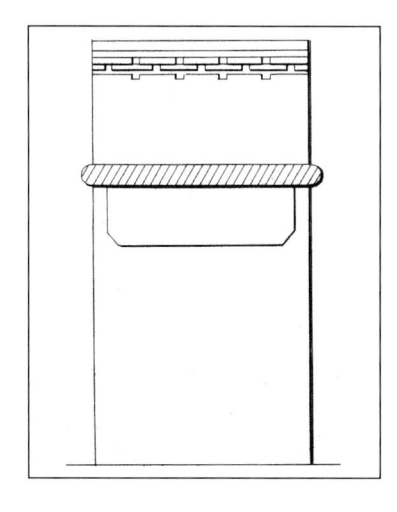

western boundary in the last bench suffered to remain, as the screen formed that to the east.

But although I argue so strongly against chairs as a rule in our communion, I am not insensible that there may be some cases where they, and they alone are admissible. There may be, and there are, numerous instances in which in this or that church it is desirable in one odd corner or other to provide supplementary accommodation, which is only procurable by chairs.

I am, your's sincerely,
A COMMITTEE MAN.

❖ ❖ ❖

The next correspondent picks up the challenge, arguing that 'A Committee Man' has exaggerated the difficulties of chairs, and made too little of the sheer effort of moving portable benches. He also introduces the need for 'pliability and elasticity' in the church space, as against 'stiffness and formality' – and here he is not only arguing the need to be able to reorganise the space, but also referring to the general impression given by the interior. This theme is picked up by later correspondents. However he leaves a door wide open towards the end of his letter, when he admits that it is not easy to kneel when using chairs.

SIR – Does 'A Committee Man' know any church seated with open benches in which as matter of fact the benches ever are removed, except perhaps upon some great and exceptional occasions? I do not; and I suspect he will find that there really are no such cases.

And this is the point upon which the whole question really turns. Do you wish to gain for our churches that pliability and elasticity, which all unite in admiring in the continental churches? or are you willing to acquiesce in the stiffness and formality of churches benched or seated continuously from side to side, and from end to end?

We shall never have the freedom and openness which so invite you into continental churches, and make you feel so much at home in them, *without* chairs. *Chairs are the right thing, – if we could only learn how to use them.*

It is said that benches economise space; and this I am disposed to admit. [But] I would prefer that upon such exceptional occasions (for how many churches are there which always have every seat filled?) – that the last comers should form a standing group at the lower [i.e. western] end of the church, women of course having chairs offered them; and this would give great ease and freedom in churchgoing to a class who dread being compelled to sit in a confined posture during the whole service. To accommodate a great number of persons upon any special day in a church, I should say, fill the east end, and rather more than three quarters of the length of your nave and aisles with chairs, then leave a vacant space at the west end, which would hold a much greater number of men *standing* than you could provide for either by chairs or forms.

But I feel very much inclined to kick against this whole idea of 'Church Accommodation' as it is called. It has been used as a test of the

Some ten years after this correspondence, an advertorial for a newly-patented folding bench appeared in the Church Builder *(no. 9 (1864), 30). Unlike previous movable benches, these benches could be folded and stacked against the side walls of the church when not required, needing only two people to move them.*

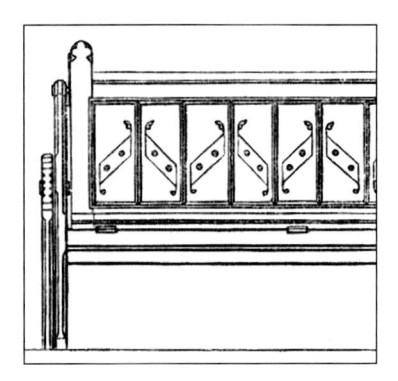

size of churches, in order that Church Building Societies may know what amount of grant they should make; but even in this point of view it is extremely fallacious; for it is well known that seats are sometimes (as the natural result of this false principle) so crowded together in new or restored churches, as to afford the very reverse of '*accommodation*' to those who occupy them; for I have known cases in which forms have been put into chancels, to hold school children on the day of consecration, so as to show the required amount of 'accommodation' and then the day after, both children and forms have been turned out (as they deserve to be), and the professed accommodation which Church Building grants had exacted, has sunk from this momentary high pressure to its real status. Surely it would be better to apportion grants by the number of square feet the area contains, leaving that area to be dealt with afterwards as convenience may suggest.

I [thus] allow that chairs may perhaps take up rather more room than benches but I do not admit the argument drawn from this, except in the case of those churches in which every seat is always occupied; and in such happy instances as those, I would say, enlarge your church, or divide and multiply your services, only do not cramp and destroy the life and elasticity of worship for the sake of a little more (misnamed) 'accommodation'.

Let me turn to the facility of removing seats after the fuller Sunday services are over. [It] is true: two men could move the seats of eight people, in bench seating, as quickly as they could move the seats of four persons in chairs; but remember they must be two men; one man would be quite helpless in moving benches. And at how many churches could two men be always found for this purpose? Moreover they must be two *strong* men, for a bench with a back to it is a tolerable weight; and two old men (such as we usually have in churches) would soon tire of such work. So that to set aside benches would be the work of two strong men; while one man, and he an old man of no great strength or activity, might be walking forwards and backwards with a light chair in each hand, for two or three hours if necessary, without any great fatigue. Chairs can be set aside easily, benches cannot be set aside without double labour and a considerable effort: consequently when chairs are used, we do find the church cleared of them and open on weekdays – where benches are used we do not.

Now to go into a church on a weekday, where there are perhaps fifty persons, [or] perhaps only five, present, and see it set out for 500 or more, has a peculiarly chilling, desolate effect – produced, not by the size of the building, but by the arrangement of seats prepared apparently for a great number of persons who have not come to occupy them.

But this is not all; there is a stiffness about churches set out with seats from end to end (for movable benches are in reality hardly ever moved on account of their weight, etc.). You have to walk straight down one passage, and then turn off at right angles into another, and the fact, of your being in the passage seems to make you feel that you *must go somewhere at once* to get out of people's way, to say nothing of the fear of a tap on the elbow from that awful personage the pew opener. Whereas in a church the area of which is open and unencumbered with seats, you may go and stand about as you please, you do not feel in any one's way, you do not feel *obliged* to fix yourself in a seat at once for the whole service, you may take a chair if you please, and where you please, nearer or further from the choir, as you like; and if you choose you may attend to the whole or part of the service without sitting down at all, if you prefer it (as many I believe would), and the group who do gather their chairs in front of the choir may have more room (I am speaking of weekday services), and fall into an easier and more natural position than if placed in rows of benches or pews.

On the continent a church is an open, inviting place; you may go in and feel at home there; you may look at the pictures if you please, or you may kneel down and say your prayers, or you may take a book and chair and sit down and read, or you may go forward and join in the service, if you wish so to do; but with us there is only one thing for it – as soon as you get inside a church door, you *must* walk into a pew, and there remain till the whole service is over, and then out you must go again.

The difficulty about kneeling is the real hindrance to the use of chairs, and our thanks would be due to any one who could get over the difficulty for us. *Two* chairs, one for sitting and one for kneeling, would I fear be too great a sacrifice of room for us, because our services seem to require that all persons should hear the words of them, which the Roman Catholic services do not of necessity require.

A cushion on the floor seems but a poor device; it is liable to get kicked about, &c. Turning the chair, and having a double seat, the under one to kneel on, would seem awkward in a full church, and a kneeler on the back of the chair in front would be worst of all, as destroying the very freedom and independence for which we wish to have chairs.

I remain, Sir, yours truly,

LONDINENSIS.

❖ ❖ ❖

The original correspondent, 'A Committee Man' gratefully walks through the wide open door left by 'Londinensis', and points out that if it is not possible to kneel when using chairs, then this more or less rules them out as an option. He mops up a few other points, but raises little that is new, except to argue that fixed benches are better for small congregations as they will scatter themselves around the whole building.

MY DEAR EDITOR – 'Londinensis' has assisted me in making good my case. This he most effectually has done by his admissions that 'the difficulty of kneeling is the real hindrance to the use of chairs', and that benches have the inferiority in the economy of space.

Any preponderating advantages, therefore, which he may able to discover in them on the other side (for of course there cannot be absolute good or bad in either chairs or benches) must be very strong indeed to strike the balance in favour of that system of seating churches which just precisely breaks down at the point where it ought to be strongest – the convenience, if not possibility, of kneeling. The question between the two parties is *all but* concluded in this passage.

[Of his other points] it is not to the use of benches rather than chairs that we owe the want of 'pliability and elasticity' in our notions of behaviour at church, which, equally with 'Londinensis', I deplore. This stiffness arises from the wretched system of locking and barring up church except during the actual service-time; of turning your congregation in, and then turning them out to suit the beadle's convenience. It arises from high pews and dry worship. Abate these evils, and then I am convinced that you will feel as much at home in a benched as in a chaired church.

Your correspondent surely draws on his imagination when he talks of the '*peculiarly* chilling and desolate effect' of a congregation of fifty or five in a church 'set out' for five hundred. No doubt so small a congregation is always chilling; but if there be benches for five hundred, the fifty will scatter themselves so as to look like a crowd, and have the effect of seventy or eighty, or it may be a hundred. But if, on the contrary, they have to cluster up to a set of chairs only just enough for their own number, they will look very few indeed – not more than twenty-five or thirty-five, perhaps. Benches permit elastic expansion to the smaller, and they give the readiest means of compression to the larger congregation. Chairs, on the other hand, militate equally against one and the other of these self-adjusting means of compensation.

The trouble and inconvenience of having to 'walk straight down one passage, and then turn off at right angles into another', in going to your seat, on which 'Londinensis' dilates, are not so very severe, methinks. Besides which, in a foreign church, thoroughly bechaired, as I have seen the Madeleine, you have, if you want a sitting, to go through the same precise evolution. One fallacy, indeed, seems to run through all 'Londinensis's' letter, which has dictated this argument in particular – that of treating all benched churches as if they *must* be benched from west wall to chancel screen. I need not point out to you that there is no such necessity.

Give free access to your churches – I repeat it – and whether they have benches or chairs in them, they will become 'open, inviting places'; 'you may go in and feel at home there,' or 'look at the pictures,' or 'kneel down and say your prayers,' or 'take a book and read': only, I warn you that the Englishman will, under no condition of things, do these things to the extent the foreigner does, for the same reason that he preferentially sits, and reads, and talks, and eats at home, when the foreigner sits, reads, eats, and talks, with or without his family, at some place of public resort. It is not a difference of religion, but of national habit; not peculiarly to be blamed, nor praised, nor yet accounted for, but simply acknowledged as a fact, and as a fact provided for.

I am, yours truly,
A COMMITTEE MAN.

❖ ❖ ❖

Our next correspondent signs himself 'A Curate'. Behind a pleasant if not ingratiating manner, he puts the knife into 'Londinensis', citing examples where chairs have not worked, and pointing out that Continental examples are not appropriate because we are not Continentals, and unlike them, we are stiff and unelastic.

DEAR SIR – Agreeing with much that 'Londinensis' says in his letter entitled, 'Chairs in Churches,' I still think that he ought *first* to have applied himself to the kneeling difficulty. Now I happen to be acquainted with a large church, where pews have been ejected, and the area entirely filled with chairs. The result, as clergy and people both allow, is anything but satisfactory, the congregation has become a sitting body, whereas formerly a fair proportion used to kneel. The reasons are, I think, obvious; for, first of all, a chair in itself is suggestive of sitting, and our people are not accustomed to view it in any other light. And then a change of position, either from sitting to kneeling, or from kneeling to standing, requires some such steady support as a bench indeed affords, but which a chair does not. They tell me this is especially the complaint with old and infirm persons. Another inconvenience arises from the natural tendency of sitters to gradually push and edge backwards.

I was amused to find, at the church to which I am referring, that two or three elderly gentlemen, who have not quite entered into the spirit of the new arrangement, have screwed down their own chairs, taking care to do the same kind service for their neighbours *in front*. At S. Ninian's, Perth, the bench-like device of a ledge attached to the back of each chair, for the use of the worshipper behind, has been found useless, and is now abandoned.

When abroad, I can fully admire all that 'Londinensis' does. Take, for example, a cathedral or other large church, with its varying round of services. Mass will be celebrated now at the high altar, now in a transept; sometimes two or three masses will be going on together in different parts of the same church. Under such a system benches would clearly be a mistake; chairs are the very thing. But the same does not apply to us. Our services – and, what is more to the purpose, our habits as a people – are stiff and unelastic. It is disagreeable and unromantic to be compelled to say so, but the omitting to mention it does not make it the less true.

Our Prayer Book, again, contemplates, to say the least, a congregation taking part in its different services: not so the offices of the Romish Church: and until the two are assimilated, I would not be a party to turning our churches into a lounging place, or even a picture gallery, to the disturbance of the regular worshippers, however few in number they might be.

When service is begun, an Englishman's plain duty is to remain and join in it, as long as he can; when there is no service, he may stand about, or read, or pray, or anything else that 'Londinensis' can teach him to do, for his soul's good; and every thoughtful man must wish to see our churches more used in this way than they are. But I don't think that chairs, as such, will much contribute to this. A church benched from end to end presents, if anything, a more inviting look to a reserved, undemonstrative Englishman, than a large open area, with only a number of chairs piled up in one corner. The having somewhere to go to at once, not so much to get out of other people's way, as, to quickly escape from an undue measure of isolation and conspicuousness, is, I venture to say, no ground of complaint against our use of benches. Still, with foreigners, such arguments would be meaningless, simply because their characteristics and sensibilities are wholly different from our own.

[I agree that] there is perhaps no greater mistake than the too common one of benching out a church, without an idea of the real wants of the parish. This is constantly being done. Within the last few days, an instance has come under my own observation. A village church is to be re-pewed from side to side and end to end, and every expedient resorted to for increasing the number of seats, while the fact that the church never has been, nor in probability ever will be, anything like full, is admitted by every one.

I am, yours faithfully,
A CURATE.

❖ ❖ ❖

At last 'Londinensis' finds a friend in favour of chairs, who argues (against 'A Committee Man') that chairs are not in fact that bad at packing people in, and that unlike benches they hit the button exactly when it comes to personal space. He argues that the kneeling problem with chairs is not insurmountable. He also queries whether a pile of portable benches is not far more off-putting than a pile of chairs. He raises several new points: the fact that fixed benches are difficult for the poor, the undesirable way in which people spread out when there are benches, and the inherent fitness for purpose of self-organised seating.

DEAR SIR – I am not at all convinced but that, in cases where on special occasions it is desired to accommodate a crowd, a larger number of persons may find room on chairs than on long benches. Each individual will gladly concede a little space to his neighbours, and it is quite unnecessary to reserve gangways or alleys as a person may thread his way out. So that, I believe, on special occasions, a larger crowd might assemble, to hear, for instance, a celebrated preacher, in a church with nothing but chairs, than in one with both benches and chairs. But 'Londinensis' is perfectly right in saying, that, after all, such unmanageable crowds are rarely collected, and perhaps not very often wanted, in our churches. If, then, we get rid, to some extent, of the question of accommodation, we may discuss the matter more allowably on the grounds of convenience and aesthetics.

I, for one, cannot understand how 'A Committeeman' can gravely argue that it is less disagreeable to 'jam' oneself into close personal contact with one's neighbours on a bench, than to bring adjacent chairs into contact. For my own part, I should feel no difficulty whatever in making my *chair* join my neighbour's chair, whenever necessary. On the other hand, anything more disagreeable than close *personal* contact with strangers, I cannot imagine. 'A Committeeman' must have had, I should think, but little acquaintance with the special discomforts of an omnibus or a second class railway carriage, or he would hardly have ventured on this opinion.

That each worshipper should have his own chair seems to me to hit the exact mean of comfort and propriety in church arrangement. It secures to each person a certain independence and isolation, which seem necessary for one's individual acts of worship; while at the same time there is nothing like pew doors or pew walls to cut one off from the common prayer of the congregation.

I am sure also that nothing will be found so convenient in actual use, as for each individual to be able to range or shift his chair at his pleasure. One could only rejoice to see a large area occupied, however confusedly, by worshippers arranged as convenience and freedom may have dictated; in fact, the chairs become actually invisible when a nave is densely crowded by a closely packed congregation.

And this brings me to speak of the outcry made by 'A Committeeman' against the untidy appearance of a large pile of chairs not in use, such as one often sees in a foreign church. No one can say, of course, that such a pile is what one would desire to see. But, at the same time, a pile of chairs, however unsightly, is so obviously temporary and easily removed an obstruction, that, whatever the eye may suffer, the mind at once perceives that they form no part of the essence of the building, and consequently abstracts them at once and without difficulty from its conception of the interior. This objection to piled up chairs comes with the less reason from 'A Committeeman', because he advocates not fixed, but movable, benches. Has he ever pictured to himself the barricade that a hundred movable benches would make, if packed up at the west end of a nave or aisle? It would be a thousand times worse than a pile of chairs. [In addition] one of the greatest advantages of chairs over benches is that the latter must be carried into their places before Service; whereas, if need be, each person on entering may carry his own chair and put it down wherever he can find room on the skirts of the congregation already assembled.

I must confess that I pine, with 'Londinensis', for more 'freedom and elasticity' in our method of attending public worship. I feel acutely what he so well describes as the grim necessity of at once finding a seat in a benched church. Whatever may be true of the 'respectable' classes, I am quite sure that the poor will not be attracted to our churches until they find therein a perfectly open area and a perfect equality of seat and place – which can only be attained by the use of chairs. I am accustomed, myself, to worship in a church with quite open benches, with (nominally) no appropriated seats. In spite of this, I observe the poorer people, when they attend, instinctively avoiding benches which they imagine to be appropriated, and, as a general rule, slinking into the furthest seats, and leaving an unoccupied space between themselves and the rest of the congregation. But summon a meeting in (for instance) a schoolroom, with no seats at all, or the children's benches ranged 'promiscuously' as people may place them for themselves, and, unless my experience is wrong, you will then find a real equality established and recognised.

One more remark before I leave the instance of the church, with the practices of which I am most acquainted. I observe the universal preference for the end seat of a bench – the outside seat. It is a very rare thing for any one to go in at once to the middle or the furthest end. The practical result of this is that the people are most inconveniently scattered over the church; the more bold alone venturing to push by a person who may already have taken the end seat.

I believe that [these effects], ought to be, as [they] easily can be, got rid of by the entire equality of a perfectly open area, in which each person will take, and place where he chooses, his own chair. The bench plan, though infinitely preferable to closed pews, is after all only a half measure, and accordingly fails

I [would have] shirked the most important part of the subject, if I did not add a word about the kneeling difficulty. I cannot, do all I will, perceive any great evil in each person having two chairs, one to sit upon and one to kneel upon, provided always that the area and the number of the congregation permit it, without injury to other worshippers. I for one should always be an advocate for much larger churches, and for much more frequent services; so that the space of two chairs might perhaps be allowed for each worshipper. But where this could not well be, I cannot, and never could, see the force of objections made against the practice of turning round the chair when needed for sitting upon. It is only for the Lessons and the Sermon that any one needs a seat; and the noise and bustle of turning the chairs – only *four* times altogether, for between the Lessons no change is needed – would be no great inconvenience.

I am, dear Sir, Yours faithfully,
RURICOLA.

❖ ❖ ❖

Enter 'A Practical Man', whose knockabout style can still raise something of a smile. But half way through matters get serious as he points out the severe shortage of parish churches, and thus (in his eyes) the foolishness of introducing chairs which would mean that at a very time when space is at a premium, it would be used less efficiently. He finishes with a bravura description of the chaos which will ensue if chairs are rotated for prayer.

SIR – [It is said] that a church in which chairs are used looks better when there is nobody inside it, than a benched church. The author of this argument would, I presume, buy a hack [horse] because he went well, except when somebody was on his back. Churches, I submit, are made to look well when they are full, not when they are empty: their decorations are intended to impress worshipping congregations, not lionising connoisseurs. And no one asserts that a congregation seated in chairs looks better than one in benches.

The next argument is easy to state, very hard to interpret. It is said that chairs give 'life and elasticity to worship'. Now if locomotion were part of our ritual or if it were desirable that we should go and chat with our acquaintances 'between the acts', I quite see the advantage of chairs. Velocipedes would be better still. But as for the sake of his neighbours, if not his own, it is desirable that a man should stick to his place when he has once chosen it, as long as he remains in church, I cannot comprehend how the fact of its continuity or discontinuity with that of his neighbour's can affect the 'life and elasticity of his worship'.

The last argument is one which I must leave to the surprise of your readers. 'Londinensis' is explaining how the chair system makes the continental churches more attractive than our own: 'On the continent a church is an open, inviting place; you may go in and feel at home there; you may look at the pictures if you please, … or you may take a chair and sit down and read' – or light a cigar possibly? These are comfortable uses for a church, which are not sufficiently remembered. We are in want of a National Gallery just now, and the cry is all for public libraries; and just in the nick of time there are the city churches waiting to be demolished. Was there ever a happier adaptation of the supply to the demand?

And now I will turn from these equivocal advantages to the very formidable objections. Your correspondents admit that 'benches economise space'. But I hardly think they duly appreciate the extent to which this is the case. Pack a number of square chairs as you will and they will occupy much more room than benches. But, if you leave this packing to the chance will and whim of each new comer, the amount of space wasted by interstices, and crannies, and diverging angles will be incalculable. But beyond this, the great difficulty of a provision for kneeling will halve the remaining available room, whether you give two chairs to each worshipper, or compel each man to turn his own chair round; for in the latter case you must allow him in addition at least his own area to revolve in. So that you will buy your 'life and elasticity' by at least halving the church accommodation.

Your correspondents treat this difficulty very lightly. Do they forget the fearful disclosures of the census? that counting up all religions, only 29 per cent of the metropolitan population can attend any worship at all? in other words (admitting Mr. Mann's assumption, that only 52 per cent could go to church even were there room), that half of the immortal souls in London, for want of this despised 'accommodation', are as though the Gospel had never been preached. Do not, says 'Londinensis', cramp and destroy the life and elasticity of worship for the sake of a little more misnamed accommodation. [Are then] the objects of church accommodation in his judgement, not, as we used to think, that the Gospel might be preached and the bread of life dispensed to our heathen millions, but that churches may be inviting places where people can come in and look at pictures, or sit down and read a book!

The number of churches absolutely needed in England and Wales, setting aside the luxuries of 'lively and elastic' chair worship, which as I have shown, would require double room, is 580. Assuming the cost of each to be not less than £1000, they would require £580,000; and a Priest to each at a stipend of £150 would involve an outlay of £87,000, or a capital sum of £2,871,000, which with the £580,000 for building is equal to £3,451,040. When this sum has been supplied, 'Ruricola' may begin to think of allowing space for two chairs to each worshipper. But while Churchmen are straining, and vainly straining, every nerve to double our church accommodation, we cannot consent to halve it, that our churches, when empty, may look well to the eyes of a connoisseur.

But to set aside the question of accommodation, whichever way you deal with it, the question of kneeling is a hopeless obstacle to the use of chairs. Some stern ascetics, with souls and bodies superior to rheumatism and housemaids' knees, suggest that the worshippers should kneel where they are, on the cold bare stone. But I fear this view, however exalted. is simply impracticable. It is hardly enough now that we can coax or bully our people into kneeling at all.

There remains 'Ruricola's' favoured plan, the turning the chairs to kneel. Now though you may tell people that they ought to leave room for each other to turn their chairs, they practically never will. On crowded days, here and there one will leave room to turn easily, a great number will be hopelessly jammed, and the remainder will turn, if they turn at all, only after severe collisions and desperate struggles with the adjoining furniture. The clatter of clashing chair legs, the jostle of simultaneously pirouetting worshippers, the muttered apologies, and the smothered grumblings, will make a din that will doubtless add to the 'life and elasticity of the worship', much the sort of 'life' that may be met with in the crush room at the opera. And conceive the variety of positions which these varied results will entail. Let us glance at a group of the congregation as they will appear when the Creed and the succeeding scuffle are over, and each man has subsided into the position he intends to occupy during the Litany. A., a labouring man, is one of the happy few who has succeeded in turning his chair, and is therefore kneeling in the prescribed position; while behind him B., a zealous lady, has got her chair jammed, and is kneeling on the floor, whereby she will catch the rheumatism, and gets A.'s hobnailed boots into her chest. C., whose chair is also jammed, preferring comfort to propriety, kneels on his chair with his back to the altar, and thereby brings his nose in a vertical line over D.'s head, who is kneeling forward beneath him, and whom he soon discovers to be but partially acquainted with soap and water. If, under these circumstances, C. attends to his prayers, C. is a philosopher. The mingling of rich and poor is pretty in idea, but not fragrant in practice. E. meanwhile eludes the danger by standing up and hiding his head in his hat, according to the peculiar rite of the Anglican Church. F. cuts the knot by comfortably sitting still; and G., a moderate man, who wishes to strike a mean, be reverent, and yet avoid the rheumatism, keeps his knees within two inches of the ground, maintaining the while a painful equilibrium by a convulsive adhesion to half an inch of chair. Are these postures unlikely if we consider the habits of an English congregation? or is this the elasticity 'Londinensis' pines for.

Your obedient servant,

A PRACTICAL MAN.

The pedestrian style of our next correspondent may be an anticlimax after the rumbustious humour of 'A Practical Man', but for the first time he raises the question of how the church is used outside congregational worship.

SIR – The 'Practical Man' seems to ignore every possible use of a church except for congregational worship. But let us look at a few other services.

I catechise, every Sunday afternoon, before my congregation, a class of sixteen – eight boys and eight girls. I go down into the nave to my children, and what do I find? A passage four feet wide and of indefinite length. Consequence: I ask all my questions with my back to one half the church; they give all their answers with their backs to the other half. If I catechise my own children at home, what do I do? Do I set them with their backs against a wall or a table, and stand in front of them, like one of the dots in the arithmetical mark of division? Certainly not. I put them in a circle round me, and as near as they can stand, so as to leave elbow room. Much more should I wish to do this in church, where by this natural arrangement I should have my congregation before me, and be able to talk to them as well as to my children.

So, from the very same cause, what an unreal, cast-iron affair, a funeral generally is! The relatives cannot, as natural affection would prompt them to do, get near the coffin; so they disperse up and down, like a scattered congregation, and as if they had no more concern in the matter than so many bystanders, or rather by-sitters. So, to a certain extent, is it the case with regard to Baptism.

No; to make these services come home to people's hearts, we must be able to have a given space in any part of the church we want. Imagine fixed benches in a drawing room. What an intolerably stiff set of people must they be who could have introduced, or who could tolerate, them! And is there less stiffness, grimness, coldness – or call it what else you please – in their introduction into the house of God?

And so it is in more 'public services' too. I give a lecture on Wednesday and Friday evenings in Lent and Advent. I know I shall only have a few old people to hear me. I want them near the pulpit. But that can't be. Why not? Because where you have fixed benches, there, to a certain extent, you must have appropriation. Her ladyship sits in a cushioned chair at home and she likes one in church. As she comes pretty often, the cushion is left there. Other people follow her example. On the Wednesday evening, when I get up into the pulpit and look about me, I see six or seven benches nearest to me tabooed, some by cushions, and some by nicely bound books, and beyond these [are the old people who have come to the lecture]. Whereas, if my church had chairs, [they] would have been pulled out of the way, and my poor old people have put their own just where it suited them best.

[Yours faithfully]
A MORE PRACTICAL MAN.

The next three letters appeared in a single issue. The first questions whether movable benches are in any way practical. The two following ones propose technological solutions – a swivelling chair which could be rotated where it stood in order to provide a seat for kneeling on (this did not catch on), and the use of folding camp chairs (neither did this).

SIR – [In the example of a funeral I have just quoted] it may be said, perhaps, that *movable* benches would have allowed a sufficient area to be cleared for the funeral to be decently performed. But not only would the difficulty of moving heavy benches be quite sufficient to hinder the insufficient, and insufficiently paid, staff of a small country church from ever attempting it but also in a church filled from one end to the other, as most of our churches necessarily are, with benches, where are the benches to be removed to, when it is required to leave an open area for particular purposes? Your correspondent 'Ruricola' asked whether a pile of benches at the west end would not be many times more unsightly than a heap of chairs? But I would also ask whether it is possible, physically, to pile heavy benches one upon the other? In fact, Sir, I believe movable benches to be a delusion altogether. The choice must be between benches of any kind, or chairs; and I, for one, have no hesitation in choosing the latter.

 Your's, obediently
  E.A.E.

❖ ❖ ❖

MY DEAR SIR – Let us give chairs a fair practical trial, and, if they fail, abolish them ruthlessly. I don't know why the lower parts might not be joined to the upper (i.e. the seat), in something of the same sort of way as a music stool so that the seat might be turned round for kneeling purposes, without wheeling round the whole framework.

 Your's, truly
  F.L.

❖ ❖ ❖

MY DEAR SIR – May I venture to suggest a modification of the humble 'camp stool' of ordinary life, as, first, cheap; secondly, convenient; thirdly, very portable; fourthly, easily stowed away when not in actual use? I have often thought that the ordinary congregation at cathedral service might be accommodated in this way and I think that the absence of fixtures of any kind in the nave of a cathedral is even more desirable than in a church. The camp stool which I have in my eye is nothing but a strong seat stretched across two pairs of folding legs. It might be made of oak, with a brown leather or cloth seat, and would, I think, so present a much more ecclesiastical or, at all events, unobtrusive appearance than the chair one sees in foreign churches.

 Your's, obediently,
  SEORSUM.

Our old friend 'A Curate' returns to the fray. He is clearly having second thoughts. He previously argued strongly against chairs. Here he begins in the same vein by pointing out the difficulty of controlling where people will put their chairs, then comes up with a new suggestion – having a mix of benches and chairs (the chairs at the front). Finally, he argues that we may have to live with chairs simply because they solve the major problem of informal appropriation, caused by people leaving cushions and other markers in their regular pews.

DEAR SIR – There is a disadvantage attaching itself to chairs, which will be felt, more or less, at the very times when our 'More Practical Friend' is anxious to secure them. He says, 'we must be able to have a given space in any part of the church we want'. Granted. But, with chairs, how are we to prevent such spaces from being encroached upon, and so gradually lost, whilst the congregation is assembling?

It is quite possible that a large space before the chancel arch (possibly as large as one entire bay of the nave) may be at times wanted in many of our churches, for such occasional services as those to which your correspondent refers [e.g. funerals]; we may well allow chairs to take the place of the ordinary benches in this part of the church. And such an arrangement as this would also admit of our placing the pulpit more in the centre of the congregation – a great point in a nave of some length, or of an unusually large area.

Before concluding, however, I must say how heartily I sympathise with all that 'A More Practical Man' has written on the subject of appropriated seats. In fact this is the strong point in favour of chairs; so strong indeed, that we may after all have to give up our opposition to them. It is idle to expect the humbler part of our town populations to come to church, unless we throw the entire area freely open to them: poor, ill dressed men, very naturally, shrink from the risk of being intruders at church. Let a church start with 'unappropriated' benches; in a very little while, we shall find, as your correspondent says, seats here and there 'tabooed' by cushions and nicely bound books – in fact, claimed and appropriated by the more regular churchgoers. Now chairs would, in great measure, if not entirely, put an end to this sort of thing; benches must encourage it; and without the greatest care, and a kind of constant struggle, benches, however open, or however nominally 'unappropriated', will perpetuate all the worst and most practical evils of the pew system.

Benches, I am sure, are the best kind of seats for a church, if only we can make them bona fide *open* benches: if not, let us by all means have chairs. A somewhat slovenly congregation will be, at any rate, better than no congregation at all, and a little noise and confusion here and there in the service, will be far better than the propriety and stillness which now reign supreme in our poor bepewed churches.

Your faithful servant,
A CURATE.

The correspondence closes with another letter from 'Londinensis', pointing out that as a matter of fact chairs are successfully used in some churches, and giving as an example the church of St Peter, Sudbury, Suffolk. It may surprise the modern reader that worshippers at the church knelt directly on the floor. On the other hand, it may not surprise the modern reader that some benches in the aisles were retained 'to conciliate prejudice'. Today the building is in the care of the Churches Conservation Trust, and has red plastic chairs, suitable for concerts and other events.

There was a report on the church in the Illustrated London News for 12 September, 1857. It described the recent restoration by William Butterfield (it would not have pleased him that he was accidentally referred to as 'Butterworth'), explaining that 'the point continually aimed at . . . has been the making this house of God equally free to the poor and rich throughout, and the abolishing everything which might lead to a restoration of the slightest distinctions or appropriation'. The chairs were 'of a light and inexpensive kind', and during weekdays were largely cleared away, leaving only enough for those attending weekday services, thus allowing the architecture to be appreciated.

In his letter, 'Londinensis' is explicit about the way that chairs allow interiors to be reorganised for particular services, making clear his love of formality and ritual – many low churchmen would not have been too pleased at his suggestion of large candlesticks around a coffin.

St Peter, Sudbury, Suffolk, detail of an engraving published in 1857. The full image will be found in Chapter 30, Figure 8, page 464. (The Illustrated London News, 12 September 1857, p. 261)

SIR – In a letter which you were good enough to publish in *The Ecclesiologist* for June 1854, I advocated generally the use of chairs in churches, as helping to get rid of that extremely stiff, rigid arrangement of our congregations, which gives such a character of formalism to our churches and services, and is felt to be so great a hindrance to the church's work, and which I really believe to be one of the main causes, if not the chief cause of all, why Clergymen so often turn aside from the parish church, and gather together their weekday congregations in schoolrooms, or in cottages, for prayer and praise, and religious reading and instruction.

[At] S. Peter's at Sudbury, in Suffolk, the use of chairs has been adopted in the best way, and with the best results; only in directing attention to this church, it must not be supposed that it is at all singular in its use of chairs, for they are used now in very many churches throughout England, and their use is growing more common every day.

The flooring [at S. Peter's] is left entirely free, and open, and unencumbered without any seats of any kind being fixed upon it, just like the floor of a room. Chairs of a very plain character, with rush seats, are placed upon this flooring when wanted, and those who occupy them have thus a wooden floor under their feet, on which they can kneel, resting their hands on the back of the chair in front of them, the chairs being made purposely with a flat bar at the top, which is perfectly convenient for this purpose.

When the church is very full (which is the case every Sunday evening) the last comers place their chairs partly or entirely on the tiled passage, and thus the very passages of the church become available, when needed, for congregational purposes, a very narrow passage being always left by which you may thread your way in or out if you wish to do so. A few fixed benches against the north and south walls of the church are still retained, to conciliate prejudice, &c.; but the nave and one half of each aisle is entirely open.

Now it is evident that such a church as this is really practicable for religious purposes, which two-thirds of our English churches are not; for the most part our parish churches (especially in towns) are sacred to pew-openers and the gentry. Here, if there is a funeral, the coffin can be easily deposited on trestles in the middle of the nave, and the Clergyman standing at the east end of the coffin, and the mourners and bearers standing on each side of it, the service can be conducted with ease, and nature, and reality. And if the service is choral, the men and boys of the choir can stand on each side of the coffin, or in a half circle round the east end of it; and if lights are used (which is surely very desirable) three candles in large standard candlesticks can be placed on the floor on each side of the coffin. So again at a wedding; a carpet can be spread in the middle of the nave, and plenty of room given for the whole party to stand round about, perfectly at their ease, instead of being compressed, as is usually the case, into a narrow passage with hardly room to move.

[Thus] in a very crowded church, every inch of the floor may be made available, and for thinly attended services, just so many chairs as are wanted may be set out: while for funerals or marriages, or any special service, the church might be arranged just as is really wanted, and plenty of space secured wherever space is required, and ease and freedom of posture given, which our present ideas of pews or long benches render almost impossible.

I should be very sorry to be thought to imply that there is nothing whatever to be said against chairs; but I think that the balance of advantage or disadvantage is so strongly in their favour, as to make their general adoption highly desirable.

I remain, Sir, your's truly,
LONDINENSIS.

❖ ❖ ❖

And there, two years after its start, this bout of correspondence comes to a close. Written, as 'Londinensis' says, in an age of pew-openers and gentry, would it have surprised those involved to know that the choices they were grappling with – fixed pews versus movable benches versus chairs – were still a live issue one hundred and fifty years later, in a period unimaginably different from their own? – and that many of their argument still resonate today? – and that opinions today are held as strongly as they were in the 1850s? Perhaps not, for the concerns raised by seating in church are universal, and enduring.

16. 'The same fashion as the present ancient seats': G. G. Scott and the reseating of medieval churches

Suzanna Branfoot

CENTRAL TO THE ACTIVITIES associated with church restoration in the mid and later nineteenth century was addressing the need for free and socially equal seating in the nave, all facing east, with enough seats for the whole parish; and the change of use of the chancel back into the place for the clergy and choir, to be used for the more frequent celebration of communion, so with access from the nave. This required the removal of galleries and high-backed pews, a process that our predecessor Society was in the forefront of promoting. As a side effect, the pre-Victorian state of medieval church interiors has largely disappeared, or been unrecognised or forgotten.

G. G. Scott was one of the first of the Victorian architects to be involved with medieval church and cathedral restorations, Although the reorderings mostly concerned bench seating (today sometimes called 'pews'), as that became the norm, and will be the subject addressed in this chapter, it is interesting to see a small comment in his *Faithful Restoration* which suggested the use of chairs – making new seats 'placed in situations not originally intended for them, movable, and the advantage which may often be obtained by the use of chairs instead of benches in such positions'.[1]

Changes to interiors

Great St Mary's, Cambridge was described as follows by *The Ecclesiologist* in 1845, an example of what was deplored:

> Imagine the nave of a highly-enriched and magnificent Perpendicular church thus treated: the whole area of the aisles filled with pues as thickly packed as the cells of a honeycomb, the lofty and graceful chancel arch completely concealed and overlaid by a nondescript cabinet or drawing-room of oak, with sash windows and spacious staircase, the material oak, the design Italian, ... and this box, room or retreat, recessed some twenty feet backwards into the chancel, and entirely boarded up behind, so as to exclude all sight of the altar, east window and indeed of the chancel itself. ... Imagine huge galleries, precariously supported against the slender and graceful piers, and extending round the other three sides, intercepting the aisle-windows at mid-height and making so complete a theatre of a church ... that the words 'pit' and 'gallery' are recognised and familiar terms.[2]

At this church, Scott took out the large, raked, west-facing chancel gallery with its chandeliers, and moved the pulpit to the east end of the nave, making the east window and chancel arch visible, and giving access to the altar; but the side galleries remain,

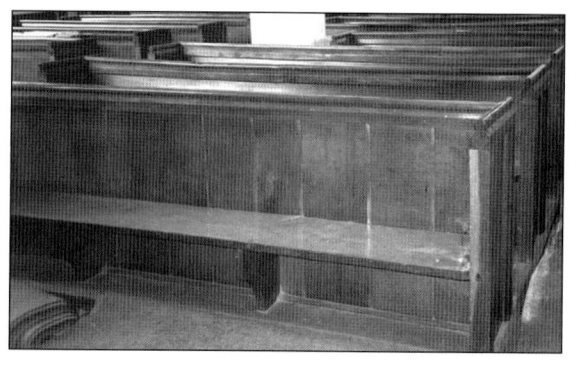

Fig. 1: St Mary, Great Milton, Oxfordshire, nave seating. On the left towards the rear of the photo the old seats, with wide, thick, horizontal oak planks; on the right the newer tongued-and-grooved woodwork.

for there was no other way of accommodating a sufficient number of students.

From the present day, it seems as if this pattern of removing galleries and pews and installing bench seating was the accepted standard at the time, but, then as now, people were unhappy with change, and it was not at first without problems affecting the architect. At St Andrew's, Bradfield (1845) he had to accommodate a single galleried pew for the Revd J. Connop, who was adamant that it should be re-installed. Scott wrote a letter strongly protesting about 'this wretched gallery' in order 'to save the Church the public dishonour which would be put upon it were that miserable feature to be re-erected'. It seems that Mr Connop 'disapproved of [the rector,] Mr Stevens' views on Church arrangements and on ritual matter' and so what Scott considered 'this hideous private gallery in the midst of a restored church' was put back, even though there was more correspondence and protest.[3]

In 1852 he was invited to restore Oundle church, including the removal of the galleries. This did not provoke just the personal reaction of a Mr Connop, but a public meeting of protest in the Town Hall, well-publicised with posters in huge black capitals, and involving the Grocers' Company and the masters of Laxton's School, whose boys occupied the galleries. Faced with such a situation, Scott withdrew and it was not until 1864 that he was invited back, the restoration went ahead, and it needed much discussion before galleries were allowed in the transepts to provide seating for up to 1500, for the parish and the school boys. A similar, though not so public, protest surrounded the reseating of Selby Abbey. It had, according to the Reverend J. Harper, 'inconvenient, very high and misshapen pews which are further rendered inaccessible to light and sound by six incongruous galleries heaped upon them'. The protest was through a local architect, James Audus, who claimed that the vicar was making himself 'obnoxious in the Parish', but Scott was invited to do the restoration and the abbey was reseated, without galleries or pews.

Use of medieval models

It is easy to assume that much of the bench seating during the nineteenth century was of similar designs, bought from a catalogue and perhaps machine-made. It is quite clear that Scott's attitude was that first, old benches in the church should be re-used wherever possible; and secondly, that if new were needed, old benches from churches of similar period or nearby be used as models, with consideration given to period styles, and particularly to local patterns and craftsmanship. In general, as his status increased, so he was more able to make these principles of conservation understood and followed, but they were generally expensive, for new pine could be cheaper than repairing, buying and carving oak; or it might be that he was chosen as architect for a scheme because the clergy involved approved of his ideas, despite their likely expense.

At Great Milton discovering the older seats inside the box pews, he decreed that they be unwrapped, the pews removed from the chancel, and the wood be used to repair and add seating where needed. The older wood is now characterised among other things by the size of the planks (Fig. 1). At Wing in Buckinghamshire, he specified 'all the seats which still retain their ancient position to be carefully repaired without being taken up or removed'.[4] However, as his report also indicated a need for considerable repairs, it must have made the task of the workmen involved much more difficult. Now it is all virtually invisible.

Fig. 2: St John the Baptist, Cirencester, Gloucestershire. On the left, the sole existing old bench end and on the right the new version, copied 350 times.

PEWS, BENCHES AND CHAIRS

Fig. 3: Church of the Assumption, Tysoe, Warwickshire. Old bench ends (left) and new (right). The old and new are used at opposite ends of the same bench.

Fig. 4: G. G. Scott notebook 23, 1847. Sketches from St Mary, Harmondsworth and St Martin, West Drayton. Scott also drew the interior of the great barn at Harmondsworth.

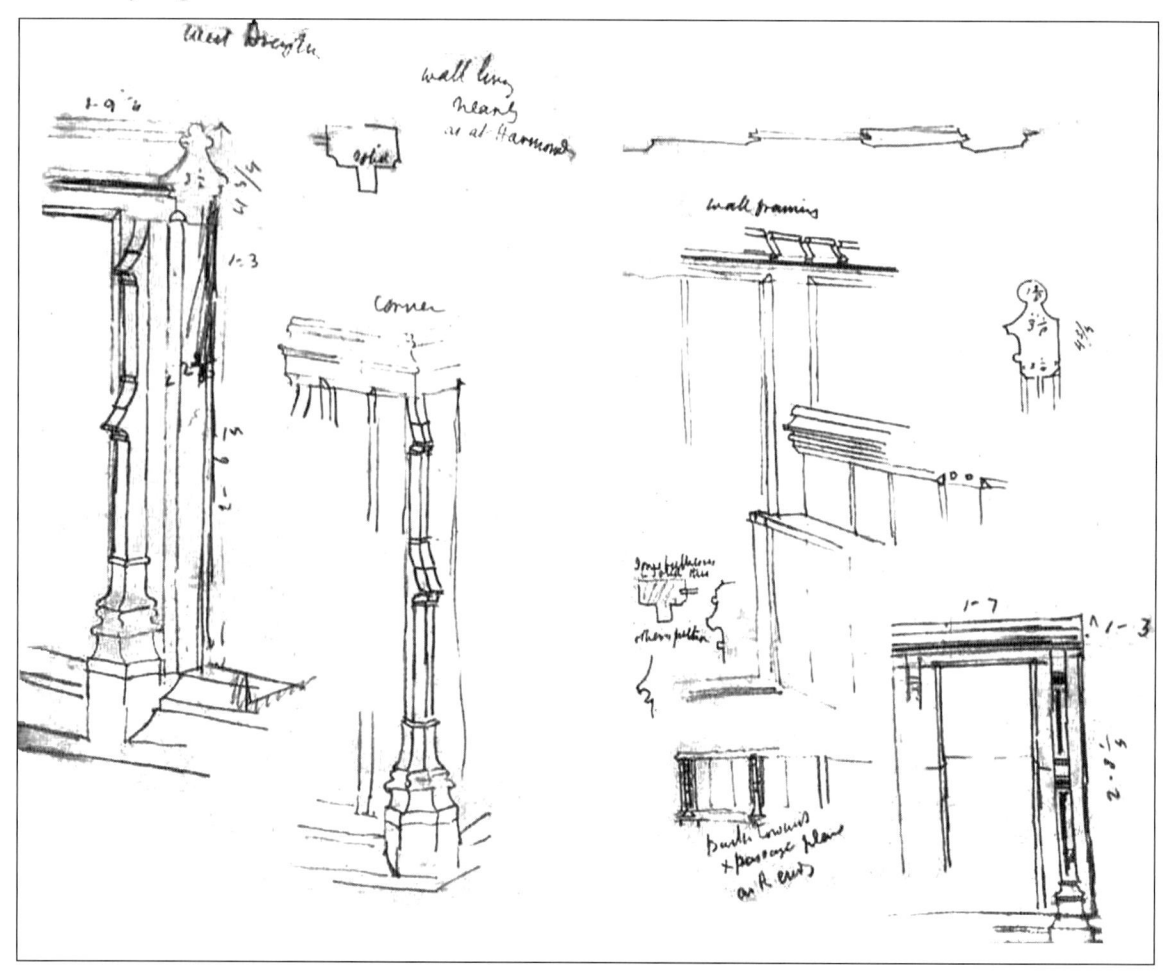

The notes for this restoration also included the sentence which became a common part of his specifications.[5]

> The new seats which are required to be made after precisely the same fashion as the present ancient seats.

So, in numerous churches all over the country, a local pattern of craftsmanship has been preserved and attention drawn to it by repetition. Cirencester's sole surviving old bench panel is now to the south of the central nave, and was, perhaps unimaginatively, reproduced 350 times for the rest of the church at a cost of £2 10s 0d each (Fig. 2). At this church there was also a request that there should be no poppy-heads, as they would be used inappropriately for hats! At Tysoe, Warwickshire (1854) the old bench ends are shared so each of the seats has one old and one new, with other new and old seating of a different design the other side of the crossing (Fig. 3). Scott's seating is almost always in oak which has now gained a patina of age, so it should be stressed here that unlike at Tysoe his work is often difficult to identify as Victorian, even when it is known that it is of the period.

It had been Scott's practice during the whole of his adult life to have a notebook with him, to record details of churches that he particularly liked or appreciated, and of those that he was working on. The details can show us where designs originated; some reflect his use of local precedent. As he said 'let them not be restored from mere conjecture or fancy… let hints be searched for from churches of corresponding age in the neighbourhood'.[6]

In 1848 when he was restoring the church at Iver, Bucks there were no old benches to copy and the pews were very dilapidated, but the notebooks show that at that time he visited a cluster of churches a few miles away at West Drayton, Hillingdon and

Fig. 5: St Peter, Iver, Buckinghamshire. A nave bench end and its back, showing the same details of buttresses, top mouldings and grooved planking as in the sketchbook shown in Figure 4.

Fig. 6: Examples of poppy-heads in churches restored by Scott, all with a variety of poppy-head bench ends throughout the nave. Left, St Mary Magdalene, Debenham, Suffolk. Centre, St Mary Magdalene, Newark, Nottinghamshire. Right, All Saints, Oakham, Rutland for which see also Figure 5c in Chapter 19, page 286.

Harmondsworth and drew panelling, benches with details of their joints, measurements and mouldings (Fig. 4). These old benches are the ones whose design and proportions were used for re-seating Iver (Fig. 5). They now look wholly unremarkable. These became some of the most commonly found designs, almost invariably in oak, in other churches of Early English and Decorated style.

Some of the new seating for enlarged churches became a celebration of woodcarving, especially of poppy-heads, being not copies of the old, but similar patterns based on the survivals. There were not always existing ones to base designs on, so they become a synthesis of many that Scott had seen and recorded in his notebooks. These resulted in forests of different poppy-heads, as at

Fig. 7: St John the Evangelist, Croxton Kerrial, Leicestershire. Left, one of the very lively old poppy-heads and, right, a new variation in the same spirit, possibly the eagle of St John (of the dedication).

Fig. 8: St James, Kilkhampton, Cornwall. The old bench end in the nave (left), the new (right) in the choir.

St Mary Magdalene, Debenham, Suffolk (1843–4), whose old bench ends became a useful precedent for Scott for other Perpendicular seating, St Mary Magdalene, Newark (1853–5), All Saints, Oakham, Rutland (1857–8) (Fig. 6), and others, all a fine exercise in iconography as well as an appreciation of woodworking. (Clearly they had no trouble with hats.)

In this style Croxton Kerrial, Leicestershire has a remarkable collection of old poppy-heads that remain in the nave. Scott restored this church in 1866–8, with a new north aisle, and

Fig. 9: Dorchester Abbey, Oxfordshire, old bench ends.

Fig. 10: St Mary, Great Milton, Oxfordshire, two old bench ends in the choir of the church.

reorganised the seating, adding extra new benches in the aisles. They have some excellent oak carving, which has been misdated as old work through its iconography and elaborate workmanship. Although there is no direct evidence available here that these poppy-heads are by Scott, they are worth seeing and typical (Fig. 7).

Many of the churches required new, additional or replacement choir seating, even though, as he wrote in 1852, chancels that were appropriated by the rector made extra difficulties for the church restorer: 'Surely the spoliator might have rested content with depriving the church of her revenues without seizing on the portion of the building which had been set apart for those who officiate in her services!'[7]

At Kilkhampton, Cornwall, a county (with Devon) of notable bench ends and woodcarving, the choir stalls were, as always where possible, based on the old existing ones. Here the bench ends that remained, though worm-eaten, were moved into the nave with some additions, and the new used for the choir stalls. They have fine animals on top, saints and bishops below; some are a direct copy of the old work, and some with dogs, squirrels and other standing figures are new designs but with the style and essence of the old (Fig. 8). At Great Milton, Oxfordshire in the choir there are some fine fifteenth-century bench ends with carved square poppy-heads and panelled sides. These Scott mended, using the designs as inspiration for the new. Other designs are based on some old work from nearby Dorchester Abbey, surely from the hand of the same medieval craftsman as at Great Milton (Figs. 9, 10 & 11). Some of Scott's finest woodwork can be found in cathedral choirs, but is outside the scope of this chapter.

Fig. 11: Great Milton, three bench ends from Scott's restoration. The leftmost is based on an old bench end in the church (compare Figure 10), the other two are based on old bench ends at Dorchester Abbey (compare Figure 9).

The role of the craftsmen

It is clear from Scott's notes, correspondence, reports and specifications that he was deeply concerned that old wood should be preserved, and old designs used. The designs become recognisable, or familiar, because of their presence in churches that he had restored, but there is little evidence that the designs are directly his own work; more that the precedents for his ideas, with measurements and details of mouldings, can be found in the medieval churches of this country, and subsequently in his notebooks. Much of the woodwork for his church restorations was done by local craftsmen, or otherwise by his favourite firms of Farmer and Brindley of London, Rattee and Kett of Cambridge which included Caroline Rattee as well as her husband, and Ruddle & Thompson of Peterborough, all of whom had craftsmen who could no doubt reproduce the kind of designs that were wanted. He clearly was concerned that there should be some recognition of the date of the church, for Perpendicular naves have Perpendicular seating, Decorated and Perpendicular poppy-heads are distinguished, though in earlier medieval styles of seating the date/style is less identifiable, probably because old seating of earlier periods is not often found.

❖ ❖ ❖

In 1843 the Cambridge Camden Society published *A Few Words to Parish Clerks and Sextons*. On the subject of 'pues', it was remarked:

> I suppose that your church is infested with some of those very ugly… things called pues or pews. … It is of course your duty to keep them clean and decent; … but when you do this you should take as much care to keep tidy the old-fashioned open seats where the poor people sit. These seats, carved in hearty four-inch old English oak, not built of miserable half-inch pieces of deal, are a great deal worthier of your care than the pues. Therefore you should not leave them dirty or greasy. They are always good in their way, and often very handsome indeed.[8]

And so, indeed, are many of those made in the nineteenth century, of good materials and high-quality craftsmanship.

Notes
1. G. G. Scott, *A Plea for the Faithful Restoration of our Ancient Churches* (London, 1852), 135.
2. *The Ecclesiologist*, 4 (1845), 253–54
3. Stevens, Connop correspondence, 1848. Family collection.
4. Report on Wing Church, Bucks, 13 September 1847.
5. Sketchbook 9.
6. G. G. Scott, *A Plea*, 31.
7. G. G. Scott, *A Plea*, 69.
8. *A Few Words to Parish Clerks and Sextons*, p. 5, paragraph 7. Reprinted in Christopher Webster (ed.), *'temples … worthy of His presence': the early publications of the Cambridge Camden Society* (Reading, 2003).

17. Some seating designs in churches by John Hayward of Exeter

Jo Cox

Author's note: The following is based on an examination of the seating in only four of the many Devon churches restored or newly built by John Hayward of Exeter. The author was persuaded by the editors that it was nevertheless worth including as a preliminary study, as it was thought to raise several points of interest.

THE THREE SEATS illustrated in Figure 1 were all erected in 1845 in Devon churches restored by the same architect, John Hayward. They establish that an architect might specify box pews and open benches with carved ends in the same year, and in the same building (seats 1b and 1c are in the same church and part of a single scheme). They raise the question of how much responsibility early Victorian church architects had for the design of congregational seating and defeat any easy assumption that an architect was likely to specify, or even favour, a particular design or set of designs for seats.

John Hayward (c.1808–91) was the leading church architect in Devon in the 1840s. He was an honorary member of and architect to the Exeter Diocesan Architectural Society (EDAS), established

Fig 1: Three pews installed in Devon in the same year, 1845, by the architect John Hayward. 1a (left): St Michael, Sowton, rebuilt for a high-church patron, the pew carved with the IHS symbol. 1b and 1c (centre and right): at Whimple, St Mary, restored the same year, a box pew and an open pew with non-symbolic carving.

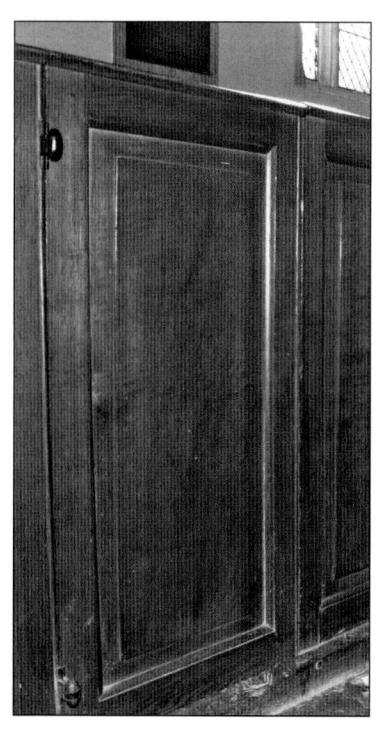

in 1841. This society functioned as a meeting point for local liturgical and architectural reformers. These were tolerated, for the most part, by the bishop of Exeter, Henry Phillpots. Hayward's first known church in Devon pre-dated the establishment of EDAS. It was built in 1839 at Tipton St John, a wide, aisleless church in the lancet style with a shallow chancel, west gallery and roof of skinny tie beam trusses. There could be no greater contrast between Tipton St John and his next church building, at Exwick, built in 1842 as a convincingly Gothic chapel of ease to St Thomas' church, Exeter. The project was promoted by the high churchman and founder of EDAS, the Revd John Medley, later bishop of New Brunswick. Exwick was described in *The Ecclesiologist* as 'the best specimen of a modern church we have yet seen'.[1] Hayward's career seemed set on the high-church course, developing his reputation and finding commissions through the network of incumbents and patrons he encountered at EDAS meetings.

In 1845 Hayward substantially rebuilt both Sowton church on the outskirts of Exeter, for the wealthy high-church patron, John Garratt, living in a former bishop's palace (later rebuilt by William White) and Whimple church, also close to Exeter in East Devon. The Whimple scheme was led by the newly-arrived rector, Lloyd Sanders.

Sowton has a splendid and very well-preserved Tractarian interior, the chancel lavishly decorated with tiles and painted colour and furnished with carved fittings (Fig. 2). There is an overriding sense of through-design to the church, from roof to heating grilles. The open benches in the nave are a good match for the chancel in elaboration, correct style and symbolism (Figs. 1a & 3). Their ends are carved with a range of Decorated Gothic tracery designs, some incorporating the symbols of the Passion (Fig. 4). The stops on the bench end mouldings are decorated, and the ends are fixed into moulded sills. The freestanding book rests at the east of the blocks of nave benches have carved ends with poppy-heads.

It comes as something of a surprise to know that, in the same year, less than 15 miles away at Whimple, Hayward was specifying box pews. (These are not the latest box pews in the county, which – as far as is currently known – are those at Cullompton, part of the 1848–50 restoration by Edward Ashworth.)[2]

The contractor for the Whimple restoration was Charles Force of Exeter. The pre-1845 seating had been a mixture of box pews and sixteenth-century open benches carved with a variety of designs but all clearly by the same hand. Lloyd Sanders, the rector, made himself personally responsible for the supervision of

Fig. 2: St Michael, Sowton, a well-preserved Tractarian interior (rebuilt by John Hayward, 1845).

Fig. 3: St Michael, Sowton, elaborate pews in the nave.

Fig. 4: St Michael, Sowton, where some of the pews of 1845 show symbols of the Passion, here the spear and ladder.

the restoration, but it is clear from the documentation that other individuals also had their say: notably T. W. Buller, the chief landowner, who had a box pew by right of faculty and promised £102 towards the cost of the restoration at an early stage and Mr Smith, another substantial landowner who, in 1822 had no fewer than eight appropriated sittings as well as his own box pew immediately beneath the pulpit. Parish subscribers to the restoration received a sitting for every £6 they contributed and also, we must presume, had an interest in what sort of seat they were getting for their money.[3]

The faculty for the Whimple restoration work includes an unusually detailed specification and a good set of drawings.[4] The

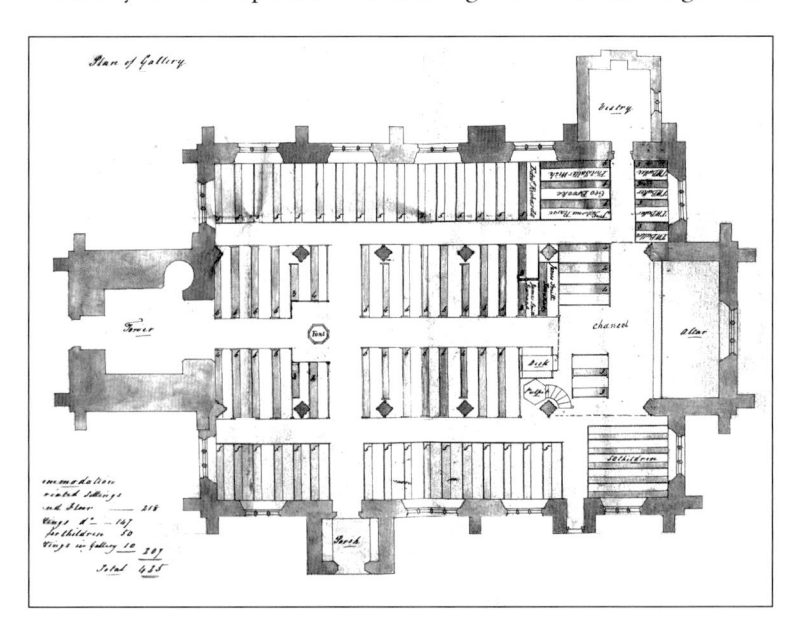

Fig. 5: The plan for the repewing of St Mary, Whimple (John Hayward, 1845). As discussed in the text, the appropriated seating in the aisles (and perhaps the chancel) was built as box pews, that in the body of the nave as open bench seating. (With acknowledgements to the Devon Record Office and Exeter Diocesan Registrar)

Fig. 6: St Mary, Whimple, the north-west block of nave seating, showing the carefully-repaired sixteenth-century bench ends.

seating plan shows that in the rebuilt church, the appropriated seats, mostly in the aisles but (according to the plan) some in the chancel, were to be box pews, with free seats in open benches in the nave (Fig. 5). The Cambridge Camden Society may have railed against box pews in their 1844 pamphlet, *Twenty-Four Reasons for Getting Rid of Church Pews (or Pues)*, but those who could afford rented seats at Whimple evidently still favoured the privacy and cachet they provided and were untroubled that the free seats at Whimple provided a much better view of the sanctuary.

Fig. 7: St Mary, Whimple, sixteenth-century bench ends. 7a (left): The making good of a flap seat is clearly visible. 7b (right): A half bench end, reframed in 1845.

271

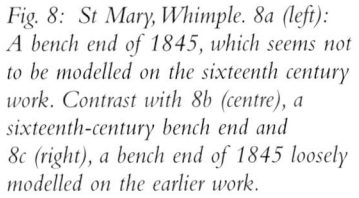

Fig. 8: St Mary, Whimple. 8a (left): A bench end of 1845, which seems not to be modelled on the sixteenth century work. Contrast with 8b (centre), a sixteenth-century bench end and 8c (right), a bench end of 1845 loosely modelled on the earlier work.

Hayward's design drawing survives for the simple 'skeleton' seats in the gallery in the west tower, which he rebuilt (subsequently removed). However his instructions to the joiners for the box pews were not accompanied by drawings. He specified the overall dimensions including the height of the partitions (lower than the previous box pews) and ordered the joiners to re-use as much as they could of the old box pew fabric, but he did not specify, for example, numbers and types of panels, for the doors and ends.[5]

> The fronts of the seats tinted blue in the plan [the box pews] except those in the chancel are to be constructed of the old wainscot framing reduced to the height of 3 feet with the deficiencies supplied with new deal framing moulded to correspond.

The specification for the new open benches with carved ends (described as 'standards' in the documentation) also required the re-use of what were existing sixteenth-century carved ends but was even more cavalier as to the decorated finish of the new seats (my italics):

> The whole of the seats tinted red as well as those in the Chancel tinted blue are to be open and are to have 3½ deal carved standards *similar to the present ones in the Church varied in Patten* framed & pinned into the oak sill before described… such of the old carved standards etc as are sound and fit to be repaired may be used in the new work with new mouldings where requisite.

Fig. 9: St Philip and St James, Ilfracombe, Devon (John Hayward, 1856), said to be 'evangelical from the start'.

Detailed drawings of the new bench end designs by Hayward may once have existed and been lost, but it seems more likely that he left the design – as the specification reads – to the joiners. Observation of the surviving seating shows that the carved ends of the sixteenth-century benches were carefully repaired (Fig. 6), in spite of being battered by age and scarred by previous flap seats (Fig. 7a); they include a half-bench end, which was re-framed (Fig. 7b). The 1845 carved ends are a robust set, using large scale designs, like their predecessors. Some closely followed the model of individual earlier benches, others are more obviously 'new' (Fig. 8). The general arrangement of the new benches placed the sixteenth-century ends at the west end of the church with the 1845 ends in pride of place, facing the nave aisle.

The contrast between Sowton and Whimple is no doubt explained by the difference between the clients, and the funding of the restorations. Whimple cost £1,500 and came in according to estimate.[6] Sowton cost just over £3,000, a huge sum (this included a scheme of stained glass by Thomas Willement).[7]

Sowton was designed for a wealthy client determined to have, and able to pay single-handedly for, a Tractarian interior of the highest quality and Hayward produced accordingly. At Whimple, he had to pay attention to funds and to the parishioners who contributed to the funding, including the four who held seats by right of faculty. This meant recycling old material and, in the box pews, old-fashioned design. The differences in the client and the funding determined the kind of seating provided and the role played by the architect. The contrast between the two projects also adds to what we understand of Hayward. He may have made his reputation from, and is best remembered for, his association with the high church movement in the Diocese of Exeter, but he was a man of business,[8] and that meant pleasing his clients, whatever the complexion of his own theology. Hayward's first church after Exwick was St Mark's, David Place, St Helier, Jersey (1842–4) with a gallery, for the low church minister the Revd Francis Jeune, later bishop of Peterborough. Taking a wider view, it seems that, at Whimple, at any rate, having specified the dimensions of the seating, he left the decorative design of those with carved ends up to the contractor.

A small sample of congregational seating in later Hayward churches, both new and restored, shows a wide range of seat design, though no more box pews. His large new 1856 church of

Fig. 10: St Philip and St James, Ilfracombe, relatively plain bench ends, complete with numbers and umbrella holders.

Fig. 11: St Peter, Bratton Fleming, Devon, restored by Hayward in 1861. Very simple bench ends.

St Philip and St James at Ilfracombe (evangelical from the outset, according to the recent churchwarden) has plainer bench ends than either Sowton or Whimple, with chamfered sides, a roll-moulded top rail and sunk panels with blind traceried heads with minor variations in the tracery (Fig. 9). The benches are numbered (Fig. 10) and pew rents continued to be charged until World War II (information from the churchwarden).

At Bratton Fleming, a small village church in North Devon, Hayward's restoration of 1861 included what can best be described as 'budget benches' with shouldered ends. The whole set (over 45 in all), including the flooring, cost only £180. The design of the ends was possibly chosen from a catalogue (Fig. 11) but satisfied the customer, the rural dean commenting that the seating was 'quite a pattern for any church in the Deanery'.[9] At the specific request of the churchwardens Hayward designed a charming version of an old-fashioned west gallery with seats with tall backs 'for the purpose of an Orchestra'.[10] This conservative element seems never to have been used for a church band, a harmonium being installed as part of the restoration, and may have been requested out of sentiment for things past.

It would be interesting to know whether other contemporary architects are associated with a similar variety of seating or whether they, or later architects, can be seen to have exerted more influence over their clients in the design of seating.

Acknowledgements

The author is very grateful to research on Sowton undertaken by the late Professor Chris Brooks, and to the following for discussion that has contributed to this chapter: Dr Stuart Blaylock, Dr Geoff Brandwood, Dr Martin Cherry, Trevor Cooper, Hugh Harrison, and Francis Kelly.

Notes

1. *The Ecclesiologist*, 2 (1843), 23.
2. *ex info* Dr Stuart Blaylock.
3. Whimple Vestry minutes, 1843–1972, Devon RO 1418A add2/PV1; and Whimple Churchwardens' Account Book, 1791–1859, Devon RO 1418A add/PW1.
4. Devon RO 1418A add2/PW1 and Whimple Faculties.
5. Devon Record Office, 1418A add2/PW1, folios 7–9.
6. Notes in the back of the Whimple burial register, Devon RO 1418A/PR6.
7. Photocopied pages from John Garratt's 1845 ledger in the Devon nineteenth-century churches project archive, gathered by Professor Chris Brooks, no reference to source. The archive is currently looked after by Jo Cox, to whom application may be made to for its use.
8. Hayward was a stickler for punctuality and advised his pupil, Robert Medley Fulford 'never let pleasure interfere with business' (Devon RO, recollections by Fulford, uncatalogued deposit, 2604).
9. Rural Dean's Book, held at Bratton Fleming.
10. North Devon RO, 1506A/P1.

18. Church seating: a view from Suffolk

James Bettley

THE HIGH QUALITY of the medieval woodwork in Suffolk's churches is well known. 'For open timber roofs', wrote Pevsner, 'Suffolk stands supreme', and the county's font covers and screens are equally famous.[1] Pevsner also praised Suffolk's medieval benches, with the best to be found at Fressingfield and Dennington; indeed he pointed out that Munro Cautley (not, it must be conceded, an altogether impartial judge) considered Fressingfield's to be 'perhaps the most beautiful in the country'.[2] These have all the usual features that one would expect: richly traceried ends of varying patterns, poppy-heads, little figures on the arms, and carved seat backs. In addition, the back of the westernmost bench on the north side is carved with emblems of the Passion, and the corresponding bench on the south side with emblems of St Peter and St Paul – to whom the church is dedicated – and of St Andrew, Peter's brother. In 1887 the interior of the church was restored by Bottle & Olley, a firm of architects from Yarmouth, in the course of which a west gallery was removed, together with a number of box pews, and the old benches were restored. This work was skilfully executed – to the extent that it is not always easy to see what is old work and what is new – by Robert Godbold, a woodcarver from Harleston, just across the county border in Norfolk. As well as restoring the nave seating, he also made new choir stalls that imitate the old benches and are, in their own way, every bit as good as their medieval precedents, and a new pulpit (Fig. 1). In 1908, Bottle & Olley also designed a new reredos and lectern, and the same high standard

Fig. 1: St Peter & St Paul, Fressingfield, Suffolk, looking from the fifteenth century through to the nineteenth and twentieth (see text).

Fig. 2: All Saints, Laxfield, Suffolk. A medieval bench converted to a box pew.

was continued here and in further sanctuary panelling which was added in 1922. The identity of the maker of the later work has not yet come to light.

What the work at Fressingfield illustrates is the way in which some nineteenth-century craftsmen respected and worked with the achievements of their medieval predecessors. Is this something that did not happen to the same extent in previous centuries, and how widespread was the practice in the nineteenth century? At Laxfield, close to Fressingfield, the nave seating demonstrates a certain continuity, but one based more on expediency than on respect. Here there are, towards the back of the nave, a few rows of medieval benches some of whose ends, still with poppy-heads, have Early Renaissance patterns that show them to be early sixteenth rather than fifteenth century. Further east more of these benches were turned into box pews in the seventeenth or eighteenth century by adding panels and doors on top of them in a very practical sort of way (Fig. 2). Right at the front are new-built box pews, although even these incorporate Early Renaissance panels that are probably domestic in origin. The early nineteenth century further contributed a block of tiered seating at the back of the nave, labelled 'For Young Men and Boys', but fortunately there seems not to have been the money for a thorough restoration.

The later nineteenth century frequently and unobtrusively took what there was of medieval work and made use of it to provide the seating that churches by then required. At Blundeston, near Lowestoft, restored by J. J. Scoles in 1849–50, we find that the medieval bench ends were reused, and placed against the walls as one end of new benches; the new work has poppy-heads to match the old (Fig. 3). At Great Bealings, near Woodbridge, new benches

Fig. 3: St Mary, Blundeston, Suffolk. Nineteenth-century benches with fifteenth-century bench ends against the wall.

with poppy-heads, carved with birds, animals, and human figures, were modelled on surviving medieval benches that were gathered together at the west end – a frequent practice, although seldom done with such elaborate skill as is demonstrated here. Choir stalls were introduced at the same time, the finials designed by Major Edward Moor of Bealings House (Fig. 4). The work was executed in 1845–50 by Henry Ringham, who was probably Suffolk's foremost woodcarver of the nineteenth century and whose importance was first highlighted by Cynthia Brown in 1980.[3] Ringham (1806–66) was based in Ipswich and is said to have been involved in the restoration of more than 160 churches, 80 of them in Suffolk. Architects for whom he worked included Gilbert Scott, Benjamin Ferrey, and, in particular, R. M. Phipson, but he was also sufficiently experienced in church restoration work to act on occasion as architect, for example at Swilland, Tuddenham St Martin and Wetheringsett.

The confidence of nineteenth-century architects and craftsmen in handling medieval work did not always, of course, achieve such good results as those of Godbold and Ringham, and their twentieth-century successors were usually more cautious. This did not necessarily mean, however, that the tradition had died. Tuddenham St Martin also contains woodwork made by Ernest Barnes of Ipswich in the 1940s and 50s, designed by H. M. Cautley. The collaboration of these two experts can best be seen at Mildenhall, where the nave is filled with their benches that replace seating of 1850–53 by Thomas Farrow of Bury St Edmunds. Barnes's benches were made to a high standard in the best Suffolk tradition, with carved ends and poppy-heads, and were designed by Cautley as a memorial to his wife, Mabel Seaman

Fig. 4: St Mary, Great Bealings, Suffolk. Choir stalls of 1845–50, made by Henry Ringham.

Fig. 5: St Mary & St Andrew, Mildenhall, Suffolk. Twentieth-century benches, the continuation of a 500-year Suffolk tradition.

Cautley, who died in 1958 (Fig. 5). Cautley himself died before the work was completed. On the backs of the westernmost benches are the initials MSC and HMC, and modest inscriptions recording E. E. Barnes, makers, Ipswich, and H. Brown, carver. Their names deserve to be remembered.

Notes

1. N. Pevsner, *Suffolk* (1974), 37.
2. H. M. Cautley, *Suffolk churches and their treasures* (London, 1937; Ipswich, 5th edn, 1982), 145.
3. C. Brown, 'Two Victorian woodcarvers: the benches in the churches of Tuddenham St Martin, St Mary's Great Bealings and Rushmere St Andrew', *Proceedings of the Suffolk Institute of Archaeology and History*, 34 (1980), 285–86. I am also grateful to Cynthia Brown for information on Godbold's work, and to Charles Tracy for enlightening visits to Fressingfield and Laxfield in June 2009.

19. Victorian church seating: variations upon a theme

Geoff Brandwood

MONDAY 30 SEPTEMBER 1844 was an important day in the Wiltshire village of Dilton Marsh where the big new church of the Holy Trinity, designed in Norman Revival style by T. H. Wyatt, was being consecrated. Its predecessor was a medieval building that was both too small and too far away. It was also too old-fashioned as it was stuffed with box-pews, a three-decker pulpit and a pair of galleries – precisely those things that were being excoriated in the pages of *The Ecclesiologist*. Happily the old church still survives, cared for by the Churches Conservation Trust, with one of the most complete Georgian village church interiors anywhere in England. For us it is quite charming but not to people with advanced taste in the 1840s. Back then, those who would worship at the new church in Dilton Marsh could look forward not only to its convenient location and greater capaciousness but a further novelty – open bench seating (Fig. 1). The Dilton Marsh seating, with its little elbows, now looks unremarkable enough because it is the kind of thing, with many variations, which by the 1890s had displaced the old box-pews in all but a tiny percentage of churches and which is still a dominant visual feature in many thousands of them today.

No one has yet done the detailed research to show when, where and by whom this new style of seating was introduced and exactly what its design sources were. Nor has any in-depth work been carried out on the evolution of such seating schemes. Perhaps it all seems too familiar and the amount of surviving work too daunting. But nonetheless it is important. Consequently, I make no special claim for the importance of the Dilton Marsh

Fig. 1: Holy Trinity, Dilton Marsh, Wiltshire. An early example of open Victorian seating from 1844. These benches are labelled 'Free' and thus intended for the poor.

seating, other than to say it is a fairly early example of the new ways of doing things.

This chapter claims to be no more than an introductory exploration of some aspects of Victorian and Edwardian congregational seating schemes and I hope it may encourage others to work on what is, to my mind, a most interesting subject.[1] It is based on many years of looking at Victorian churches and on two specific pieces of research. The first of these is my PhD research in the early 1980s on church-building and restoration at 387 Anglican churches in Leicestershire and Rutland in the period 1800–1914.[2] Seating did not receive particularly close attention but I did studiously note the shape of the bench ends and, in all but a handful of cases, established when the seating was installed. In 2003 I pulled together such information as I could into a report for one of the editors of this volume who was then Head of Research Policy for Places of Worship at English Heritage. The present chapter reworks much of that material. The second piece of work was commissioned in 2008 in connection with a partnership project between English Heritage and the diocese of Salisbury in which I headed a small team looking at the heritage aspects of 78 churches in the deaneries of Heytesbury (Wiltshire) and Sherborne (Dorset) in that diocese.[3] As this was a rapid survey, time for primary documentary research was limited, but we were able to plan ahead to collect data which I had not recorded in Leicestershire.

Using the information derived from these two studies this chapter will look at a number of matters. It will briefly discuss the survival rates of Georgian and earlier seating schemes, before considering when Victorian schemes were put in, which, of course, is much the same thing as plotting a graph of the rise and decline of the wider ecclesiological church-building and restoration movement. Then, after a few comments on Victorian versus medieval types, it will attempt a tentative, broad classification of bench ends and give some idea of the relative numbers of different types. A number of miscellaneous aspects of congregational seating will then be briefly examined. The next chapter takes a look at the information available on seating from the pages of church furnishers' catalogues.

Ancient or modern?

Relatively few churches are wholly or predominantly seated with pre-Victorian seating schemes. Of the 78 churches in the Salisbury study just two (Trent and Yetminster, both Dorset) have extensive medieval seating, while nine have seventeenth- or eighteenth-century schemes. Box-pews were only encountered at

Holnest, Dorset and Maiden Bradley, Dorset. Detailed figures are not available for Leicestershire but I estimate the number of churches with extensive seventeenth-century or earlier seating at less then ten and those with box-pews at about a dozen.

When were Victorian seating schemes put in?

Graph 1 plots the known (or very probable) dates of surviving seating schemes installed in Leicestershire and Rutland between 1830 and 1914.[4] It shows a fairly predictable pattern. Little happened in the early 1830s. Even in the 1840s these counties were slow off the mark, with the first 'correct' schemes not appearing until 1845–6. Then things took off rapidly, with a peaking of activity in the 1860s, a pattern met with in many other counties.

Graph 2 is from the Salisbury project. The number of churches in the sample was far smaller than in the Leicestershire study and the number was reduced further by the fact that the rapid survey approach did not allow for the in-depth research into the historical sources that might have thrown up precise dates. Nonetheless, the pattern is the same as for Leicestershire with work peaking in the 1860s.

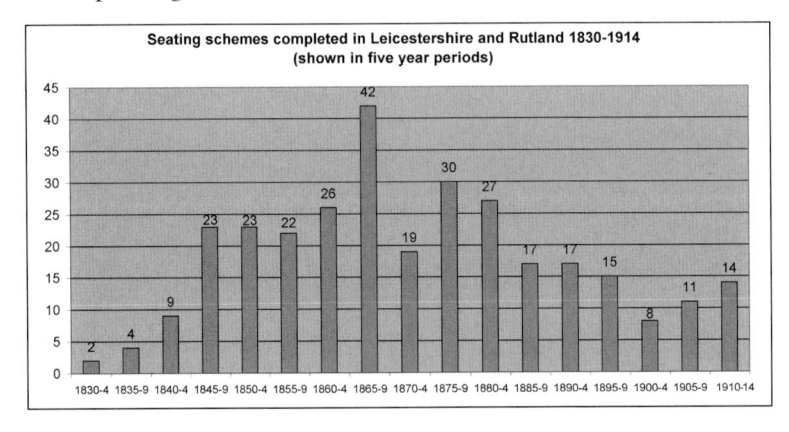

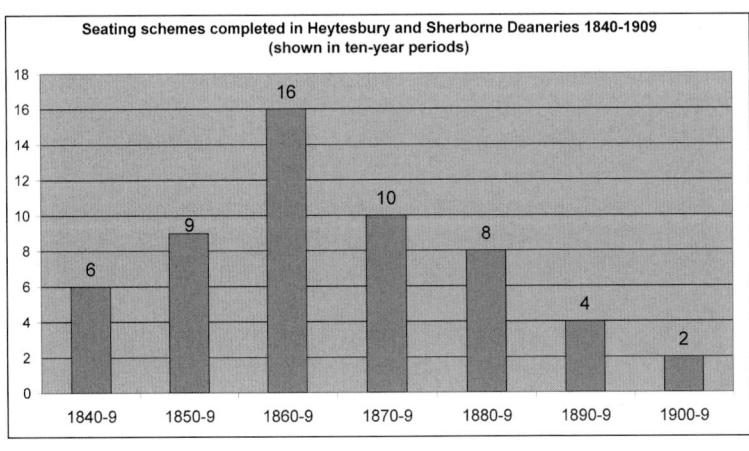

Graph 1 (above) shows the number of seating schemes installed in Leicestershire and Rutland between 1830 and 1914 in five-year periods. For example, there were 42 such schemes completed in the five years from 1865.

Graph 2 (below) shows similar information for two deaneries in the diocese of Salisbury, presenting the number of seating schemes for each decade. For example, 16 schemes were completed in the 1860s.

A useful comparator from another part of the country comes from Devon in 1861. In that year *The Ecclesiologist* was pleased to print a report on the 'progress of the anti-pew movement in the archdeaconry of Exeter'. Here the archdeacon's charge revealed that out of the 193 churches and chapels, 74 (38 per cent) displayed 'the satisfactory progress of better church arrangement' with 'more or less uniform' seating.[5] The 'progress', it has to be said, was patchy with just one church out of sixteen in Dunsford deanery being properly appointed, rising to twelve out of fifteen in the right-minded deanery of Plymtree. The benefits were palpable, with the writer having been told that at one church with the new, approved seating, 'the congregation are now to be seen regularly on their knees during the time of prayer'.

The sources of Victorian church-seating design

J. C. Cox's classic study of 1916, *Bench-ends in English Churches*, presents a selection of the riches to be found in our churches.[6] The focus is chiefly on medieval examples although attention is also given to work down to the early seventeenth century. Many of Cox's examples are extraordinarily lavish and have a richness that in Victorian times was usually only reserved for chancel seating. It is reasonable to suppose that such cases were always exceptional in medieval times and that their survival is due to the recognition of this special quality by successive generations of parishioners. The overwhelming majority of old bench ends illustrated by Cox are of two types – square-headed and those with poppy-heads. He illustrates about thirty schemes of each. Both reappear in Victorian times but in very different proportions (see below). One medieval type that was not resurrected by the Victorians, so far as I know, except in chancels, was that incorporating figure-carving either in the place of the poppy-

Fig. 2: St Michael, Garway, Herefordshire. Late thirteenth-century (Bond) or sixteenth- or seventeenth-century (Pevsner) – such is the near impossibility of dating such elemental, functional work short of dendrochronological investigation. The round-topped end made a reappearance in the Victorian age. (Photo: J. C. Cox, Bench-ends in English Churches *(London, 1916), 104)*

head or balanced on a flat surface of the bench end and found in some numbers in East Anglian churches. By the nature of his book, Cox illustrated the finest and most elaborate examples in the land but he also included a few simple examples which have characteristics taken up in abundance by Victorians when equipping or re-equipping their churches (Figs. 2 & 3).

Victorian bench ends – a typology

Attempting a classification of Victorian bench ends is dangerous since the designs are myriad and often shade into one another. It is therefore a subject where minute statistical precision is pointless and the aim here is to give an overview of what appear to be the main types. Apart from a few broad comments I have not attempted to give a historical account of typological development, partly because I have not carried out the necessary analysis and partly because any suggestion of chronological progression is undermined by the fact that same types can be seen to run and run for decades – a point which is very evident from Chapter 20. The following broad types have emerged from the Leicestershire and Salisbury studies.

Square-headed ends

By far the most common bench ends are those with a square, or flat, head (Figs. 4a–c). They account for 30 per cent of all seating schemes in Leicestershire; in the Salisbury study some 40 per cent of the 59 Victorian schemes have them. The top is usually moulded and there is typically a sunk panel taking up much of the surface area. Small, elongated buttresses are often positioned towards the edges. Just as in medieval times, when the budget would stretch to it, the sunk panel was an ideal place for embellishment in the form of blind tracery.

Fig. 3: St Michael, Clapton-in-Gordano, Somerset. Variously dated to the thirteenth or fourteenth centuries, these rugged, thick bench ends have double elbows. A great many Victorian ends have elbows but always, so far as is known, just on the eastward edge of the ends. (Photo: Cox, 9)

Fig. 4a (left): Holy Trinity, Crockham Hill, Kent. Plain yet stylish square-ended oak benches of 1842.
Fig. 4b (centre): St Mary the Virgin, Goldington, Bedfordshire. Square-ended benches with recessed panels and mini-buttresses were very popular. These ones date from the 1860 restoration by a local architect, James Horsford.
Fig. 4c (right): St Andrew, Biggleswade, Bedfordshire. Square-ended benches with tracery in the central panel and dating from Habershon & Pite's restoration of 1870.

Figs. 5a & b: St Mary, Beddington, London Borough of Sutton. Poppy-headed ends in both traceried and plain versions, probably dating from 1869 and Joseph Clarke's restoration. This date is quite late for poppy-heads for congregational seating.

Fig. 5c: All Saints, Oakham, Rutland. An array of poppy-heads can appear impressive. This fine set was installed at Gilbert Scott's restoration in 1857–8. See also Figure 5 in Chapter 16 (page 262).

Poppy-heads

Poppy-headed bench ends (Figs. 5a & b) were certainly used in Victorian churches but not nearly as often as square-headed ones. Just under 10 per cent of Leicestershire churches have Victorian poppy-heads but only two of the churches in the Salisbury project have them. If the Leicestershire evidence is to be trusted, they were quite popular in the 1830s but could appear rather crude if the head was not carved. To get round this particular problem, in a couple of cases the heads are made of cast-iron (Congerstone, 1834; Barkby, 1838), presumably to reduce cost through a factory-made product. In a large church the sea of poppy-heads can look most impressive, as, for example, Oakham, Rutland (Fig. 5c), refurnished by G. G. Scott in 1858. Poppy-headed ends do not seem to have been used extensively for congregational seating after the mid-Victorian years although they remained popular for chancel stalls.[7]

Ends with elbows

Both the Leicestershire and Salisbury studies suggest that, after square-headed bench ends, the next most popular type had small elbows. Nearly 20 per cent of Leicestershire churches have them and the picture is the same from the Salisbury study. Medieval examples of this type can be found, and Cox illustrates an example from Clapton-in-Gordano in Somerset which he believed dated back to the late thirteenth century (Fig. 3). In Leicestershire they were not used until the 1850s and even then there were only a couple of examples but from then on they started to enjoy massive popularity. However, as the Dilton Marsh case shows, they were certainly being employed earlier than the Leicestershire evidence

Fig. 6a: St Michael, Beer Hackett, Dorset. These seats with rounded elbows probably date from the restoration by Crickmay & Son of Weymouth in 1881–2.

PEWS, BENCHES AND CHAIRS

Fig. 6b: St Michael & All Angels, Blackheath, London Borough of Greenwich. The bench ends have elbows, a concave upper surface on the eastern edge, numbers painted on them, and brass holders and cast-iron drip trays for umbrellas. This church, built in 1828–30, was reseated in 1881–2 under architect Edward Drury.

Fig. 7a (below left): St Hippolytus, Ryme Intrinseca, Dorset. Bench ends combining round tops and elbows. The date is uncertain.

Fig. 7b (below right): St Mary Magdalene (R.C.), Mortlake, London Borough of Richmond-on-Thames. A chunkier version of a round-top end with elbows. The seating probably dates from the building of the church in 1852 by G. R. Blount. The framing of the end, top rail and seat itself is expressed in the small rectangular features. The seating is now movable and stands on a carpeted floor.

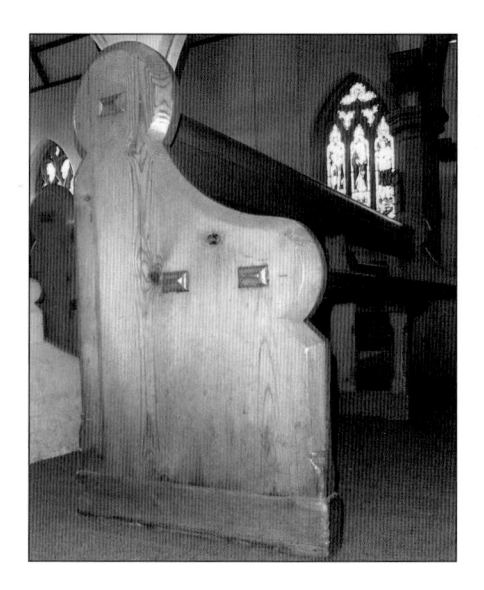

would suggest. In terms of the details of the designs the variations on this particular theme could be enormous (Figs. 1, 6a & b, 10a, 13).

Round-headed ends
It is arguable whether round-headed ends should be thought of as a separate category but a small proportion of ends have a prominent round-headed top which makes for a very distinctive appearance (Figs. 7a & b). In the two cases illustrated here the ends also have elbows.

Round-shouldered ends
In the case of round-shouldered ends, the eastward edge of the end has a large curving element (Figs. 8a & b). Some 10 per cent of Leicestershire churches have them while the figure rises to 15 per cent for the Salisbury study. In Leicestershire, apart from Butterfield's benches of 1851 at Ashwell (actually in Rutland), the type is not found before the 1860s but then they enjoyed a reasonable degree of popularity to the end of the nineteenth century.

Concave-sided ends
Sometimes the eastward edge of the bench end is scooped out to produce a concave curve but has no defined elbow (Figs. 9a & b). There are very few instances in Leicestershire but three churches out of 59 in the Salisbury study have them.

Angular ends and jagged profiles
Occasionally bench ends with a jagged, angular profile are to be found. They are often encountered from the 1860s which was a

Fig. 8a (left): Holy Trinity, Folkestone, Kent. This seating in Ewan Christian's splendid church of 1866–8 has round-shouldered ends. Note also the pew numbering and the pull-out seat.

Fig. 8b (right): All Saints, Benhilton, London Borough of Sutton. These benches with gently rounded shoulders and low-set elbows were installed in S. S. Teulon's church of 1863–6.

Fig. 9a (left): St Mary, Hermitage, Dorset. Concave-sided ends installed at Crickmay & Son's restoration of 1889.

Fig. 9b (right): St Cuthbert, Oborne, Dorset. The benches are very similar to those in Figure 9a except that the tops have small chamfers, the concave element is rather more pronounced, and the side mouldings run out more neatly. The seats are original to the church which was built in 1861–2 by William Slater.

time of strong, often wilful design where architects sought unusual, original effects. The four illustrated here (Figs. 10a–d) are by no means the extreme examples of their type.

Inverted Y-shaped ends

More than any other type of bench end, the Y-shaped form expresses the structure and this type of seating was no doubt used when the budget was tight (Fig. 11). The variations could be considerable as the catalogues show (see the next chapter). The form certainly enjoyed longevity and was still available for purchase as late as 1939, from Geo. M. Hammer & Co.'s catalogue.[8]

Other characteristics of bench seating

Oak or pine?

While oak was the material of choice for Victorian seating schemes when the budget would run to it, there seems to have been no shame attached to the alternative – pine of various kinds. I have no figures of the relative proportions other than of 61 churches in the Salisbury study of which 45 were benched in pine. The parishes in the Sherborne deanery seem to have gone for oak more regularly than Heytesbury ones.[9] Whether this is meaningful (in theory indicating greater prosperity) must remain speculation, given the small size of the sample. Certainly the choice had nothing to do with the architect responsible – even the biggest names accepted pine, as did G. G. Scott at Cattistock in Dorset (1857), G. E. Street at Chapmanslade in Wiltshire (1867) and William Butterfield at Heytesbury, also Wiltshire (and also in 1867).

Raised or flush?

Bench seating can be placed on a timber platform, be flush with the floor or have a rail at the entrance. The figures for Victorian/Edwardian treatments derived from the Salisbury study are shown in the table overleaf.

VICTORIAN CHURCH SEATING: VARIATIONS UPON A THEME

Fig. 10a (left): St Dunstan, Cheam, London Borough of Sutton. Angular ends with elbows whose vigorous design seems appropriate in Frederick Pownall's High Victorian Gothic church of 1862–4.

Fig. 10b (right): Holy Trinity, Wallington, London Borough of Sutton. Another forceful design of the 1860s, in this case in a church of 1866–7 by Edward Habershon and E. P. Loftus Brock.

Fig. 10c (left): St John the Evangelist, Ford End, Essex. Cheap but quite dramatic seating was installed in Frederic Chancellor's church of 1870–71.

Fig. 10d (right): Holy Trinity, Stevenage, Hertfordshire. This is a church of 1861–2 from the early years of A. W. Blomfield when he was interested in polychromy and exotic detail. The seating appears to reflect such interests. It seems to have been raised a couple of inches by timbers under the ends. The design could be seen as an elaborated variant of that in Figure 11.

Table: Contact between bench seating and floor (Salisbury, two deaneries)

Type of Contact	Deanery		
	Heytesbury	Sherborne	Total
Platform	13	21	34
Flush	17	12	29
Rail	0	10	10
Total	30	43	73

These figures are presented without any attempt at interpretation and it is probably unwise to read too much significance into the very different proportions between the two deaneries, especially as the number of sites is relatively small. However, in the language of modern-day health and safety, was the area around Victorian Heytesbury more conscious of trip hazards?!

Fixed or movable

In the Salisbury study no data was collected systematically as to whether benches were fixed or movable but it was noticed that a few seating schemes have movable benches. G. E. Street used them at three Wiltshire churches: Chapmanslade; St John, Warminster and Upton Scudamore.

The flooring beneath

The Salisbury study suggested that wooden boards are overwhelmingly the commonest form of flooring beneath benching. Very occasionally the floor is of stone or tiles. G. E. Street, for example, placed his benches at St John, Warminster, Wiltshire, on a tiled floor.[10] A very different and extraordinary case is at Upton Scudamore, also in Wiltshire, where, at his 1855–9 restoration, Street provided the body of the church with a truly remarkable all-over wood-block floor consisting of c.6-inch square blocks made from the heartwood of squared-off tree

Fig. 11: St Mary Magdalene, Thornford, Dorset. Inverted Y-shaped ends to the seating installed at Slater & Carpenter's restoration in 1866.

branches or small trunks. No comparable example is presently known. Wood-block floors, which became such a common and visually significant feature of churches from the last quarter of the nineteenth century, were invented, so he claimed, by the architect William White. This would have been in the early 1850s according to his reckoning although it is not known where he first used them.[11]

Kneeling boards

From the limited Salisbury evidence it seems that relatively few Victorian seating schemes were equipped with kneeling boards. Only three were encountered on the project in a sample of 60 churches.

Doors

Box-pews were an early casualty of the ecclesiological revolution and we think of Victorian bench seating in our churches as being doorless. This is, of course, generally true but it is worth noting that occasionally doors can be found. In Leicestershire there were no less than fifteen such cases between 1840 and 1847, one of c.1850, and two (Edmondthorpe and Husband's Bosworth) dating from as late as the mid-1860s.[12] The latest cases known to me are both on the Isle of Man and date from 1885 (Kirk Rushen) and 1886 (Kirk Arbory). But such late cases are very different from the box-pews of Georgian days. The doors are lower than the bench ends which are otherwise of normal square-ended type (Fig. 12a). Even that paragon of ecclesiological virtue, William Butterfield, added, or more likely was talked into adding, low doors to his seats at Trumpington, Cambridgeshire, in the mid-1850s ('unfortunately' said *The Ecclesiologist*)[13] and at Scottow, Norfolk, in 1858 (Fig. 12b). Gilbert Scott too had to sacrifice what he no doubt considered a principle when he came to seat his new church at Sewerby in the East Riding in 1846–48. In all

Fig. 12a (left): St Mildred, Whippingham, Isle of Wight. Seating with doors. The architect for the rebuilding of the nave in 1861–2 was the little-known London architect Albert Jenkins Humbert (1822–77). However, Prince Albert, who suddenly died in December 1861, was closely involved with the development of buildings in the village and the church served the royal family when it was in residence at Osborne House. It seems inconceivable that the Prince Consort was not party to (or, indeed, the instigator of) this very conservative style of seating.

Fig. 12b (right): All Saints, Scottow, Norfolk. William Butterfield's seating of 1858.

probability the low doors to the benches were one of the 'difficulties [that] arose from the fads of my employer', the squire, Yarburgh Graeme, and to which Scott tantalisingly refers to in his *Recollections*.[14] No doubt similar considerations were at work for John Hayward as Jo Cox suggests in Chapter 17.

Flap seats

In his book on bench ends Cox noted a 'curiosity of early seating in which flap seats, as they are usually termed, were attached to the ends of the substantial standards of the more permanent seating'. He goes on to say that 'many instances of this kind of seating could be quoted from Wardens' Accounts of the seventeenth century' and provides an illustration of flaps attached to bench ends of 1511 at Tintinhull in Somerset (illustrated in Chapter 7 (Figure 10, page 103), which discusses a number of other surviving examples). These seats were, Cox says, assigned 'for the most part to the maids of the occupants of the permanent pew, or in some cases to children'.

Flap seats continued to appear occasionally in Victorian churches (Fig. 13). I have not met with any documentation concerning their nineteenth-century usage and it is uncertain if they continued to be used in the same way as Cox describes or were simply a means of achieving a little extra seating at busy services, although it is difficult to imagine the owners of appropriated seats welcoming the close presence of a stranger on the end of their bench. Flap seats have been observed to be to be quite common in Victorian Roman Catholic town churches.[15] A rather neater variant is the pull-out seating at Holy Trinity, Folkestone (Fig. 8a). Another kind of occasional seating is shown in Figure 14.

Fig. 13: St Mary Magdalen, St Leonards, East Sussex (now Greek Orthodox). Rows of benches, each with a flap seat. The ends have small elbows and also rounded tops inclined towards the east. The church was built in 1852 under London architect Frederick Marrable.

Umbrella holders

Another, more common appendage to bench ends are umbrella holders and drip-trays (Fig. 6b). The umbrella started to come into general use in the middle of the eighteenth century but I am unaware of any instances of holders and drip-trays being fitted to bench ends before Victorian times. The holders are of brass or iron, and the trays of iron or enamelled metal. In the Salisbury study only one set of umbrella fittings was noted. Does this mean the hardy folk of the south-west eschewed the umbrella? Conversely church seats of all denominations in Liverpool and other parts of urban south Lancashire often have provision for umbrellas – but then the rain in that county is legendary![16]

Free or appropriated?

Victorian church-builders and restorers, and those giving grants for the purpose, were much exercised by the provision of free seating as a means of encouraging the ungodly poor to come to church. Nonetheless appropriated seating was still commonplace and at many churches pew rents were collected well into the twentieth century, very occasionally even lingering on until after the Second World War: Christ Church, Cheltenham, for example, kept them until 1954, while at St Paul, Halliwell Road, Bolton, the final rents are said to have been collected in 1964 when the final renter was paying 2s a year.[17] This latter was no doubt a relic of nineteenth-century pricing and fits within the scale of charges levied, for example, at St Andrew, Nottingham, a new church where, in 1872, the rent for the 352 appropriated seats varied from 1s to £1 a year (the average was 13s).[18] Here the total revenue amounted to £234 and paid the vicar's quarterly stipend.

In Georgian churches there was a clear visual distinction between the appropriated box-pews and the humble open benches for the poor. Victorian Britain may have been deeply class-conscious but there was also a passionate belief, at least in theory, that 'all men are equal in the House of Prayer'.[19] This underpinned the fact that bench seating in a church all looked alike, irrespective of who was using it. Some free seating, as at Dilton Marsh (Fig. 1), is marked 'Free' while many seating schemes still display the numbers given to each bench (Fig. 6b) and which is usually indicative of appropriation. Figure 15 shows seats with the name of the occupying family painted on: these date from 1842 and such an overt declaration of ownership is something one would not expect to meet in later Victorian work.

Occasionally one comes across small holders screwed to bench ends and which would have held cards with the name of the pew-renter. These, and the umbrella holders and drip trays, and bench end numbers, were all available from church-fitting catalogues.

Fig. 14: St Peter, Wrecclesham, Surrey. An unusual tip-up seat, supported in the up position by folding iron brackets. The nave was rebuilt and the north aisle added in 1876–7 under the relatively little-known architect C. H. Howell (1823 or 1824–1905) of Leatherhead, Surrey, and the seat probably dates from then.

Fig. 15: Seats at St Thomas, Exeter, dating from 1842 and bearing the name of the Franklyn family. The reseating was part of a refitting undertaken by the Revd John Medley. He was secretary of the Exeter Diocesan Architectural Society founded in 1841 and the first such society established outside Oxbridge. It avidly promoted the ecclesiological agenda and Medley probably did not approve of such overt evidence of appropriation. However, like clergy before and since, he had to deal with attitudes as he found them.

Chairs

Benches were, of course, not the only way to seat a church. Chairs were far cheaper (see Chapter 20, Figure 11) and were standard practice in cathedrals. In addition to the 1854–6 correspondence reproduced in Chapter 15, there was also an interesting and wide-ranging discussion at the Ecclesiological Society's annual meeting in 1859 prompted by the chairs at All Saints, Margaret Street.[20] The cost of these was £80, it was noted, whereas benches would have cost £300. But here economy was hardly an issue and Alexander Beresford-Hope, the chief benefactor of the church and also in the chair at the meeting, described them as 'an experiment'. His own attitude seems to have been cautious, remarking that 'while he thought chairs preferable for cathedral naves, he was more doubtful about parochial churches'. G. E. Street spoke up in their defence. In language reminiscent of that used today he 'argued that it was only with chairs that worshippers could have full liberty of action'. William White, while preferring benches for small areas, favoured chairs for large ones. The attitude of grant-giving bodies could vary markedly. Beresford-Hope noted that the London Diocesan Society had no rule against chairs whereas the Incorporated Church Building Society did (something Street 'spoke forcibly against'). The Leicestershire survey showed chairs being used in 13 per cent of the churches, a significant number. There may have been a high-church bias towards chairs, though this requires further research: it is notable that Father Wagner's distinctly high-church churches in Brighton all have chairs, and cost would not have been a factor in that case.

Children's seats

Children – especially those who attended a National School or the church Sunday school – were commonly provided with their own block of seating. Favoured locations were a chancel aisle, under the tower or in part of a nave aisle. Very little physical evidence of such seating seems to remain today. In many cases, I suspect, this is because such seating looks no different from that for adults but where it was of smaller size many examples will have been destroyed, as the idea of such grouped seating for children has long been unfashionable.

The children's seating at North Kilworth church, Leicestershire, from the 1864–5 restoration, involved a block of seats in the north-west part of the nave and north aisle: not only were they smaller than the adult versions but the bench ends were plainer too. Young worshippers at Clipsham, Rutland, found themselves accommodated on small movable benches of two different sizes from about 1860. A block of seating was sometimes called the 'children's gallery' even though it might not be elevated in the way of a normal Georgian gallery, and this was the case at the west end of All Saints, Blaby in Leicestershire at the reseating in 1846.[21] The same was true at Twyford, also Leicestershire, where the 'children's gallery' of 1849 under the tower consisted of seven smaller-than-normal benches.[22] A similar location was chosen during William Butterfield's early restoration (1845–7) at Hellidon, Northamptonshire, but here the seating was raked. Butterfield, or whoever was responsible for this, got short shrift from *The Ecclesiologist* which berated it thus: 'The tower is seated; unfortunately with forms rising one above the other, on the plea of bringing the children under the Priest's eye. But nothing can justify the arrangement'.[23] So much for that seemingly sensible idea.

Physical remains of children's seating are now rare and, where practicable, it would seem well to retain what we have as a reminder of former ways of accommodating children in our churches.

Choosing a design

Who decided on a design and why? How many schemes were architect-designed and how many were chosen 'off the shelf' from church furnishers' catalogues? Sadly I can offer no general answers to these questions, for which much more research is needed – the chapters by James Bettley, Suzanna Branfoot and Jo Cox in this book are important as a first step in this direction (Chapters 16–18). It might be thought that particular architects would favour particular styles, but, based on published studies and the material in this book, that does not seem to be the case. As we have seen, even eminent practitioners like Butterfield and Scott were not above having seats with doors in their churches, something of which they would surely have heartily disapproved (Fig. 12b). There must have been client pressure at work here. Leafing through Paul Thompson's study of Butterfield shows his churches to contain a wide range of types and the same can be said of J. L. Pearson's churches, as illustrated in Anthony Quiney's book on the architect.[24] Gilbert Scott was as busy in Leicestershire as he was everywhere else and we find his churches fitted up with widely varied seating – Suzanna Branfoot discusses how he would often use local medieval survivals as precedents. In the year 1858 square-ended benches appeared at Theddingworth while Oakham (Rutland) got poppy-heads. Other new or restored churches by Scott received bench ends with elbows and angular designs. Although poppy-heads seem to have rather fallen out of favour by the 1860s, they found their way relatively late into the Scott-restored church of Whissendine, Rutland, opened in November 1870.[25]

Information about design choices for churches in general, and seating in particular, is not particularly common. It seems quite possible that in many cases architects designed the building and major items like fonts or reredoses but left building and restoration committees free to chose what form of seating they preferred or could afford.

Completeness

In terms of generally accepted heritage protection criteria, the intactness of a building or its furnishings and fittings carries extra weight. But how many intact seating schemes have survived? Unfortunately, I have no data to offer but based on the Salisbury study and visits I have made to churches subsequently, I would suggest that the answer is very, very few.

This is not to imply a criticism of subsequent generations and the changes they have wrought. It seems wholly reasonable to adapt seating schemes to changing times. For example, a great many Victorian seating plans were so concerned to maximise the numbers of 'sittings' that seats were installed in positions that would be thought to be, quite rightly, unacceptable today – for instance, seats at the east end of aisles where the occupants would have had to stare at a wall and a window. Many benches have been removed from the west end of churches to free up circulation and create meeting space, while others have been taken away from the east end of naves to accommodate forward altars. Where accommodation in aisles has been found superfluous, many benches have been removed, sometimes to good effect, but sometimes with bad, such as creating an unsightly storage area for, say, children's playthings.

Adaptations of seating schemes to meet modern circumstances are clearly necessary but it seems reasonable to expect that in future where a truly complete Victorian seating scheme is encountered, the presumption is that it should be retained as such.

Conclusion

It is easy to take Victorian and early-twentieth-century bench seating for granted thanks to its sheer ubiquity. It is *still* a dominant element in the appearance and character of a majority of our churches and this is true of all denominations, not just the Anglican communion. In places where it has been removed or in those where it never existed, the feel of the church is totally different. This, indeed, is the very intention on the part of those congregations who cannot get rid of their benches fast enough. On the other hand, as the writer's experience of the Salisbury project has shown, most rural congregations seem keen to keep what they have and love.

Figs. 16a & b: St Mary, Clipsham, Rutland. A complete and very fine oak seating scheme of 1862 which, with other woodwork, was carved by Rippin Bros. who worked for the contractor, J. Richardson of Stamford. Overall view, showing the pierced backs, and a detail of a bench end in which small male and female heads form terminals to a pair of cusps.

This chapter has tried to show something of the variety of Victorian seating and provide a few tentative facts about it. As yet, we would be hard put to say which are the most important Victorian seating schemes throughout the country. And we might even find it difficult to set out definitive criteria for judging importance. A set of beautifully carved, richly ornamented benches such as that at Clipsham, Rutland, of 1862 (Fig. 16), are surely fine enough to be kept in all but the most pressing of circumstances. But there is more to heritage than winners of beauty contests. Things can have significance that we do not yet understand and, for examples, I take two case studies from this chapter. The Dilton Marsh seating mentioned at the start is the earliest Victorian scheme with its particular type of bench ends known to me. Also, not a bench-scheme but associated with it, the floor at Upton Scudamore might well be unique and dates from the very time when William White claimed to have just invented wood-block flooring (but of the now-familiar rectangular block variety). The floor is functional, not beautiful, and is starting to show its 150-year age: it could so easily end up in a skip to be replaced by shiny boards and a nice blue carpet.

The Victorian refitting of our churches was a massive enterprise which is historically significant on many levels, touching as it did religious convictions, social attitudes, art, industry and much more besides. Its material products are, for the most part, still with us and have lasted well, threatened more by changing ideas and fashions about the use of ecclesiastical spaces than by being physically worn out. Like any other aspect of our heritage, surviving Victorian church furnishings deserve respect with thoughtful, sensitively managed change. To help the latter we could well do with more knowledge about Victorian seating schemes and, as this chapter has set out to show, there is still so much we do not know. Any prospective PhD student seeking a fruitful subject in the realms of ecclesiology need look no further.

Acknowledgements
As explained, some of this chapter uses the results of work commissioned by English Heritage. The Ecclesiological Society gratefully acknowledges financial support from English Heritage towards the costs of publication.

The author would like to thank Sarah Brown, Trevor Cooper, Jean Fryer and Chris Webster for reading a draft of this chapter and making many helpful suggestions.

Notes

1. Henceforth 'Victorian' for brevity. The chapter does not take chancel seating into consideration.
2. 'Church-building and Restoration in Leicestershire and Rutland, 1800-1914', (PhD Thesis, Leicester University, 1984). A condensed version was published as *Bringing them to their Knees: Church-building and Restoration in Leicestershire and Rutland, 1800-1914* (Leicester, 2002).
3. This was part of a wide-ranging project undertaken by the diocese, called 'Rediscovering our Parish Churches' which at the time of writing was still in progress examining all aspects of parish life in the areas under study.
4. The figures are reduced by the fact that the handful of churches built in the 1830s mostly had their seating schemes replaced during later nineteenth-century restorations.
5. *The Ecclesiologist,* 22 (1861), 61. The article has 'anti-pew' in its title yet goes on to refer to the modern seating as 'pews' too, an interesting and relatively early example of the shift in meaning from the early Victorian 'pew' (sometimes 'pue') as the name for box pews to its modern one which simply indicates bench seating in a church.
6. J. C Cox, *Bench-Ends in English Churches* (London, 1916).
7. Paul Thompson says of Butterfield's seating 'Poppyheads are very common in the 1840s and 1850s' although he adds that they appear 'more often in stalls than seats' (*William Butterfield* (London, 1971), 482).
8. See Chapter 20. All other benches illustrated in that catalogue would have looked entirely at home in a church of 1870.
9. The two deaneries each had eight churches benched in oak: Heytesbury deanery has 28 with pine as against only 17 in Sherborne. No doubt other woods were used from time to time. St John's, Woodbridge, Suffolk, is said to have been reseated in teak in 1901-2 (Anne Riches, *Victorian Church Building and Restoration in Suffolk* (Woodbridge, 1982), 429).
10. Street's third movable bench scheme mentioned above at Chapmanslade stands on a conventional wooden floor.
11. White wrote in *Building News*, 58 (1890), 224: 'It is now not far from 40 years ago that I first invented the flat wood-block paving'. Originally at Upton Scudamore the floors were to be boards laid on joists but by October 1855 an extra £90 16s 10d had been agreed for wood-block paving on a concrete bed (Wiltshire Record Office, PR/Upton Scudamore, St Mary the Virgin/1741/21, Addition A to specification). I am most grateful to Gill Hunter for documentary details on Upton Scudamore.
12. Full details are given in my article 'Anglican churches before the restorers: A study from Leicestershire and Rutland', *Archaeological Journal*, 144 (1987), 383-408 (p. 394).
13. *The Ecclesiologist*, 18 (1857), 197.
14. G. Stamp (ed), *G. G. Scott, Personal and Professional Recollections* (originally published London, 1879, reprinted Stamford, 1995), 148.
15. I am grateful to Sarah Brown for this observation.
16. My thanks also to Sarah Brown for pointing out the frequency of umbrella holders in Liverpool churches.
17. The Cheltenham rents brought in £170 a year at the time of their abolition (guidebook). My source for the Bolton case is Dorothy Isherwood who says her mother, Bertha Isherwood (commemorated in a nave window), paid the 2s a year until her death on 27 May 1964.
18. Nottingham Record Office, PR 10, 445.
19. Quoted from the section dealing with the evils of pews in the Cambridge Camden Society's *A Few Words to Churchwardens on Churches and Church Ornaments, II, suited to Town and Manufacturing Parishes*, 5th edn, (Cambridge, 1842), 5.
20. *The Ecclesiologist,* 20 (1859), 274.

21 Incorporated Church Building Society (ICBS) papers, file 3771, plan at the Society of Antiquaries.
22 ICBS papers, Lambeth Palace Library, plan in file 4168.
23 *The Ecclesiologist* 5 (1846), 126. Of course, as with the seats with doors, it is possible this arrangement had little to do with Butterfield himself and was something insisted upon by the parishioners.
24 For Thompson, see note 7 above. A. Quiney, *John Loughborough Pearson* (New Haven and London, 1979).
25 During the period 1867–70 G. G. Scott junior was acting for his father on this restoration (information kindly provided by Gavin Stamp).

20. Spoiled for choice: seating from the catalogue

*Geoff Brandwood and
Trevor Cooper*

THE GREAT EXPLOSION of church building and restoration from the 1840s led to the rise of specialist firms of church furnishers and decorators. Some concentrated on a specific medium such as stained glass, others offered a wider range of work. When considering Victorian church furnishing and embellishment we tend to think, as we do with the architecture itself, in terms of the big names: Clayton & Bell for stained glass, Francis Skidmore for metalwork or Thomas Earp for stone carving. But a great deal of church furnishing came, not as bespoke, architect-designed work from art studios, but from the trade catalogues of companies that could offer a complete, pre-designed package. We do not know how many Victorian pews were purchased in this way, but it is likely to have been a substantial proportion of the whole.

Church furnishing firms

James Bettley has investigated the growth and activities of the church furnishing companies.[1] He shows that *Kelly's Post Office Directory* for London introduced the new category of 'church furnishers' in 1859, and the increasing numbers over the following years led Kelly's to subdivide the classification – church plate manufacturers, church embroiderers etc. By 1865 there were nine entries under the general category or one of its subdivisions. By 1875 there were twenty-six and by 1885 thirty-four and the number of entries peaked in about 1895 when there were forty-two. This continued rise in numbers runs rather counter to the downward trend in *major* church restorations towards the end of the nineteenth century as there were progressively fewer churches left to restore. It is to be explained, probably, by improved transport and mechanisation encouraging centralisation of manufacturing; by the fact that new churches of all denominations were still being built in large numbers, and that considerable additions of furniture continued to be made in those that already existed, even if it was only a screen here or a lectern there (much of it to do with memorialisation); and by the increasing richness of liturgical furnishings as the higher tone of worship instigated by the Oxford Movement and the ecclesiologists permeated through the main body of the established Church.

Church furnishing firms – at least the larger ones – worked in a variety of ways. They produced work to order for architects, and used this to advertise the quality of their craftsmanship. They also used their own designers who would design bespoke items (Figure 9 may be an example) for particular customers – often not very dissimilar from the architect-designed work! And finally, they designed their own stock items which were illustrated in trade catalogues and could be ordered as seen, or perhaps used as a stimulus for discussion with the customer as to exactly what was wanted.

A few of these trade catalogues have survived.[2] These include a number for the firm of Jones & Willis, based in Birmingham, but later with showrooms in London and Liverpool. This was one of the biggest and most prolific firms, which produced anything and everything needed in church, from altar coverings to church silver to lecterns and notice boards, while their signature can be found upon numerous stained glass windows and brass memorial tablets. Naturally, seating could be supplied too. As well as a few of the Jones & Willis trade catalogues, discussed in the following paragraphs, there survives, for this firm a large – and largely unexplored – archive, consisting both of drawings and of photographs of their executed work.[3] The photographs seem to be mostly of architect-designed work, often in major churches. The drawings, in contrast, are unsigned and often marked 'please return to Jones & Willis', and seem therefore to be in-house designs sent for approval to potential customers. Some of the drawings reappear as woodcuts in the trade catalogues. There are unquarried riches here, but our brief investigation of the many drawings of furnishings showed that, for reasons unknown, there are remarkably few of bench ends.[4]

Benches in trade catalogues

The first Jones & Willis trade catalogue was published in 1846, though no copy is known to survive. Catalogues illustrating bench ends do survive from 1870 (an estimated date), 1875, 1879, 1883 (abridged), 1893, 1899, and 1905, a thirty-year span.[5] In the following pages we have illustrated the stock bench designs shown in these catalogues (Figs. 4–6, 10–12) to give a flavour of what could be bought off the shelf in the latter part of Victoria's reign. Not all styles are illustrated in every catalogue – presumably the company could always refer the customer to the previous edition to show a design not illustrated in the current issue, or lend a drawing (see Figures 7 & 8). As so few catalogues survive, it is not possible to follow the date at which any one style of bench end was introduced, or later dropped, but the general impression is that nothing much changed, mid-Victorian Gothic preserved in aspic, with just a hint of Arts and Crafts towards the end.

We have also shown some benches (Figs. 1–3) from another major supplier, Cox & Son(s), to show how essentially similar in style their products were to those of Jones & Willis. At the other end of this period, as late as 1939 similar items could still be bought off the peg from some church furnishers (Fig. 13). This can perhaps be interpreted as dull resistance to innovation *or* that the mid-Victorians had developed functional, widely approved designs which did a practical job very well.

The 1875 Jones & Willis catalogue is worth discussing in some detail (Fig. 5). It shows half a dozen different designs, and has prices for three kinds of wood for bench ends and for four kinds of wood for the seats themselves. The cheapest wood – red deal – was on offer only for the seats while the ends could be supplied in pine, pitch pine (a tough American wood) and oak. Ordinary pine was cheapest, with pitch pine ends being between 12 and 25 per cent more expensive; oak was generally 40 to 50 per cent dearer than pine. The simplest ends with the least timber (no. 1) had a list price of 11s 6d in pine, rising to 16s 6d in oak. The shaped ends with a moulding (no. 5) – and thus representative of immense amounts of Victorian seating – were twice the price. The fancy poppy-headed end shown as no. 7 was priced at six times the cost of the plainest choice, reflecting the fact that it was carved, not moulded.[6] These prices were for single ends (an unlikely purchase!) with a 10 per cent discount for a dozen or more. But, no doubt, just as with price lists today, the actual price paid was a matter of negotiation, with the phrase 'Special Estimates given for large quantities' in the 1883 catalogue saying as much.

In 1893 the choice was between deal, pitch pine and oak. The catalogue price list (not reproduced here) shows that pitch pine ends were priced at about 15 to 20 per cent more than deal, and oak ones at between 70 and 95 per cent more than deal. This catalogue explains that deal and pitch pine seating came varnished while oak was plain, with wax polishing offered as an extra. Probably reflecting the fluctuations in the relative price of different woods, by 1905 the oak ends were being priced at about 50 per cent above deal.

Based on the list prices, in 1875 a ten-foot bench (a typical length) with two ends could cost as little as £3 13s 6d in cheap wood with cheap ends – roughly 12s per person, assuming that it would seat six people (using the guidelines for space per person provided by the Incorporated Church Building Society, printed in Chapter 14, page 224). At the luxury end of the market, one could pay as much as £15 7s 6d for oak seats with carved oak ends (about £2 11s per person). In the middle, if pitch pine were chosen, and the very typical bench end no. 5, then the cost would be £6 15s (about £1 2s per per person). A much cheaper alternative to pews was individual chairs. These could be purchased for less than 2s each, based on the 1893 catalogue (Fig. 11).

Acknowledgements
The authors would like to thank Roy Porter for alerting them to the survival of the c.1933 Geo. M. Hammer catalogue; him and James Bettley for useful comment and sharing their work on the role of church furnishing catalogues; and David Gazeley of Watts & Co. for access to the Geo. M. Hammer catalogue possessed by the company, and for stimulating discussion.

The reproductions from church furnishing catalogues

These notes provide background information to the illustrations of pews and other seating reproduced here from a range of church furnishing catalogues, dating from 1866 to the 1930s.[7]

Cox & Son(s) catalogues (Figs. 1–3.) The first of these (Fig. 1) is the earliest surviving illustrated catalogue of bench ends known to us, produced by Cox & Son (later Cox & Sons) of London in 1866. As discussed in Chapter 21 by Jo Cox (no known relation), in the 1860s and 1870s and perhaps later, Cox & Son(s) were using machines to carve church furniture, probably including bench ends.

In about 1881 the firm merged with Buckley & Co. to form Cox, Son, Buckley, & Co.,[8] and Figure 3 is from a catalogue produced by the merged firm, of unknown date. This contains the latest examples of poppy-heads we have encountered in a catalogue of congregational bench ends.

Jones & Willis catalogues (Figs. 4–6, 10–13). These represent most of the known surviving illustrated editions of the Jones & Willis catalogue, the earliest survivor (Fig. 4) being of about 1870, the latest (Fig. 13) of 1905. That for 1883 (Fig. 6) is an abbreviated edition, and shows only a few bench ends.

The main catalogues were printed on large paper, and most of the reproductions given here are approximately two-thirds size. By 1899 the paper had grown larger still (and the illustrations expanded to fit the space), but the bench ends are much the same. In 1905 the catalogue acquired a hard cover and a more pretentious title, becoming *A Book of Designs of Ecclesiastical Art* – was this a tardy response to the emphasis of the Arts and Crafts movement on individual design and workmanship?

The *c.*1870 and 1875 catalogues share five designs, but with different numberings. The 1883 catalogue is too abbreviated to be very helpful. By 1893 there is an entirely new set of bench-end designs (and the catalogue itself is described as being in 'new and revised form'); these were still available with the same numbering in 1905, though not all items were illustrated in each catalogue. Many or all of the 1905 designs would have been entirely at home in the catalogues produced decades earlier. Note that there are no designs from Jones & Willis for poppy-heads for congregational seating after the 1875 catalogue.

The 1893 catalogue contains a page showing chairs (Fig. 11). In the accompanying text, most of these are said to be for church use, but numbers 17, 26, 27 and 28 are for 'public halls'. The difference is not entirely clear to the authors, but may be the presence of a flat top to the back of most (not quite all) of the church chairs, presumably to aid prayer. The entry-level church chair (no. 1), with a rush seat cost £1 1s 0d per dozen, and if a hat rest and book rest were added (no. 4), the price rose to £1 14s 0d per dozen. The most expensive church chairs were number 14, which in varnished white wood cost £2 14s 0d per dozen, or could be obtained in oak for £4 2s 0d the dozen. Numbers 20 and 21 were also available in oak if required, though were a little cheaper, the former being the only seat with any hint of gothicisation. Number 4 is, of course, a *prie dieu*, and number 18, perhaps less obviously, a harmonium chair.

Jones & Willis drawings (Figs. 7–9). Figures 7 and 8 are typical of the generality of drawings in the Jones & Willis archive, fairly quick work, done on tinted paper. In this archive, there are many such drawings of general church furnishings but, for some reason, very few bench ends. Four of the bench ends illustrated in these particular drawings were reproduced in catalogues from 1893 onwards (item numbers 27, 30, 36 & 38 in Figures 10, 12, 13), and another is similar to a catalogue item (number 35). Figure 7 is priced up, and has a note at the bottom, 'For prices of seats and backs, see sheet', so was probably intended to be sent out to customers. Figure 8 was probably used in the same way, but may possibly have been prepared for the lithographer.

Figure 9 is of of entirely different quality, fine and detailed pen and ink draughtsmanship. It shows three bench ends, one of foliate design and two with blind tracery, one with linenfold. It seems likely these are one-off designs, though there is no reason to suppose they were in any way unusual – they were probably entirely typical of other quality work commissioned from, or provided by, the firm.

Geo. M. Hammer catalogue (Fig. 14). This edition of the Hammer catalogue was printed some time after 1932, and was being offered to customers at least as late as 1939. The company appears to have had a policy of keeping older items available, and many of the church furnishings in this 1930s catalogue would seem to have been designed in the latter half of the nineteenth century (the company was founded in 1858). Certainly the range of bench ends available in 1939 is identical to that provided by the company some twenty years earlier (in a catalogue not shown here), and few if any of the designs would have looked out of place fifty years before that.

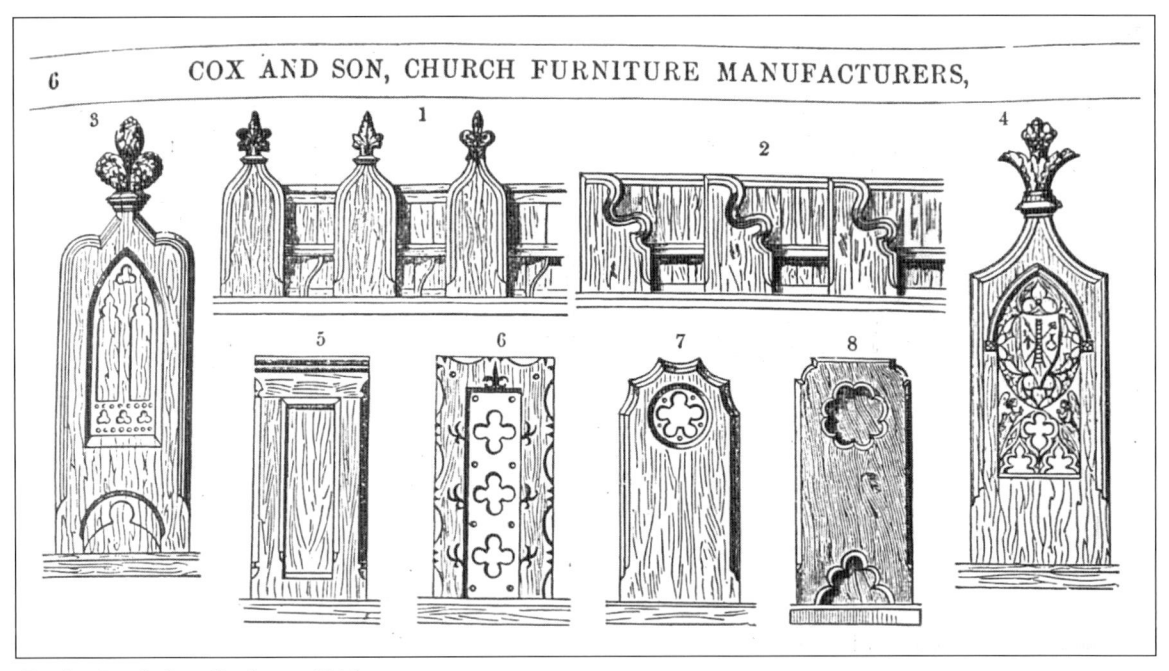

Fig. 1: Cox & Son Catalogue, 1866.

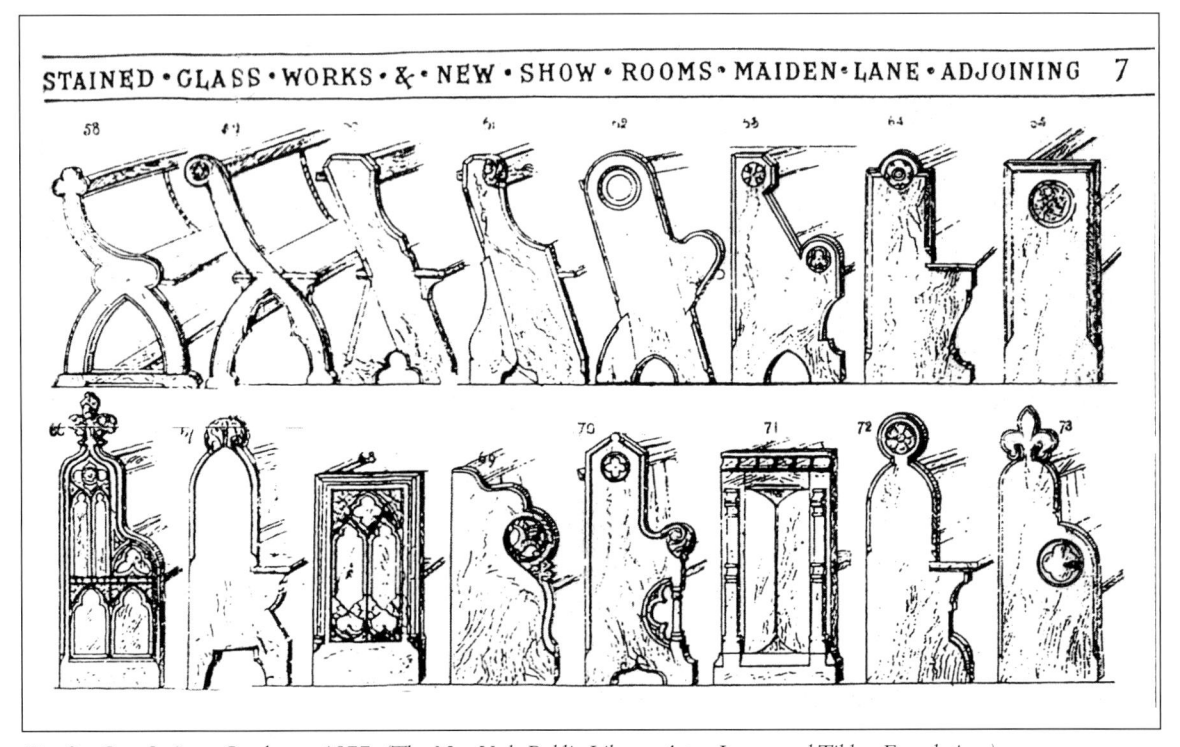

Fig. 2: Cox & Sons Catalogue, 1877. (The New York Public Library, Astor, Lenox and Tilden Foundations)

PEWS, BENCHES AND CHAIRS

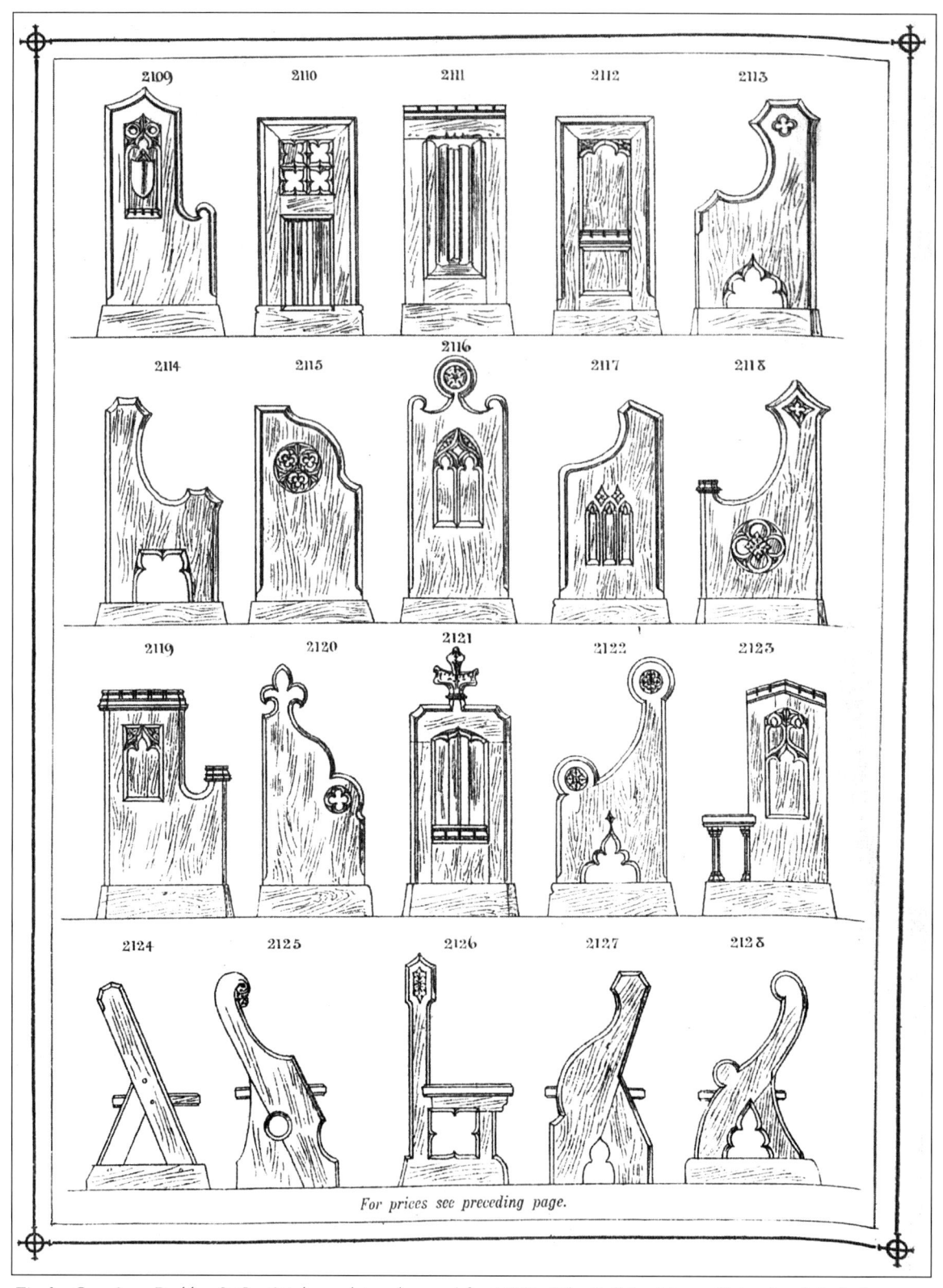

Fig. 3: Cox, Sons, Buckley, & Co. Catalogue, date unknown (after 1881). (The Bodleian Library, University of Oxford)

SPOILED FOR CHOICE: SEATING FROM THE CATALOGUE

Fig. 4: Jones & Willis Catalogue, 48th edition, date unknown (probably c.1870). (Special Collections, Princeton Theological Seminary Libraries)

PEWS, BENCHES AND CHAIRS

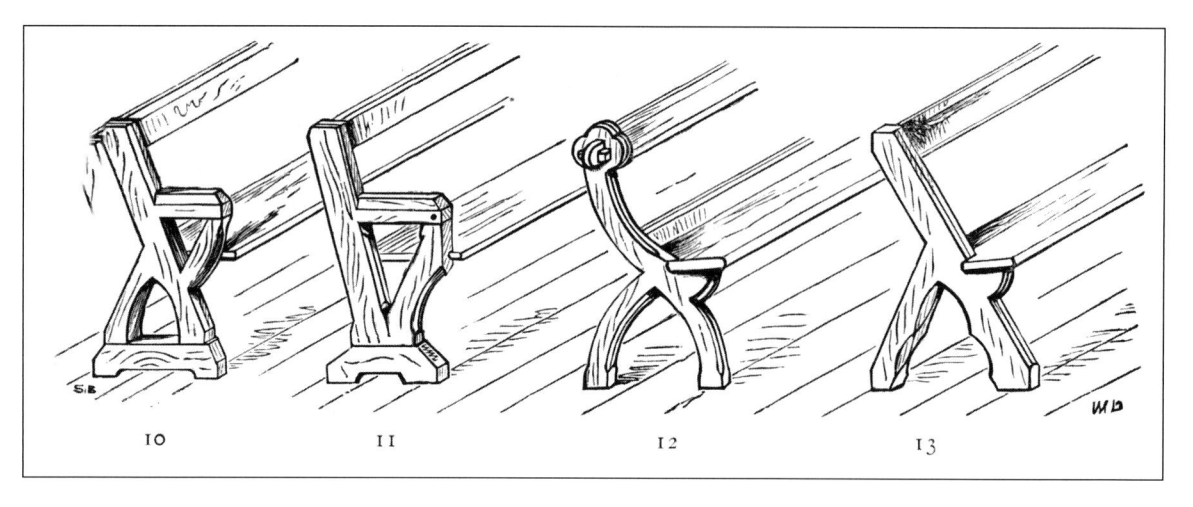

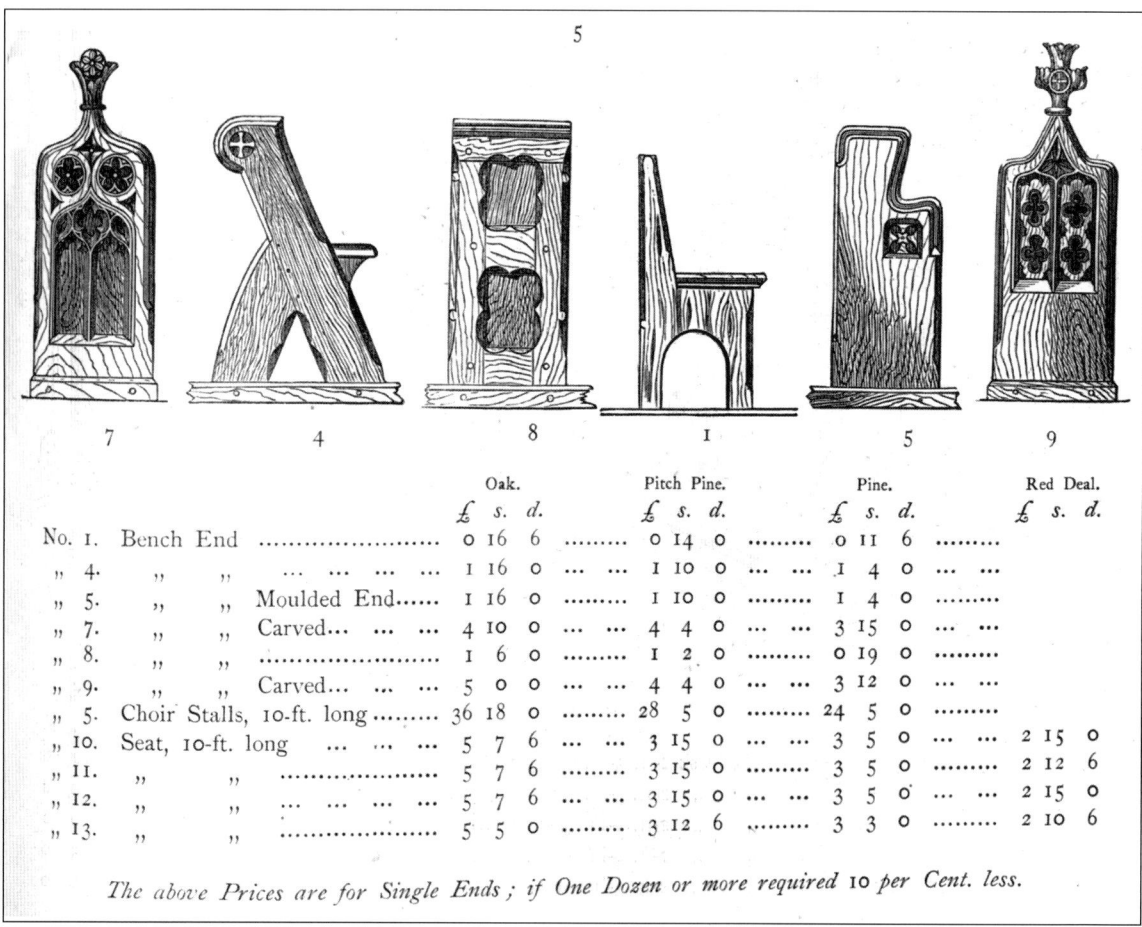

		Oak.	Pitch Pine.	Pine.	Red Deal.
		£ s. d.	£ s. d.	£ s. d.	£ s. d.
No. 1.	Bench End	0 16 6	0 14 0	0 11 6	....
" 4.	" "	1 16 0	1 10 0	1 4 0	....
" 5.	" " Moulded End.....	1 16 0	1 10 0	1 4 0	....
" 7.	" " Carved... ...	4 10 0	4 4 0	3 15 0	....
" 8.	" "	1 6 0	1 2 0	0 19 0	....
" 9.	" " Carved... ...	5 0 0	4 4 0	3 12 0	....
" 5.	Choir Stalls, 10-ft. long	36 18 0	28 5 0	24 5 0	....
" 10.	Seat, 10-ft. long	5 7 6	3 15 0	3 5 0	2 15 0
" 11.	" "	5 7 6	3 15 0	3 5 0	2 12 6
" 12.	" "	5 7 6	3 15 0	3 5 0	2 15 0
" 13.	" "	5 5 0	3 12 6	3 3 0	2 10 6

The above Prices are for Single Ends; if One Dozen or more required **10** *per Cent. less.*

Fig. 5: Jones & Willis Catalogue, 57th edition, 1875. (© V&A Images/Victoria and Albert Museum, London)

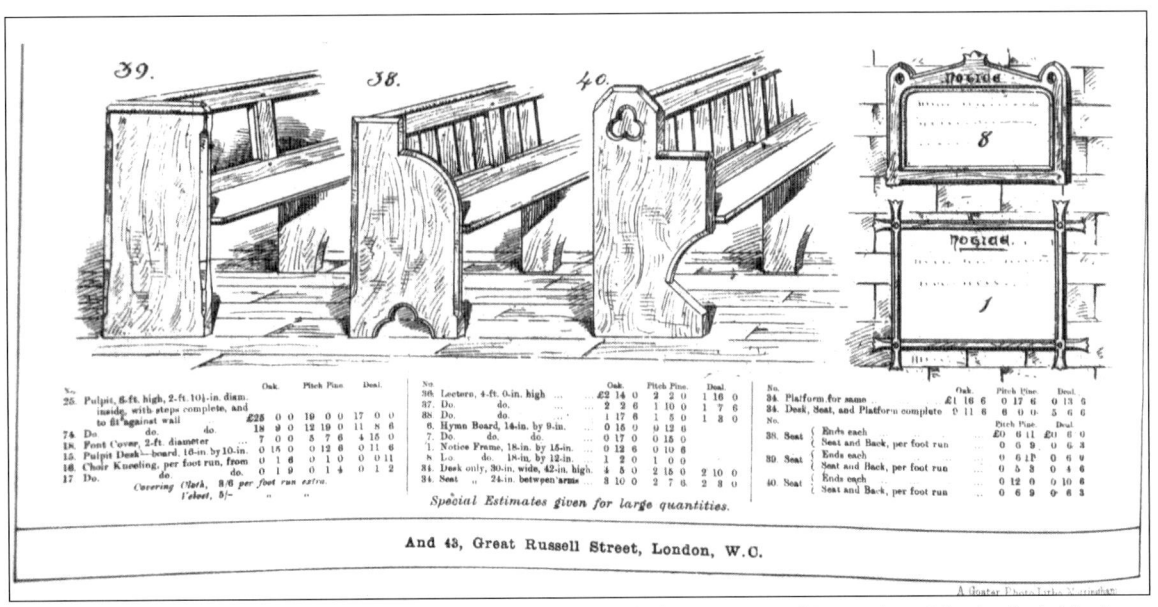

Fig. 6: Jones & Willis abbreviated Catalogue, 1883. (Reproduced with the permission of Birmingham Libraries & Archives)

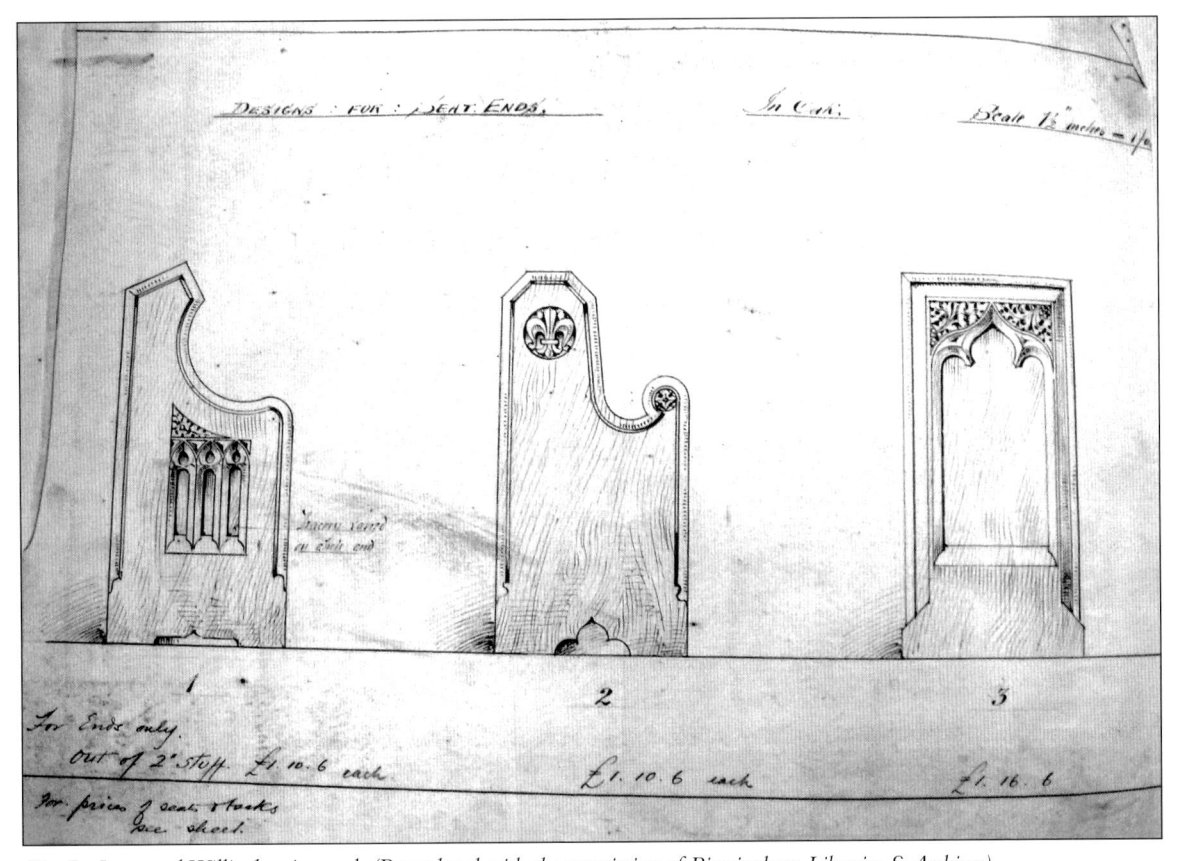

Fig. 7: Jones and Willis drawing, n.d. (Reproduced with the permission of Birmingham Libraries & Archives)

PEWS, BENCHES AND CHAIRS

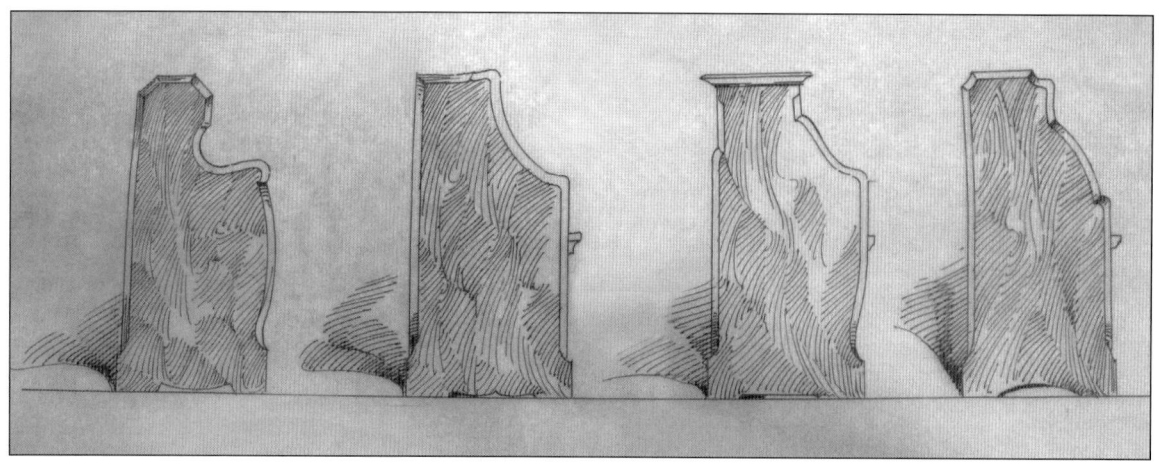

Fig. 8: Jones and Willis drawing, n.d. (Reproduced with the permission of Birmingham Libraries & Archives)

Fig. 9: Jones and Willis pen and ink drawing, n.d. (Reproduced with the permission of Birmingham Libraries & Archives)

SPOILED FOR CHOICE: SEATING FROM THE CATALOGUE

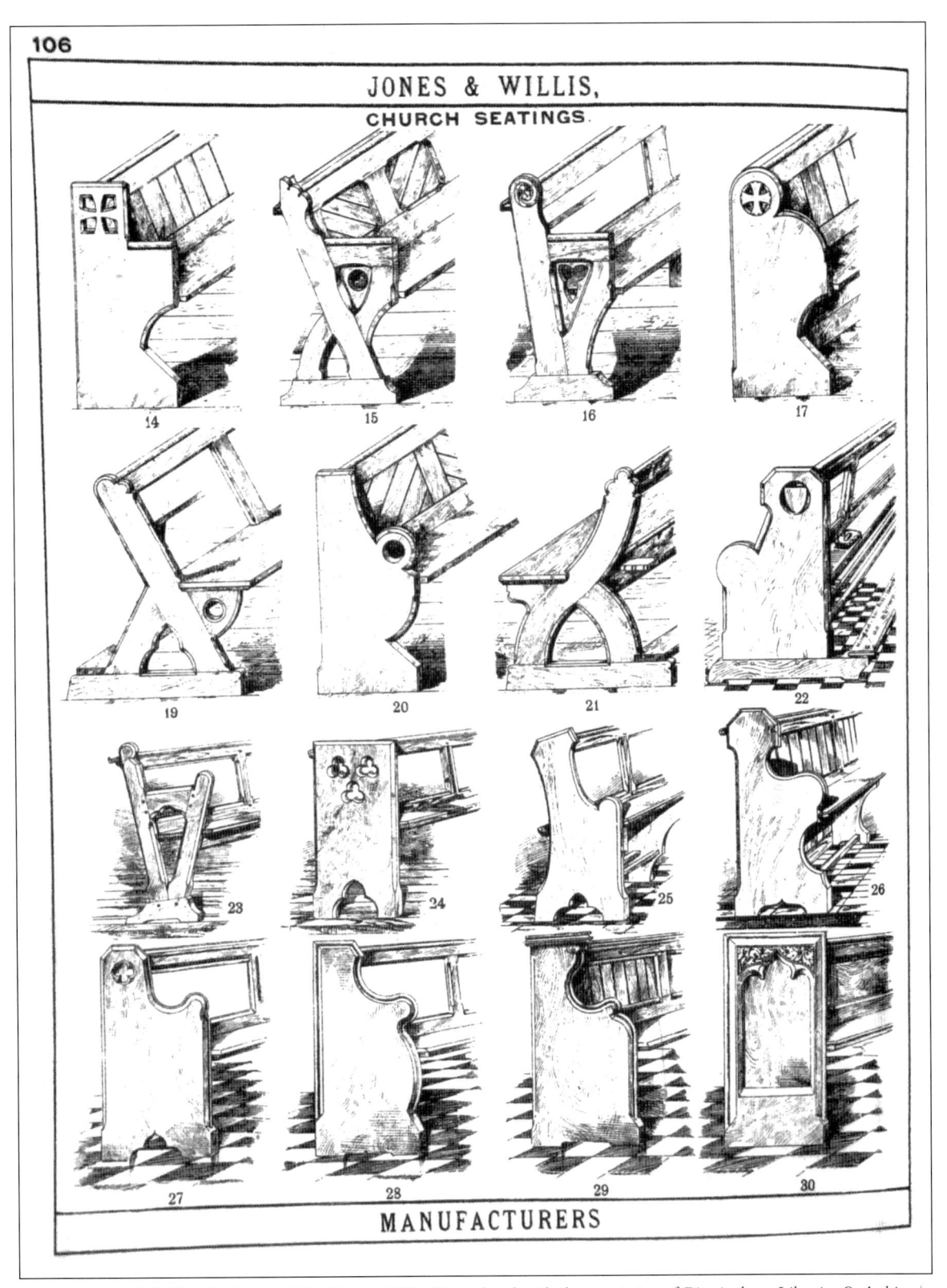

Fig. 10: *Jones & Willis Catalogue, 64th edition, 1893. (Reproduced with the permission of Birmingham Libraries & Archives)*

PEWS, BENCHES AND CHAIRS

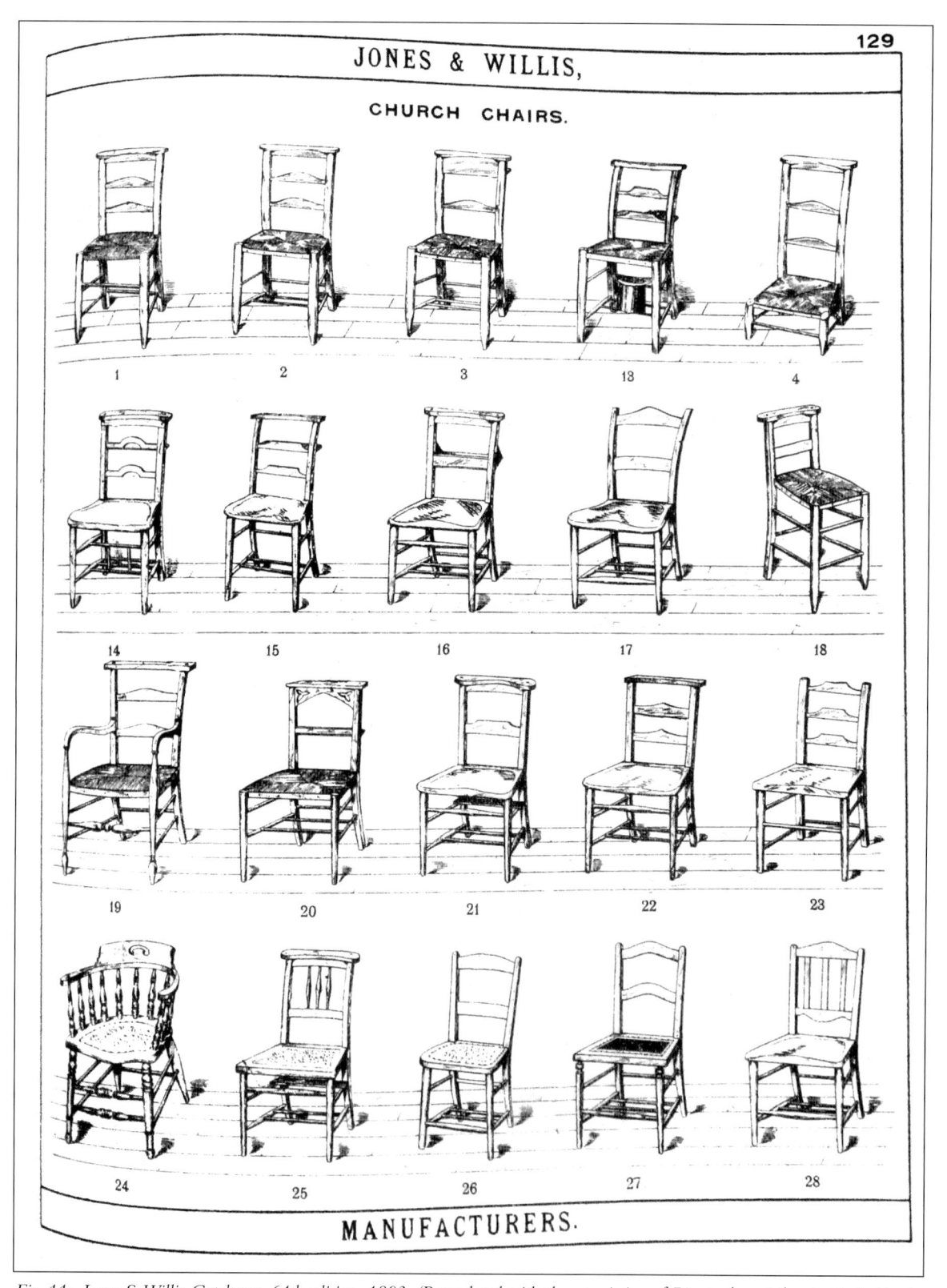

Fig. 11: Jones & Willis Catalogue, 64th edition, 1893. (Reproduced with the permission of Birmingham Libraries & Archives)

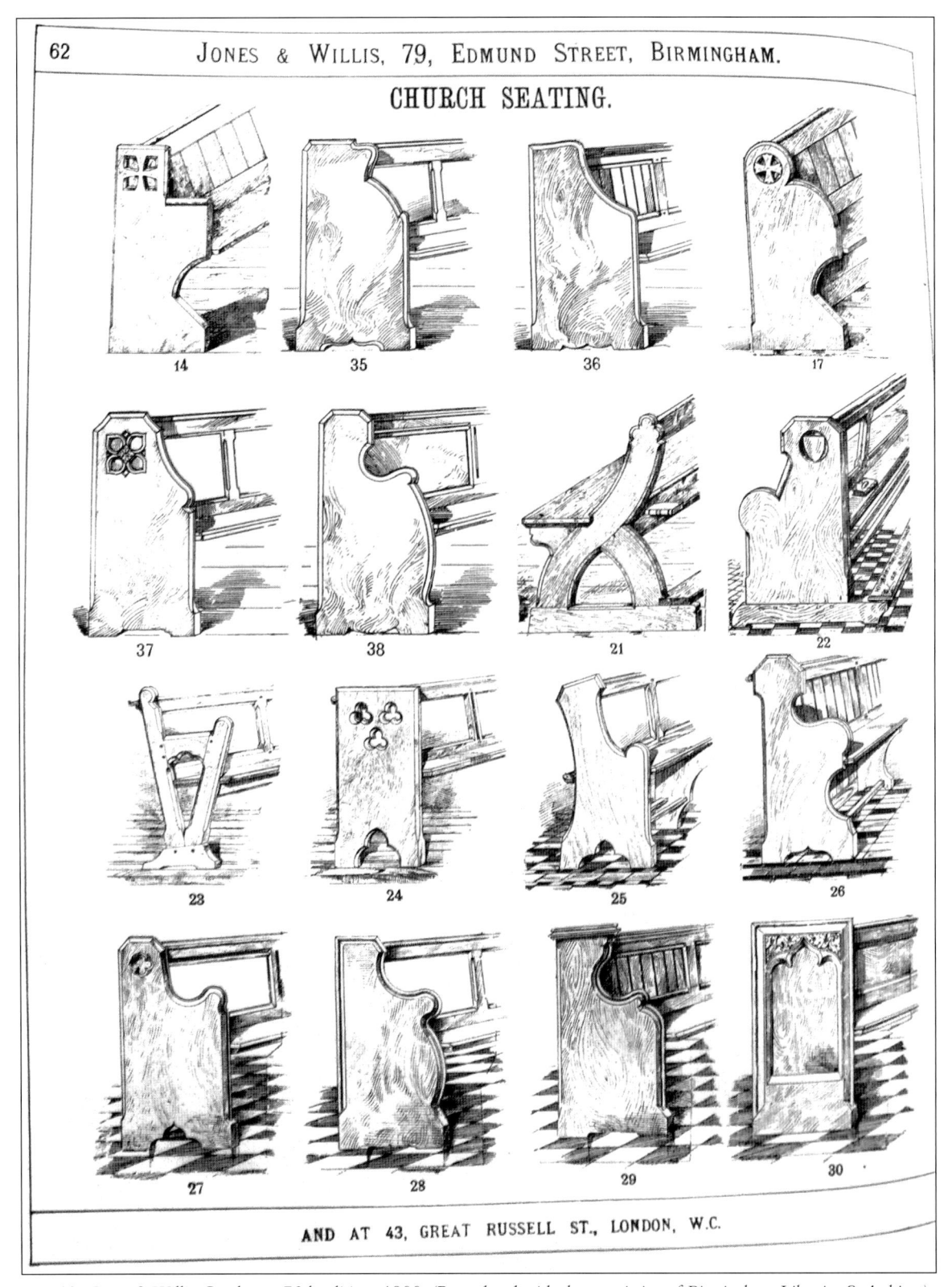

Fig. 12: Jones & Willis Catalogue, 70th edition, 1899. (Reproduced with the permission of Birmingham Libraries & Archives)

PEWS, BENCHES AND CHAIRS

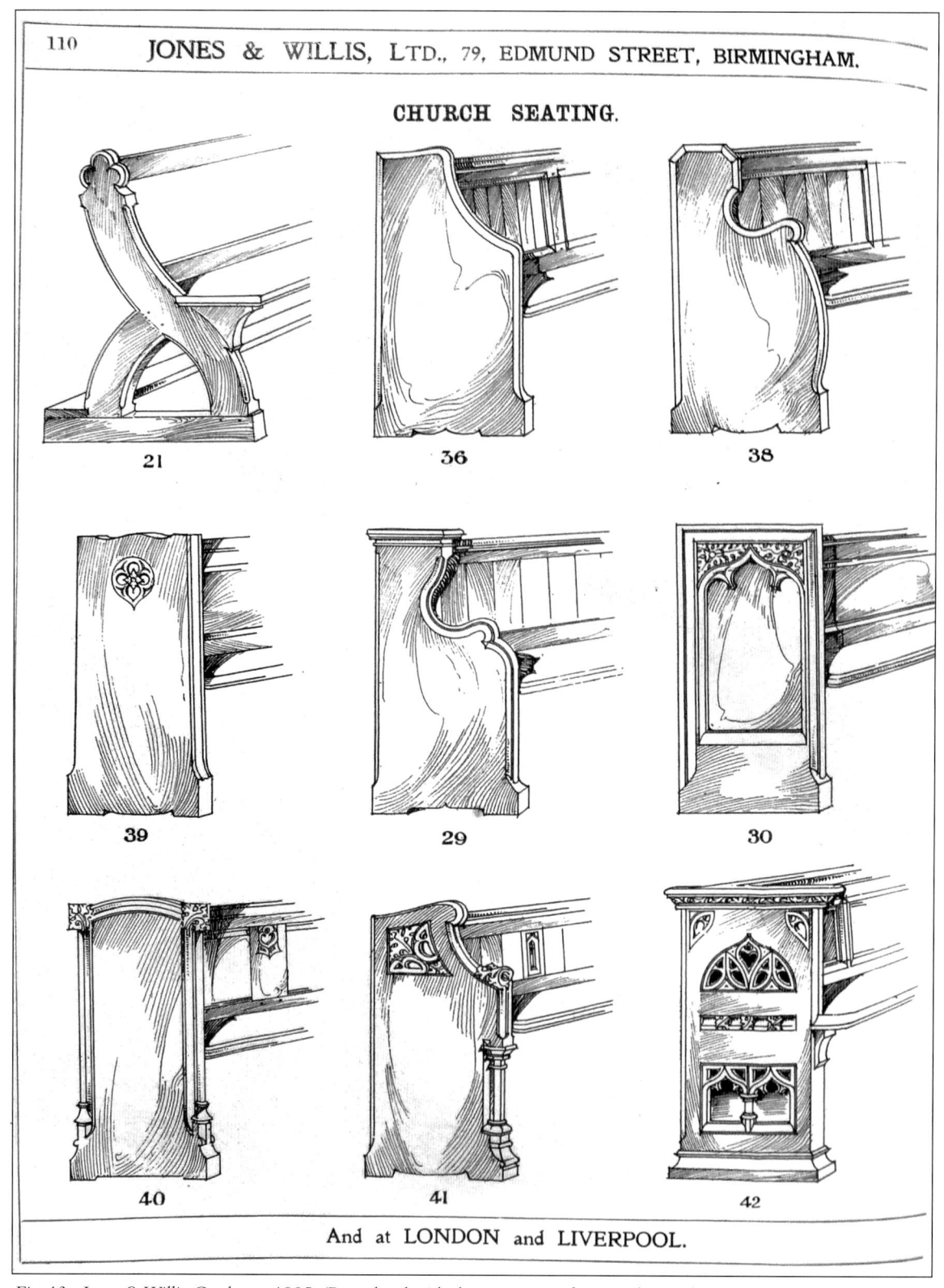

Fig. 13: Jones & Willis Catalogue, 1905. (Reproduced with the permission of Birmingham Libraries & Archives)

SPOILED FOR CHOICE: SEATING FROM THE CATALOGUE

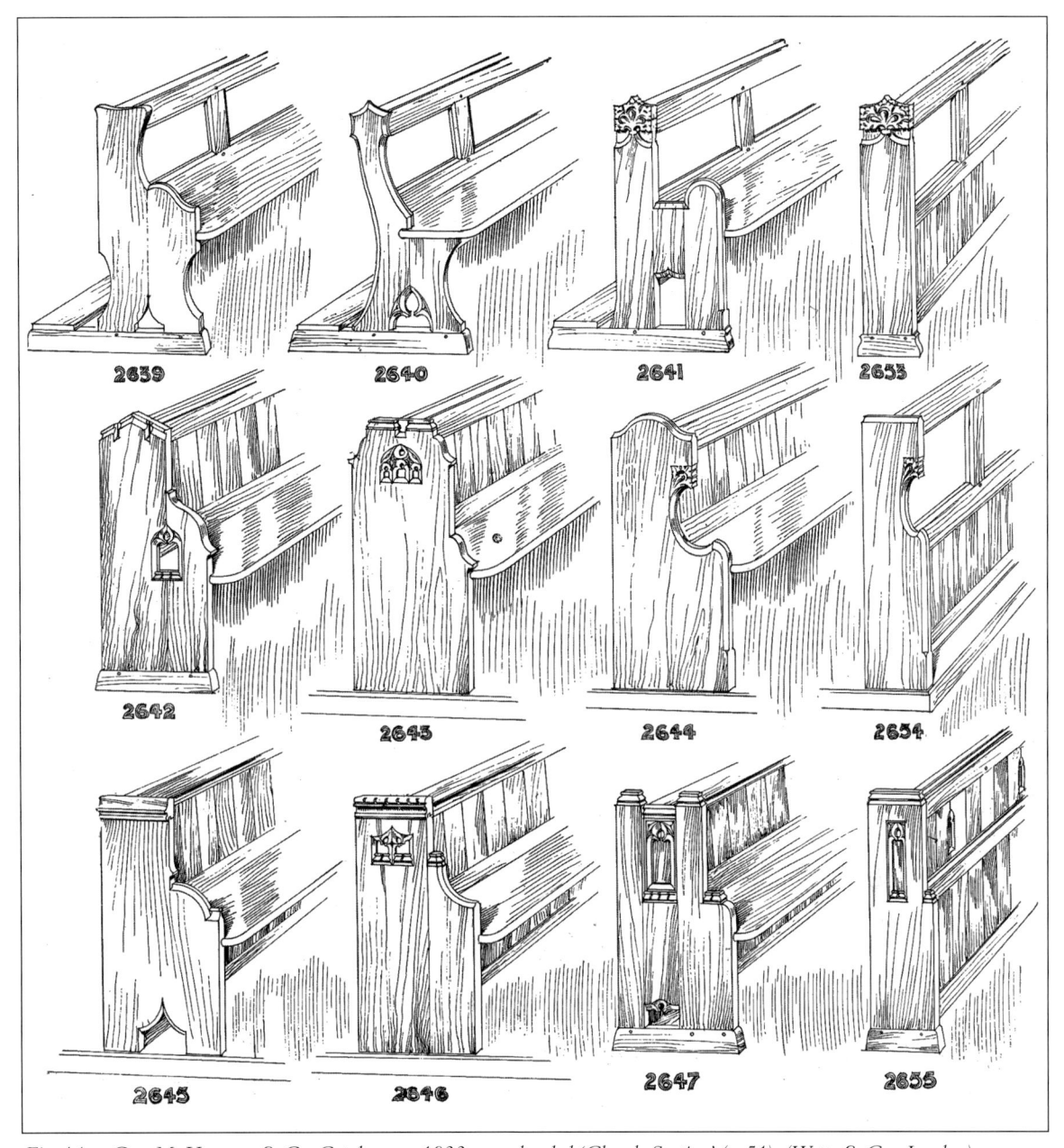

Fig. 14a: Geo. M. Hammer & Co. Catalogue, c.1933, page headed 'Church Seating' (p. 51). (Watts & Co., London)

PEWS, BENCHES AND CHAIRS

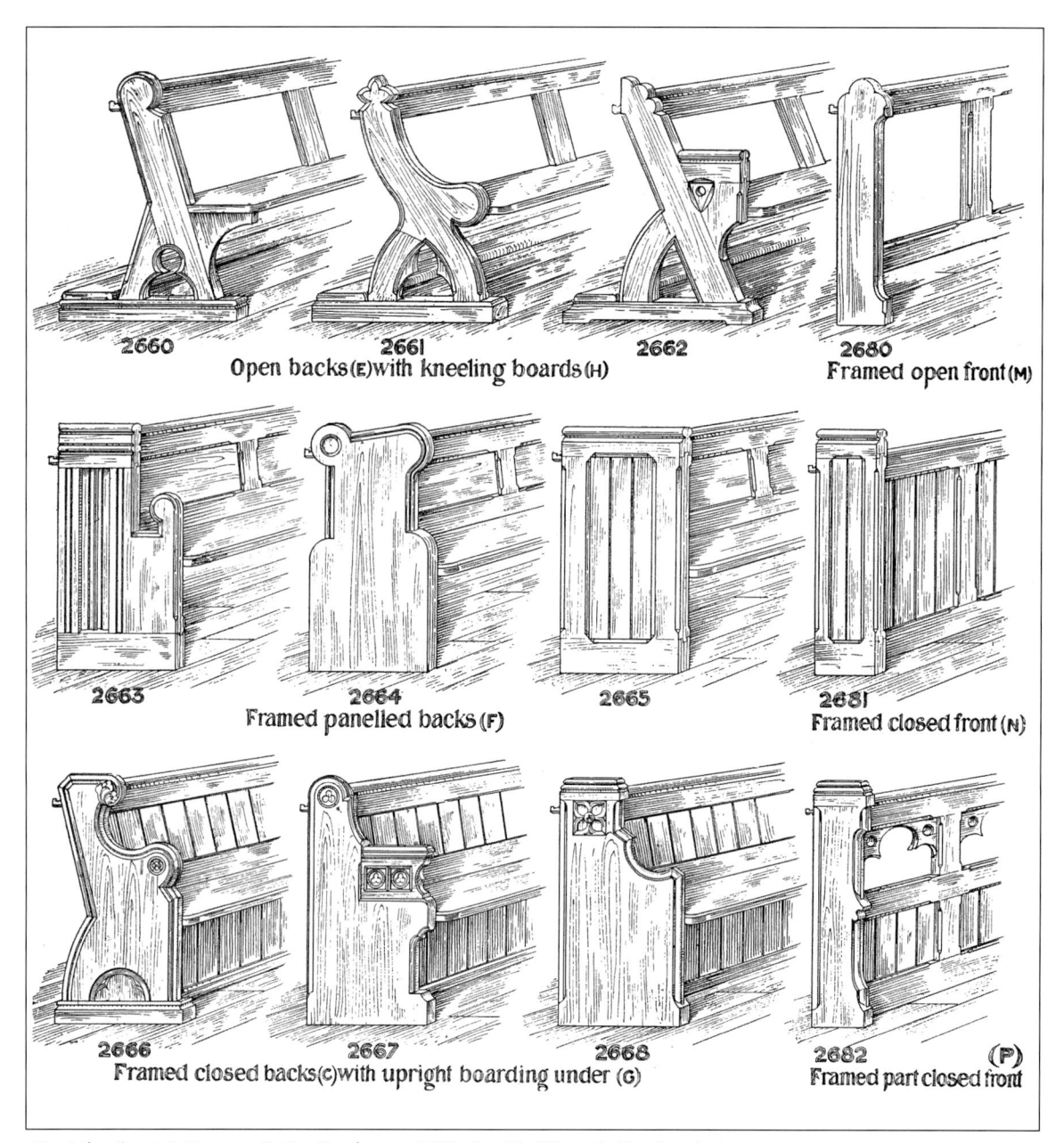

2660 **2661** **2662** Open backs (E) with kneeling boards (H)   **2680** Framed open front (M)

2663 **2664** Framed panelled backs (F) **2665**   **2681** Framed closed front (N)

2666 **2667** **2668** Framed closed backs (C) with upright boarding under (G)   **2682** (P) Framed part closed front

Fig. 14b: Geo. M. Hammer & Co. Catalogue, c.1933, (p. 52). (Watts & Co., London)

SPOILED FOR CHOICE: SEATING FROM THE CATALOGUE

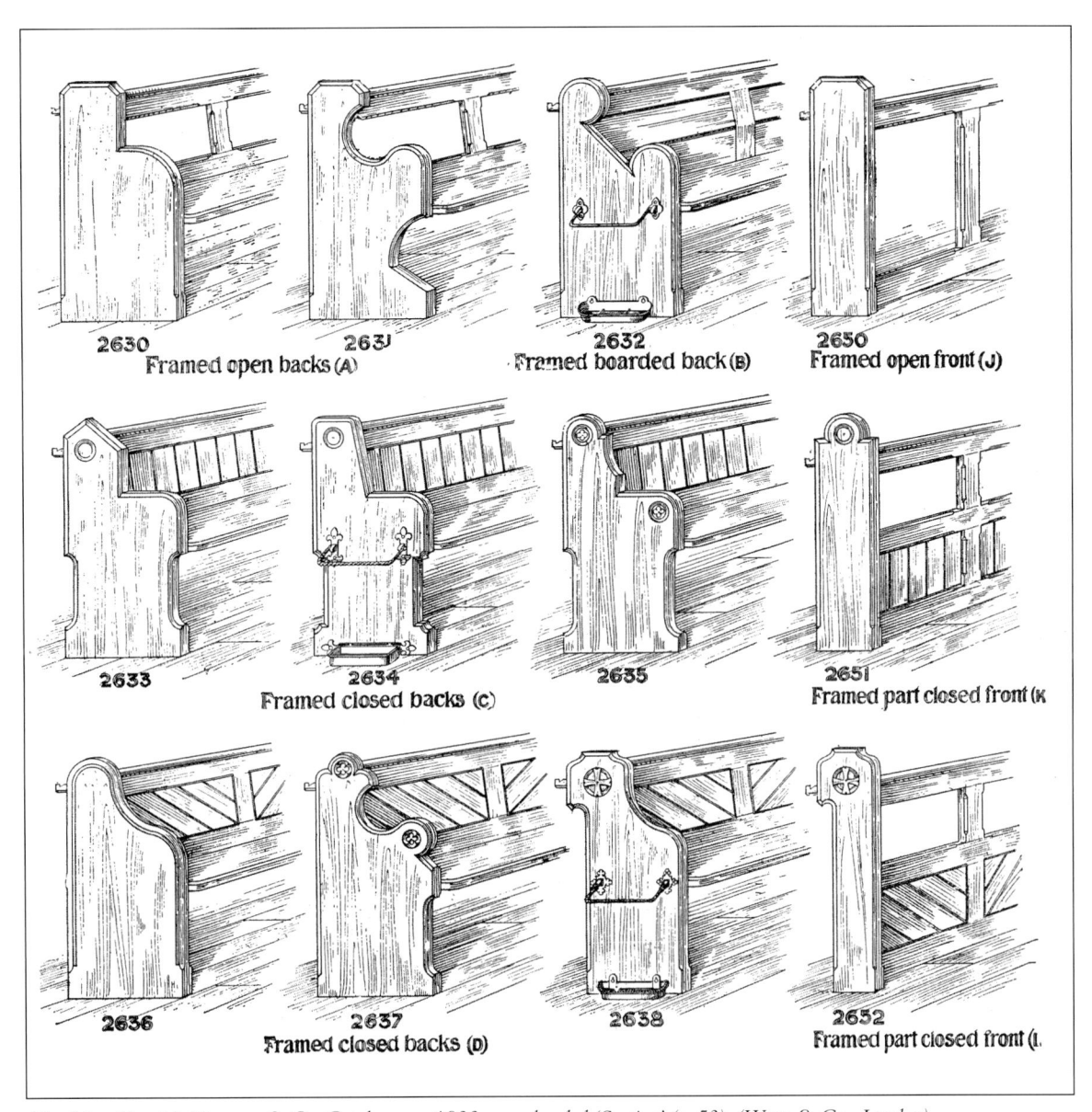

2630	2631	2632	2650
Framed open backs (A)		Framed boarded back (B)	Framed open front (J)
2633	2634	2635	2651
	Framed closed backs (C)		Framed part closed front (K)
2636	2637	2638	2652
	Framed closed backs (D)		Framed part closed front (L)

Fig. 14c: Geo. M. Hammer & Co. Catalogue, c.1933, page headed 'Seating' (p. 53). (Watts & Co., London)

Notes

1. In Chapter 7 of his PhD thesis, 'The Reverend Ernest Geldart (1848-1929) and Late Nineteenth Century Church Decoration' (Courtauld Institute of Art, University of London, 1999). This paragraph and the next rely heavily on Dr Bettley's work.
2. Bettley lists surviving catalogues known to him for four firms of church furnishers (Bettley, 'Geldart', Annex 7.1 to Chapter 7).
3. Birmingham Central Library, Archives and Heritage, catalogued as 'overZZ281'. The volumes are numbered 1–36, but some volumes are in more than one part, and there is no volume 5. The first six volumes are of drawings, the remainder of photos of executed work.
4. Drawings of bench ends in ibid., vol. 1(a), fols. 133, 134, 188; and of umbrella holders in vol. 6, fols. 310, 355, 358, 359.
5. The list of copies and references are given in Bettley, 'Geldart', Annex 7.1 to Chapter 7, except for the two additional copies, one of which we assume to be of 1870, and the other which is of 1879. The former is held by Princeton Theological Seminary Library, and is available online at www.archive.org/details/illustratedcatal00jone (accessed 10 August 2009; it is reproduced here as Fig. 4). The 1879 edition is in a bookseller's hands (Best Buy Books, 10 August 2009) and we have not seen it. Note that the Princeton copy is described on the title page as the 48th edition but has no date, though from internal evidence it must be later than 1862 (personal correspondence, the librarian); as the 1875 version is described as the '57th edition', we have estimated the date of the 48th edition to be about 1870. However, the 1879 edition (which we have not seen) is described by the bookseller as the 49th edition ('with many new designs'), so there appears to be some discrepancy. Additional note: shortly before going to press, we located a further edition (the 56th, catalogued as 1873) in the New York Public Library (ref: 3-MRBV Jones & Willis, Ltd., London. Illustrated catalogue).
6. There seems an anomaly in the pricing in that no. 9 is (understandably in our view) cheaper than no. 7 when in pine, the same price in pitch pine and yet (presumably mistakenly) 10s dearer in oak.
7. The bibliographical references are as follows. Fig. 1: Cox & Son, *Illustrated catalogue of church furniture, painted glass, and monuments* (1866), 6; Fig. 2: Cox & Sons, *Illustrated catalogue of church furniture, decoration, Gothic metal work, including church plate and lighting arrangements, altar cloths, carpets, hangings, &c.* (1877), 7; Fig. 3: Cox, Sons, Buckley, & Co., *Illustrated catalogue of art manufactures* (n.d; after 1881 when Buckley & Co. merged with Cox & Sons), 26; Fig. 4: *An illustrated catalogue of some of the articles in church furniture, clerical robes, &c. manufactured by Jones and Willis*, 48th edition (n.d., ? 1870), 80; Fig. 5: *An illustrated catalogue of some of the articles in church furniture, manufactured by Jones and Willis (Willis Brothers* (57th edn, 1875), 134 & 135; Fig 6: *Abridged illustrated catalogue of art furniture hangings & embroidery suitable for church purposes manufactured by Jones & Willis* (1883), 38; Figs. 7, 8 & 9: Birmingham Central Library, Archives and Heritage, Jones & Willis Pattern Books (catalogued as 'overZZ281'), volume 1a, fols. 133, 134 & 188; Figs. 10 & 11: *An illustrated catalogue of some of the articles in church furniture ... &c* (64th edn, in new and revised form, 1893), 102, 129; Fig. 12: *An illustrated catalogue of some of the articles in church furniture, manufactured by Jones & Willis, church furnishers to Her Most Gracious Majesty...* (70th edn, 1899), 62; Fig. 13: *A book of designs of ecclesiastical art by Jones & Willis Ltd* (80th edn, 1905), 110; Figs. 14a, b, c: Geo. M. Hammer & Co. Ltd., *Church Furniture* (n.d., c.1933), 51, 52, 53 (the Watts & Co. copy having an inserted letter of 1939); not illustrated here but referred to, Geo. M. Hammer & Co. Ltd., *Church Furniture* (n.d., c.1920), in possession of one of the authors.
8. Bettley, 'Geldart', 156.

21. Machine carving of Victorian pew ends: some initial findings

Jo Cox

Author's note: My investigation into machine-carved pews is still far from complete. I was persuaded by the editors that these initial findings were worth publishing, not least to alert readers to the existence of such objects. I plan to write a more extended study at a later date, and would welcome further examples of Victorian bench ends, or other church woodwork, carved by machine.

ALTHOUGH VICTORIAN MACHINE-CARVING has received some attention in general books on furniture,[1] it is rarely, if ever, remarked upon in respect of nineteenth-century church seating.

This may be because the identifying characteristics of machine carving are not likely to be visible unless the woodwork is stripped of varnish and/or stain. By happy accident this was the condition of one of the carved bench ends at St Mary's church, Bridgwater, Somerset before the PCC commissioned a study of its nave seating from the author, in connection with a proposal to remove some, or all, of the Victorian pews. By an even happier accident, the study was undertaken with the help of two parishioners, Tony Woolrich and Dr Peter Cattermole, who not only brought their knowledge of the church and its documentary history to the project, but who both happened to be vastly knowledgeable about nineteenth-century machinery. Their knowledge and advice has been fundamental to this investigation; indeed, without their assistance, the author would probably not even have noticed the machine marks on the stripped bench end at St Mary's.

The repewing of St Mary's church, Bridgwater

The congregational seating at St Mary's, Bridgwater, Somerset was produced as part of a major restoration of 1847–52, the latter part overseen by the architect William Hayward Brakspear (1818–98). An Oxford-educated, and presumably reforming incumbent, the Reverend T. G. James had arrived at St Mary's in 1848, rapidly followed by a competition for restoration and reseating. Architects who could combine 'correctness of architecture with the smallest outlay and greatest increase in accommodation' were invited to compete.

According to the building committee, at this time the church interior was 'disfigured by an unsightly mass of pewing, varying in height, and concealing from view some of the most striking features of the building'.[2] Furthermore, only fourteen of the

200 box pews at St Marys were for the poor, providing free seating for only 56 people.[3] The number of seats and percentage of free seats was to be massively increased and the work received grant-aid from the diocese and the Incorporated Church Building Society on this basis.

The Manchester architects Dickson and Brakspear won the competition and were contracted by June 1849. Their plans promised to increase the number of sittings in the church from 583 to 1,383, half of which were to be free. Once the competition was won, it was Brakspear alone who undertook the design work.

Little has been discovered about Brakspear. He and Dickson had designed the Commissioners' church, Christchurch, Ashton-under-Lyne, in 1847–8. According to his own account in *The Builder*, illness forced him to give up the Manchester practice and he decided to move to London. Indeed, the Bridgwater commission seems to represent Brakspear's separation from Dickson. He clearly lived in Bridgwater during the work on the church, which he supervised personally, but was 'impatient to get to London' and by 1852 his address was given as 1, Adelphi Terrace, London.[4]

By October 1849, some four months after Brakspear's appointment, the old box pews at St Mary's had been removed and, by inference, temporary seating installed. A letter to *The Bridgwater Times* was published that month, and nicely illustrates local dissatisfaction with the alterations to the church. It is a reminder that liturgical and architectural changes were often imposed on a reluctant and conservative congregation by zealous incumbents. The correspondent (probably a newspaper fiction) bewails the loss of the box pews:

> I don't like the going on in our old church. I'd as sooner sit in a barn as there just now. I used to have a cosy comfortable seat, where as sure as Sunday came I used to go without let or hindrance and where I looked round and saw lots of neighbours met together for public worship in decent and respectable order, and now I cannot find a place for myself or see where my old neighbours are poked to but am poked about on some rickety stool jostling against nobody knows who in a most uncomfortable manner.[5]

Tenders for the new nave seats at St Mary's were received in December 1849. John Wainwright of Bridgwater was awarded the contract, price £461, and the leader in *The Bridgwater Times* stated that 'the works are to be prosecuted with the greatest vigour and activity, and that the whole of the reseating is to be completed by Easter next' [i.e. Easter 1850].

The actual completion date for the reseating is not entirely clear. By early April 1850 it was reported that there had been objections because the new pews were not so comfortable as the old, but it was not fair to judge as they were unfinished.[6] In December 1850 a newspaper account refers to 'unfinished seats' below the tower arch[7] and in 1851 the Diocesan Church Building Association reported 'extensive variations' in the plan for reseating. The nave seating is recorded as finished by 31 March 1852 when the Revd James wrote to the Diocesan Society stating that 'The Nave of the Church was now completed and the whole of the seating fixed, stained and varnished'.[8]

It is worth noting that neither the surviving primary sources,[9] nor the newspaper reports and letters on the restoration at St Mary's, nor correspondence regarding the work in *The Builder* mentions the use of machine-carving for the benches.[10] If this absence of information in the records is typical, observation may be the most productive route to identifying machine-carving in other churches.

It has not yet been possible to establish whether any of Brakspear's later church work used machine-carved seating. He rebuilt the medieval church of St Mary the Virgin at Bowdon, Greater Manchester, 1851–61. This is listed Grade II★ and, as far as research so far has been able to establish, appears to represent his major surviving church work. No information to date has been gleaned on the seating there, or in the medieval church of St Bartholomew in Wilmslow, which he restored 1861–5. He also

Fig. 1: Congregational seating at St Mary, Bridgwater, Somerset.

designed the Wesleyan church of St Paul in Bowdon, Greater Manchester, built in 1874. This had a large dome and was described as 'a gothic monstrosity' by Sir Nikolaus Pevsner, who nevertheless regretted its demolition in 1968.

The pew ends at St Mary's

Brakspear's design drawings for the existing benches at St Mary's have not been found. An undated long section of the church drawn by Brakspear does show bench ends, but these are of a different design (shouldered on one side) than those actually installed. During discussion about the design of the new seating at St Mary's in October 1849, the Diocesan Architect had commented: 'I would however suggest whether the seat ends might not be treated more in accordance with medieval examples',[11] and it may be he was referring to the shouldered design.

The surviving Victorian pews are indeed loosely based on late medieval models, of the kind published as inspiring line drawings in *The Builder* in the 1840s (Fig.1). They are of deal, with oak ends. The ends are typically 14½ inches wide. They have concave corners and are carved with two tiers of blind tracery and a hollow-chamfered border. There are two types of ends, though the differences between them are minor (Figs. 2a & b). In the lower tier Type One has quatrefoils rather than the trefoils carried by Type Two; and in the top tier, Type 1 has spandrels which are foliage-carved rather than simply moulded. In addition, the westernmost bench in the north-west block has an end which is a wider version of a Type One bench. It may be a survivor (re-sited) of the churchwardens' benches, which are shown as stalls on Brakspear's plan, tucked against the responds of the tower arch. This design of only two variations in the types of carving on the ends would have provided enough repeated elements to make the manufacture of metal patterns economical.

The Type 1 bench end which had been cleaned of stain and varnish was in the south aisle and exhibited circular marks and plugged holes noticed by Dr Cattermole (Fig. 3), proof of some form of machine-assisted work. Both he and Tony Woolrich are confident that these are the marks of carving machinery. Dr Cattermole considers that the marks on the bench end are consistent with a moving tool rather than a moving piece and thus more likely to be evidence of an Irving process than from a Jordan style machine (the distinction is discussed later).

If Irving's machine, or something like it, was employed at Bridgwater, there would have been an element of hand-finishing, presumably undertaken by Wainwright, the contractor for the seating, at Bridgwater (Fig. 4). Nothing on Wainwright, apart from

Fig. 2: Bridgwater bench ends: (a) top, Type 1; (b) bottom, Type 2. See text for details.

Fig. 3: A detail of the marks on the Type 1 bench end that had been stripped of stain and varnish.

his Bridgwater address, has been found, and nothing to suggest that he may have had a carving machine in his workshop.

The use of machinery may possibly help explain the hard-edged character of the bench ends. This does not have the same appeal for the twenty-first-century eye as hand-carving, but is a typical early Victorian quality. It has parallels with other mass-produced objects and features in an age of huge progress in technology, e.g. the shiny and even character of encaustic tiling in contrast to medieval two-colour tiles.

Types of machine carving

There were a number of patent carving machines with a reputation for producing Gothic woodwork (and carving in soft stone) by 1849, the date of the commencement of the reseating at St Mary's. William Irving took out a patent on a carving machine in November 1843, and, according to one contemporary description, the machine was particularly suited to work in one plane, 'such as the mouldings of Gothic tracery, whether straight, curved, or undercut, and of all sections; the work is generally executed from templates or pattern plates'.[12] Irving worked in partnership with Samuel Pratt of Bond Street, who seems to have marketed the output of Irving's machine, to which Pratt's name

Fig. 4: The spandrel carving of the bench end would have been a hand-finished element.

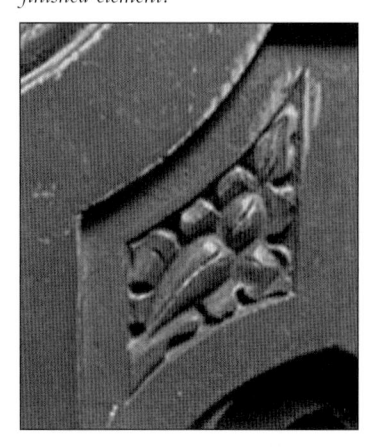

was often attached, with no reference to its inventor.[13] Thomas Jordan's carving machine was patented in 1845.[14] It was steam-driven. Two other carving machines were patented in the same year. Both Irving and Jordan's machines used rotating cutting heads and controlled the carving by following the contours of a master pattern or template, made of metal. One way in which the machines varied was whether the cutting head moved over the wood being carved (Irving's machine), or whether the material to be carved was moved while the cutting tools remained virtually stationary (Jordan's).[15]

Jordan's machine seems to have become the market leader. Enquiries to the Science Museum by Dr Cattermole established that the museum had held a 1:4 scale model of Jordan's machine for carving wood and other materials, but it was removed from the collection in the 1950s and destroyed.[16]

Machine carving was only economical for repetitive work, so bench ends made in this way are likely to be uniform or of just one or two types. This may aid identification, especially if an off-centre element were found repeated. Although the carving was hand-finished, it may be that the marks of the rotating cutting tool will still be visible in places, though the Bridgwater example shows that stain and varnish can render such marks invisible. Irving's specification drawings show the timber to be carved fixed in a kind of press, so the fixing itself may leave no marks.

The use of machine carving for pew ends and other church carving

Irving's machine was being actively marketed by Pratt as a means of carving pew-ends not long after its invention. In April 1845 some specimens of his carving in oak were exhibited to the Lincolnshire Society for the Encouragement of Ecclesiastical Architecture, for their inspection.[17] In November the previous year, Pratt personally exhibited specimens of his work to the Oxford Society for Promoting the Study of Gothic Architecture. One item, a 'rich bench end', was said to have been prepared for St Peter's church in the city (now the college library of St Edmund's Hall), copied from an original in Steeple Aston, Oxfordshire.[18] Bench ends carved by 'Pratt's machine', as it was called, were also installed in the newly-erected St Giles, Camberwell, London, consecrated in November, 1844 (Fig. 5). *The Ecclesiologist* did not like them: 'they are heavy and tame'.[19]

Both Irving's and Jordan's machines were well-publicised in various editions of *The Builder*. In particular, it reported in 1847 the use of Jordan's machine to carve woodwork in the new Palace of Westminster, by which date it had been used there for eighteen months, having been recommended by Charles Barry. The report

Fig. 5: Machine-carved bench ends at St Giles's church, Camberwell, London (discussed in the text). The blind tracery is found in a small number of variants, associated randomly with three styles of poppy-head. Was the whole bench end machine-carved? – or just the poppy-head and edge mouldings? Top row: three of the variants of the blind tracery. Bottom row: two of the three styles of poppy-head. Their faces are flat, with no attempt at three-dimensionality; the only interest arises from the concave edge mouldings.

in *The Builder* includes engravings of the House of Lords, one showing panels of blind tracery in the screens to the chamber.[20] As Edwards explains, Irving's machine (called Pratt's) and Jordan's machine were both used in this exciting national project which must have given carving machines respectability in the 1840s.[21] Brakspear, who was a fine draughtsman, provided what may have been the first contract drawings (exterior elevations) for the Palace of Westminster, presumably when working for Barry, and is likely to have encountered carving machines through connection with this project.[22]

In the years that followed, Jordan's machine undoubtedly became better known than those of Irving and Pratt. A firm of ecclesiastical suppliers, Cox & Son, purchased a machine in about 1859, and their advertising material showed it was used for 'seating' in St Barnabas, Pimlico and stalls in Streatham church.[23] They exhibited the machine at the International Exhibition 1862.[24] Their 1866 church furnishing catalogue had the following words of explanation:

> The wood work is for the most part prepared in the first instance by wood-carving machinery: in reference to which it is necessary to correct a misapprehension as to the extent to which the machinery is employed. It is used solely for the purpose of preparation, by the removal of superfluous parts of the material, and shaping it for subsequent hand-carving. The wood so prepared is then removed to hot-air chambers, in which it is thoroughly dried; and is then handed over to the carver, who finishes the work by hand. . . . the mere manual labour of the hand-carving is greatly diminished by the preparatory manual process, without the artistic excellence of the work being in the slightest degree impaired.[25]

A shortened version of this explanation appeared in the 1877 catalogue (and perhaps later ones – none have been located), indicating the continuing use of machine carving for ecclesiastical furnishings by this company.

It is not known, however, what volume of ecclesiastical work was machine carved by the Jordan machine owned by Cox & Son, nor over what period, nor how much of that might have been bench ends, nor how many bench-end patterns they had available. Nor is it known whether other ecclesiastical furnishers had their own machine, or subcontracted work to Cox and Son or to others with a carving machine. In short, the author at present has no real idea whether the quantity of machine-carved church seating was tiny, or whether the examples known to her (listed in the Table) are the tip of a large – possibly very large – iceberg.[26] She would very much welcome any further sightings of ecclesiastical examples, either of the objects themselves, or of documentary references to them.

Table: Machine-carved church seating known to the author

Date	Location	Item	Machine	Status	Note
about 1844	St Giles, Camberwell, London	Bench ends	Pratt	Extant	
about 1845	St Peter, Oxford	Bench ends	Pratt	Not extant	1
about 1849	St Mary, Bridgwater, Somerset	Bench ends	? Pratt	Extant	
by 1859	St Barnabas, Pimlico, London	'Seating'	Jordan	Not known	2
by 1859	Streatham, South London	Stalls	Jordan	Not known	3

1. It is not currently known whether the bench ends were installed in St Peter's.
2. Machine-carved 'seating' in the church was mentioned in an advertisement in 1859 and probably consisted of free standing chairs or stalls (on the assumption, not yet tested, that the pews, which are of simple repetitive blind tracery with some hand-carving, were installed by the time the church was consecrated in 1850).
3. The church has not yet been identified.

Acknowledgements

I would like to thank Dr Peter Cattermole and Tony Woolrich, who alerted me to the significance of the pew ends at Bridgwater, and have been generous in sharing their great knowledge of machine carving in Victorian times. My thanks are also due to Dr James Bettley for so readily sharing his material on Cox and Sons. I am grateful to Trevor Cooper for helpful comment on an earlier version of this chapter, and for taking the photographs of the bench ends at Camberwell. Other photographs are by the author, who may be contacted through Keystone Historic Buildings Consultants, 3 Colleton Crescent, Exeter, EX4 6TB, e-mail: keystonehb@aol.com.

Notes

1. For example in Clive Edwards, *Victorian Furniture: Technology and Design* (Manchester, 1993).
2. *The Bridgwater Times*, 7 June 1849.
3. *The Bridgwater Times*, 4 April 1850.
4. Record of works to chancel, Somerset RO, D\DWB f8/2. For *The Builder*, see note 10.
5. *The Bridgwater Times*, October 1849.
6. *The Bridgwater Times*, 4 April, 1850.
7. *The Bridgwater Times*, 5 December 1849.
8. Somerset RO, D\DWB f8/2.
9. Although plans and drawings of the seating by Brakspear survive, they need to be treated with some caution as they are not all consistent with one another, or with what survives. A plan dated 1854, at least two years after the seating was completed, labelled 'Accommodation' is believed to show what was actually done. A copy of this plan was sent to the Incorporated Church Building Society.

10 Criticism of both the character of Brakspear's scheme and his fees appeared in *The Builder* in the 1850s, with Donaldson, the President of the then recently established Royal Institute of Architects, commenting on his fees. Brakspear responded. (*The Builder*, no. 450, 20 September 1851, p. 597 and no. 646, 23 June 1855, p. 298.)

11 Somerset RO, D\DWB f8/2.

12 Charles Holtzapffel, *Turning and Mechanical Manipulation*, 2nd edn, 1846, Vol. 2 note J. William Irving was granted three patents: No. 9,962 on 25 November 1843; No. 10,517 on 10 Feb 1845; and No. 12,073 on 23 Feb 1848. They all related to methods of cutting mouldings in wood and soft stone.

13 The development of carving machines is described in detail in an article by Clive Edwards 'The mechanization of carving: the development of the carving machine, especially in relation to the manufacture of furniture and the working of wood' in *The History of Technology*, Vol. 20, 1998, ed. Graham Hollister-Short, pp. 73–102.

14 Thomas Brown Jordan was granted three patents for woodworking machines: No. 10,377 of 2 November 1844; No. 10,523 of 17 February 1845; and No. 11,564 of 8 Feb 1847. The second concerned his famous carving machine, and the third concerned a machine for making mouldings. According to Holtzapffel, *Turning*, Vol. 2 (note K) the machine described in the second patent was more in use for machining figures and shapes than for making mouldings. A detailed account of the machine, written by Jordan and too long to include here, was published in 1852 in the *Transactions of the Society of Arts*. A search for illustrations of Irving's machine by Tony Woolrich in nineteenth-century publications drew a blank, but a description of Jordan's formed a major part of the article 'Carving by machinery' in Tomlinson's *Cyclopaedia* (1854) (which did not mention Irving's method at all).

15 A fourth known machine, Braithewaite's, need not concern us as its system for repeatedly charring damp wood in a shaped mould and scraping away the charring was too laborious to have been used for church seating.

16 A *Country Life* article of 1954 reproduced a photograph of the model (G. B. Hughes, 'Mechanical carving machines', *Country Life*, 23 Sep 1954, 980-81).

17 *The Second report etc. of the of the Lincolnshire Society for the Encouragement of Ecclesiastical Architecture*, 1845, 18.

18 *Proceedings of the Oxford Society for Promoting the Study of Gothic Architecture*, Michaelmas term 1844, p. 22. The name of the exhibitor is given as S. Pratt.

19 *The Ecclesiologist*, New Series 1 (Old Series 4) (January 1845), 59.

20 *The Builder*, No. 213, 6 March, 1847, 108; No. 220, 3 April, 1847, 189–90.

21 Edwards, 'Mechanizaton', 85–87.

22 Photographic copies of two of these drawings signed by Brakspear, are in the Parliamentary Archives. The originals were sold at Sotheby's in 1990, the photographs acquired for the HLRO in 1996.

23 *Catalogue* of the Architectural Exhibition Society, 1859.

24 A recent discussion with Dr James Bettley (who has been most generous in sharing his information with the author) has revealed that Jordan's machine was certainly used for church pews. Dr Bettley has kindly provided a number of references, including the *Catalogue* of the Architectural Exhibition Society for both 1859 and 1860; Cox & Son, advertising leaflet, 1862, in NAL 86.ZZ.123 (Gimingham album).

25 Cox & Son, *Illustrated catalogue of church furniture, painted glass, and monuments* (1866), preface.

26 In addition to the church seating listed in Table 1, the following examples of other machine-carved ecclesiastical woodwork have also been noted, mostly from the secondary literature. 1. Carved with Pratt's machine: the pulpit and reading desk at St John's, St John's Wood, London (not extant); the roof and the screen at Great Malvern Abbey; stone work for St John's Church, Stratford. 2. Carved by Cox & Son, using Jordan's machine: 'works' for the chapel of the Middlesex Industrial School at Feltham; the pulpit of St Mary's church, Plympton; an altar table for Sydenham church; work at Westminster Abbey and Canterbury Cathedral. (For St John's, *Gentleman's Magazine*, July to December 1846, 191; for the remainder, Edwards, 'Mechanization', 81, 89 and n.70 on p. 101.)

Part 4

CONSIDERING CHANGE

22. Seats in church

Robert Maguire

Among the most difficult problems of rejuvenated Catholic and Reformed architecture is the space to be filled with seats and pews – in contrast to a church which is empty, to which one brings one's own kneeling cushion. Stuffing a church full of furniture is indefensible, not only aesthetically, since it destroys every architectonic line and makes illusory the effect of space, but also theologically, since the house of God is not an auditorium....To arrive at movable church furniture is one of the most pressing problems to be answered by architects and technicians.
   (Gerardus van der Leeuw, Sacred and Profane Beauty, *1963*)

It were to be wish'd there were to be no Pews, but Benches.
   (Sir Christopher Wren, 'Letter to a Friend' quoted in Parentalia)

THE PROBLEM ARISES DIRECTLY from the decision to have seats. A church with seats *tends to become a different kind of building* from one without; a tendency towards a building which is not a church. Such a statement requires some justification, and I will take what I believe to be the effects of seating one by one. It also requires a definition of what a church is. I believe that a church is a building (a *place*) set apart by the Christian people – set apart, given over, for the gathering together of the Christian people for the corporate doing of various things: to baptise, to hear the word of God read and preached, to celebrate the Eucharist, and to give praise. It is also a place of private prayer and spiritual counselling, but these are *a result of its being set apart*. Its main purposes are corporate.

   At this point already there will be those who will interject that, certainly since the 1960s, there are churches built with outreach mainly in mind, in which the main congregational space is also given over to functions of a social service and recreational nature. Observably, however, these buildings resonate, 'speak of', their general-purpose nature, and come outside the above definition of a church. The concept is perfectly valid, but the distinction has to be made. And for such buildings there is no problem about seating: a tough lightweight stacking chair (and plenty of storage) is all that is needed, and to be consistent, a trestle table for the Eucharist and a good basin for baptisms.

Seats stand in lieu of absent people
It is one of the main characteristics of architecture that the better a building serves that aspect of life for which it is designed, the

more it speaks of, reflects, or becomes the symbol of that purpose. This can be illustrated most easily in our living-rooms. Moving into a new house, we move things about, throw things out and bring things in until we are happy about the room as our living space. We feel the room now responds in some way to us. For others, the room corresponds to us; it speaks to them about us and our way of life. A house that looks like a small Town Hall is felt to be pretentious. A Town Hall, however, rightly reflects civic pride, and while probably being rather grand is not felt to be pretentious.

Because the church is the place of the People of God, its interior will speak of the nature of the worshipping community, even when empty. And two or three people who have come together in the church *are* the worshipping community, at that time and in that place. They are not just 'a disappointingly small congregation', aware mainly of their inadequacy; or at least they should not be, for they are completely sufficient for what is to be done, which is not quantitative. And they have, or should be able to have, a special relationship to the building, a relationship in which the building is brought to life by their presence, and amplifies for them the meaningfulness of what they are doing. This is the nature of a good church – that it responds to the people at any one time whether they are two or three, or two or three hundred.

A church without seats, if it is a good church, acts in this way because it is the architectural character of the *whole space* which gives it the quality of placeness, of being the place of the People of God. This character, which I have termed 'inclusive space', has an effect on each individual person. It *contains* him or her, and contains that person together with whomever is there as well, and brings them together in its purpose, which is their purpose. The place is no longer empty, because they are there: *they fill it.*

Two or three people, or twenty or thirty, cannot fill a church with two or three hundred seats. There is a level below which the building will appear empty. The seats have taken over, they have changed the architectonic character of the whole interior, and while there are seats unfilled, they stand unavoidably as symbols of emptiness, of people missing. With certain kinds of seating in a building which has a really strong – and appropriate – spatial character (and I will return to this phenomenon later) this effect can be reduced. But in varying degrees it will always be so. The emphasis has shifted from the sufficiency and completeness of the people present, to a quantitative measurement of them against an arbitrary norm. The effects on them are all too familiar: lonely in an empty building, they may feel themselves to be an inadequate corpus, or else that the liturgy is a private affair conducted for them as the stalwart faithful. Both attitudes need little encouragement to gain strength, and neither can be said to be advancing the work of the Church.

Seats make barriers

Liturgies involve a number of different kinds of relationship, generated in varying ways, between president or minister, congregation, choir, candidates for baptism, godparents, and so on. The relationship between preacher and people in a sermon, for example, is quite different to that between president and people at the Offertory. The singing of praise in a hymn has a different character from the solemn statement of the Creed. These relationships are expressed (although sometimes not very appropriately) by the physical attitudes we take up; standing, sitting, kneeling, walking in procession. Movement may seem not always to be actual but there is always something further, a movement of the mind or spirit. The use of the word 'outgoing', for example, shows by the metaphor this movement. When the president greets the people ('the Lord be with you') there is a movement to and fro.

Such movement is sufficiently associated for us with physical movement as to be hampered by physical arrangements of various kinds. I suffer from sciatica, and there comes a moment in a longish service when standing is difficult to bear, but it feels quite wrong not to be standing when standing is wholly appropriate to the liturgical action. It is hard to say with conviction the response to the president's greeting if he was looking at his wristwatch when he said the words; that is, it is difficult to respond to *a movement which has never reached you*. The *intention* may have been unequivocal, but the result is as though there were no intention to greet. Similarly it is difficult to achieve, for example, a full sense of offering at the altar when line upon line of physical barriers intervene.

An awareness of this is quite common. Some parishes (of various communions) instituted an Offertory procession in the 60s and 70s in an attempt to overcome just this difficulty. Offertory processions, however, pose a new problem: what do people do afterwards? Unless there is room (and the leadership and the consensus) for them all to remain standing around the place of the altar – which would be symbolically the appropriate 'movement' – they have to get back to their seats, and in a seated-out church this is not only unwieldy but effectively cancels out the advantages of the procession and tends to make the action appear meaningless. But the attempt shows the need to free people from the passivity imposed by barriers, to enable them to reach out, in body and in spirit, across the space of the church.

Imagine yourself walking through a park, and that you have some small, not overbearing reason not to walk on the grass but to keep to the path; pushing a friend in a wheelchair, for instance. The grass begins at the path edge, stretching away into the distance, green and rolling. It is a pleasant walk. Now imagine the same circumstances, except that the Borough Council has constructed a close-boarded fence three feet high on both sides of all paths. You can still see the green rolling grass of the park, which is even more beautifully kept for you to look at by the Council. Your enjoyment is less? But be reasonable, *you never actually went onto the grass* before!

It is not so much the execution of the physical movement, but the knowledge that the physical movement is possible, that frees the mind and perhaps the spirit to make the movement for itself.

Much has been said and written in the last fifty years about the 'long narrow medieval plan' and its unsuitability for modern worship on the grounds that people cannot see and hear the 'liturgical action'. Yet a great number of medieval churches are not particularly long and narrow. But they have been equipped, for historical reasons to be found elsewhere in this book, with high pews in serried ranks, two or four blocks of repetitive barriers, and no free space between them except minimum gangways. Many modern, reputedly 'enlightened' buildings have the same arrangement of pews, and for all their shortness and breadth, the feeling in them is similar.

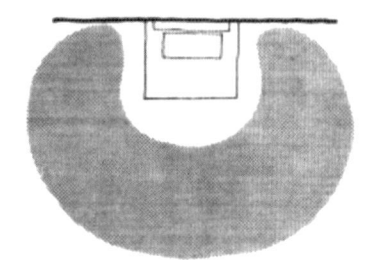

Fixed seats set up fixed patterns of relationship

Some years ago – for all I know they still do, but I now live in Scotland – the Polish community in London used a large and seatless side-chapel in Brompton Oratory as their own church. The altar had a large footpace which served, without rails, as a communion step. This was before Vatican II, and the altar was of course hard up against the wall, and people stood around, and their distribution was always as shown to the left.

This is the usual pattern people take up when unconstrained by any dominant architectural or furnishing arrangements. In fact, if the Eucharist is celebrated in a field, the same pattern can be seen despite the fact that the back wall is not there, and the reason is wholly to do with *relationship*: the priest cannot *greet* people who are behind his back.

Now it has been suggested many times that some of the main problems of new church design can be answered by sitting people down in this 'natural' distribution, and then housing its outline in a building of approximately similar shape. Seats, however, are subject to their own rules of layout, one of which demands rows or lines of some kind, and the results are very different to the random scatter that people put themselves into when standing around. The choice of possibilities is restricted to minor variants of the arrangements shown on the right.

In each case the result can be described as an increase in focusing power. Something that was formerly the result of the freedom to gather around and to gather *together* in a natural pattern of relationship (one person to another and each to the altar) is now formalised into a fixed relationship: an obligatory concentration inward as part of a focusing entity. The significant thing theologically about this is the loss of 'gathering together', particularly in the two concentric arrangements: the intensity of the focus on the one hand, and the formalisation into line on the other, makes one's neighbour no longer a person but a unit in an audience.

There are of course times when the intensive one-way focus produces the appropriate relationship. The giving of a sermon may be one of these, or the reading of the Gospel. But in such cases some flexibility of focus-point is required. The inflexibility of focus-point produced by fixed seating has led some clergy and architects to advocate the close lumping-together of altar or communion table, pulpit, lectern, font, clergy seats and paschal candlestick. Even without the addition of microphones and cables, and perhaps a music group with loudspeakers (which is not uncommon) you are getting close to the ultimate stage in the abolition of distinctions of relationships within the Church's worship.

The decision to have seats – and obviously this decision is already made for us in all but very exceptional circumstances – will always bring with it the problem of inappropriate over-focusing, and the designer's task in this respect is to mitigate the effect. Fortunately it is not only seating which has determining effects on relationships within worship, nor even is it the prime mover, unless the whole space of the building takes its cue from the plan-shape of the seats, whereupon all negative effects are amplified. Modern examples of such effects, at opposite poles, are to be seen in Coventry Cathedral and the Roman Catholic cathedral in Liverpool. The answer to mitigation lies in the design of the whole space of the church, and in the case of existing churches, in observation of the intrinsic spatial characteristics of the building (usually obscured by later furnishings) and putting them to positive use. This is a matter to which I will return.

Seats themselves tend to become the place of the people

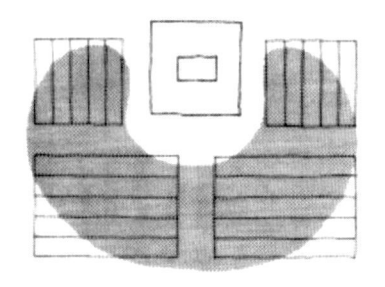

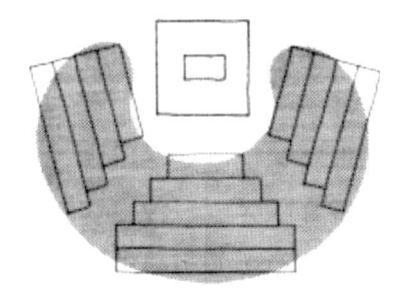

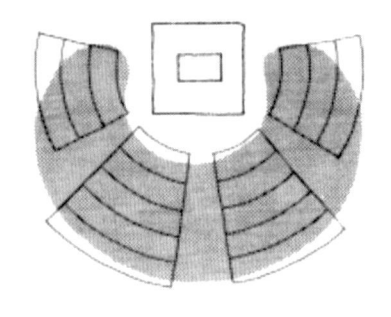

Currently, as noted at the beginning of this chapter, we have two rather different views of the nature of a church, and as I have said, I am starting from the premiss that a church is first of all the place of the Christian people, and for many who are even slightly theologically informed this is now such an established idea as to be beyond further investigation.

Most people, asked – even of a modern church – 'What do you understand by the place of the people?' would answer 'The nave' or 'The seats'. Our churches still shout this. There still seems to be no commonly held feeling that the whole church space is *their place*, they who are the 'royal priesthood ... a people belonging to God'. And there will be no commonly held *conviction* that it is in fact so – however much people are told, and expected to appreciate it as an intellectual idea – while our churches continue to speak of something different.

Church seating tends to impose this harmful misunderstanding of the nature of the church building, and hence of the nature of the Church, by a combination of the three effects I have described so far. Empty seats represent absentees and may engender feelings of inadequacy, seat-rows tie people into immobility physically with consequent mental, even spiritual passivity, and the blocks of seats reinforce the attitude *here you are in your place and that is going on over there in its place; concentrate on it.* By association with all the other seated-out places we know, the cinema, the theatre, the lecture-hall, seating encourages a 'front of house' attitude: *this is the public's part of the building.*

So what can we do about it?

All very well, you may say, but what can be done about it now? People *expect* seats in churches, standards of comfort rise continually along with the standard of living, people would not be willing to stand that long, nor to kneel without some support, not even the young and fit; and what of the aged and infirm?

Allowing that we will usually have to accept seating, and recognising its negative effects, there are ways in which these effects can be mitigated.

New churches

Taking the case of new churches first, the most urgent thing is to stop designing churches around seating layouts. This almost invariably hardens the already inflexible relationships set up by the seating. Often the desire to extend this idea to produce a building which is structurally 'exciting' leads to a more dramatic, overpowering inflexibility. This is not to decry structural inventiveness in church design – we are in need of some inspiration here – but to emphasise that more care is required in the choice of structural form in a church than in any other building type. The characteristics of space and of structure in architecture are intimately bound together, and particularly in a church, *it is the spatial organisation of the building which gives symbolic form*, which speaks of the nature of its purpose, of the nature of the Church, of the People of God for whom it exists, and of the relationships inherent in their use of it. The organisation of the whole three-dimensional space, in terms of material, structural form and light, is the true *means* of architecture, a dynamic means by which subtle distinctions can be made, distinctions which allow relationships to *happen through use*; in the case of a church, to develop *through worship*.

The basic element in the spatial organisation of a church is the floor. The floor is a datum to which each one of us relates directly, the level at which we are, and from which we act. It is the most important contributor to the quality of a church as a *place*, our place, and it runs throughout the building, uniting (unless cut up into patches of different materials and textures) the whole space. I invite the reader to look back at pages 32 & 33 of *Ecclesiology Today, Issue 40, July 2008*, to the two views of the interior of Brompton Oratory, to appreciate the architectonic strength of the floor and, by contrast, the effect of densely obscuring it.

It is significant that the floor is now generally neglected in church design, more attention being given to the seating which

Fig. 1: All Saints, Crewe, 1965 (architects Robert Maguire & Keith Murray). The church has a square plan and there is a processional ambulatory around all four sides. Natural lighting does not attempt the dramatic, but is so arranged that the whole space seems to include anyone within it. A five-seat version of the architects' early 'bench-pew' is used, designed with a view to allowing the floor to flow through as a uniting continuum. There is space for the whole congregation to stand forward, if they wish, for the Synaxis.

obscures it. There is a clear case for a lightness of touch in the design of seating, whether chairs or some form of pew or bench, and for flexibility of seating layout along with the ability to move the seating easily. The plan of the building should allow this flexibility actually to be exercised, which means that the 'space left over' from any predetermined (but hopefully provisional) seating layout should not be in the form of narrow gangways, hugging that arrangement.

This suggests the use of chairs rather than pews. For many years and in several of our early church designs, my partner Keith Murray and I used a four-seater low-backed 'bench pew', which I designed specially and seemed to us to answer to these requirements (Fig. 1). But while it could be moved about easily yet stayed put where you placed it without being fastened down, I have to concede that it does not give very great flexibility of layout. It does have the advantage that it sits on only two fin-like legs, which makes cleaning the floor easier than with the sixteen chair-legs which are needed to seat the same four people. It also has no pew-ends – verticals which visually diminish the horizontal continuum of the floor.

Chairs are far more flexible both in layout and – if stacking – in meeting different sizes of gathering. But they have many problems, and we still await a chair which acknowledges them, let alone solves them. The first problem arises because safety concerns may require that they be fixed together in groups. If this is done in an undemountable manner, as with the wooden battens used with the once ubiquitous rush-seat church chair, then you have the same limited flexibility as the four-seater bench pew. Modern designs use connecting clips of various kinds, but almost invariably these are attached to both front and back legs so that straight rows of chairs are the only option. It is entirely possible to attach connectors to the front legs only, so that chairs may be set up in curved rows.

Stacking poses great limitations on design, especially with wooden chairs, because no stiffening rails between legs are possible and this imposes large dimensions on the top joints, resulting in the ungainly boxy look which typifies the products of the main church-chair makers. These firms have however achieved chairs at prices many parishes can afford; but the obvious problem here is that the designers are quite unaware of the considerations raised by the nature of worship, particularly Eucharistic worship, and are still designing mere pew-replacements – their combined effect is usually of a kind of straight pew demanding arrangement in serried ranks and with a back too high for comfortable kneeling and no lumbar support.

At both high and low cost levels, there are stacking chairs with metal frames, and seats and backs varying from cheap polypropylene to good-quality upholstery. They all suffer from rigid straight-line interconnection, but the general design principle does in my view hold out hope for a suitable church chair. Their designers appear to assume a use for concert seating or public meetings, and hence the seat and back are shaped to tilt the body back into a comfortable listening position, guaranteed to produce passivity in any congregation.

It is at present an unsatisfactory situation, and we await an inspired chair designer who understands the nuances of the Church's worship, has a great sympathy for the architectural characteristics of church interiors old and new, and can work towards a price that churches can afford; also a manufacturer who is prepared to recognise that there is a market for anyone who can solve these problems with style.

Existing churches

Following the general liturgical reawakening of the 1960s, nave altars, experimental at first but soon hardening into permanent arrangements on largely insensitive platforms wrapped up like parcels in carpet, appeared in many old – mostly medieval but also nineteenth-century – churches. This was soon followed by a rush to do away with pews, and as one involved from the start in the reordering of churches, I observed with some apprehension that a simplistic principle had become adopted by many clergy, parishes and architects: *nave altar, chairs instead of pews, and the parish has become progressive*. I realise that this may seem rather unkind, and that many parishes had approached reordering as the necessary *outcome* of a new vitality in their worship; but more often than not a parish's first approach to me was accompanied by this simplistic 'solution' as a predetermined brief that I was merely, in their view, to do the drawings for.

From what I have written in this paper it will be evident that this quick solution, while probably bringing some immediate relief to a situation of unacceptable remoteness, does little to rectify the distortion of relationships in liturgical worship. Moreover, it leaves out of account the particular characteristics of the individual church interior. In the case of almost all of our medieval churches, the nineteenth-century over-furnishing of them destroyed the intrinsic architectonic nature of the interior space, and a first recognition and appreciation of that character – difficult except to the trained eye because of the powerful effect of the furnishing – is the key to minimising harmful effects of any refurnishing. The building itself needs to be allowed to speak, and more often than not, in my experience, the building's inherent

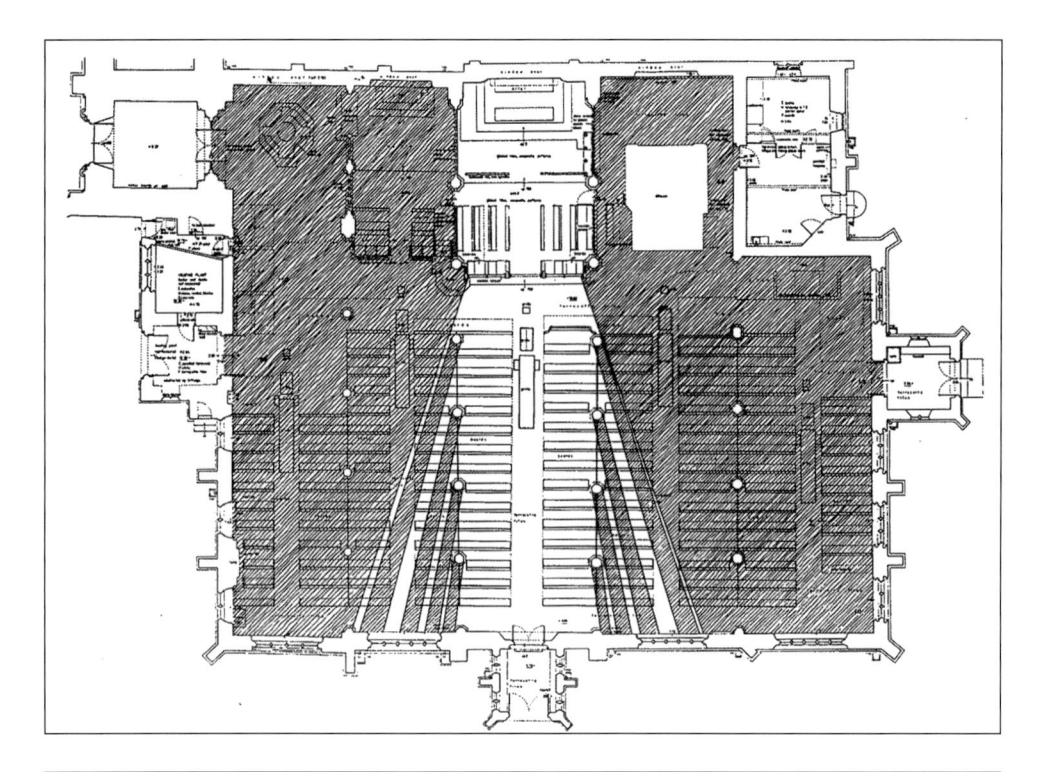

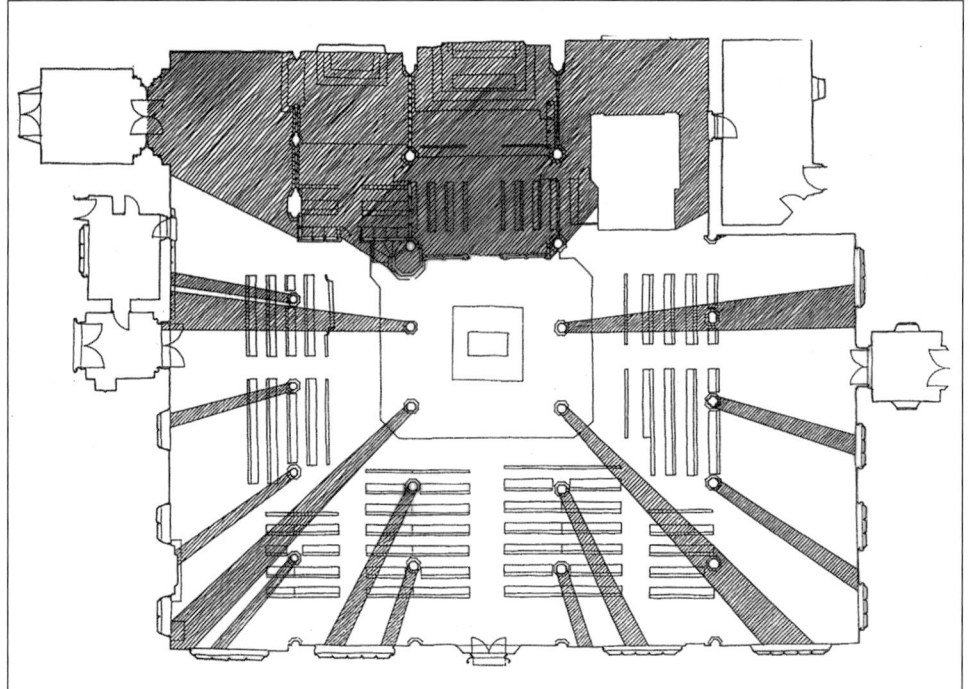

Fig. 2: Two plans of St Helen's church, Abingdon, Oxfordshire, as it was furnished in the late nineteenth century, and as reordered, 2001 (architects Maguire & Co). The plans show 'sight shadows', i.e. parts (shaded) where the seated congregation has no view of the president at the Eucharist. One aberration which resulted from the earlier plan was that a significant body of people considered that they 'worshipped separately at the Lady altar' during Parish Communion – a fact only discovered during discussions about reordering. The reordered plan uses existing pews.

spatial characteristics can be used to emphasise the relationships we are looking for in modern worship.

Every church is a different case. We are apt to think churches conform to stereotypes, like 'medieval': nave, two lower aisles ending perhaps in chapels, a chancel arch and a chancel ending in a railed-off sanctuary. Or the eighteenth-century so-called 'preaching box': a big squarish hall with columns and a gallery around three sides, windows at ground and gallery levels, and an altar-table backed by a wooden reredos, a neat fence of a communion-rail rather close to it and a high pulpit on a stick. We have probably pre-classified the first as a difficult thing for modern liturgy because of it being a long two-room thing essentially, with the aisles as second-class spaces, and the second as a one-room thing with the galleries as second-class spaces.

Yet even within these familiar prototypes there is a wide variation in spatial character.

St Andrew's, Old Headington, Oxford, has a Norman chancel arch only eight feet wide, so that the chancel is literally another room, while St Thomas's, Heptonstall, in Yorkshire, has a chancel arch so wide and a chancel so akin to the nave that there is almost no spatial subdivision.

Fig. 3: The reordered interior of St Helen, Abingdon, looking south from the (main) north entrance.

Nineteenth-century pewing-out has treated most of our medieval churches in the same manner irrespective of their differing spatial characters. Solid pew-ends form narrow fenced gangways driving the eye resolutely eastwards (with theological intention). The space west of the chancel arch therefore ceases to be a wide room stretching from outer wall to outer wall with columns standing on the floor within it, space flowing north-south as much as from west to east, but a first-class long box with second-class long boxes attached, columns ankle-deep in woodwork. How difficult it is to perceive this great spacious place with the existing furnishings within it! Sometimes, as at St Helen's, Abingdon Oxfordshire (Figs. 2–4), this great hall is actually wider than long.

While one must beware of generalising, in many cases the nave-with-aisles hall freed from the unnatural strait-jacket of long seating blocks will have a strong enough character to overcome the inherent disadvantages of any arrangement of seating that avoids extreme directional emphasis, whether with chairs or 'quiet' pews (pews with high horizontals and even higher pew-ends are to be avoided if at all possible).

Fig. 4: The 'sanctuary' at St Helen's, looking south-east across the nave. Beyond is the screen and the original chancel.

This raises again the question of pews against chairs, discussed above under *New churches*. But there remains the issue of the retention or discarding of existing pews.

First, there is obviously the question of their condition, and also of the comfort (so often discomfort) they provide. Often pews are mounted on boarded platforms built over the bare earth, and from this direction rot may be setting in, in both platforms and pews. There is no convincing case (except the value, if relevant, of genuine antiquity) in embarking on costly treatment and restoration here. A new start can yield the advantage of being able to lay a new tile or flag floor over underfloor heating, which is the only effective way of heating an old church.

Comfort really is a major consideration: liturgical worship does not demand hair shirts, and sermons do not command attention if one is suffering from backache. Long pews, those seating six or more people, will generally militate against advantageous rearrangement.

St Helen's, Abingdon was an extreme case of the necessity of reordering. Fortunately the pews are in short lengths, their pew-ends are simple returns of their backs – which are not very high – and their seats are generous. The quite extraordinarily powerful spatial character of the 'five-aisled' wider-than-long hall permitted a new arrangement with a spacious nave sanctuary in which these

Fig. 5: St Mary, Thame, Oxfordshire. View from the north aisle looking south-east towards the crossing, with the south transept visible in the centre distance. The chairs were designed specially for the church and made by a local craftsman; they do not stack, since the full seating is always in use. They are linked only by the front legs, which permits much flexibility of layout.

pews set up no conflicting tensions. There was no case for the use of chairs, except for stacking chairs brought out only for civic occasions and full-capacity concerts.

St Mary's, Thame, Oxfordshire was a very different case. As a former minster church it has a long quire; this has a fenced and gated tomb in the middle of it, added to which there is a crossing-tower with massive piers effectively forming two 'chancel-arches', and a quire screen. So for years the parish had used a little table in the nave for the Eucharist, tucked away from sight at all other times; so the church gave no indication – did not 'speak' – of the nature of the actual Christian community it served. Rather, with its rigid rows of (rotting) pews, it had the atmosphere of a carefully-tended museum. Its spatial characteristics, with delightful diagonal views, are powerful and unusual and after careful assessment of the possibilities, permitted a rearrangement using chairs in an extremely flexible manner (Figs. 5–7). This very lively parish has since used its church for a wide range of services, large and small, and re-arranges its seating frequently.

Lastly, the general case of the eighteenth-century 'preaching-box' church needs looking at. These churches are frequently filled with box pews, often high and effectively forming a horizontal visual plane which not only obscures the floor, but takes over from it. This plane then forms the base of the architectural interior, and this is usually acknowledged and reinforced by the fact that the bases of the classical columns do not sit on the floor but on square

Fig. 6: Plan of the reordered St Mary, Thame, 1995 (architects Maguire & Co). This shows the manner in which the chairs are set up for the Eucharist and family services. A number of other arrangements are also used. The extremely dynamic character of the medieval space permits great freedom of layout, since seating arrangements are always more akin to people simply standing around freely in the space. Realising this freedom required the initial recognition that the minster quire was a separate room.

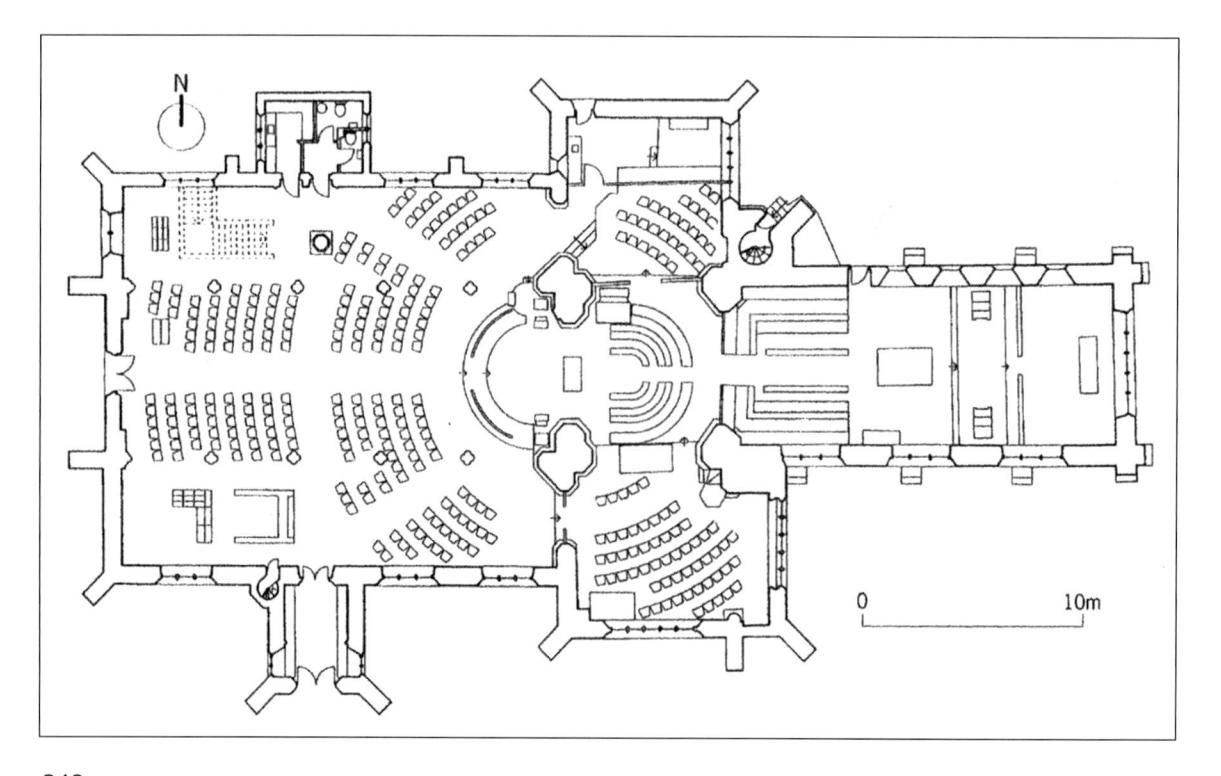

Fig. 7: St Mary, Thame, looking south-east into the crossing. The communion table is a seventeenth-century table continuously used in the church since that time, formerly in the quire. The photograph shows the south transept beyond; the clearing of nineteenth- and twentieth-century furnishings allowed the medieval space to come to life with long diagonal views into light-filled spaces.

pedestals of more or less the height of the pews. If you take away the pews to anything but the slightest extent, the architectonic characteristics of the interior are destroyed; the columns appear perched on ungainly blocks and the proportions of the structure, probably finely calculated at that period, are distorted. It is perhaps something of a blessing that such churches usually require little adjustment if any to make them suited to modern worship. They are most usually buildings which possess a quality which I have called 'inclusive space', that is, the internal space is such that anyone in it feels included in whatever is going on, and wherever they are. This is a very special quality, and sensitivity to it is needed when making any changes. Often some quite small adjustment to the position or height of the altar table is sufficient. Of course, the matter of comfort within box pews may need some attention, but (the strictures of preservation bodies apart) there is some freedom here because the visual and spatial qualities of the seats themselves do not impact upon the space of the church.

Conclusion

There is obviously no easy or ready-made solution, particularly as each building has its own characteristics and sets its own problems. This being so, great care should be taken in choosing professional help; designing or reordering for worship is a very different art to that (although noble in its own right) of keeping old stones standing or treating timber decay.

This article is based on one of the same title published in the magazine Churchbuilding *(which has no connection with a current publication of a similar name) in April 1964, much edited and considerably expanded.*

Acknowledgements
The photo of All Saints, Crewe is by John Whybrow; those of St Helen's, Abingdon are by Trevor Cooper, taken, he tells me, in poor light under somewhat rushed conditions. The other images are by Nicholas Meyjes.

23. Pews: the view from a DAC Secretary

Jonathan MacKechnie-Jarvis

IT'S A DISTINCTLY THREADBARE TITLE, but maybe one day I will pen a Diocesan advice sheet called *So you want to get rid of your pews? Some issues which may arise...*

As any DAC (Diocesan Advisory Committee) Secretary will confirm, much time is spent discussing reorderings – radical or modest – in which removal of pews is a central consideration. Arguments advanced in favour of removal commonly include comfort, sight lines, flexibility, creation of space, and sometimes a conviction that they are 'out of keeping' or 'speak of another age'.

It has to be admitted that some pews are undistinguished or uncomfortable, or both, and/or that there are far too many of them for the present needs of the congregation. But one sometimes senses that the Parochial Church Council (PCC) may be blaming the pews, irrationally, for reduced congregational support or, equally irrationally, hoping that their replacement with comfortable chairs will magically solve more fundamental problems.

As it happens, Gloucester DAC has not (yet) attempted an advice sheet on the 'pew question'. I am not convinced that it would be all that helpful, because there are so many variables, and generalised advice tends to be maddeningly vague and bland. My own role is actually that of an animated advice sheet. I sometimes feel that I am acting as a sort of preliminary litmus test, to give the parish my best guess as to how the DAC may react, based on our corporate experience, but bearing in mind that every new case presents different considerations with which to juggle. Very often I sense, or am told, that the project group members have already decided that the pews must go. I may then find myself talking as a devil's advocate, trying to ensure that quality material is not thrown out unless the case has been very carefully thought through. These are some of the points I am likely to put to the parish.

Playing Devil's advocate

Once they are gone, they are gone

Even if your pews are plain and uncomfortable, they are probably made of good timber, which is now virtually unobtainable. You will not get very much for them, and replacement furnishing will be expensive and may not be as durable as you think. So think long and hard before you discard. (N.B. This argument has rather less force if the pews are not only mean and uncomfortable in their design, but are also made of splintery, worm-eaten softwood!)

Fig. 1: St Mary, Flaxley, Gloucestershire (listed Grade II★), before and after limited removal of pews at the west baptistery. The former arrangement was very congested and made baptisms difficult. The surplus pew platforms were removed and floors made good in tiles.

Fig. 2: St Mary, Charlton Kings, Gloucestershire (listed Grade II*). Another example of limited thinning of pews to create space for nave altar, music groups and so forth at the front of the nave.

How many pews do you really need to discard?

Bearing in mind the first argument above, don't discard more pews than you really need to (Figs. 1 & 2). This applies especially to small reorderings, e.g. where pews are to be cleared in a baptistery corner, or to create space at a congested west end. An area of cleared pews can make the church look bare and impoverished, and it may be helpful to retain some of the pews as perimeter seating, for which purpose it can easily be adapted and mitred to fit into corners. This is simple joinery and can provide attractive seating while still allowing the desired unblocking of space. In Gloucester diocese we have many examples where this has been done.

How about shortening pews instead of discarding them?

Very long pews can be a menace, impossible to move, even if freestanding, and oversailing the line of the arcade, doing few favours to the architecture. Sometimes there are cross-partitions built in, making the 'inflexibility' argument even more justified. Shortening the pews, reusing or selling the surplus timber, and possibly retaining them as movable benches, is a suggestion that has sometimes been seized upon by a PCC which feels that change is needed, but which does not wish to alienate a pro-pew lobby.

Why not adapt rather than discard?

If pews are to remain as the principal form of seating, removal or remodelling of a small number may be all that is wanted. A little ingenuity may work wonders. For example, a small area to accommodate children's work can be created by remodelling, say, two pews, forming a three-sided arrangement rather like an old family pew. The pew plinth for this section can then be carpeted, with bean bags provided, and so forth.

It's not just a case of removing pews – what are you going to do about the floor?

Very often people have not thought through this detail, and typically expect to leave a two-inch trip hazard in the form of a cleared pew plinth. My DAC is not at all keen on this, and normally looks for a proper scheme for making good the area to be cleared of pews (Figs. 3 & 4). There are, of course, many ways of doing this, but a typical raised timber pew plinth might be reconstructed to match the level of the adjoining stone aisle floor – or the PCC might be lucky enough to have flush floors already. The area must not be left with evidence of removed pews; tenon holes, a mixture of fresh softwood repairs or scuffed, former 'traffic areas' all combine to give a depressing and unfinished look. Alternatively the PCC may be considering a solid floor. There are serious concerns here about the architectural detail: all too often in the recent past, impervious concrete base material has forced dampness up into adjoining walls or arcade piers. DACs now look for ways of mitigating this, perhaps by the use of limecrete or by arranging breathable details at junctions with walls.

Fig. 3: A typically cluttered arrangement at St Bartholomew, Redmarley, near Ledbury (listed Grade II). The western block of pews on the north side of the nave makes for very cramped access to the font. The PCC planned to remove the front pew in this block, and to make the necessary changes to the floor. In fact, consideration is now being given to more extensive rearrangement of this area of the church. Note also the spaces which have been cleared at both ends of the north aisle. At the west end the aim was to create a corner for children's work, but unfortunately it has itself become badly cluttered with loose chairs, tables, posters and soft toys. At the east end, loose seating (a donated set of dining chairs) contrasts with the more formal pews behind.

Don't say they are falling apart!

PCCs sometimes argue that pews must go because they are full of rot or worm. I always gently counsel them not to pursue this argument with the DAC. If they are not worth keeping on account of quality, comfort, space considerations and so forth, so be it, but a few scattered worm outbreaks are not going to persuade the DAC – or our consultative partners (English Heritage, the amenity societies, the Church Buildings Council, and others) – that the pews are past it. Joinery repair can be grant-aided, and there are plenty of good craftsmen who will give the pews a new lease of life, possibly cannibalising one or two surplus ones if need be.

Ditto the 'dingy appearance' argument

Pews are not helped by a scuffed and sad appearance. We had a long debate over a pretty set of gothic-ended pews in one of our churches, in a depressing scuffed black finish. A coat of flat-finish, olive green paint, chosen after a lot of advice and application of paint to trial areas, has transformed the appearance of the pews, and after ten years is holding up well to the inevitable knocks. Perhaps the painting option should be considered more often?

Have you thought about seating capacity?

By and large pews can accommodate peak congregations more effectively than chairs. Small children can squeeze in with their

Fig. 4: Mean and uncomfortable pews at St George, Brockworth, Gloucestershire (listed Grade I), probably dating from 1845 when the church was restored by John Jacques. The arrangements are cramped and the pews are of minimal quality and interest. Surplus pews of better quality from elsewhere may be the answer, but the floors will need to be remade flush with the aisles.

parents. The usual response to this caveat tends to assume stackable chairs, but where are they to be stored when not in use?

You say you want flexibility – have you ever physically shifted 150 loose chairs?

There are some interesting replies to this one, and usually people admit that in practice the chairs may not be moved around all that much, despite their supposed 'flexibility. This may be a good moment to ask if thought has been given to movable (even stackable) benches: 'Would you rather move 150 chairs or 30 benches?' The fact is that whereas a cathedral has the staff to rearrange seating back into the Sunday morning format as if by magic after (for instance) a big concert, most parishes do not, and in practice the chairs will spend most of their life in their serried semi-circular ranks.

Not infrequently, if people are open-minded, a good talk through the pros and cons of compromise schemes, liberally illustrated by reference to casework elsewhere in the diocese, may result in some rethinking. After all, a wholesale migration to chairs is a major investment, and often a divisive one. Sometimes the solution is all or nothing and the option of a radical reordering needs to be confidently espoused. But in many cases a minor adaptation of pews or removal of a few may work wonders. Let it also be acknowledged that there have been cases where minor adaptation has provided only a stop-gap solution to stave off an eventual radical approach. But even here, it may give a cheap and effective breathing space during which useful experience can be obtained before irrevocable decisions are made.

Occasionally the DAC has found a PCC project group to be too timid in its thinking, and has suggested that more 'elbow room' is needed, for example when creating a space at the front of a nave. It may be that two rows of pews, rather than one, need to be removed, and there are also arguments to be addressed whether a pew frontal is still needed.

Outstanding pews

In the diocese of Gloucester surprisingly few of our churches have pews of such quality that any alteration or thinning out is unthinkable. Even the best pews have usually undergone more tinkering and rearrangement than is at first apparent. Where the PCC is considering what may become a controversial reordering of really good furnishings, it may be helpful to suggest that a serious study should be commissioned from someone with nationally-acknowledged art-historical and technical knowledge. In our own diocese, parishes have approached experts of national standing for this sort of report. The PCC should be warned, however, that while the authoritative study will always enhance the statement of needs as well as the statement of significance, and the mere fact of it being commissioned will show that the PCC is serious about finding the right solution, it may not necessarily signal a green light for a particular course of action. The conclusion that an item has already been adapted, for example, does not mean that it is in order to adapt it further, let alone to discard it altogether.

New pews

A few churches have bucked the trend over the years by investing in 'new' pews. Usually this means refurbished secondhand ones, but in one case in our diocese – Blockley, near Chipping Campden – a brand new set was commissioned in American oak, comfortably designed with a decent seat and a generous rake. The cost in 1990 was about £15,000 for 16 pews of about 10 feet length each, and two matching frontals. At about the same time Sherborne church near Northleach replaced its rush-seated wooden chairs (*c.*1920s?) with a good set of pine pews from the redundant church of All Saints, Gloucester. Twenty years later the tiny church at Tarlton near Cirencester is about to replace a motley collection of secondhand chairs with some good pews made surplus by a major reordering at Holy Apostles, Charlton Kings.

I am thinking also of a church between Gloucester and Cheltenham in a once-rural setting, but now serving nearby housing estates. A small cruciform building, it is blessed with pews of the meanest quality, no rake, and constructed of poor timber, in places now splintering and wormy. A change to upholstered loose chairs would significantly reduce the seating capacity, and I cannot but feel that refurbished shortened pews from elsewhere would be their best bet, at a fraction of the price either of loose chairs or new stackable benches. Such a scheme would also need to address the pew plinths, which could be rebuilt as timber floors flush with the aisles, or as solid floors with stone paving.

Summary

Reviewing casework nationally (for example reading the monthly casework of the Church Buildings Council), one may sometimes be forgiven for thinking that by the middle of this century there will scarcely be a pew left in our churches. In fact, so far as our own diocese is concerned, I think it is surprising what a large majority of churches still rely on pews for their main form of seating. Ours is a largely rural diocese, and the typical small to medium sized village church is more than likely to retain its pews, but you will probably find that some may have been removed at the front or back of the nave, or perhaps in the aisle, in an attempt to create some clear space for one reason or another. In this short chapter, I have set out the typical arguments for and against what I might call 'pew compromise' as opposed to radical schemes of replacement. The Gloucester DAC has found that parishes are in many cases receptive of such arguments which I hope will be of wider interest.

24. The appropriate alternatives to fixed seating

Anthony Russell

The opportunities

IF CHURCHES ARE INDEED amongst the most important buildings in the centre of any community, whether urban or rural, there is now an overriding need to re-establish that primacy. The church should be of service to all, so that its very space becomes a pair of open hands, to receive the whole community. Churches can become vital, flexible, living spaces, with services of different type, perhaps even of different denomination, through the week, and in addition have the opportunity of being a place for presentations, lectures, exhibitions, meetings and receptions, and of offering wider services such as community advice, or a 'caretaker' living within the environment and providing a constant presence.

In this way churches also benefit from an additional potential for income generation, although despite the claims of some, there is little evidence that the driving force behind the current popularity of these reorderings is solely economic. There exists a genuine desire to instigate fresh ideas and approaches.

It is to meet these (admittedly not universally celebrated) aspirations, that many seek to clear the existing fixed seating and general clutter of inherited furniture. (Though it should be said that for a variety of reasons removing fixed pews generally appeals less to Roman Catholics.) Much existing seating creates rigidity in every sense, while cluttering the simple lines of the architecture. After what may be years of deliberation by a church, one is constantly met with startled delight at the sense of space, clarity and opportunity that sweeping away the fixed seating has provided (Fig. 1). Add to that flexible lighting, to support different activities and moods, or under-floor heating to give a constant welcome and no amount of planning can prepare for the result.

It is sometimes pointed out that churches have removed their fixed seating and then barely ever changed the position of their new flexible seating. But this may not be an indication of the pointlessness of the exercise but of an inability to follow through the thinking and maximise the new potential.

Benches and chairs

While the most appropriate seating solution for any church depends upon churchmanship as well as architecture, forms of worship can and do change. Surveyors and architects, keenly aware of their long-term responsibility to the fabric, may live through a constant flow of incumbents and refurbishments. So in an ancient

Fig. 1: Interior of St Michael & All Angels, Kingsnorth, Kent, before and after reordering.

church, there is an argument for maintaining a set of traditional style seating, perhaps modern movable benches, in the central nave. This can provide constant seating for regular services with a minimal visual impact, while providing a clear indication of purpose to the casual observer when the church is not is use. Additional lightweight, stacking chairs, perhaps steel framed, can then be brought in when required (Fig. 2). With this arrangement, a stacking timber bench and a lightweight chair should provide for most church needs.

In general, the traditionally heavier timber chair (of the type originally designed by Gordon Russell for Coventry Cathedral) has a greater visual impact and can distract from the architecture and more important furniture (Fig. 3). Arguably, therefore, timber chairs are more appropriate to side chapels, where regular reconfiguring does not require the lighter more flexible form of seat.

There are fine stacking benches that have the lowest possible visual impact of any seating (Figs. 4a and 4b). There is also a question of cost, as the timber chair can be the most expensive option per person. The best designs in stacking benches can currently be obtained for around £200 per person and have a life expectancy of at least fifty years. No chair of equal quality can compete on price or longevity.

Fig. 2 (left): One example of modern light weight, steel-framed, high stacking and comfortable seating with minimal visual impact (the 'Daylight' chair, by KI). Fig. 3 (right): Well-designed stacking oak seating in Canterbury Cathedral Chapter House. Designed by Luke Hughes, this chair's ancestry can be traced back to the seating designed by Gordon Russell for Coventry Cathedral.

Diocesan Advisory Committees and their equivalents in other denominations should discourage upholstered seating (and many do). It usually appears inappropriate in ancient churches, and the refurbishment costs soon become apparent to compound the aesthetic defects. Timber seating if well designed can be remarkably comfortable without upholstery.

Design

Good design is a balance between achieving minimal visual impact and harmony with the existing fabric. Modern CNC (Computer Numerical Control) routers ensure a flexibility of design never imaginable in the early days of mass production. Complex and original designs can be achieved by machine and hand finished, to provide unique effects at relatively low costs. It is a golden rule of minimalist design within a church setting that diagonals should be avoided in favour of horizontals and verticals, while detailing should show a structural integrity that is never gratuitous. The spirit of existing architectural detail is better emulated than slavishly copied and the best designers can achieve this by simply echoing a rhythm or a subtle curve.

Skill is also required in achieving a balance of scale. Too often modern seating designs have a heaviness reminiscent more of driftwood off the beach, while too spindly designs look inconsequential and apologetic.

Error can occur in the design of arms that may not even be necessary and will affect the stackability of benches. It is possible to design benches with a solidity that allows anyone requiring additional support to use the top rails in front and behind to lever themselves up and avoid completely the need for arms. Additionally, it is possible to design book rests under the seat that do not affect the stackability or spoil the appearance. However, many now argue that it is more practical to collect books and papers after a service and store them separately.

Weight is an important consideration in what is another balancing trick. Seating must obviously be substantial enough to last at least fifty years, while substance will also help a bench hold its position without the need for cumbersome looking or expensive linking devices. This increases safety but also avoids the need for time consuming repositioning of disordered seating. However, to remain a flexible space, the seating must be light enough to move easily. It must also be remembered that while an individual might carry a single chair, two may be able to handle a six-seater stacking bench, thereby vastly speeding up a reconfiguring process.

Unfortunately, as a result of ignoring a time-honoured tradition whereby only the finest craftsmanship was permitted in any church, we are now confronted by a wide range of inferior and ugly furniture. It fails on every level, as it will not last and confuses the visual and liturgical clarity within the space. Furthermore, it offends basic economic sense by throwing hard-earned cash at temporary measures.

Colour

Colour is a much underestimated factor in the success of any reordering. The first guiding principle is that careful attention should be paid to the intensity of hue. It is an inescapable fact that reorderings using high colour hues do not have the effect of lifting a dull interior. On the contrary, they will increase it by contrast. The low hues that time places upon the architectural fabric require subtle colour ranges to allow the natural richness to be revealed. This is particularly relevant to upholstery but also significant for timber, where oak has the colour traditionally considered most harmonious with the hues of an ancient church. Because of its fine figuring, richness of colour and durability, the appeal of oak is obvious but beech is also a strong contender, particularly as it is considerably cheaper.

Similarly, there is a tendency to consider staining new seating to match existing panelling or liturgical furniture. Staining can give a 'reproduction' effect and therefore appear somewhat apologetic, thereby compromising good design. Good reorderings adhere clearly to a strict hierarchy within any church, where the altar is at the pinnacle and the seating somewhere near the bottom. Although a full congregation might reduce the unfortunate visual impact of bad seating, churches are more often viewed empty and must therefore read best liturgically when so. Therefore slight variation in colour between seating and other furniture is not important. Also, as a rule, pale coloured timbers darken in time, while dark timbers bleach in the sun. However, there is an argument for applying a slight overall stain, to given an evenness of effect, where individual timber pieces might otherwise initially stand out.

Making the change

The length of time required from conception to achieving a reordering is not only affected by available funds but by the level of understanding within each church community.

Admittedly, there are churches where consultation is kept to a minimum and 'patriarchal' traditions prevail, but many require a lengthy process, perhaps over several years, to allow for consensus,

Fig. 4a: Interior of St George's, Bloomsbury, London, before the recent major refurbishment.

THE APPROPRIATE ALTERNATIVES TO FIXED SEATING

Fig. 4b: St George's, Bloomsbury on completion of the work, with the new Luke Hughes mobile bench seating. The liturgical axis has been rotated through ninety degrees, and the previous position of the altar is off the photograph to the left.

and this itself can promote a consultative and open culture. It is important to consider other points of view and remain inclusive, as it is equally important to advise the appropriate authorising bodies of the proposals at the earliest stage. Incumbents regularly acknowledge that even the lengthy or laborious discussion of new plans is a worthwhile process in itself.

In conclusion. . .

The past few years have witnessed a sea change in attitudes to removing fixed seating in parish churches. Increasingly, the arguments don't have to be made for revitalising a church building in this way. Churches can become vital, flexible, living spaces. As never before, the church needs to reach out not only to those suffering particularly in these difficult times, but to all in the community.

25. Pew platforms

Will Hawkes

Introduction

SOMETHING THAT IS OFTEN OVERLOOKED, in the continuing debate over whether pew removal can ever be acceptable in the interests of wider and more flexible use of churches, is the significance of the humble platform on which the pews stand. This significance has several elements.

This article first appeared in the Annual Report *of the Advisory Board for Redundant Churches for 2005. The Ecclesiological Society is grateful to the author and the Archbishops' Council of the Church of England for permission to reprint it.*

Historical and architectural quality

The historical and architectural quality of the pew platform will depend very much on the hand of fate, for age and decay will usually have taken its toll. Occasionally, particularly with medieval examples of pewing, the original solid floor will still be present; the pew itself being essentially independent with the bottom timber rail set on and above the floor finish. More often the flooring to the pews is raised, a kerb at the edge acting as a base to the pew ends into which they are tenoned. Raised platforms can be of solid construction, but are more commonly later replacements, of plain boarding on suspended timber joists with a shallow void beneath. The latter, with its rich compost of broken fragments of the past (not to mention the prospect of evidence of earlier walling lines) can reveal new aspects of the history and evolution of the building in the hands of the archaeologist (Fig. 1).

Fig. 1: St Mary, Stoneleigh, Warwickshire in 2005, showing the void and supporting pillars underneath a pew platform.

The floor

In considering the difficult question of whether the pews can or should be removed, similar careful thought needs to be given to the platform that lies beneath. It does not follow that, if the pews are to go, the floor must necessarily follow; something significant may then be lost. Raised kerbs and platforms can present problems if the pews are taken out, as the motivation for clearance is usually a desire to create a level and uniform floor space across nave and aisles to allow a wider range of use, reflecting the current shift to a variable liturgy and expanding community involvement.[1] Even with the pews gone, the surviving platform can help to allow the past patterns of use to be read, and the colour, texture and scale of flooring material will all affect the present character and appearance of the building. If the platform has to be lowered it is often possible to reuse or match the original materials. Small scale material can appear fussy when exposed to full view (wood parquet and Granwood composite blocks were much in vogue for re-flooring pews in the mid twentieth century). More generously scaled wider oak and fine-sawn softwood boarding can provide a successful and straightforward solution.

Schemes for the complete removal of existing pew flooring and the introduction of a single uniform material overall can have a disturbing effect on established character and appearance. The early church may well have had open unfurnished naves and only a stone bench round the perimeter, but in most churches the accretion of history has created something more complex. Even a dignified and carefully conceived scheme of replacement in natural uniform stone flags, for instance, can urbanise and harshen the character of the interior. Fitted carpet, usually introduced with the intention of making the interior warmer and more welcoming, can, with its absence of any sense of scale, radically alter the interior and change the acoustic.

Technical aspects

The technical aspects of the existing or proposed pew platform also need to be considered. The degree of intervention and replacement needs to be nicely judged to ensure the satisfactory future performance of the floor. The importance of allowing the floor area to breathe cannot be over-stressed. Even established stone paving, bedded directly on the ground, will have allowed the evaporation of moisture through the lime mortar or open joints and through the flags themselves. Changing this pattern can have serious results. The introduction of solid *in situ* concrete in place of suspended timber floors can trap moisture below and force water up the walls or arcade piers of the building, leading to accelerated decay and efflorescence in plaster and masonry

Experiments to avoid this have included leaving an evaporation slot to the perimeter around new solid concrete floors and (despite some scientific evidence to the contrary)[2] seem to have ameliorated this problem. Preference must always be to find a solution that follows the nature and performance of what is being removed. Stone flags can be laid in the traditional manner without a damp-proof membrane directly on sand blinded hardcore. A reworking of traditional construction but using modern permeable materials can be achieved through the use of 'limecrete' solid floor construction, composed of Leca expanded clay granular aggregate and hydraulic lime, which seems successful in removing the problem of rising damp and still allowing breathability.[3] Timber suspended floors can be installed successfully with modern building techniques and damp-courses, but good subfloor ventilation must be provided. Suspended concrete floors are also an option but need careful detailing to avoid the sort of problem seen in old stone floors laid over voids or vaults, where interstitial condensation can result in disfiguring patterns of moisture on the floor surface (Fig. 2).

Conclusion

Thus the preservation or removal of the pew platform should be considered carefully in conjunction with the pews. The platform may well have architectural or historic interest and make a contribution to the quality of the church interior. Any

Fig. 2: An example of the effect of moisture on the boundary between an old solid floor and a pew platform.

replacement needs to take account of the characteristics of what is being replaced so that new and old can continue to coexist in harmony, but wherever possible schemes should aim to preserve and conserve the pew flooring *in situ*.

Notes
1 As reflected in the Church of England's *Mission-shaped Church* report (Church House Publishing, 2004).
2 Brain Ridout, 'Damp damage in stone', *Conservation Bulletin*, published by English Heritage, 45 (Spring 2004), 36–37.
3 See Alison Henry, 'New developments in ... lime floors', *Context*, published by the Institute of Historic Building Conservation, 90 (July 2005), 11–12.

26. Assessing the importance of Victorian and other congregational seating

Roy Porter

Introduction

THIS CHAPTER DISCUSSES some of the factors which should be taken into account when assessing the importance of congregational seating. It is based on the author's experience with Church of England churches being considered for closure,[1] but it is hoped the discussion will be useful when considering changes to seating in churches still in use, of all denominations.

The importance of 'importance'

To obtain permission to make any change to a *listed* Church of England church in use, a Statement of Significance is required which 'should draw attention to features of special importance and record the introduction of fittings and furnishings such as pews, which may have particular historic or aesthetic merit in their own right'. Furthermore, if the proposed change will make a 'significant' difference to the church, then consultation with amenity bodies is required, and the guidance indicates that 'significant' would include 'removal of pews, or other items of furnishing, which have particular historic or aesthetic merit or were introduced as part of a composite scheme at some stage in the history of the church'.[2] Thus when contemplating making changes to pews (or other seating) in listed Church of England churches, an assessment of their importance and historical and aesthetic merit is fundamental.

Similarly, the legislation which governs the process of closing Church of England churches requires that the Statutory Advisory Committee of the Church Buildings Council make an assessment of the historic and archaeological interest and architectural quality of a church, and of the historic and architectural interest and aesthetic qualities of its contents.[3] (In passing, it is worth commenting that this is equivalent to the evidential, historical and aesthetic values of heritage assets identified in English Heritage's *Conservation Principles*, which in addition recommends evaluation of communal value in assessments of significance.)[4]

The other exempt denominations have different, but analogous, processes and criteria for considering changes to listed churches still in use. They have no requirement to carry out an assessment of listed or other churches which are being closed, though at least one denomination does carry out a formal evaluation. A church from one of these denominations that has been sold falls under secular planning legislation, and decisions will need to take into account the quality of the seating if the proposed change of use following the sale affects it significantly.

Thus, when contemplating change to seating in a listed church or chapel, it is essential to assess its historic and aesthetic merits, and determine whether a change or removal to the seating would make a significant difference to the building. Informed assessment of significance is crucial not only if seating of importance is to be identified and preserved, but also if the future of both living and former churches is not to be unnecessarily inhibited – and thereby potentially put at risk – by seating of little merit.

How should this assessment be done? Many listing descriptions say little about seating, and congregations and their advisers may thus be starting from scratch. This article sets out the author's view on some of the considerations which should apply.

The historical value of early seating

Perhaps the simplest assessment of historical interest is the case of medieval and early modern seating. A case in point is St Botolph's church at Shingham, Norfolk, a simple building of the twelfth century, altered in the fourteenth and fifteenth centuries (Fig. 1). As well as a medieval font, Jacobean pulpit and altar rails, the church contains a set of late medieval benches. Of obvious historical value on account of their age, the benches are simple in form with fairly rudimentary carved ends sporting fleur-de-lis finials ('poppy-heads') which are a common type of adornment in this region. Compared with some of the similarly dated examples of seating to be found in Norfolk, Shingham's benches can hardly be considered outstanding as examples of late medieval

Fig. 1: St Botolph, Shingham, Norfolk. Late medieval benches, the bench ends with poppy-heads.

craftsmanship. On the other hand, as examples of the simple seating one might find in a small unexceptional parish church in the fifteenth century, their relative ordinariness might be said to increase their historical value.

A similar example is the set of late-eighteenth-century pews at St Giles's church, Shermanbury, West Sussex (Fig. 2).[5] Again, perhaps the pews are not of exceptional aesthetic quality: they are provincial pieces, functional, fit for their purpose but hardly exceptional as pieces of manufacture. They are, of course, evidence of local handiwork, and their historical value is increased by the fact that they are inscribed with the names of local farms. Each pew has been assigned to either a single farm or a number of farms, and their relative position in the church might suggest the position of their original occupants in the social hierarchy of the parish. Many of the farms and houses inscribed on the pews can be identified today. Removal and relocation of the pews would have seriously diminished the significance of the church, and its ability to communicate past social arrangements to the present. Yet the retention of the seating in the event of closure would render practically impossible the consideration of any alternative uses other than for worship or as a monument. Indeed, without its seating, and evaluated on its own merits, the church at Shermanbury would have been an unlikely candidate for preservation unaltered as it is architecturally undistinguished, and was restored or partially rebuilt on several occasions. In general, while individual benches bearing no relation to other fixtures and fittings, either in terms of period or association, might be removed from a closed church, it has been usual for schemes of pre-Victorian fixed seating in closed churches to be retained *in situ*.

Fig. 2: St Giles, Shermanbury, West Sussex. Late-eighteenth-century pews, inscribed with the names of local farms.

The historical value of Victorian and Edwardian seating

While making a case for the retention of pre-Victorian box pews and benches on historical grounds is relatively straightforward, things become more problematic with nineteenth- and twentieth-century benches. The majority of churches contain Victorian or Edwardian seating, and the ubiquity of such seating can diminish claims for its possessing special historic interest.

Nevertheless, assessments of historical value should take account of how congregational seating can illustrate aspects of the social history of worship provided by nineteenth- and twentieth-century seating. Umbrella holders, and the occasional surviving devices for holding hats, point to the fashionable and practical accessories which members of the congregation might bring with them. Card holders and numbered seats should remind us of how seating might continue to be appropriated in some parishes throughout the nineteenth century and into the twentieth, and the relative position of numbered and free seats may be indicative of some of the social assumptions of parish communities (Fig. 3).

Another thing to be borne in mind is that while nineteenth-century benches may appear socially and politically innocuous to modern eyes, they were occasionally subjects of vexatious dispute. In national terms the campaign for the removal of pews and their replacement with benches was overwhelmingly successful and probably supported by most parishioners but the removal of pews during the nineteenth century was not inevitable and traditional pews had their defenders. For the anonymous author of a tract entitled *The Wooden Walls of England in Danger*, removal of pews was the harbinger of the end of Protestantism. To this person, pews

Fig. 3: An example of a Victorian bench end with umbrella holder and card holder.

were 'sturdy, significant, outward and visible Protestant Bulwarks'.[6] For another self-proclaimed 'pewite', the removal of pews not only pointed to the dangers of popery but also hinted at political agitation from abroad as it was a sign that an 'American, Republican, levelling spirit' was abroad.[7] '[The church of England] is the grand shield of Protestantism; we see popery leaguing herself with Socinianism, and anything and everything else is undermining that shield'.[8] The effect of de-pewing churches would be to undermine the social order.

> The English country-gentleman, whose forefathers, perhaps, built the village church, and whose Saxon predecessors undoubtedly secured Church-rates and tithes, by a charge on the estate, for ever – he, who directly or indirectly supports half the parish, must be displaced by those who eat his bread.[9]

Occasionally passions ran so high as to disrupt the religious life of the community. When the vicar of Tuxford, Nottinghamshire informed his parishioners that a change in the seating arrangements was intended, he provoked a passionate response. A placard was posted in the church warning the parishioners that 'Your country has long been menaced by the intrigues of Popery, but now your own sanctuary is polluted by popish superstition; your seats, to which yourselves and ancestors have liberally contributed, are now about to be wrested from you by Jesuitical intolerance'.[10]

What can be seen from all of this is that the decision of each parish to replace pews with benches was to engage in a national debate, albeit one in which the supporters of benches appear heavily to have outnumbered the supporters of pews. Nationally, the success of the movement to replace pews with benches was relatively swift and, for many contemporaries, irresistible. But the impassioned outbursts noted above show us that pews and benches were neither neutral nor universally accepted pieces of ecclesiastical furniture in nineteenth-century England, and that the date of the adoption of benches or the case of the retention of pews in a particular church might provide an indication of either the changing or inflexible attitudes and beliefs of the leading members of the parish. While such considerations alone are unlikely to make a material impact on the decision as to whether or not a set of seating should be retained, an awareness of the historical significance of the seating is essential if decisions regarding its future are to be fully informed. They should certainly inform recommendations about an appropriate level of recording and documentation before any changes are made.

Given the rapid change in fashion occurring in the 1840s, complete sets of box-pewing after about 1840 are likely to be of some historical importance (Fig. 4), and particularly so for those inserted after 1850. This, of course, ignores local and particular factors. Similarly (and again ignoring local factors) complete sets of bench seating inserted during the 1840s are probably of some historical importance, and probably more so if before 1840. Even for later Victorian and Edwardian seating, complete schemes may not survive quite as commonly as sometimes assumed, and are perhaps worthy of note and recording.

Fig. 4: St Nicholas, Saintbury, Gloucestershire. The linear box pews date from 1840–42.

Historical value can also derive from association with architects or designers of distinction, quite apart from aesthetic value. The church of St Michael & All Angels at Lowfield Heath in Surrey is a case in point. Until relatively recently Lowfield Heath was a rural village on the Surrey/Sussex border, but it has now all but disappeared due to the expansion of Gatwick Airport during the 1970s. The church was designed in 1867 by William Burges and as well as being the last remaining building of the original village, it is a building of architectural distinction by a leading Victorian architect employing all his skill on a limited budget. Of the original contents designed by Burges, the chancel stalls, the font and the pulpit (with carved and painted panels) are perhaps the most noteworthy, and all are objects of interest and quality. The nave is filled with benches on raised timber platforms (Fig. 5). Of softwood construction, they are far simpler than the chancel furnishings but are a complete set, probably installed under the architect's direction. Although of no particular aesthetic significance, as an integral part of Burges' surviving scheme for the church the historical significance of the benches *in situ* is high.

Of course, schemes of overall distinction or interest do not have to have been designed by prominent architects to make the retention of the benches desirable. Just as with the late medieval benches at Shingham, there are nineteenth-century schemes of seating which, together with the other fixtures and fittings within the church, represent such a statistically rare complete example of what we might call the ordinary face of Victorian worship in its original context that their historical interest is sufficiently high for their retention to be in the public interest. One such scheme of seating can be found at St Helen's church, Little Cawthorpe,

Fig. 5: St Michael & All Angels, Lowfield Heath, Surrey. The church of 1867 is by William Burges. The nave seating, shown here, was probably installed under the architect's direction, although otherwise is of no particular interest.

Lincolnshire (Fig. 6). The present church, which is at least the third to stand on the site, was designed by R. J. Withers in 1860 and attracted much praise from the Committee of the Ecclesiological Society, being described as 'a truly excellent design … for cheaply rebuilding a small rural church'. When the church was proposed for closure in 1996 it was noted that it retained its original fittings, including the plain pine benches in the nave, and the Church Commissioners were advised that as an unaltered ecclesiological rural church it was of considerable historic interest and that the removal of its contents would necessarily destroy an unusually complete example of minor church building of the nineteenth century. St Helen's was duly vested in the Churches Conservation Trust.

The important point to note here is that the benches at both Lowfield Heath and Little Cawthorpe are regarded as being an integral part of an overall scheme of liturgical ordering of some historic importance, which survives relatively intact. A high value is placed on them because they are part of an entity greater than their individual selves, but in another church and in a different context the desirability of the retention of the very same benches might be viewed differently.

Fig. 6: St Helen, Little Cawthorpe, Lincolnshire. The church was designed by R. J. Withers in 1860, and retains its original fittings, including nave seating, pulpit and chancel furniture.

The aesthetic value of seating

Assessing the aesthetic value of a particular set of seating involves consideration of craftsmanship, the use of materials and the contribution the seating makes to the overall character of the church. Particular consideration should be given to cases where seating forms part of a complete and comprehensive furnishing scheme, for example where pews are contemporary with, and match, other furnishings in the building, such as pulpits, choir stalls and altars. A coordinated group of fittings may have particular aesthetic value over and above the quality of the individual pieces.

With post-1840 schemes, a distinction might be made between examples of bespoke design and catalogue pieces, although identifying which category into which individual examples fall is not always easy, with many seemingly pedestrian designs being the product of architects working on restricted budgets.

The Incorporated Church Buildings Society was to a significant extent instrumental in this, in that its grants were assessed in relation to the number of seats provided. As a result architects seem quickly to have realised the ergonomic relationship between kneeling human beings and bench spacing and design with the result that 'architect designed' seating may often have rather less individuality than one might expect. Indeed, for much if not most of the nineteenth century, many – though, of course, not all – 'architect designed' seating schemes are rather unexceptional. In contrast, Arts and Crafts seating schemes and seating created by skilled craftsmen, such as Dan Gibson or 'Mouseman' Thompson, are likely to rate highly in an assessment of aesthetic significance.

Staking a claim to preservation on the grounds of association with a notable architect without also assessing aesthetic quality would be irresponsible: the seating in question should also be a distinctive example of the designer's work and notable in his oeuvre or be, as already explored, an integral part of an important overall scheme. Consideration has to be given to the quality of any scheme's design, and its execution.

A hypothetical 'aesthetic value league table of bench types' would surely place benches with plain ends and boarded backs below those with panelled backs and shaped or carved ends, while those constructed in oak would probably be regarded as finer than any parallel design executed in the far more common pine. This reflects the approach of the liturgical furnishing companies that flourished in the later Victorian and Edwardian periods. The catalogues of firms such as Cox & Sons or Jones & Willis presented the reader with a range of bench types available in oak, pine and deal, with backs and frames priced per linear foot and offering a choice of various types of shaped and rectangular bench ends, the latter being considerably cheaper than the former.[11] The ubiquity of square buttressed bench ends in Victorian schemes of seating is explained as much by their being generally the cheapest form of bench available from the liturgical furnishing companies as by any reference to medieval exemplars.

It is important to appreciate that many of these standard designs for bench end had a very long life, together with their associated fittings, such as card holders. Some basic designs travel through from the 1860s up to World War II,[12] of which the square end with recessed central panel is the most common.

The value of church seating in providing evidence about the past

In addition to historical and aesthetic importance, benches and pews may also have value through their ability to provide evidence about the past. Both below and above ground they can be regarded as an archaeological resource. Furthermore, it needs to be borne in mind that removal of seats can affect the building from which they are taken, by having an impact on those surfaces to which the seating was formerly attached. These surfaces can include historic wainscot, panelling and plaster on walls (themselves perhaps concealing wall paintings) and flooring.

Investigation will reveal what the seats are made of, how they are put together and (perhaps) when they were constructed. Schemes of seating which appear at first glance to be a complete piece from a single date may be the result of several building campaigns or may retain within them evidence of former schemes. For example, the benches at Woodcote, Shropshire were installed in the medieval church in the 1880s. While most of them sit on timber platforms installed at the same time, a group at the rear of the nave appear to stand on platforms previously used for box pews. Again, analysis of the benches at the vested church of St Thomas, Bristol revealed that they incorporated substantial amounts of material from the earlier box pews and allowed an intellectual reconstruction of their original form. There are similar examples elsewhere in this book, for example in the chapters by Hugh Harrison and Charles Tracy (Chapters 8 & 12).

Furthermore, removal of the seating may require disturbance of the floor surface, and this often has archaeological implications. Whilst buried archaeological evidence is unlikely to be an absolute constraint on most proposals, professional guidance must be incorporated into any scheme that involves re-flooring in a church standing on an archaeologically sensitive site. Proposals that involve disturbance of the floor on such a site should be preceded by archaeological assessment and, if necessary, physical evaluation, carried out by archaeologists competent and experienced in church archaeology. At sites of lesser but identifiable sensitivity, precautionary archaeological attendance may be advised.

Overall, the capacity of seating and its adjacent surfaces to yield information about the past must be taken into account when decisions are made, and underlines the importance of appropriate investigation, recording and analysis of all the relevant elements if change is made.

The closure of Church of England churches

The remainder of this chapter considers the special case of the closure of Church of England churches, in which some painful and polarised decisions may sometimes need to be made.

The aim in such cases is to seek an alternative use for a closed church which does not have an unacceptable adverse impact on the building's overall heritage value. This demands that the significance of its fixtures and fittings as well as its architectural character and quality are taken into account.

Of those contents a church might contain, its congregational seating will normally enjoy a spatial if not a qualitative predominance. However, the closure of a church can be devastating for schemes of seating as most alternative uses seek to maximise the available space by removing fixed seats and benches. Seating schemes recognised as being of outstanding historic or aesthetic importance can thus present serious constraints on the potential of a closed church to sustain an alternative use. It follows that the understanding of the significance of the seating and the values placed upon it will, to some extent, dictate the type of future use of the building in which it is located.

For former Anglican churches that are regarded as being of outstanding heritage value there is the possibility of being vested by the Church Commissioners in the Churches Conservation Trust. However, this is an option only for those churches regarded as presenting extremely little or no opportunity for alteration by virtue of their intrinsic interest, and where an alternative use involving no change has failed to be found. For this reason, only a minority of closed Anglican churches are vested in the Churches Conservation Trust.

The priority for most churches is to secure an alternative use for the building. There are many occasions when only the removal of the seating and the subsequent clearance of floor space can make possible an alternative use which will ensure the future of the building. Thus at its most brutal, the question which must be asked is what is more expendable, the seating *in situ* or the church?

This can be particularly true with churches which contain galleries. As well as housing schemes of seating, galleries can be an integral part of an historic ordering and may provide evidence of the early use of industrial materials such as cast iron. However, galleries can also seriously inhibit alternative use. If they are incorporated within a new scheme thought has to be given to primary and secondary means of access and egress, and the introduction of lifts and staircases. Galleries with raked floors full of seating are unlikely to survive unscathed within schemes for alternative use. It is more likely that applications will be made to remove the seating, level the flooring and thus free up the space contained within the gallery. And yet the seating in galleries might be older than that in the body of the church. At St John's church in Bollington, Cheshire (Fig. 7), for example, the galleries hold seating of the mid nineteenth century while the nave has lost its benches and now contains twentieth-century chairs.

In situations where the removal of the seating is proposed, it is essential to assess the material and visual impacts of removal. In those cases where the distribution of the seating is itself significant, for example because it reflects historic socio-economic patterns of use or where it illustrates development through time, a comprehensive record should be drawn up for deposit in the Diocesan Record Office and the National Monuments Record. Seating which is regarded as being of special aesthetic quality can often be recommended for re-use within another church. Where this is not the case, it is sometimes possible to re-use elements of seating within proposals for alternative use as a means of retaining some of the historic contents within the building.

In the final analysis, most would probably concede that in the exceptional circumstances of church closure the securing of a viable alternative use that will ensure the conservation of the building will outweigh the claims of the seating for preservation. Exceptions include those cases where the seating itself makes a significant contribution to the heritage value of the church. This is generally recognised in pre-Victorian seating, but schemes introduced in the wake of the ecclesiological movement and the campaign for free seating demand greater judgement of their significance.

Critical decisions affecting the future of closed churches must be properly informed in this respect, which requires the deployment of resources for basic research, analysis and recording. This may seem a tall order in the febrile atmosphere of finding a use for a closed church within the statutory use-seeking period (currently two years) but is a prerequisite for the responsible management of change. That way the historical evidence of vulnerable schemes of seating can be captured, seating of outstanding significance can be preserved and explained for the benefit of a wide range of audiences, and the future of closed churches need not be encumbered by the retention of seating of negligible heritage value.

Fig. 7: St John, Bollington, Cheshire. The seating in the galleries is from the mid nineteenth century, but the nave now has twentieth-century chairs sitting on earlier pew platforms.

Conclusion

This chapter has discussed some of the factors which should be considered when assessing the importance of church seating. It has concentrated on the issues raised by Victorian and Edwardian pews, as these are extremely common, and often proposed for partial and complete removal. The principles apply both to living churches and those closed for worship, though the latter can bring particular challenges through the need to balance the survival of the building against the survival of the seating. Overall it is hoped that the discussion will be useful to those responsible for assessing the importance of seating schemes, and the ability of church interiors to absorb change.

Acknowledgements
I am indebted for help and advice to many people, but especially to former members of the Advisory Board for Redundant Churches (ABRC) and to Sarah Brown, who encouraged my engagement with pews and benches. I am grateful to Trevor Cooper for discussion of an earlier version of this chapter. Finally, special thanks are due to Jeffrey West, my former boss at the ABRC, for his extensive help, advice, good humour and friendship.

Notes

1. The specific cases discussed in this chapter are drawn from the casework of the Advisory Board for Redundant Churches, the statutory advisers to the Church Commissioners from 1969 to 2008 on the significance of closed churches and their contents, and of those churches for which closure was considered. It should be noted that closure did not necessarily follow inclusion in the Board's casework.
2. The quotations are from *Making Changes to a Listed Church, Guidelines for Clergy, Churchwardens and Parochial Church Councils* (January 1999), available at www.churchcare.co.uk (accessed 6 June 2009).
3. The relevant legislation is the *Pastoral Measure 1983* and the *Dioceses, Pastoral and Mission Measure 2007*. The requirement described here is found in the latter document, Section 56 (1)(b).
4. English Heritage, *Conservation Principles* (2008), 27–32.
5. Closure of St Giles's church was briefly considered in 2003–4 but the church remains in use.
6. *The Wooden Walls of England in Danger: A Defence of Church Pews* (London, pub. J. Ridgway, 1844), 14.
7. *Pew Abolition: Its Impossibility, As Shewn in the Following Letters to the Editor of the Midland Monitor. By a Pewite* (Birmingham, pub. B. Hunt, 1843), 5.
8. *Pew Abolition*, 9.
9. *Pew Abolition*, 12.
10. Incorporated Free and Open Church Association, *Free and Open Church Chronology; including authorities and landmarks of the movement: a manual for the use of preachers, speakers and writers in the public press* (London, 1892), 22.
11. See for example Cox & Sons, *Trade Catalogue* (1862); Jones & Willis, *Illustrated Catalogue of Church Furniture* (1875); Jones & Willis, *An Illustrated catalogue of Some of the Articles in Church Furniture, Manufactured by Jones & Willis* (1899).
12. Geo. M. Hammer & Co. Ltd., *Church Furniture* (n.d., *c.*1933), (a copy held by Watts & Co. having an inserted letter of 1939 showing the catalogue still in use).

27. Considering changes to church seating

*Trevor Cooper and
Sarah Brown*

Introduction

THIS CHAPTER IS INTENDED TO BE HELPFUL if you are considering making any changes to the seating of a church still in use, whether the seating is simple or complex and the proposals straightforward or controversial.[1] It suggests a systematic series of steps and gives a number of checklists to help you work out a sensible proposal. It gives no answers, but provides a process for obtaining them.

Though much of what we say is widely accepted, it does not replace guidance or procedures from your own denomination (see Box 1, 'Denominational advice and requirements'), statutory bodies and expert groups. In particular, we do not describe the relevant law, and the chapter has no authority beyond any good sense it may contain.[2]

> **BOX 1: Denominational advice and requirements**
>
> Several denominations provide guidance to those considering changing church seating, including the following (the websites where these documents may be obtained are listed in 'Further Reading' at the end of this book).
>
> *Furnishings in listed churches* (Baptist Union).
>
> *Removal of pews from historic chapels* (Methodist Church)
>
> *Seating in churches* (Church of England).
>
> *Statements of significance and need: guidance for parishes* (Church of England).
>
> *Choosing new seating* (Church of England).
>
> *Making changes to a listed church: Guidelines for Clergy, Churchwardens and Parochial Church Councils prepared by the Ecclesiastical Rule Committee* (Church of England)
>
> We understand that the Statutory Advisory Committee of the Church Building Council (Church of England) may be publishing proposed *Criteria for Assessing the Heritage Significance of a Church*. An earlier version, 'Assessing heritage value and determining the scope for change in closing and closed Anglican churches' by David Baker, last Chair of the former Advisory Board on Redundant Churches, appears in *Church Archaeology*, 11 (2007 [published 2009]) pp. 61–81.
>
> *In addition, see*: English Heritage, *New Work in Historic Places of Worship* (2003).
>
> *See also* the list of 'Further reading' at the end of this book for other material which might be useful.

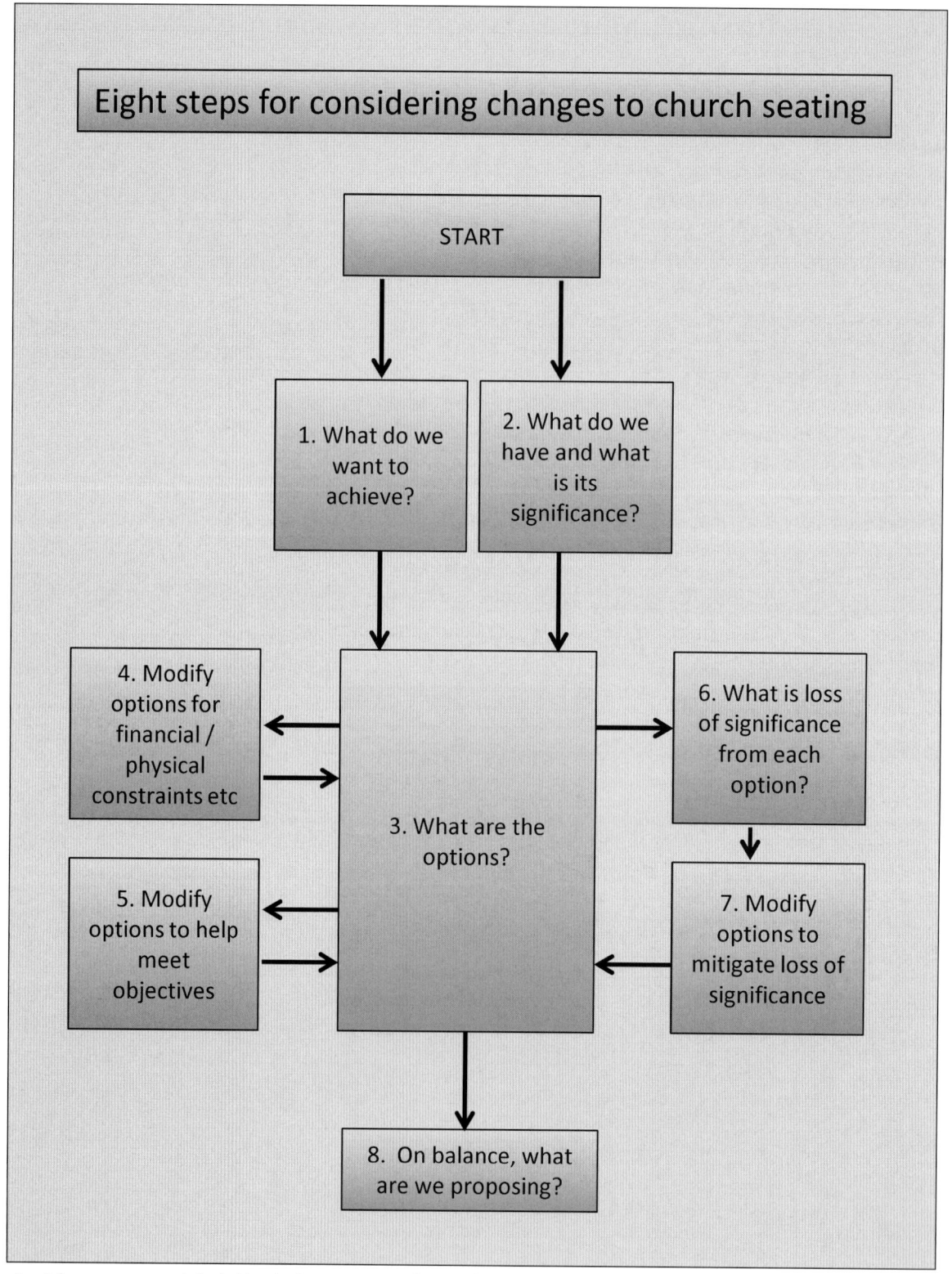

Eight steps for considering changes to church seating

```
                        START
                    ↓         ↓
        1. What do we    2. What do we
        want to          have and what
        achieve?         is its
                         significance?
                    ↓         ↓

4. Modify                              6. What is loss
options for        →  3. What are  →   of significance
financial /           the options?     from each
physical           ←                ←   option?
constraints etc

5. Modify          →                ←  7. Modify
options to help                        options to
meet               ←                   mitigate loss of
objectives                             significance

                    ↓
            8. On balance, what
            are we proposing?
```

An eight step process to help decide whether you want a change of church seating, and, if so, what change you will propose. See text for details.

Eight step process

In Figure 1 we show an eight step process to take you to the stage of deciding whether you want a change of seating, and, if so, what change you are proposing.

This requires you to be open-minded. Your 'vision' – which can usefully drive seating projects – must include, not exclude, these steps. If you come to this with a fixed solution in mind and force that one solution through the various stages so that it simply emerges unchanged at the other end, then we will have been wasting our time (and, to be frank, you will be wasting yours). The eight-step process is a way of generating options and choosing the most satisfactory one, taking everything into account and being as creative as possible; it is not a way of getting to the answer you already want. In our experience, missing out or muddling these steps often leads to unnecessary disappointment and rework.

At relevant points in the process, you should consider whether you need to call on expert advice (for example, an architect or woodwork specialist), and you may find it useful to talk to people in your position who have been through the process before. Your denominational authorities will probably be pleased to give informal guidance, and to help you obtain expert opinion where needed. You will also need to follow your denominational procedures for involving the amenity societies and other stakeholders; this may involve a site visit.

1. What do we want to achieve?

This first step encourages you to ask what it is you want to be able to do that the current seating does not allow. What are the range of things you do now in the building, and what would you like to do differently – and why? Focus on the *nature* of what you want to do, the objective itself (for example, 'we want to drink coffee together after the service') rather than the means of achieving it by any particular *solution* (for example 'we want to clear the pews at the back of the church and build a kitchenette for after-service coffee').

Think carefully whether this objective is realistic and reasonable – if not, it weakens any case for change. After-service coffee is quite likely to be seen as realistic and reasonable; the ambition to become a centre for classical music concerts every Saturday night may be, but would need rather more evidence to make the case. An important part of this step is ensuring that the objective is shared by the worshipping congregation or parish and any other local stakeholders.

From our observation, this step is often missed out, as people are keen to move straight to the solution. The result can be confusion about why the proposed change is required, whether it will actually achieve the objective, whether it is fully supported, and whether other, overlooked options might have been better.

It may take a little time to do this step, but it will pay dividends. Later on the output from this stage will probably be used to feed into what is called a 'Statement of Need', depending on your denominational requirements.

2. What do we have and what is its significance?
This second step is crucial – what is it that we have now and what is its significance? This word 'significance' is a convenient piece of jargon, broadly meaning 'importance' – why does the present seating matter? This covers both the seating itself and also its setting and relationship to the rest of the interior of the church, with its other furniture and fittings. *There is important further detail on this step in Appendix 1.*

The significance of the seating will reflect the different values people attach to it – historical, artistic, architectural, archaeological, liturgical, social and communal, and so on (this is not meant to be a complete list, and the categories overlap). In your discussions you will often find that different organisations and individuals will find significance in different aspects, so (especially in the more critical cases) at some stage a dialogue may be needed so that each party has a chance to understand and take on board what the others are saying about the importance of the seating and the interior, in a two-way process. Of course, not all of these interests are involved in every case, especially with relatively small changes, but it is useful to be aware that they can exist and be relevant. Your denomination should be able to advise.

Unfortunately there is a strong temptation to skip this step, on the assumption that you know the answer already. But experience shows that it has be done and done properly, making sure you look really carefully at the seating and its setting in detail and with a fresh eye. At the very least ask someone who is not familiar with the church to look with you; in some cases you may need to bring in an expert. You may find the results surprising, or it may confirm what you already thought. Either way, if you do this step properly you will be well placed for the next stages; skimp or ignore it and you may find those later stages throw up unanticipated problems.

3. What are the options (including the little-change and no-change options)?
After steps 1 and 2, you should generate a list of options. These will take into account both your objectives and the significance of what you currently have.

Try and cast your net widely and include both radical and minimal ideas (you will probably find some interesting ideas in this book, including in the case study section). Amongst the ideas, make sure to include a no-change, or little-change, option, as this gives you a baseline, and can be very helpful in understanding the relative strengths and weaknesses of the other options. At this stage do not rule anything out unless you are certain it is impossible for clear reasons, such as finance or obvious physical restrictions in the building. It is a common mistake to consider just one option rather than several, when the evidence suggests that forcing yourself to consider different possibilities almost always improves the final solution. *In our experience, the first option you think of is not always the best.*

Minimal options for seating which are sometimes overlooked include repairing, restoring or refurbishing the existing seating and making the existing seating more comfortable by adapting it or adding cushions. These simple solutions are often ignored, or discarded without proper consideration (or testing). Other minimal approaches include making the existing seating more flexible by making some fixed elements mobile, shortening or removing just a few fixed benches to make space as required, and having primary and secondary seating with the latter used only when necessary.

For example, if your aspiration is for the seating in the church to be comfortable enough for adults to listen to a one-hour concert without discomfort, then the radical option might be to remove all the pews and replace them with modern seating. More minimal options might be to purchase tailor-made cushions, or adjust the seat backs of the pews to make them more comfortable. As another example, some churches find that the minimal option of a 'tea-cupboard' at the back of the church meets their needs, without the scale or expense of a separate kitchen or kitchenette.

When creating the different seating options (including the no-change or little-change option) you may like to use Box 2 'Thinking about different types of seating'. This is a neutral list, encouraging you to think for yourself. It is also worth checking whether your denomination provides guidance on seating: we are aware, for example, of denominational guidance regarding fabric-covered chairs in ancient interiors, and the lightness or darkness of the wood from which the seating is made.

You need also to consider the question of flooring. This is a huge subject in its own right, and outside our scope, but some of the high-level questions which are likely to arise can be found in Box 3 labelled 'Flooring'.

BOX 2: Thinking about different types of seating

This check list can be used to establish the relative pros and cons of any seating arrangement: pews, movable benches, and chairs of various kinds. It can be used to compare options; when doing this, it is useful to compare the new options with what you have now. The check list is in no particular order.

1. Visual and aesthetic impact in the context of the architecture, lighting, the other furniture and the floor – matters such as colour, shape (including architectural references), materials, style, solidity, craftsmanship, variation versus uniformity, beauty
2. How the interior will be read and interpreted when full, when half full, when empty; including cultural references, liturgical and social relationships, implied purpose and meaning of the space
3. Quality of seat in comparison with quality of other furnishings (and if a change of seating, in comparison with current seating)
4. If more than one type of seating, the visual relationship between the various types and sizes
5. How tidy will the interior be and how much does this matter
6. What level of comfort is required, for how long, by whom, with what expectations
7. Environmental sustainability over the longer term
8. How seating arrangements will cope with congregations of different types and sizes (given that benches can usually seat more people than individual chairs)
9. Ability (if desired) to create curved or angled lines (if desired, can this be achieved if chairs clipped together for safety reasons – and if clipped together, impact on capacity)
10. Ability of seats to make good use of sightlines, cope with different foci (if desired), and allow movement (if and when desired)
11. Ease of trying out different seating arrangements even if intending finally to settle on one
12. Possible need for seating to be used in other contexts, e.g. concerts, seminars, groups, circles, squares, around a table, café style or other informal setting
13. Movability and stackability and storage requirements (if relevant): people and effort required, storage space and height, possible need for trolleys for movement and storage, storage for books when seats stacked, wear and tear when moving or stacking (seats and floor), ease of placing seating back in correct position
14. Health and safety matters (e.g. flammability, exit in emergency)
15. Likely breakage rate, and rate of degradation over time and consequent impact on appearance e.g. fading, wear and tear, scuffing, scratching, staining
16. Long-term cost - capital cost now, expected life and replacement cycle, maintenance costs (e.g. replacement fabric)
17. Physical support provided for those who find difficulty in standing up and sitting down (e.g. via seat arms, or the seat in front)
18. If removing pews, impact (if any) of draughts

19. Ability to cope with kneeling (if appropriate)
20. What will be done with books etc. before, during and after the service
21. What will be done with coats and umbrellas
22. What cushions are intended to be used (if any), how do they relate to the seat, how will they be stored
23. How will parents with children cope with the seat (controlling children crawling away, standing on the seat, slipping back through the seat, accidentally moving the seat)
24. Cleanability of seat
25. Acoustic impact of the seat when church empty and full
26. If seat movable, impact on floor surface, especially if dragged or scraped
27. Likelihood of seat accidentally being kicked over or pushed back, associated noise levels
28. Ease of cleaning floor when seats present
29. How easily is the seat stolen
30. How tempting is the seat as a target for arson

BOX 3: Flooring

This is a complex area and these are merely some of the issues.

- Will levels need to be changed? If so, is it better to level up or level down (e.g. effect on door thresholds)?
- What is the structure under the pew? Can the existing structure be lowered so that existing flooring can be reused at lower level?
- What are the archaeological implications of decisions made about new flooring, particularly proposals to lower floor levels or remove pew platforms and re-floor underneath them?
- Do the existing floor finishes reflect the previous seating layout and thus reduce flexibility?
- If a new floor finish, should or could it be laid over existing flooring? (be aware of conservation considerations e.g. for brasses; and of the risk of damp, for example with foam-backed carpet).
- If a new finish, should it be soft or hard?
- If soft, is carpet desirable in this space? How will it relate to the seating? How quickly will it wear out or become shabby?
- If hard, should it be timber, stone, composition wood, linoleum, tiles, slate, or other material? What should be its directionality? Note that a hard finish may be perceived to be colder underfoot.
- Should the flooring be uniform or divided into areas to provide visual relief or partitioning of the space?

You may also want to think hard about the quality of any new seating you are considering acquiring, and how that relates to the overall interior. Think too about how the new seating would reflect your values. For example, if your current seating is pleasing to the eye, how willing are you to replace it with anything less attractive?

The next three stages set out to modify and improve the options, without as yet deciding between them.

4. Modify options for financial, physical and other constraints
Money may well be a constraint, and could affect the way you think about your options. Also think about any physical constraints there are on making changes to the seating. These include such things as the heating system, the junction between seating and the wall (e.g. panelling), difference in flooring between the aisles (in the sense of alley ways) and under the seats, pew platforms and what is underneath them, a sloping floor, the flooring area being marked or a tatty floor being hidden by the existing seats. In step 2 you will already have identified any archaeological implications of the changes you are considering, such as the existence of memorials in the floor. The location of water and drains may affect your wider plans, whilst such items as stone fonts and war memorials may come into play. Think too about access. All these factors may make you modify some options, or even strike some out.

5. Modify options to help meet objectives
Draw up a list of pros and cons for each option, showing how well each one meets your objectives, and for each of the cons, think whether you could modify the option to manage the difficulty. This will not only improve the options but is important at the later stage (step 8), when you need to take a balanced approach in deciding between them.

6. What is the loss of significance caused by each option?
For each option, think carefully about what significance will be lost. This is only possible, of course, if you have carried out step 2. You may need to take advice for this step.

7. Modify options to mitigate or reduce loss of significance
Once you know what significance will be lost for each option, think what might be done to mitigate or reduce this loss of significance. Each case needs to be considered individually, but the earlier stage (step 2) in which you assessed the significance of the seating and the interior may provide pointers.

For example, if it is the appearance of a group of seating which has value, you might maintain a coherent block of the seating in its original place. If individual seats have historical significance, but their present location and layout does not, then you might change the placement of the seating or the way it is used, or incorporate it in new structures. If the seating carries evidence about the past (for example, in the way the seating has been altered), you might carry out an expert investigation before changing or removing it.

In all cases where a change is planned to seating of any heritage significance (further discussed in Appendix 1), an appropriate record should be made of it before that change takes place, with copies deposited in the church records and the local Historic Environment Record, held by the local authority. Making this record does capture some (usually not all) of the archaeological and other evidence which can be derived from the seating, but does little else to preserve its heritage significance, so cannot usually be put forward as a fundamental reason why change can take place. When change is decided, you may want to keep a selection of the seating for posterity, for example if it is the design or the manufacture which is of interest. It is also not uncommon to offer unwanted seating for sale or re-use elsewhere to avoid wanton destruction.

These are generalised suggestions, which may or may not apply to particular cases. The important point is you consider each option in turn, and see whether and how you can reduce or counter the loss of significance. This may involve changing some of the options, perhaps in relatively small ways.

Back to step 3: What are the options?
At this stage you have probably modified the options during steps 4, 5, 6 and 7, and may need to go around the loop again. In complex cases you may need to go round this loop several times.

8. On balance, what are we proposing?
Finally you will be ready to choose between the options. You (and others) will be looking at the trade-off being made between loss of significance and the genuine benefits from the change. You may want to ask, 'Which of the options would best help us achieve our reasonable aims without a disproportionate loss of significance?', or 'Which option would have the best balance between meeting our (well-founded) aspirations and the loss of what is significant about the seating, and the interior?' For example, if you were looking to accommodate those who use wheelchairs, you would want to ensure that any loss of heritage significance to the wider public was proportionate to the present and future need for improved access.

Whatever the precise format of proposal required by your denomination, the steps you have been through mean you will be able to make a clear case. If you need to provide a Statement of Need and a Statement of Significance, you will have done all the work necessary for these. Putting all your cards on the table in this way can be a good way of bringing others up to speed – whether the denominational advisors and decision-makers, local authorities, English Heritage or the amenity Societies – because the range of options and the pros and cons of each of them help those people to understand very quickly what you as a congregation may have been mulling over for months or years. In addition, if those bodies are not entirely happy with the eventual proposal, they will at least know what the rejected options were and why they have not been put forward.

None of this provides any guarantee that your proposal will be acceptable to all of those who have a say in the outcome, but the systematic, transparent way you have approached this will almost certainly speed up any subsequent discussions and make them more productive.

❖ ❖ ❖

APPENDIX 1: Heritage significance

Step 2 asks 'What do we have and what is its significance?' As explained earlier, the idea of 'significance' brings together a variety of ways in which the seating matters, or is important. This includes not only the seats or pews themselves, but also their relationship to the rest of the interior of the church.

This appendix deals with *heritage* significance, which is one part – often the major part – of the overall importance of the seating. A recent document defines heritage significance as follows: 'The value of a heritage asset [in our case, the church seating] to this and future generations because of its heritage interest. That interest may be archaeological, architectural, artistic or historic'.[3] Your professional advisers and denominational authorities should be aware of how thinking is developing in this area and how it affects proposals to change seating, and you should take early advice.[4]

Given the importance of heritage significance, we have provided in Box 4, 'Assessing heritage significance of seating' a list of matters often taken into account for church seating. We have divided our list up into three broad categories. One is 'architectural and artistic' factors (to do with the appearance of the seating and its relation to the interior, whether designed or accidental; some people prefer to talk of 'aesthetic' value).

A second category is 'historical' factors (how the seating and the interior illustrates the past or brings it to mind, or is associated with it in some particular way). The third category is 'archaeological' factors (how the seating could or does provide evidence about the past – note that archaeology is not just about digging, but will include the structure and materials of the seating itself; some people prefer to refer to this rather more generally as 'evidential' value). Finally there is a category in our list dealing with non-seating elements, such as the floor and what is beneath it.

Our list of factors comes with three warnings. First, it is pitched at a fairly general level. To take just one example, because our list does not delve into detail, it does not include explicit mention of seat-flaps attached to bench ends, or of prayer-book boxes or hat sliders underneath seats, all of which are somewhat uncommon, and would increase the heritage significance of that seating. However, in the present state of knowledge it would be quite impossible to provide a complete list at a more detailed level, and we thought that an incomplete detailed list could do more harm than good, as absence from the list might mistakenly have been taken to imply lack of significance.

Secondly, we are concerned that the list of factors may encourage an individual case to be assessed in isolation, when significance often requires comparing a particular case with a large sample of other cases. This will often require expertise and wide experience, in the same way that the assessment of a piece of silver or an antiquarian book requires the services of someone who knows silver or knows books. So this is not a do-it-yourself kit. Many denominations can help provide expertise and advice through one means or another, to allow the significance of your seating to be compared with others.

Finally it is important that the list of factors does not encourage a tick-list or reductionist approach, where the whole is seen simply as the mechanical sum of its parts, and not as a totality. Worse still, the list could be manipulated to arrive at a predetermined outcome. For these reasons, the list should be used as the *starting point* for an informed assessment of the overall significance of the seating and its setting, and should not simply be used to create an additive scoring system which is then used to make final judgements. Note too that seating in a listed building (especially if highly-listed, Grade I or II★) may gain in significance from that association, depending on the circumstances.

In Appendix 2 we provide some personal comment on the heritage significance of church seating, based on this list.

> **BOX 4: Assessing the heritage significance of church seating: some matters to consider**
>
> *Matters likely to affect the architectural and artistic significance of church seating*
>
> - Seating scheme making distinctive architectural or artistic or liturgical contribution to church interior (perhaps as part of a wider more comprehensive liturgical scheme or ensemble still showing overall integrity; often, though not necessarily, the product of a single mind or single building phase). For example:
>   - Designed by a notable architect (taking into account the design-quality of this instance of that person's work, the personal control exercised, and the relation of the seating to the rest of the building)
>   - Constructed by a notable craftsman (and the quality of this instance of the work, its rarity, whether uniform or not in this building, and its place in the craftsman's development)
>   - Rare in nature or of especially high quality or aesthetic appeal
>   - Illustrative (whether through the seating or its fittings) of the distinctive style of a period of art or architectural or liturgical history, and rarity in so doing
>   - Notable historicism (looking back to the past) in design or decoration of the seating, and rarity in so doing
> - Seating, which may be from the hand of numerous independent 'designers', whose unselfconscious simplicity or higgledy-piggledy and adaptive character give it charm
> - Individual seating or groups of seats acting as a vehicle for figurative or decorative carving, and quality of that work
>
> *Matters likely to affect the historical significance of church seating*
>
> - Complete seating schemes (which may include galleries) put in place at a single point of time (or through a planned phasing), especially:
>   - Pre-Reformation seating scheme (taking into account completeness, whether seating is in original location, and extent to which it is a Victorian rebuild or reframing of earlier elements in new structure)
>   - Seating scheme of the period after the Reformation up to the 1840s (taking into account completeness, whether seating is original to the church, whether in its original location, modified or reconstructed)
>   - Post-Victorian & modern seating scheme which is the product of a single designer and of high quality, especially if by the build architect and not from the catalogue
>   - For all the above, whether the seating scheme forms part of a wider liturgical scheme or suite of furniture or fittings (for example with reading desk, ambo, pulpit, screen, altar rail or altar enclosure, gallery)
> - Multi-period seating scheme (which may include galleries) illustrating adaptive change, liturgical, social or stylistic development, social distinctions, continuity of church use

(often through the modification or re-use of seating elements, and/or their piecemeal replacement); and the rarity of this
- Seating as an indicator of social, gender and age gradations (e.g. indicated by design, location, labelling, provision of seat furniture); and its relative historical importance
- Local or national historical associations, e.g. memorial seating, association of seating with particular event or individuals; and the importance of those associations
- Use of materials, or constructional techniques, unusual for the period of construction; and the importance of those features
- Individual items regardless of place in the overall ensemble, but dependent on rarity, including:
  - Medieval bench ends and carvings (which may be framed up in later work)
  - Seventeenth-century carving associated with the church (which may be framed up in later work)
  - Squire's pews and similar
  - Box pews (that is, pews with doors), especially if high box pews and seating is not all facing east
  - Historic graffiti

Matters likely to affect the archaeological significance of church seating
- Seating scheme (single-phase or multi-phase) whose organisation provides evidence about social relationships and the use of the building; and the importance of that evidence
- Multi-phase seating scheme (which may include galleries) providing evidence of changes over time, including the modification and re-use of seating elements (especially early ones); and the importance of that evidence
- Seat or seating (probably single-phase) with evidence of use of unusual materials or unusual constructional techniques; and the importance of that evidence

Significance of non-seating elements, where relevant
- The role of the floor and floor material(s) in the aesthetic value of the interior (many of the above questions regarding the architectural and artistic value of seating apply equally to flooring e.g. being associated with a notable architect or craftsman or manufacturer)
- The historical value of the floor, for example its age and originality (including medieval tiles, whether in original or displaced positions), and whether it is an early or rare example of its type. Note that later tiles may have historical value of their own, and may sometimes replicate existing or lost medieval patterns.
- Archaeological or other value from wear patterns in the floor
- Historical and evidential value from tomb slabs, monumental brasses etc., where relevant allowing for the originality of positioning, and possible relationship to burials
- Likelihood of significant below-ground archaeological evidence being affected by changes to floor, pew platforms etc.
- Historical value (e.g. through age or originality) of any wall panelling / dado likely to be affected

APPENDIX 2: Heritage significance of church seating – personal views

This appendix discusses our personal views on the heritage significance of church seating, and can safely be skipped by readers simply looking for practical suggestions.

It seems to us that there are three difficulties in deciding on the heritage significance of a particular example of church seating. The first is the lack of a formal systematised body of knowledge; the second is that we may have to make piecemeal, independent decisions; the third is the risk of over-definition.

Despite various efforts (not least in this book), there is no formal, systematised body of knowledge on church seating. Because the assessment of the heritage significance of seating often requires one to decide how unusual or important the seating is in comparison with seating elsewhere, in some cases the lack of a body of knowledge will make this difficult. For example, for none of the major Victorian architects do we know in how many churches they designed seating, nor how often it has survived intact. As there is no body of agreed knowledge in certain areas we have to rely on expert opinion, which can work well but may bring problems of consistency between cases.

Secondly we may have to make piecemeal, independent decisions, having no knowledge or control over what other people will decide in similar circumstances. Your decision to allow removal of pews designed by a particular architect may be perfectly sensible in your circumstances, but if everyone makes the same decision (perhaps using yours as a precedent) then we lose all the work of that architect. The fundamental difficulty is that no-one is taking an overview – not surprisingly, as no-one has the authority or the control mechanisms or the resources to do this. (The Methodist Church is an exception: here an overview is taken.) Indeed, for many types of seating, we do not even know our present position. Any individual decision to allow one particular example to be removed or compromised may be perfectly rational, but may over time lead to the loss of most examples of that type of seating. Examples of this have already occurred, as in the loss of simple 'preaching' interiors of the 1830s and 1840s in Liverpool, which were once common, but of which few now survive.

The final difficulty with church seating is the risk of over-definition. As we learn more and more, we will have more and more reasons to realise that something is unique or unusual. For example, as knowledge of the minor Victorian architects grows, we might find the seating of each of them being picked out for notice. Thus an increase in knowledge can lead to a gradual inflation in heritage value. This would not matter except that there can be economic and social costs attached to conservation, and those costs are not borne by the statutory bodies making the final decisions but by the volunteers who support the maintenance of the building.

These difficulties cannot be wished away. We must all learn to live with them, and manage them as best we can. Increasing our knowledge of church seating will gradually help with the first and second difficulty; we will need to be careful that it does not increase the third. We will continue to need expert opinion, and we must take a risk-based approach based on broad principles rather than a mechanistic one that deals with apparent certainties. We must make quite sure to carry out proper recording, and retain appropriate examples. We need to improve the ways in which difficult decisions are shared and used for learning, and our approach must be as systematic and transparent as possible, especially where there is legitimate public interest in the outcomes. And when there are good reasons we should not be afraid of changing our minds or not following precedent.

Given this, we thought that some broad generalisations as to our own views may be useful, not least to stimulate discussion. Each case must of course be taken on its merits.

1   Any pre-Reformation seating scheme is likely to be regarded as having considerable historical value, especially if it has never been moved and has not been significantly rebuilt (this is less common than might be thought).

2   Considerable historical value may also be attached to any seating scheme predating the changes in fashion of the 1840s, depending on its completeness and integrity, especially if there is associated liturgical furniture in place, or indications of status through design of the seating.

3   Any complete eighteenth- or nineteenth-century seating designed for a particular building by an architect or designer of national note may well be assessed as of high artistic or architectural significance, if it represents his or her better work or demonstrates that person's development. In these cases, it is usually the design which is of interest, not necessarily the seats-as-objects.

4   Regardless of architect, any ensemble which is of outstanding architectural or other aesthetic quality should be recognised as such.

5   Any multi-period seating arrangements illustrating development and continuity of use (or re-use) may have high evidential value, and some such arrangements have a historical

or aesthetic value associated not with a particular period or person but with the idea of continuity through local adaptive change, particularly if much of the church is filled with that seating.

6   Of somewhat lesser historical value are seating systems which indicate status through signage or similar on the seats; so too with bench-end furniture.

7   Seating arrangements where there is a single-phase, deliberate, extended re-use of earlier elements to create a planned interior may also have aesthetic, historical or evidential value (though it seems to us that there is growing evidence that such reworkings may have been relatively common in Victorian times), and the individual elements themselves may have considerable value, and will almost always do so if they are pre-Reformation.

We emphasise that these are our own views, based on our experience and knowledge, and certainly require further debate. We would welcome vigorous, reasoned discussion on these rather tricky matters.

Notes

1   We are grateful for helpful informal discussions with David Baker, Sara Crofts, Ian Dungavell, Joseph Elders, Diana Evans, Jonathan Goodchild, Richard Halsey, Russell Hanslip, Hugh Harrison, Linda Holder, Linda Monckton, Matthew Saunders, Ian Serjeant, Charles Smith, John Thewlis, and Jeffrey West, and comments from many of these individuals on an earlier draft of this chapter. They should not be taken to agree with what we put forward here either on a personal basis or on behalf of any organisation to which they are or have been attached. A particular concern has been to make this chapter of practical value, as far as possible avoiding jargon or theoretical discussion, yet providing a reasonable degree of rigour.

2   In drawing up this chapter, we have reviewed all the guidance listed in the box 'Denominational Advice and Requirements', and other useful unpublished material of a similar nature kindly provided to us. Account has been taken of the various principles and the proposals for managing change in the English Heritage document *Conservation Principles*, 2008 (details of which are in the list of further reading at the end of this book), and we have followed the spirit of the Burra Charter Process (available at http://australia.icomos.org/wp-content/uploads/BURRA_CHARTER.pdf, accessed August 2010), adapted for the fact that in the life of most churches, significance is only assessed when change is being considered. We have also consulted the *Standard and Guidance for Stewardship of the Historic Environment*, 2008, published by the Institute for Archaeologists and available from www.archaeologists.net (accessed September 2010), and *Planning Policy Statement 5: Planning for the Historic Environment* (The Stationery Office, 2010) and the associated *PPS5 Planning for the Historic Environment: Historic Environment Planning Practice Guide* (Department for Communities and Local Government and others, March 2010).

3   *Planning Policy Statement 5*, 14. Although even the briefest survey of the literature shows that the notion of 'significance' has no universally-agreed definition or scope, this makes little difference for the purposes of this appendix, where our aim is a practical discussion of the types of factor which may affect the heritage significance of church seating.

4   For example, in *Conservation Principles* 'communal value' is also included as one of the matters which can affect the assessment of significance (31–32).

28. Pews: why do they matter?

Trevor Cooper

The aim of this chapter is to tease out some of the different values and priorities that people attach to pews. For more factual issues, see Chapter 27, especially the checklist in Box 2.

PEWS DO SEEM TO RAISE PASSIONS, and this is perhaps not surprising. There are questions of historical significance, and aesthetic worth. There are practical matters of comfort, health and safety, flexibility, and cost. There are functional issues to do with the circulation of people, the amount of gathering space in the building, and opportunities for wider community use.

Crucially, the seating and its arrangement – including the space *not* filled by seating – will affect the way that congregations are able to worship, and thus the way that they do worship. Pews may affect the way people interact, and may be thought to give messages about what interaction is expected. Less tangibly, pews may provide familiarity and the sense of an unchanging and purposeful place, or be interpreted less charitably as showing resistance to change, and a congregation happy with fixed arrangements.

So pews, and church seating in general, lie at the intersection of many different priorities and values, which will sometimes be in conflict, even within the mind of the same individual.

This piece tries to tease out some of those issues. It is hoped that this will clarify things a little when the removal of pews is being discussed, and make debate that much easier. The chapter tries hard not to lean one way or the other, and if any bias is discerned it is as likely to be due to over-compensation as to reflect the actual views held by the author.

❖ ❖ ❖

Before reading further, you might like to do the **self-assessment questionnaire** overleaf. The rest of this chapter refers back to that questionnaire.

Pews: your values and priorities
Self assessment questionnaire

Think about a particular church which has got fixed pews, then complete each statement with the phrase which most closely reflects your values and priorities. If a statement is irrelevant, move on to the next one.

	Topic	Complete the statement with the phrase that most closely reflects your values and priorities		
1	Fitness for purpose	The pews . . .	. . . are more or less in the right place	. . . are in the wrong place, and stop the church from doing what it wants
2	Flexibility	If the church had movable seating . . .	. . . it would in practice hardly ever be moved around	. . . it would be reconfigured frequently
3	Experimental adaptability	The re-arrangement of seating which the church desires . . .	. . . is more or less understood already, and will not change much over time	. . . needs some experimentation, and/or may change over time
4	Utilisation	Most of the pews are unused at most services . . .	. . . but this does not matter	. . . and this is a strong argument for removing some of the pews
5	Permanent sense of purpose	The pews in this church speak of the permanent purpose of the building . . .	. . . and this is to be valued	. . . but this is not very important and may even be undesirable
6	Holiness or homeliness	Ideally, the seating in this church . . .	. . . should support the building as a holy place, transcendent, pointing to something beyond itself	. . . should support the building as a homely place, comfortable and familiar
7	Tradition	The pews present the church as traditional and unchanging . . .	. . . and this is valuable	. . . and this is unhelpful

	Topic	Complete the statement with the phrase that most closely reflects your values and priorities		
8	Cultural norms	Pews are not found in the secular world and their style may be regarded as 'quaint ecclesiastical' . . .	. . . but this does not matter	. . . and this adds unnecessary baggage to those not brought up in life of the church
9	Social interaction during worship	As regards social interactions between worshippers during church services . . .	. . . the pews are not a problem	. . . the pews are a problem
10	Implied social relationships of the church community	The arrangement of the pews in this church . . .	. . . implies nothing about the social relationships of the church community, or what it implies is not a problem	. . . carries unhelpful implications about the social relationships of the church community
11	Comfort	The pews are not particularly comfortable . . .	. . . and for purposes of worship that may be no bad thing	. . . and there ought to be comfortable seating for worship
12	Privacy	Sitting in a pew . . .	. . . gives a welcome sense of having arrived, of being secure, of having a place	. . . gives an unwelcome sense of being separate from other worshippers in one's own space
13	Practicality for the sitter	As regards practicality, . . .	. . . the pews are practical, for all sorts of reasons	. . . the pews are unpractical, for all sorts of reasons
14	Historic value	The pews have historic value . . .	. . . and for this reason should be kept by the church	. . . though preserving the nation's history should not be the church's priority
15	Aesthetic value	The pews complement the architecture, or are aesthetically pleasing in themselves . . .	. . . and for this reason should be kept by the church	. . . but the aesthetic value is not helping the church do its job

Qn 1: Fitness for purpose

Whether the present seating seriously constrains the congregation may sound like a factual question, but is in fact is one of priorities and values, as the answer depends on the importance attached to the things which cannot now be done. So there may be a range of strongly-held views about whether the seating is constraining – or not. Alongside this may be a concern that a change to the seating will open the door to future changes which have not yet been discussed or agreed.

With fixed seating, the congregation is in the hands of the person who installed the seating, who may be long dead, so a more fundamental question may arise – who is to have control of the seating arrangements in the building? – the Victorian restorer? today's congregation? the public and their representatives? the next generation?

Qns 2 and 3: Flexibility and experimental adaptability

One of the most common arguments for the removal of fixed pews is 'flexibility'. This is usually taken to mean *frequently reconfiguring the seating*. However, many churches who have acquired movable seating have found that they do not (or cannot realistically) make frequent changes, so the movable chairs or benches stay more or less in one position. For this reason, the desire for 'flexibility' is nowadays often subject to some challenge.

This may be to miss what is really being asked for, which is *adaptability* and the ability to *experiment*: that is, being able to explore various configurations, not necessarily the same throughout the building (discrete spaces may benefit from different layouts), before settling on what works; and to be able to repeat the experimental process in future if necessary.

Qn 4: Utilisation

A particular problem is that many churches have far too much seating, much of it due to subsidised over-seating in Victorian times.

Over-pewing is thought to have various behavioural effects. It can make people spread out rather than sitting in a communal group; some people may, of course, welcome this, and the resulting sense of privacy. It can encourage leaders to maintain a form of worship suited to a largish congregation (rousing hymns, for example) which is perhaps inappropriate to the actual number of people. The acres of empty pews may not be encouraging to the casual attendee.

Large numbers of empty seats may create a sense of a failing enterprise – perhaps quite unfairly, given the general overcapacity

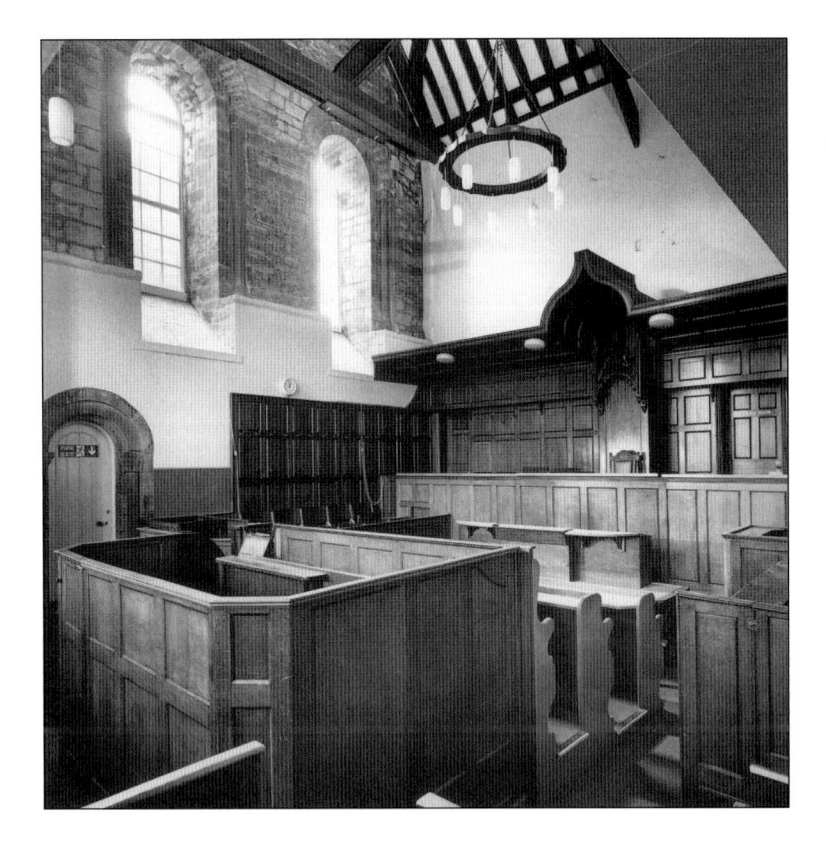

Fig. 1: Georgian woodwork in the old court room in the Great Hall at Leicester Castle, giving a clear sense of purpose to this space. (From Silence in Court: the Future of the UK's Historic Law Courts *(published by Save Britain's Heritage, 2004), p. 98)*

existing by late Victorian times. Indeed, might it be possible that opposition to the removal of pews may sometimes be due to the sense that removing seating capacity will epitomise this 'failure', or be the thin edge of the wedge in raising questions about the future of the building?

Over-seating wastes space, in an obvious way. On the other hand, a church might wish to provide enough seating for the occasional big event, which might be an argument for retaining pews, as it is very often the case that pews seat more people than chairs would.

Qn 5: *Permanent sense of purpose*

In an archetypal court room, it can be argued that the fixed wood furniture gives the building a permanent sense of purpose – that this is a building where particular and important things happen (Fig. 1). Some argue that, in the same way, solid wooden seating in a church sends a strong message that this is, in Philip Larkin's words, 'a serious house' (in his poem 'Church Going', in e.g. his *Collected Poems*).

Furthermore, formal pews may make even an empty church seem settled and ready for its purpose, quietly waiting for people to fill the spaces and fulfil their role.

Many will value this. Others may wonder if it does not lead too easily to the building (or its designer) imposing too much on the worshipping community. They may be uneasy if the building is interpreted as anything more than a neutral vessel for conveniently holding worshippers, who recreate their real purpose each time they meet.

Qn 6: Holiness or homeliness

One view is that a church building should signal transcendence, pointing to something greater than itself. In contrast, others would prefer to see churches as non-symbolic but comfortable, warm, and welcoming spaces, bringing, perhaps, the advantages of familiarity and the suggestion of human contact.

One wag has elegantly described this as the contrast between the 'beauty of holiness' and 'the beauty of homeliness'. Church seating will inevitably affect the nature of the interior, perhaps pushing it towards holiness or homeliness. There can be real (and difficult) choices to be made.

Qn 7: Tradition

Many people value pews because they embody *tradition*, though perhaps a less loaded term would be *continuity*: participation in the life of the Church in a way which respects the past and seems permanent and unchanging. The feeling may be deep rooted, even if not clearly articulated. A mild form of this is attachment to a particular pew.

In complete contrast, some will feel that seating unchanged for more than a hundred years may give the impression that the congregation is fixed in its ways and thus closed-minded.

Qn 8: Cultural norms

Pews are not part of everyday secular life, and some people argue that they give the impression that worship is a heritage activity, done in seating from a bygone age. Wooden pews may then be regarded as cultural baggage from the past, a factor to be explained away to those born outside the life of the Church.

In response it may be argued that it is not the job of the Church to go with the ebb and flow of modern culture, and that being up to date would imply continual change to avoid being out of date. It might be said that anyway most people quite successfully inhabit more than one culture; that in a postmodern age, being different matters little and may actually be a selling point; and that the demands for cultural adjustment made by pews are hardly more and probably less than that which people will meet when they first go to a football match or a pop festival and encounter the seating provided at those venues.

This type of debate is not particular to religion: consider the discussions over the appropriate clothes for Judges, or dignitaries in the Houses of Parliament.

Qn 9: Social interaction during worship

Fixed pews are normally in a straight line. Such seating suits a proscenium theatre or a public lecture, where the front of the building is the single focus, and visual contact with others is not especially important. Some people find this traditional arrangement also works well for them in church, and may rather dislike being forced into eye contact during a service. For some people, too, the ability to see the speaker's lips clearly may help them hear what is said, and there may be a degree of practical advantage in straight lines when using projector screens. Some people may also value the fact that they can slip into a service without being pressured into engaging with others.

On the other hand some people are looking for greater interaction during church services, more than can be provided with straight rows of seating facing the front. Furthermore the arrangement encourages a single focal point during the service, which not everyone thinks is desirable.

Qn 10: Implied nature of the church community

The arrangement of seating can encourage or discourage different types of social interaction. This means it can be taken to signal what social interaction is expected, and the nature of authority within the group. Think, for example, of the hierarchy of tables and chairs at a public enquiry; or the horse-shoe arrangement at a board interview; or the circle of chairs for a self-help group.

Traditionally-pewed churches, with straight lines of fixed seating, may therefore be taken to imply formality, not only in worship (which may or may not be thought desirable) but also, by implication, in the ongoing life of the people who worship there.

Some will deny straight away that people think in these terms, saying that the average person hardly notices the layout of the seating, and anyway will be so used to it being the normal arrangement in churches that he or she thinks nothing of it.

It can also be argued that even if the seating does give that impression, it is irrelevant. For, unlike the audience at the theatre or the public lecture, the congregation at a church service is part of a continuing, living community. Whatever the church seating implies is unimportant as it is not necessarily a good indicator of what their community is *truly* like and how it *actually* behaves. Any misleading message given by the seating will be swamped by what is actually experienced by those worshipping at the church.

Others will worry, though, that if the seating is misleading, it will discourage those without a church upbringing from attending in the first place.

Qn 11: Comfort

Comfort may seem an obvious requirement. But comfortable for whom and for how long, doing what? – a point raised in Box 2 in Chapter 27.

To complicate matters, there is a long tradition of regarding comfort in church as relatively unimportant, or even undesirable: as the *Daily Telegraph* put it a few years ago (26 July 2009, p. 19, third leader), 'the pews in our churches may be uncomfortable, but a little hardship can be good for the soul'. This assumes, of course that pews are uncomfortable, which is not always true.

Qn. 12: Privacy

There appears not to be any formal study of people's attitudes to pews, but anecdotal evidence would suggest that the sense of privacy and having one's own space is important to some people, whereas others read this as isolation. Are these reactions caused by the presence of the solid barrier provided by the pew in front?

Qn 13: Practicality for the sitter

There is a host of detailed questions about the practicality of the different forms of church seating – how easy it is for families with children, how likely it is to be shifted around and make a noise, does it give something to grab hold of when standing up and sitting down, how easy it is to kneel (if this is relevant) and so on. Many of the items in the checklist in Box 2 in Chapter 27 are of this nature.

Qns 14 and 15: Historic and aesthetic value

The issues are not only the historical and aesthetic value of the existing pews, but how these will be balanced against other factors when a decision is made. We explore this at some length in Chapter 27, and provide a systematic process for reaching a proposal.

Part 5

CASE STUDIES

29. Case Studies

Edited by Trevor Cooper

Introduction

These case studies show some of the ways in which people are trying to ensure that their church seating is fit for present purposes, whilst taking due account of its contribution to our heritage. These cases have been chosen simply because we thought them of interest and because they show something of what is going on, not because we necessarily support them or regard them as exemplars. Nor are they a statistically representative collection, which would have consisted mostly of partial removal of Victorian pews from the front or back of the church, with one or two cases of pews being entirely replaced by chairs.

We hope that the studies will be stimulating and useful to those thinking about seating in their own church.

The word 'pew' is mostly used with its normal colloquial meaning, to refer to fixed wooden seating. When no author is named, the study has been written by Trevor Cooper with the support of a representative of the church.

List of case studies

1. Take a pew: recycling pews for local domestic use
     by Anni Holden
2. Improving the comfort of medieval pews, reversibly: Wellow, Somerset
     by Hugh Harrison and Peter Ferguson
3. Replacing chairs with Victorian pews from another church: London
     by Charles Smith
4. Removing chairs, replacing with stackable benches:
    All Saints, Carshalton *by the Revd Dr John Thewlis*
5. Partial removal of pews: the New Room, Bristol (Methodist)
     by Ian Serjeant
6. New pews: Our Lady & St Thomas of Canterbury, London (RC)
     by Martin Goalen
7. Using old bench ends to make short benches: Wortham, Suffolk
8. Removing Victorian pews, replacing with locally-designed substantial but movable benches: Willand, Devon
9. Keeping pews in a community church: Thorpe Market, Norfolk
10. Using the church, keeping the pews: Redgrave, Suffolk
    (CCT church) *by Bob Hayward*
11. Moving seventeenth-century pews: Haughton-le-Skerne, Darlington, County Durham
12. Moving medieval pews: Haddenham, Buckinghamshire
13. Replacing Victorian pews with two types of chair: Kirtlington, Oxfordshire
14. Making Victorian pews movable: Addiscombe, South London
15. Putting a loo in family pew: Slaidburn, Lancashire

1. Take a pew: recycling pews for local domestic use
by Anni Holden, Director of Communications, Diocese of Hereford

This article is reproduced by permission from Country Way, *51 (2009) (www.countryway.org.uk)*

The phrase 'Take A Pew' has a new meaning in Herefordshire where a unique scheme is not only recycling old church seating but ensuring parishes get a better deal, and giving work to people with special needs.

Take A Pew is a positive spin-off from the diocese of Hereford's groundbreaking work in developing church buildings for community use while ensuring they remain open for prayer and worship.

The scheme has been set up by the diocese in partnership with the Local Authority and EnviroAbility, a not for profit company that works on projects that benefit the community and are good for the environment. It enables a church to benefit from the re-use of pews that are removed to create more flexible spaces. Congregation members and others whose church is removing some pews, get the chance to buy a pew cut to their requirements for use in their own homes (Fig 1).

Martin Neicho of EnviroAbility, who is administering the scheme, said: 'The result is a unique and functional piece of furniture that incorporates an element of local history'.

Fig. 1: Some of the Take a Pew team at work shortening and refurbishing pews, and an example of the finished article in a home setting. (© Take a Pew)

The Diocesan Community Partnership and Funding Officer, Wendy Coombey, said the scheme would bring benefits all round. 'We are leading the way in the Church of England in the development of our buildings for the use of the community and schemes sometimes include the removal of some or all the old pews,' she said. 'People are often sad to see them go but don't have room for one in their homes because they're so big. Now we have a solution that works for everyone,' she added.

Examples of Take A Pew in action include St Peter's Church in Peterstow where pews in the nave are being removed and a screen erected to allow a kitchen and toilet to be installed. The rest of the nave space will be used for lunch clubs, yoga, play sessions for under-fives and meetings of the village gardening club. The chancel will remain a space for regular worship, which can overflow into the nave for special occasions. At nearby Peterchurch, in another unique collaboration, the Parochial Church Council were handed a cheque for £1,500 after the recycling of their pews; the nave is to be home to a local authority Children's Centre.

Churches taking part in the scheme will be able to sell the pews to those who want them at a reasonable price, rather than, as happens now, selling unwanted pews at less than their market value to companies that go on to make a big profit.

'This project, the first of its kind anywhere in the country, will mean that a church will get a fair price and at the same time create opportunities for people with disabilities and others facing difficulties in the job market,' added Martin. Under the project they work alongside carpenters from Herefordshire day care centres, giving them the opportunity to improve their confidence and self-esteem.

'It also means that pews are likely to stay in the local area. We will put a plaque on the recycled piece and supply information about the church it came from,' Martin added. The next church for Take A Pew in the diocese of Hereford is just over the Welsh border at Discoed.

This project is a joint venture between the diocese of Hereford, EnviroAbility and Herefordshire Council and is supported by Advantage West Midlands through Herefordshire Access to Services Partnership and Community First.

For further details see www.enviroability.org.uk or contact Take-A-Pew, The Ryefield Centre, Grammar School Close, Ross-on-Wye, HR9 7QD or email: info@takeapew.org.uk

2. Improving the comfort of medieval pews, reversibly: Wellow, Somerset

by Hugh Harrison and Peter Ferguson

This short account of one West Country church's solution to its problems relates to one of our earlier surviving pew schemes, dating from the mid fifteenth century. The problem for the twenty-first-century parishioner is predominantly one of comfort, possibly the commonest concern encountered where there is continued use of early medieval benches. Quite simply, the seats are too shallow and the backs too vertical to comfortably support the average-sized adult of today (Fig. 2a).

The fourteenth-century parish church of St Julian, Wellow, in north-east Somerset, is, in Pevsner's words in the North Somerset volume of the *Buildings of England*, 'strikingly uniform in character and internally well-appointed', and it has historic connections of national importance. The nave is fitted with many sets of unaltered medieval pews. Their magnificent, matching, carved bench ends are filled with panel tracery over quatrefoiled bases, and the robustly-moulded edges culminate in impressively large foliated poppy-heads set back from the centre of the pew end. The bench seats are very solid and shallow, whilst the seat backs are plain panelled under a heavily moulded and projecting top rail. Consequently, worshippers are required to perch precariously on the edge of the seat and are pushed ever closer to the edge by the discomfort of the top rail digging into their backs just under the shoulder blades, a fact well understood by the Revd L. W. Fussell, who was appointed Vicar of Wellow in 1944. He wrote of the benches in his book, *Via Old England,* published two years later, 'over fifty of these fine benches have received Wellow folk for worship in five centuries . . . there is no comfort in them, but much joy that they are among the best in Old England'.

Fig. 2a: St Julian, Wellow, Somerset. One of the fifty or so medieval benches in the church. They are very uncomfortable with narrow seats, upright backs, and projecting, moulded top rails.

This problem has dogged vicar and churchwardens for over a hundred years, with past attempts to make the pews more bearable meeting with very little success. In 2004 the church's newly-appointed Quinquennial Surveyor, Alan Hardiman, was asked by the Parochial Church Council to try and come up with a solution and in September that year he approached Hugh Harrison, one of the authors of this study. Replacing the pews and moving them to another part of the church was not an option. Nor was physical alteration of the pews, though this might well have been carried out in the nineteenth and early twentieth centuries, when the 'minimal intervention' philosophy of today was not adhered to with the same conviction. Wellow's pews are of major historical significance and any alterations must, of necessity, be reversible and as minimally-invasive as technically possible.

There are twenty medieval pews located in the nave, with other medieval pews in the north and south aisles. Presumably based on considerations of cost and use, the Parochial Church Council decided that just the twenty nave pews were to be modified, with one pew to be adapted in an initial trial before fund-raising for the completion of the other nineteen was undertaken. By December 2004, Hugh Harrison Conservation had produced a design solution for the seat, with three alternatives for the pew backs for further discussion with the parish, the Diocesan Advisory Committee and English Heritage. It was clear from inspection of the pews that the problem of comfort could be got over if the seats could be made deeper and the backs filled in at a slight rake below the projecting top rail. The question was how to achieve this without alteration or loss to the configuration of the medieval pews, and without physically moving the pews from their present positions.

How far the seat could be brought forward, in order that leg-room would not be seriously compromised, depended upon the distance between the seat nosing and the back of the pew in front. Careful measurements were taken and a projection of 75 mm decided upon (Figs. 2b & c). New seat support brackets were introduced under the existing seat boards; these projected in front to pick up the new nosing which was screwed to the brackets from the underside with stainless steel screws. The seat brackets were skew-screwed to the floor and attached to blocking pieces screwed to the underside of the medieval seats, this being the only intervention required into the original fabric (Fig. 2d). The nosing projected above the level of the original seat board sufficiently to be rebated on the back edge to receive a false seat board laid over the original seat, loose wedged to overcome undulations in the original boards. A seat back support, split into panels and muntins to match those of the original seat back, was designed to drop into a slot in the back of the new false seat board and neatly fitted in under the projecting top rail of the pews. The false back panel would be held in position at the top by thin stainless steel pins into the original muntins. Thus the false nosing, seat and back become part self-interlocking, achieving minimal intervention into the original fabric by requiring only one screw and one pin at each new seat-bracket position to provide a fixing. Stained and polished English oak to match the original pews was specified for

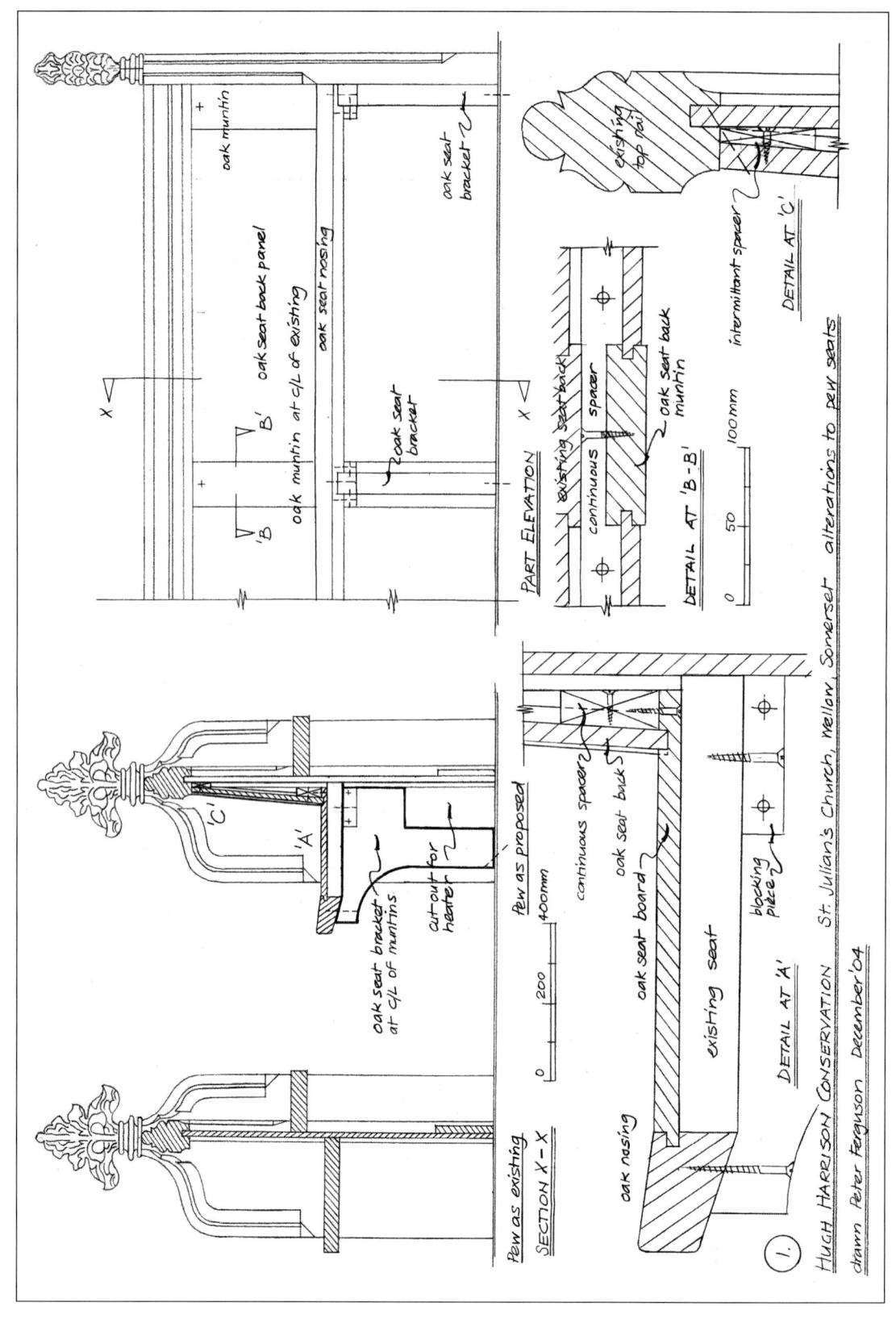

Fig. 2b: *The proposed alterations to the medieval benches at Wellow, designed to improve their comfort whilst being reversible.*

CASE STUDIES

the new seat and back which were designed to look like the original construction.

Perhaps for reasons of cost, the parish decided against trialling the proposed seat back, opting for the less visually pleasing, but cheaper, alternative of forming a wedge-shaped, foam-filled cushion to straddle the back of the pew. This meant that, to hold the new false seat in position, pins had to be used at the back, driven into the existing seat board. Constructionally this arrangement involved no more intervention into the existing fabric than that required by the full scheme, where the pins would have been driven into the back panel muntins.

The trial of the modified seat (Fig. 2e) ran for some months so that it could be fully tested and appraised. As a result of the trial, it was decided that the false nosing could be extended by a further 13mm without loss of leg-room, and this is to be incorporated into the work on the remaining nineteen pews. At the time of writing, a decision is yet

Fig. 2c (left): The new seat 'nosing' on the trial bench at Wellow, placed on top of the original seat, projecting 75 mm.
Fig. 2d (right): As discussed in the text, brackets were introduced to support the new 'nosing' on the seats.

Fig. 2e: The trial seat at Wellow in its final, modified form.

417

to be reached on the implementation of the oak seat backs, but there is no doubt in the mind of the authors that these should be fitted even though the foam cushions would undoubtedly provide some level of comfort, though for a shorter time span. It is, of course, a matter for debate, but unless wardens and sidespersons place and remove the cushions for each service, there will be visual disruption to the enjoyment of Wellow's fine medieval pews as part of that 'uniform character' commented upon so favourably by Pevsner. As for the wider implications of this experiment, the authors are confident that the method used to improve the comfort of the Wellow pews while protecting their historic fabric could also be applied with equal success to early medieval bench pews anywhere else in the country.

3. Replacing chairs with Victorian pews from another church: London, Hammersmith and Stoke Newington
by Charles Smith, previously of the Diocese of London

A listed church building is to be made redundant. Its furnishings are a complete set designed by a major architect. No new use for the building can be found without their removal. None of the interested parties can agree what to do. The diocese of London faced this familiar predicament in dealing with a significant historic church building in Hammersmith, London. But in this particular case – that of St John's, Glenthorne Road, Hammersmith – the ending was not perhaps the one that might have been expected.

St John's is a Grade II★ Gothic Revival church designed by the great Victorian architect William Butterfield in 1857–9 (Fig. 3a). The church is unmistakably Butterfieldian. The polychromatic brickwork – yellow brick with bands and patterns of red brick and stone – and the

Fig. 3a: The exterior of St John, Glenthorne Road (1857–9), a church by William Butterfield.

saddleback roof to the tower (added in 1877, instead of the originally intended spire) give very clear clues as to the date and architect. The building's provenance becomes even clearer on entering the building. The use of coloured marbles, tiles and mastic in inlay, and architectural timber are everything you would expect of Butterfield, who by this stage had already established his reputation as a master of High Victorian Gothic. Later alterations were largely carried out under the auspices of J. F. Bentley, who remodelled the chapel in 1898 and extended the building one bay east, as well as adding the east vestry and designing the organ case.

However it became clear some years ago that, with Hammersmith already well endowed with churches, St John's no longer had a viable future as an Anglican place of worship. The church was to be made redundant and new uses for the building sought. During the statutory 'waiting period', the only feasible new use put forward came from the nearby Godolphin and Latymer School. They wished to convert the building into a school hall facility, providing space for assemblies, concerts, examinations and other school-related events. Such a use would secure the future of the listed building and still allow its volume and general spatial qualities to be appreciated. In February 2006, a 125-year lease was entered into, covering the church, vicarage (which is listed Grade II, by William Butterfield, 1865) and surrounding land, to accommodate the school's pressing need for extra space.

As the building was redundant, Listed Building Consent was necessary and was duly granted for the conversion scheme, subject to the main furnishings not being removed from the church until an acceptable future location had been agreed. The furnishings comprised all the usual items you would expect in a church of this period. Crucially, the congregational benches (Figs. 3b & c), choir stalls, clergy stalls, pulpit (Fig. 3d) and communion rails (Fig. 3e) were all designed by Butterfield and, as in many new nineteenth-century churches, were part of an harmonious scheme of furnishing. The benches are lengthy, open backed, made of softwood and darkly stained. Broadly Gothic in detail, the ends are somewhat eccentric and typical of Butterfield's High Victorian style. The benches contain integrated wooden kneelers which is not surprising considering Butterfield's fierce opposition to the hassock. The choir stalls and clergy stalls are solid oak and well

Fig. 3b (left): The interior at St John's, showing Butterfield's seating in place.

Fig. 3c (right): Details of Butterfield's seating. Note the kneeling board.

Fig. 3d: Butterfield's pulpit at St John's.

Fig. 3e: Butterfield's communion rail at St John's.

constructed, comprising a range of Gothic motifs including cusped arches, integrated buttresses and turned shafts. The oak pulpit on a stone base and oak communion rails are of the same ilk.

Finding a new home for small movable furnishings, such as candles and crucifixes, is often easy: in this case the successor parish church – Holy Innocents, Hammersmith – took such items on. Fortunately, the school was happy to accommodate the octagonal Butterfield font with coloured marbles as part of its reordered space. With the timber Butterfield altar table also being retained, the two primary sacramental symbols – font and altar – were remaining in their original setting. But anyone who has worked on such projects will sympathise with just how difficult it can be to find a new home for benches, clergy stalls, choir stalls, pulpits and communion rails. Not only are these furnishings heavy and bulky, but they are often regarded as no longer fashionable in church settings. To advertise the furnishings is often a lengthy, and ultimately fruitless, process. If there are any takers, they are usually only interested in one or two items, meaning the set is broken up.

Sometimes, a more direct approach can yield results. More out of hope than expectation, the diocese decided to contact the incumbent of every church in the diocese designed by William Butterfield. And lo and behold the Revd David Lambert – the first to pick up the phone – expressed interest. His church, St Matthias, Stoke Newington, was designed by Butterfield in 1849–53 and is listed Grade I. Like St John's,

St Matthias is typically Butterfieldian: its powerful silhouette is defined by a steep saddleback roof of the tower over the chancel (Fig. 3f) and the west window is eccentrically divided by a central buttress. Inside, however, most of the original interior had been lost due to incendiary bombs in the Second World War. Although no original drawings of the furnishings have come to light, the two remaining original fittings – the font and the lectern (Fig. 3g) – suggested the style of design would have been very similar to those found in St John's, Glenthorne Road.

The existing furnishings in St Matthias were mostly inserted in the 1950s. The choir furnishings consisted of two rows of choir stalls made from hardwood and painted black and gilded, with additional priests chairs decorated in the same manner. The sanctuary rails and pulpit matched the design. The nave seating, originally benches, now comprised linked wooden chairs of c.1950 (Fig. 3h). In essence, this was a low budget post-war refit. Although simple, solidly constructed and practical, none of these furnishings were deemed to be of particular historic or architectural significance by the Diocesan Advisory Committee, English Heritage or the national amenity societies. The desirability of saving the Butterfield furnishings far outweighed the interest of saving the existing furnishings.

It was hard to imagine a more stylistically appropriate new location for the furnishings than here. Both churches were built by the same architect and at the same period of his career. Although the general dimensions of the two churches differed considerably, the width of the nave and the span of the arcades were sufficiently similar for the furnishings to fit. The benches, being free-standing, required no adaptation in order to be used in their new location.

The Parochial Church Council (PCC) met the idea of taking on the furnishings with considerable enthusiasm, as did the statutory consultees. More than sixty years since bombing had virtually obliterated the original scheme of furnishing, there was now an opportunity to enhance the status of this important Grade I listed church by returning its interior to something more respectful of Butterfield's intentions.

The choir stalls (Fig. 3i), clergy stalls and benches (Fig. 3j) have now been slotted into place at St Matthias and are well used. The transformation is not yet complete: before assuming their intended positions, the pulpit requires its base to be reformed and the communion rails need some sensitively-designed supports to enable them to be free-standing.

The net result is that a redundant Grade II* church has found a sustainable use which will ensure its care and preservation for future generations, a fine group of furnishings have been kept together as a set in a new sympathetic environment and a parish has benefited from the transfer. Father David commented that 'the congregation is delighted with the furnishings from an aesthetic point of view and have even noticed the increased levels of comfort since the pews arrived'. Butterfield would have been proud of this last observation as during his career he took particular interest in designing the ideal pew, publishing several articles about their utility and comfort (one of which is reprinted on pages 231–5 above).

Fig. 3f: The tower at Butterfield's St Matthias, Stoke Newington (1849–53).

Fig. 3g: The lectern at St Matthias.

Fig. 3h (top): Chairs at St Matthias before they were removed and replaced with the benches from St John's.

Fig. 3i (middle): Choir stalls from St John's, in their new position at St Matthias.

Fig. 3j (bottom): Nave benches from St John's, shown here in their new location at St Matthias.

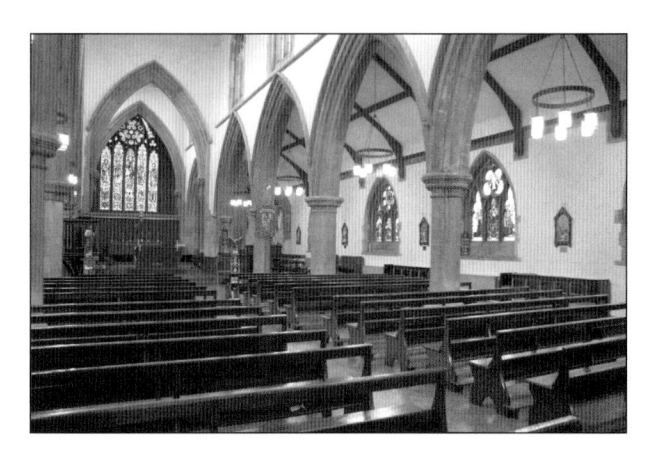

Update Autumn 2009 by Trevor Cooper

Final completion of the project has unfortunately been held up through lack of funds. The School paid to transport the furnishings from Hammersmith to Stoke Newington, but there were no funds to pay for full installation of all the furniture and, although various grant-giving bodies were approached, none was able to provide support. So the aisles still contain the pulpit and altar rail which the PCC cannot at present afford to put in place, and the choir stalls are not as yet properly installed.

4. Removing chairs, replacing with stackable benches: All Saints, Carshalton, Surrey

by the Revd Dr John Thewlis, incumbent of All Saints

Our medieval church was extended and enlarged between 1894 and 1914, but money ran out before the seating could be tackled. Routine Victorian pitch-pine benches were adapted for the aisles, and two different styles of even more routine chairs filled the nave (Fig. 4a). Three years ago we decided to do something about it. We resisted upholstery, and went for stackable oak benches.

We have found that benches are more adaptable than any chair. They allow a congregation to expand and contract in a very natural way. It is easy to huddle together on a bench, which is good for families and schoolchildren. It is also easy, unobtrusively and perhaps unconsciously, to gain a little extra space without making a big issue of it. Two people on a bench gives a much better visual message than two people in a row of seats. Big congregations look bigger – five-seaters at a pinch will accommodate seven, at least in summer.

The flexibility of benches is as great as chairs, but different. They cannot be arranged into a tight circle; café style worship would not be easy – but perhaps that is better solved by inexpensive folding metal chairs, easily stored and sometimes giving lumbar support in excess of more complicated designs. Benches can go in squares, octagons, and longitudinally down a nave or along a table. We move them with ease – one man can easily move them, using a dedicated trolley – and can stack them temporarily or semi-permanently. Though they are not fixed, there are no worries about their stability; it is easy and natural to grab on to them when you stand up. Unlike many chairs they are safe for children: firm to stand on next to their parents, presenting rounded edges and having far fewer gaps to get stuck in or fall through.

Fig. 4a: The interior of All Saints, Carshalton, before the replacement of the chairs with benches.

Fig. 4b: The new benches at All Saints.

Benches look good (Fig. 4b). Instead of an astonishingly complex tangle of uprights, the immediate impression is of calm, clear lines. They present a better theology. Shared seating echoes our membership of one body, and the fact we are branches of a single vine, much better than lines of rigidly individualistic chairs.

Their workmanship and materials involve a greater initial outlay, but they represent a better investment. Their construction is simpler, and they will last much longer. It has also to be said that even adequate chairs never come cheap.

And they are comfortable. We were at pains to provide kneelers that could double as cushions. Astonishingly, no member of our congregation – not even the most infirm – has made use of them for anything other than kneeling. Being wooden, benches are easily kept clean. The modern child seems to come to worship (*experto crede*) equipped with fruit juice, raisins and bubblegum – ruination to cushions and carpets, but shrugged off by wood.

Benches have released our church interior for all sorts of adaptations. Proof of the pudding, though, is really on the ordinary days, when the lines of the building can be experienced as the architects intended, without a stuttering congeries of chairs (Figs. 4c & d). We are really pleased with our decision.

Fig. 4c (left): The interior of All Saints, after the introduction of the new benches.

Fig. 4d (below): The interior of All Saints, looking down from the gallery, showing the new benches in one of their many possible layouts.

5. Partial removal of pews: the New Room, Bristol (Methodist)
by Ian Serjeant, Methodist Property Office

A controversial scheme to remove all the ground floor box pews from the Grade I listed chapel at the New Room, Bristol was refused by the Methodist Connexional Property Committee. A subsequent appeal resulted in a decision to allow the removal of the first two pews. The issues were varied and complex.

Background

The New Room was originally built in 1739 and enlarged and rebuilt in 1748. John Wesley was associated with the building from its outset and it was the location of the second Methodist Conference in 1745. There is a worship area and gallery (Fig. 5a) with, above, various rooms formerly used as living accommodation, now for exhibition purposes. In 1808 the building was sold to the Welsh Calvinistic Methodists who retained possession until 1929 when it reverted to Methodist use. A major restoration was carried out at this time by Sir George Oatley. It has worldwide significance as the first purpose-built Methodist building. Although still used for worship there is no resident congregation and the building is managed by a body of trustees.

The Managing Trustees of the building first suggested the removal of the pews in 1998 but a formal application was not submitted until August 2000. The scheme involved the removal of the ground floor box pews and their replacement with backless benches and, when required, chairs which would normally be kept in storage. The purpose was to restore the building to its original appearance and to accommodate a wider range of events such as music, drama, debates, receptions and media events. A decision was delayed until June 2004 because of a requirement that a Conservation Plan be prepared for the whole site.

Fig. 5a: The chapel of the New Room, Bristol, the first purpose-built Methodist building.

The report on the application concluded with the following statement:

> In many cases permission has been granted for the removal of pews from important listed buildings. But this is an exceptional, if not unique, situation.
>
> This is a Grade I building of national or wider importance. It has a singular status as Methodism's oldest purpose-built building and reflects different aspects of the life, growth and fluctuating fortunes of Methodism. The presumption therefore must be that it should be preserved without significant alteration unless a convincing case can be made. The present ground floor layout has appeared in its current form for at least two-thirds of the life of the building, albeit with changes to the actual fabric of the pews. The character of the worship area is difficult to define but it is certainly special and also fragile. The proposed change would perceptibly change its appearance by leaving a void at the centre and isolating the pulpit. It is therefore considered that the case put forward for the removal of all the ground floor box pews is not sufficient to override the presumption in favour of their retention.

The Managing Trustees lodged an appeal against the decision under the Methodist Church's own appeals procedures. The basis of the appeal was that 'The present pews do not have historical, liturgical, aesthetic or missiological inheritance and are a hindrance to our understanding of modern day mission'.

Issues
One of the main issues at the heart of the case is the fact that the New Room is not a local church although it is a place of worship. It is maintained by the Methodist Church because of its enormous historic significance. One argument against the removal of pews was that the spatial needs of a local church differ from those occurring in a building such as this which has a much broader function. It is not just a place of worship as acknowledged by the Managing Trustees. Among other things it is a shrine, a place of pilgrimage and a museum. The introduction of additional activities may be desirable, but not at the cost of a feature which gives the building part of its special interest.

The building was greatly enlarged and rebuilt in 1748, the Conference Room added after 1748, a large pipe organ was installed and subsequently removed at the 'east' end, the upper part of the pulpit is a reconstruction from 1930 and the Snetzler organ added in 1939. All of these and other changes reflect different stages of the building's history. When Oatley carried out the restoration, including the wholesale rebuilding or replacement of the pews, he sought to return the building to its eighteenth-century form, based on the understanding of conservation techniques and practices of his day. This work in itself is now an established part of the history and character of the building and is of significance in its own right.

The desire to return a building to its 'original' state is often an influence on schemes of alteration. As demonstrated above there have been many previous interventions in the building. Without overwhelming evidence of the original design and layout it was argued that the introduction of any type of bench would be speculative and should therefore be resisted.

At the hearing the appellants made much of the fact that two consultees, English Heritage and Bristol City Council, had given different responses to the two consultations carried out (these were necessitated by the submission of additional information by the Managing Trustees). Although the first responses were opposed to removal, the second response raised no objection subject to dismantling and storage. The other consultees, the Ancient Monuments Society and the Georgian Group remained opposed to the proposal.

At the appeal hearing all of these issues were considered. The Appeals Panel noted there were two distinct points of view and there is a tension between the needs of mission, and preservation and heritage. In making their decision the Panel emphasised that the building does reflect its history and evolution, and not only its historical connection with John Wesley, although the latter is of paramount importance. However, the Welsh Calvinistic Methodist phase is an important period in the life of the New Room and this had to be recognised.

The arguments for and against the removal of the pews was finely balanced. On the one hand there was an acknowledgement of the needs of the Managing Trustees to use the building for public worship and events; on the other hand both parties stressed the uniqueness of this, the most important Methodist building in the world.

The decision of the Panel was to allow the removal of the front two pews only (Fig. 5b).

Conclusions

This case underlines the fact that the case for the removal of pews, even from highly graded buildings, is not straightforward and that each case has to be examined in detail. General guidelines, such as issued by the Victorian Society and the Methodist Church are useful but can only have limited application. Where complex cases arise there may be a need for a greater forensic approach.

Much criticism has been levelled at Ecclesiastical Exemption, yet if this scheme had been dealt with by the secular system it is most likely that permission would have been given for the removal of the ground floor box pews, given the lack of opposition by English Heritage and the local planning authority.

Fig. 5b: The front two rows of pews at the New Room have been removed, as discussed in the text.

6. New pews: Our Lady & St Thomas of Canterbury, London
by Martin Goalen, architect

Those charged with reconciling a church by A.W.N. Pugin with the revived post-conciliar Roman liturgy would seem to face a paradox. Pugin's strong articulation of his buildings' structure and decoration – emphasising what he argued was 'the mystical separation between the sacrifice and the people' (*True Principles* (1841), 50) – would seemingly be denied in the exercise. The Roman Catholic Church of Our Lady and St Thomas of Canterbury at Fulham was designed in the years following that 'astute and calculated' attack on his work in *The Ecclesiologist* in 1846, the story of which is so touchingly told by Phoebe Stanton (*Pugin* (London, 1971), 185 ff.), and it received neither the rich painted decoration of St Giles, Cheadle, nor the 'solid stone walls and moulded work' of his own church at Ramsgate. Some colouring was started in the decade after Pugin's death, but, aerial bombardment in the Second World War, and other vicissitudes, left no strong overall character surviving when, in 2005, the parish took up the task of liturgical reordering.

It seemed that one answer to the dilemma was to devise a scheme that, while welcoming the post-conciliar gathering together of 'the sacrifice and the people', sought to return to the vividness of Pugin interiors at their best. Accordingly, motifs used by Pugin and his immediate followers are worked together in a new scheme which, starting at its simplest furthest from the altar with painted bands and stencilled flowers, becomes more intense towards the chancel, and, in the immediate area of the tabernacle, the decoration – stencilled diapered lozenges and fleurs-de-lis; marble and encaustic flooring; stencilled starbursts and monograms of the holy name in the ceiling – combine to form 'a splendid whole' (*The Present State of Ecclesiastical Architecture* (1843), 26n).

The new benches and sanctuary furniture reflect this same articulation. Benches in the nave – replacing the 1960s metal framed ones shown in Figure 6a – are an essay in the simple timber construction used by Pugin in some of his plainer furniture, and taken up by his followers and successors (Figs. 6b–d). The work was completed through

Fig. 6a: Our Lady & St Thomas of Canterbury, Fulham, London. The metal-framed benches dating from the 1960s, before the recent reordering.

a happy collaboration with the Anglican diocese of London when redundant plaster Stations of the Cross from a nearby church were cleaned of elaborate over-painting, each nimbus lightly gilded and the panels mounted on oak brackets matching the remaining joinery.

Reviewing the scheme, *True Principles: The Journal of the Pugin Society* (vol. III, no. iv (Winter 2007–8), 56), concluded that:

> The whole scheme is indicative of a happy reassessment of the aesthetic setting of the reformed liturgy, where recourse to historical richness and elaboration can be displayed and celebrated, rather than consciously stifled on the premise of liturgical necessity casting off a garb of obsolete superfluous distractions.

Fig. 6b: One of the new benches at Our Lady & St Thomas of Canterbury.

Fig. 6c: Our Lady & St Thomas of Canterbury, a view of the nave looking north-west, showing the new seating.

Fig. 6d: The chancel at Our Lady & St Thomas of Canterbury, newly-decorated, and with new liturgical seating.

7. Using old bench ends to make short benches: Wortham, Suffolk

Wortham is a village in north Suffolk, a few miles west of Diss. The medieval church, St Mary's, lies a mile north of the main road through the village.

Until recently, St Mary's was full of pews. There were far too many pews for the average congregation and more than enough for all but the most well attended of funerals. The construction of kitchen and toilet facilities in one corner had further reduced the available gathering space, and there was no room to meet for fellowship, for example after services.

In order to create more room the church explored the possibility of selling a number of pews, to open up the north aisle. However the St Edmundsbury and Ipswich Diocesan Advisory Committee (DAC) was concerned that the majority of the pew ends, although not necessarily the pew seats, were of medieval origin. They wished these ends to be retained in the church, perhaps by cutting down the pews to form seats.

It was agreed to attempt the conversion of one pew, which would have to be inspected and approved before any further work could be done. A cabinet maker resident in the village carried out the pilot, which was accepted by the DAC, and led to a faculty being granted for up to a maximum of eight pews being altered in this way. At the time of writing, the parish has created three 'chairs' (Fig. 7), and this has greatly increased gathering space in the building.

Fig. 7: St Mary, Wortham, Suffolk. One of the new seats, made up of a cut-down bench, thus preserving the bench ends.

8. Removing Victorian pews, replacing with locally-designed substantial but movable benches: Willand, Devon

Willand is a growing village of some three thousand inhabitants situated in mid Devon, some seventeen miles north of Exeter. The parish church, St Mary's, is medieval, and is a small, rather intimate building with congregational space consisting of a nave and north aisle. Stretching across the nave, though not the aisle, is a fine medieval rood screen and loft, said to be of the early fifteenth century, which retains some of its original gilding and colouring. There is an early-nineteenth-century two-decker pulpit against the south wall of the church, abutting the screen. The church is listed Grade I.

Until recently the church was seated with square-ended straight-back pews probably dating from the 1850s, with loose wooden kneelers in a different, rather lighter wood (Fig. 8a). The pew ends retained their umbrella stands, and were fixed to the carpeted floor. The church was pewed in both the nave and north aisle, except for a baptismal space on the north side of the chancel, which also served as a gathering area for after-church fellowship, next to the kitchen/toilet (built as an annex in matching stone in the 1980s). The pews were in poor condition, worm-eaten, and not particularly comfortable.

It was decided to reseat the church as part of a larger reordering. At the wish of the congregation, the decision was taken not to use chairs but benches especially designed for the church, for their practical benefits. In 2007 a trial was carried out of a new bench based on the design of bench end introduced into Milton Abbey, Dorset when it was restored by Sir George Gilbert Scott in 1865 (the abbey church is now used by a school). The core measurements were used by a member of the congregation (a professional artist) to produce a draft design which was refined by the reordering architect, Jo Hibbert (Fig. 8b).

Fig. 8a: St Mary, Willand, Devon. The interior before reordering, showing the Victorian pews.

Fig. 8b: One of the new movable benches at Willand.

The trials were successful, and in 2008 all the Victorian pews were removed from the nave, and replaced with the new free-standing benches which rest on the freshly-carpeted floor (Fig. 8c). (The floor is of concrete, laid in 1972, and there were problems with damp rising up the pillars and walls, so substantial works were carried out to deal with this, with trenches being dug around the pillars and along the walls.) As part of the reordering, the font was moved to the west end, which was not only more appropriate liturgically, but also increased the space for gatherings at the east end of the north aisle.

The new benches are of inverted Y-frame construction, made of insect-repellent English yew. They incorporate book troughs. Most are 75 inches (190 cm) long, seating four people, or 70 inches (178 cm) long, making a wide three-seater. In addition, there are a small number of shorter benches. Previously the church could in total seat about 100 people; the new benches seat a little over this number (108 people) whilst a further 36 can be accommodated on folding chairs, stored in new purpose built yew cupboards at the east end of the north aisle, where the font used to be.

In practice the changes have made the Church a more welcoming and comfortable place and have been part of the reason for the growth in congregation numbers. Because the new seating is movable it can be reconfigured to suit a particular use; this has seen concerts, social events and both baptisms and weddings take place in formats that best suit their needs. The flexibility provided by the additional temporary seating is also a useful asset.

All this was Phase I of a two-phase project. The second phase was carried out in 2009, to substantially extend the church hall with a new room for meetings, and for work with the large number of children in the church family. As a result of these improvements, Willand now has a church and ancillary buildings fit to meet the challenging demands of the twenty-first century. Further details can be found at the church's website, www.stmaryswilland.org.uk.

Fig. 8c: The interior at Willand after reordering, looking north-east across the nave. In the far corner is the fellowship space at the east end of the north aisle.

9. Keeping pews in a community church: Thorpe Market, Norfolk

Thorpe Market is a village in rural north Norfolk, some twenty miles north of Norwich, and a few miles from the coast. It has a population of about 300. There is a village hall, but the village no longer has a post office. The church of St Margaret lies a little way from the centre of the village. It is open almost every day for visitors – for more more details of the church, see www.thorpemarket.org.uk.

The church was built in 1796 and is an early example of Gothic Revival, listed at Grade II★. The main structure is a small rectangular box (Fig. 9a), overtly symmetrical, with four corner turrets, twin porches to the south, and a balanced set of ancillary rooms on the north. Internally, the church still has its coved and ribbed ceiling. It also retains two original screens of wood and latticed metal and painted glass ('gimcrack' Pevsner calls them). One of these is at the west, where the medieval font from the original church is placed, and the other divides the nave from the chancel area, which now has Victorian furnishings. The church has recently undergone a major restoration to re-roof it, refurbish the water-damaged ceiling, and carry out interior redecoration – possibly for the first time ever.

Since the mid 1990s the church has been establishing itself as a centre for musical activities in its area of rural north Norfolk. Despite the small size of the village, in the course of a typical year the church hosts an average of twenty musical events, and photographic and art exhibitions, attracting more than five thousand attendees. At the time of writing, an additional venture, a film club has just been started. Unsurprisingly with this level of activity, the church was runner up in the first *Country Life* 'Village Church for Village Life' competition a couple of years ago.

To provide the necessary facilities for these activities, in 2002 an extension containing kitchen, toilets and a meeting room was built on the north side of the church. This replicated an earlier coach-house in that position which had been demolished fifty years earlier, thus restoring the original symmetry of the building on the north. The money (some £40,000) was raised locally over a period of four years and

Fig. 9a: St Margaret, Thorpe Market, Norfolk, from the south. The church was built in 1796.
(© copyright Simon Knott www. norfolkchurches.co.uk)

Fig. 9b: Staging in place in the chancel of Thorpe Market.

the work was carried out and supervised by local residents. In addition, the church now has level access, and adequate parking.

A modern, high-quality demountable stage was also acquired. The stage can, for example be set up in the chancel area, with a small apron into the nave, and in this position is large enough to hold forty or more singers (Fig. 9b). As the screens in the church are light and open they hardly obstruct the view of the stage. The church also possesses display stands (Fig. 9c), and a full range of audio visual equipment, including blackout blinds.

It is notable that despite this range of activities, the church has retained all its Victorian pews, which are of oak, and locally made. The church takes the view that it is not trying to replicate the facilities provided by a village hall, but is making use of its strengths – good light and acoustics – and that the pews provide both safe (and, with cushions, reasonably comfortable) concert seating, and a level platform for exhibition screens. With the building already being used to the maximum that a small village can cope with, the church cannot see any need to remove the pews.

Fig. 9c: An exhibition being held at Thorpe Market.

10. Using the church, keeping the pews: Redgrave, Suffolk (CCT church)

by Bob Hayward, Chairman, Redgrave Church Heritage Trust

Redgrave lies about roughly half way between Norwich and Bury St Edmunds. The church of St Mary's, which is Grade I listed, lies about half a mile from the current village of Redgrave, which has a population of some five hundred. It is a medieval church, mostly built in the Decorated style, and contains a large number of monuments and hatchments to the Bacon family, together with other notable memorials.

St Mary's is redundant, and was placed in the care of the Churches Conservation Trust (CCT) about five years ago. Local residents have formed the Redgrave Church Heritage Trust (RCHT), and that trust and the CCT have signed a Local Management Agreement which enables the RCHT to arrange events and deal with minor problems quickly and locally. The two trusts have also worked closely and raised over £40,000 to install a toilet block in the base of the tower and a kitchenette in the south-west corner of the church, together with an electric heating system. This has helped to transform the church into a community venue capable of hosting a range of events, services and concerts.

Both the CCT and the RCHT have a very simple policy at St Mary's – that no pews are going to be removed but, paradoxically, that those activities which require clear space will be encouraged.

The first reason for retaining the pews is to conserve an almost complete 1850 pew layout, which will become progressively rarer as other churches continue to remove pews. There are, however, other equally valid reasons for retaining them that are often not considered.

All of the people who are alive today and their parents, grandparents, and great grandparents would have known the church complete with its pews and sat in them for what would have been important events in their lives. It is one of those rare timeless places that has looked and felt the same for all of their lives. We aim to keep it that way.

From a more practical point of view why would anyone throw out a magnificent set of 350 seats which do not have to be purchased, put out, put away, and stored? If they were taken out a huge space would have to be heated consuming 140 kW versus the much less costly 10 kW needed to just keep the people in the pews warm. It is usually argued that wooden pew seats are uncomfortable: so we just put in removable cushions to make them comfortable.

We had to consider how to achieve the apparently impossible task of keeping the pews whilst running all manner of events which require clear space. In our case putting the pews on concealed wheels was not a feasible solution as they would have needed to be completely rebuilt in sections and a whole new floor would have been required as the pew structure currently rest on sand.

We therefore decided to build around them, build in them, and build above them in temporary configurations specific to each usage. Almost every event is different so flexibility is essential. The key to being able to do this is having highly flexible modular staging which can be configured differently for each event and is adjustable in height so that it can be used either in existing spaces or above the pews.

It is possible to buy or hire staging, and almost anything is possible using scaffolding companies, but it can become very expensive. We therefore designed and built our own 2 metre by 1 metre steel-framed decks clad with plywood. These take pieces of scaffold pole for legs and adjustable scaffold jacks for feet. The decks bolt together to give the required continuous floor space and are so solid that nothing moves, even when a piano is lifted onto them. There are several sizes of leg so that the floor space can be either at stage height, over the top of the pews, or tiered as for a choir (Figs. 10a–d). Because everything is standardised on scaffold pole diameter any configuration of steps and safety rails and kick boards is possible using tube and scaffold clips which are relatively inexpensive to buy. The floors are protected using free carpet samples and offcuts of the plywood which was used to make the decks. When pew space is required for instruments and soloists, thick plywood and timber platforms are put into the pews covering the seat so that the whole pew becomes a raised floor.

This approach of building round and over the pews means that we have been able to accommodate plays, concerts, lectures, church services, bands, and an art exhibition without the pews presenting any problem. It takes a couple of days to assemble staging and less than a day to remove it – after which anyone coming into the church would be unaware that any event had ever taken place.

We find that having such a fine set of pews is actually a huge advantage – many thanks to our Victorian ancestors!

Fig. 10a: St Mary, Redgrave, Suffolk. Stage set up for a jazz concert.

Fig. 10b: Under the stage, showing the individual floor decks bolted together.

Fig. 10c: A staging module above the pews, demonstrating the adaptability of the modular system.

Fig. 10d: A platform in a pew for a musician or soloist.

11. Moving seventeenth-century pews: Haughton-le-Skerne, Darlington, County Durham

The village of Haughton-le-Skerne is now a suburb in north-east Darlington. It contains Darlington's oldest church, St Andrew's, which dates from Norman times, with the Norman church consisting of a west tower, nave and chancel. The church is Grade I listed.

St Andrew's has a fine set of furnishings from the seventeenth century, including box pews (Fig. 11a) and a twin pulpit and reading desk at the chancel arch. The pews date from the 1630s (one has '1639' scratched on it), whilst the pulpit and reading desk are probably from the 1660s. All are of particular importance for their association with John Cosin, a key figure in the religious arguments of the pre-Civil War period, who had two stints in the diocese of Durham, first from the 1620s into the 1630s, and later as bishop of the diocese from 1660. Cosin was famous for his introduction of what were then regarded as extreme forms of church ceremonial. He also promulgated the return of Gothic forms to church furnishing, and those at Haughton-le-Skerne are important as being amongst a small number of surviving furnishings introduced by him or (as here) by those under his influence.

The church was restored in 1895. A new floor was introduced, north and south transept built, chancel furniture installed, the pulpit and reading desk modified, and the gallery removed. At the back of the church, four new rows of pews were inserted where there had previously been none, utilising old pew ends, possibly from the gallery. These made-up pews did not have doors.

St Andrew's is a lively and growing church, and some years ago it reached the conclusion that changes were needed to the interior. The church wanted to bring the communion table closer to the congregation, and it needed a space at the front to allow groups of people to be seen (for example for nativity plays and music groups). In addition, a number of those who belong to the church use wheelchairs. They were unable to receive communion with everyone else at the front, and their leadership role in the service (such as reading the scriptures or leading prayers) had to be carried out from where they were sitting.

It was propose proposed to clear the north and south transepts of their Victorian oak pews, thus providing room for the music group in the

Fig. 11a: St Andrew, Haughton-le-Skerne, Durham. One of the seventeenth-century box pews

south transept. More controversially, it was also proposed to remove four rows of seventeenth-century pews from the front of the church to release space for a dais or platform in the nave, extending from the chancel, to hold the nave altar. The platform would have wheelchair access via a ramp in the north transept, and would provide enough space for singers and other groups. This is, of course, a fairly standard approach to re-ordering, but the sensitivity of the interior meant that any changes to the front pews, and their subsequent reuse, had to be given very careful consideration, though all the pews had, of course, already been (carefully) reordered once before, in 1895, when a brand new floor was laid.

Although the plans reduced the total seating in the church, from about 220 to about 160, it was felt that the church would cope well enough at normal services, and that the chancel and the transept areas could be used for overflow when needed.

There was some debate about what should happen to the pews removed from the front. The initial proposal was to remove their doors and place these doors on the made-up pews at the rear of the church (which did not have doors); and then use the old pew ends from the front to create four freestanding short pews for use in the south transept. After some discussion, a different solution was adopted: the four rows from the front were placed in their entirety at the back of the church, replacing the four made-up rows already there. To fit the space they had to be lengthened slightly, and the doors widened slightly with fillets of wood. The four made-up rows were dismantled, and the early pew ends (the ones which may have come originally from the gallery) converted into seats, now placed in the south transept and used by the musicians.

As the Society for the Protection of Ancient Buildings (which supported the proposals) noted, 'This case clearly highlights the tension between the significance of historic church furnishings and the needs of a modern congregation spurred on by the principles of the Disability Discrimination Act 1995' (SPAB *News*, June 2006). It is probably true to say that English Heritage was of the same mind. One learning point for the church was the need to satisfy the Council for the Care of Churches (now the Church Buildings Council) that proper investigation had been made into the history of the pews and their current state, and that a conservator's report and method statement had been produced which would ensure that the pews could withstand their removal, repair, alteration, and reinstatement, and not be irreparably damaged in the process.

A faculty was sought in December 2008, and granted in September 2009, and work started almost immediately (Fig. 11b). This included the introduction of a bespoke altar and other liturgical furniture for the nave platform. Particular care was taken with detailing, for example with the railings for the wheelchair ramp. As a result of the work, the church now feels that the building is now not only more practical for worship, and meets the needs of those who use wheelchairs, but reflects what the worshipping community is trying to say about itself and its beliefs. An informative panoramic photograph of the reordered interior can be seen on the church website, at www.standrewshaughton.org.uk.

Fig. 11b: The interior of Haughton-le-Skerne after the reordering, looking east. The twin pulpits can be seen, and the new altar platform and altar to the west of the screen

The pews at Haddenham are discussed in depth by Charles Tracy on pages 113–14 and 120–30 above, where photographs will also be found.

12. Moving medieval pews: Haddenham, Buckinghamshire

Haddenham, which lies in the Aylesbury Vale, is a flourishing village of some 5,000 inhabitants. The parish church building is medieval, of various build dates, and has nave and chancel, north and south aisles, north Lady Chapel and a west tower. It lies in an attractive setting of church, churchyard, duck pond, village green and pub (see www.haddenhamstmarys.org). It is listed Grade I.

The church is flourishing. The style of worship is broad-based, with Book of Common Prayer and Common Worship services each Sunday, together with informal evening services, and a variety of occasional services. In addition there is a range of youth and children's services in the St Mary's Centre and other buildings, including Caféplus, an innovative monthly Sunday drop-in café held in the village community centre (www.cafeplus.org.uk/).

In addition to its architectural interest, the church contains a Norman font, an extensive set of medieval benches ('pews'), and a medieval rood screen, clearly carved by the same workshop as the benches. The screen was built in sections (see Fig. 12a): the central section (shown as K on the plan) is now located under the tower arch, the south section (B on the plan) now divides the north chapel from the chancel, and the north section (A) is still in situ, dividing the north aisle from the north chapel (though the 1960 edition of Pevsner's *Buildings of England* recorded it as lying against the west wall of the south aisle — perhaps this was connected with the introduction of a pulpit in 1955).

In 1849 it was reported that 'there are some good open seats' (by which was meant medieval benches) and an engraving of a poppy-head from a medieval bench end in the church was published a few years before (referred to in *The Ecclesiastical and Architectural Topography of England: Buckinghamshire* (1849), entry 183). However by mid-Victorian times, some of the original seating had clearly either been removed or converted to box pews, as the *Bucks Herald* reported in October 1864 after the interior had been restored (by David Brandon) that 'the whole of the seats have been taken up and replaced, the contrast being very striking between the present sittings, which are roomy and open, and the old, large "horse boxes" as they were facetiously but not inaptly designated. They are now all uniform, whereas previously they were almost all sorts and sizes'.

As part of this Victorian restoration, the medieval benches were sensitively restored and replaced, and the church is now extensively pewed. Many of the bench ends are medieval, together with substantial portions of the frontals and the terminal seat backs at the rear of the blocks. Some of the seats and backs of the benches are also medieval. The remainder of the work is Victorian, sometimes incorporating surviving medieval elements. (This is discussed in more detail on pages 113–14 and 120–130 in this book.) Referring to the plan in Figure 12a, the highest proportion of medieval work is at the rear of the nave (areas E and G on the plan), with less at the front of the nave (areas F & H), a pattern commonly found in Victorian restorations. The aisles have less medieval work still, particularly areas C and D, and area J had none.

CASE STUDIES

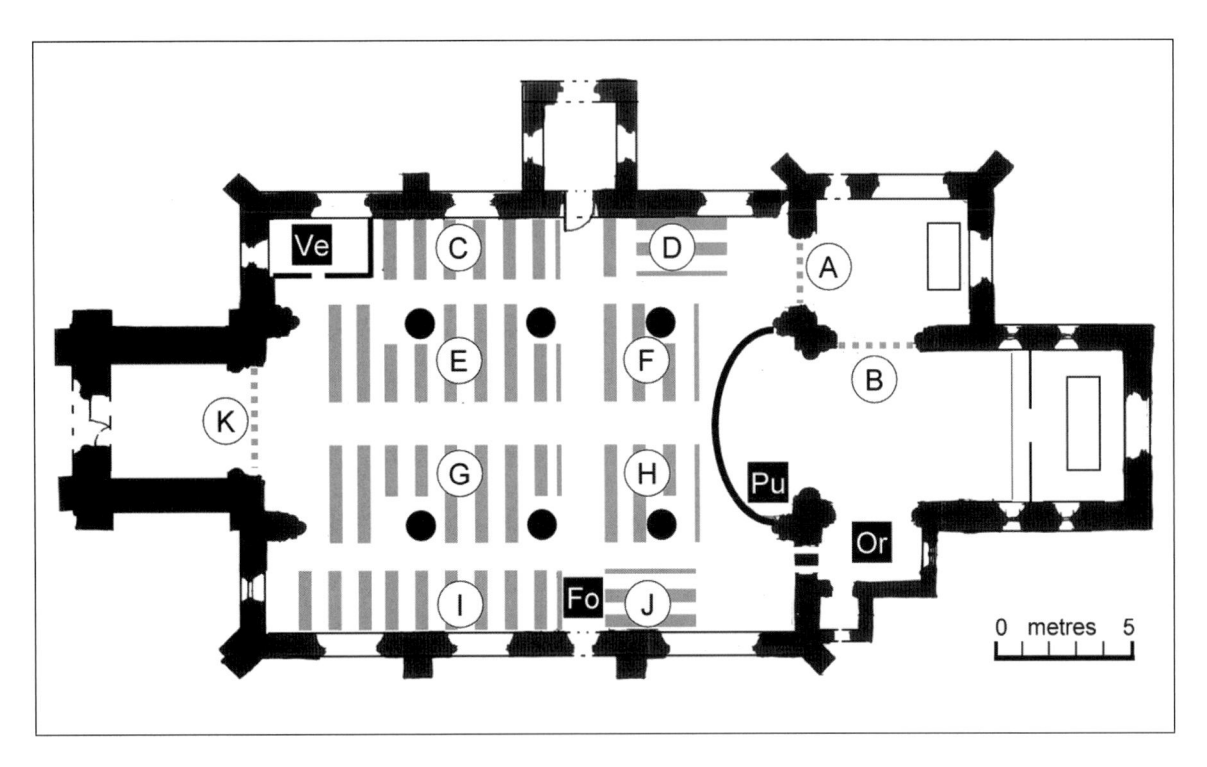

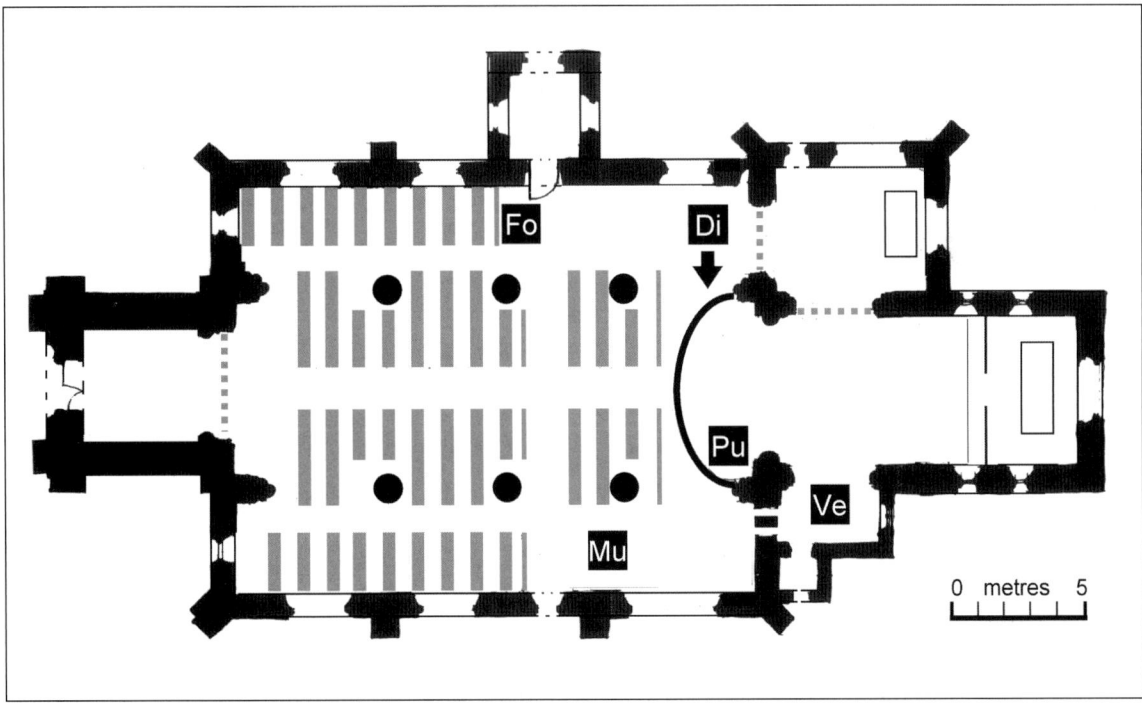

Fig. 12a: This sketch plan of St Mary, Haddenham is redrawn from one created by Julian Munby. It shows the position of the seating as in the year 2000. Individual benches are shown, but are not to scale, and their position is approximate. See text for discussion. Key: Ve: Vestry; Fo: Font; Pu: Pulpit; Or: Organ.

Fig. 12b: St Mary, Haddenham, after reordering in 2007. See text for discussion. Key: as for Plan 1, and also: Mu: Musicians area and console for electronic organ; Di: disabled access to platform.

443

The church has undergone a number of changes since the Victorian period. In 1955 a new pulpit was introduced. In 1970 the font was moved from the south-west corner to a position close to the south door (entrance is via the north door), and there was some adjustment of the pewing at the back of the south aisle. And in the 1980s the two front rows of pews in the nave were removed to enable a curved platform to be constructed, and the chancel was cleared of its undistinguished Victorian furnishings. Some pews, incorporating medieval work, were removed from the north-west corner, and in their place a screen was built, to create a vestry. A collegiate style pew arrangement was introduced in place of an east-facing one at the east end of both the south and north aisles (areas D and J), utilising some or all of the pews that had been removed.

As regards the church building, to use its own words, the church believes that 'present day culture, lifestyle and forms of worship differ greatly from those of previous generations', so that 'modifications made in the nineteenth century no longer fully meet the needs of those seeking to worship God in the twenty-first century'. In the light of this, a substantial reordering was conceived for the Millennium. This was to be in two phases. Phase I was completed in 2001, and saw a crèche inserted in the first floor of the tower, with a kitchen and toilets beneath. For the second Phase, the underlying wish was to create a welcoming and comfortable environment, and a flexible space, as well as to improve the audio-visual facilities, and provide more space for musicians. The initial thought was to clear the seating from the church and replace it with modern seating, ensuring the preservation of the medieval bench ends by displaying them on the walls of the building. A factor lying behind this is the fact that the pews are uncomfortable, despite the use of cushions. In the words of one user, 'the principal problem comes from a ridge running horizontally along the back, which does not correspond to anyone's lumbar curve and effectively narrows the depth of the seat'.

In order to gain a better appreciation of the significance of the medieval benches, in 2003 the church commissioned a report from Charles Tracy on their art-historical significance. This highlighted the unusually good quality of construction and design of the medieval benches, and emphasised that the seating was a remarkably well preserved example of a set of high quality parochial benching of the later middle ages. A second, briefer, report was written in 2004 by Julian Munby, assessing the extent to which each of the various elements of the seating were Victorian or medieval, and it is from this report that our Figure 12a has been redrawn (and from which we drew the *Bucks Herald* comment quoted earlier).

In the light of these reports, a number of other options were discussed, including various combinations of enlargement of the vestry area to create space, the removal of some of the restored benches at the front of the nave, the movement of some of the benches into the chancel, the enlargement of the platform, and the reinstatement of the screen. There was wide consultation both with statutory bodies, and within the congregation and with those on the electoral roll.

In the event, the final proposal, which was carried out in 2007, was more modest, but adapted the space in creative ways, whilst preserving the coherence of the seating as a whole. The organ, which was of no historic interest and in a poor state, was removed, and a new vestry was inserted in the space thus released (Fig. 12b). This made available the space taken up by the 1960s vestry, allowing the pews removed at that time to be replaced there, and the adjacent pew block to be moved westward. This freed up space as a welcome area around the north (entrance) door, large enough for the font to be moved there, and for a disabled person's ramp to link to the nave platform. At the same time, the Victorian pews near the south door were removed, and this, together with the relocation of the font, provided space for a music group and electronic organ console. Modern audio equipment was installed (the church is still thinking about the best way to meet its requirements for screens and monitors). The chancel was freshly carpeted, and made more suitable for informal events, with individual chairs providing flexible seating.

The net effect of Phase 2 has been to make the church more welcoming at initial entrance, to provide a little more circulation space, to make room for the musicians, to provide disabled access, and to support an audio system which meets modern needs. The church can seat about the same number of people as before, and can thus continue to support civic events and other large services. The chancel has been given new life as a small space for informal worship. On the other hand, there is not the total flexibility which was originally hoped for. And the pews are still uncomfortable.

13. Replacing Victorian pews with two types of chair: Kirtlington, Oxfordshire

The village of Kirtlington lies some nine miles due north of Oxford and has a population of about 900. It is the largest village in the seven-parish Akeman benefice, its parish church the largest church, and at the moment the church life possibly the strongest in the group: future developments are likely to place increasing emphasis on Kirtlington as a main centre for worshipping life in the benefice, partly as a result of the reordering of the church.

St Mary's, the medieval parish church, is listed Grade II★. It consists of a nave with north and south aisles, a central tower with south chapel, and a chancel. The east and west tower arches are of the early twelfth century and the nave and its aisles of the mid thirteenth century. The original tower was taken down in the late eighteenth century, and rebuilt in neo-Norman style by Benjamin Ferrey in 1853, and the chancel restored by George Gilbert Scott in 1877 with original medieval features.

People walk through the churchyard and past the church all day long to visit other parts of the village, and the churchyard is also constantly visited by families from the village and elsewhere tending graves. There is much affection for the church building in the village.

However, until recently the church had deficiencies. The heating was increasingly inadequate as the boiler neared the end of its life. The dark Victorian pews in the nave, unlike those in the chancel, were of poor quality, unattractive and uncomfortable; moreover, both pews and pew platforms had woodworm. The red and black floor tiles in the aisles were cracked, and worms had been seen coming up between them. The font stood on a large base so near to the main entrance that it was impossible for the door to be opened fully, and it blocked access to the children's area. Coffee after the service had to be served in the north aisle because of the blockage caused by the font, whilst visitors departed on the other side of the church. Water for the coffee had to be brought in large plastic bottles, as none was laid on; naturally, there was no lavatory.

With typical attendance on a Sunday about twenty-five to thirty, the greater part of the congregation in its seventies and eighties, and no young people or children coming, it was realised that the future of the church was in doubt unless the decline in church-going could be first halted and then reversed.

It was decided that the building had to be made more welcoming (better heating being an important consideration in this) and more flexible in use. This would allow activities other than services to be held there. The Parochial Church Council (PCC) believed that a widely-used church building would not only provide an important link with the non-churchgoing population but would help the church and village become more closely integrated, and contribute to the overall sense of being a single community.

After extended debate, a plan was agreed. The pews were removed, and the floor of the nave (but not the chancel or chapel) completely re-laid in York stone, laid east to west in random lengths with uniform width. Underfloor heating was installed, with top-up radiators by the doors and children's area. Care was taken to provide a good number of power points in the new floor, concealed under stone lids; these have been found a boon for purposes as disparate as lighting the Christmas tree and vacuum cleaning. The font, minus the ugly and inconvenient base, was relocated in the north aisle opposite the south door, where it draws the eye on entrance. The children's corner, better equipped and furnished, was also moved to the north aisle. A large oak cupboard was built-in down the whole of one side of the tower area, behind folding doors covered in a fine brass mesh: this lightens the look of a previously dark space. A lavatory and running water were installed at the north-west corner behind a purpose-built partition of light oak and lightly-tinted blue-green glass; this area includes a sink and storage cupboards for flower arranging. Coffee is now served in the space newly accessible in the south-west corner, making it easy and natural for visitors to pause and stay instead of leaving; it is intended in another phase of work to install a servery against the walls in this corner, concealed when not in use by folding doors matching those under the tower.

The primary seating is on sixty cushioned, stackable (in threes) chairs of American white ash, with a flower motif from Scott's altar rail carved into the back rest of each chair. The chairs were individually sponsored by local people. The chairs clip together at the front, so can be arranged in curves or straight lines, as needed, though as the chairs are heavy and do not shift on the stone floor it has been found unnecessary to use the clips. Two chairs with arms were initially purchased, and a further four have since been obtained, as some of the more elderly members of the congregation find them helpful when raising and lowering themselves. Most people do not kneel during services; but nor did they when there were pews.

The reordering is somewhat unusual in that it uses two types of chairs (Fig. 13a): in addition to the cushioned chairs, the church has some eighty lighter metal-framed stacking chairs, with the seats and backs also in white ash, and the same motifs carved on the backs. These chairs are used as secondary seating. They are normally kept stacked high on three trolleys at the rear of the building (Fig. 13b), and can then easily be set out for weddings, funerals, and other special occasions. These chairs can be set up or stacked by two people in around twenty minutes. The total seating capacity is thus about 140 people, more or less the same as provided by the pews that were removed.

Perhaps the cushioned chairs are also unusual in the colour of their fabric, being neither blue nor red! – rather, a light turquoise was chosen, colourful but not bright or garish or drawing attention to itself, and halfway between the colour of the organ pipes (a deep blue-green) and the faint blue-green of the glass wall of the new partition in the opposite corner. The chairs thus unify the interior.

Another unusual feature of the relaying of the floor is the preservation of a large and ornate Victorian cast-iron heating grill under the central tower. The grill is covered with thick glass which can be

Fig. 13a: St Mary, Kirtlington, Oxfordshire, the interior after re-ordering, looking west. Note the two types of chair.

Fig. 13b: Some of the metal-framed chairs at Kirtlington, stacked at the rear of the church.

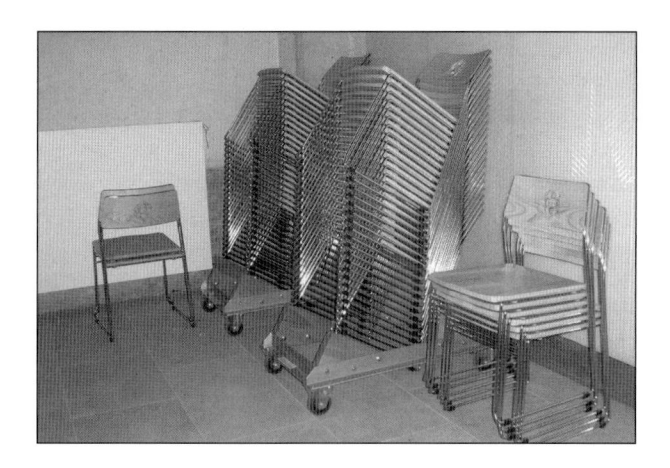

walked over: not only does this preserve a decorative object, but from the nave the whole length of the large east window – good Victorian stained glass – can be seen reflected on the tower floor (Fig. 13c). The effect is visually stunning; moreover the reflection in the glass lightens up the whole of the tower area, and draw the eye up to the chancel and altar, which previously seemed rather cut off from the body of the church.

Interestingly – and these days, perhaps to some extent unusually – the congregation are (at present) no longer using a nave altar. Instead, for the consecration the priest moves up to the chancel, and the congregation is invited to follow: most stand in informal groups, while those who need to sit use the choir stalls. The intermediate tower space emphasises that this journey is for a serious and special purpose. The chancel itself retains the furnishings and Minton tile flooring introduced by Scott.

The work, not long completed, has made the church look lighter and more spacious, ensured it is warm, and provided a space which can be used in a variety of ways. The building is now regularly used during the week by a yoga class and a pre-school music group. A painting exhibition has been arranged, and a local musician wishes to start a choral group rehearsing weekly in the church. A number of concerts have been held there (the acoustics are now excellent as the result of removing the pews), and some mission events – the church is becoming the *de facto* meeting place for the seven benefice churches. For one concert the seating was rotated through 180 degrees to face west, a measure of the flexibility of the new arrangements. A week-long benefice Holiday Club for children culminated in a service in a church magically transformed into a tropical island (the theme for the week), with dramatic and other activities as part of the service: without the reordering this could not have happened.

Although further work remains – not least the lighting and the servery – the PCC feel they have already achieved their primary objective of creating a comfortable, welcoming space which will allow the church to play a central part in community life, and provide an attractive, unobtrusively modern, yet timeless setting for worship.

Fig. 13c: St Mary, Kirtlington, looking through the central tower to the east window, showing the reflections from the glass placed over the Victorian grating under the tower. The new storage cupboards in the tower can be seen to the left.

14. Making Victorian pews movable: St Mary Magdalene, Addiscombe, South London

The church

St Mary Magdalene's church, which is listed Grade II★, was built in 1869 for a cleric seceding from the Church of England, but became Anglican in 1878 when the original congregation, which had by then seceded from the seceder, purchased the building from him. Details of this unusual story can be found on the church's website, www.stmmm.org.uk.

The architect of the building was E. B. Lamb, and the church is typical of him in having a centralised plan and featuring a complex roof (Fig. 14a).

The church is a suburban one, in South London. It is open evangelical in persuasion, with attendance on Sundays of about one hundred adults and some thirty young people and children. On Sunday mornings there is both a relatively traditional service and an informal one.

Reordering

In 1973 there was a major reordering of the interior by the leading church architect, George Pace. A new communion table and rails were commissioned and placed into the crossing to create worship 'in the round'.

The floors and aisles, which had previously been a mix of black and white tiles and herringbone wood-blocks, and were on different levels, were raised to a single level and given a stone covering.

Fig. 14a: St Mary Magdalene, Addiscombe, built in 1869 by E. B. Lamb.

The pews

As part of this major change, the Victorian pews from the nave were discarded whilst pews from the aisles were placed in the nave and transepts, but without being fixed in place. The original pew furniture of umbrella rail, drip tray and the pew rent payer's plaque were removed at this time, but the marks are still visible. As a result, the church now has the benefit of Victorian pews which can be moved (Figs. 14b–d).

Although they are heavy, moving them is relatively straightforward, currently using a pair of garden-centre pot-plant trolleys, one at each end. Two people can shift them easily, and one person if need be. In practice they are moved several times a year, for example to change the seating arrangements for a concert, or, as recently, to clear space in the church for a week of prayer when prayer stations and a temporary labyrinth were installed. On this occasion, the pews were moved into space in the transepts. The pews do not, of course, stack.

The pews are reasonably comfortable, though perhaps not perfect for concerts where long periods of concentrated sitting are required. The pews are flexible in use – they can accommodate large numbers of people when needed, and are particularly suitable for families with small children. The feeling is that the church was far-sighted in the early 1970s in keeping its solid, well-made furniture whilst introducing a degree of flexibility in layout, and there are no current plans to change these arrangements.

Figs. 14b–d: St Mary Magdalene, the Victorian pews, now removed from their fixed positions and free to be moved on trolleys.

15. Putting a loo in a family pew: Slaidburn, Lancashire

The parish of Slaidburn, lying some ten miles north of Clitheroe in the Forest of Bowland, is said to be the parish with the largest geographical area in England, yet with a population of only around 800 people in three villages. The parish church, St Andrew's, lies on the outskirts of the village.

The church building is medieval and is listed Grade I. It consists of a west tower, and a nave and chancel without architectural division, with north and south aisles extending the full length of the building. There is a chantry chapel, the Hamerton chapel, on the south side of the chancel. The church is particularly famous for its post-Reformation woodwork. The font cover is said to be Elizabethan, there is a rood screen of 1634 similar to that at St John's, Leeds (and said to be by the same hand, that of Francis Grundy), and a stately three-decker pulpit of 1740 in the middle of the south side of the nave (Fig. 15a). There is also a profusion of pews, using the term to mean gated, enclosed seating: there are small family pews in the south side of the chancel ('Smelthwaites' and 'Parkers'); the rector's and squire's pew on the east of the rood screen with further family pews to the west of the screen in an undisturbed Georgian arrangement; pews in the aisles and chapels; and three very large family pews at the west end of the church. There are also open

Fig. 15a: St Andrew, Slaidburn, Lancashire. The interior, showing the eighteenth-century triple-decker pulpit.

benches, of a similar date, perhaps from a single building campaign. Some of the seating is dated: 1616, 1676, 1749. Many seats have attached to them the name of the farm or of the family to whom they were appropriated – 'Bleazards House in Croasdale', 'Thomas Oakes, Harrop Hall'.

The congregation is typically between twenty and twenty-five in number (reduced by the presence of a chapel of ease not far away), with few children. They make the best they can of what is necessarily a restrictive environment. One of the pews at the west of the church, the 'Peel' pew, is used to contain children of kindergarten age, and also for Parochial Church Council (PCC) meetings – it can seat up to twelve people. Overall the seating is exceptionally uncomfortable, with narrow seats and vertical backs, and this restricts the use of the church for concerts and similar events, though the church has acquired some staging which can be placed inside a couple of the box pews, and hopes to experiment further with its use.

For some time the PCC have been aware of the need for a toilet and simple kitchen area, both for their own use after service, when they gather in a space at the west end which has been cleared of some Victorian (or possibly Edwardian) seating, and also for the 8,000 or so visitors who make their way to the church every year. At the same time the PCC were very conscious of their duty to maintain as far as possible the unique character of their much-loved church.

The agreed solution was in two parts, with work being carried out a couple of years ago. It utilised two of the western pews, which were at that time largely unused and in rather poor condition (Figs. 15b & c). The 'Parker' pew in the south-west corner was widened slightly to allow safe movement (reducing space in the next door Peel Pew), the floor lowered, and the interior converted into a kitchenette (Fig. 15d). At the same time, in the 'Rudd' pew in the north-west corner of the church a disabled toilet with changing facilities was installed (Fig. 15e). The floor in this pew was also lowered, the walls insulated for sound, ventilation installed, and a roof fitted. Pelmet curtains were then added to help the new toilet blend in and become (literally) part of the

Fig. 15b: The Parker pew at St Andrew's, Slaidburn in the south-west corner of the church, showing its shabby state before its recent conversion to a kitchenette.

Fig. 15c: The poor state of the interior of the Parker pew before conversion.

Fig. 15d: The Parker pew at Slaidburn after conversion to a kitchenette.

Fig. 15e: The Rudd pew at Slaidburn after conversion to a toilet.

furniture; the curtains are not only a reference to the room's original function as a pew, but make a visual link with curtaining on the nearby organ and north door. The only difficulty encountered with this pew was that a change in plan led to the unexpected need to dig into the underlying floor, which had archaeological implications.

In both cases the original pew panelling was largely maintained and the new work was of the highest craftsmanship, restoring the structures to a good condition as well as giving them a new purpose. The total cost was of the order of £70,000, approximately two-thirds being raised locally. There is a strong feeling that the work has been well worth the cost and effort, and that the church and community have gained valuable facilities whilst retaining a very special church interior.

Part 6

POSTSCRIPT & FURTHER READING

30. Postscript: One hundred years hence

Trevor Cooper

Author's note: This is neither a summary nor a synthesis, but a series of informal, free-ranging reflections picking up some of the themes in the book. I have allowed myself a fairly loose rein.

IT WOULD BE HARD TO ARGUE from the photographic evidence that the seating at St Paul's, Eastchester, USA is entirely fit for purpose (Fig. 1).

During the nineteenth century the original box pews at this church were removed and the interior was reordered and remodelled for sacramental worship. However in 1941-2 the parish restored the nave to more or less its 1790s appearance, including the reintroduction of high box pews facing the pulpit, with the altar to the side.[1] Ceremonial eucharistic worship continued, but now in an interior designed for listening to the Word.

Fig. 1: Conflict between church seating and the form of worship. St Paul, Eastchester, New York State, shown after the box pews were reinstated. The photo was probably taken in the 1950s; the church ceased regular services in May 1977. It is open for guided tours. (Photo: www.clipart.com)

Fig. 2: The Sermon of St Peter, *by Hans Suess Kulmach (c.1480–c.1522). This image is not from England (Kulmach was active in Nuremberg and also worked in Krakow), but some of the details may reflect English practice in church. The gentleman on the right appears to be wearing a sword. (From a polyptych depicting scenes from the Lives of St Peter and St Paul (oil on panel), Galleria degli Uffizi, Florence. Image: the Bridgeman Art Library)*

I cannot help wondering, when did the congregation realise things were not exactly right? How much did they mind? Did they feel the need to explain things to guests? When did it all become normal to them, and cease to register?

Normality
Standing and sitting

It is perhaps worth using a series of vignettes to remind ourselves how much has changed over the years in English parish churches, and how many different things have been 'normal' during that time.

Consider Figures 2 and 3. The first of these (Fig. 2) shows a pre-Reformation sermon (although the painting is not English, some of the details may well reflect English late medieval practice). There is a range of stools and portable chairs, and some seating against the wall-panelling (representing misericords in the choir, perhaps). The women sit, in reasonably tidy rows – are they on benches? Men mainly stand, some wearing their hats, one of them seemingly wearing a sword. Is it my imagination, or do these informal huddles of standing people listening to a sermon seem more natural and welcoming to modern eyes than sitting in straight lines?

The second image (Fig. 3) also shows people listening to a sermon, in an English church interior of the 1680s. The men stand. Although their hats are off, they wear swords. The women sit, in linear box pews (pews with doors). The communion table is to their side. For the occasional communion service, men and women kneel together at the altar rail.

Fig. 3: A church service, images from the frontispiece of an English book first published in 1682, shown here slightly larger than the original size. 3a (left): A sermon; all are focused on the preacher. The women sit together in pews with doors, a child sitting with them in the front row. The men stand, hatless, wearing their swords. 3b (right): The sacrament is taken kneeling. Men and women kneel together. (Lancelot Addison, An introduction to the sacrament *(London, 1682), frontispiece)*

PEWS, BENCHES AND CHAIRS

Fig. 4: Box pews in two eighteenth-century churches, dating from the time the churches were built. Both show a mix of linear box pews facing east, with a small number of square box pews.
4a (above): St Margaret, Babington, Somerset. Built in 1750, a parish church, though built in front of the great house. The apse is decorated with eucharistic imagery.
4b (below): St Mary, Stoke Edith, Herefordshire. The body of the church was rebuilt in the early 1740s by the owners of the big house. Early soft furnishings survive in what is presumably the family pew, opposite the pulpit. Most of the other box pews are linear.

The congregation in both instances would probably have seen all this – the men standing, the women sitting in straight lines, the swords, the wearing of hats, the separation of the sexes – as normal. Would they also have seen it as 'traditional'? Would that notion even have crossed their mind? I do not know.

The box pew

It may not be coincidence that the growth in popularity of box pews, which are relatively cosy and warm, roughly corresponded with the so-called Little Ice Age, running from the sixteenth to the nineteenth centuries, when England's climate was the coldest

Fig. 5: The Ferneley Family Pew, 1828, *by John Ferneley (1782–1860). This shows Mrs Ferneley and her six children in Melton Mowbray church, together with the faint unfinished outline of Mr Ferneley, with (possibly) the artist's father, William Ferneley. All are listening, or meant to be listening, to Dr Ford, the vicar, preaching. Note the curtains to protect the box pews from draughts. The church is now seated with chairs. (Oil on canvas, 130 cm x 112 cm, 1828, Leicester County Museums Service)*

in its recent history, though no doubt there were other factors at play. Box pews can be linear or square often representing differences of status (Figs. 4–5).[2] Facing each other in a square box pew has the obvious disadvantage that some people have to turn their back on the action (Fig. 6), but much the same happens today in a secular context with the round-table seating arrangements we have at award ceremonies and business conferences, so perhaps it was not too disruptive. Nevertheless it incurred the displeasure of the Victorian church reformers, for all the obvious reasons. Are we returning to the idea with the café church?

The insertion of pews by private individuals in an uncontrolled way could lead to a disorganised interior, and this was happening at least by the 1630s, when some Laudian bishops re-exerted control over the height and directionality of pews.[3] However, the continued unplanned insertion of box pews and

Fig. 6: St Clydog, Clodock, Herefordshire, looking east from the gallery, a photograph taken before the tidying-up of the interior. The pews and other furnishings were mostly built at various dates in the latter half of the seventeenth century, and their piecemeal insertion has created something of a jumble. Note the unusual communicants' bench with kneeling board on the south side of the three-sided chancel rail. The interior has since been altered, but is still atmospheric. (Photograph hanging in the church under glass, reproduced by kind permission of the church authorities)

other seating meant that by the early nineteenth century some churches were not only hierarchical in their seating but were becoming rather chaotic, as in Figure 7. This is caricature – but *recognisable* caricature. The church is huddled and crowded with people, occupying what seems a random mix of pews, with benches in the aisle, and the band and probably other folk in the gallery; some men stand, a bonneted lady peers out of the window, and an old lady sits dozing in a chair in the aisle, her prayer book on the floor beside her.[4]

How much of a growing sense was there by this time amongst ordinary villagers that the interior of these churches was really not up to the job? Or did it all simply seem part and parcel of the normal Sunday experience?

Victorian tidiness

Either way, the mid and later nineteenth century saw a grand tidying-up of church interiors, a major hiatus to congregational seating. Imagine your church looking like Figure 7, closing down for a few months, and when it reopened finding it had changed to Figure 8. It must have been startling. Not that ordinary parishioners necessarily had much say in the matter, with both the money and the decisions often flowing from a relatively small number of people, a major difference from today.

Of course, rather than the chairs shown in this picture, many Victorian reorderings introduced fixed bench pews, at least partly to allow some seats to be appropriated (that is, be reserved for the use of particular individuals). I have included this particular

Fig. 7: 'Our pew at church', an engraving published in Charles Dickens's David Copperfield *(Chapter 2), published in parts from 1849. This is loosely based on 'The Sleeping Congregation' from Hogarth's* The Rake's Progress. *(Engraving by Hablot Knight Browne (Phiz) (1815–92))*

Fig. 8: St Peter, Sudbury, Suffolk in 1857 shortly after the restoration and reordering by William Butterfield. During weekdays the chairs were largely cleared away. For more details, see page 255. (Engraving, The Illustrated London News, *12 September 1857, p. 261)*

illustration as a reminder that some first class Victorian architects were happy to introduce chairs into medieval churches. Here it was a deliberate ploy to avoid any risk of appropriation. However there was also an aesthetic bonus: the removal of most of the chairs on weekdays resulted in 'the open floor of the pavement and the full length of the columns being left unencumbered'. The Victorians have made pews so normal that we perhaps forget that some of our medieval church interiors were almost certainly designed to be seen without them.

The second half of the twentieth century

Figure 9 brings us forward almost exactly one hundred years, to 1953. This is an affectionate, gently ironic drawing, contrasting the hymn's claim that the church building is a house of particular honour, with the reality of a building which has seen better days. Indeed, it seems hardly to have changed in the hundred years or so since its Victorian restoration, and the War and subsequent austerity have led to delays in repairs and maintenance. Unlike the congregation's own homes, the building is still lit by oil.

The pews are the typical square-headed Victorian shop-work, probably in pine. Note how well the drawing catches the way pews allow people to choose how closely they place themselves to their neighbour. It is this flexibility in space allocation which usually allows benches to seat more people than chairs (Fig. 10). It is chilly in the church, and everyone wears their overcoats, for at that date a church was roughly half-way between being indoors and outdoors, and one always kept one's coat on. In some churches one still does, but expectations have been changing. One day this church may start to think about introducing underfloor heating. What would be the implications for the seating?

Here in 1953 they are standing to sing a hymn (written in 1854) and soon they will kneel to pray. A hassock can just be seen. One of the results of the move to bench pews in the nineteenth century was that kneeling became normal in Church of England churches; however, during the latter part of the twentieth century it has become less common.[5] There are probably many reasons for this change, which I do not propose to discuss here, but the result is that when new church seating is being considered today, it may well not need to provide a means of kneeling. Looking ahead, this congregation may still have hassocks at the end of the twentieth century, but there is a good chance they will be beautifully embroidered and serve not so much for kneeling as to decorate the church.

"We love the place, O God,
Wherein Thine honour dwells..."

Fig. 9: 'We love the place, O God, Wherein Thine honour dwells'. The title is the first two lines of a hymn written in 1854. The drawing is from the 1953 Christmas issue of Punch *(p. 744) accompanying an appeal by John Betjeman for the newly-formed Historic Churches Preservation Trust (active today as the National Churches Trust). (Reproduction of drawing by E. H. Shepard (1879–1976))*

Fig 10: A view of a recent General Synod of the Church of England, taken from above. It is worth studying carefully to see how people occupy the chairs. Note how some wider people take up more than one chair, encouraging people to leave an empty seat next to them (or to take various types of evasive action). In contrast, narrow people do not always quite take up all their allotted space. This sort of behaviour varies with the width of the people, the spacing of the chairs, and how well people get on together. (Photo © Geoff Crawford)

The image (Fig. 9) accompanied an appeal by John Betjeman for the then (1953) newly-formed Historic Churches Preservation Trust (active today as the National Churches Trust). In passing he pointed out that 'people may not go to church today in such numbers as once [they] did' but that those who attend do so 'because they believe, not because they want to be thought respectable conformers'.[6] As this trend continues from 1953 and onward into the twentieth century, as wealth gradually increases, as choices become wider, as churchgoers take greater and greater financial responsibility for all aspects of church life, how will the congregation at this imaginary church start to develop their church building? How will they want to worship? And what role will the seating arrangements play in this? For illustrations of the various directions they might choose to take forty or fifty years later, we need only look at the case studies in Chapter 29.

As our vignettes emphasise, over the years change has been fitful but significant, with different generations remodelling their church seating to meet the needs of the moment. Each of these arrangements in its turn has become normal, until supplanted by the next development.

Secular seating, ecclesiastical seating

The changes discussed so far are the obvious ones. Another more subtle one has crept up over the last hundred years or so: church seating and secular seating have diverged.

For hundreds of years, ecclesiastical church seating and secular public seating often had a family resemblance, based on the wooden bench. Thus the late medieval model of a seat in Figure 11 is not a church pew, but looks very much like one. Similarly, although secular, the eighteenth-century high-backed settle in Figure 12 is similar enough to a church pew for this style to be called a 'pew group' in the ceramic literature.[7] As a later example, Figure 13 shows a selection of designs of benches sold by an early-twentieth-century church furnisher as being suitable for 'mission and Sunday school seating'.[8] All of these designs could be secular.

Until at least the end of the nineteenth century it was normal to sit on wooden benches in many public places – for example, the pub, the school, the lecture theatre, the public meeting, the waiting room and various forms of public transport. Wooden bench seating was also found in the theatre, where right through to late Victorian times the cheap seats in the pit could consist of un-upholstered wooden benches, as shown in Figure 14.[9]

POSTSCRIPT: ONE HUNDRED YEARS HENCE

Fig. 11: A relief statuette in oak, St Anne (on the right) with Virgin and Child, probably Brabant (Netherlands), c.1500–1510. At first glance this looks like a church pew, though closer inspection shows that the boarding underneath the seat is at the front, making kneeling impossible. Nevertheless there is an obvious similarity between this and church pews of the period. (Photo © Victoria and Albert Museum, London)

Fig. 12: A salt-glazed stoneware pew group, with applied brown details, Staffordshire, c.1750. Although known generically in the literature as 'pew groups', the figures are in fact sitting on a high-backed settle, typical of inns and rural houses of the period, but the confusion illustrates the fundamental similarity at this time between everyday group seating and church seating. (Photo © Victoria and Albert Museum, London)

469

Fig. 13: A selection of four benches from a church furnishing catalogue of about 1920, presented as suitable for 'schools and mission chapels'. There are another eight such designs not shown here; of the total of twelve, only three have any Gothic elements. It is likely that some or all of these designs were current in the 1880s.
(Geo. M. Hammer & Co. Ltd., Church Furniture *(n.d., c.1920)*, 58–59)

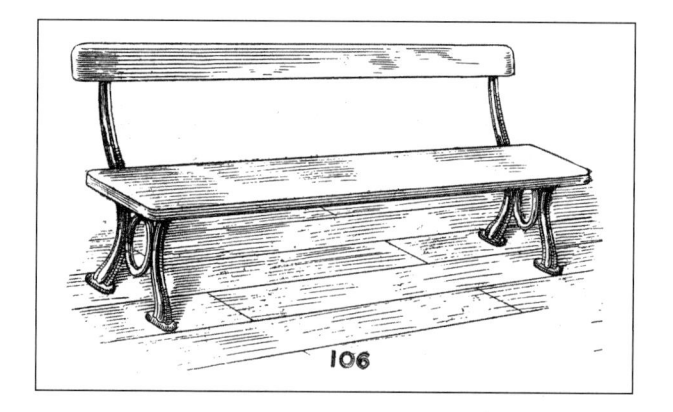

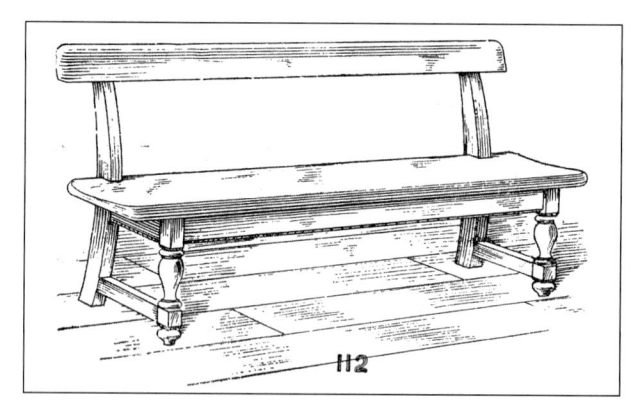

No. 35—PIT SEAT.
Upholstered in Utrecht Velvet or Railway Rep; Seat 11 inch × 1½ inch Pine;
Back 6 inch × 1 inch. N.B.—Supported by strong Iron Standards,
One to every 4 feet 6 inches run.
3/6 per Foot Run.
Ditto, with Polished Seat and Back,
1/9 per Foot Run.
Ditto, Upholstered in good American Leather,
2/11½ per Foot Run.

Fig. 14: A seat for the pit of a theatre, from a catalogue of about 1898. Even at this relatively late date, it is available if required as a hard wooden bench, without upholstery – a form of seating entirely familiar to those attending public venues at that time. Compare with Figure 13, number 106. (From a Catalogue of A. R. Dean of c.1900)

In addition, as theatre historian John Earl has pointed out, wooden seating was also found in early music halls. Furthermore – because of its familiarity and practicality – it was equally fitted for use in a mission chapel.

> The earlier, boozier music halls had flat floors, encircling promenade, supper tables near the stage and rows of benches toward the rear. The two sole surviving examples of this were both saved from demolition by being converted to mission halls when music hall use ceased around the 1870s. The physical alterations that had to be made were minimal, as the working requirements of a music hall and a mission hall are remarkably similar: a big room with a raised stage and acoustics suitable for vocal music; a number of private dining (activity) rooms and an apartment for the landlord (minister).
> The benches in a music hall of the period would have had a little shelf on the back to accommodate the glasses of the drinkers in the next row. Mission hall benches often instead had a shelf for hymn books. They were otherwise largely indistinguishable. The benches in the illustration (Fig. 15), taken in 1979, at Wilton's music hall, are leftovers from mission hall days, but could equally well have served the music hall.[10]

So right through to the late nineteenth century, wooden benches were familiar and unremarkable in those places where people congregated, whether secular or religious.

Indeed one particular form of seat has shown a remarkable longevity, the bench-with-open-back-and-arms. Seventeenth-century examples can be found in several churches (Fig. 16, and see Figure 9 in Chapter 11, page 181)[11] and similar benches were still in use in the early nineteenth century for free church seating for the poor; we have just seen them in use in mission halls. It is not long since they were provided in large numbers at railway termini for the convenience of waiting passengers. And the form survives today as outdoor seating in parks and gardens.

Fig. 15: Wilton's Music Hall, London, photo of 1979. As explained in the text, this was converted to a mission hall, and thus preserved much of its essential layout. What look to our eyes like garden seats are the wooden benches used in the mission hall, very similar to the music hall seating they replaced (compare Figure 13 number 1460). Wooden bench seating was ubiquitous, and unremarkable.

Today wooden benches are not very often found indoors, though they have made a somewhat self-conscious return in pubs and wine-bars. This may partly be a nostalgic gesture, and the seating may also be associated with notions of conviviality and good fellowship. Any problems with comfort are resolved partly by the provision of cushions, and partly by being free to lounge back or lean forward on a table, with no requirement to remain still for any length of time.

But on the whole, wooden benches are now the exception rather than the rule. Thus within a few generations church pews have diverged from secular seating, and have moved from being an unremarkable example of public seating of a type in continuous use for hundreds of years, to being one of its last representatives.[12]

Does that mean that pews have had their day? Of course not. That simply does not follow. But it is a fact which it would be sensible not to ignore.

Fig. 16: St Mary, Monnington-on-Wye, Herefordshire. The church was rebuilt in 1679, and the seating dates from then or soon after. Nikolaus Pevsner in the Herefordshire *volume of his* Buildings of England *series describes the benches as 'quite domestic'. The kneeling boards are later.*

'The gorgeous pew had vanished'

LONDON ONE HUNDRED YEARS HENCE: *I looked into the churches and places of worship, and there I saw the gorgeous pew – screened off, cushioned, and private – had vanished; and with it had vanished the hard, narrow plank that was once the poor man's purgatory.*[13]

That was written in 1857, and the author's generation did indeed make both the 'gorgeous pew' and the poor man's 'hard, narrow plank' vanish.

This was a revolution. But it happened in slow motion: only a few per cent of existing churches made the change each year, and it took much more than a generation to see things through, though rather less than the 'one hundred years hence' the author allowed himself to peer ahead.[14]

I wonder, would it have surprised the writer that – rather more than 'one hundred year's hence' – some people wish that the new bench pews put in place by his and succeeding generations should vanish in their turn? Are we in fact already seeing the early stages of a second revolution, also in slow motion, with fixed pews 'vanishing' and being replaced by movable seating? And if this is a revolution, will it be all-embracing, or limited to a relatively small

Fig. 17: The Pew Fairy (aka Helen) has secretly removed all the pews from the church, freeing up the space, and provoking a series of reactions. This cartoon (originally in colour) appeared in The Church Times *for 5 June 2009, in the* St Gargoyle's *series by Ron Wood.*

number of churches – if so, which ones? Where, in short, will be 'one hundred years hence'?

I really do not know. But it may be relevant that, to the extent there is a shift going on, it seems to a large extent to be happening from the bottom up. Unlike the changes of the mid nineteenth century, it is not being pushed by a clerical elite. Nor is it being bolstered by the cast-iron certainties of a Cambridge Camden Society, or the distorting financial subsidies of an Incorporated Church Building Society. On the other hand the removal of pews may to some extent be encouraged by institutional support for the wider use of church buildings.

Of course, as with any organisation relying on voluntary support, things may not happen very fast – pews can arouse strong feelings, and the need even to consider change may not be agreed by everyone involved. Even where there is agreement on this point, quite what the change should be can take a good deal of working out, both internally and with a range of stakeholders, especially if there are heritage implications. So it is not surprising that there is sometimes a certain caution even about starting the process rolling.

All of which provides the context for the final image (Fig. 17). This shows a mix of reactions to the discovery that a set of pews has vanished overnight. Like many cartoons, it can only be appreciated because of the unstated background assumptions. As is the way with most humour, I doubt this will seem terribly funny 'one hundred years hence'. I wonder, will it even be understood?

Notes
1. Eastchester is in the State of New York in the USA. I do not know if there are any similar English mismatches between worship and seating. For Eastchester, see the brief account at www.nps.gov/sapa/index.htm under 'history and culture', and for a fuller account with detailed drawings, http://loc.gov/pictures/item/ny0861/; an interior plan is reproduced at http://historicpelham.blogspot.com/2007/08/plan-of-pews-in-st-pauls-church-1790.html; for a collection of recent photographs, see www.andrewcusack.com/2004/12/28/st-pauls-eastchester/ (all accessed July 2010). The photograph used here was obtained from www.clipart.com. I am grateful to Andrew Cusack for a brief discussion of the church, and how to source this photograph.
2. The impression I have is that if a church was reseated from scratch in the earlier seventeenth century that linear box pews were the norm, whilst by Georgian times a neat and tidy mix of linear and square pews was typically introduced when an interior was reordered. I hope at some stage to carry out a systematic review of surviving seventeenth-century church seating plans, which may provide confirmation on the first of these points.
3. See e.g. Kenneth Fincham and Nicholas Tyacke, *Altars Restored: the Changing Face of English Religious Worship, 1547–c.1700* (Oxford, 2007), 243–45.
4. For a useful discussion of this image, including the working drawing on which it is based, see Michael Steig, *Dickens and Phiz* (Indiana, 1978), 115–17.
5. The point was first drawn to my attention by Keith Lovell. I am grateful to Diana Evans for helpful discussion of this change.

6 *Punch*, 23 December 1953, 744.
7 Julia Poole, *English Pottery* (Cambridge, Fitzwilliam Museum Handbooks, 1995), 56–57.
8 The illustrations are from a catalogue printed in the 1920s (Geo. M. Hammer & Co. Ltd., *Church Furniture* (n.d., *c.*1920)). No earlier editions of this catalogue have been located. However one design in the catalogue (not shown here) is advertised in the *Church Builder* for 1884 (p. 116), and it seems likely that many if not all of the designs in the 1920s edition dated from the later nineteenth century. Other images from the same company will be found on page 319–21.
9 I am grateful to John Earl for Figures 14 & 15. His book *British Theatres and Music Halls* (Princes Risborough, 2005) has images of wooden benches being used for seating on page 10 (restored seating in Georgian circuit theatre), page 5 (pit seating in Victorian theatre), and page 18 (Victorian music halls). As well as the seats themselves, there are, of course, parallels in the *layout* of the seating between church and theatre in Georgian and Victorian times.
10 John Earl, personal correspondence.
11 I am aware of similar seating in churches at Letton, Herefordshire (where the backs have been filled in subsequently, I think), Leighton Bromswold, Huntingdonshire (early 1630s), nearby Barham (probably of similar date), Puddletown, Dorset (early 1630s, see Figure 9 in Chapter 11), and in the Barnardiston pew at Kedington, Suffolk (probably early seventeenth century). There are probably many others of similar date, and I would be interested to know of them: their use deserve further investigation.
12 Is this due to a difference in investment cycle? In the past, serious church re-ordering seems to have had a cycle of several generations (is it now speeding up?), much longer than the replacement cycle for seating in many other public places.
13 The *Leisure Hour*, 10 December 1857, quoted in *Free and open church chronology including authorities and landmarks of the movement* (published by the Incorporated Free and Open Church Association, 1892), 31.
14 Simon Bradley, 'The roots of Ecclesiology: late Hanoverian attitudes to medieval churches' in Christopher Webster and John Elliott, *'A Church as it Should be': The Cambridge Camden Society and its Influence* (Stamford, 2000), 22–44, (p. 40). See also the long time periods implied in Graph 5 on page 42 above, and on page 283 above.

Further reading

This list of further reading is intended to provide a point of departure rather than be complete. Most of the references are to books, but articles and unpublished theses are mentioned when they are of particular importance. Local studies, or those relating to particular churches, are not listed unless they are of general applicability. Website addresses were checked early in 2011.

Changing seating: guidance

Several denominations provide guidance to changing church seating, including the following.

Baptist Union. *Furnishings in listed churches*. Available online at www.baptist.org.uk/resources/leadership_admin.html, under 'buc guidelines', item LB7.

Church of England. *Choosing new seating*. Available online at www.churchcare.co.uk/contents.php, under 'seating', then scroll down to bottom of page to 'seating guidance'.

— *Making changes to a listed church: Guidelines for Clergy, Churchwardens and Parochial Church Councils prepared by the Ecclesiastical Rule Committee*. Available online at www.churchofengland.org/media/51391/mctlc.doc.

— *Seating in churches*. Available online at www.churchcare.co.uk/contents.php, under 'seating'.

— *Statements of significance and need: guidance for parishes*. Available online at www.churchcare.co.uk/legal.php, under 'statements of significance and need'.

— (forthcoming) Statutory Advisory Committee of the Church Building Council (Church of England) may be publishing proposed *Criteria for Assessing the Heritage Significance of a Church*, likely to be available on www.churchofengland.org/about-us/our-buildings.aspx. An earlier version, 'Assessing heritage value and determining the scope for change in closing and closed Anglican churches' by David Baker, last Chair of the former Advisory Board on Redundant Churches, appears in *Church Archaeology* 11 (2007 [published 2009]) pp. 61–81.

Methodist Church. *Removal of pews from historic chapels*. Available online at www.methodist.org.uk/index.cfm?fuseaction=churchlife.content&cmid=1382 and scroll down the page.

See also the very useful general document produced by English Heritage, *Caring for Places of Worship* (2010), available at www.english-heritage.org.uk/publications/caring-for-places-of-worship.

Changing seating: conservation principles

Clark, Kate. *Informed Conservation: Understanding Historic Buildings and their Landscapes for Conservation*, London, English Heritage, 2001.

Earl, John. *Building Conservation Philosophy*, third edition, Donhead St Mary, 2003. Useful annotated bibliography.

English Heritage. *New Work in Historic Places of Worship*, 2003. Available online from www.english-heritage.org.uk.
— *Conservation Principles, Policies and Guidance for the Sustainable Management of the Historic Environment*, 2008. Available online from www.english-heritage.org.uk
— *Conservation Bulletin*, 60 (Spring 2009), entitled 'Conservation Principles in Practice'. This provides commentary on English Heritage's Conservation Principles, and a range of case studies.

Changing seating: principles for the arrangement of church interiors

The books listed here are a tiny selection from the extensive current literature on how to organise a church interior. They represent a range of advocacy and polemic. The lecture by Sir Roy Strong calls for the destruction of pews to allow naves to be used as village halls.

Giles, Richard. *Re-Pitching the Tent: Re-ordering the Church Building for Worship and Mission in the New Millennium*, Norwich, 1996.
Hammond, Peter. *Liturgy and Architecture*, London, 1960.
Schloeder, Steven J. *Architecture in Communion: Implementing the Second Vatican Council through Liturgy and Architecture*, San Francisco, 1990.
Strong, Roy. 'The beauty of holiness and its perils: what is to happen to 10,000 parish churches?', Lecture at Gresham College, 30 May 2007, available at www.gresham.ac.uk.

Changing seating: disabled access

Several denominations provide information about the Disability Discrimination Act and its implications, including the following.
Baptist Union. *Disability Discrimination Act 1995*. Available online at www.baptist.org.uk/resources/resource_downloads/196.pdf.
Church of England. Discussion and links to useful sites at www.churchcare.co.uk/legal.php?GL.
Methodist Church. *Disability Access Provision in Historic Chapels*. Available online at www.methodist.org.uk/static/rm/accessforhistoricbuildings.pdf.
See also the more general discussion in the English Heritage publication, *Easy Access to Historic Buildings* (2004), available at www.english-heritage.org.uk/publications/easy-access-to-historic-buildings.

History: the arrangement of the interiors of churches in England and Wales

This is a small selection of the various books which describe the history of the arrangement of church interiors.
Addleshaw, G. & Etchells, F. *The Architectural Setting of Anglican Worship: an Inquiry into the Arrangements for Public Worship in the Church of England from the Reformation to the Present Day*, London, 1948.
Anson, Peter. *Churches: their Plan and Furnishing*, Milwaukee, USA, 1948. Deals with Roman Catholic interiors.

— *Fashions in Church Furnishings, 1840-1940*, London, 1960. Deals with Church of England interiors.
Chatfield, Mark. *Churches the Victorians Forgot*, second edition, Ashbourne, 1989. Deals with unrestored Church of England churches.
Drummond, A. L. *The Church Architecture of Protestantism: an Historical and Constructive study*, Edinburgh, 1934.
Whiting, Robert. *The Reformation of the English Parish Church*, CUP, 2010.
Yates, Nigel. *Buildings, Faith and Worship: the Liturgical Arrangement of Anglican Worship, 1600–1900*, second edition, OUP, 2000.

History: the use of church buildings for secular purposes

Davies, J. G. *The Secular Use of Church Buildings*, London, 1968.

History: use and allocation of church seating

The book by Heales is the most recent attempt at a book-length documentary history of church seating. The studies by Flather and by Dillow, and the articles by Marsh, have a particular focus on the way in which the arrangement of church seating might reflect social structures. The article by Aston is a seminal study of the separation of the sexes in churches. In addition, see the book by R. L. Brown and the thesis by Timothy Parry referred to in the section on Victorian debates.

Aston, Margaret. 'Segregation in Church', *Women in the Church: Studies in Church History* 27 (1990), pp. 237-294.
Dillow, Kevin. 'The social and ecclesiastical significance of church seating arrangements and pew disputes, 1500–1740', unpublished DPhil. dissertation, Oxford, 1990.
Flather, Amanda. 'The politics of place: a study of church seating in Essex, c.1580-1640', *Friends of the Department of English Local History, Friends' Papers*, No. 3, Leicester, 1999.
Hardy, W. J. 'Remarks on the history of seat-reservation in churches', *Archaeologia* 53 (1892), pp. 95-106.
Heales, Alfred. *The History and Law of Church Seats, or Pews*, 2 volumes, London, 1872.
Marsh, Christopher. 'Order and place in England 1560-1640: the view from the pew', *Journal of British studies*, 44.1 (January 2005), pp. 2-27. A substantial extract from this is reprinted in Chapter 9 above, which also references the two other articles on the topic by Marsh.

History: Victorian debates on church seating

The only recent survey of the Victorian arguments on church seating is that of Brown, listed first here, which, despite the title, is mostly about the Victorian period and contains much English material. Neale's initially anonymous *History of Pews* ('Pues' in some editions) was regarded at the time as being an important polemic, but is biased as regards history. An interesting retrospect on the history of the (ultimately successful) movement to make church seating free is the booklet by the

Incorporated Free and Open Church Association, published in 1892. Chapter 2 of the work by Parry discusses the role of the Incorporated Church Building Society in encouraging free seating. In addition, see Chapters 14 and 15 above which reprint Victorian discussion from the *Church Builder* and *The Ecclesiologist*.

Brown, Roger Lee. *Pews, benches and seats, being a history of the church pew in Wales*, Welshpool, 1998.

Incorporated Free and Open Church Association. *Free and open church chronology including authorities and landmarks of the movement*, 1892.

Anon., [J. M. Neale]. *The History of Pews*, (Paper read to the Cambridge Camden Society, 22 Nov 1841, enlarged edns Cambridge 1842, 1843). This is available from Google books. There were two ancillary papers, often bound or published with the main paper (a) *An appendix containing a Report presented to the Society on the Statistics of Pews, etc* and (b) *A Supplement to the History of Pues*.

Parry, Timothy. 'The Incorporated Church Building Society, 1818-1851', unpublished M. Litt. Thesis, Trinity College Oxford, Trinity Term, 1984. Copy in Lambeth Palace Library, class mark H5194.P2.

Historic artefacts: church and cathedral choir stalls

The subject of chancel and choir seating is outside the scope of this volume. The books listed here deal with medieval seating.

Bond, Francis. *Wood Carvings in English Churches: I – Stalls and Tabernacle Work*, OUP, 1910. Has a chapter on the parish church.

Tracy, Charles. *English Gothic Choir Stalls 1200-1400*, Woodbridge, 1987. General survey.

Tracy, Charles & Harrison, Hugh. *The Choir-Stalls at Amiens Cathedral*, Reading, 2004. This book updates the bibliography of Charles Tracy's book.

Historic artefacts: misericords

There are a number of monographs on misericords. However most misericords were made for choir seating, and are thus outside the scope of this volume. The book below provides a recent survey and bibliography.

Grossinger, Christa. *The World Upside-Down: English Misericords*, London, 1997.

Historic artefacts: medieval congregational seating, including carved bench ends

The following is a more or less complete list of books on medieval congregational seating. Howard & Crossley have a good introduction to the structure of this seating.

Agate, John. *Benches and Stalls in Suffolk Churches*, Suffolk Historic Churches Trust, 1980.

Cox, J. C. *Bench Ends in English Churches*, London, 1916.

— *English Church Fittings, Furniture and Accessories*, London, n.d. [*c*.1923], chapter 5.

Cox, J. C. & Harvey, A. *English Church Furniture*, second edition, London, 1908, chapter 8.
Gardner, Arthur. *Minor English Wood Sculpture 1400–1550: an Essay on Carved Figures and Animals on Bench-ends in English Parish Churches*, London 1958.
Howard, F. E. & Crossley, F. H. *English Church Woodwork: A Study in Craftsmanship during the Medieval Period, AD 1250–1550*, second edition, London, 1927, chapter 6.
Randall, Gerard. *Church Furnishing and Decoration in England and Wales*, London, 1980, especially chapter 4.
Smith, J. C. D. *Church Woodcarvings: a West Country Study*, Newton Abbott, 1969.
— *A Guide to Church Woodcarvings*, Newton Abbott, 1974.
Wright, Peter Poyntz. *The Rural Benchends of Somerset: a Study in Medieval Woodcarving*, Amersham, 1983.

Historic artefacts: Victorian and later carving on bench ends

The study of Victorian and later church woodcarvers is in its infancy, and there is relatively little literature.

Brown, C. 'Two Victorian Woodcarvers', *Proceedings of the Suffolk Institute of Archaeology & History* 34 (1980).
Davidson, Eleanor. *The Simpsons of Kendal, Craftsmen in Wood 1885-1952*, University of Lancaster, 1978.
Lennon, Patricia and Joy, David. *Mouseman: the Legacy of Robert Thompson of Kilburn*, second edition, Ilkley, 2008.
Olding, Simon. 'The indefatigable Mr Hems of Exeter', *Devon and Cornwall Notes and Queries*, 33:8 (1977), pp. 290–94. Harry Hems ran a workshop in Exeter of some one hundred people, executing carving in both stone and wood. See also www.exetermemories.co.uk/EM/_people/hems.php and www.devonheritage.org/Places/Exeter/HarryHems1.htm.
Pinwill, Violet. Obituary notice to Violet Pinwill in *The Times* 10 Jan 1957. The Pinwill sisters (Violet was the key player) were encouraged by Sedding and did considerable work in the West Country.
Stead, Harold. *The Ecclesiastical and other Woodwork of H. P. Jackson*, London, n.d. (c.1927). Jackson (d. 1931) was a Yorkshire wood carver.
Stephenson, Joyce. *The Wood Carvings by William Gibbs Rogers for St Michael's Church, Cornhill*, 2009. Published by the author (ISBN: 978-0-9812354-0-0). Includes a biography of Rogers. Available from the author at jstephenson2@cogeco.ca.

Historic artefacts: church floors and related items

A change to congregational seating often requires changes to floors, and may raise issues regarding artefacts resting on or embedded in the floor. As far as possible, the books in this section have been chosen because they contain material on maintenance and conservation.

Beulah, Kenneth & Van Lemmen, Hans. *Church Tiles of the Nineteenth Century*, Princes Risborough (Shire Books), 2001.

Egan, B.S. and Stuchfield, M. *The Repair of Monumental Brasses*, Newport Pagnell, 1981. And also see the useful conservation section of the Monumental Brass Society website: www.mbs-brasses.co.uk/conservation.html.

Fawcett, Jane. *Historic Floors: their History and Conservation*, new edition, London, 2001. And see her useful short chapter 'Floors' in Peter Burman (ed.), *Treasures on Earth: a Good Housekeeping Guide to Churches and their Contents*, Wimbledon, 1994.

Field, Robert. *Geometric Patterns from Churches and Cathedrals*, Diss (Tarquin Publications), 1996, for the short section on Victorian floor gratings.

Greenhill, F. A. *Incised Effigial Slabs: a Study of Engraved Stone Memorials in Latin Christendom, c.1100 to c.1700*, two vols, London, 1976.

Ryder, Peter. *The Medieval Cross Slab Grave Covers in Cumbria*, Cumberland and Westmorland Antiquarian and Archaeological Society, 2005. One of several works by this author. Includes wider bibliography.

Van Lemmen, Hans. *Medieval Tiles*, Princes Risborough (Shire Books), 2004. A brief introduction, with select bibliography to the wider literature.

Archaeology and the evidential value of churches

The standard introduction to the archaeology of churches is Rodwell, who also deals briefly with burials within the church, and explains the importance of recording strata when excavating. For a wider survey, see Blair and Pyrah.

Blair, J. & Pyrah, C. (eds.). *Church Archaeology: Research Directions for the Future*, CBA Research Report 104, York, 1996.

Rodwell, Warwick. *The Archaeology of Churches*, Stroud (Tempus), 2005.

Novels focusing on pews

As far as we are aware, there is only one novel focusing on pews. First published in 1842, it was popular enough to require a second edition. As the story develops it becomes clear that, in the author's eyes, appropriated box pews are bad and free open seating is good, and that the blame for introducing the former is to be laid firmly at the door of the early-seventeenth-century Puritans (of which the novel contains a number, including the mellifluously named Mahalaleel Mumgrizzle). The book does not take long to read, and usefully illuminates the views of a body of churchmen in the 1840s.

Paget, Francis. *Milford Malvoisin: or, Pews and Pewholders*, London, 1842. There was a second edition of 1847, which is available to download from Google Books.

Notes on Contributors

P. S. BARNWELL teaches architectural history at Oxford University and is a Fellow of Kellogg College. He has published extensively on the pre-Reformation parish church. He is a member of the Council of the Ecclesiological Society.

JAMES BETTLEY is working on a new edition of the Pevsner Architectural Guide to Suffolk. His revision of the volume on Essex was published by Yale University Press in 2007.

GEOFF BRANDWOOD is an architectural historian with a long-standing interest in Victorian and Edwardian churches and their fittings, on which he has published widely.

SUZANNA BRANFOOT is Hon. Treasurer of the Ecclesiological Society. Her doctoral thesis was on G. G. Scott's restoration of parish churches and cathedrals.

SARAH BROWN is a lecturer in the History of Art at the University of York, and Course Director of the MA in Stained Glass Conservation and Heritage Management. Previously she was Head of Research Policy for Places of Worship at English Heritage. She is a member of the Council of the Ecclesiological Society.

TREVOR COOPER is Chairman of Council of the Ecclesiological Society. He recently retired from a career in business. He has a lifelong interest in churches, with particular interests in church interiors of the first half of the seventeenth century and in the future of church buildings, attempting to place current debates on this topic on a firm factual basis.

JO COX is a partner in Keystone Historic Buildings Consultants. She has a long-standing interest in Victorian church buildings, and in the 1970s was a co-founder with Chris Brooks and Martin Cherry of the Nineteenth-Century Churches Project, with the aim of documenting and assessing all nineteenth-century Anglican church work in Devon.

PETER DOLL is Canon Librarian of Norwich Cathedral, previous to which he was team Vicar in the Parish of Abingdon. He has an active interest in historical, ecumenical, and liturgical studies.

HUGH HARRISON leads a specialist company of consultants, designers and contractors in the surveying and conservation of historic structural and decorative woodwork and the design and manufacture of new bespoke work in conservation settings. He is often called upon to help parishes assess historic church woodwork.

WILL HAWKES recently retired from architectural practice at Stratford upon Avon after a lifetime of involvement with churches of all sorts and conditions, both at the practical and advisory level.

ANTHONY RUSSELL has for a number of years been a consultant to Luke Hughes & Co., the prestigious furniture designer, travelling the country advising significant buildings on their furniture needs, including museums, palaces, schools and cathedrals, whilst continuing his work as a professional artist and lecturer. He recently joined Aegistra, the on-line sister company to Luke Hughes. He has recently held an exhibition of paintings, "Idyllic Illusions", and is currently writing a book on moral philosophy.

FRANCIS KELLY is an architectural historian employed by English Heritage as an Inspector of Historic Buildings, here writing in a personal capacity.

BOB MACHIN read History at Oxford and until 1994 was Bristol University Resident Tutor in Dorset, where retirement has provided him with an opportunity to reconsider thirty years of historical research in the county.

ROBERT MAGUIRE OBE, FRSA is a retired architect, formerly of the partnership Robert Maguire & Keith Murray and subsequently Chairman of Maguire & Co. His firms specialised in university and school buildings as well as church work, for which he is perhaps better known. He was Head of the Oxford School of Architecture 1976–85, and a founder-member of the New Churches Research Group in 1958. His first building was St Paul's Church, Bow Common.

CHRISTOPHER MARSH is a reader in early modern history at the Queen's University of Belfast. He is a social and cultural historian, working mainly on England during the sixteenth and seventeenth centuries. His first projects all concerned aspects of popular religion, but he is now completing a book entitled *Music and Society in Early Modern England*.

JONATHAN MACKECHNIE-JARVIS has been Secretary of Gloucester DAC since 1986, and a member of the Church Buildings Council (formerly Council for the Care of Churches) since 2001. He is a Fellow of the Society of Antiquaries and a member of the IHBC. In 1992 he published a history of the Gloucester DAC, covering its first seventy years of operation.

PETER MOGER is National Worship Development Officer for the Church of England, working with the Liturgical Commission to enable good practice in the preparation and leading of worship

ROY PORTER was formerly Casework Officer for the Advisory Board for Redundant Churches, and his chapter in this book is based on his experience there. He subsequently joined English Heritage, where he is Territory Properties Curator for the South of England.

JERRY SAMPSON is the archaeological consultant to the conservation architects Caroe and Partners and to the Dean and Chapter of St David's Cathedral. He specialises in medieval stone buildings, and has worked on eight English and Welsh cathedrals, and numerous church and vernacular sites. With the rise in the number of church reorderings, he is increasingly involved in assessing medieval seating assemblages in Somerset.

ODDBJØRN SØRMOEN is Director of the Department for Church Buildings and Heritage Management in KA, the church's employer and interest organisation in Norway. For sixteen years he was Senior Adviser with the Directorate for Cultural Heritage, Norway, and for two years Special Adviser with English Heritage. He is an art historian, and as well as writing widely on Norwegian churches has edited the series *Kirker i Norge* (*Churches in Norway*).

CHARLES TRACY PHD, FSA is a specialist in historic church furniture. He is the author of several books, including a two-volume study of English Gothic choir stalls, and another on European church furniture in England. He is often consulted by parishes facing difficult reordering decisions which hinge on the significance of their furnishings.

CHRISTOPHER WEBSTER is an architectural historian. He is a member of the Council of the Ecclesiological Society, and Reviews Editor of *Ecclesiology Today*, the Society's journal.

Index

Entries in *italic* refer to illustrations (chapter and figure number), normally indexed by location, not subject matter. Except where necessary to avoid ambiguity, churches are listed by place name only, without the dedication. 'Seating' refers to church seating, 'pew' refers to any fixed wooden bench seating (often without doors), and 'box pew' to any pew with doors, of any shape. The term 'Victorian' should be taken to encompass some years either side of the reign of Queen Victoria.

A Book of Designs of Ecclesiastical Art, 307
'A Church as it Should Be', 13
A Few Words . . ., (pamphlets), 197, 204, 205, 266; *see also* anti-pew publications
A Plea for the Faithful Restoration …, 257
Abingdon, Oxon
    Abbey, 17
    St Helen, 346, 347, *22.2, 22.3, 22.4*
    St Michael & All Angels, Chapter 3, *3.1–3.4*
accommodation, *see* capacity
Addison, Lancelot, 459, *30.3*
Advantage West Midlands, 413
aesthetic value, *see* significance
age of seating, *see* date of seating
aisle (i.e. alley), required by ICBS, *see under* ICBS
Albert, Prince, and box pews, *19.12a*
Alldridge, Nicholas, 136
allocation (of seating, by churchwardens; mainly pre 19th century; for later periods, and for rights to seating, *see* appropriation): 83, Chapter 9 *passim*, Chapter 11 *passim* (esp. 175–9)
    churchwardens' role, Chapter 9 *passim* (esp. 132–8)
    criteria (for allocation)
        general discussion, 134–8
        for children and youth, 104, 135, 136, 179, 294; *see also* children and their seating
        by area of dwelling, 138
        for elderly and deaf, 136, 138, 225
        by gender, 69, 79, 94, 104, 106, 135–6, 152–3, 178, 459–60
        by moral worth, 136–8
        by social status and wealth (including servants), 75, 78–82, 94, 104, 108, 133, 134–6, 156, 174, 175–82, 257, 294
        for the poor (explicitly), 111, 134, 175, 178, 197, 199; *see also* appropriation, free seats
        see also appropriation, basis
    medieval (various), 75, 79–80, 83
    pew disputes, Chapter 9 *passim* (esp. 132, 139–42, 145–6, 171–2; infrequency of, 142, 146
    plans (post-Reformation), 133–42 *passim*, 150–53, 175–9, 180
    purchase and rent of seats, *see* appropriation, basis
    use of spare places, 143–4, 178
    see also appropriation
Altarnun, Cornwall, 76, 112, 143
altars, *see* communion tables and rails
angel on bench end, 87
anti-pew publications, 197, 204, 205–6, 257, 266, 281, 284, 293, 374–5
appearance of seating (attractiveness)
    Victorian discussions, *see* Victorian seating, appearance
    current discussions, 24, 390, 392, Chapter 22 *passim*, 355, 357, Chapter 24 *passim*
    for aesthetic value in a heritage context, *see* significance
appropriation (formal rights to seating, often 19th century; for allocation of seating by churchwardens esp. in earlier periods, *see* allocation): 37, 45–9, Chapter 13 *passim* (esp. 198–203), 255, 258, 264, 271, 295, 374
    basis
        by faculty or other title, 65 n.15, 132, 208, 270, 274
        by link with property, 45, 132, 137, 138
        with rent, 45, 47 (incl. Table 4), 132, 201, 208, 222, 275, 295
        without rent, 178–9
        sale and purchase, 49
    free seats (unappropriated) and poor seats, 45–9 *passim*, 107, 198, 199, 201–207 *passim*, 227, 232, 266, 271, 295, 324, 374, *19.1, rear cover*; *see also under* allocation, criteria
    informal and unofficial, 37, 248, 252, 254, 406
    percentage appropriated and free, 41 (Table 1), 42 (Graphs 7 & 8), 45–9 (incl. Tables 3 & 4)
    and pews
        pressure for pews not chairs, 37, 49, 208, 226, 255
        numbering on pews, *see* bench ends, identifiers
    disappearance (of appropriation), 45–6, 49, Chapter 13 *passim*, 295, 474
    see also allocation; children and their seating
archaeology and other evidence from seating (for below ground archaeology, *see under* floors)
    methods and results
        medieval, Chapter 7, 120–130; *see also* medieval seating, date of (assessing)
        post-medieval, 114–119, Chapter 10, Chapter 12, 380
    preserving evidence, *see* significance
architects, involvement in church seating, *see under* Victorian seating
Architectural and Church Building Societies, subcommittee, 213
Ardleigh, Essex, 231
arguments over seating, *see* allocation, pew disputes
Arma Christi, on bench end, 151
Armitage Bridge, 207
Arts and Crafts seats, 304, 307, 379
Ashby St Ledgers, Northants, 78, 128, *8.A17*
Ashcott, Somerset, 87, 98
Ashton, Mersey, 144
Ashton-under-Lyne, Tameside, Greater Manchester, 324
Ashwell, Derbyshire, 289
Ashworth, Edward, 268
Aspley Guise, Beds, 204
assembly notation, *see under* structure of pews
Aston, Margaret, 69
Atherston, Warwicks, 204
attachment to particular pew, *see* appropriation, informal and unofficial
attendance at church (numbers), *see* sittings, utilisation
attitudes to seating today, discussions, 23–4, 298–300, Chapter 28 *passim*, Chapter 30 *passim*
    for heritage values, *see* significance
Audus, James, 258
Aurland, Norway, *4.A1*
Ave Maria, on bench end, 75

487

INDEX

Babington, Somerset, *30.4*
backs of pews
  effect on comfort, *see* pews, comfort
  part of pew structure, *see* structure of pews
Bacon family, 438
Baltonsborough, Somerset, 104, *7.10*
Banks, Robert, 139
baptism, implications for seating, 10
Baptist Union
  advice from, *see* denominational advice
  data on, 43 (Table 2)
Barkby, Leics, 287
Barnes, Ernest, 279, 280
Barry, Charles, 328
Bath, Wife of, 83
Battes, Mrs, 103
beadle, 245; *see also* pew opener
Bealings House, 279
Beaumont family, 76
'beauty of homeliness', *see* church interiors, today, domestication v. transcendence
Bedford Hours, 162
Bedfordshire, style of bench ends in, 128
Beer, Hants, *19.6a*
Beguinage, Ghent, 226
bench ends
  assembly notation, *see under* structure of pews
  carvers, *see* contractors and craftsmen
  carving, non-symbolic, 88, 100–101, 117–18, 125–6, 160–62, 206, Chapter 17 *passim*, 277, 279, 326–7; poppy-heads, 262–3, 264, 265, 268, 277, 278, 279, 284, 287, 297, 307, 372, 414, (risk of stowage of hats on, 261)
  dates on, 76, 115, 118; *see also* date of seating
  iconography on, 74, 75–6, 79, 87–8, 106–107, 151, 156–8, 162, 163, 164, 263, 264, 268, 277
  identifiers and signs
    initials, names, rebuses, coats of arms, 76, 96, 106, 107, 117, 118, 151, 156, 158, 160–62, 165, 280, 295
    numbers and other signage, 46, 107–108, 151, 156, 159, 189, 275, 278, 295, *7.14, 8.4, 19.15*
  reusing as chairs, *see* reuse of old seating
  sliding and hanging seats, *see under* structure of pews
  umbrella holders and other fixtures, 107–109, 117, 219, 230, 236, 274, 295, 374, *8.9, p.238, 17.10, 19.6b*
    opposed, 236

see also books, stowage of; hats, stowage of
Victorian shapes
  categorised, 285–90
  examples, 106–107, 222, Chapter 16 *passim*, Chapter 17 *passim*
  persistence, 285, 290, 304–5, 307, 308, 380
bench assembly and location notation, *see under* structure of pews
Bench-ends in English Churches (J. C. Cox), 69, 70, 72, 284, 287, 294, *6.5, 10.15, 19.2, 19.3*
benches (*see also* pews)
  assembly and location notation, *see under* structure of pews
  movable benches
    medieval, *see* medieval seating, portable
    Victorian, *see under* Victorian seating, flexibility
    today (modern light benches), *see* stackable benches
    today (other), *see under* reordering examples, types of change
  'open' benches
    i.e. no backs, 179, 198, 199, 202; *see also under* poor, seating for
    i.e. open backs, 472
    i.e. without doors, *see* Victorian seating, 'open' benches
  wooden secular, 227, 468–72
Bentley, J. F., 419
Beny, John, 96
Bere, Abbot, 88
Beresford-Hope, Alexander, 296
Betjeman, John, 171, 468
Bettley, James, 303
Bicknoller, Somerset, 93, 97, 105, *7.6, 7.12*
Biggleswade, Beds, *19.4c*
Bilston, 203
Birmingham, St Philip's Cathedral, *p.238* (illustration)
Bishops Lydeard, Somerset, 87, 93, 98, 101, *7.7, 7.12*
Biteford, Devon, *10.3*
Blaby, Leics, 297
Black Book of Swaffham, *see* Swaffham
Blakey, Simon, 144
Blakstad & Munthe-Kaas, *4.8*
Bleazards House, 453
Blessed Virgin Mary
  on bench end, 75, 79
  statuette, 468, *30.11*
Blithe, Henry, 141
Blockley, Glocs, 357
Blomfield, A. W., *19.10d*
Blount, G. R., *19.7b*
Blundeston, Suffolk, 278, *18.3*
Blunham, 128
Bodley, G. F., 211

Bodmin, 78
Bodø Cathedral, Norway, *4.8*
Boethius, 17
Bollington, Cheshire, 382, *26.7*
Bolton, Halliwell Road, St Paul, 295
Bond, William, 138
books, stowage of
  in boxes, 159, 230
  in chairs, 227, *p.238* (illustration)
  in pews, *see* structure of pews, back rail
Boston, Lincs, St Botolph, 4, *1.4*
Bottle & Olley, 277
Bowdon, Greater Manchester, 325, 326
box pews (pews with doors, whether linear or square), *frontis*, 172–9 *passim*, Chapter 12 *passim*, 198, 199, 208, 293–4, 348–9, 425, 441–2, 460–62
  and appropriation, *see* appropriation, pews
  comfort, or not, 221, 234, 350, 453
  creation of
    by panelling-over earlier seating, *frontis*, 220, 221, 259, 278, 442
    by simple addition of doors, 105
    other, 155
  doors and hinges, 105–106, 189, 190
  curtains with, 206, 453–4, *30.5*
  examples by period
    pre Georgian, 115, 116, 155, Chapter 12 *passim*, 268, 440–41, 452–4; contemporary illustration, *30.3*
    long 18th century ('Georgian'), *frontis*, 3, 373, 375, 425–7, 461; contemporary illustrations, *13.1, 30.5*
    19th century, 108, 201, 208, 267, 268, 270, 271–2, 274, 293–4; latest known, 268, 293; contemporary illustrations, *13.2, 13.3*
  interiors jumbled with, 198, 203, 206, 257, 323, 462, *front cover*
  panelling, *see* structure of pews, panels
  survival of, *see under* liturgical assemblages
  Victorians (creation and destruction), *see* Victorian seating, box pews
  see also family pews
boys, seating for, *see* children and their seating
Brabant, Netherlands, *30.11*
Bradfield, Berkshire, 258
Bragernes, Drammen, Norway, *4.5, 4.6*
Brakspear, William Hayward, 323–6
Brandon, David, 211, 442
Bratton Fleming, Devon, 275, *17.11*
Braunton, Devon, 143, 155, 160–69, *10.13–10.25*
Brereton, Sir William, 144

INDEX

Bridgwater, Somerset, 323–7, 328, 331, *21.1–21.4*
Bright, John, 76
Bristol City Council, 427
Bristol
    All Saints, 79
    New Room (Methodist), 425–7, *29.5*
    St Thomas, 380
British people, habits of, Victorian views, 246, 247
Brock, E. P. Loftus, *19.10b*
Brockworth, Glocs, *23.4*
Brompton Ralph, Somerset, *7.11b*
Broomfield, Somerset, 100, 101, 102, 104, 108, *7.15*
Brown, Cynthia, 279
Brown, H., 280
Browne, Hablot Knight, *30.7*
Browning, Edward, *13.5*
Buckley & Co., 307
Bucks Herald, 442, 444
Builder, The, 326, 328–9
Buller, T. W., 270
Bunbury, Cheshire, 144
Burges, William, 377, *26.5*
burial in church, 2, 80, 81, 83
Burroughes, Thomas, 145
Burton, Wiltshire, *6.1*
Butleigh, Somerset, 106, 108
Butterfield, William, 6, 107, 289, 290, 293, 297, 418–22 *passim*, *19.12b*, *30.8*
    article by, 5–6, 231–5
'By piety's due rites...', *13.1*
Byfield, Northants, 128, 130, *8.A16*
BVM, *see* Blessed Virgin Mary

Caféplus, 442
Cambridge Camden Society (founded 1839, renamed Ecclesiological Society 1845)
    general influence, 3–4, 6, 13, Chapter 13, 212, 219, 237, 293, 296, 378, 382
    no agreed view on seating, 239
    anti box pew campaign, Chapter 13 *passim*; *see also* Victorian seating, box pews
    chairs, discussion, Chapter 15, 296
    publications of, 197, 204, 205, 266, 271; *The Ecclesiologist*, 7, 205–6, Chapter 15, 257, 268, 281, 284, 293, 297, 328, 378, 428
    for current Ecclesiological Society, *see* Ecclesiological Society, present
Cambridge
    Little St Mary, 136
    St Mary the Great, 77
Cambridgeshire, bench ends in, 128
camp chair, for cathedrals, 253
candle-prickets on pews, 108

Canterbury Cathedral Chapter House, *24.2b*
Canterbury, St Andrew, 77
capacity
    ability of seating types to provide Victorian views, *see* Victorian seating, capacity
    today, *see under* seating compared
    total numbers catered for, *see* sittings
carpenters' marks, *see* structure of pews, assembly and location notation
carpets, *see under* floors
Carshalton, Surrey, All Saints, 423, *29.4*
Carter, Ann, 103
carvers, *see* contractors and craftsmen
carving machines, *see* machine carving
Cassington, Oxon, 74, *6.3*
cast iron (pews), 206, 287
catalogues, Chapter 20
    role of church furnishing firms, 303–4, 379–80
    seating in catalogues
        reproductions, 307–21, 470; chairs, 306, 307–8
        use of catalogues (or not) for seating, 259, 275, 297–8, 379–80
    other church goods in catalogues, 295, Chapter 20 *passim*, 330, 379
Catcott, Somerset, 103, *7.8*
catechising, in Victorian times, 252
cathedrals, seating for, Victorian suggestion, 247
Cattermole, Peter, 323, 326, 328
Cattistock, 290
Cautley, H. M. (and M. S.), 74, 279–80
CBC (Church Buildings Council, formerly Council for the Care of Churches), 355, 357, 371, 441
CCS, *see* Cambridge Camden Society
Census, Religious, *see* Religious Census
chairs
    compared with other forms of seating, *see* seating compared
    not easily used with appropriation, *see under* appropriation, pews
    mixed with other seating, *see* mixed seating
    use in 19th century, *see under* Victorian seating
    use today
        planned by architect, 20–23
        used in reordering, *see* reordering examples
chancel
    out of scope, vii
    furniture, 115, 264, 279, 428–31
    congregation in
        historic, 49, 80, 134, 136, 175, 204, 206, 207, 243, 254, 257, 271–2, 296
        today, *see* worship, today

Chancellor, Frederic, *19.10c*
changing seating, considerations (for examples, *see* reordering examples): Part 4 (esp. 343–50, 385–94)
    advice, *see* denominational advice
    checklists when considering change
        general and practical, 390–91
        heritage significance, 396–7
        pews 'your values and priorities' questionnaire, 402–3
    steps to take (flowchart), 386
    building, taking account of, 343–50
    capacity, *see under* seating compared
    colour, *see* colour of seating
    comparison of seating types, *see* seating compared
    flexibility, *see under* seating compared
    floors and pew platforms, 353–4, Chapter 25 *passim*, 380–81, 391, 434, 446; *see also* floors
    impression given by seating, 346, 403, 407–8
    pews, keep or remove?, *see under* pews
    process for considering change, 385–94 (flowchart), 386
    relationships, effect of seating on, 37–9, 338–9, 403, 407, 408
    significance (heritage), need to consider, 371, 372, 388, 392–4; *see also* significance
    wider use of church building, Chapter 24
    worship, *see* church interiors, today
Chantrell, R. D., 201, *13.3*
Chapman, John and Catherine, 77
Chapmanslade, 290, 292
Charismatic renewal, 9
Charlton Kings, Glos, 357, *23.2*
Chartres Cathedral, 16
Chatteris, Isle of Ely, 136, 142
Chaucer, Geoffrey, 83
Cheadle, Staffs, St Giles (RC), 428
checklist for seating, *see under* changing seating, considerations
Cheddar, Somerset, 102
Chedzoy, Somerset, 103
Chelmsford, diocese of, seats in churches, 55
Chelsey, Jocosam, 143
Cheltenham, Christ Church, 295
chest, oak, 17th-century, 116
Chester, diocese of
    bishop, 136
    frequency of pew disputes in, 144–5
Chester, St Michael, 136
Chevington, Suffolk, *6.6a*
children and their seating
    historical, *see under* allocation, criteria; Victorian seating, children
    contemporary illustration, *30.3*

489

INDEX

children and their seating (*cont.*)
  in today's church, 168, 298, 353, 424, 435, 446, 448; suitability of pews and benches for, 353, 355, 391, 408, 423, 424, 451, 453
Chislehampton, Oxon, 209
choice of seating (today), *see* seating compared
Cholmondley, Viscount, 145
Christian, Ewan, 211, *19. 8a*
church ales, 182
church bands, 9, 275
Church Builder, *see* ICBS
church buildings
  capacity, *see* capacity
  closure, *see* closure of churches
  interiors, *see* church interiors
  listed (number), 43 (Table 2), 54, 60
  mission chapels, *see* mission chapels and halls
  number at various times
    general, 38 (Graphs 1, 4), 40
    Anglican, Chapter 5 *passim* (esp. 38 (Graph 4), 40, 41–44 (incl. Graphs 5–6), 56 (Graph 23), 58–9 (incl. Table 7), 199–200, 250–51
    Nonconformist, 37, 40, 41 (Table 1), 56 (Graph 23), 57–60 (incl. Table 7)
    Roman Catholic, 39, 40, 41 (Table 1), 56 (Graphs 23 & 24), 58 (incl. Table 7), 60
  for number of seats, *see* sittings
  restorations (number), 43–4
  size *see* sittings, number per church
Church Buildings Council, *see* CBC
Church Commissioners, *see* Commissioners' Churches
church furnishing firms, *see* catalogues
church interiors
  historic (general)
    coherent (incl. sets of seating), *see* liturgical assemblages
    unplanned, *see* box pews, interiors jumbled with
  historic (by period)
    different periods, vignettes, 457–68
    medieval, *see* medieval seating
    post-Reformation, *see* post-Reformation seating
    Victorian, *see* Victorian seating
  today
    attitudes, *see* attitudes to seating
    possible requirements discussed, Chapter 2, Chapter 3, 19–21, Chapter 22, Chapter 23, Chapter 24; *see also* worship, today
    domestication v. transcendence, 11–12, 402, 406
    for changes to seating, *see* changing seating, considerations
church rates, *see* funding of seating
church running costs
  general pre-Reformation, 172–4, 182
  paying for seating, *see* funding of seating
Church Times, *30.17*
churches, *see* church buildings; church interiors
Churches Conservation Trust, 255, 281, 378, 381
Churches of Cambridgeshire, 205
churchwardens
  accounts, 74, 77, 79–81, 160, 167
  encouraged to be agents in Victorian changes, *see A Few Words . . .*
  presentments, 171, 172; *see also* allocation, pew disputes
  role in allocating seating, *see under* allocation
cill (of pews), *see* sill
cinemas, number of seats in, 55
Cirencester, Glocs, St John the Baptist, 261, *16.2*
City of London, *see* London
Clapton-in-Gordano, Somerset, 74, 287, *19.3*
Clarke, Joseph, articles by, 220–26
Clarke, Kate, *see Informed Conservation*
class (social), *see* allocation, criteria
Clayton & Bell, 303
cleaning, *see under* floors
Clevedon, Somerset, 87, 100, 108, 109
Clipsham, Rutland, 296, 300, *19.16*
Clodock, Herefordshire, *30.6*
closure of churches
  number, *see* church buildings, number
  examples, *see* Churches Conservation Trust
  heritage considerations, 371–2, 381–3
Clovelly, Devon, 150
CNC, *see* Computer Numerical Control
coats of arms on bench ends, *see* bench ends, identifiers and signs
coats, storage of, *see* bench ends, umbrella holders
Cocke, Thomas, 77
Colne, Lancs, 137, 144
colour of seating, 30, 353, 363, 447
comfort of seating, *see* seating compared
Commissioners' churches, 200–202, 324, 378
  sittings, number and type funded by, 47, 48 (Graph 11), 49–51
  size of churches, 47, 48 (Graph 9), 51, 201
Common Worship, 10
communion tables (altars) and rails
  historic, 9, 13, 70, 174, 175, 199, 257, 298, 345, 372, 419–22 *passim*, 450, 457–9
  current considerations, 9, 14–17, 20, 26, 158, 335, 337, 343, 363, 428, 440, 441, 448, 450; *see also* changing seating, considerations; foci of seating; worship, today
companions, unpleasant, *see* vermin
comparison of seating types, *see* seating compared
complete furnishing or seating schemes, *see* liturgical assemblages
Computer Numerical Control, 362, 363
Congerstone, Leics, 287
congregational sizes
  attendance, *see* sittings, utilisation
  catering for different, *see* size of congregation, catering for
Connop, Revd J., 258
consecrations, rate of (historic), 38 (Graph 3), 43
Conservation Principles, 2, 371
contemporary seating needs discussed, *see* church interiors, today
continental comparisons (Victorian)
  churches, 237, 242, 244, 245, 246, 248, 250, 253
  habits of the continentals, 247
contractors and craftsmen
  pre-19th-century (individual), *see*: Beny, John; Glosse; Grundy, Francis; Taylor, Edward; Werman, Simon; for 'I. B.', 106
  19th-century
    role, *see* Victorian seating, craftsmen
    individual, *see*: Bottle & Olley; Clayton & Bell; Earp, Thomas; Farmer & Brindley; Farrow, Thomas; Godbold, Robert; Halliday, William; Rattee & Kent; Ringham, Henry; Ruddle & Thompson; Skidmore, Francis
  20th-century (individual), *see* Barnes, Ernest; Gibson, Dan; Thompson, 'Mouseman'
Coombey, Wendy, 413
Copperfield, David, *30.7*
Cosin, John, 440–41
Cothelstone, Somerset, 97
Cottenham, Cambs, 139
Council for the Care of Churches, *see* CBC
Country Life, 436
court room, 405
Coventry Cathedral, 339, 361
Cox & Son(s), and Cox, Son, Buckley, & Co., 305, 307, 330, 379, *20.1*, *20.2*, *20.3*; for general discussion, *see* catalogues
Cox, J. C. *see Bench-Ends in English Churches*
craftsmen, *see* contractors & craftsmen

INDEX

'cramming' of seating in 19th century, *see* Victorian seating, cramming
Crewe, Cheshire, *22.1*
Crickmay & Son, *19.6a, 19.9a*
Croasdale, Lancashire, 453
Crockham Hill, Kent, *19.4a*
Crossley, F., *see* English Church Woodwork
Crowcombe, Somerset, 106, *7.16*
crowned 'M' on bench end, 75, 163
Croxton Kerrial, Leics, 263, *16.7*
Cullompton, Devon, 268
cultural associations of seating, 23–4, Chapter 28 *passim*, Chapter 30 *passim*
current seating needs discussed, *see* church interiors, today
Curry Rivel, Somerset, 109
curtains in pews, *see under* box pews
cushions
   historic use, 197, 252, 254, 474, *30.4*
   today with new seating, 424
   use of with old pews, *see* pews, comfort, improving

DACs, 159, 351, 354, 362; *see also* Gloucester DAC
Daily Telegraph, 408
Dartmouth, 75
date of seating
   dates on seats, *see under* bench ends
   dendrochronological (tree ring) dating, 74, 164, 167, *19.2*; need for more, 74, 84
   by period (assessing and discussing)
      medieval and distinguishing from Victorian, *see under* medieval seating
      post-medieval, 162–5
      19th century, *see under* Victorian seating
David Copperfield, 462, *30.7*
Dawes, Perigan and Josse, 103
deafness, *see* hearing difficulties
deal (type of wood), *see* wood
Dean, A. R., catalogue, *30.14*
Deane, Lancs, 117–19, *8.6, 8.7*
Debenham, Suffolk, 263, *16.6*
decorative panelling used on pews, 115–17
dendrochronological dating
   for seats, *see under* date of seating
   roof and spire, 160
Dennington, Suffolk, 277
denominational advice, 385, 387, 394, 395
Derby, diocese of, *see* Derbyshire
Derbyshire, church seats etc, 45, 51–7 *passim* (incl. Graphs 15–22)
Dickson and Brakspear, 324
Dillow, Kevin, 132, 136, 141
Dilton Marsh, Wilts, 281, 287, 295, 300, *19.1*

Diocesan Advisory Committees, *see* DACs
direction of seating, *see* foci of seating
disabilities, providing for those with, 407, 413, 440–1, 445, 453, 478; *see also* elderly, seating for
Discoed, Powys, 413
discomfort (of seating) a moral good (or not), *see under* seating compared, comfort
disputes over seating
   17-century *see under* allocation
   Victorian, *see* Victorian seating, reordering, contested
domestication, *see under* church interiors, today
doors on pews, *see* box pews
Dorchester Abbey, Oxon, 265, *16.9, 16.11*
dragons on bench ends, 156–8
draughts, *see* keeping warm
Drury, Edmund, *19.6b*
Dunsfold, Surrey, 74, *6.4*
Dunsford, deanery of, 284
Durandus of Mende, 79
Dymond, David, 142

Earp, Thomas, 303
East Anglia, bench design in, 75, 81, 126, 128, 277, 285
East Quantoxhead, 104, 107
Eastchester, New York State, USA, 457, *30.1*
Ecclesiastical and Architectural Topography of Britain, 442
Ecclesiastical Exemption, discussed, 427
Ecclesiological Society
   original (founded 1839 as Cambridge Camden Society, renamed 1845, defunct by 1870s), *see* Cambridge Camden Society
   present (founded 1879 as St Paul's Ecclesiological Society, publishers of this book), vii, 13; *Ecclesiology Today* (journal), 341
Ecclesiologist, The, *see* Cambridge Camden Society
Ecclesiology Today, 341
EDAS, *see* Exeter Diocesan Architectural Society
Edmondthorpe, Leics, 293
Edwards, Clive, 330
eighteenth-century seating, *see* box pews
elderly, seating for
   historic separation of elderly, *see* allocation, criteria
   Victorian discussion, *see under* Victorian seating
   today, *see* seating compared
Elmsted, 77
Eltoft family pew (Edmund Eltoft), 115, *8.4*

Ely, St Mary, 135, 136
emptiness of churches, *see* sittings, utilisation
England, population, *see* population
Englesen, Gurly, 35
English Church Woodwork, 69, 111, *8.A11*
English Heritage, viii, ix, 1, 2, 282, 300, 355, 371, 415, 421, 427
EnviroAbility, 412–13 *passim*
evidential value of seating, *see* significance; for archaeology of seating, *see* archaeology
Exeter, archdeaconry of, 284
Exeter, bishop of, 268
Exeter Diocesan Architectural Society, 268
Exeter, St Thomas, 268, *19.15*
Exwick, 268
Eynsham, Oxon, 213, *14.4*

family pews, 115, 201, 204, 206, 452–4, 474, *30.5*
   galleried pews, 184, 257, 258
   see also appropriation; box pews
Farmer & Brindley, 265
Farrow, Thomas, 279
Fauntleroy, William, 171–2
Ferneley family pew, *30.5*
Ferrey, Benjamin, 211, 279, 445, *13.6*
Fet, Norway, *4.9*
Flamstead, Herts, 2, *1.1*
flap seats, *see* structure of pews, sliding and hanging seats
Flaxley, Glocs, *23.1*
fleur-de-lis, on bench ends, 125
flexibility
   of liturgists, 27
   of seating
      Victorian views on, *see* Victorian seating, flexibility
      today, *see under* seating compared
floors (including pew floors), 353–4, Chapter 25, 391
   archaeology
      methods and results, 193, 367–8, 381
      preserving evidence, *see* floors, significance
   burial under, *see* burial in church
   carpets, 368
   cleaning, 234, 236, 342, 391
   considerations if changing seating, 354, 368–9, 392, 434; checklist, 391
   importance of visually, 229, 341–2
   material and construction issues today, 354, Chapter 25, 434
   platforms (for pews), 290–92, Chapter 25; Victorian discussions, 226, 229, 236
   post-Reformation, 193

INDEX

floors (including pew floors) (cont.)
  significance (heritage), 300, 380, 391, 397
  Victorian
    nature, 290–93, 300
    Victorian discussions, 226, 229
  warmth of, 229, 368, 446
foci of seating (direction facing)
  medieval, 70, 71, 79, 459
  post-Reformation, 171, 192, 221, 457, 459, 461
  19th-century arrangements, *see under* Victorian seating
  today (incl. implications), 4–5, 9, 15, 156, 339, 407, 461; *see also* church interiors, today
Folke, Dorset, 171–2, 182
Folkestone, Kent, 294, *19.8a*
font covers, 174, 277
football league, number of seats in stadia, 55
Force, Charles, 268
Ford End, Essex, *19.10c*
Ford, Dr, *30.5*
foreigners, nature of *see* continental comparisons (Victorian)
forms (backless benches), *see* benches, open
Foster family, 141, 142
Foster, Richard, 231, 234–5
Franklyn family, *19.15*
free seating, *see under* appropriation
French, K. L., 69, 79, 82
Fressingfield, Suffolk, 112, 277, 278, *18.1*
fullness of churches, *see* sittings, utilisation
funding of seating (initial)
  medieval, *see under* medieval seating
  post-Reformation, 174–9
  Victorian seating, *see* Victorian seating, financing and cost
  for ongoing costs, *see* appropriation, basis, rent
furnishing schemes, *see* liturgical assemblages
Fussell, Revd L. W., 414
fustian, 189
Fyllingsdalen, Bergen, Norway, *4.3, 4.4*

Gager, judge of Consistory Court, 140, 141
galleries
  children's, 203, 258, 296
  galleried pews, *see* family pews
  contemporary illustrations, *13.1, 13.3, 30.7, 30.8*
  implications for use of building today, 345, 382, 425
    using space under, 27, 184
    significance (heritage), 382, 396, 397

insertion
  pre-19th-century, 173, 175, 179, *11.5, 11.6, 11.9*
  19th-century, 201–2, 208, 258, 268, 272, 274, 275; in principle, 219
removal, 49, 208–9
  contested, 258
  examples, 184, 257, 258, 277, 281, 440
  Victorian dislike expressed, 199, 205
Garrratt, John, 268
Garway, Herefordshire, *19.2*
Gatwick Airport, 377, 378
General Synod, *30.10*
Gentleman's Magazine, 204
Georgian box pews, *see* box pews
Germany, North, 23
Gibson, Dan, 379
Giles, Richard, 1
Gill, Robin, 40, 59
Girrie, Mr, 136
Glastonbury Abbey, Somerset, 88
Gleadall, Jeremy and family, 137, 142
Glosse, 101
Gloucester, All Saints, 357
Gloucester DAC, Chapter 23
Glynne, Sir Stephen, 192
Godbold, Robert, 277
Godmersham, Kent, 77
Godolphin & Latymer School, 419, 422
Goffman, Erving, 143
Goldington, Beds, *19.4b*
Goodwin, Francis, 203
Gough, Richard, 134
Graeme, Yarbugh, 294
grants, Victorian, *see* Victorian seating, financing and cost
Granwood composite blocks, 368
Great Bealings, Suffolk, 278–9, *18.4*
Great Chalfield, Wilts, 213, *14.4*
Great Haseley, Oxon, 213, *14.3*
Great Milton, Oxon, 259, 264–5, *16.1, 16.10, 16.11*
Great Tew, Oxon, 117, 128, *8.A12*
Greater London, *see* London
Gregory, Ann, 171
Grigg, John, *1.1*
Grocers' Company, 258
Grundy, Francis, 452
Guilden Morden, Cambs, 128
Guilden Sutton, Cheshire, 134, 135, 136, 145
Gunton, William and relations, 137, 139–40, 141, 142, 143

Habershon & Pitt, *19.4c*
Habershon, Edward, *19.10b*
Haddenham, Bucks, 113–14, 117, 120–30, 442–5, *8.1a, 8.1b, 8.A1–8A10, 30.12*
Halliday, William, 88, 100, 106, *7.4*

halls & rooms, Victorian worship in, 40
Haltham, Lincolnshire, *6.2a*
Hamerton chapel, 452
Hammer, Geo. M., catalogue, 290, 308, 468, *20.14a, b, c*; for general discussion, *see* catalogues
Hampton Poyle, Oxon, 128
hanging seats, *see* structure of pews
Hardiman, Alan, 415
Harper, Revd J., 258
Harrap Hall, 453
Harrison, Hugh, 165
Hartland, Devon
  church and seating, 143–59, 160, 169, *10.1–10.10, 10.12*
  Abbey, 151, 169
Haslingfield, Cambs, 205
hassocks
  Victorian discussions, *see* Victorian seating, kneeling
  use today, 465
  see also kneeling
Hastings, Henry, *see* Puddletown and Waterson, Lords of
Hatch Beauchamp, Somerset, 101
hats, stowage of, 108–09, 156, 178, 219, 230, 234, 236; poppy-heads not for use for, 261
Haughton-le-Skerne, Darlington, County Durham, 440–41, *29.11*
Hayward, John, 4, Chapter 17
Headington, Oxon, 213, *14.2*
Heales, Alfred, 69
hearing difficulties, 225, 407
Hearth Tax, 178
heating
  deleterious effect, 29
  keeping warm, *see* keeping warm
Helen, aka the Pew Fairy, *30.17*
Hellidon, Northants, 297
Heptonstall, West Yorks, 345
Hereford, diocese of, 413
Herefordshire Council, 413
heritage significance of seating, *see* significance; *see also* floors, significance
Hermitage, Dorset, *19.9a*
Heytesbury, Wilts, 290
  deanery of, seats in, Chapter 19 *passim* (esp. 282)
Hibbert, Jo, 433
hierarchy in seating, *see* allocation, criteria, social status
High Commission, 136
Higham, Thomas, 139, 141
Historic Churches Preservation Trust, *see* National Churches Trust
Historic Environment Record, 393
historical value of seating, *see* significance
History and Law of Church Seats, 69
History of Pues/Pews, 3, 69
Hjertholm, *4.3, 4.4*

492

Hobbs, Steve, 150, 169, *10.3*
Hogarth, William, *30.7*
holiness, beauty of, *see* church interiors, today
Holnest, 283
homeliness, beauty of, of *see* church interiors, today
Horsford, James, *19.4b*
Hoskins, Mr, 235
Houses of Parliament, 328–9
Howard, Frank, *see English Church Woodwork*
Howell, C. H., *19.14*
Hughes, Luke (furniture), *24.2, 24.4b*
Hughes, P., 167
Humbert, Albert Jenkins, *19.12a*
Hunslet, 203
Husband's Bosworth, Leics, 293
Husday, Susan, 171, 172, 180
hymn books, *see* books, stowage of

ICBS, 43–4, 200, 202–3, 211–14, 296, 324
  advice on seating from *Church Builder*, Chapter 14 *passim*
  aisle (i.e. alley) required by, 219, 220, 224, 227
  and box pews, 219, 220, 221, 224, 227; *see also* Victorian seating, box pews
  and chairs, 213, 225–7, 235, 296; *see also under* Victorian seating
  committee of architects, 211, 220, 226, 231, 235
  data, 42 (Graphs 5, 6, 8), 46, 48 (Graph 11), 49
  grants, 43–4, 46, 49, 211, 212–13, 379; *see also* Victorian seating, financing and cost; for the resulting cramming, *see* Victorian seating, cramming
  medieval exemplars, promotion of, *see under* Victorian seating
  model pews at ICBS offices, 219, 220, 231
  rules and 'Suggestions', 212–13, 219–20, 221, 222, 224, 235
iconoclasm (possible example), 162
iconography
  as aid to dating, *see* date of seating, by period
  on bench ends, *see under* bench ends
identifiers (e.g. names, numbers) on bench ends, *see under* bench ends
IHS on bench end, 163
Ilfracombe, Devon, 275, *17.9, 17.10*
Illustrated London News, *30.8*
impression given by seating
  Victorian views, *see under* Victorian seating
  today, *see under* changing seating, considerations

Incorporated Church Building Society, *see* ICBS
Informed Conservation, 2
initials on bench ends, *see under* bench ends, identifiers
Innvik, Norway, *4.A2*
interior of churches, *see* church interiors
international developments in seating, 20
International Exhibition, 330
Introduction to the Sacrament, 459, *30.3*
Irving, William, *see* machine carving
Isle of Man, 293
Iver, Bucks, 261, *16.5*

Jacques, John, *23.4*
James, Revd T. G., 323, 325
Jensen & Skodvin, 20, *4.1, 4.2*
Jersey, 274
Jeune, Revd Francis, 274
Jones & Willis, 304–306, 307, 308, 379
  catalogues and drawings, *20.4–20.13*; for general discussion, *see* catalogues
Jordan, Thomas, *see* machine carving
Jordayne, Hester, 171, 172, 180

keeping warm, 29, 347, 359, 390, 392, 438, 446, 465
  introduction of box pews, 460
  see also curtains; floor, warmth of
Kelly's Post Office Directory, 303
Kent, church building in, 57
Kettle, Margaret, 144
Kildwick, West Yorks, 114–17, *8.2, 8.3, 8.4*
Kilkhampton, Cornwall, 162, 264, *16.8*
King, Gregory, 176
Kingsnorth, Kent, *24.1*
Kingston, Dorset, 6, *1.5*
Kirk Arbory, Isle of Man, 293
Kirk Rushen, Isle of Man, 293
Kirkstall, Leeds, West Yorks, 201, 203, 207, *13.3*
Kirtlington, Oxon, 445–9, *29.13*
kitchen in a pew, *see* reordering examples
kneeling
  medieval period, 70, 78
  19th century, *see under* Victorian seating
  issues today, 335, 337, 340, 342, 391, 408, 424, 447, 465
Kulmach, Hans Suess, 459, *30.2*
Kyrbye, Edward, 135, 143

labyrinth, 16–17
Lamb, E. B., 450
Lambert, Revd David, 420–21
Lancashire, South, 295
Landbeach, Cambs, 128, 130, *8.A13*
Laneast, Cornwall, *6.7b*
Langman, John and Agnes, 77

Larkin, Philip, 405
Laud, William and Laudian changes, 146, 461
Launcells, Cornwall, 143, 162, *6.6b*
Laxfield, Suffolk, 278, *18.2*
Laxton's School, 258
Leamington, All Saints, 203
Leca aggregate, 369
lectern, 277
Leeds, West Yorks
  parish church, 206
  St John, 116, 452, *8.5*
Leicester Castle, *28.1*
Leicestershire and Rutland, bench ends in, Chapter 19 *passim* (esp. 282)
Leweston, 172
lily and chalice, on bench end, 75
Lincolnshire Society for Encouragement of Ecclesiastical Architecture, 328
listed churches, number *see under* church buildings
Little Cawthorpe, Lincs, 377–8, *26.6*
Little Ice Age, 460
Littleport, Isle of Ely, 135, 142
liturgical assemblages
  furnishing schemes (more than seats)
    medieval examples, 109, 125, 167, 442, 452
    post-medieval examples, 3, 151–9 *passim*, 171–182 *passim*, 184, 425–7, 440–41
    end of 18th & 19th century, 277, 377–8, 418–22, 436–7
  importance, *see under* significance
  seating schemes, number surviving
    pre-Victorian, 4, 282–3, 375–6
    Victorian, 208, 296–7, 298, 376, 377
Liturgical Movement, 343
liturgical requirements, *see* church interiors, today
liturgical texts, revised, 9–10, 19–20
liturgy on bench end, 75
Liverpool, 295; Roman Catholic Cathedral, 339
location notation, *see* structure of pews, assembly and location notation
locking churches (Victorian), *see* beadle
London Diocesan Society, 296
London, including Westminster and the City of London, and Greater London
  Addiscombe, St Mary Magdalene, 450–51, *29.14*
  Beddington, Sutton, St Mary, *19.5a & b*
  Benhilton, Sutton, All Saints, *19.8b*
  Bermondsey, Southwark, Christ Church, 203
  Blackheath, Greenwich, St Michael & All Angels, *19.6b*
  Bloomsbury, St George, *24.3a & b*

INDEX

London (cont.)
    Camberwell, St Giles, 328, 331, *21.5*
    Cheam, Sutton, St Dunstan, *19.10a*
    City of London
        St Bride, Fleet Street, *13.2*
        St Dunstan in the West, Fleet Street, *13.4*
        St Martin Outwich, Bishopsgate Street, 81
        St Mary Magdalen, Old Fish Street, 231
    Fulham, Our Lady & St Thomas of Canterbury (RC), 428–31, *29.6*
    Hammersmith
        Glenthorne Road, St John, 418–22 *passim*, *29.3*
        Holy Innocents, 420
    Harmondsworth, Hillingdon, St Mary, 262, *16.4*
    Hillingdon, 261
    Kensington, Brompton Oratory, 338, 341
    Marylebone, Margaret Street, All Saints, 6, 296
    Pimlico, St Barnabas, 330, 331
    Stoke Newington, St Matthias, 418–22 *passim*, *29.3*
    Streatham, 330, 331
    Tottenham, All Hallows, 231
    Wallington, Sutton, Holy Trinity, *19.10b*
    West Drayton, Hillingdon, St Martin, 261, *16.4*
    Westminster
        St Margaret, 79
        St Martin in the Fields, 81
        St Stephen, Rochester Row, *13.6*
loo in a pew, *see* reordering examples
Lopham, Norfolk, 76
Lowfield Heath, Surrey, 377, 378, *26.5*
Lydeard St Lawrence, Somerset, 105
Lyme Regis, 171

'M', crowned, on bench end, 75, 163
machine carving, 198, 259, 307, Chapter 21
Madeleine, Paris, 245
Maguire, Robert and Keith Murray and related architectural firms, 342, *22.1, 22.2, 22.6*
Maiden Bradley, Wilts, 283
Manchester
    diocese of, 55
    Greater Manchester, *see* Bowdon
Mann, Horace, 250
Mannerist style, 186
Marrable, Frederick, *19.13*
Martin, John, 145
Mary (Mother of Jesus) *see* Blessed Virgin Mary
Massie, James, 144
materials for seating, *see* wood

maze, *see* labyrinth
Meacock, John, 145
medieval seating (for some topics not listed here *see under* pews)
    archaeology, *see* archaeology
    appropriation of seats (through rental, etc.), *see* allocation, medieval
    date of (assessing)
        methods and results, 74–6, Chapter 7 *passim*, 123, 259, 261
        possible confusion with Victorian work, 88, 99–101, 259–61, 277; *see also* Victorian seating, medieval exemplars, copying
        for dates on bench ends, *see under* bench ends; for date of introduction, *see* medieval seating, introduction
    examples discussed, Chapter 7, Chapter 8 (esp. 113–14, 120–30), 277
    funding and installation, 74–5, 76–8
    historiography, 69–70
    identifying, *see* medieval seating, date of
    introduction
        date of, Chapter 6 *passim* (esp. 74–6)
        causes, Chapter 6 *passim* (esp. 82–4)
    part of church structure (possibly) (e.g. pillars, walls), 70–72
    portable, 72–4, 78, *30.2*
    reuse in later periods, *see* reuse of old seating
    standing, *see* standing in church
    structure, *see* structure of pews
    style (incl. regional variants), 75–6, 126–30
    as Victorian exemplars, *see* Victorian seating, medieval exemplars
Medley, Revd John, 268, *19.15*
Melton Mowbray, Leics, *30.5*
men, segregated, *see under* allocation, criteria
Methodist Church, 43 (Table 2), 398, 425–7 *passim*; advice from, *see* denominational advice
Meyer, Richard, 20
Micklethwaite, J. T., article by, 235–6
Middleton & Son, 184, 191
Middlezoy, Somerset, 87, 93, 95, 96, 98, 100, 104, 106, *7.1, 7.7, 7.11a*
Midlands, bench ends in, 126–30, *8.A11*
Mildenhall, Suffolk, 279, *18.5*
Milton Abbey, Dorset, 433
Minster Lovell, Oxon, 128, *8.A15*
mission chapels and halls, 44, 53
    nonconformist, 44
    number and sittings provided, 42 (Graph 6), 44, 48 (Graphs 10 & 12), 53

seating types, 227–8, 232, 468, 471–2, *30.13, 30.15*
mixed seating (different types in one church)
    adaptive through time, *see* box pews, interiors jumbled with Victorian, *see under* Victorian seating
    today, discussed, 361; for examples, *see* reordering examples
model pews, *see under* ICBS
monks on bench ends, 75
Monksilver, Somerset, 102, 106, 108
Monnington on Wye, Herefordshire, *30.16*
Moor, Edward, 279
Mortensrud, Oslo, 20, *4.1, 4.2*
Mortlake, Richmond-on-Thames, London, *19.7b*
Morwenstow, Cornwall, 75, 158, *6.7a, 10.11*
mouldings, medieval, *see* medieval seating, date of (assessing)
movable seating
    benches, *see under* benches
    Victorian, *see* Victorian seating, flexibility
    today, *see under* seating compared, flexibility
movement in worship, *see* worship, today
Mullion, Cornwall, 75
Munby, Julian, 444
Murray, Keith, *see under* Maguire, Robert
music hall, *see* benches, wooden secular
music stool, twirled for praying, 253
Myddle, Shropshire, 134

names on bench ends, *see* bench ends, identifiers
Nantwich, Cheshire, 145
National Churches Trust, 55, 468, *30.9*
National Monuments Record, 382, *see also* English Heritage
nave altars, *see* communion tables and rails
Neale, J. M., 2, 69, 205
Neicho, Martin, 412
New Brunswick, bishop of, 268
New Room, Bristol (Methodist), 425–7, *29.5*
Newark, Notts, St Mary Magdalene, 263, *16.6*
Newent, Glocs, Chapter 12, *12.1–12.19*
nineteenth-century seating, *see* Victorian seating
Nonconformity
    out of scope of this book, ix
    data, 37, 38 (Graph 1), 40, 41 (Table 1), 43 (incl. Table 2), 50 (Graph 13), 55, 56 (Graph 23), 57–60 (incl. Table 7)

Nonconformity (cont.)
  mission chapels, see mission chapels
  concern in Church of England, 200
  seating, 5, 37, 39, 45, 55, 57–60
    case study, 425–7
  see also Baptist church; Methodist church
Norfolk, see East Anglia, 126
Norgrenn, *4.5, 4.6*
North Aston, Oxon, 130
North Cadbury, Somerset, 76
North Kilworth, Leics, 296
Northamptonshire, bench ends in, 128
Northlew, Devon, 166
Norwegian churches, Chapter 4
  worship and liturgical development, 19–20, 23–24
Nottingham, St Andrew, 295
number
  of churches, see under church buildings
  of pews and people accommodated, see capacity
numbers on pew ends, see bench ends, identifiers

oak, for seating, see wood
Oakes, Thomas, 453
Oakham, Rutland, 263, 287, 297, *16.6, 19.5c*
Oates, William, 139
Oatley, Sir George, 425–7 passim
Oborne, Dorset, *19.9b*
occupancy of seats, see sittings, utilisation
Old Headington, Oxon, 345
old seating, use of, see reuse of old seating
open benches, see under benches
order in church, maintaining, 83, Chapter 9 passim
organic arrangements of seating
  Victorian discussions, see under Victorian seating, chairs
  today (discussion), 338–9
Osborne House, Isle of Wight, *19.12a*
Oslo, 20
Othery, Somerset, 87–91, 93, 106, *7.2, 7.3, 7.4*
Ottery St Mary, Devon, 98, 101, 107
Oundle, Northants, 258
Our Lady of Pity, see Blessed Virgin Mary
Over, Cambs, *6.1*
over-filling churches with seating, see Victorian seating, cramming
ownership of seating, see appropriation
Oxford Architectural Society (Oxford Society for Promoting the Study of Gothic Architecture), 328
Oxford
  city
    St Michael, 75, 77
    St Peter, 328, 331
  University
    St Edmund's Hall, 328
    Sheldonian Theatre, 183
Oxfordshire, style of bench ends in, 126

Pace, George, 450
painting pews, see colour of seating
Palace of Westminster, 328–9
Palmer, Thomas, 107, *7.14*
papier mâché (pews), 206
Parentalia, 335
Paris, the Madeleine, 245
Parish Communion movement, 9
Passion, Instruments of, on benches, 75, 163, 277
patina and surfaces, see date of seating
paying for seating, see funding of seating
Pearson, J. L., 211, 297
pegs, for hats, see hats, stowage
Pelican on bench end, 88
persistence of Victorian seat design, see under bench ends, Victorian shapes
Personal and Professional Recollections (G. G. Scott), 294
Perth, 246
Peterborough, bishop of, 274
Peterborough, unspecified church, 81
Peterchurch, Herefordshire, 413
Peterstow, Herefordshire, 413
Pevsner, Nikolaus, 87, 150, 162, 277, 326, 414, 418, 436, 442, *19.2, 30.16*
pew disputes, see under allocation
pew ends, see bench ends
Pew Fairy, 475, *30.17*
pew opener, 243, 256; see also beadle
'pew', use of word, x, 235
pews: many topics not listed here will be found under separate headings; in addition, see also box pews; medieval seating; Victorian seating, pews
  adaptation from earlier form, see reuse of old seating
  advantages and disadvantages, see pews, keep or remove?
  attachment to particular pew, see appropriation, informal
  comfort
    an issue, 5, 23, 30, 96, 229, 347, 350, 351, 414, 433, 444, 445, 446, 453, *11.8, 23.4, 30.2*
    not an issue, 421, 428, 437, 438, 451
  improving (including use of cushions), 23, 30–36, 96, 149, 389, 391, 413–18, 437, 438, 444, 473
  comfort a Victorian design factor, see under Victorian seating, pews
  compared to other seating, see seating compared
  construction, see structure of pews
  cramming, see Victorian seating, cramming
  disputes, see allocation
  family and galleried pews, see family pews
  keep or remove?, 347–50, Chapter 23, Chapter 24, 390–91, Chapter 28, 474–5; see also seating compared
  medieval, see medieval seating; for medieval pews as exemplars, see under Victorian seating
  modern, see under reordering examples
  number, see sittings
  private, see appropriation; see also family pews
  recycling, 412–13
  removal (and other reordering)
    case for and against, see pews, keep or remove?
    examples, see reordering examples
    general reordering considerations, see changing seating, considerations
    rate of removal, see under sittings, post-19-century changes
  shortening, see reordering examples
  values attached to, 23–4, Chapter 28
  Victorian approaches to seating etc, see Victorian seating
Phillpots, Henry, 268
Philpot, William, 77
Phipson, R. M., 279
'Phiz', *30.7*
pilasters, 183, 193
pilgrimage, see worship, today
pillars, seat-ledges at base, see medieval seating, part of church structure
pitch pine, see wood
plans (spatial diagrams)
  to allocate post-Reformation seating, see under allocation
  to aid Victorian re-ordering, 201, 211, 221, 271–2, 298, 324, 325, 326
plaster, wall, 193
platforms (for seating,) see floors, platforms
plinths for pews, see floors, platforms
Plowenan, Agnes, 171, 172, 180
Plymtree, deanery of, 284
Polish community in London, 338
Pontefract, West Yorks, All Saints, 204
poor (those with little money)
  attendance at church, 180, 248, 251, 252, 254, 255, 295; see also mission chapels
  seating for
    pre 19th century, see under allocation, criteria

poor, seating for (*cont.*)
    19th century, *see* appropriation, free seats
poppy-heads, *see* bench ends, carving
population of England (part or all), 37, 39, 58 (Table 7)
post-Reformation seating, Chapters 8–12, 440–1, 452–4
    box pews, *see* box pews
    date, *see* date of seating
    funding, *see* funding of seating
    pew plans and pew disputes, *see under* allocation
    for other topics, *see under* pews
posture when sitting, 228–30 *passim*
Pownall, Frederick, *19.10a*
Pratt, Samuel, *see* machine carving
Prayer Book (and its revisions), 9–10, 246
preaching (medieval), 82, 83
preaching box, as spatial stereotype, 345
pre-Reformation seating, *see* medieval seating
present seating needs discussed, *see under* church interiors today
Present State of Ecclesiastical Architecture (A. W. N. Pugin), 428
Prestbury, Cheshire, 135
principles of arrangement of interiors, *see* church interiors
private pews, *see* appropriation; *see also* family pews
procession in worship
    on medieval bench end, 75
    today, *see* worship, today
projectors, 11
Protestantism (extreme) and seating, 238, 245, 246, 374–5
provision of seating, *see* allocation
Prust, Hugh, 151
Puddletown and Waterson, Lords of, 178
Puddletown, Dorset, Chapter 11, 136, 150, *11.1–11.9*
pues (archaic spelling of 'pews'), *see* pews
Pugin, A. W. N., 428–31 *passim*
pulpits, *see* liturgical assemblages
Punch, *30.9*
punches, use of, 100–101

Quantock group of bench ends, 100
Quiney, Anthony, 297

Råholt, Norway, *4.A3*
Rake's Progress, *30.7*
rank, seating by, *see* allocation, criteria
rates, *see* funding of seating
Rattee and Kett (and Caroline Rattee), 265
Reade, John, 144
reading desk, *see* liturgical assemblages
Reading, St Lawrence, 79
recycling of pews, 412–13

Redgrave, Suffolk (Churches Conservation Trust), 438–9, *29.10*
Redmarley, Glocs, *23.3*
redundancy of churches, *see* closure of churches
reframing of old seating by Victorians, *see* Victorian seating, reuse
relationships, effect of seating, *see under* changing seating, considerations
Religious Census of 1851, Chapter 5 *passim* (esp. 40, 41, 44, 58, 60), 250
removal of pews, *see under* pews
rental of seats, *see under* appropriation, basis
reordering examples (modern) (for principles of reordering, *see* changing seating, considerations): 15–17, 158–9, 347–9, Chapter 29
    purpose
        for wider use of building, 15–17, 413, 419, 425–7, 436–7, 438–9, 442–5, 445–9
        for worship or post-worship fellowship, 15–17, 347–9, 418–22, 423–4, 428–31, 432, 433–5, 440–1, 442–5, 445–9
    type of change
        full pew removal, replace with chairs, 15–16, 17, 348–50, 413, 445–9
        full pew removal, replace with fixed or movable benches, 279–80, 357, 428–31, 433–5
        full pew removal, replace with mix of seating, 435, 445–9
        partial pew removal, 27, 113–14, 117–19, 158–9, 184, 425–7, 440–1, 442–5
        keeping or adapting existing pews (incl. making pews movable), 26, 27, 346–8, 413–18, 436–7, 438–9, 450–51; shortening, 432; with mix of seating, 348
        chair removal, replace with benches or pews, 418–22, 423–4
        toilet and kitchen in a pew, 452–4
        denomination other than Anglican, 425–7, 428–31
repair of old seating, *see* Victorian seating, reuse
responsibility to provide seating, *see* allocation, churchwardens' role
restoration of churches, number *see under* church buildings
reuse of old seating
    to create box pews, *see* box pews, creation
    in Victorian period, *see* Victorian seating, reuse
    modern use of bench ends to make church chairs, 161, 168, 432

recycling of pews, 412–13
Reynard the Fox, 76
Richardson, J., *19.16*
Rideout, Walter, 180, 171–2
Ringham, Henry, 279, *18.4*
Rippin Bros., *19.16*
Rivers, Robert, 139
Rivingtons, 231
Roberts, Richard, 136–7
Roman Catholic church (post-Reformation)
    out of scope of this book, ix
    data, 38 (Graph 1), 39, 40, 41 (Table 1), 43 (incl. Table 2), 50 (Graph 13), 55, 56 (Graphs 23 & 24), 58 (Table 7), 60
    liturgical renewal, 9
    seating, 1, 5, 39, 45, 60, 294, 339, 359
    case study, 428–31
Romayne style, 158, *10.10, 10.11*
Rome, 20
rotating chair, designed to pray on in church, 240, 253
Rudding Park, 204
Ruddle & Thompson, 265
Russell, Gordon, 361, *24.2*
Ryme Intrinseca, Dorset, 171, *19.7a*

Sacred and Profane Beauty, 335
Sadler, Elihonor, 2
St Andrew on bench end, 277
St Anne with Virgin and Child, 468, *30.11*
St Brannock on bench end, 163
St Christopher, painting, 77
St Columb Major, Cornwall, 143, 162
St Gargoyle's (imaginary church), *30.17*
St Helier, Jersey, 274
St Katherine altar, 75
St Leonards, East Sussex, *19.13*
St Margaret on bench end, 87
St Mark on bench end, 74
St Michael on bench end, 87
St Paul on bench end, 277
St Paul's Ecclesiological Society, *see* Ecclesiological Society, present
St Peter
    on bench end, 277
    sermon of, 459, *30.2*
St Teath, Cornwall, 75
Saintbury, Glocs, 2, 10, *26.4*
sale of seats, *see under* appropriation, basis
Salisbury
    diocese of, seats in, Chapter 19 *passim* (esp. 282)
    St Edmund, 79, 103
Sanders, Lloyd, 268
Sauland, Norway, *4.A4*
schemes of seating with other liturgical furniture, *see* liturgical assemblages
scholars, seating for, *see* children and their seating

schoolroom, adults meeting in, 248, 255
Schüssler, *4.9*
Scoles, J. J., 278
Scott, G. G. and his seating, 4, 13, Chapter 16, 279, 287, 290, 293, 294, 297, 433, 445, *19.5c*
Scottow, Norfolk, 293, *19.12b*
screens (chancel) *see* liturgical assemblages
screens (for projection), *see* projectors
seasons, in worship, 10
seating allocated for particular groups, *see* allocation, criteria
seating, appropriate for today's needs, discussed, *see* church interiors, today
seating compared (different types today), 342–3, Chapter 23, Chapter 24, 390–91, Chapter 28
    advocacy for types of seating
        chairs, 342–3, 359–61, 362; *see also* chairs
        stackable benches, 356, 359–61; *see also* stackable benches
        pews (i.e. fixed benches), 346, Chapter 23; *see also* pews, keep or remove?
    capacity, 355–6, 390, 465
    checklist for comparison, 390–91
    comfort
        what sort of comfort?, 233–4, 343, 390, 408
        discomfort a moral good (or not), 347, 408
        of pews in particular, *see* pews, comfort
    elderly, needs of, 340, 362, 390, 408; examples, 423, 447
    flexibility
        discussed, 342, 353, 356, 361, 390–91, 402, 404
        examples: by moving not stacking, 27, 433–5, 450–51; by moving and stacking, 361, 423–4, 445–9; flexibility without moving seating, 436–7, 438–9
        for examples of reordering with different types of seating, *see* reordering examples
secular seating, *see* benches, wooden secular
Seddon, J. P., 211
segregation of sexes, *see* allocation, criteria, by gender
Selby Abbey, North Yorks, 258
self-organising seating, *see* organic arrangements of seating
servants, seating for, *see under* allocation, criteria
seventeenth-century seating, *see* post-Reformation seating
Sewerby, East Yorks, 293

Shaw, Norman, 211
Shelton, Beds, 128
Shepard, E. H., *30.9*
Sherborne, Dorset
    deanery of, pews in, Chapter 19 *passim* (esp. 282)
    church at, 79
Sherborne, Glocs, 357
Sherburne family, Stoneyhurst, Lancs, *8.8*
Shermanbury, West Sussex, 373, *26.2*
Shingham, Norfolk, 372, 377, *26.1*
significance (heritage), Chapter 26, 394–400
    importance of assessing, 347, 356–7, 371–2, 381–3, 384, 388–94, 408
    meaning discussed, 394–5; types of heritage value, Chapter 26 *passim*, 394–400
    and Statements of significance and need, 357, 371, 385, 388, 394
    of floors, 300, 380, 391, 397
    of liturgical assemblages, 373, 377–8, 379, 396–7 *passim*, 399
    of seating, Chapter 26, 394–400
        assessing (principles), 298, Chapter 26, 396–400
        assessing (practicalities), 111–12, 356–7, 388
        assessing (difficulties), 87–92, 300, 398–9
        assessing (examples), 113–14, 114–17, 117–19, 125–30, 156–9, Chapter 12, Chapter 26 *passim*
        some factors influencing, 396–7
        mitigating loss of, 356–7, 381–3, 392–3
        views expressed on significance of seating, 24–6, 209, 266, 300, 375–6, 379–80, 399–400
sills (of pews)
    role as part of pew, *see under* structure of pews
    role as pew floor, *see* floor, platforms
sitting, posture, *see* posture
sittings (places to sit), Chapter 5
    19th-century provision, 37–9, 40–41, 48 (Graph 11), 49–53 (incl. Graph 19), 58 (Table 7)
    concerns about lack of, 51, 200, 203, 250–1
    cramming of seating, *see* Victorian seating, cramming
    post-19th-century changes and present pew removal
        general, 37, 53–4
        present rate of pew removal, 39, 54 (incl. Table 5), 357–8, 474–5
    number today (overall)
        all churches, 37, 41 (Table 1), 48 (Graphs 10, 12)

        Anglican, 41 (Table 1), 53–5, 58 (Table 7)
        Nonconformist (general and specific), 37, 40, 41 (Table 1), 55, 57–60 (incl. Table 7)
        Roman Catholic, 39, 40, 41 (Table 1), 45, 55, 58 (Table 7), 60
    number per church, 37–9 (incl. Graph 2), 48 (Graph 9), 50 (Graphs 13–16), 51–53 (incl. Graphs 17, 18, 20), 55, 59
    utilisation and attendance, all denominations, 37, 39, 40, 41 (incl. Table 1), 44, 50 (Graph 14), 54–7 (incl. Graphs 21 & 22), 58 (Table 7), 59, 402, 404–5
    see also church buildings
size of church buildings, *see* sittings, number per church
size of congregation, catering for
    Victorian discussion, *see under* Victorian seating
    today (discussed), 336–7, 390
Skidmore, Francis, 303
Skipton, North Yorks, Christ Church, 204
Slaidburn, Lancashire, 452–4, *29.15a–e*
Slater & Carpenter, *19.11*
Slater, William, *19.9b*
sliding seats, *see under* structure of pews
Slindon, Sussex, *6.5*
social implications of seating
    historic, including status, *see* allocation; *see also* appropriation
    current concerns, *see* changing seating, considerations, relationships
Socialism, 375
Society for the Protection of Ancient Buildings, 44
Somerset, benches in, Chapter 7
South Creake, Norfolk, *6.2b*
South-Hole, Hartland, 151
Southworth family, 135, 144
Sowton, Devon, 268, 273–4, 275, *17.1a, 17.2, 17.3, 17.4*
SPAB, 441
space per person on Victorian pews, *see* Victorian seating, pews
Spaxton, Somerset, 95, 106, 107
Spofforth, North Yorks, 204
squires' pews, *see* family pews
stackable benches (modern), 356, Chapter 24 *passim*
    compared with other forms of seating, *see* seating compared
    examples of use, *see* reordering examples
    flexibility, moving and stacking, *see* seating compared, flexibility
    mixed with other seating, *see* mixed seating

stackable benches (modern) (*cont.*)
  for historic movable benches, *see under* benches
Staffordshire 'pew' group, 468, *30.12*
staging, 436–7, 438–9
staining woodwork, *see* colour of seating
Stamford, Lincolnshire, St Martin, *13.5*
'standards' (i.e. bench ends), *see* bench ends; use of word, 272, 294
standing in church, 70, 78, 80, 83, 156, 175, 242, 244, 246, 338, 340, 448, 459; *see also* worship, today
Stanton Harcourt, Oxon, 213, *14.4*
Stanton, Phoebe, 428
Statements of significance and need, *see under* significance
status reflected in seating, *see* allocation, criteria; *see also* appropriation
Stavanger, Norway, 35, *4.A5*
Steeple Aston, Oxon, 128, 213, 328, *8.A14, 14.1*
Stevenage, Herts, *19.10d*
Stevens, Mr, 258
sticks, stowage of, *see* bench ends, umbrella holders
Stockport, Cheshire, 134
Stogumber, Somerset, 72, 80, 87, 93, 94, 95, 101, 103, 104, 105, 106, *7.9, 7.12*
Stogursey, Somerset, 93, 95, 101, 103
Stoke at Hartland, Devon, *see* Hartland
Stoke Edith, Herefordshire, 142, *30.4*
Stoke St Gregory, Somerset, 96
Stoneleigh, Warwicks, *25.1*
Stoneyhurst, Lancs, *8.8*
stools, medieval use, of *see* medieval seating, portable
Street, G. E., 6, 211, 290, 292, 296, *1.5*
Stringston, Somerset, 107, *7.14*
Strong, Sir Roy, 1, 15
structure of pews (medieval and general) (for Victorian pews in particular, *see* Victorian seating, pews): Chapter 7 *passim*, 123–30, 149, 186–193
  assembly and location notation, 101–102, Chapter 10
  back of pew, 96, 123
  back rail ('book rest'), 94, 95, 96, 107, 149, 159, 208, 219, 223–5, 227, 229, 230, 236, *7.5, 7.6, 10.7, 11.8*
  bench ends, *see under* bench ends
  dimensions, 91, 92–3, 94, 95, 117, 125, 201, 415
  doors and hinges, *see under* box pews
  form of the timber, 96
  lining of, 189, *30.4b*
  materials, *see* wood
  panels, 186–193 *passim*; dividing into sections, 227
  pegging (pinning), 91, 94–6, 149, 186, 187, 191

repairs (identifying), 91
sills, 95, 120–21, 143, 155, 165, 167, 268, 272
sliding and hanging seats, flaps, etc, 103–104, 179, 225, 273, 294
top rail, 91, 94, 95, 108, 126, 149, 156, 191, 222, 229, 236, *7.5, 7.6*
Styward, Thomas and Cecily, 77
subscriptions, *see* Victorian seating, financing and cost
Sudbury, Suffolk, St Peter, 255–6, 462, *p.255, 30.8*
Suffolk, bench ends in, 4, 78, 126, 128, Chapter 18
Suffolk, Right Hon. Earl of, *see* Puddletown and Waterson, Lords of
Sunday School children
  effect on attendance numbers, 44, 57
  seating for, *see* children and their seating
survival of extended seating schemes, *see under* liturgical assemblages
Sussex, church building in, 57–8
Sutton Mallet, Somerset, 108, *7.17*
Sutton, Isle of Ely, 132–143 *passim*
Swaffham, Norfolk, 76–7
Sweden, Lutheran liturgical movement in, 23
Swift, Jonathan, 115
Swilland, Suffolk, 279
symbolism
  of seating arrangements, 23–4, 424; *see also* impression given by seating
  on bench ends, *see* bench ends

Taft, Robert, 15
'Take a pew', 412–13
Tarvin, 199
Taylor, Edward, 183
Temperance, as Christian name, 140
temperature, *see* heating
Temple Newsam, Leeds, West Yorks, exhibition at, 116
Temple of Solomon, 14
Teulon, S. S., *19.8b*
Thame, Oxon, 77, 348, *22.5, 22.6, 22.7*
theatre seating, *see* benches, wooden secular
Theddingworth, Leics, 297
Theseus, 17
thirty pieces of silver, on bench end, 162
Thompson, 'Mouseman', 379
Thompson, Paul, 297
Thornfalcon, Somerset, *7.5*
Thornford, Dorset, *19.11*
Thorpe Market, Norfolk, 436–7, *29.9*
Tintinhull, Somerset, 104, 294, *7.10*
Tipton St John, Devon, 268
today's seating needs discussed, *see* church interiors, today

toilet in a pew, *see* reordering examples
Tong, 206
Tor Tre Teste, Rome, 20
Torbryan, Devon, *frontis*
Towneley, Mrs, 144
Tractarian interior, 197, 268, 274
tradition
  maintenance of old styles, Chapter 18
  sense of, associated with seating, *see* attitudes to seating
transcendence, *see under* church interiors, today
tree-ring dating, *see* dendrochronological dating
Trent, Dorset, 75, 282
Trondheim, Norway, 26, *4.7*
True Principles (A. W. N. Pugin), 428
True Principles (Journal of Pugin Society), 429
Trull, Somerset, 75, 93, 96, 100, 108
Trumpington, Cambs, 293
Tuddenham St Martin, Suffolk, 279
Tuxford, Notts, 204
Twenty-four Reasons for Getting Rid of Church Pews (or Pues) (pamphlet), 271
Twyford, Leics, 297
types of seating compared, *see* seating compared
Tysoe, Warwickshire, 261, *16.3*

Ufford, Suffolk, 112
umbrellas, *see* bench ends, umbrella holders
United Reformed Church, 43 (Table 2)
unplanned seating arrangements, *see* box pews, interiors jumbled with
Upchurch, Richard, 137
Upton Lovell, Wilts, 143
Upton Scudamore, Wilts, 292, 300
utilisation of seating, *see under* sittings

values attached to seating
  for heritage significance, *see* significance
  for attitudes, *see* attitudes to seating
van der Leeuw, Gerardus, 335
Vår Frue, 26, *4.7*
Vatican II (Council), 9
velocipedes, 250
vermin, 227, 232
Vernacular Architecture Group, 74
Via Old England, 414
Victorian churches, number, *see* church buildings
Victorian seating (incl. earlier 19th century)
  accommodation, *see* Victorian seating, capacity
  architects, role of, Chapter 16, Chapter 17, 293–4, 297–8, 303–4, 325–6, 377, 379

498

Victorian seating (*cont.*)
  appearance (attractiveness) discussed, 225, 227, 229, 237, 239, 241, 249, 323
  bench end, shapes, *see* bench ends, Victorian shapes
  box pews (including move away from), Chapter 13 *passim*, Chapter 17 *passim*
    creation by Victorians, *see under* box pews, examples by period
    faculties for removal, 208
    liking for box pews, 204, 208, 258, 324, 374–5
    not liking box pews, 3–4, 197, Chapter 13 *passim* (e.g. 204), 219, 220, 221, 224, 227, 245, 266, 271, 281, 323, 374; *see also* anti-pew publications
    move away from, to benches without doors, Chapter 13 *passim*, 213–14, 220, 221, 281–2, 375–6
  capacity (ability of seating types to provide), discussed, 219, 220, 237, 239–40, 242, 243, 247, 250
  capacity (total numbers catered for) *see* sittings, 19th-century provision
  catalogues, *see* catalogues
  chairs
    attitudes to, 213, 225–7, 235, Chapter 15 *passim*, 257, 296, 306, 452–6; early opposition, 225; need to 'conciliate prejudice' against, 256
    designs (practical and impractical), 227, 238, 240, 253, 307–8, *p.238* (illustration), *p.240* (illustration), 20.3
    moving and stacking, discussed, 227, 241, 243, 248, 253, 256
    organic arrangements discussed, 237, 244, 248, 249, 254
    price, 225, 296, 306, 307–8
    see also Victorian seating, flexibility
  children
    seating for, 203, 208, 220, 224, 243, 278, 296, 468
    'galleries' for, *see under* galleries
    survival of seating for, 208, 296–7
  comfort, *see* Victorian seating, pews (construction), principles
  craftsmen, role of, 265–6, 272–3, 274, 279; for list, *see* contractors and craftsmen, Victorian
  cramming of seating (often encouraged by financing arrangements), 13, 202–3, 212, 222, 235, 236, 237, 243, 245, 247, 298, 343; *see also* ICBS, grants; Victorian seating, financing and cost

date of move to open seating, *see* Victorian seating, box pews, move away from
dating Victorian seating by style, difficulties because of persistence of style, *see* bench ends, Victorian shapes, persistence of style
direction facing, *see* Victorian seating, foci
elderly needs, discussed, 225, 236, 246, 237, 252
financing and cost, 37, 200, 202–3, 204, 211, 270, 273–4, 275, 295, 305–6, 379; *see also* ICBS, grants
fixtures to bench ends, *see* bench ends
flexibility of arrangement
  contemporary discussion, Chapter 15 *passim* (esp. 237, 239, 242, 243, 252, 253, 254, 256), 296
  movability and stackability: general discussion, Chapter 15 *passim* (esp. 237, 241, 243, 248, 253); of chairs, *see* Victorian seating, chairs; of benches, 202, 257, 224, 292, *p.242* (illustration)
  see also Victorian seating, chairs
foci (direction faced), 121, 192, 199, 201–202, 204, 207, 208, 209, 257, 271; ICBS rules, 219, 220, 224, 227
hats, *see* hats, stowage of
identification (as against medieval), *see* medieval seating, date
impression given by seating, discussed, 237, 241, 242, 243, 245, 246–7, 248, 255, 346, 403, 408
kneeling
  and chairs, Chapter 15 *passim*
  designing for, *see* Victorian seating, pews (construction), principles
  mode: hassocks, 219, 220, 230, 465 (argued against, 223, 232, 234–5); kneeling-boards, 6, 219, 220, 223, 230, 231–5, 236, 293, 419–21; kneeling chair, specialist, 240, 253; kneeling mats, 230; on floor, 255 (argued against, 251)
  provision and concern for, 199, 204, 208, 212, 237, 239, 240; required by ICBS, 199, 219, 220, 224
materials, *see* wood
medieval exemplars
  general guide to style or technique, 94, 106, 213–18, 220, 222, 229, Chapter 16 *passim*, 279, 281–90 *passim* (esp. 284–5), 326; working drawings provided, 213–18

  copying of particular local examples, 88, 93, 106, 117, 229, Chapter 16 *passim*, 272–3, 277–8, 279, 328; failure to, 106
medieval work, confusion with, *see under* medieval seating, date of
mixed types of seating in one church, 235, 236, 242, 247, 254
model pews, for copying, *see under* ICBS
'open' benches (i.e. without doors), 19th-century move to, *see under* Victorian seating, box pews
persistence of Victorian designs, *see under* bench ends, Victorian shapes
pews (construction)
  principles (incl. comfort and kneeling), 96, 202–3, 219, 220, 222–3, 224, 225, 226, 227–230, 232–4, 236, 272, 346, 379; *see also* structure of pews
  surviving specifications and drawings, 201–204, 270–73, 326
  for bench ends, *see* bench ends, Victorian shapes; *see also* pews
plans (seating*)*, *see under* plans
platforms for pews, *see* floors, platforms
poor, seating for *see* poor, the
rate of pew removal today, *see under* sittings, post-19-century changes
reordering, Victorian, examples, 201, 203, 204, 255–6, Chapter 16 *passim*, Chapter 17 *passim*, 281, 323–6, 375, 462
  contested, 204, 208, 258, 324, 374–5
plans (spatial diagrams), *see under* plans
reuse or reframing of earlier seating, 96–99, 113–14, 115–17, 117–18, 120–30, Chapter 12, 220, 221, 222, 229, 259, 272–3, 274, 278, 279, 380, 442; significance, 400
significance (heritage), *see* significance
sittings provided, *see under* sittings
size of congregation, catering for, 237, 245, 249
survival, extent of, *see under* liturgical assemblages
umbrellas, storage of, *see under* bench ends
wood
  choice of type, 261, 272, 290
  price, 259, 305–6
  other materials for seating, 206, 287

499

view from seating, *see* foci of seating
Virgin & Child with St Anne, 468, *30.12*
visual impact of seating, *see* impression given by seating; appearance of seating

Wagner, Father, 296
Wainwright, John, 324
Wales, Church of, disestablishment, 39
walls, seat-ledges on, *see* medieval seating, part of church structure
Walpole St Peter, Norfolk, 3, *1.1, 1.3*
Warkworth, Northants, 75
Warminster, Wilts, St John, 292
warmth, *see* heating
Warrington, Lancs, 135, 144
'We love the place, O God', 465, *30.9*
Weever, John, 221
Wellow, Somerset, 413–18, *29.2*
Welsh Calvinistic Methodist church, 427
Werman, Simon, 100, 102
Wesley, John, 425–7 *passim*
West and Collier, 227
West Country, style of bench ends in, 128, 143, 160
Wetheringsett, Suffolk, 279
Whalley, Lancs, Abbey and church, 117, 118, *8.8, 8.9*
Whimple, Devon, 166, 268, 270–73, 274, *17.1b & c, 17.5, 17.6, 17.7, 17.8*

Whippingham, Isle of Wight, *19.12a*
Whissendine, Rutland, 297
Whitby, North Yorks, St Mary's, 209
White, William, 268, 293, 296, 300
  article by, 226–30
wider use of church buildings, *see under* changing seating, considerations; reordering examples
width of pews, *see* space per person on seating
Wife of Bath, 83
Wiggenhall St Mary, Norfolk, 79
Willand, Devon, 433–5, *29.8*
Willement, Thomas, 273
Wilmslow, Cheshire, 325
Wilton's Music Hall, 471, *30.15*
Wing, Bucks, 259
Withers, R. J., *26.6*
women, segregated, *see* allocation, criteria, by gender
Wood, Ron, *30.17*
wood
  for Victorian seating, *see under* Victorian seating
  today, 363
Woodcote, Shropshire, 380
wooden seating (secular), *see under* benches
Wooden Walls of England in Danger: A Defence of Church Pews, (tract), 374–5
Woolrich, Tony, 323, 326

Woolsery, Devon, 162
working drawings of medieval pews, 213–8
worship
  changes at and after Reformation, 9, 151
  today
    recent developments, 9–11, 19–20, 23–24, 27–8, 468
    movement during worship, 10–11, 13–18, 250–51, 337–8, 448; worship as journey, 14–17
  see also church interiors, today
  reordering to meet needs of, *see* changing seating, considerations
Wortham, Suffolk, 432, *29.7*
Wraxall, Somerset, 100
Wrecclesham, Surrey, *19.14*
Wren, Sir Christopher, 183, 335
Wright, Charles, circle of, *13.1*
Wyatt, T. H., 211, 281

Yates, Nigel, 4, 13
Yetminster, Dorset, 282
Yorkshire churches, furniture and carving in, 116–17